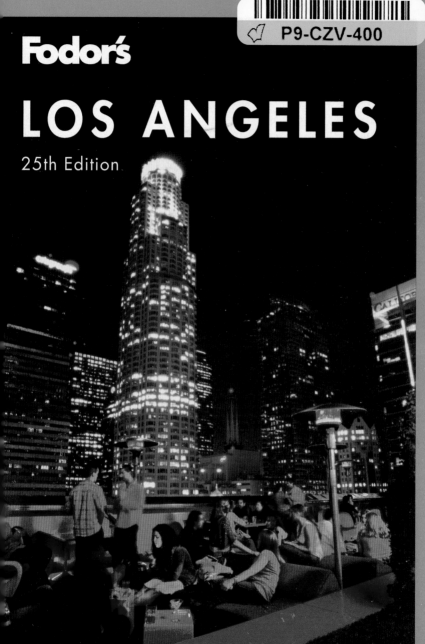

Fodor's

LOS ANGELES

25th Edition

Fodor's Travel Publications   New York, Toronto, London, Sydney, Auckland
www.fodors.com

P9-CZV-400

Eugene Fodor:
The Spy Who Loved Travel

As Fodor's celebrates our 75th anniversary, we are honoring the colorful and adventurous life of Eugene Fodor, who revolutionized guidebook publishing in 1936 with his first book, *On the Continent, The Entertaining Travel Annual.*

Eugene Fodor's life seemed to leap off the pages of a great spy novel. Born in Hungary, he spoke six languages and graduated from the Sorbonne and the London School of Economics. During World War II he joined the Office of Strategic Services, the budding spy agency for the United States. He commanded the team that went behind enemy lines to liberate Prague, and recommended to Generals Eisenhower, Bradley, and Patton that Allied troops move to the capital city. After the war, Fodor worked as a spy in Austria, posing as a U.S. diplomat.

In 1949 Eugene Fodor—with the help of the CIA—established Fodor's Modern Guides. He was passionate about travel and wanted to bring his insider's knowledge of Europe to a new generation of sophisticated Americans who wanted to explore and seek out experiences beyond their borders. Among his innovations were annual updates, consulting local experts, and including cultural and historical perspectives and an emphasis on people—not just sites. As Fodor described it, "The main interest and enjoyment of foreign travel lies not only in 'the sites,' . . . but in contact with people whose customs, habits, and general outlook are different from your own."

Eugene Fodor died in 1991, but his legacy, Fodor's Travel, continues. It is now one of the world's largest and most trusted brands in travel information, covering more than 600 destinations worldwide in guidebooks, on Fodors.com, and in ebooks and iPhone apps. Technology and the accessibility of travel may be changing, but Eugene Fodor's unique storytelling skills and reporting style are behind every word of today's Fodor's guides.

Our editors and writers continue to embrace Eugene Fodor's vision of building personal relationships through travel. We invite you to join the Fodor's community at fodors.com/community and share your experiences with like-minded travelers. Tell us when we're right. Tell us when we're wrong. And share fantastic travel secrets that aren't yet in Fodor's. Together, we will continue to deepen our understanding of our world.

Happy 75th Anniversary, Fodor's! Here's to many more.

Tim Jarrell, Publisher

FODOR'S LOS ANGELES
Editor: Rachel Klein

Editorial Contributor: Erica Duecy
Writers: Cindy Arora, Tanvi Chheda, Alene Dawson, Elline Lipkin, Lea Lion, Susan MacCallum-Whitcomb, Laura Randall

Production Editor: Evangelos Vasilakis
Maps & Illustrations: Mark Lindroth, *cartographers;* Bob Blake, Rebecca Baer, *map editors;* William Wu, *information graphics*
Design: Fabrizio La Rocca, *creative director;* Guido Caroti, *art director;*
Tina Malaney, Nora Rosansky, Chie Ushio, *designers;* Melanie Marin, *associate director of photography*
Cover Photo: (Hollywood): Alveiro Leiva/age fotostock
Production Manager: Angela L. McLean

25th Edition

ISBN 978-0-679-00971-9

ISSN 1095-3914

SPECIAL SALES
This book is available at special discounts for bulk purchases for sales promotions or premiums. Special editions, including personalized covers, excerpts of existing books, and corporate imprints, can be created in large quantities for special needs. For more information, write to Special Markets/Premium Sales, 1745 Broadway, MD 3-1, New York, NY 10019, or e-mail specialmarkets@randomhouse.com.

AN IMPORTANT TIP & AN INVITATION
Although all prices, opening times, and other details in this book are based on information supplied to us at press time, changes occur all the time in the travel world, and Fodor's cannot accept responsibility for facts that become outdated or for inadvertent errors or omissions. So **always confirm information when it matters,** especially if you're making a detour to visit a specific place. Your experiences—positive and negative—matter to us. If we have missed or misstated something, **please write to us.** Share your opinion instantly through our online feedback center at fodors.com/contact-us.

PRINTED IN SINGAPORE

10 9 8 7 6 5 4 3 2 1

CONTENTS

CONTENTS

ABOUT
THIS BOOK

Our Ratings

At Fodor's, we spend considerable time choosing the best places in a destination so you don't have to. By default, anything we recommend in this book is worth visiting. But some sights, properties, and experiences are so great that we've recognized them with additional accolades. Orange Fodor's Choice stars indicate our top recommendations; black stars highlight places we deem Highly Recommended; and Best Bets call attention to top properties in various categories. Disagree with any of our choices? Care to nominate a new place? Visit our feedback center at www.fodors.com/feedback.

Hotels

Hotels have private bath, phone, and TV, and do not offer meals unless we specify that in the review. We always list facilities but not whether you'll be charged an extra fee to use them.

> For expanded hotel reviews, visit **Fodors.com**

Restaurants

Unless we state otherwise, restaurants are open for lunch and dinner daily. We mention dress only when there's a specific requirement and reservations only when they're essential or not accepted—it's always best to book ahead.

Credit Cards

We assume that restaurants and hotels accept credit cards. If not, we'll note it in the review.

Budget Well

Hotel and restaurant price categories from ¢ to $$$$ are defined in the opening pages of the respective chapters. For attractions, we always give standard adult admission fees; reductions are usually available for children, students, and senior citizens.

Listings
- ★ Fodor's Choice
- ★ Highly recommended
- ⊠ Physical address
- ✛ Directions or Map coordinates
- ⌂ Mailing address
- ☎ Telephone
- 🖶 Fax
- ⊕ On the Web
- ✉ E-mail
- ✉ Admission fee
- ☉ Open/closed times
- Ⓜ Metro stations
- ▭ No credit cards

Hotels & Restaurants
- 🏨 Hotel
- ⤵ Number of rooms
- ⚲ Facilities
- ⦿ Meal plans
- ✕ Restaurant
- ⚶ Reservations
- 🎩 Dress code
- ⤢ Smoking

Outdoors
- 🏌 Golf
- ⛺ Camping

Other
- ☾ Family-friendly
- ⇨ See also
- ⊠ Branch address
- ☞ Take note

1

Experience
Los Angeles

LOS ANGELES TODAY

Starstruck . . . excessive . . . smoggy . . . superficial . . . There's a modicum of truth to each of the adjectives regularly applied to L.A. But Angelenos—and most objective visitors—dismiss their prevalence as signs of envy from people who hail from places less blessed with fun and sun. Pop Culture, for instance, *does* permeate life in LaLaLand: a massive economy employing millions of Southern Californians is built around it.

However, this city also boasts highbrow appeal, having amassed an impressive array of world-class museums and arts venues. America's second-largest city has more depth than paparazzi shutters can ever capture. So set aside your preconceived notions and take a look at L.A. today.

Downtown's Upswing

Los Angeles has been archly described as "72 suburbs in search of a city." Hence the renaissance its once-desolate Downtown is experiencing may come as something of a surprise. Long-neglected neighborhoods here have been spruced up, and streets even the police deemed irredeemable have been revitalized.

Even taking an ailing economy into account, in the last decade Downtown saw a remarkable development boom—most notably L.A. LIVE: a 27-acre, $2.5-billion entertainment complex, which includes the Nokia Theatre and the innovative Grammy Museum.

And there's plenty more to come in the next few years. The Autry National Center in Griffith Park will expand its space by an additional 25,000 square feet, to house its collection of artifacts from the American West. And Downtown L.A. will get Southern California's only museum dedicated to the Italian-American experience, due to open in 2012 in the historic Italian Hall near Olvera Street.

State of the Art

SoCal's beauty-obsessed citizens aren't the only ones opting for a fresh look these days: esteemed art museums are, too. Take the Huntington Library, Art Collections, and Botanical Gardens' recent $20-million makeover of its galleries, a "must-see" for lovers of European art.

The biggest news in L.A.'s museum world today puts the spotlight on Downtown. Plans for The Broad Foundation's new, 120,000-square-foot, three-story contemporary art museum, simply called "the Broad" is in the works, to be built across the street from Walt Disney Concert Hall and the Los Angeles Museum of Contemporary Art (LACMA).

The museum is being designed by architectural firm Diller Scofido + Renfro, expected to cost more than $100 million, and is scheduled to open in 2013. In 2008, the Broad Contemporary Art Museum at LACMA was built, designed by starchitect Renzo Piano.

Access Hollywood

Hollywood may disappoint tourists looking to overdose on glitz: after all, most of its moviemakers departed for the San Fernando Valley decades ago, leaving the area to languish. Even after the much-hyped 2001 debut of the Hollywood & Highland Center, the area remained more gritty than glamorous.

Yet new life continues to be pumped in. In the last few years, Vintage venues such as the Hollywood Palladium have been refurbished; the popular Madame Tussauds constructed a movie-theme museum adjacent to Grauman's Chinese Theatre; and Cirque du Soleil began a show with a decade-long run at the Kodak Theatre.

The newest addition to the heart of Tinseltown will be the Academy Museum of Motion Pictures (AMMP), which will highlight how film and the moviemaking business has woven its way into pop culture over the course of time since its creation. The museum, said to cost around $400 million, is due to open in 2013.

New Lights on the Coast

Having fun in the sun isn't relegated to the beaches and other outdoor activities alone in L.A., when you consider the number of amusement parks close to the city.

One of the first sites you see driving into Santa Monica is a tremendous Ferris wheel at Pacific Park out on the Santa Monica Pier—and now it stands out even more. The wheel was recently replaced, and the new one is covered with about 160,000 dazzling LED lights that shine much brighter than the 5,000 or so red, white and blue bulbs on the old one.

Food for Thought

Star chefs continue to flock from across the country to make their mark on Los Angeles. Recent big openings have included Red O, a classic Mexican eatery in West Hollywood, from Chicagoan TV chef Rick Bayless, and The Royce, in the Langhan Hotel in Pasadena, with its menu created by David Feau. Thomas Keller's recent launch of L.A.'s outpost of Bouchon is just as popular as ever, and other big names including Gordon Ramsay, José Andrés, and Michael Mina are on the list as well for noteworthy additions to the dining scene.

Nevertheless, eats in L.A. remain relatively equalitarian. Even posh places seldom require jackets, so the dress code is casual. Ditto for the menu. (In the city that invented fast food, it's no coincidence Govind Armstrong flips gourmet burgers or that Wolfgang Puck built his reputation on pizza!)

Of course, if you want to go budget, you can easily justify chowing down at McDonald's, Carl's Jr., and In-N-Out Burger because all, having started in the Five-County Area, qualify as "indigenous cuisine." Alternately, you can savor L.A.'s international flavor by grabbing some sushi in a *kaiten-zushi* restaurant or ordering carne asada from an old-school taco truck.

L.A. Free Ways

Though high-profile Angelenos have elevated conspicuous consumption to an art, you can still spend time here without dropping a dime. Visiting culture vultures will be relieved to learn the Getty Center and Getty Villa offer free entry, and that the Los Angeles County Music Center hosts complimentary tours, plus no-cost programs under the "Active Arts" banner.

Frugal movie fans can get reel on Hollywood Boulevard's star-paved Walk of Fame or in the forecourt of Grauman's Chinese where celebs have been pressing hands, feet, and other body parts into cement since 1927 (time it right and you may catch a premiere, too).

Music buffs, meanwhile, can view memorabilia from past headliners at the free Hollywood Bowl Museum. Interested in a different kind of stargazing? There is no fee to see the Griffith Observatory's stellar exhibits or peer through its giant telescope.

—Susan MacCallum-Whitcomb

WHAT'S WHERE

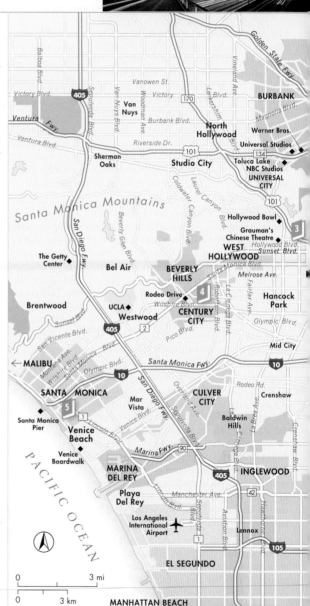

Numbers correspond to chapters.

2 Downtown Los Angeles.
Downtown L.A. shows off spectacular modern architecture with the swooping Walt Disney Concert Hall and the stark Cathedral of Our Lady of the Angels. The Music Center and the Museum of Contemporary Art anchor a world-class arts scene, while Olvera Street, Chinatown, and Little Tokyo reflect the city's history and diversity.

3 Hollywood and the Studios. Glitzy and tarnished, good and bad—Hollywood is just like the entertainment business itself. The Walk of Fame, Grauman's Chinese Theatre, Paramount Pictures studio, and the Hollywood Bowl keep the neighborhood's romantic past alive. Universal Studios Hollywood, Warner Bros., and NBC Television Studios are in the Valley.

4 The Westside and Beverly Hills. Go for the glamour, the restaurants, and the scene. Rodeo Drive is particularly good for a look at wretched or ravishing excess. But don't forget the Westside's cultural attractions—especially the dazzling Getty Center. West Hollywood's an area for urban indulgences—shopping, restaurants, nightspots—rather

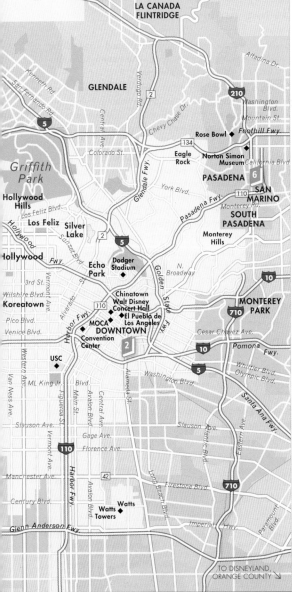

than sightseeing. Its main arteries are the Sunset Strip (Sunset Boulevard), and Melrose Avenue, lined with shops ranging from punk to postmodern.

5 Santa Monica and the Beaches. In Santa Monica, a lively beach scene plays out every day. Venice, just south of Santa Monica, is a more raffish mix of artists, beach punks, and yuppies, most of whom you can see on the Venice Boardwalk. Drive up PCH (the Pacific Coast Highway) to Malibu, where the rich and famous reside. An extravagant residence of a different kind, the Getty Villa Malibu is filled with exquisite antiquities.

6 Pasadena and Environs. Like Santa Monica, Pasadena may appear to be an extension of L.A. but it's actually a separate city with a strong sense of community. It's a quiet, genteel area to visit, with outstanding arts and crafts homes, good dining, and a pair of exceptional museums: the Norton Simon and the Huntington Library, Art Collections, and Botanical Gardens in adjoining San Marino.

LOS ANGELES PLANNER

When to Go

Any time of the year is the right time to visit Los Angeles. From November to May, you can find crisp, sunny, unusually smog-free days. December to April is the rainy season, but storms are usually brief, followed by brilliant skies. Dining alfresco, sailing, and catching a concert under the stars—these are reserved for L.A. summers, which are virtually rainless (with an occasional air-quality alert).

Prices skyrocket and reservations are essential when tourism peaks July through September.

Southern California is a temperate area, moderated by the Pacific Ocean. In addition, mountains along the north and east sides of the Los Angeles coastal basin act as buffers against the extreme summer heat and winter cold of the surrounding desert and plateau regions.

Pasadena and the San Fernando Valley are significantly hotter than Beverly Hills or Hollywood, while coastal areas can be dramatically cooler. Late spring brings "June gloom," when skies tend to be overcast until afternoon.

Getting Around

In L.A., where the automobile is worshipped—and will be, no matter how high gas prices go—the freeways are the best way for you to get around town.

Renting a Car. Definitely plan to do it at the airport. And if you want to cruise around in a convertible—a quintessential L.A. experience that allows you to catch some sun while sitting in traffic—reserve well in advance. It's also a good idea to spring for a GPS system.

Parking. With the exception of inside Downtown high-rises, where parking costs can be exorbitant—look for flat-rate surface lots instead—parking in L.A. is not expensive and there are plenty of garages and lots. Avoid rush hour (before 10 am and between 5 and 7 pm) if at all possible, and remember that even-numbered freeways run east–west, and odd-numbered ones run north–south.

Taking Taxis. There are, however, ways to get around Los Angeles without a car. Taxis are not as plentiful as in New York or San Francisco, but you can always find one at a major hotel. From LAX to downtown, a cab ride runs about $42, and shuttle vans cost about $16 per person.

Dining and Lodging

Chefs in L.A. are frontrunners in the farm-to-fork mentality, and scour the city's many farmers' markets for the freshest of locally grown ingredients. For lodging, there's everything from ultra-luxe, swanky hotels in Beverly Hills to quiet beachfront resorts along the coast in Santa Monica, with a wide range of prices in every area.

WHAT IT COSTS

	¢	$	$$	$$$	$$$$
Restaurants	under $10	$10–$17	$18–$24	$25–$35	over $35
Hotels		under $100	$100–$199	$200–$299	$300–$399	over $400

Restaurant prices are per person for a main course or equivalent combination of smaller plates (e.g., tapas, sushi), excluding 9.75% sales tax. For hotels, taxes (10%–15.5%) are extra. In listings, we always name the facilities available, but we don't specify whether they cost extra. When pricing accommodations, always ask what's included.

Tips for the Freeway

Pick a lane. The car-pool lane, the "fast lane," the truck lane, the merge lane—this isn't your typical freeway. First of all, keep out of the two far right lanes, which buses and trucks are restricted to. To drive the speed limit, pick the middle lane; the fourth lane moves about 5 mi over the speed limit. Newbies should stay out of the far left lane. Speeds here range from 75 to 90 mph and you've got to deal with car-pool-lane mergers. And what about that car-pool lane—also known as the diamond lane? Use it if you have two or more people in your car and it's moving faster than the speed of traffic.

Signaling is a must. You might be able to get away with a quick lane-change in other cities, but don't try it in L.A. People may try to merge into the same spot as you from three lanes away.

Get a freeway map. The small, laminated maps that just cover the jumble of freeways are indispensable if you merge onto the wrong freeway, get lost, or get stuck in traffic and want to find an alternative route. Nearly every gas station sells them; you can get a decent one for a few bucks. ■TIP→ You can also find one on the inside back cover of this guide.

Don't pull over. Short of a real emergency, never, ever, pull over and stop on a freeway. So you took the wrong ramp and need to huddle with your map? Take the next exit and find a safe, well-lighted public space to stop your car and get your bearings.

L.A. Driving Times

From LAX to Downtown L.A.	30–75 min/19 mi
From LAX to Beverly Hills	30–75 min/15 mi
From LAX to Santa Monica	20–60 min/18 mi
From Downtown L.A. to Beverly Hills	20–45min/11 mi
From Downtown L.A. to Pasadena	15–25 min/11 mi
From Downtown L.A. to Burbank	18–30 min/12 mi
From Downtown L.A. to Universal City	15–40 min/10 mi
From Santa Monica to Redondo Beach	25–55 min/15 mi
From Santa Monica to West Hollywood	25–50 min/10 mi
From Santa Monica to Malibu	32–75 min/25 mi

Visitor Resources

There are two L.A. visitor information centers, on Figueroa Street downtown and on Hollywood Boulevard in Hollywood. The Santa Monica CVB runs a visitor information center on Main Street and several kiosks throughout the city, including the Santa Monica Pier and Third Street Promenade.

CITY AND STATE CONTACTS

California Office of Tourism 🕾 916/444–4429, 800/862–2543 ⊕ visitcalifornia.com.

L.A. Inc./The Convention and Visitors Bureau 🕾 213/624–7300, 800/228–2452 ⊕ discoverlosangeles.com.

NEIGHBORHOOD CONTACTS

Beverly Hills 🕾 310/248–1000, 800/345–2210 ⊕ beverlyhillschamber.com.

Hollywood 🕾 323/469–8311 ⊕ www.hollywoodchamber.net.

Long Beach Area 🕾 562/436–3645 ⊕ www.visitlongbeach.com.

Pasadena 🕾 626/795–9311 ⊕ www.pasadenacal.com.

Redondo Beach 🕾 310/374–2171, 800/282–0333 ⊕ www.visitredondo.com.

Santa Monica 🕾 310/319–6263, 800/544–5319 ⊕ www.santamonica.com.

West Hollywood 🕾 310/289–2525, 800/368–6020 ⊕ www.visitwesthollywood.com.

LOS ANGELES
TOP ATTRACTIONS

Disneyland
(A) "The Happiest Place on Earth" continues to delight children and all but the most cynical adults. A visit here can be enchanting, exciting, romantic, or nostalgic, depending on your age and experience. Disneyland, the original vision of Walt Disney, is now paired with Disney's California Adventure, showcasing more recent Disney characters and Hollywood-oriented attractions. Outside the theme parks, Downtown Disney supports a wide range of restaurants, bars, and clubs.

Walt Disney Concert Hall
(B) Designed by Frank Gehry, the voluptuous curves of this stainless steel-clad masterpiece located Downtown is a signature of the modern metropolis. One of several venues of the Music Center, the 2,265-seat Disney Hall is home to the Los Angeles Philharmonic. It features unrivaled acoustics and a stunning pipe organ, which is as much a work of art

as a musical instrument. For a truly opulent evening, pair a concert with dinner at Patina, located inside the building.

Grauman's Chinese Theatre and the Walk of Fame
(C) An iconic metaphor for Hollywood, this elaborate Chinese-theme theater opened in 1927 with the premier of Cecil B. DeMille's *King of Kings*. That's when the tradition of stars imprinting their hands or feet into the cement began with an "accidental" footprint by Norma Talmadge. More than 160 stars have contributed, and among the more unique prints are the nose of Jimmy Durante and hoofs of Trigger. The theater is adjacent to the Hollywood & Highland center. Then of course there's the Walk of Fame that runs a mile along Hollywood Boulevard, with the handprints of more than 1,600 stars.

The Getty Center

(D) On a hillside above Brentwood, the $1-billion-plus Getty Center is not only a museum, but a statement that L.A. has taken its place in the art world. The Richard Meier–designed complex has a skin of travertine marble and natural light floods the galleries filled with impressionist masterpieces, Greek antiquities, and jaw-dropping exhibits of furniture and decorative arts from French monarchy. Pedestrian plazas and gardens abound, and a sunset dinner at the restaurant, with its panoramic views, is the stuff of scrapbook memories.

Rodeo Drive

(E) Dominated by the exclusive names of Gucci, Versace, and Cartier, Rodeo Drive is a shoppers' paradise. Along the cobblestoned, Mediterranean-inspired Via Rodeo, you can drop a thousand dollars on python pumps or nosh on a $500 sushi dinner. Fortunately, Rodeo Drive doesn't cater exclusively to the rich and famous, and more moderate shops and restaurants are interspersed with the iconic boutiques.

The Santa Monica Pier

(F) Spend a sunny day oceanside riding the Ferris wheel, eating cotton candy, and playing dozens of games for prizes at this popular family destination.

The Venice Boardwalk

(G) The bohemian lifestyle of this famous boardwalk is constantly threatened by the rapid gentrification of Venice. Still, the magicians, fortune-tellers, and Muscle Beach weight lifters still survive. Struggling artists sell their paintings, infiltrated by tackier purveyors of cheap watches and sunglasses. Rent a bicycle or in-line skates, grab a hot dog, and enjoy the sights and the sunset.

LOS ANGELES TOP EXPERIENCES

The Best Drives

Considering that the greater L.A. area sprawls over more square mileage than some small countries, it comes as no surprise that residents clock a lot of road time. Contrary to popular belief, however, stand-still freeway traffic is only part of the picture. In Los Angeles, the popular 1950s-era pastime of cruising is still alive and well.

One of the premier ways to see the L.A. hot spots so often captured on the silver screen is to take a drive down **Sunset Boulevard.** The famed thoroughfare runs from the **Pacific Coast Highway** in Malibu to downtown Los Angeles, but the most well-known stretch is the **Sunset Strip,** in West Hollywood.

Heading east on Sunset Boulevard, pass by legendary music venues including the **Roxy,** the **Whisky-A-Go-Go,** and the **Viper Room.** Continue a little father to glimpse movie star magnet of yesteryear the **Sunset Tower Hotel** (formerly the Argyle Hotel) and current celebrity hangout the **Chateau Marmont.**

The famous roadway, **Mulholland Drive,** snakes along the ridge separating L.A. from its suburban neighbor, the San Fernando Valley. Like Sunset Boulevard, Mulholland Drive starts at the ocean and extends all the way into Hollywood, but unlike its urban counterpart, Mulholland forgoes street scenes for mountain views and traffic lights for unpaved stretches of road.

Another not-to-be-missed scenic stretch is the winding road that climbs through **Laurel Canyon,** a nexus of the 1960s music scene and former home to rockers Joni Mitchell and Neil Young among many others. At its apex, **Laurel Canyon Boulevard**

meets up with Mulholland Drive, so be sure to fuel up before you start the climb.

L.A. Outdoors

While Los Angeles' car culture is well-publicized, its bike culture is a little more under-the-radar, but that is not to say there isn't a healthy cycling scene. With seemingly endless days of summer, Angelenos love to spend time outdoors.

One of the quintessential L.A. activities is to rent an old-school beach cruiser and bike along the 22-mi-long **Strand,** which stretches from Santa Monica's **Will Rogers State Beach** to **Torrance County Beach** in Venice.

If you are an outdoor enthusiast, don't forget to pack your hiking boots alongside your stiletto heels so that you can **hike the Santa Monica Mountains.** Popular routes include the Backbone Trail, a 43-mi-stretch of chaparral-covered hillsides, oak woodlands, and creeks that links Will Rogers State Historic Park to Point Mugu, anchored in the middle by **Malibu Creek State Park** and **Topanga State Park.** The highly accessible **Griffith Park,** just north of Hollywood, is technically part of this mountain chain as well.

For some solitude and rural terrain, visit **Angeles National Forest,** in the northern reaches of L.A. County. The mostly flat and shaded **Gabrielino Trail** (☎ *626/574–5200 forest service*) along the upper Arroyo Seco is a favorite of mountain bikers, runners, birders, and horseback riders. To get there, exit the 210 Freeway at Arroyo Boulevard–Windsor Avenue in Altadena. Drive three-quarters of a mile north and look for the small parking lot just before you reach Ventura Avenue.

Eat with the Locals

With residents hailing from all over the world, Los Angeles is famous for its varied ethnic cuisine. One of the best ways to sample a variety of foods is to take a trip to 75-year-old **Farmers Market at Third and Fairfax.**

Some of the international eats to be found: A Mexican taco stand, a French crepe company, a Korean barbeque, a Mediterranean falafel stall, and a Brazilian grill. For dessert, pick up some fresh-cut fruit from one of the colorful produce stands.

Of course, there's also L.A.'s famous local chains, including '20s-era Hollywood hot spot the **Pig 'N Whistle** and comfort food mecca **Roscoe's House of Chicken and Waffles,** as well as **In 'N Out** burger haven.

Get Starstruck

Seemingly floating above downtown Los Angeles like a Jetsons-age oasis, the rooftop **bar at the Standard Hotel** attracts everyone from buttoned-up office workers, who flock to the space for happy hour drinks, to the swanked-out, late-night crowd.

A surefire way to see stars (or at least the constellation they call home) is by **purchasing a star map** from vendors on street corners around the city. If you keep up with celeb gossip, check the places they eat and shop, and the playgrounds they take their kids to, to increase chances of a star sighting.

Save yourself a lot of pavement-pounding by signing up to be a part of a live audience, **watching a TV show being taped or taking a studio tour.**

In Los Angeles, moviegoing is elevated to an art form. Instead of seeing a flick at the multiplex, catch what's showing at the **Hollywood Forever Cemetery** (aka "Resting Place of Hollywood's Immortals"), surrounded by the graves of Cecil B. DeMille, Jayne Mansfield, Rudolph Valentino, Douglas Fairbanks, and hundreds of other screen legends.

The Best Views

Perch yourself high above Hollywood Hills and have a **picnic at the Hollywood Bowl.** Choose your soundtrack from a lineup of rock concerts sponsored by local radio station KCRW or time it with a Los Angeles Philharmonic concert.

Top off any trip to Los Angeles—literally—by taking in the **view from the Griffith Observatory.** Located on the southern slope of Mount Hollywood in Griffith Park, the 75-year-old icon offers stellar views of the heavens thanks to the observatory's original 12-inch Zeiss refracting telescope as well as a trio of solar telescopes.

This is also one of the best vantage points to see the **Hollywood Sign.**

For a view of the sign from the ground, walk, run, or bike around **Hollywood Reservoir (aka Lake Hollywood) Trail.** The 4-mi flat walk around also offers great views of hillside mansions. The reservoir was built by the god of Los Angeles water, William Mulholland; its dam has a memorable movie cameo in Roman Polanski's *Chinatown.*

In addition, the 3-mi **Mt. Lee Trail,** which begins in Hollywood near the junction of Beachwood and Hollyridge drives, climbs 500 feet to the Hollywood Sign itself. You can't walk around the sign, but you can get about 100 yards from it, which is pretty good for snapshots.

GREAT ITINERARIES

The trick to having a decent quality of life in Los Angeles, claims one longtime Angeleno, is to live near where you work. The same adage holds true for visitors in that staying put in a single area of the city—being in a car for as short a time as possible—is a good rule of thumb. The best way to explore is one neighborhood at a time. Here are a few of our favorite itineraries to try.

Downtown Los Angeles

■ TIP➔ Best for fans of modern architecture and ethnic cuisine lovers.

If you have a half day: Formerly an unwelcoming neighborhood dominated by the glass and steel office buildings of Bunker Hill on one side and the poverty and despair of Skid Row on the other, downtown Los Angeles has staged a major comeback in recent years.

While the skyscrapers and tent cities still exist, there is also a middle ground that lures visitors with the promise of high art and historic architecture.

Don't miss the gems of Grand Avenue the Walt Disney Concert Hall and the Museum of Contemporary Art. At the concert hall, be sure to take the hour-long self-guided audio tour, which includes a walk through the venue's second-story hidden garden.

If you have a whole day: After checking out MOCA and Disney Hall, see the Art Deco icon Union Station to admire the heavy wood beam ceilings, leather upholstered chairs, and inlaid marble floors.

Then, walk across Alameda Street to stroll past the shops and restaurants of L.A.'s historic Olvera Street, where you'll find traditional Mexican fare. Other ethnic eats can be found venturing into Little Tokyo for a wide variety of Japanese cuisine or to Chinatown, especially for dim sum.

Hollywood

■ TIP➔ Best for first-timers to L.A., as well as film and music history buffs.

If you have a half day: Tourists flock to Hollywood Boulevard to see old movie palaces such as Grauman's Chinese Theatre, where movie stars have left their mark, literally, in the concrete courtyard of the theater since 1927.

These days the theater's entrance is also graced by dozens of impersonators—from Marilyn Monroe to Spiderman—who are more than happy to pose for photos with visitors.

Go to Hollywood & Highland Center for lunch, followed by a tour of the Kodak Theatre, which hosts the annual Academy Awards ceremony.

Wander the Walk of Fame, a 5-acre stretch of bronze stars embedded in pink terrazzo that lines Hollywood Boulevard to pay homage your favorite movie stars. Or visit independent record store Amoeba Records for just about everything a music lover could want.

If you have a whole day: Some of the historic movie palaces, including Grauman's, still show films, but the real movie buffs should opt to see a movie at the ArcLight, a state-of-the-art theater on Sunset Boulevard that features gourmet food and reserved seating. The ArcLight also boasts an in-house café bar that is perfect for a quick meal before a film or an après-show martini.

West Hollywood

■ TIP➔ Best for trend-savvy shoppers, farmers' market foodies, and parents pushing strollers.

If you have a half day: Thanks to its central location, West Hollywood is the ideal place to spend a couple of hours without committing an entire day—not that there isn't a day's worth of things to do in this neighborhood.

A shopping hub in its own right, visitors can choose to stroll around the outdoor pedestrian area, The Grove, or at the mammoth indoor Beverly Center. There are also countless small boutiques and specialty shops lining Beverly Boulevard, Third Street, and Melrose Avenue.

For lunch, grab a corned beef sandwich or some matzo ball soup at Canter's Delicatessen, a Los Angeles landmark since 1931, or to the Farmers Market for a collection of ethnic food stalls and local products.

If you have a whole day: Tack Robertson Boulevard onto your shopping agenda to find boutiques ranging from the local favorite American Apparel to the celebrity magnet Kitson.

West Hollywood is known for its buzzing nightlife, so afterward choose from hundreds of small restaurants for dinner, then follow up with a drink from one of the area's many bars.

Beverly Hills and the Westside
■ TIP→ Best for high-end shoppers, ladies who lunch, and contemporary art museum -goers.

If you have a half day: Depending on how hardcore of a shopper you are, you can easily check out the boutiques of Beverly Hills in a couple of hours. In fact, with all of the designer flagships and tony department stores, it might be dangerous to spend too much time (translation: too much money) in this ritzy neighborhood.

Hit Rodeo Drive for all of the runway names, such as Chanel, Christian Dior, Dolce & Gabbana, Fendi, Gucci, Prada, Valentino, and Versace.

Of course, not all of the action is on Rodeo; don't forget to wander the side streets for more high-fashion. The department stores—Barneys New York, Neiman Marcus, and Saks Fifth Avenue—are located nearby on Wilshire Boulevard. After you finish shopping refuel with a dose of sugar at local dessert favorite Sprinkles Cupcakes.

If you have a whole day: After all that shopping, jump in the car to get some culture by heading east to the Miracle Mile, a stretch of Wilshire Boulevard that's home to the mammoth Los Angeles County Museum of Art as well as smaller museums, such as the Craft and Folk Art Museum.

Santa Monica and the Beaches
■ TIP→ Best for families with kids of all ages, sun worshipers and surfers, and anyone who likes cruising in a convertible.

If you have a half day: With a couple of hours on your hands, it's a quick trip (if there's no traffic) to the beaches of Santa Monica or Venice. While they may not offer quite as much in the natural beauty department as their Malibu counterparts, they have plenty of sights of a different variety.

Don't miss the boardwalk vendors who hang out on Venice Beach or the street performers who frequent the Santa Monica Pier. Grab a snack at one of the beach-themed restaurants on the Strand such as divey Big Dean's Oceanfront Café or dressy Shutters on the Beach.

If you have a whole day: The ideal way to see Los Angeles' most beautiful beaches

is to set aside an entire day for Malibu. Driving down the scenic Pacific Coast Highway is a treat in and of itself with sheer cliffs on one side of the road and ocean views on the other.

Topanga State Beach, Malibu Lagoon State Beach, and Malibu Surfrider Beach are all beautiful and popular spots to pass the day, but it's worth the extra drive time to see Point Dume State Beach, which is nestled away from the hustle and bustle of the highway.

Be sure to seek out the single-track trail that winds its way up a nearby coastal bluff revealing breathtaking views of Santa Monica Bay, the Malibu Coast, and Catalina Island. Stop for lunch at any of the seafood shacks that line PCH.

Los Feliz, Silver Lake, and Echo Park

■TIP➜ Best for scene-seeking hipsters and young professionals looking to blow off steam.

If you have a half day: Venture out to Silver Lake hot spot Sunset Junction for off-beat finds such as one-of-a-kind threads at Matrushka Construction, handmade leather bags at Dean Accessories, and quirky home goods at Reform School.

Grab a cup of joe at Intelligentsia Coffee and some tasty treats at the Cheesestore of Silverlake next door. For lunch, check out one of many sidewalk cafés that line Sunset Boulevard.

If you have a whole day: After you check out Sunset Junction, jump in the car and drive to Los Feliz for more shopping and sightseeing on the bustling Hillhurst and Vermont avenues.

In the evening, catch a show at one of the area's famed live music venues, The Echo in Echo Park or Spaceland in Silver Lake, followed by a drink at local hang El Prado.

Pasadena and Environs

■TIP➜ Best for multigenerational groups, as well as art and architecture aficionados.

If you have a half day: Aside from spending time pouring over the massive collection of rare manuscripts and books at the Huntington Library, be sure to set aside a couple of hours for the Botanical Gardens to explore the more than a dozen themed areas, including authentic examples of both Japanese and Chinese gardens.

The Huntington has a beautiful outdoor café, as well as the Rose Garden Tea Room, where you can grab a tasty treat.

Another must-see museum is The Norton Simon Museum, with a collection that includes everything from ancient Asian art to 20th-century works.

If you have a whole day: Take a tour of Charles and Henry Greene's 1908 masterpiece the Gamble House, followed by a trip to the Castle Green, the architects' Moorish Colonial and Spanish style building.

Then, walk around into Old Town Pasadena, a revitalized shopping area with boutiques and eateries housed in historic buildings.

If you happen to be here during the once-a-month, massive Rose Bowl Flea Market, which takes over the Rose Bowl parking lot, you can browse around roughly 2,500 vendors' stalls.

FREE AND ALMOST FREE

Even in this town—where money seems to ooze from every hill and corner—there are plenty of fun things to do that are free and appeal to everyone from kids to art-lovers to movie and film buffs. These are some of our top picks.

Be Part of the Audience. Watching one of your favorite television or awards shows being filmed is an exciting experience that will make you feel as if you're part of the entertainment industry. **Audiences Unlimited** (⌧ *100 Universal City Plaza, Bldg. 153, Universal City* ☎ *818/260–0041* ⊕ *www.tvtickets.com*) helps fill seats for television programs (and sometimes for televised award shows). The free tickets are distributed on a first-come, first-served basis to those 16 and older.

See the Great Grunion Runs. The most popular and most unusual form of fishing in the L.A. area involves no hooks, bait, or poles, and is absolutely free. The grunion runs, which take place from March through July, occur when hundreds of thousands of small silver fish called grunion wash up on Southern California beaches to lay their eggs in the sand. The fish can be picked up by hand while they are briefly stranded on the beach. All that's required is a fishing license and a willingness to get your toes wet.

Spend the Evening on the Griffith Observatory's Rooftop Observation Deck. Known for stunning and famous views of Los Angeles, this rooftop deck is open until 10 pm every night except Monday, when the Observatory is closed.

Watch Rehearsals at the Hollywood Bowl. There's no charge to visit the Hollywood Bowl and the grounds that surround it, but an even better tip is that in the summer, from 9 am to noon on Tuesday, Thursday, and Friday, it's possible to watch rehearsals for free. Take a snack and enjoy the view. If you can't make a rehearsal, seeing stark-white amphitheater with the Hollywood sign set against the mountains in the background is worth the trip alone.

Visit the Paramount Ranch. One least-known way to experience an on-location studio set is also completely free. Just a short drive from Hollywood up into the hills of the Santa Monica Recreation Area is this the Paramount Ranch (⌧ *2813 Cornell Rd., Agoura Hills* ☎ *818/260–0041* ⊕ *www.tvtickets.com*), 2,700 acres of land that Paramount Pictures bought in 1927 as a real ranchland getaway for its stars. It later became used for filming, and today you can tour many of the backlots used in movies such as Oscar-nominated *I Married a Witch* from 1942, and from the television show *M*A*S*H*.

Check Out Free Days and Nights at Museums. The best freebie is without a doubt the Getty Center, but just about all the other major museums in Los Angeles have free days, including the Geffen Contemporary and the Museum of Contemporary Art, free on Thursday evenings from 5–8 pm. Also, several museums stay open as late as 9 pm some nights.

Visit the Hollywood Forever Cemetery. Inside the Hollywood Memorial Park right in the center of Hollywood, the Hollywood Forever Cemetery (⌧ *6000 Santa Monica Blvd., Hollywood* ⊕ *www.hollywood forever.com*) is where several of the film industry's famous are buried. Pick up a free map just inside for a self-guided tour.

LOS ANGELES WITH KIDS

With seemingly endless sunny days, Angeleno kids almost never have to play indoors. There are a few things to keep in mind, however, when navigating the City of Angeles with your pint-size angel: If possible, avoid the freeways by exploring no more than one neighborhood each day; and you can never have too much sunscreen (L.A. moms don't leave home without the stuff).

Aquarium of the Pacific

A huge tank with shimmering schools of fish and swaying kelp forest? Check. Shark lagoon featuring more than 150 varieties, including gray nurse, sand tiger, and whitetip? Check. Tropical reef habitat filled with zebra sharks, porcupine puffers, and a large blue Napoleon wrasse? Check. Head down to this Long Beach–based epicenter for all things aquatic and to learn tons of interesting facts about the Pacific Ocean.

California Science Center/ Natural History Museum of Los Angeles County

Don't miss your chance to test ride a high-wire bicycle or catch a film on the seven-story IMAX theater. Then, just down the road is the Natural History Museum, where kids can explore everything from diamonds to its new dinosaur hall. In spring, don't miss the outdoor butterfly habitat, fittingly named the Pavilion of Wings, which makes way for the Spider Pavilion come fall.

The Disneyland Resort

Experience all the classic attractions that you may recall from your own childhood visit, such as the "It's a Small World" ride, a meet-and-greet with Tinkerbell, or a Mickey Mouse home tour, who, unlike less amenable celebrities, makes a daily appearance for fans.

Griffith Park

It's the largest municipal park and urban wilderness area in the United States, and the kids will go wild for the pony rides and the classic 1926 merry-go-round. But the pièce de résistance is the Griffith Park and Southern Railroad, a circa-1940s miniature train that travels through an old Western town and a Native American village. Other highlights are the Los Angeles Zoo and the Griffith Observatory, an L.A. icon in its own right.

Kidspace Children's Museum

Little ones can pan for gold in a small creek, play Spiderman on a weblike climber, or race around a trike track (helmets are provided). Indoor activities include a walk-through kaleidoscope, two climbing towers—one mimicking raindrops, the other modeled after a wisteria vine—a bug diner (think: banana worm bread and roasted cricket pizza), and a contraption that lets kids generate their very own earthquake.

Santa Monica Beach

The best way to check out Santa Monica's beachfront is by renting bikes or roller skates at any one of the shacks on the Strand (a stretch of concrete boardwalk that snakes along the beach toward Venice). Some must-sees along the way: The roller dancers of Venice Beach, the body builders of Muscle Beach, and the Santa Monica Pier, a 100-year-old structure that's home to a vintage 1920s carousel, an oversized Ferris wheel, and old-time amusement park games. After hitting the beach, drive over to the pedestrian-only Third Street Promenade to grab a bite and do some shopping.

BEST GARDENS AND ZOOS

Thanks to its Mediterranean climate, Los Angeles can simulate a host of other environments ranging from lush tropical to bone-dry desert. So forgo the round-the-world plane ticket that you have been dreaming about and tour L.A.'s eclectic mix of gardens instead.

Descanso Gardens

Tucked away in the foothills of the San Gabriel Mountains in La Cañada Flintridge, Descanso Gardens is a plant-lovers paradise. Wander past the Craftsman-style entrance and find yourself winding through Japanese-theme gardens complete with bubbling fountains, koi ponds, and a traditional teahouse. The trail continues through a shady grove of native oaks under-planted with hundreds of varieties of camellia trees. Other highlights include a California native plants garden, a mini-railroad that runs on the weekends, and a scenic outdoor café.

Huntington Gardens

On more than 200 acres in the tony neighborhood of San Marino, the Huntington Gardens and Library is one of Los Angeles' most beautiful locales. With more than a dozen theme gardens, it is almost impossible to see the Huntington in one day. Don't miss the impressive bonsai collection and rock garden housed in the Japanese-theme garden, or the floating pagodas and lyrically named bridges of the Chinese garden. The water features of the children's garden are a hit with the kids as are the curvy paths that wind through the rainbow-hue succulent garden.

Los Angeles Zoo

Across from the Western-theme Autry Museum in Griffith Park, the L.A. Zoo is the perfect place to spend a couple of hours (unlike its bigger, badder San Diego counterpart, which demands an entire day). Of course, the L.A. Zoo's smaller size doesn't mean that its animals are any less impressive—simply that you can see more of them in a shorter amount of time. Be sure to check out the chimpanzee compound, the giraffe corral, the new and expanded elephant forest, and a lion and lioness dozing in the sun.

Rancho Santa Ana Botanic Garden

True or false: The palm tree is native to California. Surprisingly, the answer is false. Despite the city's iconic tree-lined boulevards, the palm was actually imported from more tropical locales. For the native plant aficionado, the Rancho Santa Ana Botanic Garden offers a sneak peek into what the region may have looked like before nonindigenous species were introduced. Think stately old oak trees stretching their branches over manzanitas and lots of lilac and sage bushes.

Murphy Sculpture Garden/UCLA Hannah Carter Japanese Garden

The UCLA campus offers a shady haven from the sun-drenched concrete corridors of Los Angeles—not to mention a top-notch outdoor sculpture collection that includes 70 sculptures by artists such as Alexander Calder, Henry Moore, Isamu Noguchi, Auguste Rodin, and Richard Serra. UCLA also runs a little-known Japanese garden located off-campus on a hillside plot in Bel Air. This classical Japanese garden features authentic water basins, stone carvings, and a five-tiered pagoda. But be forewarned: Reservations are required, so plan ahead.

L.A. LIKE A LOCAL

Hordes of tourists descend on Los Angeles each year with visions of seeing stars—of the Hollywood Boulevard and celebrity variety that is—but before you purchase that star map there are a few things you should know about how to live like a local.

For starters, never bat an eye when you encounter a movie star. Remember they are real people, too (albeit real people who live like royalty). Here are a few activities to help you fit in with the natives.

Bike the Strand

Despite urban myths that claim otherwise, Angelenos do abandon their cars every now and then—especially if it's to rent an old-school beach cruiser and bike down the 22-mi-long Strand, which stretches from Will Rogers State Beach in Santa Monica to Torrance County Beach in Redondo.

The Strand runs parallel to the Pacific Ocean through Santa Monica and Venice. Don't miss one-of-a-kind sights, including the oversize Ferris wheel on the Santa Monica Pier, the greased up bodybuilders of Muscle Beach, and the roller dancers (think disco on roller skates) of Venice Beach. And if biking isn't your thing, there are plenty of roller-bladers and walkers as well.

Drive-Through In-N-Out

It's no secret that the people of Los Angeles love their cars. In fact, they're famous for driving convertibles, scoffing at the idea of public transportation, and spending an inordinate amount of time on freeways.

But what the casual observer may not know is that Angelenos have another passion—for the local burger chain In-N-Out—that, thankfully, is perfectly car-friendly. Of course, Angelenos don't get out of their cars to make this magical moment happen. Easy directions: Drive up to an In-N-Out window, order from the secret menu (available online), and enjoy your "Animal Style" in the car.

Eat at the Farmers Market

At 3rd and Fairfax, the Farmers Market is pretty much Los Angeles' version of a community center. Everyone comes here to eat, drink and, most importantly, people-watch. Founded by a collective of farmers in 1934, the Farmers Market now houses more than 85 shops and restaurants—you can find everything from a Brazilian grill to a French creperie to a Lebanese kebab stand—in an open-air bazaar ringed by stalls and stands.

The Farmers Market and the adjacent shopping area, The Grove, are also low-key places to spot celebrities going about their everyday business.

Try a Taco Truck

It seems that everyone in Los Angeles has a taco truck that they swear by. Typically, these taco stands on wheels have a regular corner and semi-regular hours. The only way to find a good one is to ask a local—or do some research on a foodie Web site.

Not all taco trucks are created equal and it pays to know the specialty of the house—or truck, that is. A few things that most taco trucks share in common: tasty tacos, cheap prices, and a locals-only peek into L.A.'s hometown cuisine.

See a Show at the Hollywood Bowl

No doubt you've seen the iconic dome in movies, but nothing compares to spending a summer evening in a bleacher seat (or, better yet, one of the coveted boxes) at the Hollywood Bowl. To really get your local on, pack a picnic complete with bottle of wine and wicker basket

and don't be afraid to share goodies with your neighbors.

Performances run the gamut from reggae night to rock concerts to Los Angeles Philharmonic performances. But as most Angelenos would agree, the experience is as much about sitting outside under the night sky as it is about the music.

Hike in Griffith Park

The park, extremely accessible from the city, offers a 53-mi network of trails, roads, and bridle paths. One of the most popular routes is up Mount Hollywood, which boasts panoramic views of the Los Angeles basin, the Griffith Observatory, and the Hollywood Sign along the way.

Stop at a Seafood Shack

There may be nothing that epitomizes Los Angeles more than a drive down the scenic Pacific Coast Highway, or PCH, as locals call it. After taking in the sweeping views and turquoise waters, stop at a seafood shack, such as Malibu Seafood or the Reel Inn, for some ahi burgers or fish-and-chips.

Afterward, check out one of Malibu's most beautiful beaches: Topanga State Beach, Zuma Beach, or the small and secluded La Piedra, El Pescador, and El Matador beaches.

Go to a Dodger or Lakers Game—or Both

One way to blend in with the locals is to surround yourself with them—literally.

Get out to Dodger Stadium for a baseball game, and don't forget to dress in all blue and eat a Dodger Dog while you're there. Unless it's a big game, Dodger tickets are easy to come by—especially if you're willing to sit in the cheap bleacher seats. You can also spend a bit more to sit in one of the special sections such as the All-You-Can-Eat Pavilion.

It's much harder to procure Lakers tickets when they play at Staples Center, but if you plan ahead, a Lakers game is a sure-fire way to see big celebrities and even bigger feats of aerodynamics.

Catch a Movie at the ArcLight

It would be an understatement to say that Angelenos take their movies seriously. Considering that the entertainment industry is many locals' bread and butter, it's no surprise that moviegoing ups the ante here, too. Look no further than the ArcLight in Hollywood for a signature L.A. moviegoing experience. The ArcLight has all the fixin's: stadium seating, gourmet food, and authentic costumes from films on display in the lobby.

But what sets the ArcLight above the rest is that each movie is introduced by a live announcer schooled in movie trivia. If you're super lucky, you might catch the directors as they frequently make appearances here to discuss their work.

If you want to *really* do it like a local, catch a flick in the middle of the day—remember, Angelenos have sunny days to burn.

MUSEUMS AND GALLERIES

Despite its long-standing reputation as a second-rate art capital after New York, Los Angeles easily vies for the top spot when it comes to its museum exhibitions and gallery shows.

The undisputed heavyweights are the **UCLA Hammer Museum**, the **Getty Center**, the **Los Angeles County Museum of Art**, and the **Museum of Contemporary Art**.

On the gallery front, the scene is no less colorful. Four major epicenters—Chinatown, Culver City, Santa Monica, and West Hollywood—boast hundreds of art spaces.

MUSEUMS

On a busy stretch of Wilshire Boulevard in Westwood, the **UCLA Hammer Museum** (✉ *10899 Wilshire Blvd., Westwood* ☎ *310/443–7000* ⊕ *www.hammer.ucla. edu*) is known for cutting-edge exhibitions with a special emphasis on "the art of our time," as they put it. The Hammer also has an extensive library dedicated to the study of video art.

In a modernist compound of rough-hewn Italian travertine on a hilltop in the Santa Monica Mountains, the Richard Meier–designed **Getty Center** (✉ *1200 Getty Center Dr., Los Angeles* ☎ *310/440–7300* ⊕ *www.getty.edu*) has fabulous views of the Pacific Ocean and the San Gabriel Mountains, as well as an extensive garden designed by Robert Irwin. The permanent collection includes works from the 19th century to the present.

Also, don't miss the **J. Paul Getty Museum at the Getty Villa** (✉ *17985 Pacific Coast Hwy., Pacific Palisades* ☎ *310/440–7300* ⊕ *www.getty.edu*) in Pacific Palisades for Greek, Roman, and Etruscan antiquities.

Claiming the crown of the largest art museum in the western United States, the **Los Angeles County Museum of Art** (✉ *5905 Wilshire Blvd., Miracle Mile* ☎ *323/857– 6000* ⊕ *www.lacma*.org) is a complex of seven buildings with more than 100,000 objects dating from ancient times to the present.

Two of the newest attractions, both designed by Renzo Piano are the **Broad Contemporary Art Museum**, which features work by Richard Serra, Cindy Sherman, Jean-Michel Basquiat, Damien Hirst, Robert Rauschenberg, and many other top names, and the Resnick Pavilion for special exhibitions. LACMA may be the biggest museum in the West, but the **Museum of Contemporary Art** is certainly in the running in the best category, and is *the* place to go to see blockbuster exhibits. It has three buildings: **MOCA Grand Avenue** (✉ *250 S. Grand Ave., Downtown* ☎ *213/626–6222* ⊕ *www.moca.org*) and the **Geffen Contemporary** (✉ *152 N. Central Ave., Little Tokyo* ☎ *213/626–6222* ⊕ *www.moca.org*) are downtown; and the **Pacific Design Center** (✉ *8687 Melrose Ave., West Hollywood* ☎ *213/626–6222* ⊕ *www.moca.org*) is in West Hollywood.

GALLERIES

Chinatown

The pedestrian walkway, Chung King Road, becomes a block party during an evening of multi-gallery openings. Festive red lanterns zigzag overhead. The must-sees include **Telic Arts Exchange** (✉ *951 Chung King Rd., Chinatown* ☎ *213/229– 8907* ⊕ *www.telic.info*).

Culver City

Formerly a sleepy enclave populated by movie studios, Culver City is making a name for itself with dozens of world-class

galleries located within a three-block radius of each other. The tree-lined neighborhood also hosts regular art walks.

Be sure to stop at **Blum & Poe** (✉ 2727 S. La Cienega Blvd., Culver City ☎ 310/836–2062 ⊕ www.blumandpoe.com) and **Roberts & Tilton** (✉ 5801 Washington Blvd., Culver City ☎ 323/549–0223 ⊕ www.robertsandtilton.com).

Downtown

What started as a grassroots organizational effort with three galleries in the city's downtown Historic Core's Gallery Row neighborhood is now a monthly free event held on the second Thursday of every month, with 40 galleries that participate.

The largest concentration of galleries is in the area called "Gallery Row." Approximately 30 galleries and museums are within a short walk of one another.

The **Bert Green Fine Art** (✉ 102 W. 5th St., Downtown ☎ 213/624–6212 ⊕ www.bgfa.us) on the ground floor of the Rosslyn Hotel was one of the pioneering spaces in the district, and specializes in contemporary California artists.

The **Gallery at REDCAT** (✉ 631 W. 2nd St., Downtown ☎ 213/237–2800 ⊕ www.redcat.org) in Walt Disney Concert Hall is another must-see.

Santa Monica

Constructed in 1875 as a stop for the Red Line trolley, the industrial complex known as **Bergamot Station** (✉ 2525 Michigan Ave., Santa Monica ☎ 310/829–5854 ⊕ www.bergamotstation.com) is now Southern California's largest art gallery complex and cultural center, with more than 30 contemporary art galleries, the **Santa Monica Museum of Art** (✉ 2525 Michigan Ave., Santa Monica ☎ 310/586–6488 ⊕ www.smmoa.org), several architecture and design firms, and a café.

West Hollywood and Beverly Hills

When Angelenos talk about art galleries the buzz is always about Chinatown, Culver City, and Bergamot Station. Yet West Hollywood and Beverly Hills have more than 40 noteworthy galleries, many of which are West Coast outposts of major New York counterparts.

The best include the **Gagosian Gallery** (✉ 456 N. Camden Dr., Beverly Hills ☎ 310/271–9400 ⊕ www.gagosian.com), **Margo Leavin** (✉ 812 N. Robertson Blvd., West Hollywood ☎ 310/273–0603 ⊕ www.margoleavingallery.com), **New Image Art** (✉ 7908 Santa Monica Blvd., West Hollywood ☎ 323/654–2192 ⊕ www.newimageartgallery.com), **Otero Plassart** (✉ 820 N. Fairfax Ave., Los Angeles ☎ 323/951–1068 ⊕ www.oteroplassart.com), **Prism** (✉ 8746 W. Sunset Blvd., West Hollywood ☎ 310/289–1301 ⊕ www.prismla.com), and **Regen Projects** (✉ 633 N. Almont Dr., Los Angeles ☎ 310/276–5424 ⊕ www.regenprojects.com).

GREAT ARCHITECTURE

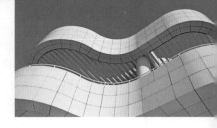

Sorry, New York, you may offer the best of the best in other categories, but when it comes to groundbreaking new architecture, Los Angeles takes the prize (the Pritzker, that is).

Amid the patchwork of California bungalows and stucco Caliterraneans that dot the cityscape dwell some of the last century's most notable architectural feats. Here are a few examples that no architecture buff should miss.

Downtown

A stone's throw from the blaring ranchero music of South Broadway, the circa 1880s **Bradbury Building** (✉ *304 S. Broadway, Downtown*) designed by George H. Wyman lays testament to downtown's halcyon days.

This Victorian-style office building, best known for the intricate cast iron metalwork that details its soaring, light-filled atrium, is a mecca for architecture students. Don't be surprised if you see a few artsy types soaking up the ambience.

Just a short walk away, join the horde of photographers snapping photos on Grand Avenue. No, it's not a celebrity-fueled paparazzi gathering, just the day's crew of people snapping photos of Frank Gehry's **Walt Disney Concert Hall** (✉ *111 S. Grand Ave., Downtown* ☎ *323/850–2000* ⊕ *www.laphil.com*). Wrapped in curving stainless steel, the music hall possesses a clothlike quality reminiscent of a ship's sails billowing in the wind.

And then there's L.A.'s other major Gehry favorite, the **Geffen Contemporary** (✉ *152 N. Central Ave., Downtown* ☎ *213/626–6222* ⊕ *www.moca-la.org*), which opened in the early '80s as a temporary space for works housed inside the **Museum of Contemporary Art** (✉ *250 S. Grand Ave.,* *Downtown* ☎ *213/626–6222* ⊕ *www.moca.org*), designed by Arata Isozaki. MOCA, located on Grand Avenue, retained the Geffen as an exhibition space and also has the Pacific Design Center, located on Melrose Avenue.

Echo Park

Resembling a street from another era (if not another city entirely), the **1300 block of Carroll Avenue** in Angelino Heights claims the city's highest concentration of Victorian houses.

After a series of major renovations in recent years, the homes lining both sides of the block are textbook examples of the intricate, brightly painted styles popular at the turn of the last century.

Considering that several of the houses are designated historical monuments, it may come as no surprise that they are often rented for film shoots. Look for the **Sessions House (No. 1330)** and the **Haunted House (No. 1345)**—the latter seen in Michael Jackson's Thriller video.

To get to Carroll Avenue from Downtown, take Temple Street west to Edgeware Road, turn right onto Edgeware, and go over the freeway. Carroll Avenue is on the left.

Hollywood, Los Feliz, and Silver Lake

A fine example of Frank Lloyd Wright's work, the '20s-era **Hollyhock House** (✉ *4800 Hollywood Blvd., Los Feliz* ☎ *323/644–6269* ⊕ *www.hollyhockhouse.net*) can be found in scenic Barnsdall Art Park.

These hilly neighborhoods also feature countless examples of work by Richard Neutra, such as his 1928 ode to steel columns and casement windows, the **Lovell House** (✉ *4616 Dundee Dr., Los Feliz*), and his former studio space on Glendale Boulevard.

Other must-sees are Rudolf Schindler's hillside **W. E. Oliver House** (⊠ *2236 Micheltorena St., Silver Lake*) and the much-photographed **Stahl House, Case Study House No. 22** (⊠ *1635 Woods Dr., Hollywood Hills* ⊕ *www.stahlhouse.com*) by Pierre Koenig.

Santa Monica and Venice Beach

Aside from his heavy-hitters downtown, Frank Gehry spread his architectural talent all over the city of Los Angeles, including buildings along the coast. Two of note are the **Gehry House** (⊠ *1002 22nd St., Santa Monica*), built in 1978 in Santa Monica, and the colorful **Venice Beach House** (⊠ *2509 Ocean Front Walk, Venice* ⊕ *www.stahlhouse.com*), which was completed in 1986.

Pasadena

Home to countless examples of the California Craftsman, Pasadena lays claim to the quintessential example, Charles and Henry Greene's **Gamble House** (⊠ *4 Westmoreland Pl., Pasadena* ☎ *626/793–3334* ⊕ *www.gamblehouse.org*). Built in 1908, the house is heavy on stained glass and teak woodwork.

If the Gamble House doesn't satiate your appetite for all things Greene and Greene, check out the **Castle Green** (⊠ *99 S. Raymond Ave., Pasadena* ☎ *626/793–0359* ⊕ *www.castlegreen.com*), a seven-story Moorish Colonial and Spanish-style building on a palm-tree lined site in Old Town Pasadena.

South Los Angeles

Few tourists make it to the neighborhood formerly known as South Central Los Angeles (the City officially changed its moniker to South Los Angeles in 2003), thanks in large part to the infamous Watts Riots of 1965 and the well-documented gang violence of the early '90s.

But those who do will not be sorry. Simon Rodia's **Watts Towers** (⊠ *1761–1765 E. 107th St., Watts* ⊕ *www.wattstowers.us*) consist of 17 sculptures constructed of steel and covered with a mosaic of broken glass, seashells, and pieces of 20th-century American ceramics.

Other architectural highlights are the **Bailey House, Case Study House No. 21** (⊠ *9038 Wonderland Park Ave., Los Angeles*) in the Hollywood Hills, and the **Eames House** (⊠ *203 Chautauqua Blvd., Pacific Palisades* ⊕ *www.eamesfoundation.org*) in Pacific Palisades.

L.A.'S BEST
BEACHES

You're in L.A., so seeing the coast is a must. Before you pack your picnic, do some planning and pick a beach that suits your needs.

The Pacific can be cold, but swimming is not the only attraction along the coast. Santa Monica Pier is nostalgic fun, with old-school amusement-park rides. Nearby you can rent bikes to ride along the Venice Boardwalk. Or, with more time, take that convertible up the Pacific Coast Highway to Malibu.

Best All-Around Beach

Santa Monica. A wide swath of sand, plenty of people-watching, good swimming, great views from the bluffs—other than its surfing (nil), this beach hits the key marks. Plus it has the added benefit of adjoining Santa Monica Pier, fun for families during the day and hordes of teenagers at night.

Best For Activities

Redondo and Zuma. Both have volleyball, snorkeling, and fishing. Zuma has a playground, while Redondo's got a pier with places to eat and shop.

Easiest Parking

Venice at Ocean Front Walk. This beach is at the west end of Rose Avenue, and if you're looking for a quick hop in the ocean or a brief surf run, it's your best bet.

Best for People-Watching

Venice City Beach. Check out the scene on its boardwalk, volleyball courts, and nonstop parade of characters. Runner-up: Manhattan Beach, though the people are more cookie-cutter. Note that the crowds here (and the traffic) can be a bit crazy and overwhelming on weekends.

Best for Kids

Mother's Beach/Marina del Rey. A protected lagoon, barbecue pits, and a cool playground mean you can easily make a full day of it. If your kids want to go in the water, though, you should check the water conditions first, as pollution's been on the rise.

In Orange County, Huntington State Beach stands out for its family-friendly facilities and relatively easy parking.

Best Surfing

Malibu Lagoon/Surfrider. The waves are awesomely steady; an annual surfing competition is held here. Looking south to Orange County, the north side of Huntington City Beach is another surfing hot spot with consistent peaks.

Best for Walking

Malibu Lagoon. While it's not a large beach, the natural lagoon here is a bird sanctuary, and the trails are perfect for romantic sunset walks beneath the rocky bluffs.

Quietest Beach

Western end of Leo Carrillo. If it's seclusion you're after, it's worth braving the steep concrete steps of Staircase Beach; the descent leads to an idyllic crescent of sand and water that's rarely crowded. Runner-up: Robert H. Meyer, a trio of rocky coves. (Watch out for high tide.)

L.A.'S BEST FARMERS' MARKETS

A great way to get a taste of Southern California's bounty is to visit its farmers' markets, where hundreds of family farmers, sustainable ranchers, and artisan producers sell their products. A cross-section of the city—chefs, foodies, families, and seniors—mingle and sample their way through the best of the region's fresh produce, meat and fish, baked goods, and specialty products. Fruits and vegetables both recognizable and exotic get scooped up by the bag-full and local vendors offer tantalizing snacks like grilled corn, crepes, omelets, and tacos.

Markets are held every day of the week, but weekends are the most popular. Many have special events such as cooking demonstrations, pony rides, and live music. Get there early to avoid a crowd.

Southland Farmers' Market Association. Check with the Southland Farmers' Market Association for locations, days, and times of the more than 70 local markets. ⊕ *www.cafarmersmarkets.org.*

Here are a few of the best:

Beverly Hills Farmers' Market. Held Sunday 9–1, the Beverly Hills Farmers' Market showcases more than 60 farmers and vendors every week. ⊠ *Civic Center Dr. between Alpine Dr. and Foothill Rd.* ☏ *310/550–4796.*

West Hollywood Farmers' Market. The West Hollywood Farmers' Market, on Monday 9–2, is as busy and cheerful as a street fair. ⊠ *1200 N. Vista St., at Fountain Ave.* ☏ *323/845–6535.*

Hollywood Farmer's Market. This farmer's market is held Sunday 8–6. ⊠ *Ivar and Selma Aves.*

Santa Monica Wednesday Market. The best farmers' market in L.A. hands down is the Santa Monica Wednesday Market. Running from 8:30 to 1:30, it draws all the area's top chefs and amateur foodies alike. Depending on the time of year, you might be tempted by heirloom tomatoes, Chinese long beans, Persian cucumbers, or blood oranges. On Saturday 8:30–1, there's an organic produce market at this same location. Other Santa Monica markets are held Saturday at Pico and Cloverfield boulevards (8–1) and Sunday at Main Street and Ocean Park Boulevard (9:30–1). ⊠ *Arizona Ave. at 2nd St.* ☏ *310/458–8712.*

Los Angeles Farmers Market. If it's authentic tacos, award-winning pies, or other snacks you're after, visit the landmark Los Angeles Farmers Market, crammed with prepared foods from all corners of the globe. Most spots are fast-food–style eateries sharing a common seating area—good for people-watching. An authentic *croque monsieur* sandwich, as well as crepes both savory and sweet, are available at the **French Crepe Company** (☏ *323/934–3113* ⊕ *www.frenchcrepe. com*). Some of the city's best tacos, wrapped in freshly made tortillas, are found at **Loteria! Grill** (☏ *323/930–2211* ⊕ *www.loteriagrill.com*). Folks line up for the bold flavors of Louisiana—including jambalaya and one of the few authentic New Orleans–style muffuletta sandwiches in L.A.—at the **Gumbo Pot** (☏ *323/933–0358* ⊕ *www.thegumbopotla.com*). **Bob's Coffee & Doughnuts** (☏ *323/933–8929*) is legendary for its raspberry-filled "Bismarck" donuts, and some of L.A.'s most beloved pies are peddled at **Dupar's** (☏ *323/933–8446*). ⊠ *3rd St. and Fairfax Ave.* ☏ *310/993–9211* ⊕ *www. farmersmarketla.com.*

L.A. SPORTS ACTION

Los Angeles is a serious sports city, with many of its professional and college teams in playoffs. It's a great way to hang with the locals—if you can score tickets to games, that is.

Baseball

Dodgers. Watch the Dodgers take on their National League rivals while munching on pizza, tacos, or a foot-long "Dodger dog" at one of baseball's most comfortable ball parks, **Dodger Stadium** (⊠ *1000 Elysian Park Ave., exit off I–110, Pasadena Fwy.* ☎ *866/363–4377 ticket information* ⊕ *www.dodgers.com*).

Los Angeles Angels of Anaheim. The Los Angeles Angels of Anaheim won the World Series in 2002, the first time since the team formed in 1961, and play at the **Angel Stadium of Anaheim** (⊠ *2000 Gene Autry Way, Anaheim* ☎ *714/663–9000* ⊕ *www.angelsbaseball.com*).

Basketball

L.A.'s pro basketball teams play at the **Staples Center** (⊠ *1111 S. Figueroa St., Downtown* ☎ *213/742–7340 box office* ⊕ *www.staplescenter.com*).

Los Angeles Lakers. It's not easy to get tickets, but if you can don't miss the chance to see this championship-winning team. ☎ *310/426–6000* ⊕ *www.nba.com/lakers*.

Clippers. L.A.'s "other" team, the much-maligned but newly revitalized Clippers, sells tickets that are generally cheaper and easier to get than those for Lakers games. ☎ *888/895–8662* ⊕ *www.nba. com/clippers*.

Los Angeles Sparks. After the 2010 retirement of WNBA superstar Lisa Leslie, the Los Angeles Sparks have put the spotlight on rookie forward Candace Parker. ☎ *310/426–6031* ⊕ *www.wnba.com/ sparks*.

University of Southern California. The Trojans of the University of Southern California play at Galen Center. ☎ *213/740–4672* ⊕ *usctrojans.cstv.com*.

University of California at Los Angeles. The University of California at Los Angeles Bruins play at Pauley Pavilion on the UCLA campus. ☎ *310/825–2101* ⊕ *uclabruins.collegesports.com*.

These schools go head-to-head in Pac 10 competition.

Football

Since the L.A. Avengers are now no longer, football in Los Angeles is all about the college teams. Fortunately, because they're some of the best matchups in the league, stadiums are packed and the games are well worth the price of admission.

USC Trojans. The USC Trojans play at the **L.A. Memorial Coliseum** (⊠ *3939 S. Figueroa St., Downtown* ☎ *213/748– 6136*), both a state and federal historic landmark. ☎ *213/740–4672* ⊕ *usctrojans. collegesports.com*.

UCLA Bruins. The UCLA Bruins pack 'em in at the **Rose Bowl** (⊠ *1010 Rose Bowl Dr., Pasadena* ☎ *626/449–7673*). ☎ *310/825– 2101* ⊕ *uclabruins.collegesports.com*.

Hockey

L.A. Kings. The National Hockey League's L.A. Kings are sometime playoff contenders at the Staples Center. ☎ *888/546–4752* ⊕ *www.lakings.com*.

Anaheim Ducks. The Anaheim Ducks push the puck at **Honda Center** (⊠ *2695 E. Katella Ave., Anaheim* ☎ *714/704–2500*). Long an underdog team, they became the first Southern California team to win the Stanley Cup in 2007. ☎ *877/945–3946* ⊕ *ducks.nhl.com*.

PLAYING GOLF IN L.A.

Given the near-perfect weather year-round in Southern California, golf is incredibly popular in Los Angeles. Beautiful public courses can be found in just about every area of the city.

Nissan Open. For those who love to watch the pros in action, the hot golf ticket in town each February is the PGA Northern Trust Open. The $6.4-million purse attracts the best golfers in the world to its week of competition at the Riviera Country Club in Pacific Palisades. ☎ 800/752–6736.

City Courses

Rancho Park Golf Course. The City Parks and Recreation Department lists seven public 18-hole courses in Los Angeles, and L.A. County runs some good ones, too. Rancho Park Golf Course is one of the most heavily played links in the country. It's a beautifully designed course, but the towering pines present an obstacle for those who slice or hook. There's a two-level driving range, a 9-hole pitch 'n' putt, a snack bar, and a pro shop where you can rent clubs. ✉ 10460 W. Pico Blvd., West L.A. ☎ 310/838–7373.

Griffith Park. Griffith Park has two splendid 18-hole courses along with two challenging 9-hole courses. **Harding Municipal Golf Course** and **Wilson Municipal Golf Course** (✉ 4900 Griffith Park Dr., Los Feliz ☎ 323/663–2555) are about 1½ mi inside the park entrance, at Riverside Drive and Los Feliz Boulevard. Bridle paths surround the outer fairways, and the San Gabriel Mountains make a scenic background.

Holmby Park Pitch 'n' Putt. The Holmby Park Pitch 'n' Putt is truly cozy: the longest hole is 68 yards. ✉ 601 Club View Dr., near Beverly Glen ☎ 310/276–1604.

Los Feliz

Los Feliz Municipal Golf Course. You may recall the 9-hole pitch 'n' putt Los Feliz Municipal Golf Course from the movie *Swingers.* ✉ 3207 Los Feliz Blvd., Los Feliz ☎ 323/663–7758.

Roosevelt Municipal Golf Course. The 9-hole Roosevelt Municipal Golf Course can be reached through the park's Vermont Avenue entrance. ✉ 2650 N. Vermont Ave., Los Feliz ☎ 323/665–2011.

The Valley

Sepulveda Golf Complex. Several good public courses are in the San Fernando Valley. The Sepulveda Golf Complex has the Balboa course (par 70) and the longer Encino course (par 72), plus a driving range. ✉ 16821 Burbank Blvd., Encino ☎ 818/995–1170.

Woodley Lakes Golf Course. Five lakes and occasional wildlife spottings make the Woodley Lakes Golf Course fairly scenic. It's flat and thus somewhat forgiving, but the back 9 is more challenging, with only one par 4 under 400 yards. ✉ 6331 Woodley Ave., Van Nuys ☎ 818/780–6886.

Pasadena and Environs

Los Verdes Golf Course. If you want a scenic course, the county-run, par-71 Los Verdes Golf Course has fierce scenery. You get a cliff-top view of the ocean—time it right and you can watch the sun set behind Catalina Island. ✉ 7000 W. Los Verdes Dr., Rancho Palos Verdes ☎ 310/377–7370.

Scholl Canyon Golf Club. Sitting on landfill, the Scholl Canyon Golf Club may only be a par 60, but it's fun and challenging, attractive for its top condition as well as its ups and downs and elevated views. ✉ 3800 E. Glenoaks Blvd., Glendale ☎ 818/243–4100.

SOUTH-OF-THE-BORDER FLAVOR

From Cal-Mex burritos to Mexico City–style tacos, Southern California is a top stateside destination for experiencing Mexico's myriad culinary styles.

Many Americans are surprised to learn that the Mexican menu goes far beyond Tex-Mex (or Cal-Mex) favorites like burritos, chimichangas, enchiladas, fajitas, and nachos—many of which were created or popularized stateside. Indeed, Mexico has rich, regional food styles, like the complex mole sauces of Puebla and Oaxaca and the fresh ceviches of Veracruz, as well as the trademark snack of Mexico City: tacos.

In Southern California, tacos are an obsession, with numerous blogs and Web sites dedicated to the quest for the perfect taco. They're everywhere—in ramshackle taco stands, roving taco trucks, and strip-mall taquerias. Whether you're looking for a cheap snack or a lunch on-the-go, SoCal's taco selection can't be beat. But be forewarned: there may not be an English menu. Here we've noted unfamiliar taco terms, along with other potentially new-to-you items from the Mexican menu.

THIRST QUENCHERS

Spanish for "fresh water," *agua fresca* is a nonalcoholic Mexican drink made from fruit, rice, or seeds that are blended with sugar and water. Fruit flavors like lemon, lime, and watermelon are common. Other varieties include *agua de Jamaica*, flavored with red hibiscus petals; *agua de horchata*, a cinnamon-scented rice milk; and *agua de tamarindo*, a bittersweet variety flavored with tamarind. If you're looking for something with a little more kick, try a *Michelada*, a beer that has been enhanced with a mixture of lime juice, chili sauce, and other savory ingredients. It's typically served in a salt-rimmed glass with ice.

DECODING THE MENU

Ceviche—Citrus-marinated seafood appetizer from the Gulf shores of Veracruz. Often eaten with tortilla chips.

Chile relleno—Roasted poblano pepper that is stuffed with ingredients like ground meat or cheese, then dipped in egg batter, fried, and served in tomato sauce.

Clayuda—A Oaxacan dish similar to pizza. Large corn tortillas are baked until hard, then topped with ingredients like refried beans, cheese, and salsa.

Fish taco—A specialty in Southern California, the fish taco is a soft corn tortilla stuffed with grilled or fried white fish (mahimahi or wahoo), pico de gallo, and shredded cabbage.

Gordita—"Little fat one" in Spanish, this dish is like a taco, but the cornmeal shell is thicker, similar to pita bread.

Mole—A complex, sweet sauce with Aztec roots made from more than 20 ingredients, including chiles, cinnamon, cumin, anise, black pepper, sesame seeds, and Mexican chocolate. There are many types of mole using various chiles and ingredient combinations, but the most common is *mole poblano* from the Puebla region.

Quesadilla—A snack made from a fresh tortilla that is folded over and stuffed with simple fillings like cheese, then toasted on a griddle. Elevated versions of the quesadilla may be stuffed with

sautéed *flor de calabaza* (squash blossoms) or *huitlacoche* (corn mushrooms).

Salsa—A class of cooked or raw sauces made from chiles, tomatoes, and other ingredients. Popular salsas include *pico de gallo*, a fresh sauce made from chopped tomatoes, onions, chiles, cilantro, and lime; *salsa verde*, made with tomatillos instead of tomatoes; and *salsa roja*, a cooked sauce made with chiles, tomatoes, onion, garlic, and cilantro.

Sopes—A small, fried corn cake topped with ingredients like refried beans, shredded chicken, and salsa.

Taco—In Southern California, as in Mexico, tacos are made from soft, palm-sized corn tortillas folded over and filled with meat, chopped onion, cilantro, and salsa. Common taco fillings include *al pastor* (spiced pork), *barbacoa* (braised beef), *carnitas* (roasted pork), *cecina* (chile-coated pork), *carne asada* (roasted, chopped beef), *chorizo* (spicy sausage), *lengua* (beef tongue), *sesos* (cow brain), and *tasajo* (spiced, grilled beef).

Tamales—Sweet or savory corn cakes that are steamed, and may be filled with cheese, roasted chiles, shredded meat, or other fillings.

Torta—A Mexican sandwich served on a crusty sandwich roll. Fillings include meat, refried beans, and cheese.

top left photo: ceviche; top right: fish taco; bottom left: tamales

DOWNTOWN CULINARY WALK

In the last few years, Downtown has blossomed into the dining "it" girl everyone wants to see, with so many ethnic eats, new upscale hot spots, and tasty classics. Traffic is ever-present, so park your car and walk.

Chinatown to Grand Central Market

Chinatown is a colorful fusion of the city's long-time Chinese community and a burgeoning artists' scene of art galleries and clothing boutiques. Along North Broadway you can find Central Plaza, a bright red Pagoda-esque shopping and dining hub home to the **Hop Louie** (⊠ *950 Mei Ling Way* ☎ *213/628–4244*), a Los Angeles dining relic loved for its Chinese food and cozy dive bar. For classic dim sum turn north on Hill Street to **Ocean Seafood** (⊠ *747 N. Hill St.* ☎ *213/687–3088*). For a bite of L.A. baking history, stop into **Phoenix Bakery** (⊠ *969 N. Broadway* ☎ *213/628–4642*), which has been baking its famous whipped strawberry cake since 1938. On Broadway, turn left toward the 100-year-old **Phillipe: The Original Restaurant** (⊠ *1001 N. Alameda* ☎ *213/628–3781*), which claims to have invented the French dip sandwich. Order your sandwich "single dip," "double dip," or "wet," corresponding to the amount of au jus you want on the bun.

Continuing on Broadway, pass the last remaining Chinese stores and step onto Olvera Street—L.A.'s Latino hamlet. Walk through the leather shops, past stores blaring mariachi music.

Take a snack break at **La Noche Buena** (⊠ *12 Olvera St.* ☎ *213/628–2078*), where tasty tacos and tamales beckon. For a sweet treat, try **Mr. Churro** (⊠ *15 Olvera St.* ☎ *213/680–9036*) for a $3 caramel, strawberry, or sweet cream stuffed fritter rolled in cinnamon sugar.

On Broadway, turn right to walk into the center of downtown. At about 1.2 mi you can find the **Grand Central Market** (⊠ *317 S. Broadway*), L.A.'s oldest open-air market and ethnic eats food court. This is a great place to come for buying spices, herbs, and produce from the specialty Latino and Asian markets.

7th Street to Little Tokyo

From the Grand Central Market your best bet is the Red Line to South Park—exit at 7th Street—the area's Financial District. Start at 7th Street/Metro Center and turn south toward Figueroa Boulevard, then straight toward the Staples Center. You'll walk past a number of chain eateries until you come upon L.A.'s oldest restaurant, the **Original Pantry Cafe** (⊠ *877 S. Figueroa* ☎ *213/972–9279*), which is known for its hearty breakfasts of pork chop and eggs or buckwheat pancakes. Continue south on Figueroa until you see the new loft developments and leafy courtyards that make up South Park. Stop off at **Rivera Restaurant** (⊠ *1050 S. Flower St.* ☎ *213/749–1460*), a block up from Figueroa, for a taste of excellent modern Latin cuisine and tasty mojitos.

Walk east down Olympic and make a left on Broadway. Just past W.7th St. is the entertainment complex **L.A. Live** (⊠ *800 W. Olympic Blvd.*) and **Staples Center** (⊠ *1111 S. Figueroa St.*), the sports arena that's home to the NBA's L.A. Lakers.

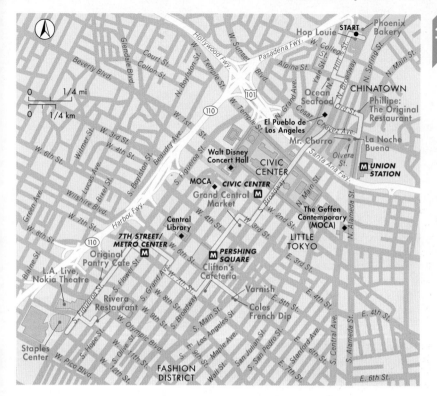

Highlights:	The historic charm of Chinatown and Olvera Street, and Downtown's artist core.
Where to start:	Chinatown; take a combination of bus and LA's Metro Line to see all the sights.
Length:	Duration depends on how quickly you get from spot to spot. Take half a day to really get a taste of the city.
Best time to go:	Daytime allows you to see all the sights, and you can enjoy the working community of Downtown. But at night you can enjoy the bustling happy hour, nightlife, and dining scene.
Worst time to go:	Early morning and after work hours because of traffic congestion.
Editor's choices:	The Historic Core has become such a lively center in Downtown, full of wonderful restaurants, gourmet markets, dessert shops

Clifton's Cafeteria (✉ *648 S. Broadway* ☎ *213/627–1637*), a historical landmark that's pure old-school kitsch. Order the hand-carved brisket and green Jell-O with a swirl of whipped cream. On Broadway head toward 6th Street and make a right. After a few blocks you pass Main Street and find **Coles French Dip** (✉ *118 6th St.* ☎ *213/622–4090*), now a hipster hangout, which has pastrami, lamb, turkey, or beef dips topped with "atomic pickles" or crumbled blue cheese. Get a side of excellent bacon-potato salad. The space is also home to the cocktail speakeasy **Varnish.**

CRUISING THE STRIP

For more than half a century, Hollywood's night owls have headed for the 1¾-mile stretch of Sunset Boulevard between Crescent Heights Boulevard on the east and Doheny Drive on the west, known as the Sunset Strip. The experience of driving it from end to end gives you a sampling of everything that makes L.A. what it is, with all its glamour and grit, and its history of those who rose fast and fell faster.

Left and top right, two views of Sunset Boulevard. Bottom right, Mel's Drive-in Diner.

In the 1930s and '40s, stars such as Errol Flynn and Rita Hayworth came for wild evenings of dancing and drinking at nightclubs like Trocadero, Ciro's, and Mocambo.

The Strip's image as Tinseltown's glamorous nighttime playground began to die in the '50s, and by the mid-'60s it was the center of L.A.'s raucous music-and-nightlife scene. Bands like the Doors and the Byrds played the Whisky a Go Go, and the city's counterculture clashed with police in the famous Sunset Strip curfew riots in the summer of 1966.

In the '70s, the Strip was all about glam rock, with David Bowie, T. Rex, and Queen hitting the venues. But this was when it began a decline that would last almost two decades, until it became a seedy section of the city where hookers hung out on every corner.

It's only been in the last five to seven years that the Strip has seen a true revitalization, with new hotels, restaurants, and bars opening that have become haunts for celebs and A-listers. It retains its rough-and-tumble image in some sections but overall is a much classier spot to spend a night out.

A CLASSIC DRIVE THROUGH L.A.

Depending on the time of day, driving the Strip is a different experience. In the afternoon grab lunch at a hotel and hobnob with industry types. At night, drive with the top down and come to hear music, hit a club, or have cocktails at a rooftop bar. Either way, it's good to park the car and walk (yes, walk!).

WHERE TO EAT & DRINK

See and be seen at **Skybar at the Mondrian Hotel** (✉ 8440 Sunset Blvd. ☎ 323/848–6025), the luxe outdoor lounge and pool deck. The bar opens to the public at 8 pm daily. Come early to enjoy sweeping views of the city before turning your gaze inward to the beautiful people milling around.

Laid-back hipsters and the occasional celebrity gather at the **Standard Hotel's Cactus Lounge** (✉ 8300 Sunset Boulevard ☎ 323/650–9090) and adjacent pool deck for mojitos and burgers. DJs and live bands play on some nights.

For a taste of L.A.'s swanky side, reserve a table at **Asia de Cuba** (✉ 8440 Sunset Blvd. ☎ 323/848–6000), a sleek restaurant inside the Mondrian Hotel. The all-white, Philippe Starck–designed dining room is a minimalist backdrop for the restaurant's colorful Latin-Asian fusion fare.

TIPS FOR PARKING

Parking and traffic around the Strip can be tough on weekends. Although there's some parking on side streets, it may be worth it to park in a lot and pay $10–$25. Most of the hotels have garages as well.

Gordon Ramsay at the London Hotel (✉ 1020 N. San Vicente Blvd. ☎ 310/358-7788) is one of the more glamorous dining experiences in town. Jeans and sandals are replaced by stilettos and sparkly dresses. For a more casual vibe, head to the bar or the adjacent Boxwood Café.

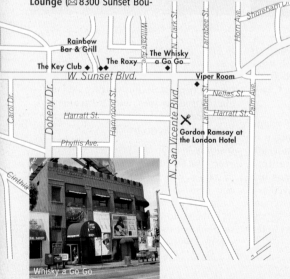

Whisky a Go Go

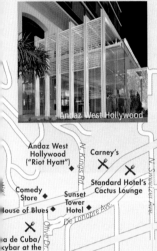

The Roxy

The Key Club

The Chateau Marmont

Sunset Blvd.

Andaz West Hollywood

Andaz West Hollywood ("Riot Hyatt")

Carney's

Comedy Store

Standard Hotel's Cactus Lounge

House of Blues

Sunset Tower Hotel

De Lonopre Ave.

a de Cuba/ kybar at the drian Hotel

Fountain Ave.

SIGHTS TO SEE

The Chateau Marmont
(8221 West Sunset Boulevard). Greta Garbo once called this castle-like hotel home. It's also where John Belushi died.

Comedy Store (✉ 8433 Sunset Boulevard). David Letterman and Robin Williams rose to fame here.

Sunset Tower Hotel (✉ 8358 Sunset Boulevard). Where Clark Gable, Marilyn Monroe, and John Wayne once lived.

Andaz West Hollywood ("Riot Hyatt") (✉ 8401 Sunset Boulevard). Led Zeppelin, the Rolling Stones, and the Who stayed and played here when they hit town.

Rainbow Bar & Grill (✉ 9015 Sunset Boulevard). Jimi Hendrix and Bob Marley began their climb to the top of the charts here.

The Whisky a Go Go (✉ 8901 Sunset Boulevard). This venue opened in 1964 and is credited as the first place go-go dancers danced in cages.

The Roxy (✉ 9009 Sunset Boulevard). Neil Young was the opening act here in 1973; it's been a Strip anchor and front-runner in revitalization.

The Viper Room (✉ 8852 Sunset Blvd.) This always popular, always booked venue was where River Phoenix OD'd in 1993.

The House of Blues (✉ 8430 Sunset Boulevard). This relative newcomer has hosted top acts such as Tupac Shakur and Prince with Maceo Parker.

The Key Club (✉ 9039 Sunset Boulevard). On the site where Gazzari's stood in the '60s (known as Billboard Live from 1996 to 1998), it's the place hard-rock bands like Bon Jovi and Def Leppard favor.

Stop in for a burger and shake at **Mel's Drive-In** (✉ 8585 Sunset Blvd. ☎ 310/854-7201), open 24 hours a day. The iconic 1950s-inspired diner in the heart of the Strip is a fun place to people-watch, day or night.

For the city's best hot dogs, chili fries, and frozen chocolate-dipped bananas, head to **Carney's** (✉ 8351 Sunset Blvd. ☎ 310/654-8300), a popular spot for a quick bite. You can't miss it—look for the yellow railcar.

A DRIVE BEYOND THE STRIP

California's Pacific Coast Highway at dusk

There's more to see along Sunset Boulevard than the Strip. If you have time and want to take another classic L.A. drive, you'll understand how Sunset Boulevard got its name if just before dusk you continue west until it ends at the ocean, where it hits the Pacific Coast Highway (PCH) in Pacific Palisades.

WHEN TO GO

If you time it right, you can catch that famous L.A. sunset. If that's not possible, late morning after rush hour is good as well. Arrive just in time for lunch at a waterfront restaurant or a picnic on the beach.

The PCH is also known for its fresh seafood shacks along the roadside. For a cocktail with a great view, try **Gladstone's 4 Fish** (✉ *17300 Pacific Coast Hwy.*), where Sunset Boulevard hits the PCH.

TRIP TIPS

While it's hard to tear your eyes away from sites along the way, there are hairpin turns on the Boulevard, and driving is challenging. Also stop-and-go traffic—especially along the Strip—means lots of fender benders. Be careful and keep a safe distance.

Sunset view from Gladstone's

Downtown
Los Angeles

WORD OF MOUTH

"If you have a chance, consider taking the guided walking tours organized by LA Conservancy. Most of the tours are on Saturday 10 am. We took one last year (Art Deco) and loved it."

—yk

GETTING ORIENTED

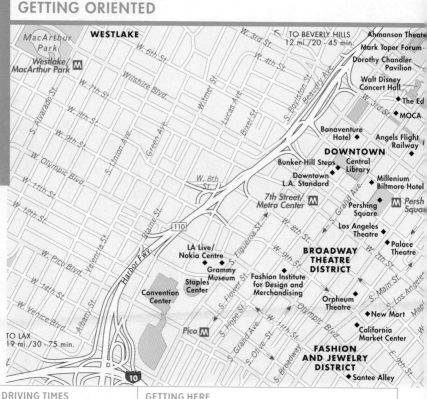

DRIVING TIMES AND DISTANCES

Minimum times listed below represent little to no traffic; maximum times assume the worst.

Adjust accordingly taking rush hour and peak weekend travel time into account.

■ **From LAX:** 30–75 min/19 mi

■ **From Los Feliz/Silver Lake:** 15–30 min/8 mi

■ **From Beverly Hills:** 20–45 min/12 mi

■ **From Pasadena:** 15–25 min/ 12 mi

■ **From Burbank:** 18–30 min/ 12 mi

GETTING HERE

Driving Strategy. The good news is that freeways 5, 101, 110, and 10 all get you there—but the bad news is that the traffic can be horrendous. If you're coming from the Los Feliz/ Silver Lake area, skip the freeways altogether and take Sunset Boulevard, which turns into César Chávez Boulevard. Make a right on South Grand Avenue, and after a few blocks you'll be in the heart of Downtown. If you're coming directly from LAX, take the 105 E to the 110 N exit to the 6th Street/9th Street exit toward Downtown/Convention Center/Figueroa Street.

Parking. If staying at a hotel downtown with a garage, keeping your car there and getting around by foot, cab, or even the metro is a better option than driving. If you must take your car, there are several options including lots and street parking, the latter being less convenient and ideal.

2

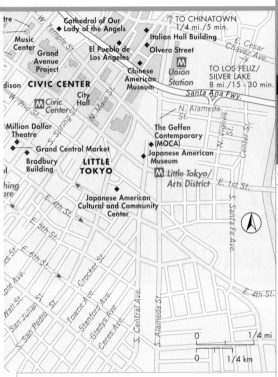

Map labels:
tre
W. Temple St.
Music Center
Grand Avenue Project
Cathedral of Our Lady of the Angels
El Pueblo de Los Angeles
Italian Hall Building
Olvera Street
TO CHINATOWN 1/4 mi./5 min.
E. Cesar Chavez Ave.
ison **CIVIC CENTER**
Chinese American Museum
Union Station
TO LOS FELIZ/ SILVER LAKE 8 mi./15 - 30 min.
N. Main St.
City Hall
Civic Center
Santa Ana Fwy.
N. Alameda St.
Million Dollar Theatre
Grand Central Market
Bradbury Building
LITTLE TOKYO
The Geffen Contemporary (MOCA)
Japanese American Museum
Little Tokyo/ Arts District
E. 1st St.
Japanese American Cultural and Community Center
E. 4th St.
E. 5th St.
Crocker St.
S. Santa Fe Ave.
E. 4th St.
0   1/4 mi
0   1/4 km

TOP REASONS TO GO

Visit Frank Gehry's Walt Disney Concert Hall. Be wowed by the genius architecture and grab tickets for a performance led by passionate conductor Gustavo Dudamel.

See a Lakers Game. Catch the action at the Staples Center and possibly rub elbows with stars such as Jack Nicholson and Leonardo DiCaprio.

Get Interactive at the Grammy Museum. Set your inner Rock God free playing virtual drums or learn about folk music from Bob Dylan at this highly interactive museum.

Take an Historic Walking Tour. The L.A. Conservancy offers several tours, such as of Olvera Street, where you can see traditional Mexican culture, eat, and shop for hand-crafted wares.

Soar Sky High at the Bonaventura Hotel. Sure, it's a bit retro, but the restaurant rotates and offers a stunning view. Then have a cocktail in a Hollywood Golden Age setting at The Edison.

PLANNING YOUR TIME

Visit weekdays during the day, when the area is bustling and restaurants are open for lunch. It's easy to find street parking on weekends, but with the exception of Chinatown, L.A. Live, Olvera Street, and destination-bars such as The Edison at night, the area shuts down.

Seeing everything in one day is possible, but it's best to spread it out over two. For art lovers, the Museum of Contemporary Art, MOCA at the Geffen Contemporary, the African American Museum, the Japanese American Museum, and the Chinese American Museum are worthy of more than just a pass-through.

Plan your visits around specific areas you can walk to in one circuit. Parking lots run $4–$12 so if you're on a budget, you don't want to be moving your car around too much.

The entertainment industry loves to use Downtown for movie backdrops, so when film crews take over entire blocks for shooting, traffic jams up in every direction.

BROADWAY'S HISTORIC THEATERS

From the late 19th century to the 1950s—before malls and freeways—Broadway glittered with the finest shops and the highest number of luxurious theaters in the world, making it a rich, cultural haven.

(above) The Palace Theatre, which opened in 1911. (lower right) The Orpheum Theatre. (upper right) The Million Dollar Theatre.

Though it remains the main road through Downtown's Historic District, the area has changed dramatically over the years.

Currently bustling with stores and businesses catering to a mostly Mexican and Central American immigrant community, between 1st and 9th streets you can find mariachi and *banda* music blaring from electronics-store speakers, street-food vendors hawking sliced papaya sprinkled with chili powder, and fancy dresses for a young girl's *Quinceañera* (15th birthday).

But to see the glory of its golden years, you merely have to look "up," above the storefront signs, to see the marvelous architecture and theater marquees of the majestic buildings they reside in.

FOR A GUIDED TOUR

The **Los Angeles Conservancy** regularly conducts Saturday-morning walking tours of Downtown architectural landmarks and districts.

Tours begin at 10 am, last about 2½ hours, and are offered rain or shine. Call for schedule and fees.

For information, call ☎ *213/623-2489* or visit ⊕ *www.laconservancy.org.*

THE MILLION DOLLAR THEATER

Million Dollar Theater. The Million Dollar Theater opened in 1918 as part of Sid Grauman's famed chain of movie theaters. This Spanish Baroque–style venue had the special feature of having its own organ. Film stars such as Gloria Swanson, Rudolph Valentino, and a young Judy Garland frequently made appearances. In the '40s, the venue swung with jazz and big-band performers including Billie Holiday.

The theater is open for special events and it's worth a stop if you're walking past to inspect the lavish exterior with entertainment figures carved into the molding. ⊠ *307 S. Broadway, Downtown* ☏ *213/617–3600* ⊕ *www.milliondollartheater.com.*

THE ORPHEUM THEATRE

Orpheum Theatre. Opened in 1926, the opulent Orpheum Theatre played host to live attractions including burlesque dancers, comedians, jazz greats like Lena Horne, Ella Fitzgerald, and Duke Ellington, and later on rock-and-roll performers such as Little Richard.

After massive renovation and restoration work, the Orpheum now books a variety of concerts and special events. It's worth the ticket price just to see the interior, with its stunning white marble lobby, majestic auditorium with fleur-de-lis sidewall panels, modern seating refurbished in vintage styling, exquisite detailed moldings, and two dazzling oversize chandeliers.

A thick red velvet and golden-trimmed curtain signals "Showtime," and a white Wurlitzer pipe organ (one of the last remaining organs of its kind from the silent movie era) is at the ready, as the original 1926 Orpheum rooftop neon sign again shines brightly over a new era for this theater. ⊠ *842 S. Broadway, Downtown* ☏ *877/677–4386* ⊕ *www.laorpheum.com.*

THE PALACE THEATRE

Palace Theatre. Built in 1911, the Palace Theatre is loosely styled after an Italian Renaissance palazzo. Though only the entrance is viewable through the locked gates, you can see the multicolor terra-cotta swags, flowers, fairies, and theatrical masks. Now the oldest remaining Orpheum Theatre in the country, the Palace still hosts occasional shows. ⊠ *630 S. Broadway, Downtown* ☏ *213/629–2939.*

THE LOS ANGELES THEATRE

Los Angeles Theatre. The Los Angeles Theatre, built in 1931, opened with the premiere of Charlie Chaplin's *City Lights.* Full of glorious French Baroque–inspired decor, the six-story lobby is awe-inspiring with its dramatic staircase, enormous fountain, grandiose chandeliers, and ornate gold detailing. Officially closed to the public, you can still witness the old Hollywood glamour by catching a special movie screening. ⊠ *615 S. Broadway, Downtown* ⊕ *www.losangelestheatre.com.*

Sightseeing
★★★★★
Nightlife
★★★
Dining
★★★
Lodging
★★
Shopping
★★★

If there's one thing Angelenos love, it's a makeover, and city planners have put the wheels in motion for a dramatic revitalization. Downtown is both glamorous and gritty and is an example of Los Angeles' complexity as a whole. There's a dizzying variety of experiences not to be missed here if you're curious about the artistic, historic, ethnic, or sports-loving sides of L.A.

Updated by
Alene Dawson

Glance in every direction and you'll see construction crews building luxury lofts and retail space aimed at making Downtown a one-stop destination to work, live, and play.

Two massive entertainment complexes are further transforming the area: The long-awaited Frank Gehry–designed Grand Avenue Project is in the works, to be built around the **Music Center** performance complex, and the newly built **L.A. Live/Nokia Theater** project, anchored around the **Staples Center** sports arena.

For art lovers, the **Geffen Contemporary at MOCA** is known for having one of the world's most important modern and contemporary art collections, and those who are fans of architecture should make a point to see another Gehry creation, the **Walt Disney Concert Hall**, or the massive, geometrically-designed **Cathedral of Our Lady for the Angels**.

As you venture into the ethnic enclaves of Downtown—**Chinatown, Little Tokyo,** and **El Pueblo de Los Angeles**—take advantage of the tastes, sounds, and sights. Eat duck in Chinatown, red bean cakes in Little Tokyo, or pickled cactus on **Olvera Street**. Spend time browsing at the **Grand Central Market**, where stalls are filled with colorful locally-grown produce and homemade treats such as tamales and olive bread.

Visit neighborhood cultural institutions including the **Chinese American Museum**, the **Japanese American National Museum**, and the **California African-American Museum**.

If traveling with kids, check out the **California Science Center** as well as the **Natural History Museum of Los Angeles County**, with its brand-new Dinosaur Hall.

TOP ATTRACTIONS

Fodor'sChoice **Cathedral of Our Lady of the Angels.**
★ A half block away from the giant rose-shaped steel grandeur of Frank Gehry's curvaceous Disney Concert Hall sits Cathedral of Our Lady of the Angels. It's a spiritual draw and an architectural attraction as well. The exterior is all strict soaring angles and the building is as heavy, solid, and hunkering as the Gehry building is feminine and ethereal.

Controversy surrounded Spanish architect José Rafael Moneo's unconventional, costly, austere design for the seat of the Archdiocese of Los Angeles. But judging from the swarms of visitors and the standing-room-only holiday masses, the church has carved out a niche for itself in Downtown's daily life.

Opened in 2002, the ocher-concrete cathedral looms up by the Hollywood Freeway. The plaza in front is relatively austere, glaringly bright on sunny days; a children's play garden with bronze animals helps relieve the stark space.

Imposing bronze entry doors, designed by local artist Robert Graham, are decorated with multicultural icons and New World images of the Virgin Mary. The canyonlike interior of the church is spare, polished, and airy. By day, sunlight illuminates the sanctuary through translucent curtain walls of thin Spanish alabaster, a departure from the usual stained glass.

Artist John Nava used residents from his hometown of Ojai, California, as models for some of the 135 figures in the tapestries that line the nave walls. Make sure to go underground to wander the bright, mazelike white-marble corridors of the mausoleum.

Free guided tours start at the entrance fountain at 1 on weekdays. Check for free concerts inside of the Cathedral on Wednesdays at noon. There's plenty of underground visitor parking; the vehicle entrance is on Hill Street. ■TIP→ **The café in the plaza has become one of Downtown's favorite lunch spots. You can pick up a fresh, reasonably priced meal to eat at one of the outdoor tables.** ⊠ *555 W. Temple St., Downtown* ☎ *213/680–5200* ⊕ *www.olacathedral.org* ✉ *Free, parking $3 every 20 min, $18 maximum* ☼ *Weekdays 6–6, Sat. 9–6, Sun. 7–6.*

Fodor'sChoice **The Geffen Contemporary at MOCA.** Frank Gehry transformed what was
★ a former police warehouse in Little Tokyo into this top-notch museum, originally built as a temporary exhibit hall while the **Museum of Contemporary Art** (**MOCA**) was under construction at California Plaza. Thanks to its popular reception, the Geffen, with 40,000 square feet of exhibition space, is the museum's main site.

The permanent collection, spanning American and European art from 1940 to the present, includes heavy hitters such as Mark Rothko, Jackson Pollack, Frank Stella, Willem de Kooning, Jasper Johns, Diane

The Cathedral of Our Lady of the Angels, one of Downtown's must-sees, is a 21st-century architectural landmark.

Arbus, and Robert Frank, among others. Much of it is housed here, as well as at two other satellite buildings. **MOCA Grand Avenue** (✉ *250 S. Grand Ave., Downtown* ☎ *213/626–6222* ⊕ *www.moca.org* ☐ *$10, free Thurs. 5–8* ⊘ *Mon. and Fri. 11–5, Thurs. 11–8, weekends 11–6. Closed Tues. and Wed.*) is a smaller space with underground galleries and the flagship MOCA Store, and in West Hollywood, the **Pacific Design Center** (✉ *8687 Melrose Ave., West Hollywood* ☎ *213/626–6222* ⊕ *www.moca.org* ☐ *Free* ⊘ *Tues–Fri. 11–5, weekends 11–6. Closed Mon.*) focuses on architecture and design.

The museum holds at least 20 top-notch, well-curated and imaginative themed shows annually, drawing crowds nationwide and internationally as well. ✉ *153 N. Central Ave., Downtown* ☎ *213/626–6222* ⊕ *www.moca.org* ☐ *$10, free Thurs. 5–8* ⊘ *Mon. and Fri. 11–5, Thurs. 11–8, Sat. 11–9, Sun. 11–6. Closed Tues.*

Grand Central Market. Handmade white-corn tamales, warm olive bread, dried figs, Mexican fruit drinks. Hungry yet? This mouthwatering gathering place is the city's largest and most active food market. The spot bustles nonstop with locals and visitors surveying the butcher shop's display of everything from lambs' heads to pigs' tails; produce stalls are piled high with locally grown avocados and heirloom tomatoes. Stop by **Del Rey**, at stall A7, for a remarkable selection of rare chilies and spices. Even if you don't plan to buy anything, the market is a great place to browse and people-watch. ✉ *317 S. Broadway, Downtown* ☎ *213/624–2378* ⊕ *www.grandcentralsquare.com* ☐ *Free* ⊘ *Daily 9–6.*

★ **L.A. Live / Nokia Theater.** Filling the void that was a no-man's-land except for the legendary Staples Center sports arena, mammoth L.A. Live/

BEST SPOTS FOR STAR-SIGHTING

■ **Courtside seats at a Lakers game during the playoffs.** Best way to see Kobe up close? Be a celebrity, know a celebrity, or be a celebrity's agent. Having an in at one of the big downtown law firms that often buy season tickets is also a winning strategy. Otherwise, hire a private concierge service and be prepared to pay—a lot. Whatever you do, don't buy tickets off the street or randomly online. Your ticket source should be well-known and trusted.

■ **Opening night galas.** Try for Disney Hall or preview opening parties at the Museum of Contemporary Art. Celebrities support their fellow artists in Los Angeles and often entry to these fêtes is as easy as paying for the ticket to get in.

■ **The rooftop bar at the Standard.** The place still has enough buzz to attract the occasional celebrity. Booking a room is the surest way to gain access to the rooftop bar and pool. Word of advice: Never name drop in Los Angeles. People who are truly connected here don't have to.

Nokia Center is the place to enjoy an evening of entertainment without driving all over town—a rare occurrence in Los Angeles!

The first things that you'll notice as you emerge from the parking lot are the giant LED screens and sparkling lights. There's a happy buzz here as people make their way to dinner before or after a sporting event, awards ceremony, or concert at the Nokia.

For a unique experience head to the wildly entertaining interactive Grammy Museum—a space that brings the music industry's history to life; there's the Conga Room, a Latin-focused nightclub owned by Jimmy Smits, Jennifer Lopez, and Paul Rodriquez; hipster Lucky Strike bowling lanes which has a café, bar, and billiard tables; the 14-screen Regal Cinemas; and in winter, an ice-skating rink.

There are also more than 10 restaurants and other eateries here, including Los Angeles favorite Katsuya, the spot for sizzling Kobe beef platters and sushi so good it's addictive (the crab rolls are not to be missed). If you're enjoying yourself so much you hate to leave, the JW Marriott/Ritz-Carlton Hotel and Spa and Ritz-Carlton Residences are adjacent to the property. And for a bit of L.A. glitz and glamour, know that this venue is home to various award shows including the Emmy and ESPY awards. ⊠ *777 Chick Hearn Court, Downtown* ☎ *213/763–6030* ⊕ *www.nokiatheatrelalive.com.*

Fodor's Choice ★ **Walt Disney Concert Hall.** L.A.'s crown jewel, designed by Frank Gehry, opened in 2003 and instantly became a stunning icon of the city. The gorgeous stainless-steel-clad exterior soars upward, seeming to defy the laws of engineering.

Inside, there's a billowing ceiling of Douglas fir, and an enormous pine-clad organ centerpiece said to have been inspired by a box of McDonald's french fries. The carpet, named "Lily," is a wild collage of petals inspired by Lillian Disney's love of flowers, as is the "Rose for Lily" fountain—made entirely of bits of Delftware, Mrs. Disney's favorite collectible—in the tranquil outdoor public garden.

Docent-led and self-guided audio tours of the Hall are available free to the public for parties of 14 and less, but note that entry to the performance space is subject to rehearsal schedules. Your chances are better in summer when the Philharmonic moves to the Hollywood Bowl.

Additional children's performances, lectures, and experimental works are held in surrounding smaller theater spaces: the indoor BP Hall, two outdoor mini-amphitheaters, and CalArts's intimate 266-seat REDCAT Theatre.

The Hall is part of the 11-acre **Music Center** campus, which has served as L.A.'s major performing arts venue since its opening in 1964, and was where the Academy Awards was held until it moved to the Kodak Theatre. It's reminiscent of New York's Lincoln Center because the buildings that house the Los Angeles Philharmonic, the Los Angeles Opera, the Center Theater Group, and the Los Angeles Master Chorale all surround a large courtyard. Glorya Kaufman presents Dance at the Music Center is another program that features the best of dance, from global to traditional ballet. At intermission, patrons spill into the plaza to drink wine and enjoy the lighted "dancing" fountain or occasional art exhibits.

The largest of the center's four theaters is the **Dorothy Chandler Pavilion,** named after the philanthropic wife of former *Los Angeles Times* publisher Norman Chandler. The **Ahmanson,** at the north end, is a flexible venue for major musicals and plays. In between these two sits the round **Mark Taper Forum,** an intimate 700-seat theater.

Activity isn't limited to merely ticketed events; free tours of the entire Music Center campus are available by volunteer docents who provide a wealth of architectural and behind-the-scenes information while escorting you through elaborate, art-punctuated VIP areas. ⊠ *135 N. Grand Ave., at 1st St., Downtown* ☎ *213/972–7211, 213/972–3688 for tour information* ⊕ *www.musiccenter.org.*

WORTH NOTING

Angels Flight Railway. The turn-of-the-20th-century funicular, dubbed "the shortest railway in the world," operated between 1901 and 1969, when it was dismantled (but saved) to make room for an urban renewal project that saw total redevelopment of the Bunker Hill district.

In 1996, 27 years later, Angels Flight returned with its two original orange-and-black wooden cable railway cars cabling people up a 298-foot incline from Hill Street (between 3rd and 4th streets) to the fountain-filled Watercourt at California Plaza. The railway closed in 2001 and after undergoing a $3.3-million repair and restoration reopened March 2010. Take the short trip and be rewarded with a stellar view of the neighborhood, a Starbucks, and MOCA, which is just on the other side of the Plaza. The railway runs every day from 6:45 am to 10 pm. ⊠ *351 S. Hill St., between 3rd and 4th Sts., Downtown* ☎ *213/626–1901.*

Frank Gehry's Walt Disney Concert Hall became an instant L.A. icon when it opened in 2003.

Avila Adobe. This residence was built as an 18-room home in 1818; today only a seven-room wing still stands. The remains have been converted to a museum space representing the oldest residential building still standing in Los Angeles. The house has graceful, simple structure that features 3-foot-thick walls made of adobe brick over cottonwood timbers, a traditional interior courtyard, and 1840s-era furnishings. Open daily 9–4. ⊠ *E-10 Olvera St., Downtown.*

★ **Bradbury Building.** Stunning wrought-iron railing, blond-wood and brick interior, pink marble staircases, a 50-foot high Victorian-style skylighted atrium, and a birdcage elevator: it's easy to see why the Bradbury leaves visitors awestruck.

Designed in 1893 by a novice architect who drew his inspiration from a science-fiction story and a conversation with his dead brother via a Ouija board, the office building was originally the site of turn-of-the-20th-century sweatshops, but now houses a variety of business that try to keep normal working conditions despite the barrage of daily tourist visits and filmmakers. *Blade Runner, Chinatown,* and *Wolf* were filmed here.

For that reason, visits (and photo-taking) are limited to the lobby and the first-floor landing. The building is open daily 9–5 for a peek, as long as you don't wander beyond visitor-approved areas. ⊠ *304 S. Broadway, southeast corner Broadway and 3rd St., Downtown* ☎ *213/626–1893.*

Bunker Hill Steps. Threading a peaceful path through Downtown's urban towers, a fountain stream spills down the center of this monumental staircase designed by Lawrence Halprin. Its quiet beauty is reminiscent of Rome's Spanish Steps (albeit more narrow). The stream originates

DID YOU KNOW?

It wasn't always the case, but over the last decade Downtown L.A. has become a hot spot for nightlife, with hotel rooftop bars and new, notable restaurants opening.

at the top of the stairs where Robert Graham's nude female sculpture *Source Figure* stands atop a cylindrical base. The figure's hands are open, as if to offer water to the city.

If you're not inclined to walk up, hop on the escalator parallel to the stairs. Halfway up there's a coffeehouse where you can fortify yourself before tackling the remaining climb. ✉ *5th St. between Grand Ave. and Figueroa St., Downtown.*

California African-American Museum. Works by 20th-century African-American artists and contemporary art of the African Diasporas are the backbone of this museum's permanent collection. Its exhibits document the African-American experience from Emancipation and Reconstruction through the 20th century, especially as expressed by artists in California and elsewhere in the West. Special musical as well as educational and cultural events are offered the first Sunday of every month. ✉ *600 Exposition Park, Exposition Park* ☎ *213/744–7432* ⊕ *www. caamuseum.org* ✉ *Free, parking $8* ☉ *Tues.–Sat. 10–5, Sun. 11–5.*

☕ **California Science Center.** You're bound to see excited kids running up to the dozens of interactive exhibits here that illustrate the relevance of science to everyday life, from bacteria to airplanes. This center provides opportunities to examine such topics as structures and communications, where you can be an architect and design your own building and learn how to make it earthquake-proof, or watch Tess, the 50-foot animatronic star of the exhibit "Body Works," dramatically demonstrate how the body's organs work together.

Air and Space Exhibits reveal what it takes to go to outer space with Gemini 11, a real capsule flown into space by Pete Conrad and Dick Gordon in September 1966. An IMAX theater shows large-format releases. ✉ *700 State Dr., Exposition Park* ☎ *213/744–7400, 323/724–3623* ⊕ *www.casciencectr.org* ✉ *Free, except for IMAX, prices vary; parking $8* ☉ *Daily 10–5.*

Chinese American Museum. In the El Pueblo Plaza adjacent to Olvera Street, you might think this museum should feature Mexican-American art. But in actuality, it's in the last surviving structure of L.A.'s original Chinatown, although it illustrates a commonality with the Hispanic experience in that it documents the lives of immigrants who settled here.

Three floors of exhibits offer a range of displays that explore the different cultures, as well as how people set up shops and paved the way for what is now the vibrant and varied Chinatown district. Rotating exhibits feature the work of Chinese-American fine artists. Note that an expansion is in the works and is slated to be completed in 2012. ✉ *425 N. Los Angeles St.* ☎ *213/485–8567* ⊕ *www.camla.org* ✉ *$3 suggested donation* ☉ *Tues.–Sun. 10–3.*

OFF THE BEATEN PATH

Carroll Avenue. Looking like a street lifted out of another era, the 1300 block of Carroll Avenue in Angelino Heights has the city's highest concentration of Victorian houses. Less than 10 minutes by car to both Downtown and the Los Feliz/Silver Lake neighborhoods, if you're in the vicinity it's worth a quick diversion by car.

CLOSE UP

El Pueblo de Los Angeles

The oldest section of the city, known as El Pueblo de Los Angeles, Olvera Street has come to represent the rich Mexican heritage of L.A. It had a close shave with disintegration in the early 20th century, until the socialite Christine Sterling walked through in 1926. Jolted by the historic area's decay, Sterling fought to preserve key buildings and led the transformation of the street into a Mexican-American marketplace.

Today this character remains; vendors sell puppets, leather goods, sandals, serapes (woolen shawls), and handicrafts from stalls that line the center of the narrow street. The quality of what you can find ranges from Tijuana-style "junkola" (donkey-shaped salt and pepper shakers) to well-made glassware and pottery.

WHAT TO SEE

At the beginning of Olvera Street is **The Plaza**, a wonderful Mexican-style park with plenty of benches and walkways, shaded by a huge Moreton Bay fig tree. On weekends, mariachis and folkloric dance groups often perform.

Not to be missed is one of city's top sites—**Cathedral of Our Lady of the Angels**, designed by architect José Rafael Moneo.

Two annual events particularly worth seeing: the Blessing of the Animals and Las Posadas. On the Saturday before Easter, Angelenos bring their pets (not just dogs and cats, but horses, pigs, cows, birds, hamsters) to be blessed by a priest.

For Las Posadas (every night between December 16 and 24), merchants and visitors parade up and down the street, led by children dressed as angels, to commemorate Mary and Joseph's search for shelter on Christmas Eve.

WHERE TO EAT

The most authentic Mexican food is at **La Luz del Dia** (⊠ W-1 Olvera St., Downtown ☎ 213/628–7495), which has traditional favorites such as chiles rellenos and pickled cactus, as well as handmade tortillas patted out in a practiced rhythm by the women behind the counter.

Another delicious option, **La Golondrina** (⊠ W-17 Olvera St., Downtown ☎ 213/628–4349), midblock, has a delightful patio, and is located in the Pelanconi House, built in 1855, which was the first brick building in Los Angeles.

GETTING HERE

This neighborhood is a few blocks north of Union Station, near the intersection of North Main Street and East Cesar Chavez Avenue. Olvera Street is just off Cesar Chavez Avenue.

BEST TIME TO GO

To see Olvera Street at its quietest, visit late on a weekday afternoon, when long shadows heighten the romantic feeling of the passageway.

TOURING TIP

For information, stop by the **Olvera Street Visitors Center** (⊠ 622 N. Main St., Downtown ☎ 213/628–1274 ⊕ www.olvera-street.com), in the Sepulveda House, a Victorian built in 1887 as a hotel and boardinghouse. The center is open weekdays and weekends 9–4. Free hour-long walking tours leave here at 10, 11, and noon Tuesday–Saturday.

Olvera Street, at the heart of the city's oldest neighborhood, is the place to experience many aspects of L.A.'s Mexican-American culture.

As a designated historical district, it's no surprise the homes here are often rented for film shoots. Look for the Sessions House (No. 1330) and the Haunted House (No. 1345)—the latter seen in Michael Jackson's *Thriller* video. To get to Carroll Avenue from Downtown, take Temple Street west to Edgeware Road, turn right onto Edgeware, and go over the freeway. Carroll Avenue is on the left.

City Hall of Los Angeles. An icon of the Los Angeles cityscape, this gorgeous 1928 landmark building has seen its fair share of stardom—from the opening scenes of the TV series *Dragnet* to serving as the "Daily Planet" building in the original *Adventures of Superman*. During an extensive renovation in the late '90s, the original Lindburg Beacon was put back in action atop the hall's 13th-story tower. The revolving spotlight, inaugurated by President Calvin Coolidge from the White House via a telegraph key, was used from 1928 to 1941 to guide pilots into the Los Angeles airport.

There are free weekday tours of the beautifully detailed building at 10 and 11, which sometimes include a visit to the observation deck. Reservations are required, but you can do a self-guide tour without a docent. ✉ *200 N. Spring St., Downtown* ☎ *213/978–1995.*

Downtown L.A. Standard. Housed in the former Superior Oil Headquarters, the Standard's interior flaunts a cool steel design bursting with bright pop art furniture that would make Andy Warhol proud. Take the elevator to the rooftop lounge for a spectacular view and a dip in the pool. Playful perks like circular waterbeds, pod couches, and S-shaped tanning chairs lend a party setting.

Chinatown

CLOSE UP

Smaller than San Francisco's China-town, this Downtown sector near Union Station still represents a slice of Southeast Asian life. Sidewalks are usually jammed with tourists, locals, and, of course, Asian residents hustling from shop to shop picking up goods, spices, and trinkets from small shops and mini-plazas that line the street.

Although some longtime establish-ments closed in recent years, the area still pulses with its founding culture. During Chinese New Year, giant drag-ons snake down the street. And, of course, there are the many restaurants and quick-bite cafés specializing in Chinese feasts.

Gallery openings and hip artists bring in a stylish, younger crowd to Chinatown, and a few choice bars are getting in on the action, too, by offering a nightlife scene without the "guest list only" culture of Hollywood. You can get a taste of it in the Central Plaza of New Chinatown, where there are a handful of lively bars, some with karaoke.

WHAT TO SEE

The **Chinese American Museum** is located in the city's original Chinatown, which today is part of the neighboring El Pueblo de Los Angeles neighbor-hood, just a short hop away. It's worth a quick detour or a visit prior to com-ing to put the history of Chinese set-tlement into context with the arrival of the city's other ethnic groups.

An influx of local artists has added a spark to the neighborhood by taking up empty spaces and opening galler-ies along **Chung King Road**, a faded pedestrian passage behind the West Plaza shopping center between Hill and Yale. Also look for galleries along a little side street called **Gin Ling Way**

on the east side of Broadway. Most galleries open when they have a show, or in the afternoon and early evenings from Wednesday through Saturday.

WHERE TO EAT

The Asian holdout **Empress Pavilion** (✉ 988 N. Hill St. ☎ 213/617–9898) buzzes with activity and is touted as one of Chinatown's best restaurants.

GETTING HERE

Bordered by Yale, Bernard, Ord, and Alameda streets, Chinatown has its main action on North Broadway. There are several garages available for parking here that range from $3–$8 per day.

BEST TIME TO GO

This neighborhood is always bustling. Weekdays are busy with residents rush-ing to and from work, picking up gro-ceries and kids from school on the way home. On weekends, restaurant are packed with locals and tourists alike.

TOURING TIP

On the first Saturday of the month, there's a walking tour called "The Undiscovered Chinatown" from 10:30 am to 1 pm. For information, call ☎ 213/680–0243.

DID YOU KNOW?

L.A.'s Chinatown has its share of Chinese restaurants, shops, and cultural institutions, but you'll also find a growing community of artists and galleries.

Nearby skyscrapers serve as video projection screens at night, as hipsters groove to an in-house DJ along with an influx of L.A.'s beautiful people. During the day, it's worth a visit for a breakfast or lunch in the screaming yellow '60s-style diner to take in the ambience without having to push through the party crowd. Look for a beer garden to open in 2012. ⊠ *550 S. Flower St.* 📞 *213/892–8080* ⊕ *www.standardhotel.com.*

Exposition Park. Originally developed in 1880 as an open-air farmers' market, this 114-acre park has a lovely sunken rose garden and three museums—the **California African-American Museum,** the **California Science Center,** and the **Natural History Museum of Los Angeles County**—as well as an **IMAX** theater. There's also the Los Angeles Memorial Coliseum and Sports Arena, where Olympic festivities were held in 1932 and 1984 and where USC games are now played. A metro line is planned to reach the park in 2012. Note that the park and neighborhood are sketchy at night. ⊠ *Between Exposition and Martin Luther King Jr. Blvds., Exposition Park.*

Italian Hall Building. This landmark isn't open to the public, but it's noteworthy because its south wall bears an infamous mural. Famed Mexican muralist David Alfaro Siqueiros shocked his patrons in the 1930s by depicting an oppressed worker of Latin America being crucified on a cross topped by a menacing American eagle. The anti-imperialist mural was promptly whitewashed but was later restored by the Getty Museum. ⊠ *650 N. Main St., Downtown.*

The Japanese American Cultural and Community Center. There's a lot offered here in terms of books as well as traditional and contemporary cultural events. Founded in 1980, JACCC is home to a number of civic and arts organizations. Call ahead or check the Web site for a schedule. Through the center's basement you can reach the James Irvine Garden, a serene sunken garden where local plants mix with bamboo, Japanese wisteria, and Japanese maples. ⊠ *244 S. San Pedro St., Downtown* 📞 *213/628–2725* ⊕ *www.jaccc.org.*

Japanese American National Museum. What was it like to grow up on a sugar plantation in Hawaii? How difficult was life for Japanese-Americans interned in concentration camps during World War II? These questions are addressed by changing exhibits at this museum in Little Tokyo. Insightful volunteer docents are on hand to share their own stories and experiences. The museum occupies an 85,000-square-foot adjacent pavilion as well as its original site in a renovated 1925 Buddhist temple. ⊠ *369 E. 1st St., at Central Ave., next to Geffen Contemporary, Downtown* 📞 *213/625–0414* ⊕ *www.janm.org* 🎟 *$9, free Thurs. 5–8 and 3rd Thurs. of month* ☉ *Tues., Wed., and Fri.–Sun. 11–5; Thursday 12–8.*

Millennium Biltmore Hotel. The wow factor hits you as soon as you walk in the door of this hotel. Dripping in Italian Renaissance style, the Biltmore's ornate details, frescoes, and golden columns are truly luxe. You might get a crick in your neck from admiring the magnificence of the ceilings alone.

Opened in 1923, a creation of the architecture firm Schultze and Weaver, which also built New York City's Waldorf-Astoria, the Biltmore is a registered historical landmark and has served presidents, royalty, and celebrities alike.

The Academy Awards were held here in the 1930s and '40s, and the hotel has also been seen in many films and TV shows, including *Chinatown*. These days, the hotel really kicks into high glamour for the holidays with special dinners, a traditional afternoon holiday tea, and New Year's bash. ⊠ *506 S. Grand Ave., Downtown* ☎ *213/624–1011* ⊕ *www.thebiltmore.com.*

2

Natural History Museum of Los Angeles County. The completed renovation of the museum's 1913 Beaux Arts building sets the stage for celebration of its centennial in 2013, with its most notable addition, the spectacular new Dinosaur Hall. The Hall features a tremendous Triceratops, a 68-foot long-necked Mamenchisaurus, as well as more than 300 fossils, 20 full-body specimens, and an impressive T. Rex series.

The museum has the same quaint feel of many natural history museums, with enclosed dioramas of animals in their natural habitats. But it mixes it up with interactive displays such as the Butterfly Pavilion in a separate small building in front of the museum; The Discovery Center, where kids can touch real animal pelts; the Insect Zoo; and their Dino Lab, where you can watch actual paleontologists work on dinosaur fossils.

In addition, there are also exhibits typifying various cultural groups, including pre-Columbian artifacts and a display of crafts from the South Pacific as well as marine-life exhibits. ⊠ *900 Exposition Blvd., Exposition Park* ☎ *213/763–3466* ⊕ *www.nhm.org* ⊠ *$9, free 1st Tues. of month* ⊙ *Weekdays 9:30–5, weekends 10–5.*

Pershing Square. The city's cultures come together in one of the oldest parks, named in honor of WWI general John J. Pershing. Opened in 1866, Pershing Square was renovated in the 1990s by architect Ricardo Legorreta and landscape architect Laurie Olin with colorful walls, fountains, and towers.

Although the massive block-and-sphere architecture looks somewhat dated, Pershing remains an icon of Downtown L.A. Nearby office workers and visitors stroll thorough or stop for a lunch break. From mid-November to mid-January, the place perks up with holiday events and the outdoor ice rink. ⊠ *Bordered by 5th, 6th, Hill, and Olive Sts.* ☎ *213/847–4970* ⊕ *www.laparks.org/pershingsquare/pershing.htm* ⊠ *Free* ⊙ *Daily.*

Richard J. Riordan Central Library. It's still known locally as the Central Library—but after fires in the 1980s precipitated reconstruction, it's become the nation's third largest public library. The original building, designed by Bertram Goodhue, was restored to its 1926 condition, with the pyramid tower and a torch symbolizing the Light of Learning crowning the building.

The mega-size of this library, with several floors and departments, can be overwhelming. The Cook rotunda on the second floor features murals by Dean Cornwell depicting the history of California, and the Tom Bradley Wing, named for another mayor, has a soaring eight-story atrium.

CLOSE UP

Little Tokyo

Originally the neighborhood of Los Angeles' Japanese community, this Downtown spot has been deserted by many of its founding immigrants, although it still remains only one of three official Japantowns in the country, all of which are in California.

However, the area has recently begun to blossom again thanks to the next generation of Japanese-Americans setting up small businesses here mixed with an influx of foot traffic coming in from neighboring redevelopment projects and newly built condos.

Little Tokyo has dozens of sushi bars, tempura restaurants, karaoke bars, and trinket shops selling electronic toys, lanterns, and Hello Kitty tchotchkes.

On 1st Street you'll find the only strip of intact buildings from the early 1900s. Look down when you get near San Pedro Street, to see the art installation "Omoide no Shotokyo" ("Remembering Old Little Tokyo").

Embedded in the sidewalk are brass inscriptions naming the original businesses, quoted reminiscences from Little Tokyo residents, and steel timelines of Japanese-American history up to World War II. Nisei Week (a *nisei* is a second-generation Japanese) is celebrated here every August with traditional drums, dancing, a carnival, and a huge parade.

WHAT TO SEE
Aside from the restaurants and shops, there's a lovely garden at the **Japanese American Cultural and Community Center**, a good resource for ongoing local events. There's also the **Japanese American National Museum**, which maintains its original site, a renovated Buddhist temple

from 1925 that has an ornately-designed entrance.

GETTING HERE
Little Tokyo is bounded by 1st, San Pedro, 3rd, and Central streets.

BEST TIME TO GO
The area tends to get a bit deserted at night, so it's best to come in the later part of the afternoon on weekdays.

TOURING TIPS
Because of its location right near other top attractions Downtown—including the Geffen Contemporary—it's the perfect spot to stop for an inexpensive and interesting lunch. Grab some sushi and pick up a bag full of authentic Japanese sweets to keep you going while sightseeing.

DID YOU KNOW?

The Geffen Contemporary, a branch of the Museum of Contemporary Art located in Little Tokyo, is one of L.A.'s top museums to visit.

The library offers frequent events and special exhibits, plus a small café to refuel. For $50 out-of-towners may apply for a one-year visitor's card by showing a valid ID to check out books. Don't ignore the gift shop, which is loaded with unique items for readers and writers. ⊠ *630 W. 5th St., at Flower St., Downtown* ☎ *213/228–7000, 213/228–7168 for tour information* ⊕ *www.lapl.org* 🖂 *Free* ☉ *Tues. and Thurs. 10–8, Wed., Fri. and Sat. 10–5:30; closed Sunday and Monday. Free docent tours are given daily; call 213/228–7168. Daily on-hour Walk-In Tours of the Central Library Tues.–Fri. at 12:30, Sat. at 11 and 2, and Sun. at 2. A self-guided tour map is also available on library's Web site.*

Staples Center. Home to the Lakers, the Clippers, the Sparks, and ice hockey team the Los Angeles Kings, the Staples Center also hosts ice shows, tennis, and superstar performers such as Bruce Springsteen and Madonna. This extravagant stadium treats its guests to high style, good sound quality, and comfortable seating.

Though not open to visitors except for events, the saucer-shaped building has made a permanent impression on the Downtown cityscape. Next to the Convention Center, the arena is now also adjacent to the newly built L.A. Live entertainment complex. ⊠ *1111 S. Figueroa St., Downtown* ☎ *213/742–7340* ⊕ *www.staplescenter.com.*

★ **Union Station.** Once the key entry point into Los Angeles prior to LAX, Union Station is worth a visit even if you don't plan to go anywhere but merely want to wallow in the ambience of one of the country's last great rail stations.

Evoking an era when travel and style went hand in hand, Union Station will transport you to another destination, and another time. Built in 1939 and designed by City Hall architects John and Donald Parkinson, it combines Spanish colonial revival and art deco styles that have retained their classic warmth and quality.

The waiting hall's commanding scale and enormous chandeliers have provided the setting for countless films, TV shows, and music videos. The indoor restaurant, **Traxx,** offers a glamorous vintage setting for lunch and dinner. ⊠ *800 N. Alameda St., Downtown.*

University of Southern California (USC). There's more to this private university than mascot Tommy Trojan and the legendary marching band. Its parklike inner-city campus dates to 1880, its film school is George Lucas's alma mater, and it fosters a fanatical cross-town rivalry with UCLA.

Free docent-led campus tours are available weekdays, as is a self-guided tour map for potential students or film buffs who just want to walk in Lucas's footsteps. ⊠ *Guest Relations, 615 Childs Way, Adjacent to Exposition Park, University Park* ☎ *213/740–6605* ⊕ *www.usc.edu/visit* ☉ *Call for tour schedule and reservations.*

OFF THE
BEATEN
PATH

★ **Watts Towers.** After many years of a much-needed restoration, the City of Los Angeles has contracted the Los Angeles County Museum of Art to maintain the jewel of rough South L.A. The Towers are the legacy of Simon Rodia, a tile setter who emigrated from Italy to California and erected one of the world's greatest folk-art structures.

THE LOS ANGELES METRO

Once upon a time, Los Angeles had an enviable public transportation system known as the Pacific Electric Red Cars, trolleys that made it possible to get around this sprawling city without an automobile. In the mid-1900s, the last of the Red Cars disappeared, and Los Angeles lost itself in the car culture. Make no mistake, the car culture is here to stay; an afternoon in rush-hour traffic will drive that point home.

But for the last few years, a sleek new rail system has emerged. You can now take a subway through parts of Downtown Los Angeles, Hollywood, Pasadena, and North Hollywood.

The Metro Red Line subway, which is the most useful for exploring parts of the city, starts at Downtown's Union Station, then curves northwest to Hollywood and on to Universal City and North Hollywood. The Blue and Green light rail lines are geared for commuters. The latest addition, the Gold Line, goes from Union Station up to Pasadena.

Though it takes some planning, using the Metro can spare you time you might otherwise spend stuck in traffic—if the stations are convenient, that is. If you're worried about being caught in the subway during an earthquake, keep in mind that stations and tunnels were built with reinforced steel and were engineered to withstand a magnitude-8 earthquake.

The Metro Rail stations are worth exploring themselves, and you can sign up for a free docent-led **MTA art tour** (☎ *213/922–2738* ⊕ *www.mta.net or www.metro. net/about/art*), which departs

from the entrances to the Hollywood & Highland and Union Stations. You'll receive a free day pass to ride the rails as you visit the colorful murals, sculptures, and architectural elements of each station, designed to carry out themes of Los Angeles history.

The Universal City station is next to the site of the Campo de Caheunga, where Mexico relinquished control of California to the United States in 1847, and the station features a timeline of the area's past done in the traditional style of colorful Mexican folk art.

The North Hollywood station also celebrates local history: native Gabrielino culture, many immigrant communities, Amelia Earhart (a local), Western wear designer Nudie, and the history of transportation in Los Angeles County.

They are recycled film reels on the ceiling of the Hollywood and Vine station as well as original Paramount Pictures film projectors from the 1930s, and floor paving that looks like the yellow brick road from *The Wizard of Oz*. Imposing, glass-clad columns juxtaposed with rock formations can be seen at the Vermont and Beverly station. The old Red Car trolley makes a guest appearance in the Hollywood and Western station.

From 1921 until 1954, without any help, this eccentric man built the three main cement towers, using pipes, bed frames, and anything else he could find. He embellished them with bits of colorful glass, broken pottery, and more than 70,000 seashells.

The towers became the centerpiece of a state historic park and cultural center, part of an effort by Watts neighborhood leaders to overcome the area's gangland and riot-zone history—but it's still best to use your street smarts while visiting.

Because of the preservation work, tours may be affected, so make sure to check ahead before booking. ⊠ *1727 E. 107th St., Take I–110 to I–105 east; exit north at S. Central Ave., and turn right onto 108th St., left onto Willowbrook Ave., Watts* ☎ *213/847–4646* ✉ *$7, includes tour* ☉ *Gallery Wed.–Sat. 10–4, Sun. noon–4; tours Thurs. 11–3, Fri. 11–3, Sat. 10:30–3, Sun. 12:30–3.*

Westin Bonaventure Hotel & Suites. In 1976 John Portman designed these five shimmering cylinders in the sky, with nary a 90-degree angle. Sheathed in mirrored glass, the now-dated building once looked like a science-fiction fantasy; this emblem of postmodern architecture has been featured countless TV shows and movies.

Take a ride in the soaring glass elevator that carried Arnold Schwarzenegger in *True Lies*. For a truly panoramic view of L.A., be sure to have a meal in the Bona Vista Lounge on the 34th floor, which features floor-to-ceiling windows and rotates 360 degrees as you dine. ⊠ *404 S. Figueroa St., Downtown* ☎ *213/624–1000* ⊕ *www.westin. com/bonaventure.*

Hollywood and the Studios

WORD OF MOUTH

"The Warner Bros. studio tour is generally considered the best of the 'pure' tours. Universal Studios is a combination tour of the Universal back lot and a theme park. It's great fun."

—dbdurand

GETTING ORIENTED

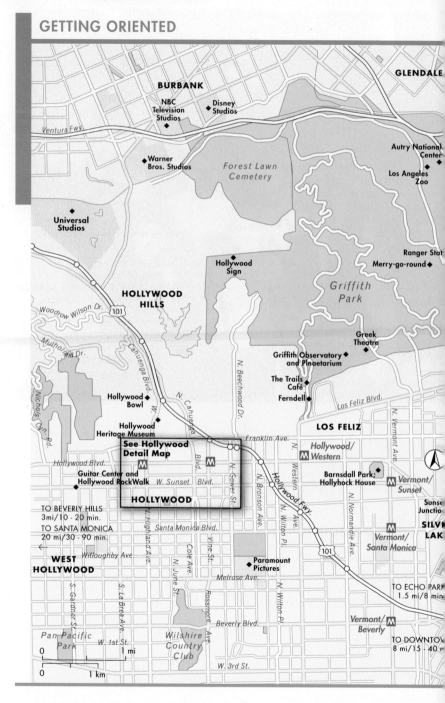

GLENDALE

BURBANK

NBC
Television
Studios ◆

◆ Disney
Studios

Ventura Fwy.

Autry National
Center

◆ Warner
Bros. Studios

*Forest Lawn
Cemetery*

Los Angeles
Zoo

Universal
Studios

Ranger Stat

Merry-go-round ◆

Hollywood
Sign ◆

*Griffith
Park*

HOLLYWOOD
HILLS

Woodrow Wilson Dr. 101

Mulholland Dr.

Cahuenga Blvd.

Greek
Theatre ◆

N. Beechwood Dr.

Griffith Observatory ◆
and Planetarium

The Trails
Café

Nichols Cnyn. Rd.

Hollywood ◆
Bowl

N. Cahuenga

Ferndell ◆

Los Feliz Blvd.

N. Vermont Ave.

Hollywood ◆
Heritage Museum

Blvd.

Ⓜ

Franklin Ave.

LOS FELIZ

**See Hollywood
Detail Map**

Ⓜ

*Hollywood/
Western*

Ⓜ

Hollywood Blvd.

Ⓜ

N. Gower St.

Barnsdall Park;
Hollyhock House ◆

Ⓜ *Vermont/
Sunset*

Guitar Center and
Hollywood RockWalk ◆

W. Sunset Blvd.

Western Ave.

HOLLYWOOD

N. Bronson Ave.

Hollywood Fwy.

Suns
Junctio

TO BEVERLY HILLS
3mi/10 - 20 min.
TO SANTA MONICA
20 mi/30 - 90 min.

Santa Monica Blvd.

N. Wilton Pl.

Ⓜ

SILV
LAK

←

N. Highland Ave.

Vine St.

101

*Vermont/
Santa Monica*

**WEST
HOLLYWOOD**

Willoughby Ave.

Cole Ave.

N. June St.

◆ Paramount
Pictures

N. Normandie Ave.

TO ECHO PAR
1.5 mi/8 min

S. Gardner St.

S. La Brea Ave.

Rossmore Ave.

Melrose Ave.

Beverly Blvd.

*Vermont/
Beverly* Ⓜ

*Pan-Pacific
Park*

W. 1st St.

*Wilshire
Country
Club*

TO DOWNTO
8 mi/15 - 40 r

0 _____ 1 mi

0 _____ 1 km

W. 3rd St.

TOP REASONS TO GO

See the Studios. Catch a glimpse of where the stars work—Paramount Pictures, Warner Bros. Studios, Universal Studios Hollywood, and NBC Television Studios

Walk in the Stars' Footsteps. There's Grauman's Chinese Theatre and the Walk of Fame, with handprints of more than 1,600 of the entertainment industry's most famous.

Picnic at the Hollywood Bowl. Even if you don't get tickets for a show, stop at this L.A. landmark just north of Hollywood for a great outdoor meal.

Get up to Griffith Park. The largest municipal park and urban wilderness in the country has a zoo, miles of trails to hike, an observatory, and one of L.A.'s best views.

Check out the Best Hollywood Memorabilia. The Hollywood Museum has an incredible collection of Tinseltown's most glamorous costumes, photos, and more.

GETTING HERE

Driving Strategy. During rush hour, traffic jams on the Hollywood Freeway (U.S. 101/Highway 170), San Diego Freeway (I-405), and Ventura Freeway (U.S. 101/Highway 134) can be brutal, so avoid trips to or from the Valley at those times.

In fact, the best way to get from Hollywood to Burbank is to skip the freeways all together and take Hollywood Boulevard to Cahuenga Boulevard heading north, and take Burham Boulevard straight to Burbank.

Parking. The best way to see the Walk of Fame is to drive to Hollywood, park the car, and walk. The best garage is located near the corner of Hollywood and Highland.

PLANNING YOUR TIME

Plan to spend the better part of a morning or afternoon taking in Hollywood, including seeing Grauman's Chinese Theatre and the Walk of Fame.

Hollywood Boulevard sometimes attracts a rough collection of homeless people and runaways; if you've got children in tow, stick to a daytime walk.

Later in the evening, you can return to Hollywood for a cabaret performance at the Roosevelt Hotel's Cinegrill, a movie at the El Capitan or the fabulous ArcLight, or a summertime concert at the Hollywood Bowl.

Expect to spend most of a day at Universal Studios Hollywood and CityWalk; studio tours at NBC and Warner Bros. last up to two hours.

DRIVING TIMES AND DISTANCES

Minimum times listed below represent little to no traffic; maximum times assume the worst. Adjust accordingly taking rush hour and peak weekend travel time into account.

■ **LAX to Hollywood:** 30–60 min/25 mi

■ **Beverly Hills to Hollywood:** 15–30 min/5 mi

■ **Hollywood to Burbank:** 20–40 min/7 mi

■ **Santa Monica to Hollywood:** 30–90 min/20 mi

3

THE HEART OF HOLLYWOOD

As much an idea as a place, Hollywood is a dream factory. Year after year, wannabe stars flock here in search of ever-elusive fame. Sure, Hollywood's top attractions are a bit touristy— but if it's your first time, you should at least make a brief stop here.

(above) The facade of Grauman's Chinese Theatre. (lower right) The marquee of El Capitan Theatre. (upper right) Handprints of the stars at Grauman's.

Be sure to check out the Walk of Fame and catch a movie in one of the neighborhood's opulent movie palaces, such as the infamous Grauman's Chinese Theatre or the El Capitan.

In the old days, the intersection of Hollywood and Vine was the hub of the radio and movie industry: film stars like Gable and Garbo hustled in and out of their agents' office buildings at these fabled cross streets.

The glamour has dimmed a bit, but the area comes alive after dark as a place for theater and nightlife. The intersection of Hollywood and Highland, another hot spot of yesteryear, is the location of a massive entertainment complex.

TIPS FOR TOURING

The best time to arrive to see this section of Hollywood is around 11 am, when there are just enough people to make it seem busy without it feeling overwhelmingly crowded. After you've seen the sites, stop for lunch at the Hollywood & Highland Center where you can get everything from pizza to sushi. If you can't get an early table, there's plenty to do to occupy your time while waiting.

TOP ATTRACTIONS

GRAUMAN'S CHINESE THEATER

Although this cinematic fantasy of Chinese pagodas and temples is best appreciated by seeing a movie in the ornate theater, admittance to the interior courtyard (where the famous footprints of the stars reside) is free. ⊠ *6925 Hollywood Blvd., Hollywood* ☎ *323/464–8111, 323/463–9576 for tours* ⊕ *www.manntheatres.com.*

HOLLYWOOD WALK OF FAME

On this mile-long stretch of Hollywood Boulevard sidewalk, the names of more than 1,600 entertainment-industry overachievers are embossed in brass, each at the center of a pink star. Contact the Hollywood Chamber of Commerce for more information about specific celebs' stars. ⊠ *7018 Hollywood Blvd.* ☎ *323/469–8311* ⊕ *www.hollywoodchamber.net.*

WORTH NOTING

EL CAPITAN THEATRE

This theater—where Orson Welles debuted Citizen Kane—originally opened in 1926. Taken over and fully restored to its former grandeur by the Walt Disney Company, the palatial venue features soaring ceilings and a lavish East Indian motif. ⊠ *6838 Hollywood Blvd.* ☎ *323/467–7674* ⊕ *disney.go.com/disneypictures/el_capitan.*

EGYPTIAN THEATRE

Impresario Sid Grauman built Hollywood's first movie palace in 1922. The nonprofit American Cinematheque now hosts special screenings and discussions with notable filmmakers, and on weekends you can watch a documentary about Hollywood history. ⊠ *6712 Hollywood Blvd.* ☎ *323/466–3456* ⊕ *www.egyptiantheatre.com.*

KODAK THEATRE

Follow the path of red-carpet Hollywood royalty to the home of the Academy Awards. ⊠ *6801 Hollywood Blvd., Hollywood* ☎ *323/308–6300* ⊕ *www.kodaktheatre.com.*

HOLLYWOOD & HIGHLAND CENTER

This hotel-retail-entertainment complex pays tribute to the city's film legacy. ⊠ *Hollywood Blvd. and Highland Ave., Hollywood* ☎ *323/467–6412 visitor center* ⊕ *www.hollywoodandhighland.com.*

ARCLIGHT/CINERAMA DOME

Plush stadium seating, reserved seats, an usher who welcomes you, and snack bars that cook fresh caramel corn—the ArcLight justifies its high ticket prices. Next door is the restored geodesic Cinerama Dome, a curved-screen architectural icon. ⊠ *6360 Sunset Blvd., at Vine St., Hollywood* ☎ *323/464–4226* ⊕ *www.arclightcinemas.com.*

3

VISITING THE STUDIOS

If you've never been to L.A.—or if you have, and are coming back with your kids—it's hard to resist the allure of being where the magic happens among the cameras, props, and backlots of Tinseltown's studios.

(above) Go to Universal Studios for a big-bang theme park experience of moviemaking. (lower right) Warner Bros. Studios. (upper right) Paramount Pictures.

Nearly 70% of all L.A.'s entertainment productions happen in the Valley. And to really get behind the scenes, studio tours are the best way for mere mortals to get close to where celebs and the industry's crème-de-la-crème work.

Most tours last several hours, and allow you to see where hit television shows are filmed, spot actors on the lot, and visit movie soundstages—some directors even permit visitors on the set while shooting.

Specific sights change daily, so if there's something in particular you're dying to see, it's best to call ahead and ask.

IT'S ALL ABOUT LOCATION

Many L.A. first-timers make the incorrect assumption that because Hollywood is where all the action takes place, it's also where the stars work.

The only studio that's still located in Hollywood is Paramount; Warner Bros., Universal Studios Hollywood, and NBC Television Studios are north of Hollywood, in Universal City and Burbank.

3

PARAMOUNT PICTURES

BEST FOR
Paramount offers an intimate—eight to 10 people at a time—two-hour tour of its 63-acre lot. It's probably the most authentic studio tour you can take, giving you a real sense of the film industry's history. Paramount is the only studio left in Hollywood—all the others are in Burbank, Universal City, or Culver City.

TOURING BASICS
Guests primarily visit sets and soundstages that are not in use—though directors occasionally allow visitors during production, so there's a decent chance of seeing a celebrity. Other stops include the New York back-lot and the studio's iconic Bronson Gate.

WHAT'S BEEN FILMED HERE
Chinatown, The Godfather, The Untouchables, Breakfast at Tiffany's, Austin Powers, Cloverfield, Titanic, Star Trek, and the most recent installment of Indiana Jones are just a few of the notable films shot here.

TIPS FOR TOURING
For an inexpensive lunch costing as little as $10, try The Café, the studio's commissary, a buffet where you can grab everything from sandwiches to pizza to Mexican food.

GETTING HERE
From Melrose Avenue, enter on Windsor Boulevard at the main gate. Parking

is just north of the gate on the left, and there's additional parking at the lot on the southwest corner of Windsor and Melrose.

VISITOR INFORMATION
Kids must be 12 or older to tour the studio. ⊠ *5555 Melrose Ave., Hollywood* ☎ *323/956–1777* ⊕ *www.paramount. com* 🎬 *Tours weekdays by reservation only, $35.*

WARNER BROS. STUDIOS

BEST FOR
If you're looking for an authentic behind-the-scenes look at how films and TV shows are made, head to this major studio center, one of the world's busiest. There aren't many bells and whistles here, but you'll get a much better idea of production work than you will at Universal Studios.

TOURING BASICS
On the VIP Tour, which lasts almost 90 minutes, you'll see the studio from inside an electric cart with 11 others. The specifics of what you'll actually see changes daily, but after viewing a short film on WB movies and shows, you'll be taken by tram to visit sets like the often-recycled Anytown U.S.A.

as well as soundstages and back-lot locations for popular films and shows. The studio's museum has a floor dedicated to Casablanca and 85 years of WB history; another belongs exclusively to Harry Potter. The tour ends here, and you can explore it at your leisure.

The Deluxe Tour is a five-hour affair that takes you onto working production sets and includes lunch at the commissary (great stargazing ops).

WHAT'S BEEN FILMED HERE
Without A Trace, *The Mentalist*, *Friends*, the original *Ocean's Eleven*, *Casablanca*, and *Rebel Without a Cause*.

TIPS FOR TOURING
Showing up about 20 minutes before the scheduled time of your tour is recommended. VIP Tours leave continuously throughout the day; the Deluxe Tour leaves daily at 10:20 am.

GETTING HERE
The studio's Web site (⊕ *www2.warnerbros. com/vipstudiotour*) provides good directions from all parts of the city, including Downtown (take 101 north).

VISITOR INFORMATION
✉ *3400 W. Riverside Dr., Burbank* 🕾 *818/ 972–8687* ⊕ *www.wbsf.com* 📧 *VIP Tour is $48 per person; the Deluxe Tour is $225 per person* ⊙ *Weekdays 8:30–4:30. Children under 8 are not admitted. Advance booking is recommended. Parking is $7 at Gate 6.*

UNIVERSAL STUDIOS HOLLYWOOD

BEST FOR
This studio is more a theme park with lots of roller coasters and thrill rides than a backstage pass, though its studio tour does provide a good firsthand look at familiar TV shows and major movie sets.

TOURING BASICS
The tour lasts about an hour and you'll sit on a tram with nearly 100 other people. You'll pass back-lots, dressing rooms, and production offices.

There's also a VIP Tour where you can explore a historic, working movie studio's back-lot and score a closer view of sets, costumes, and props. It's a full-day outing that includes a two-hour studio tour, lunch, valet parking, and front-of-the-line privileges for the theme park's thrill rides.

WHAT'S BEEN FILMED HERE

See the airplane wreckage from *War of the Worlds*, the *Desperate Housewives'* Wisteria Lane, *King Kong* miniatures, *Psycho*'s infamous Bates Motel, and the animatronic Great White Shark from *Jaws*.

TIPS FOR TOURING

You may be tempted to get the $109 pass that takes you to the front of the line. Try to resist this splurge. Once inside, you'll find that the lines, if any, move quickly. Pass on the premium and spend it on a decent lunch outside the park.

GETTING HERE

The park is located in Universal City. From Hollywood, take the 101 Hollywood Freeway north to Universal Studios Boulevard.

VISITOR INFORMATION

✉ *100 Universal City Plaza, Universal City* ☎ *818/622–3801* ⊕ *www.universalstudioshollywood.com* 🎟 *Ticket prices for the studio tour are included in park admission ($74); $239 VIP tour, parking is $15; $10 after 3 pm. Preferred parking is available for $20* ⊙ *Contact park for seasonal hrs.*

NBC TELEVISION STUDIOS

BEST FOR

In contrast to other studio tours, you get to walk on the set rather than being confined to a tram. It's the only TV studio that offers a behind-the-scenes look at production.

TOURING BASICS

The guided 70-minute tour—a rare opportunity to see the inside of a TV studio—emphasizes the history of the station from its roots in radio. You'll visit an old broadcast booth, listen to

bands rehearsing, view setups for jokes, check out rehearsals, see sets under construction, and visit the prop warehouse and the studios where shows are taped.

WHAT'S FILMED HERE

The Tonight Show with Jay Leno, Days of Our Lives, The Ellen DeGeneres Show, and *Access Hollywood.*

TIPS FOR TOURING

If you decide to take a last minute studio tour, definitely call ahead; low ticket prices and advance purchase means tickets tend to sell out quickly the day of.

GETTING HERE

The studio is located in Burbank. The best way to get here from Downtown or the Hollywood area is to take the Hollywood Freeway 101 North to Barham Boulevard, which forks off onto West Olive Avenue. Make a right on West Alameda Avenue and then a right on Bob Hope Drive. The studio is on the right.

VISITOR INFORMATION

✉ *3000 W. Alameda Ave., Burbank* ☎ *818/840–3537* ⊕ *www.nbc.com* 🎟 *Tours $8.50. There's no minimum age requirement for children; those under 4 are free.*

(below) Jurassic Park—the Ride at Universal Studios

A DAY AT GRIFFITH PARK

With so much of Los Angeles paved in cement and asphalt, 4,100-acre Griffith Park stands out as a special place. It's the largest municipal park and urban wilderness area in the United States.

(above) On the trail in Griffith Park. (lower right) A resident of the park's zoo. (upper right) The Griffith Observatory.

On warm weekends, there are parties, barbecues, maria-chi bands, and strolling vendors selling fresh fruit. Joggers, cyclists, and walkers course its roadways. There are also top attractions within the park, including the Griffith Observatory and the Los Angeles Zoo.

The park was named after Col. Griffith J. Griffith, a mining tycoon who donated 3,000 acres of land to the city for the park in 1896. It has been used as a film and television location since the early days of motion pictures. One early Hollywood producer advised, "A tree is a tree, a rock is a rock, shoot it in Griffith Park."

GETTING HERE

The park has several entrances: off Los Feliz Boulevard at Western Canyon Avenue, Vermont Avenue, Crystal Springs Drive, and Riverside Drive; from the Ventura/134 Freeway at Victory Boulevard, Zoo Drive, or Forest Lawn Drive; from the Golden State Freeway (I–5) at Los Feliz Boulevard and Zoo Drive. The park is open from 5 am to 10 pm.

TOP EXPERIENCES

VISIT THE GRIFFITH OBSERVATORY

The view from the front of the Observatory is absolutely breathtaking, and since its recent massive makeover what's inside is equally impressive. Visit during a scheduled talk or show at the Leonard Nimoy Event Horizon Theatre, look through the Zeiss Telescope on a clear night, or check out the Samuel Oschin Planetarium and its incredible dome.

It's also fun—and free—to tour the expansive grounds, which include a monument dedicated to James Dean; several scenes from *Rebel Without a Cause* were filmed here. And to see the lights of the city twinkle at night from above, stay late and head up to the Observatory Deck, open until 10 pm every evening except Monday.

CLIMB MOUNT HOLLYWOOD

There's plenty of fabulous hiking to do in this park, but the best is to the top of Mount Hollywood. Park for free at the Griffith Observatory lot and pick up the trail, which begins there. It's an easy half-hour hike to the top. On super clear days you'll be able to see all the way to the Pacific Ocean and Catalina Island. About two-thirds of the way up is Dante's View, an area with benches to stop for a break or snack.

An up-close view of the Hollywood sign from just below means hiking a little more than 6 miles round-trip from the parking lot.

CHECK OUT THE LOS ANGELES ZOO AND BOTANICAL GARDENS

Located in the northeast corner of the park, the zoo's highlights include a new gorilla reserve, a Sumatran tiger, a snow leopard, and an acre dedicated to one of the largest troops of chimpanzees in the United States. In addition, the zoo claims to have more flamingoes than any other zoo worldwide.

OTHER FUN THINGS TO DO

CATCH A CONCERT AT THE GREEK THEATRE

This 6,100-seat outdoor venue (☎ 323/665–1927 ⊕ *www.greektheatrela.com*), is where top artists such as Elton John and Paul Simon have performed.

LEARN ABOUT THE WEST

The silver-screen cowboy Gene Autry created the Museum of the American West (✉ *4700 Western Heritage Way, at Zoo Dr.* ☎ *323/667–2000* ⊕ *www.autry-museum.org*), which features paintings, sculpture, textiles, and more that help tell the story of how the West was settled. Open Tuesday–Friday 10-4 and weekends 11–5 (open until 8 on Thursday in July and August). Admission is $9; get in free the second Tuesday of the month.

BEST ACTIVE ADVENTURES

ENJOY A BIKE TOUR
There's a flat, family-friendly 4.7-mi path that runs along Crystal Springs Drive and Zoo Drive. Rentals are available inside the park at Spokes n' Stuff Bike Shop (✉ *4730 Crystal Springs Dr., at the Ranger Station Parking Lot* ☎ *323/653–4099* ⊕ *www.spokes-n-stuff.com*).

HIKE THE TRAILS
Explore the rugged hills and remote areas hiking along the park's 53-mile network of trails. Maps and other information are available at the park's Ranger Station (☎ *323/913–4688*).

GO HORSEBACK RIDING
Although riders must stay on specially marked trails, much of the park can be seen on horseback. Private stables are located in the park's northwest and southwest boundaries.

BEST FOR KIDS

TAKE A PONY RIDE
Hop on top of a pony or horse—or try a covered wagon ride—along the oval track located near the Los Feliz park entrance (☎ *323/662–5874*).

SAY ALL ABOARD
If your kids love trains, they'll be riding high at Griffith Park with a ton of options, such as seeing old locomotives and taking miniature train rides. **Travel Town** (✉ *5200 Zoo Dr.* ☎ *323/662–5874*) is a free, outdoor museum that has a fantastic collection of old locomotives, cabooses, freight cars, and more as well as a miniature train ride around the museum. **The Griffith Park Southern Railroad** (✉ *4400 Crystal Springs Dr.* ☎ *323/664–6903*) has run miniature train rides since 1948. For riding a real steam locomotive, there's the **Los Angeles Steamers Live Railroad Museum** (✉ *5202 Zoo Dr.* ☎ *323/662–8030*), although it's only open Sunday from 11 to 3.

RIDE THE MERRY-GO-ROUND
L.A.'s oldest merry-go-round (☎ *323/665–3051*). Adults and kids can ride for $2 each.

DID YOU KNOW?

Renovations to the Griffith Planetarium have made its interior nearly as spectacular as the views of Hollywood from outside.

Sightseeing
★★★★★
Nightlife
★★★★
Dining
★★★
Lodging
★★
Shopping
★★

The Tinseltown mythology of Los Angeles was born in Hollywood. But reputation aside, it's a workaday neighborhood without the glitz and glamour of places like Beverly Hills. Still, like Downtown L.A., Hollywood is undergoing a transformation designed to lure hipsters and big money back into the fold. New sleek clubs and restaurants seem to pop up every month drawing in celebrities, scenesters, and starry-eyed newcomers to create a colorful nighttime landscape (and some parking headaches).

Updated by
Elline Lipkin

Many daytime attractions can be found on foot around the home of the Academy Awards at the **Kodak Theatre,** part of the **Hollywood & Highland** entertainment complex. The adjacent **Grauman's Chinese Theatre** delivers silver screen magic with its cinematic facade and ornate interiors from a bygone era. A shining example of a successful Hollywood revival can be seen and experienced just across Hollywood Boulevard at the 1926 **El Capitan Theater,** which offers live stage shows and a Wurlitzer organ before selected movie engagements.

Walk the renowned **Hollywood Walk of Stars** to find your favorite celebrities and you can encounter derelict diversions literally screaming for your attention (and dollar), numerous panhandlers, and an occasional costumed superhero not sanctified by Marvel Comics. At Sunset and Vine, a developer-interpreted revival with sushi, stars, and swank condos promises to continue the sporadic renovations of the area. In summer, visit the crown jewel of Hollywood, the **Hollywood Bowl,** which features shows by the Los Angeles Philharmonic.

It's only a few miles north from the Hollywood Bowl on the freeway, yet some say it's worlds away. The **San Fernando Valley**—*The* Valley— has seemingly always had a bad rap. Mocked in the infamous Frank Zappa song and Nicolas Cage film, both of the same name, "Valley Girl," this area of suburban bliss is located just over the hill from the notably cooler areas of Downtown, Hollywood, and the Westside. But despite all the snickering, the Valley is home to many of the sets and artists that have made Los Angeles famous: **Disney Studios; Warner Bros. Studios; Universal Studios;** and **NBC Television Studios.**

TOP ATTRACTIONS

★ **Grauman's Chinese Theatre.** A place that inspires the phrase "only in Hollywood," these stylized Chinese pagodas and temples have become a shrine to stardom. Although you have to buy a movie ticket to appreciate the interior trappings, the courtyard is open to the public. The main theater itself is worth visiting, if only to see a film in the same seats as hundreds of celebrities who have attended big premieres here. You could also opt for a tour for $12.50 that takes you around the theaters and the VIP lounge.

And then, of course, outside in front are the oh-so-famous cement hand-and footprints. This tradition is said to have begun at the theater's opening in 1927, with the premiere of Cecil B. DeMille's *King of Kings,* when actress Norma Talmadge just happened to step into wet cement. Now more than 160 celebrities have contributed imprints for posterity, including some oddball specimens, such as ones of Whoopi Goldberg's dreadlocks. ⊠ *6925 Hollywood Blvd., Hollywood* ☎ *323/464–8111, 323/463–9576 for tours* ⊕ *www.manntheatres.com.*

Fodor's Choice **Griffith Observatory.** High on a hillside overlooking the city, the Griffith
★ Observatory is one of the most celebrated icons of Los Angeles. And now, its interior is as impressive as its exterior after a massive expansion and cosmic makeover.

Highlights of the building include the Foucault's pendulum hanging in the main lobby, the planet exhibitions on the lower level, and the playful wall display of galaxy-themed jewelry along the twisty indoor ramp.

In true L.A. style, the Leonard Nimoy Event Horizon Theater presents guest speakers and shows on current space-related topics and discoveries. The planetarium now features a new dome, laser digital projection system, theatrical lighting, and a stellar sound system. Shows are $7.

During your visit, don't miss a quick and delicious meal at the Café at the End of the Universe, which serves up dishes created by celebrity chef Wolfgang Puck of Spago.

For a fantastic view, come is at sunset to watch the sky turn fiery shades of red with the city's skyline silhouetted. ⊠ *2800 E. Observatory Rd., Griffith Park* ☎ *213/473–0800* ⊕ *www.griffithobservatory.org* ☉ *Tues.– Fri. noon–10, weekends 10–10.*

Hollywood Bowl. Classic Hollywood doesn't get better than this. Summer-evening concerts have been a tradition since 1922 at this amphitheater cradled in the Hollywood Hills. The Bowl is the summer home of the Los Angeles Philharmonic, but the musical fare also includes pop and jazz. A new much larger shell arrived in 2004, improving the acoustics and allowing the occasional dance and theater performance on stage with the orchestra.

Evoking the 1929 shell structure, the new shell ripples out in a series of concentric rings. The 17,000-plus seating capacity ranges from boxes (where alfresco preconcert meals are catered) to concrete bleachers in

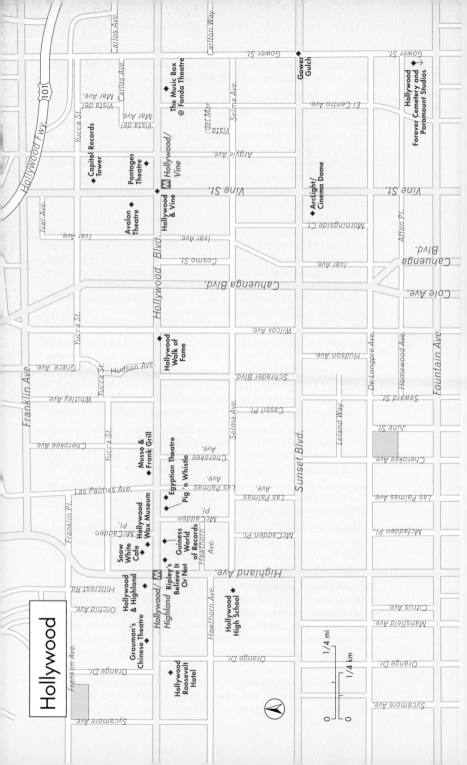

There are more than 2,000 stars honored on the Hollywood Walk of Fame.

the rear. Most of the box seats are reserved for season ticket holders, but the ideally located "super seats," with comfortable armrests and great sight lines, are your best bet. Dollar tickets are available for some weeknight classical and jazz performances. Come early to picnic on the grounds.

Before the concert, or during the day, visit the **Hollywood Bowl Museum** for a time-capsule version of the Bowl's history. The microphone used during Frank Sinatra's 1943 performance is just one of the pieces of rare memorabilia on display.

Throughout the gallery, drawers open to reveal vintage programs or letters written by fans tracing their fondest memories of going to the Bowl. Listen with headphones to recordings of such great Bowl performers as Amelita Galli-Curci, Ella Fitzgerald, and Paul McCartney. Videos give you a tantalizing look at performances by everyone from the Beatles to Esa-Pekka Salonen. Be sure to pick up a map and take the "Bowl Walk" to explore the parklike grounds of this beautiful setting. During the summer, the store stays open until showtime. ☎ 323/850–2058 ☉ *Tues.–Fri. 10–5, Sat. by appointment* ✉ *2301 N. Highland Ave., Hollywood* ☎ *323/850–2000* ⊕ *www.hollywoodbowl. com* ✉ *Museum free* ☉ *Grounds daily dawn–dusk, call or check online for performance schedule.*

Fodor's Choice ★ **Hollywood Museum.** Lovers of Hollywood's glamorous past will be singing "Hooray for Hollywood" when they stop by this gem of cinema history. It's inside the Max Factor Building, purchased in 1928. Factor's famous makeup was made on the top floors, and on the ground floor was a salon. After its renovation, this Art Deco landmark now holds more than 10,000 bits of film memorabilia.

The extensive exhibits inside include those dedicated to Marilyn Monroe and Bob Hope and to costumes and set props from such films as *Moulin Rouge, The Silence of the Lambs,* and *Planet of the Apes.* There's an impressive gallery of photos showing movie stars frolicking at such venues as the Brown Derby, Ciro's, the Trocadero, and the Mocambo.

Hallway walls are covered with the stunning autograph collection of ultimate fan Joe Ackerman; aspiring filmmakers will want to check out an exhibit of early film equipment. The museum's showpiece, however, is the Max Factor exhibit, where separate dressing rooms are dedicated to Factor's "color harmony": creating distinct looks for "brownettes" (Factor's term), redheads, and of course, bombshell blondes. You can practically smell the peroxide of Marilyn Monroe getting her trademark platinum look here, and see makeup cases owned by Lucille Ball, Lana Turner, Ginger Rogers, Bette Davis, Rita Hayworth, and others who made the makeup as popular as the starlets who wore it. ⊠ *1660 N. Highland Ave., Hollywood* ☎ *323/464-7776* ⊕ *www. thehollywoodmuseum.com* ⊠ *$15* ⊙ *Wed.–Sun. 10–5.*

★ **Hollywood Walk of Fame.** Along Hollywood Boulevard runs a trail of affirmations for entertainment-industry overachievers. On this mile-long stretch of sidewalk, inspired by the concrete handprints in front of Grauman's Chinese Theatre, names are embossed in brass, each at the center of a pink star embedded in dark-gray terrazzo. They're not all screen deities; many stars commemorate people who worked in a technical field. The first eight stars were unveiled in 1960 at the northwest corner of Highland Avenue and Hollywood Boulevard: Olive Borden, Ronald Colman, Louise Fazenda, Preston Foster, Burt Lancaster, Edward Sedgwick, Ernest Torrence, and Joanne Woodward (some of these names have stood the test of time better than others). Since then, more than 1,600 others have been immortalized, though that honor doesn't come cheap—upon selection by a special committee, the personality in question (or more likely his or her movie studio or record company) pays about $15,000 for the privilege. To aid you in spotting celebrities you're looking for, stars are identified by one of five icons: a motion-picture camera, a radio microphone, a television set, a record, or a theatrical mask. Contact the **Hollywood Chamber of Commerce** (⊠ *7018 Hollywood Blvd.* ☎ *323/469-8311* ⊕ *www.hollywoodchamber.net*) for celebrity-star locations and information on future star installations.

NBC Television Studios. In the entertainment sector of Burbank, NBC studios is home to some of TV's most popular talk shows, soap operas, and news broadcasts. An hour-long tour gives you behind-the-scenes access to many of the network's shows and news programs.

If you'd like to be part of a live studio audience, free tickets are available for tapings. ⊠ *3000 W. Alameda Ave., Burbank* ☎ *818/840-3537* ⊠ *Tours $8.50.*

Paramount Pictures. With a history dating to the early 1920s, this studio produced many of Hollywood's most luminous stars, including Rudolph Valentino, Mae West, Mary Pickford, and Lucille Ball, who filmed episodes of *I Love Lucy* here.

The lot still churns out memorable movies and TV shows, such as *Forrest Gump*, *Titanic*, and *Star Trek* on the list. You can take a studio tour (reservations required; ages 12 and up) led by guides who walk and trolley you around the back lots. As well as gleaning some gossipy history (see the lawn where Lucy and Desi broke up), you'll spot the sets of TV and film shoots in progress. You can also be part of the audience for live TV tapings. Tickets are free; call for listings and times. ✉ *5555 Melrose Ave., Hollywood* ☎ *323/956–1777* ⊕ *www.paramount.com/ paramount.php* 🎟 *Tours weekdays by reservation only, $40.*

☾ **Universal Studios Hollywood.** Despite the amusement park clichés, hard-core sightseeing and entertainment junkies will make this studio required visiting.

The first-timer favorite is the tram tour, during which you can experience the parting of the Red Sea; duck from spitting creatures in Jurassic Park, visit Dr. Seuss's "Whoville," see the airplane wreckage of *War of the Worlds* and the still-creepy *Psycho* house, and be attacked by the ravenous killer shark of *Jaws* fame. The trams have audiovisual monitors that play video clips of TV shows and movies shot on the sets you pass. ■ TIP➔ This tram ride is usually the best place to start, since it's on the lower level of the park, which gets really crowded in the afternoon.

Many attractions are based on Universal films and television shows, designed to give you a thrill in one form or another. Take your pick from the bone-rattling roller coaster Revenge of the Mummy, The Ride, or see Shrek 4-D, a 15-minute trailer of 3-D animation shown in an action simulation theater. Fear Factor Live and the House of Horrors are guaranteed to provide screams, while the Animal Actors show offers milder entertainment courtesy of some talented furry friends. The attraction based on the *Simpsons* animated series takes you on a journey like no other through their Springfield neighborhood in a ride that only the beloved, albeit cantankerous, Krusty the Klown could dream up.

Throughout the park you can wander through prop-style settings of a French Village or a travel back in time to the good ol' '50s, as costumed characters mingle with guests and pose for photos. Aside from the park, CityWalk is a separate venue, with shops, restaurants, nightclubs, and movie theaters, including IMAX 3-D. ✉ *100 Universal City Plaza, Universal City* ☎ *818/622–3801* ⊕ *www.universalstudioshollywood. com* 🎟 *$74, parking $15 ($10 after 3)* ☾ *Contact park for seasonal hrs.*

Warner Bros. Studios. This major studio center wins hands-down for the most authentic behind-the-scenes look at how films and TV shows are made.

Start with a short film on Warner Bros. movies and TV shows, then hop on a tram for a ride through the sets and soundstages of such favorites as *Casablanca* and *Rebel Without A Cause*. You'll see the bungalows where icons such as Marlon Brando and Bette Davis spent time between shots, and the current production offices for Clint Eastwood and George

TOP WALK OF FAME STOPS

Here are the sites of a few of the stars along the Walk of Fame. Seeking out a particular star? Hit the directory on the Hollywood Chamber of Commerce's Web site, ⊕ *www. hollywoodchamber.net.*

Marlon Brando: 1765 Vine St.

David Bowie: 7021 Hollywood Blvd.

Carol Burnett: 6439 Hollywood Blvd.

Charlie Chaplin: 6751 Hollywood Blvd.

Tom Cruise: 6912 Hollywood Blvd.

Bette Davis: 6225 Hollywood Blvd.

Clark Gable: 1608 Vine St.

Cary Grant: 1610 Vine St.

Ella Fitzgerald: 6738 Hollywood Blvd.

Tom Hanks: 7000 Hollywood Blvd.

Audrey Hepburn: 1652 Vine St.

Alfred Hitchcock: 6506 Hollywood Blvd.

Nicole Kidman: 6801 Hollywood Blvd.

Marilyn Monroe: 6774 Hollywood Blvd.

Jack Nicholson: 6925 Hollywood Blvd.

Mary-Kate and Ashley Olsen: 6801 Hollywood Blvd.

Clooney. You might even spot a celeb or see a shoot in action; tours change from day to day, depending on the productions taking place on the lot.

Reservations are required. Call at least one week in advance and ask about provisions for people with disabilities; children under eight are not admitted. Tours are given at least every hour, more frequently from May to September, and last two hours and 15 minutes. A five-hour deluxe tour, $225 including a VIP lunch, allows visitors to spend extended time on the sets, with more ops for behind-the-scenes peeks and star spotting. ⊠ *3400 W. Riverside Dr., Burbank* ☎ *818/972–8687* ⊕ *www2. warnerbros.com/vipstudiotour* ☜ *$48* ⊙ *Weekdays 8:20–4:30.*

WORTH NOTING

ArcLight/Cinerama Dome. Film buffs and preservationists breathed a sigh of relief when the ArcLight complex opened its doors and rewrote the book on cushy moviegoing. With plush stadium seating, reserved seats for some showings, state-of-the-art sound, an usher who welcomes you and introduces the film, and snack bars that cook up fresh caramel corn, the ArcLight justifies its high ticket prices ($11.50–$14.50, depending on the hour you go). Built next to the restored geodesic Cinerama Dome, a curved-screen architectural icon, the complex also caters to film lovers with special director's Q&A nights as well as exhibits of movie costumes and photography throughout the lobby.

Weekend nights have an especially hip buzz as film enthusiasts and Industry power couples linger in the soaring lobby. Browsing in the artfully curated lobby gift shop and bookstore is a great way to pass time and people-watch. Parking is $2 in the adjacent garage with a movie

Actor Russell Crowe at the ceremony placing his star on the Walk of Fame.

ticket purchase and validation. ✉ *6360 W. Sunset Blvd., at Vine St., Hollywood* ☎ *323/464–4226* ⊕ *www.arclightcinemas.com.*

OFF THE
BEATEN
PATH

Barnsdall Park/Hollyhock House. The panoramic view of Hollywood alone is worth a trip to this hilltop cultural center. After many years of closure as the buildings were repaired and retrofitted following the 1994 Northridge earthquake, this arts center is coming back into its own.

On the grounds is the famous Hollyhock House, designed by architect Frank Lloyd Wright between 1919 and 1923. It was commissioned by philanthropist Aline Barnsdall to be the centerpiece of an arts community on the hill, complete with theaters and an actors' dorm.

While Barnsdall's project didn't turn out quite the way she planned, the park now hosts the L.A. Municipal Art Gallery and Theatre, which provides exhibit space for visual and performance artists; affordable art classes for children and adults are also taught here.

A film chronicling the Hollyhock House runs daily in the lobby of the Municipal Art Gallery—but better yet, join a docent tour of the building. Wright dubbed this style "California Romanza" (*romanza* is a musical term meaning "to make one's own form"). Stylized depictions of Barnsdall's favorite flower, the hollyhock, appear throughout the house in its cement columns, roofline, and furniture.

The leaded-glass windows are expertly placed to make the most of both the surrounding gardens and the city views. On summer weekends, there are wine-tasting events and outdoor movie screenings that are wildly popular. There is also a small farmers' market every Wednesday (noon–6 pm) in the parking lot near the entrance. ✉ *4800*

DID YOU KNOW?

Don't worry about trying to
figure out the best seats on
the Universal Studios tram—
you'll be scared out of it no
matter where you sit!

Hollywood Blvd., Los Feliz ☎ *323/644–6269* ⊕ *www.hollyhockhouse. net* 🖥 *Gallery free, Hollyhock House tour $7* ☉ *Museum: Thurs.–Sun. noon–5; 1st Fri. of month, noon–9. Hollyhock tours: Wed.–Sun. hourly 12:30–3:30.*

Capitol Records Tower. According to legend, singer Nat King Cole and songwriter Johnny Mercer suggested that the record company's headquarters should be shaped to look like a stack of 45s, and their comment produced this lasting symbol of '50s chic. Or so the story goes. Architect Welton Becket claimed he just wanted to design a structure that economized space, and in so doing, he created the world's first cylindrical office building.

On its south wall, L.A. artist Richard Wyatt's mural *Hollywood Jazz, 1945–1972* immortalizes musical greats Duke Ellington, Billie Holiday, Ella Fitzgerald, and Miles Davis. Of course, pop icons the Beatles, who are on display in stunning photos near the Vine Street entrance, are Capitol's most treasured offering. John Lennon's star on the Hollywood Walk of Fame lies in the sidewalk out front and is often the scene of gatherings on his birthday.

The recording studios are underneath the parking lot; all kinds of major artists, including Frank Sinatra, the Beatles, and Radiohead, have filled the echo chambers with sound. At the top of the tower, a blinking light spells out "Hollywood" in Morse code. Due to tightened security, the building is not open to the public. ✉ *1750 N. Vine St., Hollywood.*

Disney Studios. Although tours of this film studio are not available, a peek from Riverside Drive shows you that Disney's innovations go beyond the big and small screens to fanciful touches of architecture (note the little Mickey Mouse heads mounted on the surrounding fence). On the Michael Eisner Building, designed by architect Michael Graves, giant figures of the Seven Dwarfs support the roof's gable. The Animation Building, meanwhile, has a cartoonish spin with an 85-foot-tall "Sorcerer's Apprentice" hat, red-and-white stripes, and the word "animation" in tall letters. You can see the colorful complex from the Ventura Freeway (Highway 134). ✉ *500 S. Buena Vista, Burbank.*

Los Angeles Zoo. A short drive from downtown Los Angeles at the junction of the Ventura Freeway (Highway 134) and the Golden State Freeway (I–5) is the 80-acre Los Angeles Zoo. You'll need good walking shoes for your visit, as distances are compounded by plenty of construction detours. Notable residents here include the endangered California condor and a trio of Sumatran tiger cubs born in June 2007. The zoo's newest exhibit—"Elephants of Asia"—opened in 2010 with three elephants in an elaborate 3.8-acre enclosure of sand, grassy hills, and waterfalls. ☎ *323/644–4200* ⊕ *www.lazoo.org* 🖥 *$14.*

Egyptian Theatre. Hieroglypics in Hollywood? Why not? Impresario Sid Grauman built Hollywood's first movie palace in 1922; the Egyptian-theme theater hosted many premieres in its early heyday. In 1992 it closed, with an uncertain future. Six years later it reopened with its Tinseltown shine restored.

The nonprofit American Cinematheque now hosts special screenings and discussions with notable filmmakers, and on weekends you can watch a documentary about Hollywood history (*Forever Holly-wood*, $7). Walk past giant palm trees to the theater's forecourt and entrance. Backstage tours, which detail the theater's Old Hollywood legacy, take place twice a month (see the schedule online at ⊕ *www.americancinematheque.com*). Films, primarily classics and independents, are shown in the evening. ⊠ *6712 Hollywood Blvd.* ☎ *323/466–3456* ⊕ *www.egyptiantheatre.com* ⊠ *$10; call for tour reservations and times.*

Pig 'n Whistle. During Hollywood's heyday, the Pig 'n Whistle was the place to stop for a bite before or after seeing a movie in the Egyptian Theatre, next door. After extensive restoration, the historic restaurant is back, with overstuffed booths, dramatic paneled ceilings, and attentive service. ⊠ *6714 Hollywood Blvd., Hollywood* ☎ *323/463–0000.*

Guinness World of Records. Saluting those who have gone the extra mile to earn placement in the *Guinness Book of Records*, this for-profit museum exhibits replicas and photographs of endearing record breakers that include such oddities as the most-tattooed human and the world's heaviest man.

An interactive simulation theater allows guests to sit in moving, vibrating seats while viewing a film to actually "experience" the force of a record being broken, and educational monitors give a hands-on approach to trivia pursuit. ⊠ *6764 Hollywood Blvd., Hollywood* ☎ *323/463–6433* ⊕ *www.guinnessattractions.com* ⊠ *$15.95* ۞ *Mon.–Sun. 10 am–midnight.*

Guitar Center and Hollywood RockWalk. If you love to rock, this store salutes you. At the Guitar Center on Sunset you can try out any musical instrument your heart desires as well as view memorabilia donated by some of the store's star customers—Led Zeppelin's set list, Jeff Beck's yellow Strat guitar, and KISS members' platform boots are memorable highlights. Be sure to check out the collection of vintage guitars in the back of the store.

A place that has provided equipment for virtually every band to have come out of Los Angeles since the 1960s, the Guitar Center pays tribute to its star clientele with a "RockWalk" out front. The concrete slabs are imprinted with the talented hands of Van Halen, Bonnie Raitt, Chuck Berry, Dick Dale, Def Leppard, Carlos Santana, KISS, and others. Two standouts are Joey Ramone's upside-down hand and Lemmy of Motörhead's "middle finger salute."

Inductees are celebrated with a ceremony that's open to the public. The adjacent mini-museum displays signed sheet music and broadsides of lyrics as well star memorabilia, such as Bob Dylan's hat and harmonica. ⊠ *7425 Sunset Blvd., Hollywood* ☎ *323/874–1060* ⊕ *www.rockwalk.com* ⊠ *Free* ۞ *Mon.–Fri. 10–9, Sat. 10–8, Sun. 11–8.*

Bob's Big Boy. Only in L.A. could a Bob's Big Boy be classified a historical landmark. Built in 1949, this Big Boy stands as the best example of streamlined coffee-shop architecture in L.A. Its signature Big Boy Combo plate stacks a double-decker burger with fries and a salad, preferably with the rich blue cheese dressing.

DID YOU KNOW?

El Capitan Theatre on Hollywood Boulevard is where Orsen Welles held the world premiere of *Citizen Kane.*

The best time to come is on Friday night, when local car clubs flood the diner's parking lot to show off their restored hot rods. Weekends from 5 pm to 10 pm are carhop nights, when waitresses will serve your burger and malt on 1950s-style window trays. ⊠ *4211 W. Riverside Dr., at W. Alameda Ave., Burbank* ☎ *818/843–9334.*

Hollywood & Highland. Bringing some glitz, foot traffic and commerce back to Hollywood, the hotel-retail-entertainment complex here has become a huge tourist magnet. The design pays tribute to the city's film legacy with a grand staircase leading up to a pair of white stucco 33-foot-high elephants, a nod to the 1916 movie *Intolerance*. ■TIP➔ Pause at the entrance arch, Babylon Court, which frames the Hollywood Sign in the hills above for a picture-perfect view.

There are plenty of clothing stores and eateries, and you may find yourself ducking into these for a respite from the crowds and street artists. In the summer and during Christmas vacation—when the complex is at its busiest—special music programs and free entertainment keep strollers entertained.

A Metro Red Line station provides easy access to and from other parts of the city, and there's plenty of underground parking accessible from Highland Avenue. ⊠ *Hollywood Blvd. and Highland Ave., Hollywood* ☎ *323/467–6412 visitor center* ⊕ *www.hollywoodandhighland.com* 🅿 *Parking $2 with validation* ☉ *Mon.–Sat. 10–10, Sun. 10–7.*

**QUICK
BITES**

Dakota at the Hollywood Roosevelt Hotel. For a good meal any time of day, stop at Dakota at the Hollywood Roosevelt Hotel. At the jazz brunch on Sundays, $10 will buy you a bottomless Bloody Mary or champagne drink. Deep brown leather booths and handsome lights fastened around the hotel's columns provide a swank, yet somehow cozy retreat from the sticky sidewalks of Hollywood Boulevard just outside the leaded 15-foot windows of this historical Hollywood landmark hotel. ⊠ *7000 Hollywood Blvd.* ☎ *323/466–7000.*

Hollywood and Vine. The mere mention of this intersection inspires images of a street corner bustling with movie stars, hopefuls, and moguls arriving on foot or in Duesenbergs and Rolls-Royces. In the old days this was the hub of the radio and movie industry: film stars like Gable and Garbo hustled in and out of their agents' office buildings at these fabled cross streets.

Now that glamour has dimmed; the area only comes alive after dark as a place for theater and nightlife. An exception is the Sunday Farmer's Market (8 am–1 pm), which covers several blocks and draws locals from all over the city. Stop by to lunch on some of California's most luscious produce and people-watch.

Even the Red Line Metro station here keeps up the Hollywood theme, with a *Wizard of Oz*–style yellow brick road, giant movie projectors, and old film reels whimsically decorating the station. The **Pantages Theatre** brings in Broadway shows such as the *Lion King, Hairspray,* and a production of *Wicked* unique to L.A. ⊠ *6233 Hollywood Blvd.*

Across the street is the opulent **Music Box @ Fonda Theatre,** built in the 1920s with an open-air palazzo. Pop-music concerts and small theater productions are both put on here. ⊠ *6126 Hollywood Blvd.* ⊕ *www.henryfondatheater.com* Just north on Vine, the **Avalon Theater** hosts rock concerts and dance nights in the space where the 1950s TV show *This Is Your Life* was recorded. ⊠ *1735 N. Vine St.* ⊕ *www. avalonhollywood.com*

★ **Hollywood Forever Cemetery.** Leave it to Hollywood to have a graveyard that feels more V.I.P. than R.I.P. With its revived grounds and media-genic approach, this celebrity-filled cemetery (formerly the Hollywood Memorial Park) is well worth a visit.

The lush gardens, lakes, and spectacular views of the Hollywood sign and Griffith Park Observatory (whose founder, Griffith J. Griffith, is buried here) make it a good spot for an afternoon walk; you can pick up a map of the grounds in the gift shop. Among the graves are those of Cecil B. DeMille, Douglas Fairbanks Sr., and Mel Blanc, voice of many Warner Bros. cartoon characters, whose headstone reads, "That's all, folks!"

Film and music fans flock here to find their recently departed idols, including King Kong's love Fay Wray and punk rockers Johnny Ramone and Dee Dee Ramone (buried under his given name, Douglas Glenn Colvin). The large Grecian tomb in the center of the lake belongs to philanthropist William A. Clark Jr., founder of the Los Angeles Philharmonic. Inside the Cathedral Mausoleum is Rudolph Valentino's crypt, stained red from many lipstick kisses. For years, a mysterious "Lady in Black" visited Valentino's tomb on the anniversary of his death.

■ TIP→ In summer, the cemetery hosts events including film screenings starring Valentino and other interred residents on the mausoleum's outer wall, and the grounds become quite a party scene. At Halloween-time the cemetery hosts Dia De Los Muertos, a Mexican festival celebrating the dead with colorful costumes, art, and music. The cemetery also has a kiosk in the main office with video memorials and digital scrapbooks of those buried here.

Note: When planning a visit, even for a festive event, maintain respect to the gravesites. Many families of the departed have voiced concerns of unruly visitors. The cemetery also still performs burials here and proper etiquette is expected. ⊠ *6000 Santa Monica Blvd., Hollywood* ☎ *323/469–1181* ⊕ *www.hollywoodforever.com* ◧ *$10 movies, $10 Day of the Dead* ☉ *Daily 8:30–5.*

Hollywood Heritage Museum. A must for Cecil B. DeMille fans, this unassuming building across from the Hollywood Bowl is a trove of memorabilia from the earliest days of Hollywood filmmaking, including a thorough history of DeMille's career.

Large sections of the original stone statue props from *The Ten Commandments* lay like fallen giants among smaller items in glass cases around the perimeter of this modest museum. A documentary tracking Hollywood's golden era is worth taking in.

The Hollywood Bowl, decked out for a Fourth of July concert.

The building itself is the restored Lasky–DeMille Barn, designated a California State Historic Landmark in 1956. Early birds can catch a 3½-hour walking tour of Hollywood Boulevard the Hollywood Heritage offers on Saturday morning at 9 ($10; call to reserve a spot; no kids or pets). ⊠ *2100 N. Highland Ave., Hollywood* ☎ *323/874–2276, 323/465–6716 walking tour reservations* ⊕ *www.hollywoodheritage. org* ✉ *$7* ⊙ *Wed.–Sun. noon–4.*

OFF THE BEATEN PATH **Hollywood High School.** Grease is the word! This stellar high school has seen a who's who of Hollywood royalty in its classrooms and many productions shot in its halls. The school's most memorable starring role was in *Grease* with Sandy and Danny dancing their way across the grassy playground during a true L.A. heat wave.

Surely no other high school has such a shining alumni list. Such names as Carol Burnett, Carole Lombard, John Ritter, Lana Turner, and Sarah Jessica Parker called HHS their alma mater.

While you can't enter the school grounds, it's easy to imagine the prece-lebs struggling over an algebra equation or being asked out to the prom. You can also see the star-studded mural *Diversity in Entertainment*, by famed local painter Eloy Torrez. ⊠ *1521 N. Highland Ave., Hollywood.*

Hollywood Roosevelt Hotel. In the hotel world, the Roosevelt's something of a comeback kid. This historical landmark opened in 1927 and hosted the first Academy Awards that same year. It was a glamour magnet during Hollywood's golden age, but its reputation then slumped until the late '90s.

New owners, a substantial face-lift, and some hip club promoters turned it around. These days, you're likely to need an insider connection to get into the celeb-filled club or the Tropicana poolside bar, where you can peek at the underwater mural by David Hockney.

Though the new management tries to play down the ghost stories of the hotel's past—including sightings of Montgomery Clift, Clark Gable, and Carole Lombard—they did put a replica of the famous "Marilyn Mirror" in every room, modeled after the original, which sparked reports of the actress's ghostly reflection. ⊠ *7000 Hollywood Blvd., Hollywood* ☎ *323/466–7000* ⊕ *www.hollywoodroosevelt.com.*

★ **Hollywood Sign.** With letters 50 feet tall, Hollywood's trademark sign can be spotted from miles away. The sign, which originally read "Hollywoodland," was erected on Mt. Lee in the Hollywood Hills in 1923 to promote a real-estate development.

In 1949 the "land" portion of the sign was taken down. By 1973, the sign had earned landmark status, but since the letters were made of wood, its longevity came into question. A makeover project was launched and the letters were auctioned off (rocker Alice Cooper bought the "o", singing cowboy Gene Autry sponsored an "l") to make way for a new sign made of sheet metal.

Inevitably, the sign has drawn pranksters who have altered it over the years, albeit temporarily, to spell out "Yollyweed" (in the 1970s, to commemorate lenient marijuana laws), "go navy" (before a Rose Bowl game), and "Perotwood" (during the 1992 presidential election). A fence and surveillance equipment have since been installed to deter intruders. Use caution if driving up to the sign on residential streets since many cars speed around the blind corners. ⊕ *www.hollywoodsign.org.*

Hollywood Wax Museum. If a walk through Hollywood hasn't yielded any star-spotting, head over to this venerable icon of a museum which has been open continuously for more than 45 years.

Get up close and personal with the trio of contemporary Charlie's Angels (Drew Barrymore, Cameron Diaz, and Lucy Liu), or pose with a dapper, lifelike Samuel L. Jackson. Vignettes from classic films recreate well-known scenes, such as Katharine Hepburn and Humphrey Bogart in *The African Queen* or Tom Hanks in *Forrest Gump*, as well as the figures from *The Wizard of Oz*, on display since 1965. There's an homage to Heath Ledger in *The Dark Knight,* alongside older icons such as John Wayne and the ever-present Charlie Chaplin.

Be sure to walk the red carpet with the latest Oscar stars and, if you're so inclined, creep along the dimly lit "horror chamber" where scenes from popular films of fright are reconstructed. The effect is heightened at night when fewer visitors are around.

Exhibits change on a regular basis, so expect new figures to join the wax family each visit. ⊠ *6767 Hollywood Blvd., Hollywood* ☎ *323/462–5991* ⊕ *www.hollywoodwaxmuseum.com/hollywood* ⊒ *$15.95* ◷ *Daily, 10 am–midnight.*

DID YOU KNOW?

The Kodak Theatre, home to the Academy Awards, has daily half-hour tours on which you can get a firsthand view of the place where Hollywood honors its own.

Musso & Frank Grill. Open since 1919, it is the last remaining Old Hollywood watering hole. Come for dinner or just stop in for a martini and soak up some atmosphere. Expect dark wood, framed photos, high prices, and some unjustified attitude. ✉ *6667 Hollywood Blvd., at N. Las Palmas Ave.* ☎ *323/467–5123* ◷ *Closed Sun. and Mon.*

Snow White Cafe. On the lighter and weirder side, the Snow White Cafe, opened in 1946, supposedly created by some of the original Disney animators and filled with murals of the film's characters, is a good stop for a quick bite. ✉ *6769 Hollywood Blvd., at Highland Ave.* ☎ *323/465–4444.*

★ **Kodak Theatre.** Taking a half-hour tour of the theater that hosts the Academy Awards isn't cheap, but it's a worthwhile expense for movie buffs who just can't get enough insider information.

Tour guides share plenty of behind-the-scenes tidbits about Oscar ceremonies as they take you through the theater. You'll get to step into the VIP George Eastman Lounge, where celebrities mingle on the big night, and get a bird's-eye view from the balcony seating.

The interior design was inspired by European opera houses, but underneath all the trimmings, the space has one of the finest technical systems in the world.

If you aren't one of the lucky few with a ticket to the Oscars, get a glimpse of the inside by attending a musical or concert performance. ✉ *6801 Hollywood Blvd., Hollywood* ☎ *323/308–6300* ⊕ *www.kodaktheatre.com* ▤ *Free; tours $15* ◷ *Daily 10:30–4.*

Ripley's Believe It or Not. "Odditorium" is a good name for it—while the ticket price may be a bit steep for these slighted faded relics of the bizarre and sometimes creepy, where else can you see a bikini made of human hair, a sculpture of Marilyn Monroe made of shredded money, a "killing kit" from 1850, and animal freaks of nature? You're asked to "believe it or not," and many of the curiosities may fail a strict authenticity test, but it still offers some goofy fun. ✉ *6780 Hollywood Blvd., Hollywood* ☎ *323/466–6335* ⊕ *www.ripleys.com* ▤ *$14.99* ◷ *Daily 10 am–midnight.*

Beverly Hills and the Westside

WORD OF MOUTH

"Saturday is the only day the restaurant at the Getty Center is open for dinner. Absolutely go there, and you must make a reservation. The food is excellent, the service is very good, and the overall experience is wonderful."

—Barbara

GETTING ORIENTED

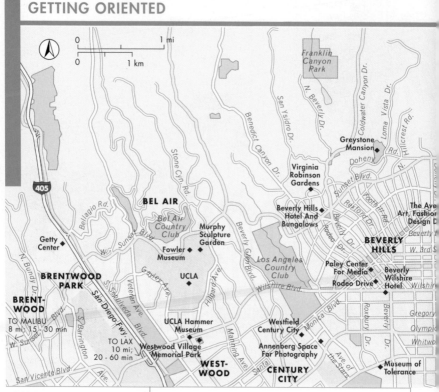

DRIVING TIMES AND DISTANCES

Minimum times listed below represent little to no traffic; maximum times assume the worst.

Adjust accordingly taking rush hour and peak weekend travel time into account.

■ **From LAX:** 30–75 min/15 mi

■ **From Downtown:** 20–45 min/12 mi

■ **From Abbot Kinney:** 20–30 min/8 mi

■ **From Malibu:** 15–30 min/8 mi

GETTING HERE

Driving Strategy

If Santa Monica is jammed up, try Pico or Olympic Boulevard, which run roughly parallel a bit farther south. Westwood Village and Brentwood's commercial district on San Vicente Boulevard come alive at night and on weekends, and the afternoon rush hour can be maddening—another good reason to plan museum trips early in the day or on Sunday.

Parking

For street parking, bring plenty of quarters; parking on residential streets is by permit only.

Finding parking along Wilshire Boulevard can present a challenge any time of the day; you can find advice on the information phone lines of most attractions.

In Beverly Hills, park your car in one of several municipal lots (the first one or two hours are free at most of them), and spend as long as you like strolling along Rodeo Drive.

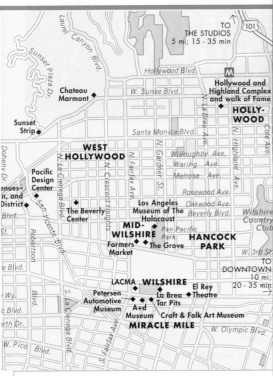

4

PLANNING YOUR TIME

Museums open between 10 and noon. LACMA is open Monday but closed Wednesday and has extended hours into the evening, closing at 8 (9 on Friday). The other museums are closed on Monday (except the Page).

Set aside a day to do this entire tour: an hour or two for the Farmers Market and The Grove, four hours for the museums, and an hour for the Wilshire Boulevard sights.

After a drive along Sunset Boulevard and a foray into the hills to see opulent homes, plan to arrive in the Golden Triangle of Beverly Hills at midday. Most stores open by 10 or 11, with limited hours on Sunday. (Some close on Sunday or Monday.)

Advance reservations are not essential but are recommended for visits to the Museum of Tolerance, closed Saturday, and the Getty Center, closed Monday—so plan accordingly. Each museum merits at least a half day.

TOP REASONS TO GO

Shop on Rodeo. Even if it's window shopping, it's a one-of-a-kind experience to watch the parade of diamonds, couture gowns, and Ferraris being fetishized.

Explore the Grounds and Gallery at the Getty. The galleries are fantastic, but go to enjoy the view, Richard Meier's architecture, and the Central Garden.

Get Artsy at LACMA. With the addition of the Eli Broad Museum of Contemporary Art, there is a breadth of artistic expression to be enjoyed.

Feast at the Farmers Market. Visit for a shopping respite or to take in and appreciate the Farmers Market 75-year-old history and atmosphere.

Cruise down Sunset Blvd to the Ocean. The quintessential Los Angeles experience—it's best to start at La Cienega headed west on Sunset so that you get to see the Sunset Strip.

Sightseeing
★★★★
Nightlife
★★★
Dining
★★★★
Lodging
★★★★
Shopping
★★★★★

If you only have a day to see L.A., see Beverly Hills. Love it or hate it, it delivers on a dramatic, cinematic scale of wealth and excess. Beverly Hills is the town's biggest movie star, and she always lets those willing to part with a few bills into her year-round party. Just remember to bring your sunscreen, sunglasses, and money for parking.

Updated by
Alene Dawson

Boutiques and restaurants line the palm tree–fringed sidewalks. People tend to stroll, not rush. Shopping ranges from the accessible and familiar (Pottery Barn) to the unique, expensive, and architecturally stunning (Prada on **Rodeo Drive**). It's hard not to imagine yourself in a film since this locale has basically become a backlot itself.

Just a few blocks west on **Santa Monica Boulevard** is Beverly Hills' buttoned-down brother, **Century City**. If Beverly Hills is about spending money, Century City is about making it. This district of glass office towers is home to entertainment companies—including two of Hollywood's key talent agencies, CAA and ICM, law firms, and investment corporations. It's a particularly precise place, with angular fountains, master-planned boulevards, and pedestrian bridges making it worth a drive down its famous "Avenue of the Stars" if only to imagine yourself amongst them.

From Los Feliz to the ocean edges of Santa Monica, privilege is on display in the City of Angeles as exemplified by the wealth of both movie star mansions of bygone eras (particularly Hollywood's Golden Age) and McMansions, especially as you cozy up to "The Hills." But the neighborhoods widely touted as chicest are the infamous **Westside** enclaves **Beverly Hills** and **Bel Air**, as well as lesser-known **Brentwood** and the **Pacific Palisades**. But don't let the glitter (and glitterati!) blind you to the Westside's other offerings. The area is rich in culture—and not just entertainment-industry culture. It's home to **UCLA** in **Westwood**, the monumental **Getty Center**, and the engrossing **Museum of Tolerance**.

West Hollywood is not a place to see things (like museums or movie studios) as much as it is a place to do things—like go to a nightclub, eat at a world-famous restaurant, or attend an art gallery opening. Since

Beverly Hills is a separate city from Los Angeles, with its own beautiful city hall.

the end of Prohibition, the **Sunset Strip** has been Hollywood's nighttime playground, where stars headed to such glamorous nightclubs as the Trocadero, the Mocambo, and Ciro's. Las Vegas eclipsed the Strip's glitter in the 1950s, but in the next decade the music industry moved into town, and rock clubs like the **Whisky-A-Go-Go** took root. While the trendiest nightclubs are orbiting elsewhere, today's Sunset Strip is still going strong, with clubgoers lining up outside well-established spots like the **House of Blues** and Hollywood insiders cued outside the members-only paparazzi stake-out **Soho House** near the Beverly Hills border. But hedonism isn't all that drives West Hollywood. Also thriving is an important interior-design and art-gallery trade exemplified by the Cesar Pelli–designed **Pacific Design Center**.

In the 1980s, a coalition of seniors, gays, and lesbians spearheaded a grassroots effort to bring cityhood to West Hollywood, which was still an unincorporated part of Los Angeles County. The coalition succeeded in 1984, and today West Hollywood has emerged as one of the most progressive cities in southern California. It's also one of the most gay-friendly cities anywhere, with one-third of its population estimated to be either gay or lesbian. Its annual Gay Pride Parade is one of the largest in the nation, drawing tens of thousands of participants each June.

The three-block stretch of **Wilshire Boulevard** known as **Museum Row**, east of Fairfax Avenue, racks up five intriguing museums and a prehistoric **La Brea Tar Pits** it to boot. Only a few blocks away are the historic **Farmers Market and The Grove** shopping mall, a great place to people-watch over breakfast.

The Farmers Market is a great place to pick up prepared food, baked goods, and more, making it a popular place for a quick meal.

Wilshire Boulevard itself is something of a cultural monument—it begins its grand 16-mi sweep to the sea in Downtown Los Angeles. Along the way it passes through once-grand but now run-down neighborhoods near MacArthur Park; Mid-Wilshire, holding some of the city's first high-rise office buildings; the elegant old-money enclave of Hancock Park along with **Miracle Mile** and Museum Row; the showy city of Beverly Hills; and the high-price high-rise condo corridor in Westwood, before ending its march at the cliffs above the Pacific Ocean.

The drive from Downtown to the ocean can be traffic clogged; Wilshire is a major thoroughfare and tends to be busy all day long. For avid urban explorers, the most interesting stretch historically is the boulevard's eastern portion, from Fairfax Avenue to Downtown.

TOP ATTRACTIONS

The Avenues: Art, Fashion & Design District. Established in 1996, the area defined by Melrose Avenue and Robertson and Beverly boulevards is The Avenues: Art, Fashion & Design District. More than 300 businesses including art galleries, antique shops, contemporary furniture and interior design stores, high-end boutiques, and about 40 restaurants are clustered here.

Note that some showrooms are reserved for design professionals and require trade credentials, and not open to the public. ☎ *310/289–2534,* ⊕ *avenueswh.com.*

Fodor's Choice **Farmers Market and The Grove.** The saying "Meet me at 3rd and Fairfax"
★ became a standard line for generations of Angelenos who ate, shopped, and spotted the stars who drifted over from the studios for a breath of unpretentious air.

Starting back in 1934 when two entrepreneurs convinced oil magnate E.B. Gilmore to open a vacant field for a bare-bones market, this spot became a humble shop for farmers selling produce out of their trucks. From this seat-of-the-pants situation grew a European-style open-air market and local institution at the corner of 3rd Street and Fairfax Avenue.

Now the market includes 110 stalls and more than 30 restaurants, plus the landmark 1941 Clock Tower. The Grove celebrated its 10th anniversary in 2012, and the outdoor mall, with its pseudo-European facade, cobblestones, marble mosaics, and pavilions has never been more popular or packed, especially on weekends.

Los Angeles history gets a nod with the electric steel-wheeled Red Car trolley, which shuttles two blocks through the Farmers Market and The Grove. If you hate crowds, try visiting The Grove before noon for the most comfortable shopping experience. By afternoon, it bustles with shoppers and teens hitting the movie theaters and chain stores such as Banana Republic, Crate & Barrel, Barnes & Noble, and J. Crew. Fashionistas find a haven at the Barney's Co-Op store.

The parking structure on the east side for The Grove handles the cars by monitoring the number of spaces available as you go up each level. The first hour of parking is free, as is the second with a validated ticket. Surface parking for the Farmers market is two hours free with validation. ⊠ *Farmers Market, 6333 W. 3rd St.; The Grove, 189 The Grove Dr., Fairfax District* ☎ *323/933–9211 Farmers Market, 323/900–8080 The Grove* ⊕ *www.farmersmarketla.com* ☉ *Farmers Market weekdays 9–9, Sat. 9–8, Sun. 10–7; The Grove Mon.–Thurs. 10–9, Fri. and Sat. 10–10, Sun. 11–8. Some vendors, bars, and restaurants are open earlier and stay open later.*

QUICK BITES

Feeling peckish? The Farmers Market is the place to be. Snag a snack at one of the fruit stands or fresh bakeries, or for something more substantial, hit the French Crêpe Company for made-on-the-spot crepes, waffles, salads, and sandwiches. (☎ 323/934–3113). In the middle of the Farmers Market is also the long-standing favorite Gumbo Pot, which steams with Cajun goodies—gumbos, jambalaya, corn bread, and beignets. (☎ 323/933–0358). Another favorite is Brazilian buffet *churrascaria* (or steak house) Pampas Grill for slowly turning steak, lamb, and bacon-wrapped chicken. (☎ 323/931–1928).

Fodor's Choice ★

The Getty Center. With its curving walls and isolated hilltop perch, the Getty Center resembles a pristine fortified city of its own. You may have been lured up by the beautiful views of L.A. (on a clear day stretching all the way to the Pacific Ocean), but the architecture, uncommon gardens, and fascinating art collection will be more than enough to capture and hold your attention.

When the sun is out, the complex's rough-cut travertine marble skin seems to soak up the light. You'll need to do some advance planning, since parking reservations are sometimes required during vacation periods, but the experience is well worth the effort.

BEST SPOTS FOR STAR SIGHTING

■ **Hit Hotel Bars and Spas.** Wait for your car at the valet stand at any of the big, insider hotels during Award Season, such as the Beverly Wilshire Beverly Hills (a Four Seasons Hotel), Chateau Marmont, or Sunset Tower. You don't have to book a room in the hotel to valet your car here, you can stop in for a meal or cocktail, as all three hotels have swanky restaurants and bars.

■ **Stroll Along Robertson Boulevard.** The paparazzi-filled street of Robertson in West Hollywood is a good bet, especially if you watch who comes in and out of the boutique Kitson or iconic restaurant the Ivy.

■ **Eat at Industry Restaurants.** There are those certain places filmmakers and celebs love—whether it's for the special treatment there or simply the food—such as Mr. Chow in Beverly Hills, Dan Tana's on Sunset in West Hollywood, or members-only Soho House.

J. Paul Getty, the billionaire oil magnate and art collector, began collecting Greek and Roman antiquities and French decorative arts in the 1930s. He opened the J. Paul Getty Museum at his Malibu estate in 1954, and in the 1970s, he built a re-creation of an ancient Roman village to house his initial collection.

When Getty died in 1976, the museum received an endowment of $700 million that grew to a reported $4.2 billion. The **Getty Villa Malibu**, reopened in 2006, is devoted to the antiquities. The Getty Center, designed by Richard Meier, opened in 1998 and pulled together the rest of the collections, along with the museum's affiliated research, conservation, and philanthropic institutes.

Getting to the center involves a bit of anticipatory lead-up. At the base of the hill, a pavilion disguises the underground parking structure. From there you either walk or take a smooth, computer-driven tram up the steep slope (make sure to glance out at the Bel Air estates across the humming 405 freeway). The five pavilions that house the museum surround a central courtyard and are bridged by walkways. From the courtyard, plazas, and walkways, you can survey the city from the San Gabriel Mountains to the ocean.

In a ravine separating the museum and the Getty Research Institute, conceptual artist Robert Irwin created the playful **Central Garden** in stark contrast to Meier's mathematical architectural geometry. The garden's design is what Hollywood feuds are made of: Meier couldn't control Irwin's vision, and the two men sniped at each other during construction, with Irwin stirring the pot with every loose twist his garden path took. The result is a refreshing garden walk whose focal point is an azalea maze (some insist the Mickey Mouse shape is on purpose) in a reflecting pool.

Inside the pavilions are the galleries for the permanent collections of European paintings, drawings, sculpture, illuminated manuscripts, and decorative arts, as well as American and European photographs. The Getty's collection of French furniture and decorative arts, especially from the early years of Louis XIV (1643–1715) to the end of the reign of Louis XVI (1774–92), is renowned for its quality and condition; you can see a pair of completely reconstructed salons.

In the paintings galleries, a computerized system of louvered skylights allows natural light to filter in, creating a closer approximation of the conditions in which the artists painted. Notable among the paintings are Rembrandt's *The Abduction of Europa*, Van Gogh's *Irises*, Monet's *Wheatstack, Snow Effects,* and *Morning,* and James Ensor's *Christ's Entry into Brussels.*

If you want to start with a quick overview, pick up the brochure in the entrance hall that guides you to 15 highlights of the collection. There's also an instructive audio tour ($5) with commentaries by art historians. Art information rooms with multimedia computer stations contain more details about the collections.

The Getty also presents lectures, films, concerts, and special programs for kids and families. The complex includes an upscale restaurant and downstairs cafeteria with panoramic window views, and two outdoor coffee bar cafés. ■TIP→ On-site parking is subject to availability and usually fills up by late afternoon on holidays and summer weekends, so try to come early in the day. You may also take public transportation (MTA Bus 761). ⊠ *1200 Getty Center Dr., Brentwood* ☎ *310/440–7300* ⊕ *www.getty.edu* ☜ *Free, parking $15* ☉ *Tues.–Fri. 10–5:30, Sat. 10–9, Sun. 10–5:30.*

La Brea Tar Pits. Do your children have dinos on the brain? Show them where dinosaurs come from by taking them to the stickiest park in town.

About 40,000 years ago, deposits of oil rose to the earth's surface, collected in shallow pools, and coagulated into asphalt. In the early 20th century, geologists discovered that all that goo contained the largest collection of Pleistocene, or Ice Age, fossils ever found at one location: more than 600 species of birds, mammals, plants, reptiles, and insects. Roughly 100 tons of fossil bones have been removed in excavations over the last seven decades, making this one of the world's most famous fossil sites.

You can see most of the pits through chain-link fences. (They can be a little smelly, but your kids are sure to love it.) Pit 91 and Project 23 are ongoing excavation projects; tours are available, and you can volunteer to help with the excavations in summer. There are several pits scattered around Hancock Park and the surrounding neighborhood; construction in the area has often had to accommodate them, and in nearby streets and along sidewalks, little bits of tar occasionally ooze up, unstoppable.

WORD OF MOUTH

"As for places to go, the Getty Museum, off the 405 freeway at Getty Drive, is a must. It's architecturally beautiful and the gardens are absolutely wonderful. It's not the type of museum that you have to just focus on the artworks as we Angelenos like to be outside, which is why the outside spaces and views are so breathtaking. Now, in February there could be a little rain, but it shouldn't be any big deal. We're outside all year here." —Guenmai

The nearby **Page Museum at the La Brea Tar Pits** displays fossils from the tar pits and has a "Fishbowl Lab," which is a glass-walled laboratory that allows visitors a rare look behind the scenes of the museum where paleontologists and volunteers work on specimens. ⊠ *5801 Wilshire Blvd., Hancock Park, Miracle Mile* ☎ *323/934–7243* ⊕ *www. tarpits.org* ⊠ *$7, Children under 5 free, free on 1st Tues. of each month.*

Los Angeles County Museum of Art (LACMA). Without a doubt, LACMA is the focal point of the museum district that runs along Wilshire Boulevard. Chris Burden's *Urban Light* sculpture, composed of more than 200 restored cast iron antique street lamps, elegantly illuminates the building's front.

Inside, visitors will find one of the country's most comprehensive collections of roughly 100,000 objects dating from ancient times to the present. Since opening in 1965, the museum has grown into a campus of several different buildings interconnected via walkways, stretching across 20 acres.

Works from the museum's rotating permanent collection include Latin American artists such as Diego Rivera and Frida Kahlo, prominent Southern California artists, collections of Islamic and European art, paintings by Henri Matisse and Rene Magritte, as well as works by Paul Klee and Wassily Kandinsky. There's also has a solid collection of art representing the ancient civilizations of Egypt, the Near East, Greece, and Rome, plus a vast costume and textiles collection dating back to the 16th century.

As part of an ambitious 10-year face-lift plan that is becoming a work of art on its own, entitled "Transformation: The LACMA Campaign," the museum is adding buildings, exhibition galleries, and redesigning public spaces and gardens.

In early 2008, the impressive **Broad Contemporary Art Museum** (BCAM) opened. With three vast floors, BCAM's integrates contemporary art into LACMA's collection, exploring the interplay of current times with that of the past. Then in 2010, the **Lynda and Stewart Resnick Exhibition Pavilion** was added, a stunning, light-filled space designed by Renzo Piano.

LACMA's other buildings include the **Ahmanson Building**, which contains African, Middle Eastern, South and Southeast Asian collections, as well as the **Gore Rifkind Gallery for German Expressionism**; the **Art of the Americas** building; the **Pavilion for Japanese Art**, featuring scrolls, screens, drawings, paintings, textiles, and decorative arts from Japan; the **Bing Center**, a research library, resource center, and film theater; and the **Boone's Children's Gallery**, located inside the Korean art galleries in the **Hammer Building**, where kids can take advantage of activities such as story-time and learning how to brush paint.

The museum organizes special exhibitions and host major traveling shows. The extraordinarily popular "Pacific Standard Time: Art in L.A. 1945–1980" involves more than 60 other cultural institutions in Southern California, and "California Design 1930–1965: Living In A Modern Way" was the first major study of California mid-century modern design.

■TIP→ Temporary exhibits sometimes require tickets purchased in advance, so check the calendar ahead of time. ⊠ *5905 Wilshire Blvd., Miracle Mile* ☎ *323/857–6000* ⊕ *www.lacma.org* 🖾 *$15* ☉ *Mon., Tues., and Thurs. noon–8, Fri. noon–9, weekends 11–8.*

Melrose Avenue. Back when alternative music was, well, alternative (and not Top 40), Melrose drew a colorful crowd of underground punks and heavy metal peacocks scouring the anti-conformist clothing shops and record stores along the "strip" between Fairfax and Poinsettia.

Today, Melrose's hip factor has been tempered with mainstream additions such as Urban Outfitters and Coffee Bean & Tea Leaf. You can find a good selection of vintage wear at resale shops Slow and Aardvarks' Odd Ark, or pre–Hot Topic alt-rock gear at Posers or Shrine, then get your designer fix by traveling farther west to higher-end shops such as Fred Segal, Paul Smith, Marc Jacobs, Vivienne Westwood, Vera Wang, Agent Provocateur, and Betsey Johnson.

QUICK BITES

Urth Café. If the buzz of L.A. gives you a hankering for a pick-me-up, stop into Urth Café. It's pumping with crowds of the beautiful people refueling on organic eats of sandwiches, salads, fresh juices, and desserts. The outdoor patio is a great place to take in the scene. It's also a good place to spot celebrities. ⊠ *8565 Melrose Ave.* ☎ *310/659–0628.*

Museum of Tolerance. Using interactive technology, this important museum (part of the Simon Wiesenthal Center) challenges visitors to confront bigotry and racism. One of the most affecting sections covers the Holocaust, with film footage of deportation scenes and simulated sets of concentration camps. Each visitor is issued a "passport" bearing the name of a child whose life was dramatically changed by the German Nazi rule and by World War II; as you go through the exhibit, you learn the fate of that child. Anne Frank artifacts are part of the museum's permanent collection as is Wiesenthal's Vienna office, set exactly as the famous "Nazi hunter" had it while performing his research that brought more than 1,000 war criminals to justice.

Interactive exhibits include the "Millennium Machine," which engages visitors in finding solutions to human rights abuses around the world; Globalhate.com, which examines hate on the Internet by exposing problematic sites via touch-screen computer terminals; and the "Point of View Diner," a re-creation of a 1950s diner, red booths and all, that "serves" a menu of controversial topics on video jukeboxes. Renovations brought a new youth action floor and revamped 300-seat theater space.

To ensure a visit to this popular museum, make reservations in advance (especially for Friday, Sunday, and holidays) and plan to spend at least three hours there. Testimony from Holocaust survivors is offered at specified times. Museum entry stops at least two hours before the actual closing time. Although every exhibit may not be appropriate for children, school tours visit regularly. ⊠ *9786 W. Pico Blvd., just south of Beverly Hills* ☎ *310/553–8403* ⊕ *www.museumoftolerance.com* 🖾 *$15* ☉ *Weekdays 10–5, Sun. 11–5, early close at 3 pm Fri. Nov.–Mar.*

The collection at the Los Angeles County Museum of Art includes more than 100,000 objects, dating from ancient times to the present.

QUICK BITES

Newsroom. If shopping on Robertson, news junkies in particular should hit the Newsroom, which streams current event headlines nonstop on several TVs hung around the café. It also has a magazine stand to browse to distract you while you wait for a table (which could take a while during peak hours). The menu's health-focused, with smoothies and vegetarian choices. ✉ *120 N. Robertson Blvd., at Beverly Blvd.* ☎ *310/652–4444.*

★ **MOCA Pacific Design Center.** World-renowned architect Cesar Pelli's vision for the Pacific Design Center was three buildings that housed designer showrooms, office buildings, parking and more—a virtual multi-building shrine to design.

The building sheathed in blue glass (known as the Blue Whale) opened in 1975; the green building opened in 1988; and the final "Red" building has a 2012 open-date at this writing.

All together, the 1.2-million-square-foot complex covers more than 14 acres and has more than 130 design showrooms as well as 2,200 interior product lines, making it the largest interior design complex in the western United States.

You'll also find restaurants such as Red Seven by Wolfgang Puck, the Silverscreen movie theater, and a myriad of special events. The PDC also has a Designer Service to help nonprofessionals shop and get access to certain designers and showrooms. ✉ *8687 Melrose Ave., West Hollywood* ☎ *310/657–0800* ⊕ *www.pacificdesigncenter.com* ⊙ *Weekdays 9–5.*

DID YOU KNOW?

Beverly Hills became a haven for the stars during the Roaring '20s, when Charlie Chaplin, Rudolph Valentino, and dozens of other film luminaries built mansions here. Today it remains one of Southern California's most coveted addresses.

★ **Rodeo Drive.** The ultimate shopping indulgence, Rodeo Drive is one of Southern California's bona fide tourist attractions. The art of window-shopping is prime among the retail elite: Tiffany & Co., Gucci, Jimmy Choo, Valentino, Harry Winston, Prada—you get the picture.

Several nearby restaurants have patios where you can sip a drink while watching career shoppers in their size 2 threads saunter by with shopping bags stuffed with superfluous delights. At the southern end of Rodeo Drive (at Wilshire Boulevard), **Via Rodeo,** a curvy cobblestone street designed to resemble a European shopping area, makes the perfect backdrop to strike a pose for that glamour shot.

The holidays bring a special magic to Rodeo and the surrounding streets, with twinkling lights, swinging music, and colorful banners. ✉ *Beverly Hills.*

Susina Bakery. Pair a shopping high with a sugar rush at Susina Bakery, a sweet, Paris-influenced pastry place offering mouthwatering tarts, tiny cookies, decadent cakes, and candied gifts. ✉ *7122 Beverly Blvd., next to boutique Veronica M.* ☎ *323/934–7900.* **MILK.** Another favorite is MILK, so popular that they've been asked to provide desserts for Emmy after-parties. Their "Warm Ooey Gooey Chocolate Sundae" and "Milky Way Malted Milk Shakes" are few of their homemade lovelies to tempt your sweet tooth. ✉ *7920 Beverly Blvd.* ☎ *323/939–6455.* **Sweet Lady Jane.** Or take your sweet tooth over to Sweet Lady Jane, where you can eat a sandwich or lemon bar while watching people jockey for the beautifully decorated cakes. ✉ *8360 Melrose Ave., at N. Kings Rd.* ☎ *323/653–7145.*

Santa Monica Boulevard. For many gay and lesbian visitors, Santa Monica Boulevard is the Main Street of modern gay America. From La Cienega Boulevard on the east to Doheny on the west, it's the commercial core of West Hollywood's gay community, with restaurants and cafés, bars and clubs, bookstores, and other establishments catering largely to gays and lesbians. Twice a year, during June's Gay Pride Parade and on Halloween, in October, the boulevard becomes an open-air festival.

★ **Sunset Boulevard.** One of the most fabled avenues in the world, Sunset Boulevard began humbly enough in the 18th century as a route from El Pueblo de Los Angeles (today's Downtown L.A.) to the ranches in the west and then to the Pacific Ocean.

Now as it winds its way across the L.A. basin to the ocean, it cuts through gritty urban neighborhoods and what used to be the working center of Hollywood's movie industry. In West Hollywood, it becomes the sexy and seductive **Sunset Strip,** then slips quietly into the tony environs of Beverly Hills and Bel Air, twisting and winding past gated estates. Continuing on past UCLA in Westwood, through Brentwood and Pacific Palisades, Sunset finally descends to the beach, the edge of the continent, and the setting sun.

Cobblestone Via Rodeo, off Rodeo Drive, was designed to resemble a European shopping street.

WORTH NOTING

Architecture and Design Museum (A+D). Unique buildings are what make Los Angeles a captivating city, so it's no wonder that one dedicated to celebrating design would open here on Museum Row.

Exhibits are themed around residential and commercial structures, interior landscaping, product design, and their creators. Everything from hanging panels of photographs to designers' models are thoughtfully displayed in the one-room, exposed-ceiling, warehouse-style space. ⊠ *6032 Wilshire Blvd., Miracle Mile* ☎ *323/932–9393* ⊕ *www.aplusd. org* ☞ *$5* ⊗ *Tues.–Fri. 11–5, weekends 12–6.*

Beverly Hills Hotel and Bungalows. The iconic "Pink Palace" has been steeped in Hollywood lore since 1912. Greta Garbo, Howard Hughes, and other movie-industry guests kept low profiles when staying at this pastel landmark.

Indulge in a lunch in the Polo Lounge where film luminaries have cut high-powered deals (note: reservations are a must) and combine it with a stroll through the hotel's neatly manicured grounds. ⊠ *9641 Sunset Blvd., 1 mi west of Doheny Dr.* ☎ *310/276–2251* ⊕ *www. thebeverlyhillshotel.com.*

Beverly Wilshire, a Four Seasons Hotel. Anchoring the south end of Rodeo Drive at Wilshire Boulevard, this hotel has been an opulent house of luxury since opening in 1928, and it's the place to splurge on a room overlooking Rodeo drive for the quintessential Beverly Hills experience in convenient proximity to all of the luxe shops.

DID YOU KNOW?

The ubiquitous palm trees that line the streets of Beverly Hills aren't native to the region. They were popularized by developers who believed the trees were emblematic of easy living.

A renovation in 2006, along with a name change, pushes it farther up the ladder as a preferred address of the rich and famous, with additions such as an 8,000-square-foot spa, a pool bar and café, and luxurious poolside cabanas.

Need a break in the day? Dip a toe in the glamour of it all and sit courtside to the parade of Jimmy Choos and Louboutins at their restaurant Boulevard on Wilshire overlooking Rodeo Drive. ⊠ *9500 Wilshire Blvd., Beverly Hills* ☎ *310/275–5200* ⊕ *www.fourseasons. com/beverlywilshire.*

QUICK BITES

Nate 'n' Al's. A longtime refuge from California's lean cuisine, Nate 'n' Al's serves up steaming classic pastrami, matzo ball soup, and potato latkes. ⊠ *414 N. Beverly Dr., at Brighton Way, Beverly Hills* ☎ *310/274–0101.*

Farm. Or stop at the Farm and grab a seat at one of the sidewalk tables. The restaurant is known for dishes such as ahi tuna appetizer, a lobster club with applewood-smoked bacon, and a luscious brownie sundae. Reserve a table on the patio, sit back with an endless glass of iced tea with mint, and take in the view; you'll have a good chance of a celeb sighting here. ⊠ *439 N. Beverly Dr.* ☎ *310/273–5578.*

Century City. A sprawling 280 acres of office buildings, a shopping center, hotels, an entertainment complex, and residential space, this complex was built in the 1960s on what used to be the back-lot of Twentieth Century Fox. (The studio is not open to the public.) The focal point of this complex is a pair of silvery triangular towers known as **Century City Towers.** ⊠ *Ave. of the Stars and Constellation Blvd.*

The **Anenberg Space for Photography** shows digital and print award-winning riveting photography exhibitions in a sleek, modern space. ⊠ *2000 Ave. of the Stars* ☎ *213/403–3000* ⊕ *www. annenbergspaceforphotography.org* ⌂ *Free* ☉ *Wed.–Sun. 11–6*

Westfield Century City is an open-air shopping center with a sparkling white exterior that makes strolling store-to-store (through places like BCBG, Apple, Banana Republic, Kenneth Cole, and Macy's) feel like a jaunt down the catwalk. ⊠ *10250 Santa Monica Blvd.* ☎ *310/277–3898*

Chateau Marmont. If we only had a dollar for every time a celebrity interview was conducted alongside the Marmont pool. This secluded hotel, hidden in greenery off the Sunset Strip, has earned its stripes as a popular hideaway for industry actors, musicians, and writers.

The ambience is chic without being frosty; most important, the hotel cultivates a sense of privacy. Stars such as Jim Morrison, Robert De Niro, Boris Karloff, Marilyn Monroe, and Dustin Hoffman liked this hotel so much that they moved in for long periods of time. In 1982 actor John Belushi checked out permanently here, of a drug overdose.

Though most areas are strictly for guests, you can visit the main-floor lounge or outdoor patio for a meal or a cocktail. ⊠ *8221 Sunset Blvd., West Hollywood* ☎ *323/656–1010* ⊕ *www.chateaumarmont.com.*

Craft and Folk Art Museum (CAFAM). This small but important cultural landmark in the city pioneered support for traditional folk arts. These days, the two-story space takes on a global scope, embracing international contemporary crafts, social movements, and long-established artisan work. The gallery space mounts rotating exhibitions where you might see anything from costumes of carnival celebrations around the world to Mennonite quilts.

The courtyard area provides a tranquil space for periodic exhibits and opening receptions. Be sure to take a look around the ground-level gift shop for unique collection of handcrafts, jewelry, ceramics, books, and textiles. ⊠ *5814 Wilshire Blvd., Miracle Mile* ☏ *323/937–4230* ⊕ *www.cafam.org* ☟ *$7* ⊙ *Tues.–Fri. 11–5, weekends noon–6.*

Greystone Mansion. L.A.'s answer to the châteaus of Europe, this 1927 neo-Gothic mansion was owned by oilman Edward Doheny (Doheny Drive is named after him). Now owned by the city of Beverly Hills, it sits on 18½ landscaped acres and has been used in such films as *The Witches of Eastwick, Indecent Proposal,* and *There Will Be Blood.*

Guided tours of the mansion are available and the gardens are open for self-guided tours, where you can get an idea of the exquisite interior by peeking through the windows. Also, look for their in-house murder-mystery drama that plays up the mansion's dramatic history.

Sporadically, concerts are held in the mansion's courtyard on summer afternoons. The grounds close for period special events; call to check hours prior to your visit during these months. ⊠ *905 Loma Vista Dr., Beverly Hills* ☏ *310/550–4796* ⊕ *www.greystonemansion.org* ☟ *Free* ⊙ *Daily 10–5.*

QUICK BITES

For the white glove treatment, take in a spot of tea at the Greystone Mansion. Afternoon tea on the terrace is served one Saturday a month May–August. The fee is $43 per person for nonresidents. Reservations are highly recommended by calling ☏ *310/550–4753*. Tea starts promptly at 4 pm. What could be more civilized?

Hancock Park. Highland Avenue marks the western perimeter of the neighborhood called Hancock Park (which is east of the park of the same name, home of LACMA and La Brea Tar Pits). In the 1920s, wealthy families came here to build English Tudor–style homes with East Coast landscaping that defied local climate and history.

Today Hancock Park is a quiet, relatively suburban neighborhood whose residents frequently venture out to the **Larchmont Village** shopping district to browse a collection of bookstores, antiques shops, and a Saturday farmers' market. ⊠ *Bordered by Wilshire and Beverly Blvds., Highland Ave., and Wilton Pl., Mid-Wilshire.*

Koreatown. Although L.A.'s sizable Korean population is scattered throughout the city, it's especially concentrated here, along Olympic Boulevard between Vermont and Western avenues, where you can find Korean specialty food stores and restaurants among many shops displaying furniture, electronics, and other items. ⊠ *Bordered by Vermont and Western Aves., 8th St., and Pico Blvd., west of Downtown.*

Miracle Mile. The strip of Wilshire Boulevard between La Brea and Fairfax avenues was vacant land in the 1920s, when a developer bought the parcel to build a shopping and business district that catered to automobile traffic.

Nobody thought the venture could be successful, but the auto age was just emerging, and the strip became known as Miracle Mile. It was the world's first linear Downtown, with building designs incorporating wide store windows to attract attention from passing cars.

The area went into a decline in the 1950s and '60s, when high-rises began to break up its cohesiveness, but it's now enjoying a comeback as Los Angeles' Art Deco architecture has come to be appreciated, preserved, and restored. The exemplary architecture includes **El Rey Theater** (⊠ *5515 Wilshire Blvd., Miracle Mile* ☎ *323/936–6400*), now a regular concert hall.

Paley Center for Media. Formerly the Museum of Television and Radio, this institution changed its name in 2007 with a look toward a future that encompasses all media in the ever-evolving world of entertainment and information.

Reruns are taken to a curated level inside the sleek stone-and-glass building, designed by Getty architect Richard Meier. A sister to the New York location, the Paley Center carries a duplicate of its collection: more than 100,000 programs spanning eight decades.

You can search for your favorite commercials and television shows on easy-to-use computers. A radio program listening room provides cozy seats supplied with headphones, playing snippets of a variety of programming, from a toast to Dean Martin to an interview with John Lennon.

Frequent seminars with movers 'n' shakers from the film, television, and radio world are big draws, as well as screenings of documentaries and short films. Free parking is available in the lot off Santa Monica Boulevard. ⊠ *465 N. Beverly Dr., Beverly Hills* ☎ *310/786–1000* ⊕ *www. paleycenter.org* ⊙ *Wed.–Sun. noon–5.*

Petersen Automotive Museum. You don't have to be a gearhead to appreciate this building full of antique and unusual cars. The Petersen is likely to be one of the coolest museums in town with its take on some of the most unusual creations on wheels and rotating exhibits of the icons who drove them.

Lifelike dioramas and street scenes spread through the ground floor help to establish a local context for the history of the automobile. The second floor may include displays of Hollywood-celebrity and movie cars, "muscle" cars (like a 1969 Dodge Daytona 440 Magnum), alternative-powered cars, motorcycles, and a showcase of the Ferrari.

You can also learn about the origins of our modern-day car-insurance system, as well as the history of L.A.'s formidable freeway network. A children's interactive Discovery Center illustrates the mechanics of the automobile and fun child-inspired creations; there is also a gift shop. ⊠ *6060 Wilshire Blvd., Miracle Mile* ☎ *323/930–2277* ⊕ *www.petersen. org* ⊠ *$10* ⊙ *Tues.–Sun. 10–6.*

🐾 **Page Museum at the La Brea Tar Pits.** This member of the Natural History Museum family is sunk, bunkerlike, half underground. A bas-relief around four sides depicts life in the Pleistocene era, and the museum has more than 3 million Ice Age fossils. Exhibits include reconstructed, life-size skeletons of mammoths, wolves, sloths, eagles, and condors.

The fishbowl-like, glass-enclosed laboratory is a real attention getter— here you can watch paleontologists as they clean, identify, catalog, and piece together bits of fossils excavated from the nearby asphalt deposits. *The La Brea Story,* a short documentary film, is shown every 15–30 minutes. A hologram magically puts flesh on 9,000-year-old "La Brea Woman." ⊠ *5801 Wilshire Blvd., Miracle Mile* ☎ *323/934–7243* ⊕ *www.tarpits.org* ⊠ *$7, free 1st Tues. of month* ⊙ *Weekdays 9:30–5, weekends 10–5.*

Skirball Cultural Center. With a mission of exhibiting the connections "between four thousand years of Jewish heritage and the vitality of American democratic ideals," this Jewish cultural institution sits, grand in scale, atop the Santa Monica Mountains.

Within, it traces Jewish life, including immigration to America in a rotating exhibit, "Visions and Values: Jewish Life from Antiquity to America," in 12 galleries using artifacts, building reconstructions, and multimedia installations. Highlights include a large collection of Judaica and a two-thirds-size replica of the torch of the Statue of Liberty.

A big draw is the Noah's Ark interactive exhibit, where children are invited to become Noah as they join the animals in the rainstorm, board the Ark, and discover how to live in harmony with each other as they recreate the famous biblical story using their own imagination. ⊠ *2701 N. Sepulveda Blvd., north of Brentwood* ☎ *310/440–4500* ⊕ *www. skirball.org* ⊠ *$10, Thurs. free* ⊙ *Tues.–Fri. noon–5, weekends 10–5.*

Sunset Plaza. With a profusion of sidewalk cafés, Sunset Plaza is one of the best people-watching spots in town. Sunny weekends reach the highest pitch, when people flock to this stretch of Sunset Boulevard for brunch or lunch and to browse in the trendy shops that offer a range of price points. There's free parking in the lot behind the shops. ⊠ *8600 block of Sunset Blvd., a few blocks west of La Cienega Blvd., West Hollywood.*

UCLA Hammer Museum. The bold murals and installations at this museum have been known to bring traffic on Wilshire Boulevard to a crawl. In the heart of Westwood, the Hammer emphasizes the here and now, luring in crowds with splashy, eye-catching displays in its glass entryway.

Focused on art and artists of our time, the museum forms a bridge between the city's artistic expression and the forward-thinking educational spirit of adjacent UCLA. Selections from Armand Hammer's

A classic Beverly Hills mansion.

permanent collection are also incorporated, including works by Claude Monet, Vincent van Gogh, and John Singer Sargent's powerful portrait of Dr. Pozzi. The 295-seat Billy Wilder Theater opened in 2006, offering selections from UCLA's Film & Television Archive. ✉ *10899 Wilshire Blvd., Westwood* ☎ *310/443–7000* ⊕ *www.hammer.ucla.edu* ✉ *$10, free Thurs.; 3-hr parking $3 with validation* ⊗ *Tues., Wed., Fri., and Sat. 11–7, Thurs. 11–9, Sun. 11–5.*

University of California, Los Angeles (UCLA). With spectacular buildings such as a Romanesque library, the parklike UCLA campus makes for a fine stroll through one of California's most prestigious universities.

In the heart of the north campus, the **Franklin Murphy Sculpture Garden** contains more than 70 works of artists such as Henry Moore and Gaston Lachaise. The **Mildred Mathias Botanic Garden,** which contains some 5,000 species of plants from all over the world in its 7-acres, is in the southeast section of the campus and accessible from Tiverton Avenue. West of the main-campus bookstore, the **Morgan Center Hall of Fame** displays the sports memorabilia and trophies of the university's athletic departments.

Campus maps and information are available at drive-by kiosks at major entrances daily, and free 90-minute walking tours of the campus are given on weekdays at 10:15 and 2:15 and Saturday at 10:15. Call 310/825–8764 for reservations, which are required several days to two weeks in advance. The campus has cafés, plus bookstores selling UCLA Bruins paraphernalia. The main-entrance gate is on Westwood Boulevard. Campus parking costs $10.

Many visitors head straight to the **Fowler Museum at UCLA,** which presents exhibits on the world's diverse cultures and visual arts, with a particular focus on those of Africa, Asia, the Pacific, and Native and Latin America. Museum admission is free; use parking lot 4 off Sunset Boulevard ($10). The Fowler Museum is open Wednesday–Sunday noon–5, Thursday until 8 pm. ☎ *310/825–4361* ⊕ *www.fowler.ucla.edu* ✉ *Bordered by Le Conte, Hilgard, and Gayley Aves. and Sunset Blvd., Westwood* ⊕ *www.ucla.edu.*

Santa Monica and the Beaches

WORD OF MOUTH

"Venice Beach is a must-see for teens, especially if it's a nice week-end day. You can also go on the Santa Monica Pier and the 3rd Street Promenade all in the same general vicinity. SM Pier and Third Street Promenade are very close to each other—you can park in one of the free SM public garages. Parking at Venice Beach is more of a challenge, but it's worth it."

—alison

GETTING ORIENTED

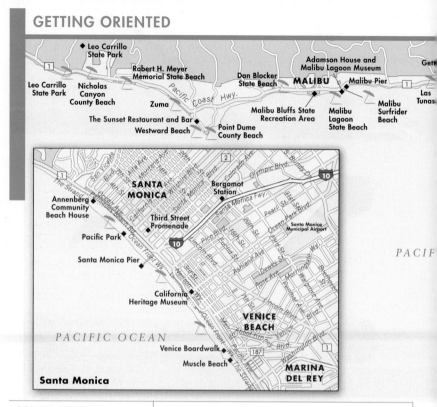

DRIVING TIMES AND DISTANCES

Minimum times listed below represent little to no traffic; maximum times assume the worst. Adjust accordingly taking rush hour and peak weekend travel time into account.

■ **LAX to Santa Monica:** 20–60 min/18 mi

■ **Santa Monica to Malibu:** 30–75 min/22 mi

■ **Santa Monica to Venice Beach:** 10–15 min/3 mi

■ **Venice Beach to Redondo Beach:** 25–40 min/13 mi

GETTING HERE

Driving Strategy. From downtown, the easiest way to hit the coast is by taking the Santa Monica Freeway (I–10) due west. Once you reach the end of the freeway, I–10 runs into the famous Highway 1. Better known as the Pacific Coast Highway, or PCH, Highway 1 continues north to Sonoma County and south to San Diego. MTA buses run from downtown along Pico, Olympic, Santa Monica, Sunset, and Wilshire boulevards westward to the coast. Driving along the coast is a quintessential L.A. experience—so is sitting in beach traffic. Avoid driving to Malibu during rush hour, when traffic along PCH moves at a snail's pace.

Parking. Public parking is usually available at beaches, though fees can range anywhere from $8 to $20; in some areas, it's possible to find free street and highway parking.

PLANNING YOUR TIME

If you've got the time, break your coastal visit into two excursions: Santa Monica and Venice on one excursion, and Malibu on the other.

The best way to "do" L.A.'s coastal communities is to park your car and walk, cycle, or skate along the bike path, known as "The Strand."

For this, of course, a sunny day is best; on all but the hottest days, when literally millions of Angelenos flock to the beaches, get started in the morning, either before or after rush hour.

Places like Santa Monica Pier, Main Street, and the Venice Boardwalk are more interesting to observe as the day progresses.

Try to avoid the boardwalk, beach, and backstreets of Santa Monica and Venice at night, when the crowds dissipate.

TOP REASONS TO GO

Bike Along the Strand. Spend the day on this 22-mile paved path, also known as the South Bay Bike Trail, that stretches from Santa Monica to Rendondo Beach.

Watch the Sun Set Over the Pacific in Malibu. Either cliff-side or parked on beach blanket, the view will stay fixed in your mind as a trip highlight.

Spend the Day at Santa Monica Pier. A fun family day or a night out, the pier's appeal is its Ferris wheel, carousel, fair food, and games galore.

Catch the Mellow Vibe in Venice Beach. Stroll along the canals, shop and grab an all-organic lunch on Albert Kinney, or watch tanned locals in tie-dye toting longboards.

Take a Surfing Lesson. The sport is said to have started on Redondo Beach in the early 1900s—learn how to hang 10 from several great schools along the coast.

Sightseeing
★★★

Nightlife
★★★

Dining
★★★★

Lodging
★★★

Shopping
★★★★

L.A.'s beaches are an iconic and integral part of Southern California, and getting some sand on the floor of your car is practically a requirement. Hugging the Santa Monica Bay in an arch, the desirable communities of Malibu, Santa Monica, and Venice move from ultrarich to ultracasual to bohemian. What they have in common, however, is cleaner air, mild temperatures, horrific traffic, and an emphasis on the fun in the sun beach-focused lifestyle.

Updated by
Elline Lipkin

Santa Monica—which, because of its liberal populace, has been dubbed the People's Republic of Santa Monica—is a pedestrian-friendly little city, about 8.3 square mi, with a dynamic population of artists and writers, entertainment folks, educators, and retired people, all attracted by the cooler, sometimes-foggy climate. Mature trees, Mediterranean-style architecture, and strict zoning have helped create a sense of place often missing from L.A.'s residential neighborhoods. This character comes with a price: real estate costs are astronomical.

Venice was a turn-of-the-20th-century fantasy that never quite came true. Abbot Kinney, a wealthy Los Angeles businessman, envisioned this little piece of real estate as a romantic replica of Venice, Italy. He developed an incredible 16 mi of canals, floated gondolas on them, and built scaled-down versions of the Doge's Palace and other Venetian landmarks. Some canals were rebuilt in 1996, but they don't reflect the old-world connection quite as well as they could.

Ever since Kinney first planned his project, it was plagued by ongoing engineering problems and drifted into disrepair. Today only a few small canals and bridges remain. On nearby **Abbot Kinney Boulevard** there's a wealth of design and home decor shops and chic cafés—plus great people-watching.

North of Santa Monica, up the **Pacific Coast Highway**, past rock slides, Rollerbladers, and cliffside estates, is **Malibu**. Home to blockbuster names like Spielberg, Hanks, and Streisand, this ecologically fragile

23-mi stretch of coastline can feel like a world of its own, with its slopes slipping dramatically into the ocean.

In the public imagination Malibu is synonymous with beaches and wealth—but in the past couple of years there's been some friction between these two signature elements. Some property owners, such as billionaire music producer David Geffen, have come under attack for blocking public access to the beaches in front of their homes. All beaches are technically public, though; if you stay below the mean high-tide mark you're in the clear.

And everyone is welcome (with reservations) to the reimagined yet still intimate seaside **Getty Villa** and its collection of Greek, Etruscan, and Roman art and artifacts.

SANTA MONICA

TOP ATTRACTIONS

5

Main Street. It's a great spot for star-sighting, and also for anyone who enjoys strolling along a street with lots of laid-back Californians. Crowds pop in and out of old-fashion, colorful and cozy boutiques that stock everything from high-end fashion to bohemian favorites. There's also a good selection of casual restaurants and cafés dotted in between shops. ⊠ *Between Pacific St. and Rose Ave., and Santa Monica and Venice Blvds., Santa Monica.*

Santa Monica Aquarium. Run by beach conservation group Heal the Bay, this live marine life menagerie contains more than 100 species of marine animals and plants, all found in Santa Monica Bay. A theater room runs education films throughout the day, and a Kid's Corner provides books, games, and a puppet-show.

Don't miss this chance learn about the area's ecology and how pollution is affecting the marine environment. The Aquarium can be tricky to find—look for it tucked under the eastern end of the Santa Monica Pier bridge along Ocean Front Walk. Follow the seascape murals that cover the outside walls. ⊠ *1600 Ocean Front Walk, Santa Monica* 🕾 *310/393–6149* ⊕ *www.healthebay.org/smpa* 🖃 *$3* ⏱ *Tues.–Fri. 2–5, weekends 12:30–5.*

☾ **Santa Monica Pier.** Souvenir shops, carnival games, arcades, eateries, an outdoor trapeze school, and Pacific Park are all part the festive atmosphere of this truncated pier at the foot of Colorado Boulevard, below Palisades Park. The pier's indoor trademark 46-horse Looff Carousel, built in 1922, has appeared in several films, including *The Sting.* Free concerts are held on the pier in summer. ⊠ *Colorado Ave. and the ocean, Santa Monica* 🕾 *310/458–8900* ⊕ *www.santamonicapier.org* 🖃 *$3-$5* ⏱ *Hours vary by season; check Web site before visiting.*

★ **Santa Monica State Beach.** It's the first beach you'll hit after the Santa Monica Freeway and it's one of L.A.'s best known. Wide and sandy, Santa Monica is *the* place for sunning and socializing: be prepared for a mob scene on summer weekends, when parking becomes an expensive ordeal.

The boardwalk of Venice Beach.

Swimming is fine (with the usual poststorm pollution caveat); for surfing, go elsewhere. For a memorable view, climb up the stairway over PCH to Palisades Park, at the top of the bluffs. Summer-evening concerts are often held here. ✉ *1642 Promenade, PCH at California Incline, Santa Monica* ☎ *310/305–9503* ☞ *Parking, lifeguard (year-round), restrooms, showers.*

Third Street Promenade. Stretch your legs along this pedestrians-only three-block stretch of 3rd Street, just steps away from the Pacific, lined with jacaranda trees, ivy-topiary dinosaur fountains, strings of lights, and branches of nearly every major U.S. retail chain.

Outdoor cafés, street vendors, movie theaters, and a rich nightlife make this a main gathering spot for locals, visitors, as well as street musicians and performance artists. Plan an evening to take it all in, or an afternoon for a long people-watching stroll.

Santa Monica Place reopened in 2010 at the south end of the promenade as a sleek outdoor mall and foodie haven. Its three stories are home to Bloomingdale's, Burberry, Coach, and other upscale retailers. Don't miss the ocean views from the rooftop food court. There's plenty of parking in city structures on the streets flanking the promenade. ✉ *Third Street, between Colorado and Wilshire Blvds., Santa Monica* ⊕ *www.thirdstreetpromenade.com.*

OFF THE BEATEN PATH

Will Rogers State Historic Park and Museum. The humorist, actor, and rambling cowboy Will Rogers lived on this site in the 1920s and 1930s. His ranch house, a folksy blend of Navajo rugs and Mission-style furniture, has become a museum featuring Rogers memorabilia.

The park's broad lawns are excellent for picnicking, and there's hiking on miles of eucalyptus-lined trails. A new visitor center with displays of the park's history and a bookstore is in the works. Free weekend games are scheduled April–October, weather permitting.

Who knows how many of Will Rogers' famed witticisms came to him while he and his wife hiked or rode horses along the **Inspiration Point Trail** from their ranch, now part of the park.

The point is on a detour off the lovely 2-mi loop, which you pick up right by the riding stables beyond the parking lot ($12 per car). On a clear (or even just semiclear) day, the panorama is one of L.A.'s widest and most wow-inducing, from the peaks of the San Gabriel Mountains in the distant east to the Oz-like cluster of downtown L.A. skyscrapers to Catalina Island looming off the coast to the southwest.

If you're looking for a longer trip, the top of the loop meets up with the 65-mi Backbone Trail, which connects to Topanga State Park.

At the museum, a short film presented in the visitor center highlights his roping technique and homey words of wisdom. Rogers was a polo enthusiast, and in the 1930s, his ranch house reopened in 2006 for docent-led tours. Featuring Rogers' stuffed practice calf and the high ceiling he raised so he could practice his famed roping style indoors, this house also holds an impressive array of Navajo rugs, saddles, and Mission-style furniture. Rogers was a polo enthusiast, and in the 1930s, his front-yard polo field attracted such friends as Douglas Fairbanks Sr. for weekend games.

✉ *1501 Will Rogers State Park Rd., Pacific Palisades* ☎ *310/454–8212* 🎫 *Free, parking $12* ⊙ *Parking daily 8–dusk, house tours Thurs. and Fri. 11, 1, 2, weekends hourly 10–4.*

WORTH NOTING

Annenberg Community Beach House. This beachfront property was originally developed in the 1920s by William Randolph Hearst as a palatial private residence and a gathering spot for Hollywood's megastars. In 1947 it was converted into a members-only beach club; the state of California bought and renamed the club in 1959, but it wasn't until after the earthquake of 2004 that the state made the property a public place.

With the help of the Annenberg foundation, it reopened as a community beach house in 2009. Feel like a millionaire lounging by the pool on one of the beachside chairs, or lunch at the café while enjoying uninterrupted ocean views. The house's Beach=Culture events series includes a variety of classes (yoga, beach volleyball), readings, and exhibits; check their Web site for the calendar. ✉ *415 Pacific Coast Hwy., Santa Monica* ☎ *310/458-4904* ⊕ *beachhouse.smgov.net* 🎫 *Free* ⊙ *Daily 8:30–5:30; Event House Gallery open Sat.-Mon., 10–4; Marion Davies Guest House open Sat. and Sun., 11–3; pool open 7 days June through August.*

Bergamot Station. Named after a stop on the Red Trolley line that once shuttled between Downtown and the Santa Monica Pier, Bergamot Station is now a depot for intriguing art. The industrial facades house more than 30 art galleries, shops, a café, and a museum. The galleries

DID YOU KNOW?

Venice Beach is part of skateboarding's Dogtown, where the Zephyr Team (or Z-Boys) created the modern version of the sport.

cover mixed-media: photography, jewelry, and paintings from somber to lurid.

Inside one of the many cavernous, steel-beamed warehouses that make up this unique area, the **Santa Monica Museum of Art** hosts exhibits of emerging artists. The museum is open Tuesday–Saturday 11–6, with a $5 suggested donation. There are also evening salons with artists, performers, and speakers (☎ *310/586–6488* ⊕ *www.smmoa.org*). ⊠ *2525 Michigan Ave., Santa Monica* ☎ *310/453–7535* ⊕ *www.bergamotstation. com* ⊙ *Galleries generally Tues.–Fri. 10–6, Sat. 11–5:30.*

California Heritage Museum. The real star of this collection is the 1894 Victorian house the museum occupies. The interior has been beautifully restored to represent four decades of design. Rotating exhibits focus California decorative and folk art including paintings, furniture, photography, sculpture, and a solid collection of California tiles and pottery. ⊠ *2612 Main St., Santa Monica* ☎ *310/392–8537* ⊕ *www. californiaheritagemuseum.org* 🖼 *$8* ⊙ *Wed.–Sun. 11–4.*

Pacific Park. Built on Santa Monica Pier, extending over the bay, this small amusement area harks back to the days of the grand Pacific Ocean Park (1957–67). Its attractions include a tame coaster, a large Ferris wheel, and a handful of rides that wildly satisfy the under-six crowd. ■ TIP→ **This isn't squeaky-clean Disneyland, so expect some litter and watch your personal belongings. Since the pier is riddled with nails and splinters, opt for sneakers over flip-flops.** ⊠ *380 Santa Monica Pier, Santa Monica* ☎ *310/260–8744* ⊕ *www.pacpark.com* 🖼 *Rides $3–$5, all-day pass $21.95* ⊙ *Hrs vary, weather permitting. Call or check Web site for schedule.*

Will Rogers State Beach. This clean, sandy, 3-mi beach, with a dozen volleyball nets, gymnastics equipment, and playground equipment for kids, is an all-around favorite. The surf is gentle, perfect for swimmers and beginning surfers. However, it's best to avoid the place after a storm, when untreated water flows from storm drains into the sea. ⊠ *17700 PCH, 2 mi north of Santa Monica Pier, Pacific Palisades* ☎ *310/305– 9503* ☞ *Parking, lifeguard (year-round, except only as needed in winter), restrooms.*

VENICE BEACH

TOP ATTRACTIONS

★ **Venice Beach Oceanfront Walk.** The surf and sand of Venice are fine, but the main attraction here is the boardwalk scene, which is a cosmos all its own. Go on weekend afternoons for the best people-watching experience. There are also swimming, fishing, surfing, basketball (it's the site of some of L.A.'s most hotly contested pickup games), racquetball, handball, and shuffleboard. You can rent a bike or some in-line skates and hit **the Strand** bike path. ⊠ *1800 Ocean Front Walk, west of Pacific Ave., Venice* ☎ *310/305–9503* ☞ *Parking, restrooms, food concessions, showers, playground.*

Continued on page 140

ALONG THE STRAND

L.A.'S COASTAL BIKE PATH

Cycling along the Strand

Venice Beach graffiti

On the Waterfront Cafe

Venice Beach café

Santa Monica Beach

When L.A. wants to get out and play by the water, people hit the Strand for the afternoon. This paved 22-mile path hugs the coastline and loops through tourist-packed stretches and sleepy beach towns. Quirky cafés, loads of souvenir stands, a family-packed amusement park on a pier, and spots for gazing at the Pacific are just a few things to see along the way.

The path extends from Santa Monica's Will Rogers State Beach to Torrance County Beach in South Redondo. It's primarily flat—aside from a few hills you encounter as you head toward Playa del Rey—and it's a terrific way for people of all fitness levels to experience L.A.'s beaches not far from Hollywood or Beverly Hills. You can explore at your own pace.

The hardest part of the journey isn't tackling the path itself—it's trying to get through it all without being distracted by the surrounding activity. With colorful graffitied murals, surfers and sailboats, weightlifters and tattoo par-

lors, local characters in carnivalesque costumes, volleyball games and skateboarders, there are almost too many things to busy youself with.

Santa Monica amusement park

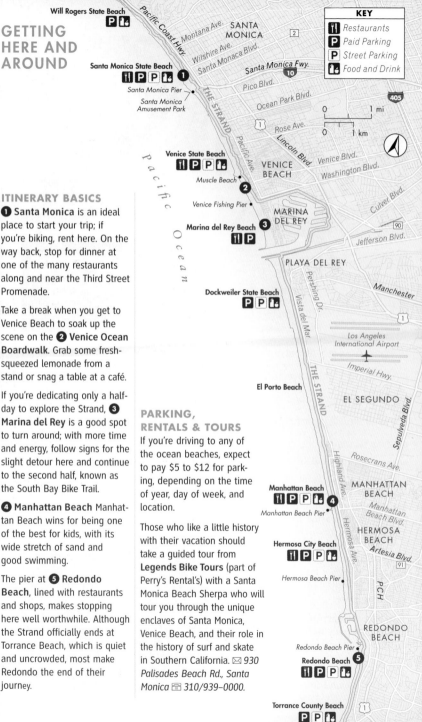

GETTING HERE AND AROUND

KEY
- **Restaurants**
- **P** Paid Parking
- **P** Street Parking
- **Food and Drink**

Will Rogers State Beach

Santa Monica State Beach **1**

Santa Monica Pier

Santa Monica Amusement Park

Montana Ave.

Wilshire Ave.

Santa Monica Blvd.

SANTA MONICA

Santa Monica Fwy. **10**

Pico Blvd.

Ocean Park Blvd.

Rose Ave.

Lincoln Blvd.

Venice Blvd.

Washington Blvd.

Culver Blvd.

Venice State Beach

Muscle Beach

Venice Fishing Pier

VENICE BEACH **2**

MARINA DEL REY **3**

Marina del Rey Beach

PLAYA DEL REY

Manchester

Dockweiler State Beach

Pershing Dr.

Vista del Mar

Los Angeles International Airport

Imperial Hwy.

El Porto Beach

EL SEGUNDO

Sepulveda Blvd.

Rosecrans Ave.

Manhattan Beach **4**

Manhattan Beach Pier

MANHATTAN BEACH

Manhattan Beach Blvd.

Highland Ave.

Hermosa Ave.

HERMOSA BEACH

Artesia Blvd.

Hermosa City Beach

Hermosa Beach Pier

PCH

REDONDO BEACH

Redondo Beach Pier

Redondo Beach **5**

Torrance County Beach

Pacific Coast Hwy.

THE STRAND

Pacific Ave.

Pacific Ocean

ITINERARY BASICS

1 Santa Monica is an ideal place to start your trip; if you're biking, rent here. On the way back, stop for dinner at one of the many restaurants along and near the Third Street Promenade.

Take a break when you get to Venice Beach to soak up the scene on the **2 Venice Ocean Boardwalk**. Grab some fresh-squeezed lemonade from a stand or snag a table at a café.

If you're dedicating only a half-day to explore the Strand, **3 Marina del Rey** is a good spot to turn around; with more time and energy, follow signs for the slight detour here and continue to the second half, known as the South Bay Bike Trail.

4 Manhattan Beach Manhattan Beach wins for being one of the best for kids, with its wide stretch of sand and good swimming.

The pier at **5 Redondo Beach**, lined with restaurants and shops, makes stopping here well worthwhile. Although the Strand officially ends at Torrance Beach, which is quiet and uncrowded, most make Redondo the end of their journey.

PARKING, RENTALS & TOURS

If you're driving to any of the ocean beaches, expect to pay $5 to $12 for parking, depending on the time of year, day of week, and location.

Those who like a little history with their vacation should take a guided tour from **Legends Bike Tours** (part of Perry's Rental's) with a Santa Monica Beach Sherpa who will tour you through the unique enclaves of Santa Monica, Venice Beach, and their role in the history of surf and skate in Southern California. ✉ 930 Palisades Beach Rd., Santa Monica ☎ 310/939–0000.

SANTA MONICA BEACH

Santa Monica Beach is the heart of the Strand—and also the most crowded section, especially on weekends.

WHAT TO SEE AND DO

No matter how old you are, there's something about a beachfront amusement park that just dazzles all five senses and then some. At the **Santa Monica Pier and Amusement Park** there's the wooden roller coaster that sends you flying just above the ocean, the Ferris wheel with a picture-perfect view of the Pacific Ocean, and carnival games for winning that stuffed animal.

Another option is to take a trapeze class through the **Trapeze School of New York** (☎ 310/394–5800 ⊕ www.Trapeze School.com), which holds classes right on the pier.

WHERE TO REFUEL

At loads of places you can pick up corn dogs, cotton candy, funnel cakes, and fresh-squeezed lemonade, but don't miss **Marisol Cocina Mexican** (✉ 401 Santa Monica Pier, Santa Monica ☎ 310/917–5050) for an oversized margarita and a platter of nachos.

For a swankier Santa Monica meal, try one of the beachfront hotels' restaurants for brunch or an afternoon cocktail. It's a perfect way to add a touch of luxury to your day on the Strand. Top choices include **Shutters on the Beach** (✉ One Pico Blvd, Santa Monica ☎ 310/458–0030) and the **Georgian Hotel** (✉ 1415 Ocean Ave., Santa Monica ☎ 310/395–9945).

WHAT ELSE IS NEARBY

Take a walk over to the **Third Street Promenade,** a pedestrian-only street lined with shops and restaurants. For some culture, check out **Bergamot Station** (☎ 310/458–7535 ⊕ www.bergamotstation.com), which was once a stop on the Red Trolley line that ran between Downtown and Santa Monica. The station contains museums, cafés, restaurants, and shops. It's home to the **Santa Monica Museum of Art** (☎ 310/586–6488 ⊕ www.smmoa.org), which has an eclectic mix of emerging artists.

Sign leading to pier

VENICE BEACH

Venice Beach—one California's uber-bohemian enclaves—is hands down one of L.A.'s best spots for dreamy escapism.

WHAT TO SEE AND DO

You won't break a sweat playing the most popular sport on the **Venice Ocean Boardwalk**, which is, of course, people-watching. It's vibrant, edgy, and packed with interesting characters such as knife jugglers, mimes, and a turban-wearing roller skater who plays his electric guitar. There are body builders who stop traffic at the beachfront Gold's Gym, found right on the Strand and known for its discovery of Arnold Schwarzenegger.

Take a peek at **Skate Plaza**, where you can join an impressive crew of disco roller skaters or jump into one of the drum circles that take place in the middle of the boardwalk.

WHERE TO REFUEL

Don't miss the fruit vendors and outdoor cafés perfect for a quick snack. Check out Washington Boulevard and try a soy latte at **The Cows End Coffee** (✉ *34 Washington Blvd., Venice Beach* ☎ *310/574–1080*), a favorite with locals. There's also the **Venice Whaler**, a beachfront bar with an amazing view and pub food, or head to **Terrace Café** (✉ *7 Washington Blvd., Venice Beach* ☎ *310/578–1530*) for alfresco dining.

WHAT ELSE IS NEARBY

Take a detour to check out the Venice Beach canals, which wind through the residential neighborhoods. Reserve a gondola ride at sunset to take you through the canals. Afterward, continue your trip into the South Bay (⊕ *www.gondolaamore.com* ☎ *310/376–6977*).

MARINA DEL REY
TO MANHATTAN BEACH

Volleyball at Manhattan Beach

The ride to the two Del Rey beach towns is the less popular leg of the Strand, as it takes you through some of LA's congested streets. But bike lanes and plenty of signs help you get right back onto the South Bay Bike Trail.

WHAT TO SEE AND DO

Make a stop at the **Fisherman's Village**, a replica of a New England seaport and fishing town. Here you can catch a harbor tour, rent a tandem bike at **Daniel's Bicycles** (⊠ *13737 Fiji Way, Marina del Rey* ☎ *310/980–4045*), or rent a sailboat, pedal boat, or kayak through the **UCLA Marina Aquatic Center** (⊠ *14001 Fiji Way, Marina del Rey* ☎ *310/823–0048*).

During the summer months you can enjoy free water-taxi rides around the marina to all the hot spots. Check out **Chance Park**; **Marina Beach**, where you can take windsurfing lessons; or **Bellona Wetlands**, for a peek into the wildlife living in the city.

If you're looking for a little adrenaline rush, check out the hang-gliding school kiosk on **Dockweiller State Beach**; class reservations can be made at (⊕ *www.windsports.com* ☎ *818/367–2430*).

WHERE TO REFUEL

For an indulgent brunch and lunch buffet, **Shanghai Reds** (⊠ *13813 Fiji Way, Marina del Rey* ☎ *310/823–4522*) serves a great spread with a memorable waterfront view. If you want to pack a picnic, hit **Rainbow Acres Natural Foods** (⊠ *4756 Admiralty Way, Marina del Rey* ☎ *310/823–5373*).

The next town, Playa del Rey, gateway to the South Bay, is a sleepy surf town with epic waves and a slew of beach shacks nestled alongside million-dollar homes. There are plenty of cantinas where you can grab a cold beer, and a number of independent restaurants beloved by locals. Check out **Señor G's** (⊠ *343 Culver Blvd., Playa del Rey* ☎ *310/822–7733*), **Cantalinis** (⊠ *193 Culver Blvd., Playa del Rey* ☎ *310/821–0018*).

WHAT ELSE IS NEARBY

The Strand continues through Manhattan and Redondo beaches, where there are downtowns and other areas to explore. The **Manhattan Beach Pier** is a fun diversion for shopping or an ideal spot to stop for for a meal. Try **Uncle Bill's Pancake House** (⊠ *1305 Highland Ave., Manhattan Beach* ☎ *310/545–5177*) for everything from banana-buckwheat pancakes to a wrap.

WORTH NOTING

Marina del Rey. Just south of Venice, this condo-laden, chain restaurant–lined development is a good place to grab brunch (but watch for price gougers), take a stroll, or ride bikes along the waterfront. A number of places, such as **Hornblower Cruises and Events** (⊠ *13755 Fiji Way* ☎ *888/467–6256* ⊕ *www.hornblower.com*) in Fisherman's Village, rent boats for romantic dinner or party cruises around the marina. There are a few man-made beaches, but you're better off hitting the larger (and cleaner) beaches up the coast.

Muscle Beach. Bronzed young men bench-pressing five girls at once, weight lifters doing tricks on the sand—Muscle Beach fired up the country's imagination from the get-go. There are actually two spots known as Muscle Beach. The original Muscle Beach, just south of the Santa Monica Pier, is where bodybuilders Jack LaLanne and Vic and Armand Tanny used to work out in the 1950s. When it was closed in 1959, the bodybuilders moved south along the beach to Venice, to a city-run facility known as "the Pen," and the Venice Beach spot inherited the Muscle Beach moniker.

The spot is probably best known now as a place where a young Arnold Schwarzenegger first came to flex his muscles in the late '60s and began his rise to fame. The area now hosts a variety of sports and gymnastic events and the occasional "beach babe" beauty contest that always draws a crowd. ⊠ *1800 Ocean Front Walk, Venice.*

MALIBU

TOP ATTRACTIONS

Fodor's Choice
★

Getty Villa Malibu. Feeding off the cultures of ancient Rome, Greece, and Etruria, the remodeled Getty Villa opened in 2006 with much fanfare—and controversy concerning the acquisition and rightful ownership of some of the Italian artifacts on display.

The antiquities are astounding, but on a first visit even they take a backseat to their surroundings, as this megamansion sits on some of the most valuable coastal property in the world.

Modeled after an Italian country home, the Villa dei Papiri in Herculaneum, the Getty Villa includes beautifully manicured gardens, reflecting pools, and statuary. The largest and most lovely garden, the Outer Peristyle, gives you glorious views over a rectangular reflecting pool and geometric hedges to the Pacific. The more modern structures blend thoughtfully into the rolling terrain and significantly improve public spaces, such as the new outdoor amphitheater, gift store, café, and entry arcade. Talks and educational programs are offered at an indoor theater. ■ **TIP→ An advance timed entry ticket is required for admission. Tickets are free and may be ordered from the Web site or by phone.** ⊠ *17985 Pacific Coast Hwy., Pacific Palisades* ☎ *310/440–7300* ⊕ *www.getty.edu* ☐ *Free, tickets required. Parking $15, cash only* ⊗ *Wed.–Mon. 10–5.*

Malibu Lagoon State Beach. Bird-watchers, take note: in this 5-acre marshy area you can spot egrets, blue herons, avocets, and gulls. (You need to stay on the boardwalks so as not to disturb their habitats.) The path leads out to a rocky stretch of beach and makes for a pleasant stroll.

The Getty Villa: a gorgeous setting for a spectacular collection of ancient art.

You're also likely to spot a variety of marine life. Look for the signs to help identify these sometimes exotic-looking creatures. The lagoon is open 24 hours and is particularly enjoyable in the early morning and at sunset. The parking lot has limited hours but street-side parking is usually available at off-peak times. ⊠ *23200 Pacific Coast Hwy., Malibu.*

Robert H. Meyer Memorial State Beach. Part of Malibu's most beautiful coastal area, this beach is made up of three minibeaches: El Pescador, La Piedra, and El Matador—all with the same spectacular view. Scramble down the steps to the rocky coves where nude sunbathers sometimes gather (although in recent years, police have been cracking down). "El Mat" has a series of caves, Piedra some nifty rock formations, and Pescador a secluded feel; but they're all very pretty and fairly private. ⊠ *32350, 32700, and 32900 PCH, Malibu* ☏ *818/880–0363* ☞ *Parking, 1 roving lifeguard unit, restrooms.*

Zuma Beach County Park. Zuma, 2 mi of white sand usually littered with tanning teenagers, has it all: from fishing and diving to swings for the kids to volleyball courts. Beachgoers looking for quiet or privacy should head elsewhere. Stay alert in the water: the surf is rough and inconsistent. ⊠ *30000 Pacific Coast Highway, Malibu* ☏ *310/305–9503* ☞ *Parking, lifeguard (year-round, except only as needed in winter), restrooms, food concessions.*

WORTH NOTING

Adamson House and Malibu Lagoon Museum. With spectacular views of Surfrider Beach and lush garden grounds, this house epitomizes all the reasons to live in Malibu.

Built in 1929 in the Moorish Spanish style by the Rindge family, who owned much of the Malibu area in the early part of the 20th century, they knew even then this was an ideal setting to settle down. Malibu was quite isolated then, with all visitors and supplies arriving by boat at the nearby Malibu Pier (and it can still be isolated these days when rock slides close the highway).

The Rindges had an enviable Malibu lifestyle, decades before the area was trendy. The house, covered with magnificent tile work in rich blues, greens, yellows, and oranges from the now-defunct Malibu Potteries, is right on the beach, but high chain-link fences keep out curious beachgoers.

Docent-led tours provide insights on family life here as well as the history of Malibu and its real estate. Signs posted around the grounds outside direct you on a self-guided tour, but you can't go inside the house without a guide. Garden tours take place on Friday at 10 am. There's pay parking in the adjacent county lot or in the lot at PCH and Cross Creek Road. ⊠ *23200 Pacific Coast Hwy., Malibu* ☎ *310/456–8432* ⊕ *www. adamsonhouse.org* ⌦ *$5* ⊘ *Wed.–Sat. 11–3; last tour departs at 2.*

Dan Blocker State Beach. Originally owned jointly by the stars of the *Bonanza* TV series, this little stretch of beach was donated to the state after Blocker (who played Hoss) died in 1972. Locals still know this as Corral Beach. Its narrow stretch of fine sand and rocks make it great for walking, light swimming, kayaking, and scuba diving. Because of the limited parking available along PCH, it's rarely crowded. ⊠ *26000 PCH, at Corral Canyon Rd., Malibu* ☎ *310/305–9503* ⌦ *Parking, lifeguard (year-round, except only as needed in winter), restrooms.*

Las Tunas State Beach. This small beach known for its groins (metal gates constructed in 1929 to protect against erosion) has good swimming, diving, and fishing conditions, and a rocky coastline. ⊠ *19444 Pacific Coast Highway, Malibu* ☎ *310/305–9503* ⌦ *Parking on highway only, lifeguard (year-round, except only as needed in winter).*

Leo Carrillo State Park. On the very edge of Ventura County, this narrow beach is better for exploring than for sunning or swimming (watch that strong undertow!). On your own or with a ranger, venture down at low tide to examine the tide pools among the rocks.

Sequit Point, a promontory dividing the northwest and southeast halves of the beach, creates secret coves, sea tunnels, and boulders on which you can perch and fish. Generally, anglers stick to the northwest end of the beach; experienced surfers brave the rocks to the southeast. Campgrounds are set back from the beach; call ahead to reserve campsites. ⊠ *35000 Pacific Coast Highway, Malibu* ☎ *818/880–0363, 800/444–7275 for camping reservations* ⌦ *Parking, lifeguard (year-round, except only as needed in winter), restroom, showers, fire pits.*

Malibu Pier. This 780-foot fishing dock is a great place to drink in the sunset, take in some coastal views, or to watch local fishermen reel up a catch. A pier has jutted out here since the early 1900s; storms destroyed the last one in 1995, and it was rebuilt in 2001. In 2004 private developers worked with the state and refurbished the pier, yielding a gift shop, water-sport rentals, burger joint, and restaurant. A surfing museum is also in the works. ⊠ *Pacific Coast Hwy. at Cross Creek Rd.* ⊕ *www. malibupier.com.*

Malibu Surfrider Beach. Steady 3- to 5-foot waves make this beach, just west of Malibu Pier, a surfing paradise. Water runoff from Malibu Canyon forms a natural lagoon that's a sanctuary for 250 species of birds. Unfortunately, the lagoon is often polluted and algae-filled. If you're leery of going into the water, you can bird-watch, play volleyball, or take a walk on one of the nature trails, which are perfect for romantic sunset strolls. ⊠ *23050 Pacific Coast Highway, Malibu* ☎ *818/880-0363* ☞ *Parking, lifeguard (year-round), restrooms, picnic tables.*

Nicholas Canyon County Beach. Sandier and less private than most of the rocky beaches surrounding it, this little beach is great for picnics. You can sit at a picnic table high up on a bluff overlooking the ocean, or cast out a fishing line. Surfers call it Zero Beach because the waves take the shape of a hollow tube when winter swells peel off the reef. ⊠ *33805 Pacific Coast Highway, Malibu* ☎ *310/305–9503* ☞ *Parking, lifeguard (year-round), restrooms, showers, picnic tables, barbecues.*

Westward Beach–Point Dume. Go tide-pooling, fishing, snorkeling, or bird-watching (prime time is late winter–early spring). Hike to the top of the sandstone cliffs to whale-watch; their migrations can be seen between December and April. Westward is a favorite surfing beach, but the steep surf isn't for novices. ■TIP→ **Bring your own food, since the nearest concession is a longish hike away.** ⊠ *71030 Westward Beach Rd., Malibu* ☎ *310/305–9503* ☞ *Parking, lifeguard (year-round, except only as needed in winter), restrooms, showers.*

QUICK
BITES

The Sunset Restaurant and Bar. This watering hole and eatery is as close to the beach as you can get without getting sand in your drink. It's a locals' secret, with breathtaking views of the ocean, dolphins, surfers, and celebrity locals taking a break on the protected patio. Stop in for a cocktail at the friendly bar or a light meal of grilled fish tacos or one of their unique salads. ⊠ *Off Pacific Coast Hwy., just north of Zuma Beach, 6800 Westward Beach Rd., Malibu* ☎ *310/589–1007* ⊕ *www.thesunsetrestaurant.com.*

Topanga State Beach. The beginning of miles of public beach, Topanga has good surfing at the western end (at the mouth of the canyon). Close to a busy section of PCH and rather narrow, Topanga is hardly serene; hordes of teenagers zip over Topanga Canyon Boulevard from the Valley. Fishing and swings for children are available. ⊠ *18700 block of Pacific Coast Highway, Malibu* ☎ *310/305–9503* ☞ *Parking, lifeguard (year-round, except only as needed in winter), restrooms, food concessions.*

Topanga State Park. This is another way into the Santa Monicas via the Trippet Ranch entrance, which gives you several options: a ½-mi nature loop, a 7-mi round-trip excursion to the Parker Mesa Overlook (breathtaking on a clear day), or a 10-mi trek to the Will Rogers park. Parking is $4 per vehicle. To get here, exit U.S. 101 onto Topanga Canyon Boulevard in Woodland Hills and head south until you can turn left onto Entrada; if going north on PCH, turn onto Topanga Canyon Boulevard—a bit past Sunset Boulevard—and go north until you can turn right onto Entrada. ⊠ *20829 Entrada Rd., Malibu* ☎ *310/455–2465.*

FROM PLAYA DEL RAY TO TORRANCE BEACH

TOP ATTRACTIONS

★ **Redondo Beach.** The Redondo Beach Pier marks the starting point of this wide, sandy, busy beach along a heavily developed shoreline community. Restaurants and shops flourish along the pier, excursion boats and privately owned crafts depart from launching ramps, and a reef formed by a sunken ship creates prime fishing and snorkeling conditions.

If you're adventurous, you might try to kayak out to the buoys and hobnob with pelicans and sea lions. A series of free rock and jazz concerts takes place at the pier every summer. ⊠ *Torrance Blvd. at Catalina Ave., Redondo Beach* ☎ *310/372–2166* ☞ *Parking, lifeguard (year-round), restrooms, food concessions, showers.*

Torrance Beach. This little-known gem of a beach, where the Strand walkway–bicycle path finally comes to an end, has no pier or other loud attractions, just a humble snack shop that's open in the summer. But it's a great place to escape the crowds of Redondo to the north and has a park with volleyball and lovely vistas. ⊠ *387 Paseo de la Playa, Torrance* ☎ *310/372–2166* ☞ *Parking, restrooms, food concessions, showers.*

WORTH NOTING

Dockweiler State Beach. The longest (4-mi) strip of beach in the county, Dockweiler has almost all the makings of a perfect beach: RV park, playground, separate bike trail, bonfire pits, mild surf, volley ball courts, and nice sand. If only the planes from LAX weren't taking off directly overhead and factories weren't puffing out fumes right behind you. But if you don't mind that, you'll find plenty of room to spread out. An additional bonus is the hang-gliding facility (right in front of the water-treatment plant). Contact **Windsports International** (☎ *818/367– 2430* ⊕ *www.windsports.com*); $120 will get you a full lesson with equipment. ⊠ *12000 Vista del Mar, west end of Imperial Hwy., Playa del Rey* ☎ *310/372–2166, 310/322–4951* ☞ *Parking, lifeguard (year-round), restrooms, showers.*

Hermosa Beach. South of Manhattan Beach, Hermosa Beach has all the amenities of its neighbor but it attracts more of an MTV crowd. Swimming takes a backseat to the volleyball games and parties on the pier and boardwalk. ⊠ *1201 The Strand, Hermosa Ave. and 33rd St., Hermosa Beach* ☎ *310/372–2166* ☞ *Parking, lifeguard (year-round), restrooms, food concessions, showers, wheelchair access to pier.*

Manhattan Beach. A wide, sandy strip with good swimming and rows of volleyball courts, Manhattan Beach is the preferred destination of muscled, tanned young professionals and dedicated bikini-watchers. There's also a bike path, a playground, fishing equipment for rent, a bait shop, and a sizable fishing pier. ⊠ *Manhattan Beach Blvd. and N. Ocean Dr., Manhattan Beach* ☎ *310/372–2166* ☞ *Parking, lifeguard (year-round), restrooms, food concessions, showers.*

Pasadena
and Environs

GETTING ORIENTED

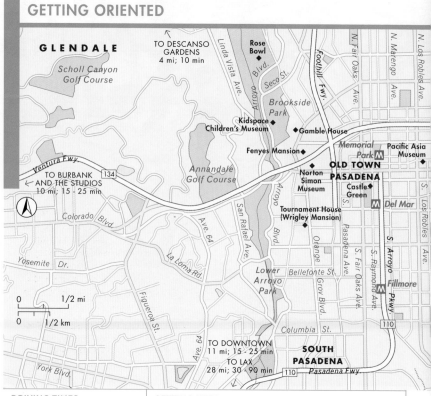

DRIVING TIMES AND DISTANCES

Minimum times listed below represent little to no traffic; maximum times assume the worst.

Adjust accordingly taking rush hour and peak weekend travel time into account.

- **From LAX:** 30–90 min/28 mi

- **From Los Feliz/Silver Lake:** 20–30 min/13 mi

- **From Beverly Hills:** 30–60 min/19 mi

- **From Burbank:** 15–25 min/ 12 mi

GETTING HERE

Driving Strategy. To reach Pasadena from Downtown Los Angeles, drive north on the Pasadena Freeway (I–110).

From Hollywood and the San Fernando Valley, use the Ventura Freeway (Highway 134, east), which cuts through Glendale, skirting the foothills, before arriving in Pasadena.

Parking. There are several city lots located in Old Town Pasadena with low rates, all close to Colorado Boulevard, the main drag. On-street parking here is also widely available with few restrictions.

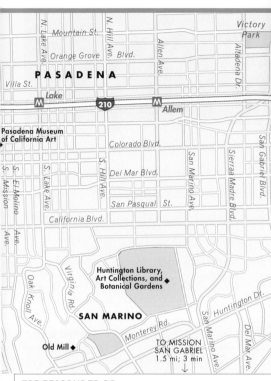

6

PLANNING YOUR TIME

Set aside most of a day for the Huntington—in summer, visit the gardens in the morning to avoid the midday heat. Keep in mind that many museums are closed Monday, though the Norton Simon and the Huntington are closed Tuesday.

If you want to see the Descanso Gardens, start early and see them first. Otherwise, get a late-morning or early-afternoon start to see the important architectural sights on this tour, saving Old Pasadena for last since it offers an outstanding evening street scene. Shops and restaurants stay open late in this relatively safe neighborhood, and it's easy to find parking in nearby garages.

A stop at the Gamble House shouldn't take more than an hour, leaving plenty of time for an afternoon visit to the Norton Simon Museum. Unless you're planning on seeing a game or hitting the flea market, you will probably want to skip the Rose Bowl.

TOP REASONS TO GO

Visit the Huntington Library. In addition to a collection of 18th-century British art, this library has 4 million manuscripts and 700,000 books, including the Gutenberg Bible.

Walk Through the Huntington's Botanical Gardens. Set aside a couple hours to enjoy the expansive lawns and stately trees surrounding the Huntington Library.

See American Craftsmanship at the Gamble House. The teak staircase and cabinetry are just a few of the highlights at this home, built in 1908.

Check Out the Norton Simon Museum. This small museum's fine collection features works by Renoir, Degas, Gauguin, and others.

Hang Out in Old Town Pasadena. Spend the afternoon walking around this 12-block historic town filled with cafés, restaurants, and shops.

Sightseeing
★★★★
Nightlife
★
Dining
★★
Lodging
★★
Shopping
★★

Although seemingly absorbed into the general Los Angeles sprawl, Pasadena is a separate and distinct city. It's most well known for the Tournament of Roses, or more commonly, the Rose Bowl, seen around the world every New Year's Day. But the city has sites worth seeing year-round—from gorgeous Craftsman homes to exceptional museums, particularly the Norton Simon and the Huntington Library, Art Collections, and Botanical Gardens.

Updated by
Laura Randall

First-time visitors to L.A. only here for a short time might find it hard to get out to Pasadena. However, if you've had your fill of city life and are looking for a nearby escape that feels much farther away than it is, with open space and fresher air, it's the perfect trip.

The **Botanical Gardens** is a great place to start, with or without plans to see the **Huntington Library** and **Art Collections**. There's also **Descanso Gardens,** which has everything from California redwoods to acres of roses, and is a smaller and often less crowded place to immerse yourself in nature than at the Huntington's gardens.

For a true small-town experience, spend the afternoon strolling around **Old Town Pasadena,** with shops and restaurants filling its 19-centruy brick buildings.

Art and architecture lovers shouldn't miss the city's top site, the **Norton Simon Museum,** most noted for its excellent collection of Degas, as well as works by Rembrandt, Goya, and Picasso. **The Gamble House** is an immense three-story house and one of the country's best examples of American Arts of Crafts bungalow architecture.

The thing that might surprise you the most about visiting Pasadena is that even the drive here—on the freeway, though not during rush hour—is a pleasant one, with lovely scenery. The Pasadena Freeway follows the curves of the arroyo (creek bed), lined with old sycamores. It was the main road north during the early days of Los Angeles, when horses and buggies made their way through the countryside to the small town of Pasadena. In 1939 the road became the Arroyo Seco Parkway, the first freeway in Los Angeles, later renamed the Pasadena Freeway.

TOP ATTRACTIONS

★ **Descanso Gardens.** Getting its name from the Spanish word for "rest," this lovely oasis is a truly tranquil setting, shaded by massive oak trees. Known for being a smaller, mellower version of the nearby Huntington, Descanso Gardens features denser foliage, quaint dirt paths, and some hilly climbs that can make for good exercise. It's the perfect place to come in search of wonderful scents—between the lilacs, the acres of roses, and the forest of California redwoods, pines, and junipers, you can enjoy all sorts of fragrances.

Once part of the vast Spanish Rancho San Rafael, these 160 acres were purchased by E. Manchester Boddy, publisher of the *Los Angeles Daily News*, in 1937. He developed the area into acres of lushly planted gardens and slopes covered in native chaparral as well as an elegant 22-room mansion, which now serves as a museum. A forest of California live oak trees makes a dramatic backdrop for thousands of camellias, azaleas, and a breathtaking 5-acre International Rosarium holding 1,700 varieties of antique and modern roses. The Japanese Tea House hosts various events throughout the year—its Zen garden is a nice spot to stop for refreshments and reflection. Classes (yoga and floral arranging, for example), night walks, and activities for families are scheduled throughout the year. The oak-framed main lawn is a lovely setting for summer concerts. A small train ride draws families on weekends. There are also a child's train, a gift shop, and a café. ✉ *1418 Descanso Dr., La Cañada/Flintridge* ☎ *818/949–4200* ⊕ *www.descansogardens.org* 🎟 *$8* ⊙ *Daily 9–5.*

★ **Gamble House.** Built by Charles and Henry Greene in 1908, this is a spectacular example of American Arts and Crafts bungalow architecture. The term *bungalow* can be misleading, since the Gamble House is a huge three-story home. To wealthy Easterners such as the Gambles (as in Procter & Gamble), this type of vacation home seemed informal compared with their mansions back home. What makes admirers swoon is the incredible amount of handcraftsmanship, including a teak staircase and cabinetry, Greene and Greene–designed furniture, and an Emil Lange glass door. The dark exterior has broad eaves, with sleeping porches on the second floor.

An hour-long, docent-led tour of the Gamble's interior will draw your eye to the exquisite details. If you want to see more Greene and Greene homes, buy a self-guided tour map of the neighborhood in the bookstore. ✉ *4 Westmoreland Pl., Pasadena* ☎ *626/793–3334* ⊕ *www. gamblehouse.org* 🎟 *$10* ⊙ *Thurs.–Sun. noon–3; tickets go on sale Thurs.–Sat. at 10, Sun. at 11:30. 1-hr tour every 15–20 min.*

Fodor's Choice ★ **Huntington Library, Art Collections, and Botanical Gardens.** If you have time for only one stop in the Pasadena area, it should be the Huntington, built in the early 1900s as the home of railroad tycoon Henry E. Huntington. You'll truly forget you're in a city here wandering the ground's 150 acres, just over the Pasadena line in San Marino.

DID YOU KNOW?

The Huntington Botanical Gardens span 120 acres and are made up of more than a dozen themed gardens—including a rose garden, desert garden, and children's garden.

Henry and his wife, Arabella (who was his aunt by marriage), voraciously collected rare books and manuscripts, botanical specimens, and 18th-century British art. The institution they established became one of the most extraordinary cultural complexes in the world.

Among the highlights are John Constable's intimate *View on the Stour near Dedham* and the monumental *Sarah Siddons as the Tragic Muse,* by Joshua Reynolds. In the Virginia Steele Scott Gallery of American Art, which reopened in May 2009 after extensive renovations, you can see paintings by Mary Cassatt, Frederic Remington, and more.

The library contains more than 700,000 books and 4 million manuscripts, including such treasures as a Gutenberg Bible, the Ellesmere manuscript of Chaucer's *Canterbury Tales,* George Washington's genealogy in his own handwriting, scores of works by William Blake, and a world-class collection of early editions of Shakespeare. You'll find some of these items in the Library Hall with more than 200 important works on display. In 2006 the library acquired more than 60,000 rare books and reference volumes from the Cambridge, Massachusetts–based Bundy Library, making the Huntington the source of one of the biggest history of science collections in the world.

Although the art collections are increasingly impressive here, don't resist being lured outside into the stunning Botanical Gardens. From the main buildings, lawns and towering trees stretch out toward specialty areas. The 10-acre Desert Garden, for instance, has one of the world's largest groups of mature cacti and other succulents, arranged by continent. Visit this garden on a cool morning or in the late afternoon; a hot midday walk may be a little too authentic.

In the Japanese Garden, an arched bridge curves over a pond; the area also has stone ornaments, a Japanese house, a bonsai court, and a Zen rock garden. There are collections of azaleas and 1,500 varieties of camellias. The 3-acre rose garden is displayed chronologically, so the development leading to modern varieties of roses can be observed; on the grounds is the charming Rose Garden Tea Room, where traditional afternoon tea is served. (Reservations required for English tea.) There are also herb, palm, and jungle gardens, plus the Shakespeare Garden, which blooms with plants mentioned in Shakespeare's works.

The Rose Hills Foundation Conservatory for Botanical Science, a massive greenhouse–style center with dozens of kid-friendly, hands-on exhibits illustrate plant diversity in various environments. (These rooms are quite warm and humid, especially the central rotunda, which displays rain-forest plants.)

The Bing Children's Garden is a tiny tot's wonderland filled with opportunities for children to explore the ancient elements of water, fire, air,

DID YOU KNOW?

Raphael's Madonna and Child with Book is part of the wide-ranging collection of the Norton Simon Museum.

and earth. A classical Chinese Garden "Liu Fang Yuan" (or Garden of Flowing Fragrance) opened in spring 2008, the largest of its kind outside China. Work on this will continue for the next several years. A 1¼-hour guided tour of the botanical gardens is led by docents at posted times, and a free brochure with map and highlights is available in the entrance pavilion. ⊠ *1151 Oxford Rd., San Marino* ☎ *626/405–2100* ⊕ *www.huntington.org* 🖃 *$15 weekdays, $20 weekends, free 1st Thurs. of month (reservations required)* ⊘ *Mon. and Wed.–Fri. noon–4:30, weekends 10:30–4:30; call for summer hours.*

Fodor'sChoice
★

Norton Simon Museum. Long familiar to television viewers of the New Year's Day Rose Parade, this low-profile brown building is more than just a background for the passing floats. It's one of the finest small museums anywhere, with an excellent collection that spans more than 2,000 years of Western and Asian art. It all began in the 1950s when Norton Simon (Hunt-Wesson Foods, McCalls Corporation, and Canada Dry) started collecting the works of Degas, Renoir, Gauguin, and Cézanne. His collection grew to include old masters, impressionists, and modern works from Europe and Indian and Southeast Asian art. After he retired, Simon reorganized the failing Pasadena Art Institute and continued to assemble an impressive collection.

Today the Norton Simon Museum is richest in works by Rembrandt, Goya, Picasso, and, most of all, Degas: this is one of the only two U.S. institutions to hold the complete set of the artist's model bronzes (the other is New York's Metropolitan Museum of Art). Renaissance, baroque, and rococo masterpieces include Raphael's profoundly spiritual *Madonna with Child with Book* (1503), Rembrandt's *Portrait of a Bearded Man in a Wide-Brimmed Hat* (1633), and a magical Tiepolo ceiling, *The Triumph of Virtue and Nobility Over Ignorance* (1740–50). The museum's collections of Impressionist (Van Gogh, Matisse, Cézanne, Monet, Renoir) and Cubist (Braque, Gris) works are extensive. Several Rodin sculptures are placed throughout the museum. Head down to the bottom floor to see rotating exhibits and phenomenal Southeast Asian and Indian sculptures and artifacts, where graceful pieces like a Ban Chiang blackware vessel date to well before 1000 BC. Don't miss a living artwork outdoors: the garden, conceived by noted Southern California landscape designer Nancy Goslee Power. The tranquil pond was inspired by Monet's gardens at Giverny. ⊠ *411 W. Colorado Blvd., Pasadena* ☎ *626/449–6840* ⊕ *www.nortonsimon.org* 🖃 *$8, free 1st Fri. of month 6–9 pm* ⊘ *Wed., Thurs., and Sat.–Mon. noon–6, Fri. noon–9.*

★ **Old Town Pasadena.** Once the victim of decay, the area was revitalized in the 1990s as a blend of restored 19th-century brick buildings with a contemporary overlay. A phalanx of chain stores has muscled in, but there are still some homegrown shops and plenty of tempting cafés and restaurants. In the evening and on weekends, streets are packed with people, and Old Town crackles with energy. The 12-block historic district is anchored along Colorado Boulevard between Pasadena Avenue and Arroyo Parkway.

Tutti Gelati. To cool off, follow the intoxicating aroma of freshly pressed waffle cones to Tutti Gelati, an Italian gelateria behind Crate & Barrel on Colorado Boulevard. Flavors include zabaglione, *stracciatella* (chocolate chip), and hazelnut; many ingredients come directly from Milan, and everything is made on the premises. ⊠ *62 W. Union St., No. 1* ☎ *626/440–9800.*

WORTH NOTING

Castle Green. One block south of Colorado Boulevard stands the one-time social center of Pasadena's elite. This Moorish building is the only remaining section of a turn-of-the-20th-century hotel complex. Today the often-filmed tower (in *The Sting, Edward Scissorhands,* and *The Last Samurai*) is residential. The building is not open to the public on a daily basis, but it does organize seasonal tours on the first Sunday of December and June. ⊠ *99 S. Raymond Ave., Pasadena* ☎ *626/385-7774* ⊕ *www.castlegreen.com.*

Fenyes Mansion. With its elegant dark wood paneling and floors, curved staircases, and a theatrical stage in the parlor, it's easy to envision how this 1905 mansion along Pasadena's Millionaire's Row once served as gathering place for the city's wealthiest residents (it also housed the Finnish Consulate until 1965). Most rooms on the ground and second floors are still fitted with original furniture; you can peek into these roped-off spaces, now home to mannequins dressed in period clothing, to get a sense of what life was like a century ago.

At this writing, the mansion and adjacent Finnish Folk Art Museum were expected to reopen in spring 2012 after major renovations. You can also visit the Historical Center Gallery, which remains open during renovations and has rotating exhibits dedicated to the art and culture of Pasadena. ⊠ *470 W. Walnut St., Pasadena* ☎ *626/577–1660* ⊕ *www.pasadenahistory.org* ⊠ *Tours $4–$8* ☉ *Wed.–Sun. noon–5. Hrs for tour vary. Call ahead.*

Heritage Square Museum. Looking like a prop street set up by a film studio, Heritage Square sticks out like a row of bright dollhouses in the Montecito Heights neighborhood. Five 19th-century residences, a train station, a church, a carriage barn, and a 1909 boxcar that was originally part of the Southern Pacific Railroad, all built between the Civil War and World War I, were moved to this small park from various locations in southern California to save them from the wrecking ball.

Docents dressed in period costume lead visitors through the lavish homes, giving an informative picture of what life in Los Angeles was like a century ago. Don't miss the unique 1893 Octagon House, one of just a handful of its kind built in California; a wraparound veranda modeled after the original was added in 2009. Guided tours are available for $10. They are also open on most holiday Mondays. ⊠ *3800 Homer St., off Ave. 43 exit,* ☎ *323/225–2700* ⊕ *www.heritagesquare.org* ⊠ *$10* ☉ *Fri.–Sun. noon–5.*

The Old Mill (El Molino Viejo). Built in 1816 as a gristmill for the San Gabriel Mission, the mill is one of the last remaining examples in Southern California of Spanish Mission architecture. The thick adobe walls and textured ceiling rafters give the interior a sense of quiet strength. Be sure to step into the back room, now a gallery with rotating quarterly exhibits in alliance with the California Art Club. Outside, a chipped section of the mill's exterior reveals the layers of brick, ground seashell paste, and oxblood used to hold the structure together. The surrounding gardens are reason enough to visit, with a flower-decked arbor and old sycamores and oaks. In summer the California Philharmonic ensemble performs in the garden. ⊠ *1120 Old Mill Rd., San Marino* ☎ *626/449–5458* ⊕ *www.old-mill.org* 🖃 *Free* ☉ *Tues.–Sun. 1–4.*

Ⓒ **Kidspace Children's Museum.** Looking like a Looney Tunes cartoon, this activity-focused, kid-centric playground with oversize replicas of familiar objects offers lessons along with some fun. Imaginative exhibits invite kids to interact, while parents can gain tidbits of knowledge on earthquakes, animals, and insects. In the towering leaf, climb inside a sunny atrium; kids assume the role of ants on their daring ascent. They can also take on a tricycle race on the "Trike Tracks." It's a place practically built to wear out the little ones out and give parents a much needed break. ⊠ *480 N. Arroyo Blvd., Pasadena* ☎ *626/449–9144* ⊕ *www. kidspacemuseum.org* 🖃 *$10* ☉ *Tues.–Fri. 9:30–5, weekends 10–5.*

★ **Los Angeles County Arboretum.** Wander through a re-created tropical forest, a South Africa landscape, or the Australian outback at this arboretum. One highlight is the tropical greenhouse, with carnivorous-looking orchids and a pond full of brilliant Chinese goldfish. The house and stables of the eccentric real-estate pioneer Lucky Baldwin are well preserved and worth a visit. Kids will love the dozens of peacocks and waterfowl that roam the property. The Santa Anita Racetrack is across the street, but you'll seldom see it as you wander these 40 acres. To get there, go east on I–210 just past Pasadena, exit in Arcadia on Baldwin Avenue and go south, and you will soon see the entrance. It's open daily 9–5 and costs $8. ⊠ *301 N. Baldwin Ave., Arcadia* ☎ *626/821–3222* ⊕ *www.arboretum.org.*

Pacific Asia Museum. Devoted to the arts and culture of Asia and the Pacific Islands, this manageably sized museum displays changing exhibits drawn from its permanent collection of 17,000 works and artifacts. It's not the place for blockbuster shows—instead, you'll find modest displays of ceramics, calligraphy, textiles, traditional robes, and the like. The building itself is worth a look: it's inspired by Han Dynasty structures and surrounds a courtyard with a koi fishpond. ⊠ *46 N. Los Robles Ave., Pasadena* ☎ *626/449–2742* ⊕ *www.pacificasiamuseum. org* 🖃 *$9, free 4th Fri. of month* ☉ *Wed.–Sun. 10–6.*

Pasadena Museum of California Art. The first thing you see when you approach this museum is the graffiti-riddled parking structure. Was it vandalized by local taggers? Nope—it's the handiwork of artist George Kenny Scharf as part of this museum's dedication to all forms of Californian art, architecture, and design from 1850 to the present. The regularly changing exhibits are focused and thoughtfully presented; you might find anything from early California landscapes to contemporary works on car culture. Subject to closures for installations; call ahead. ⊠ *490 E. Union St., Pasadena* ☎ *626/568–3665* ⊕ *www.pmcaonline. org* 🖃 *$7, free 1st Fri. of month* ☉ *Wed.–Sun. noon–5.*

DID YOU KNOW?

Pasadena's Tournament of Roses Parade, famed for its fanciful floats, has been an annual event since 1890.

Rose Bowl. With an enormous rose, the city of Pasadena's logo, adorned on its exterior, it's hard to miss this 100,000-seat stadium, host of many Super Bowls and home to the UCLA Bruins. Set in Brookside Park at the wide bottom of an arroyo, the facility is closed except during games and special events such as the monthly Rose Bowl Flea Market, which is considered the granddaddy of West Coast flea markets. If you want the best selection of items, show up early. People start arriving here at the crack of dawn, but note you will also pay a higher entry fee for having first dibs on the selection. The best bargaining takes place at the end of the day when vendors would rather settle for a few less dollars then have to lug their goods home. ⊠ *1001 Rose Bowl Dr. at Rosemont Ave., Pasadena* ☏ *626/577–3100* ⊕ *www.rosebowlstadium. com for flea market, www.rgcshows.com for shows* ⊡ *$8 from 9 am on, $10 for 8–9 am entrance, $15 for 7–8 am entrance* ☷ *Flea market 2nd Sun. of month 9–3.*

OFF THE
BEATEN
PATH

Mission San Gabriel Archangel. Wondering where the Mission District got its name? Here's the answer. Established in 1771 as the fourth of 21 missions founded in California, this massive adobe complex was dedicated by Father Junípero Serra to St. Gabriel. Within the next 50 years, the San Gabriel Archangel became the wealthiest of all California missions. In 1833 the Mexican government confiscated the mission, allowing it to decline. The U.S. government returned the mission to the church in 1855, but by this time the Franciscans had departed. In 1908 the Claretian Missionaries took charge and poured much care into preserving the rich history. The cemetery here, the first in L.A. County, is said to contain approximately 6,000 Gabrieleno Indians.

Tranquil grounds are lushly planted and filled with remnants of what life was like nearly two centuries ago. The museum underwent a renovation in 2006 to further preserve the 1812 structure that originally served as the living space for the mission fathers. Public mass is held at the mission Sunday morning at 7 and 9:30. If you're lucky, you'll hear the six bells that ring out during special services—a truly arresting experience. You can take a self-guided tour of the grounds here by purchasing a map in the gift shop or come for History Day the first Saturday of the Month. Docent led tours are also available by appointment. ⊠ *428 S. Mission Dr., San Gabriel* ☏ *626/457–3048* ⊕ *www.sangabrielmission. org* ⊡ *$5* ☷ *Daily 9–4:30.*

Tournament House (Wrigley Mansion). Chewing-gum magnate William Wrigley purchased this white Italian Renaissance–style house in 1914. Upon his wife's death in 1958, Wrigley donated the house to the city of Pasadena under the stipulation that it be used at the headquarters for the Tournament of Roses. The mansion features a green-tile roof and manicured rose garden with 1,500 floral varieties. The interior still provides a glimpse of the over-the-top style of the area in the early 20th century. Tours of the house last about an hour; fans of the Rose Parade will see the various crowns and tiaras worn by former Rose Queens, plus Rose Bowl related trophies and memorabilia. ⊠ *391 S. Orange Grove Blvd., Pasadena* ☏ *626/449–4100* ⊕ *www.tournamentofroses. com* ⊡ *Free* ☷ *Tours every Thurs. 2–4, Feb.–Aug.*

7

Nightlife

WORD OF MOUTH

"The Dresden!! We had been hearing about Marty and Elayne at The Dresden for several years. . . . How can I describe this lounge act??!! Marty and Elayne are way past their prime, their matching outfits are sort of Las Vegas style, their performance is almost self-satirizing—BUT their spirit and energy are very infectious."

—elnap29

Updated by
Lea Lion

The turnover among L.A.'s nightspots can be enough to make your head spin—it's almost as dizzying as the diversity that's available virtually every night of the week. Hollywood and West Hollywood, where hip-and-happening nightspots liberally dot Sunset and Hollywood boulevards, are the epicenter of L.A. nightlife and both buzz louder than ever.

The lines are as long as the skirts are short outside just about every club du jour citywide, although it's hard to keep track of places A-listers frequent. Indeed, competition has become so fierce—and nightclubbers so fickle—that remodeling and renaming former hot spots is de riguer these days.

Although the ultimate in velvet-roped vampiness and glamour used to be the Sunset Strip, in the past couple of years the glitz has definitely shifted to Hollywood Boulevard and its surrounding streets. Thanks to vibrant new drinking and dining spaces along Cahuenga, Las Palmas, and Ivar, Tinseltown finally feels like a lively—somewhat safe—area to stroll at night, a real barhopper zone.

That said, the Strip still has plenty going for it, too, with comedy clubs, hard-rock spots, and restaurants. West Hollywood's Santa Monica Boulevard bustles with gay and lesbian bars and clubs.

Also, after decades of neglect, downtown Los Angeles is enjoying a resurrection, with new pockets of nightlife emerging on a regular basis.

For less conspicuous—and congested—alternatives, check out the events in Downtown L.A.'s performance spaces and galleries. Silver Lake and Echo Park are best for boho bars and live music clubs.

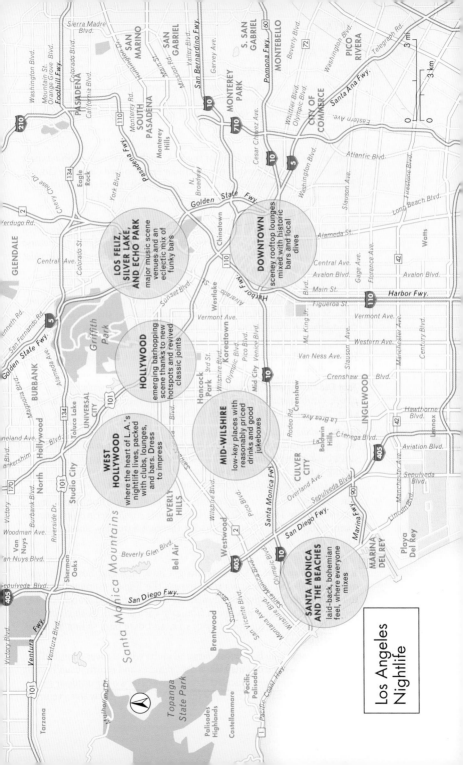

Los Angeles Nightlife

LOS FELIZ, SILVER LAKE, AND ECHO PARK major music scene venues and an eclectic mix of funky bars

DOWNTOWN sceney rooftop lounges mixed with historic bars and local dives

HOLLYWOOD emerging barhopping scene thanks to new hotspots and revived classic joints

WEST HOLLYWOOD where the heart of L.A.'s nightlife lives, packed with clubs, lounges, and bars. Dress to impress

MID-WILSHIRE low-key places with reasonably priced drinks and good jukeboxes

SANTA MONICA AND THE BEACHES laid-back, bohemian feel, where everyone mixes

NIGHTLIFE PLANNER

WHERE TO GET INFORMATION

Good sources include *Los Angeles* magazine, ⊕ *www.la.com*, and ⊕ *losangeles.metromix.com*. Also, check the *Los Angeles Times* (⊕ *www.latimes.com*) calendar section, as well as *LA Weekly* (⊕ *www.laweekly.com*).

HOURS

Despite the high energy level of the L.A. nightlife crowd, don't expect to be partying until dawn—this is still an early-to-bed city. Bars close at 2 am, and it's safe to say that by this time, with the exception of a few after-hours venues, most clubs have closed for the night.

PARKING

After 7 pm, parking is at a premium in Hollywood. In fact, it's restricted on virtually every side street along the "hot zone" of West Hollywood (Sunset Boulevard from Fairfax to Doheny). Paying $5–$20, for valet or lot parking is often the easiest way to go.

BEST NIGHTLIFE EXPERIENCES

Cocktails With a View. Tops picks are the rooftop bar at the Downtown L.A. Standard, the Hotel Erwin in Venice Beach, the Sky Bar at the Mondrian in West Hollywood, and the ABH at Thompson Beverly Hills.

Hitting the Strip. The Sunset Strip has seen a fast turnaround from its once seedy status with a wave of new hot spots.

That Old Hollywood Glamour. For an evening of this town's Golden Era, check out historic bars filled with character, such as Chez Jay Restaurant, the Formosa Café, and the Kibutz Room at Cantor's Deli.

LATE-NIGHT TRANSPORTATION

To quench your thirst in La-La Land, getting in a car is an unfortunate drawback of nightlife here. That means picking a designated driver, or taking a taxi, which can easily tack on an extra $20 to your evening going from one neighborhood to another, as rates are steep.

The exception is if you're going out along Hollywood Boulevard, which has the "Holly Trolley" (⊕ *www.ladottransit.com/other/trolley*). It runs from 6:30 pm to 2:30 am, Thursday through Saturday, and $1 tokens are available at most bars.

WHAT A NIGHT OUT COSTS

Expect to pay a $15–$20 cover to get into high-end hot spots (add another $20–$50 if you want to bypass the line by tipping the doorman). The more casual hangouts, on the other hand, rarely charge more than $5. Drink prices are similarly varied, with posh clubs asking $10 and above for specialty drinks, and dive bars selling $2 beers and well drinks.

Due to the smoking ban, most bars and clubs with a cover charge allow "in and outs"—patrons may leave the premises and return (usually with a hand stamp or paper bracelet). Some newer clubs offer outdoor smoking patios—a great way to enjoy the city's consistently warm evenings.

The Rooftop Bar at The Standard, Downtown L.A., is a swanky place to enjoy a nightcap with a view.

DOWNTOWN

From the glitzy rooftop bar at the Standard Hotel to the kitschy local dive Bar 107, downtown there's a wide variety of places to suit your every nightlife need.

BARS AND LOUNGES

Bar 107. The look of this local dive is best described as everything but the "kitsch"-en sink (religious art, taxidermy, chandeliers) and the clientele is equally mixed, which makes for a vivacious vibe whether the night's entertainment is DJs, live burlesque, or just the jukebox. ⊠ *107 W. 4th St., Downtown* ☎ *213/625–7382.*

★ **Broadway Bar.** The 1940s-style historic bar feels swanky but avoids velvet-rope syndrome. The two-level, chandeliered room is more Rat Pack than brat pack; it's got stiff drinks, a jukebox filled with rock and lounge, and a smoking balcony overlooking the boulevard. ⊠ *830 S. Broadway, Downtown* ☎ *213/614–9909* ⊕ *www.broadwaybar.la.*

Fodor's Choice **Downtown L.A. Standard.** This futuristic hotel has a groovy lounge with
★ pink sofas and DJs, as well as an all-white restaurant that looks like something out of *2001: A Space Odyssey.* But it's the rooftop bar, with an amazing view of the city's illuminated skyscrapers, a heated swimming pool, and private, podlike water-bed tents, that's worth waiting in line to get into. And wait you probably will, especially on weekends and in summer. Friday and Saturday $20 cover charge after 7 pm. ⊠ *550 S. Flower St., Downtown* ☎ *213/892–8080* ⊕ *www.standardhotels.com.*

Edison. One of Downtown's most gorgeous lounges, the Edison is at the site of a former power plant and amazingly it manages to be classy and sophisticated while still retaining much of the original look. With waitresses in beaded frocks, deco touches, and jazzy sounds, the space is '20s glam meets industrial vamp. To maintain the ambience, there's even a dress code: no sneakers, jeans, or athletic wear. ✉ *108 W. 2nd St., Downtown* ☎ *213/613–0000* ⊕ *www.edisondowntown.com.*

Golden Gopher. The old-school vibe of this urban cocktail lounge is as much about the location as the venue. Don't be surprised if you're pan-handled on your way inside this downtown spot, which manages simultaneously to be swanky (art deco columns, Victorian wallpaper), kitschy (golden gopher-shaped lamps, video games), and divey (there's a small liquor store inside the place for stocking up on your way home). ✉ *417 W. 8th St., Downtown* ☎ *213/614–8001* ⊕ *www.goldengopherbar.com.*

Redwood Bar. This downtown staple has been around since the '40s (JFK was rumored to hang there), but when new owners took over a couple of years ago and remodeled it with a nautical theme, it quickly became known as "the pirate bar" with the hipster set. Fare includes the obligatory fish-and-chips, and drinks are nice and arrrrr hearty. DJs spin faves in the back room on weekends. ✉ *316 W. 2nd St., Downtown* ☎ *213/680–2600* ⊕ *www.theredwoodbar.com.*

Seven Grand. With antlered stuffed heads peering down over leather couches and plaid carpets, this downtown newcomer has the feel of a hunting lodge. It is warm and friendly, especially after everyone's had a few glasses of the specialty here—there are more than 270 kinds of whiskey, many extremely rare. DJs spin everything from rock to country to jazz on various nights. ✉ *515 W. 7th St., 2nd fl., Downtown* ☎ *213/614–0737* ⊕ *www.sevengrand.la.*

CLUBS

La Cita. Always packed by midnight, this red-hue Mexican dive is scruffy in more ways than one—Thursday and Friday nights, La Cita comes alive with hipsters working the American Apparel–patented, disheveled-casual look on its tiny dance floor. Sounds range from ironic '80s dance hits to electro to punk and reggae. ✉ *336 S. Hill St., Downtown* ☎ *213/687–7111* ⊕ *www.lacitabar.com.*

MUSIC

Bordello. Formerly Little Pedro's, Bordello has been called the oldest bar in Los Angeles, and lore has it, it was once a brothel. So when owners Tony Gower and Elisabeth Peterson remodeled and renamed it, they decided to pay homage to its seductive past with crimson red walls, black chandeliers, and other sexy yet ornate touches. Entertainment ranges from burlesque shows to jazz to rock. ✉ *901 E. 1st St., Downtown* ☎ *213/687–3766* ⊕ *www.bordellobar.com.*

The Smell. This hidden music venue may have bands only two or three nights a week (Wednesday, Friday, or Saturday), but they're often choice—in the alternative fringe world, anyway. If they're not playing at the Knitting Factory, Spaceland, or the Silver Lake Lounge, they just might be at the Smell. There's no liquor, the cover's usually $5, and there's also an art gallery. Enter via the back alley. ✉ *247 S. Main St., Downtown* ☎ *No phone* ⊕ *www.thesmell.org.*

Rapping at the El Rey Theater.

MID-WILSHIRE

BARS AND LOUNGES

The Dime. Another dark drinkin' hole where seasoned neighborhood guzzlers, Sex on the Beach–sipping barhoppers, and even a smattering of celebs peacefully coexist is the Dime. This low-key option gets energetic on weekends—and when DJs take over the sound system with a mix of rock and chilled electro beats. ✉ *442 N. Fairfax Ave., Fairfax District* ☎ *323/651–4421.*

HMS Bounty. After-work business types frequent this elegant old watering hole in the historic Gaylord apartment building. Be sure to check out the brass plates above each booth—they bear the names of Hollywood heavies who once held court here. The reasonably priced drinks are impressive; so is the jukebox. ✉ *3357 Wilshire Blvd., Mid-Wilshire* ☎ *213/385–7275* ⊕ *www.thehmsbounty.com.*

Molly Malone's. This authentic Irish pub is a small, casual spot where the only posturing is in the pro-Irish posters on the wall. The nightly live music tends to the Irish in flavor, but snappy blues and alternative-rock bands shake up the mix; the cover is usually no more than $10. ✉ *575 S. Fairfax Ave., Fairfax District* ☎ *323/935–1577* ⊕ *www.mollymalonesla.com.*

CLUBS

Jewel's Catch One. This dance club is a lively hangout for just about anyone, with male and female dancers and lip-synching shows, karaoke, and DJs spinning hip-hop and disco. ✉ *4067 W. Pico Blvd., Mid-City* ☎ *323/734–8849* ⊕ *www.jewelscatchone.com.*

MUSIC

El Rey Theater. About eight or 10 times a month, the gloriously restored art deco theater showcases concerts, often by top-name bands on national tours, as well as an assortment of theme nights. ✉ *5515 Wilshire Blvd., Mid-Wilshire* ☎ *323/936–6400* ⊕ *www.theelrey.com.*

HOLLYWOOD

Despite its well-publicized penchant for hedonism, Los Angeles, unlike New York, Chicago, and San Francisco, has never been much of a saloon town. But Hollywood's renaissance as a true nightlife destination is changing that part of the equation.

BARS AND LOUNGES

★ **Beauty Bar.** This bar cum salon offers manicures and makeovers along with the perfect martinis, but the hotties who flock to this retro spot (the little sister of the Beauty Bars in NYC and San Fran) don't really need the cosmetic care—this is where the edgy beautiful people hang. ✉ *1638 N. Cahuenga Blvd., Hollywood* ☎ *323/464–7676* ⊕ *www.thebeautybar.com.*

Burgundy Room. The dark and groovy hot spot has been a Hollywood favorite for some time, attracting an unpretentious rock-and-roll crowd most nights. ✉ *1621½ N. Cahuenga Blvd., Hollywood* ☎ *323/465–7530.*

Cabana Club. The name of the game at this club, as the tabloids say, is canoodling, whether you want to be seen or not (curtains can be drawn for privacy around the cabanas that line this outdoor club). On Thursday through Saturday nights, DJs spin everything from lounge to rock. ✉ *1439 Ivar Ave., Hollywood* ☎ *323/463–0005* ⊕ *www.cabanaclubhollywood.com.*

Cat & Fiddle Pub. This pub is a SoCal hacienda-style venue with a touch of England. Happy hours are weekdays 4–7 and 10–11, with drink specials at the bar. You can play darts, check out the memorabilia displays, or loll on the patio, where jazz is played Sunday night 7–11 (free). ✉ *6530 Sunset Blvd., Hollywood* ☎ *323/468–3800* ⊕ *www.thecatandfiddle.com.*

Green Door. The Green Door is one of the most charming newish lounges in Hollywood. With a whimsical vintage decor (gilded lamps and mirrors, and a giant circular velvet couch in its center), a fun dinner menu, and an atmosphere that gets livelier with inventive DJ mixing and dancing later in the evening, you can find a hip yet amiable crowd behind this door. ✉ *1439 Ivar Ave., Hollywood* ☎ *323/463–0008* ⊕ *www.sunseteg.com.*

Fodor's Choice ★ **Musso & Frank Grill.** Film-studio moguls, movie extras, and those longing for a look at a Hollywood watering hole of yesteryear flock here. This former haunt of F. Scott Fitzgerald is Hollywood's oldest restaurant, established in 1919 and still at the same location. The bar serves up the Rob Roys smooth. Stick with them, or if you *must* eat (and "enjoy" the famous attitude of the waiters), go for the steaks. ✉ *6667 Hollywood Blvd., Hollywood* ☎ *323/467–7788.*

Continued on page 171

L.A. STORY

THE CITY'S HISTORY THROUGH ITS BARS

Los Angeles is known as a place where dreams are realized, but it is also a place where pasts are forgotten. Despite what people say about L.A.'s lack of memory, however, there are quite a few noteworthy old-school bars that pay tribute to the city's vibrant past and its famous patrons.

Collectively, these eclectic watering holes have hosted everyone from ex-presidents to rock legends to famed authors and, of course, a continual stream of countless movie stars.

The bars are located in virtually every corner of the city—from Downtown to West Hollywood to Santa Monica.

In terms of character, they run the gamut from dive to dressy and serve everything from top-shelf whisky to bargain-basement beer.

While it's their differences that have kept people coming back through the decades, they all have something in common: Each has a story to tell.

EIGHT OF L.A.'S BEST

Mixing at Cole's

Chez Jay

Cole's

CHEZ JAY RESTAURANT (1959)
Noteworthy for: Located down the block from the Santa Monica Pier, this steak-and-seafood joint walks the line between celebrity hangout and dive bar.
Signature drink: Martini
Celeb clientele: Members of the Rat Pack, Leonard Nimoy, Sean Penn, Julia Roberts, Renée Zellweger, Owen Wilson, Drew Barrymore
Don't miss: The little booth in the back of the restaurant, known to insiders as Table 10, is a favorite celebrity hideout.
Filmed here: *Maverick*
Join the crowd: *1657 Ocean Ave., Santa Monica, 310/395–1741*

COLE'S (1908)
Noteworthy for: Found inside the Pacific Electric building, touted as Los Angeles's oldest public house, and once the epicenter of the Red Car railway network, this watering hole has its original glass lighting, penny-tile floors, and 40-foot mahogany bar.

Signature drink: The Red Car, a heady concoction with Rittenhouse rye, ginger liqueur, and lemon juice
Celeb clientele: Bill Murray, members of the cast of *Mad Men*
Don't miss: The Varnish at Cole's is an in-house speakeasy with 11 booths that can be accessed through a hidden door marked by a tiny framed picture of a cocktail glass.
Filmed here: *Forrest Gump, L.A. Confidential, Mad Men*
Join the crowd: *118 E. 6th St., Los Angeles, 213/622–4049*

FORMOSA CAFE (1929)
Noteworthy for: You can't miss West Hollywood's iconic bright red building with black-and-white-striped awnings. Once a trolley car, this Asian-inspired restaurant is an entertainment-industry favorite, with tons of autographed photos on its walls.
Signature drink: Mai tai, martini
Celeb clientele: Marilyn Monroe, Clark Gable, Elizabeth Taylor, Humphrey Bogart

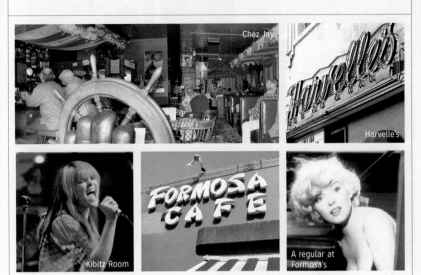

Chez Jay

Harvelle's

Kibitz Room

Formosa Cafe

A regular at Formosa's

Don't miss: Booths are named after the movie stars who sat in them during Hollywood's Golden Age.
Filmed here: *L.A. Confidential*
Join the crowd: *7156 Santa Monica Blvd., West Hollywood, 323/850–9050.*

FROLIC ROOM (1935)
Noteworthy for: This Hollywood favorite next door to the famed Pantages Theater has served actors and writers from Elizabeth Short to Charles Bukowski.
Signature drink: Cheap Budweiser ($2.75 during happy hour)
Celeb clientele: Kiefer Sutherland
Don't miss: A bowl of popcorn from the old-fashioned machine; the Hirschfeld mural depicting Marilyn Monroe, Charlie Chaplin, Louis Armstrong, Frank Sinatra, and others.
Filmed here: *L.A. Confidential, Southland*
Join the crowd: *6245 Hollywood Blvd., Los Angeles, 323/462–5890*

HARVELLE'S (1931)
Noteworthy for: Located one block off the Third Street Promenade, this dark and sexy jazz bar is said to be the oldest live-music venue on the Westside.
Signature drink: The Deadly Sins martini menu offers house-made mixes named after the seven sins, from Pride to Lust.
Don't miss: The Toledo Show is a pulse-quickening weekly burlesque-and-jazz performance on Sunday nights.
Join the crowd: *1432 4th St., Santa Monica, 310/395–1676.*

THE KIBITZ ROOM AT CANTER'S DELI (1961)
Noteworthy for: Adjacent to the famous Canter's Deli, which opened in 1948, this Fairfax District nightspot is definitely a dive bar, but that doesn't keep the A-listers away. Jakob Dylan and the Wallflowers got their start playing a weekly gig here.
Signature drink: Cheap beer
Celeb clientele: Dustin Hoffman, Tim Robbins, Kiefer Sutherland,

In golden days.

Canter's

Pastrami at Canter's

La Dolce Vita

Julia Roberts, Javier Bardem, Penélope Cruz

Don't miss: The decor is pure retro 1960s, including vinyl booths and a fall-leaf motif on the ceiling.

Filmed here: *I Ought to Be in Pictures, Entourage, Curb Your Enthusiasm, Sunset Strip, Enemy of the State, What's Eating Gilbert Grape*

Join the crowd: *1 N. Fairfax Ave., Los Angeles, 323/651–2030.*

DOLCE VITA (1966)

Noteworthy for: Located in tony Beverly Hills, this staple for northern Italian has a classy clubhouse atmosphere, round leather booths, white tablecloths, and exposed-brick walls.

Signature drink: Martini

Celeb clientele: Members of the Rat Pack; several ex-presidents, including Ronald Reagan. The place prides itself on being a safe haven from pesky paparazzi.

Don't miss: The burgundy-hued round leather booths.

Join the crowd: *9785 Santa Monica Blvd., Los Angeles, 310/278–1845*

MUSSO & FRANK GRILL (1919)

Noteworthy for: This swanky old-timer is called the oldest bar in Hollywood. While that title may spark jealousy among some of its Tinseltown counterparts, there is no doubt that this famed grill conjures Hollywood's halcyon days with its authentic '30s-era decor—and serves a mean martini.

Signature drink: The Mean Martini

Celeb clientele: Charlie Chaplin, Greta Garbo, Ernest Hemingway, F. Scott Fitzgerald, Marilyn Monroe

Don't miss: The red tuxedo–clad waiters are famous in their own right; some have been at the restaurant for more than 40 years.

Filmed here: *Ocean's Eleven, Charlie's Angels 2, Mad Men*

Join the crowd: *6667 Hollywood Blvd., Los Angeles, 323/467–7788*

Musso & Frank Grill

THE OLDEST RESTAURANT IN HOLLYWOOD
Since 1919

My House. Offering a brand-new take on the house party, this 10,000-square-foot club is dressed up to look like a swank bachelor pad with dozens of microsuede couches, leather chairs, and shag carpets. Don't miss the second-floor bedroom (aka VIP area) complete with king-size bed. ✉ *7080 Hollywood Blvd., Hollywood* ☎ *323/960–3300* ⊕ *www.myhousehollywood.com.*

Playhouse. Not for the weak of heart, this Vegas-style nightclub offers scantily clad go-go dancers, headdress-wearing hostesses, and swarms of beautiful people looking to get their drink on and hit the dance floor. While you are there, check out the in-house eatery aptly named Sweet Love Hangover. ✉ *6506 Hollywood Blvd., Hollywood* ☎ *323/656–4800* ⊕ *www.playhousehollywood.com.*

The Room. Dark and sequestered, this Hollywood spot promises some of the town's hottest DJs every night. The accent is on hip-hop, but Thursday–Saturday, *anything* is fair game. Enter on the alley. ✉ *1626 N. Cahuenga Blvd., Hollywood* ☎ *323/462–7196* ⊕ *www.theroomhollywood.com.*

★ **Three Clubs.** This casually hip club is in a strip mall, beneath a sign that simply reads "cocktails." The DJs segue through the many faces and phases of rock-and-roll and dance music. With dark-wood paneling, lamp-lighted tables, and even some sofas, you could be in a giant basement rec room from decades past—no fancy dress required, but fashionable looks suggested. ✉ *1123 Vine St., Hollywood* ☎ *323/462–6441* ⊕ *www.threeclubs.com.*

Tropicana Bar. This outdoor, poolside lounge in the Roosevelt Hotel, had so much buzz the management had to tone it down. After the hotel's revamp in 2005 and the arrival of lightning-rod promoter Amanda Scheer Demme (now gone), the place became a ridiculously fabulous hot spot for celebs and their tantalizing misbehavior. It's a good place to drink with the beautiful people and the occasional celeb. Inside the hotel, the even more exclusive **Teddy's** continues to pack in celebutants trying to avoid the paparazzi. ✉ *7000 Hollywood Blvd., Hollywood* ☎ *323/466–7000* ⊕ *www.hollywoodroosevelt.com.*

★ **Yamashiro.** A lovely L.A. tradition is to meet at here for cocktails at sunset. In the elegant restaurant, waitresses glide by in kimonos, and entrées can zoom up to $39; on the terrace, a spectacular hilltop view spreads out before you. ■TIP➔ **Mandatory valet parking is $7.50.** ✉ *1999 N. Sycamore Ave., Hollywood* ☎ *323/466–5125* ⊕ *www.yamashiroresraurant.com.*

CLUBS

★ **Boardner's.** This bar has a multidecade history (in the '20s it was a speakeasy), but with the adjoining ballroom, which was added a couple of years ago, it's now a state-of-the-art dance club. DJs may be spinning electronica, funk, or something else depending on the night—at the popular Saturday Goth event "Bar Sinister," patrons must wear black or risk not getting in. The cover here hovers around $5–$10. ✉ *1652 N. Cherokee Ave., Hollywood* ☎ *323/462–9621* ⊕ *www.boardners.com.*

Circus Disco and Arena. Ethnically mixed gay and straight crowd flocks here for two huge, side-by-side discos with techno and rock music, as

On busy nights, L.A.'s dance floors can get as crowded as its freeways.

well as a full bar and patio, open Tuesday through Sunday. Only certain nights are gay-theme. Top local and international DJs spin funk, house, trance, disco, and more until 4 am on Saturday. The cover varies but can go up to $25. ⊠ *6655 Santa Monica Blvd., Hollywood* ☎ *323/462–1291.*

Club Empire. Formerly Sugar, this Hollywood space offers sleek decor, a descent size dance floor and DJs spinning everything from rock to hip-hop. ⊠ *1716 N. Cahuenga Blvd., Hollywood* ☎ *323/836–0854* ⊕ *www. empirehollywood.com.*

Florentine Gardens. The 18-and-over set crowds into this spot on weekends. DJs from local radio stations often take over the turntables, and the crowd is usually made up of kids who drive in from Hollywood's outskirts. ⊠ *5955 Hollywood Blvd., Hollywood* ☎ *323/464–0706.*

Ivar. This swanky club has been attracting the model-actor "discover me" set with weekly hip-hop, electronic, and Top-40. It has two levels and lots of rooms to wander, including an outdoor patio and five bars. It's open Friday through Sunday. ⊠ *6356 Hollywood Blvd., Hollywood* ☎ *323/465–4827* ⊕ *www.ivarhollywood.com.*

Club Lax. The wait outside this Hollywood hot spot can often be as bad as the baggage check-in lines at its namesake, but that doesn't stop the L.A.'s party crowd from showing up. Definitely call before you come and get your name on the guest list—or better yet, reserve a table for the night. ⊠ *1714 Las Palmas Ave., Hollywood* ☎ *323/464–0171.*

★ **The Ruby.** This three-room dance venue is popular for young indie-rock and retro-loving twentysomethings. You might find anything from doomy Goth and industrial ("Perversion") to '80s retro ("Beat It") to '60s–'70s Brit pop and soul ("Bang") to trance and techno. ⊠ *7070 Hollywood Blvd., Hollywood* ☎ *323/467–7070.*

COMEDY

Acme Comedy Theater. This comedy club is really what its name suggests, the height of zaniness—mainly improv, sketch comedy, or both in the same production. The fare is consistently nutty, including an improvised game show and an improvised '40s-style radio drama. ⊠ *135 N. La Brea, Hollywood* ☎ *323/525–0202* ⊕ *www.acmecomedy.com.*

★ **Groundling Theatre.** More than a quarter-century old, this renowned theater company has been a breeding ground for *Saturday Night Live* performers; alumni include Lisa Kudrow and *Curb Your Enthusiasm*'s Cheryl Hines. The primarily sketch and improv comedy shows run Wednesday–Sunday, costing $14–$18. ⊠ *7307 Melrose Ave., Hollywood* ☎ *323/934–4747* ⊕ *www.groundlings.com.*

iO West Theater. Formerly known as Improv Olympic West, this comedy club showcases thematic improv and revues among its nightly shows, with covers from free to $10. It's known for Second City comedy troupe's long-form improv called "the Harold." ⊠ *6366 Hollywood Blvd., Hollywood* ☎ *323/962–7560* ⊕ *www.iowest.com.*

Upright Citizens Brigade. New York's UCB marched in with a mix of sketch comedy and wild improvisations skewering pop culture. Members of the L.A. Brigade include VH1 commentator Paul Scheer and *Mad TV*'s Andrew Daly. ⊠ *5919 Franklin Ave., Hollywood* ☎ *323/908–8702* ⊕ *www.ucbtheatre.com.*

MUSIC
JAZZ
Baked Potato. Powerhouse jazz and blues please crowds at this tiny club. The star of the menu is, of course, the baked potato, jumbo and stuffed with everything from steak to vegetables. The music's on every night, with a cover that usually hovers around $15 but can get more pricey for special events. ⊠ *3787 Cahuenga Blvd. W, North Hollywood* ☎ *818/980–1615* ⊕ *www.thebakedpotato.com.*

Catalina. After moving to a bigger space in 2005, this jazz club is hotter than ever, with top-notch jazz bookings ranging from classic Chicago style to Latin-flavored. ⊠ *6725 W. Sunset Blvd., Hollywood* ☎ *323/466–2210* ⊕ *www.catalinajazzclub.com.*

LATIN
Fodor'sChoice **El Floridita.** The Cuban food here is anywhere from good to great—and
★ the music (Monday, Friday, and Saturday) is anywhere from very good to through the roof. A frequent guest is the salsa bandleader Johnny Polanco, backed by the sizzling Orquesta Amistad. Watching some of the paying customers who get up to dance is alone worth the price of admission (usually $10 or $15, or free with dinner). ⊠ *1253 N. Vine St., Hollywood* ☎ *323/871–8612* ⊕ *www.elfloridita.com.*

DID YOU KNOW?

A cruise down Sunset Boulevard takes you to the heart
of Los Angeles nightlife.
Whether you're looking for
someplace seedy or swank,
you can find it here.

ROCK

Avalon. The landmark formerly known as the Palace is now the Avalon. The multilevel art deco building opposite Capitol Records has a fabulous sound system, four bars, and a balcony. Big-name rock and pop concerts hit the stage during the week, but on weekends the place becomes a dance club, with the most popular night the DJ-dominated Avaland on Saturday. Upstairs, but with a separate entrance, you can find celeb hub **Bardot,** a glamorous tribute to Old Hollywood where celebs and their entourages are frequent visitors. ⊠ *1735 N. Vine St., Hollywood* ☎ *323/462–8900* ⊕ *www.avalonhollywood.com.*

California Institute of Abnormal Arts. For the sake of pithiness, this place abbreviates its name to CIA. Its nuttiness (bands and multimedia events) is let loose several nights a week. It's been said that on "weekends it's a giant magnet for every loose screw in town." ⊠ *11334 Burbank Ave., North Hollywood* ☎ *818/506–6353* ⊕ *www.ciabnormalarts.com.*

Dragonfly. Dark and grungy, this live music venue showcases a mix of live rock and rock hybrids several nights a week. On Friday, it morphs into a dance club. On Thursday, it's drum and bass all night. When you need to cool off, there's an outdoor patio with bar. ⊠ *6510 Santa Monica Blvd., Hollywood* ☎ *323/466–6111* ⊕ *www.thedragonfly.com.*

Genghis Cohen Cantina. At this longtime music-industry hangout you can hear hopefuls and veteran performers of the singer-songwriter sort and sample the kosher Chinese cuisine at the same time. ⊠ *740 N. Fairfax Ave., Hollywood* ☎ *323/653–0640* ⊕ *www.genghiscohen.com.*

King King. Everything from Latin rhythms to electronic music to raging punk sounds can found at this roomy nightclub. Good acoustics, even better crowd. The entrance from the parking-lot side of the building helps you avoid slackjawed tourists on the Walk of Fame. ⊠ *6555 Hollywood Blvd., Hollywood* ☎ *323/960–9234* ⊕ *www.kingkinghollywood. com.*

Largo. Musician-producer Jon Brion (Fiona Apple, Aimee Mann, and others) shows off his ability to play virtually any instrument and any song in the rock lexicon—and beyond—as host of a popular evening of music some Fridays at Largo. Other nights, low-key rock and singer-songwriter fare is offered at this cozy venue. And when comedy comes in, about one night a week, it's usually one of the best comedy nights in town, with folks like Sarah Silverman. ⊠ *366 N. La Cienega Blvd., Hollywood* ☎ *310/855–0350* ⊕ *www.largo-la.com.*

WEST HOLLYWOOD

With a bar or club on what seems to be every street corner, West Hollywood is the place to be for nightlife aficionados. True late-night scenesters should head to the Sunset Strip for a taste of neighborhood's rock-and-roll glory days, while those more apt to seek out a classic cocktail should hit up one of the area's many sophisticated drinking holes. Wherever you end up, however, don't forget to dress to impress.

BARS AND LOUNGES

★ **Bar Marmont.** As at so many other nightspots in this neck of the woods, the popularity and clientele of this hotel bar bulged—and changed— after word got out it was a favorite of celebrities. Lately, it's gotten a second wind thanks to a strong DJ selection and luscious cocktails. The bar is next to the inimitable hotel Chateau Marmont, which bold-face names continue to haunt. ⊠ *8171 Sunset Blvd., West Hollywood* ☎ *323/650–0575* ⊕ *www.chateaumarmont.com.*

Barney's Beanery. Half bar, half restaurant, and home to what the owners call "L.A.'s second-best chili" and the equally touted chili burger, this casual joint serves more than 200 different beers. Established in 1920, it's second only to Musso & Frank in restaurant longevity in L.A. The funky decor, long bar, two pool tables, and assortment of air hockey, video, and even pinball games keep the relatively hip but unaffected crowd amused and coming back for more. ⊠ *8447 Santa Monica Blvd., West Hollywood* ☎ *323/654–2287* ⊕ *www.barneysbeanery.com.*

Formosa Café. Decent Chinese food and pretty good drinking are on offer at this historic locale, featured in 1997's noir *L.A. Confidential* for being a rare, still-intact remnant of that bygone Hollywood era. Its railroad-car design allows for lots of booths, and the walls are a picto-rial shrine to the film community, many of whom have frequented the place (it's across from the former Warner Hollywood lot). ⊠ *7156 Santa Monica Blvd., West Hollywood* ☎ *323/850–9050.*

Happy Ending. With a jovial hipster atmosphere, tasty gourmet menu, and saucily named signature drinks, this isn't your typical sports bar. TV screens galore, karaoke, and a colorful "drink wheel" (spin it and you can win everything from $2 shots to $10 beer pitchers) help this bar live up to its name in more ways than one. ⊠ *7038 Sunset Blvd., Hollywood* ☎ *323/469–7038* ⊕ *www.thehappyendingbar.com.*

Jones. Get up close and personal with Hollywood hipsters at Jones. It's too dark and crowded for you to be able to tell, but this is an authenti-cally preserved old showbiz haunt, with secluded booths, scrumptious food, and very loud music. ⊠ *7205 Santa Monica Blvd., West Holly-wood* ☎ *323/850–1727.*

★ **Rainbow Bar & Grill.** In the heart of the Strip and next door to the legend-ary Roxy, the Rainbow is a landmark in its own right as *the* drinking spot of the '80s hair-metal scene—and it still attracts a music-indus-try crowd. ⊠ *9015 Sunset Blvd., West Hollywood* ☎ *310/278–4232* ⊕ *www.rainbowbarandgrill.com.*

Skybar. To enter this poolside bar at the Hotel Mondrian, you must have a Mondrian room key, a screen credit, or a spot on the guest list. The view is phenomenal, as is the staying power of its cachet. ⊠ *8440 Sunset Blvd., West Hollywood* ☎ *323/650–8999* ⊕ *www.mondrianhotel.com.*

★ **The Standard.** A classic Hollywood makeover—formerly a nursing home, this spot in the happening part of Sunset Strip got converted into a smart, brash-looking hotel, the Standard, for the young, hip, and con-nected. (Check out the live model in the lobby's terrarium.) The hotel and especially the bar here is popular with those in the biz. ⊠ *8300 Sunset Blvd., West Hollywood* ☎ *323/650–9090* ⊕ *www.standardhotels.com.*

In L.A.'s bar scene, there's a place for every fashion sensibility.

Villa. Formerly Monroe's and before that the historic J. Sloan's, Villa is more exclusive than either of its prior incarnations. You must know someone associated with the bar to enter or even have the valet park your car there. The vibe is luxe but homey—it was designed to look a mansion. ✉ *8623 Melrose Ave., at Huntley Dr., West Hollywood* ☎ *310/289–8623* ⊕ *www.villalounge.com.*

Voyeur. As you may have guessed from its name, the theme is sex at this WeHo club-du-jour. Expect to see risqué photography, erotic live art installations, dancers in sequined pasties on a glass-encased stage, and a scantily clad crowd of beautiful people. ✉ *7969 Santa Monica Blvd., Hollywood* ☎ *310/255–1111* ⊕ *www.voyeur7969.com.*

Winston's. One of a slew of newer bars bringing straight crowds to WeHo's mostly gay nightlife scene, this WeHo spot is also notable for its star quota. Everyone from Britney to Paris frequent the place, and its dark, '20s-flaired opulence was featured on HBO's *Entourage* soon after it opened. ✉ *7746 Santa Monica Blvd., West Hollywood* ☎ *323/654–0105* ⊕ *www.winstonsla.com.*

COMEDY

Comedy Store. A nightly premiere comedy showcase, this comedy venue has been going strong for more than two decades, with three stages (with covers ranging from free to $20) to supply the yuks. Famous comedians occasionally make unannounced appearances. ✉ *8433 Sunset Blvd., West Hollywood* ☎ *323/650-6268* ⊕ *www.thecomedystore.com.*

Improv. Richard Pryor got his start here, a renowned establishment showcasing stand-up comedy. Reservations are recommended. Cover is $15–$20, and there's a two-drink minimum. ✉ *8162 Melrose Ave., West Hollywood* ☎ *323/651–2583* ⊕ *www.improv.com.*

Laugh Factory. Look for top stand-ups—and frequent celeb residents, like Bob Saget, or unannounced drop-ins, like Chris Rock. The club has shows at Sunday through Thursday nights at 8 pm and 10 pm, plus an additional show on Friday and Saturday at midnight; the cover is $20–$30. ✉ *8001 Sunset Blvd., West Hollywood* ☎ *323/656–1336* ⊕ *www.laughfactory.com.*

CLUBS

The Factory. True to its name, this club churns out dance music for those who like to grind. In the adjoining Ultra Suede, there's an urban dance party on Wednesday and "Living" on Friday. Saturday, the two houses combine for an event called "Cherry Pop." Covers range from $5 to $15. ✉ *661 N. Robertson Blvd., West Hollywood* ✉ *652 La Peer Dr., West Hollywood* ☎ *310/659–4551* ⊕ *www.factorynightclub.com.*

★ **Here.** Nowhere is more gregarious than here (no pun intended), where there are hot DJs and an even hotter clientele. Some weekly highlights include "Truck Stop" on Friday, "Neon" on Saturday, and "Stripper Circus" Wednesday. ✉ *696 N. Robertson Blvd., West Hollywood* ☎ *310/360–8455* ⊕ *www.herelounge.com.*

The Palms. A long-running gay-gal fave, this club continues to thrive thanks to great DJs spinning dance tunes as well as karaoke and comedy shows. There are also an outdoor patio, pool tables, and an occasional live performance. ✉ *8572 Santa Monica Blvd., West Hollywood* ☎ *310/652–1595* ⊕ *www.thepalmsbar.com.*

Rage. This spot is a longtime favorite of the "gym boy" set, with DJs following a different musical theme every night of the week (alternative rock, house, dance remixes, etc.). The cover ranges from free to $10. ✉ *8911 Santa Monica Blvd., West Hollywood* ☎ *310/652–7055.*

MUSIC

Cat Club. Slim Jim Phantom, former drummer of the Stray Cats, is the man behind this rock club. Bands play nightly, and Mr. Phantom sometimes comes out to play with buds like ex–Guns N' Roses axman Gilby Clarke. There are an upstairs and a back patio, but it's still, to euphemize, "intimate." ✉ *8911 Sunset Blvd., West Hollywood* ☎ *310/657–0888.*

House of Blues. This Delta-theme club functions like a concert venue, hosting popular jazz, rock, and blues performers. Occasional shows are presented cabaret style and include dinner in the restaurant area upstairs; you can *sort of* see from some of it. Every Sunday there's a gospel brunch. ✉ *8430 Sunset Blvd., West Hollywood* ☎ *323/848–5100* ⊕ *www.houseofblues.com.*

Key Club. This flashy, multitier rock club offers four bars presenting current artists of all genres (some on national tours, others local aspirants). After the concerts, there's often dancing with DJs spinning techno and house. ✉ *9039 Sunset Blvd., West Hollywood* ☎ *310/274–5800* ⊕ *www.keyclub.com.*

Rocking out at the Roxy.

The Roxy. A Sunset Strip fixture for decades, this live music club hosts local and touring rock, alternative, blues, and rockabilly bands. Not the comfiest club around, but it's the site of many memorable shows. ✉ *9009 Sunset Blvd., West Hollywood* ☎ *310/278–9457* ⊕ *www.theroxyonsunset.com.*

The Troubadour. One of the best and most comfortable clubs in town, this live music Mecca has weathered the test of time since its '60s debut as a folk club. After surviving the '80s heavy-metal scene, this all-ages, wood-panel venue has caught a second (third? fourth?) wind by booking hot alternative rock acts. There's valet parking, but if you don't mind walking up Doheny a block or three, there's usually ample street parking (check the signs carefully). ✉ *9081 Santa Monica Blvd., West Hollywood* ☎ *310/276–6168* ⊕ *www.troubador.com.*

Viper Room. Actor Johnny Depp sold his share of the infamous rock venue in 2004, but the place continues to rock with a motley live music lineup, if a less stellar crowd. ✉ *8852 W. Sunset Blvd., West Hollywood* ☎ *310/358–1881* ⊕ *www.viperroom.com.*

Whisky-A-Go-Go. The Whisky, as locals call it, is the most famous rock-and-roll club on the Strip, where back in the '60s, Johnny Rivers cut hit singles and the Doors, Love, and the Byrds cut their musical eyeteeth. It's still going strong, with up-and-coming alternative, hard rock, and punk bands, though mostly of the unknown variety. ✉ *8901 Sunset Blvd., West Hollywood* ☎ *310/652–4202* ⊕ *www.whiskyagogo.com.*

LOS FELIZ, SILVER LAKE, AND ECHO PARK

While the Sunset Strip may have been the place to be for music lovers in the '70s and '80s, Silver Lake and Echo Park are the indisputable heavyweight champions of the live music scene these days. Check out Spaceland or The Echo for a firsthand taste of the neighborhoods' hipster-heavy indie rock scene.

BARS AND LOUNGES

4100. A space that's as popular with nonlocals as it is with the neighborhood's bohemian barflys, this Silver Lake bar is a great place to meet and be merry. A lively jukebox mixing rock-and-roll and soul, plus seating around the bar, makes it a hip, no-hassle hookup spot. ⊠ *4100 Sunset Blvd., Silver Lake* ☎ *323/666–4460.*

Akbar. This space has retained its friendly neighborhood feel, even after an expansion brought a bigger dance floor and sound system. The largely gay crowd tends be artier than the WeHo pretty-boy set, and it's also less of a meat market. ⊠ *4356 Sunset Blvd., Silver Lake* ☎ *323/665–6810* ⊕ *www.akbarsilverlake.com.*

Big Foot Lodge. This rustic bar has a cheeky outdoors theme, with a life-size, animated Smokey the Bear, but the twentysomething crowd tends toward the rock and rockabilly set. Different DJs offer sounds from '80s metal to '60s French pop. If you're feeling campfire nostalgia, try the Toasted Marshmallow, a creamy drink topped with, you guessed it, a flaming marshmallow. ⊠ *3172 Los Feliz Blvd., Los Feliz* ☎ *323/662–9227* ⊕ *www.bigfootlodge.com.*

★ **Cha Cha Lounge.** Seattle's coolest rock bar now aims to repeat its success with this colorful, red-lighted space. Think part tiki hut, part tacky Tijuana party palace. The tabletops pay homage to the lounge's former performers; they've got portraits of Latin drag queens. ⊠ *2375 Glendale Blvd., Silver Lake* ☎ *323/660–7595* ⊕ *www.chachalounge.com.*

Dresden Room. A '40s-style bar that was rediscovered during the mid-'90s lounge craze and immortalized in the film *Swingers*, this swanky spot is still a popular hangout with old-timers and Gen X lounge lizards alike. Marty and Elayne (also seen in the film) are still burning up the joint with inimitable covers of "Staying Alive" and "Livin' La Vida Loca" (nightly, except Sunday and Monday, 9 pm–1:15 am; no cover, but there's a two-drink minimum). ⊠ *1760 N. Vermont Ave., Los Feliz* ☎ *323/665–4294* ⊕ *www.thedresden.com.*

El Prado. During its previous incarnation as a Mexican cowboy bar, this Echo Park favorite was a small dimly lighted space that served mostly beer. Now, it is still small, still dimly lighted and still serving mostly beer, but it also boasts a Dwell-worthy salvaged wood counter, a micro dance floor and every hipster's favorite accessory, a bonafide vinyl-spinning record player. ⊠ *1805 W. Sunset Blvd., Echo Park* ☎ *213/483–8609* ⊕ *www.elpradobar.com.*

Good Luck Bar. This red-lighted, Chinese-motif bar teems with young singles looking to meet someone, and the sexy vibe (helped along with soul tunes and strong spirits) means this place often lives up to its name. ⊠ *1514 Hillhurst Ave., Los Feliz* ☎ *323/666–3524.*

The Echoplex draws national acts to the basement stage of the Echo nightclub in Echo Park.

★ **Short Stop.** It got its name thanks to its proximity to Dodger Stadium, but for decades this multiroom bar was even better known for its regulars—the LAPD. Under new ownership for the past couple of years, the low-lighted three-room space still has cop memorabilia on the walls, but now it attracts artsy, fashionable locals. There's a great dance room with DJs spinning all sorts of sounds Tuesday through Sunday. ✉ *1455 Sunset Blvd., Echo Park* ☎ *213/482–4942.*

Smog Cutter. It may be in an iffy part of town, but this dive bar still attracts a fun cross-section of local barflies and Hollywood hipsters. Come for its raucous karaoke nights and cheap drinks. ✉ *864 N. Virgil Ave., Silver Lake* ☎ *323/660–4626.*

★ **Tiki-Ti.** The tiny Hawaiian-theme room is one of the most charming drinking huts in the city. You can spend hours just looking at the Polynesian artifacts strewn all about the place, but be careful—time flies in this tiny tropical bar, and the colorful drinks can be so potent that you may have to stay marooned for a while. ✉ *4427 Sunset Blvd., Silver Lake* ☎ *323/669–9381* ⊕ *www.tiki-ti.com.*

CLUBS

MJ's. This Silver Lake gay bar is laid-back enough to attract locals of every persuasion. DJs spin an array of diva disco, electro, and mash-ups. ✉ *2810 Hyperion Ave., Silver Lake* ☎ *323/660–1503* ⊕ *www.mjsbar.com.*

MUSIC

★ **The Echo.** This Echo Park mainstay sprang from the people behind the Silver Lake rock joint Spaceland. Most evenings this dark and divey space's tiny dance floor and well-worn booths attract artsy local bands and their followers, but things rev up when DJs spin reggae, rock, and funk. Opened in the club's basement in 2007, **the Echoplex** books bigger national tours and events. ⊠ *1822 Sunset Blvd., Echo Park* 🕾 *213/413–8200* ⊕ *www.attheecho.com* ⊠ *1154 Glendale Blvd.*

Silver Lake Lounge. Neighborhoody and relaxed, this lounge draws a mixed collegiate and boho crowd. The club is very unmainstream "cool," the booking policy an adventurous mix of local and touring alt-rockers. Bands play three to five nights a week; covers vary but are low. ⊠ *2906 Sunset Blvd., Silver Lake* 🕾 *323/663–9636.*

★ **Spaceland.** The hottest bands of tomorrow, surprises from yesteryear, and unclassifiable bands of today perform at this low-key Silver Lake venue, which has a bar, jukebox, and pool table. Monday is always free, with monthlong gigs by the indie fave du jour. Spaceland has a nice selection of beers and a hip but relaxed interior. ⊠ *1717 Silver Lake Blvd., Silver Lake* 🕾 *323/661–4380* ⊕ *www.clubspaceland.com.*

SANTA MONICA AND THE BEACHES

Santa Monica and Venice are known for their relaxed beachy atmosphere, but that is not to say that it is all bikinis and flip-flops at local nightlife spots. A good rule of thumb to follow: If you are within sight of the sand and sea, a casual look will probably suit you just fine, but if you are stepping out on artsy Abbot Kinney, don't be afraid to dress the part.

BARS AND LOUNGES

The Brig. The retro charm of this Abbot Kinney watering hole suits the beachy locals just fine, but with DJs spinning cool sounds and stylish drinks (including a tasty blood-orange martini), it has become a destination for commuting clubbers, too. ⊠ *1515 Abbot Kinney Blvd., Venice* 🕾 *310/399–7537* ⊕ *www.thebrig.com.*

Chez Jay. This saloon, near the Santa Monica Pier, has endured since 1959. With 10 tables, checkered tablecloths, and sawdust on the floor, it's a shabby but charming setting for inventive seafood fare and regular celebrity sightings. ⊠ *1657 Ocean Ave., Santa Monica* 🕾 *310/395–1741* ⊕ *www.chezjays.com.*

Circle Bar. This Main Street hang gets its name from the bar's circular-shape, a setup that helps make it a see-and-be-seen beachside "it" spot. On most nights DJs spin electronic dance beats, hip-hop, and rock for casually dressed twentysomethings. ⊠ *2926 Main St., Santa Monica* 🕾 *310/450–0508* ⊕ *www.thecirclebar.com.*

Duke's Barefoot Bar. If it's surfer boys or girls you're after, this beachy locale will be your new favorite hangout. The tiki-decorated oceanside drinking spot—named after famed surf god Duke Kahanamoku—is a casual place, with a patio right near the waves and an adjoining restaurant offering tasty finger foods. ⊠ *21150 Pacific Coast Hwy., Malibu* 🕾 *310/317–0777* ⊕ *www.dukesmalibu.com.*

The Galley. Thick with nautical mementos, this tiny restaurant/bar is recommended for nostalgics who want to recapture Santa Monica circa 1940. ⊠ *2442 Main St., Santa Monica* ☎ *310/452–1934* ⊕ *www. thegalleyresraurant.net.*

The Lighthouse Cafe. This café has a full bar and live music weeknights (music starts at 9). A $5–$10 cover is charged on Friday and Saturday; jazz is on offer every Thursday and Sunday evening. ⊠ *30 Pier Ave., Hermosa Beach* ☎ *310/376–9833* ⊕ *www.thelighthousecafe.com.*

Monsoon. Carved wooden tribal masks and other Indian and Southeast Asian items make this one of the most elegant spots on the always-jumping Promenade. The restaurant serves South Asian cuisine, and there's live music (from so-so to pretty good) in the upstairs bar most nights. ⊠ *1212 3rd St. Promenade, Santa Monica* ☎ *310/576–9996* ⊕ *www.globaldiningca.com.*

Moonshadows. Famous locals (Britney Spears, Mel Gibson) frequent the restaurant side of this Malibu favorite due to its location, but it's the adjoining Blue Lodge that steals the spotlight with nightly DJs spinning mostly atmospheric electronic grooves. ⊠ *20356 Pacific Coast Hwy.* ☎ *310/456–3010* ⊕ *www.moonshadowsmalibu.com.*

Otheroom. Dark and spacious, this relative newcomer may be a har-binger of Abbot Kinney's gentrification, but it's still got that laid-back Venice vibe. In fact, it fits into this neighborhood well enough that you'd never guess the original's from Manhattan. There's an impressive selection of microbrews and wines. ⊠ *1201 Abbot Kinney Blvd., Venice* ☎ *310/396–6230* ⊕ *www.theotheroom.com.*

The Underground. This British pub and sports bar offers imported beers and alcohol-absorbing greasy food, plus darts, pool, and DJs spinning dance hits on the weekends. ⊠ *1332 Hermosa Ave., Hermosa Beach* ☎ *310/318–3818* ⊕ *www.undergroundpub.com.*

MUSIC

Café Boogaloo. This Hermosa Beach venue has live blues on tap nearly every night, not to mention more than two-dozen microbrews. Its cozy, down-to-earth, Louisiana-style restaurant and bar scene is especially popular among O.C. locals. The cover charge hovers around $5 on most nights. ⊠ *1238 Hermosa Ave., near Pier Ave., Hermosa Beach* ☎ *310/318–2324* ⊕ *www.boogaloo.com.*

Harvelle's. A young crowd, many of them regulars, packs this art deco–style club on the weekends; come early or be prepared to stand in line. Watch from the back if you want, but down front, you'll be dancing. The cover's usually less than $10 weekdays, but can be higher on the weekends; a two-drink minimum is sometimes enforced. ⊠ *1432 4th St., Santa Monica* ☎ *310/395–1676* ⊕ *www.harvelles.com.*

Little Temple. The funky people behind Santa Monica's Zanzibar and now-closed Temple Bar moved east for this warm, more intimate spot. The DJs and live acts focus on soul, Latin, and reggae music. ⊠ *4519 Santa Monica Blvd., Santa Monica* ☎ *323/660–4540* ⊕ *www. littletemple.com.*

McCabe's Guitar Shop. This famous guitar shop is rootsy-retro-central, where all things earnest and (preferably) acoustic are welcome—chiefly folk, blues, bluegrass, and rock. It *is* a guitar shop (so no liquor license), with a room full of folding chairs for concert-style presentations. Shows on weekends only. Make reservations well in advance. ✉ *3101 Pico Blvd., Santa Monica* ☎ *310/828–4497, 310/828–4497 for concert information* ⊕ *www.mccabes.com.*

Rusty's Surf Ranch. When you're not gawking at the many vintage surf-boards on the walls and ceiling of this beach-theme venue, you can watch rock-and-roll bands, singer-songwriters, or blues boppers. ✉ *256 Santa Monica Pier, Santa Monica* ☎ *310/393–7437* ⊕ *www. rustyssurfranch.com.*

CABARET AND VARIETY

Beyond Baroque. This performance space and bookstore in the old Venice Town Hall is dedicated to the literary arts, with popular poetry and literature readings that have included the likes of Viggo Mortensen. They also offer free poetry and writing workshops for aspiring scribes. ✉ *681 Venice Blvd., Venice* ☎ *310/822–3006* ⊕ *www.beyondbaroque.org.*

★ **Highways Performance Space.** With seating for 120, this Santa Monica–based spot is one of the primary venues for avant-garde, offbeat, and alternative performance art as well as theater, dance, and comedy programs. It also has a gallery space. ✉ *1651 18th St., Santa Monica* ☎ *310/453–1755, 310/315–1459* ⊕ *www.highwaysperformance.org.*

CLUBS

Zanzibar. Funk and hip-hop rule at this DJ-driven dance club, a warm and inviting spot from the people behind now-closed Temple Bar. Sounds ranging from Latin jazz to soul to deep house attract a mix of locals and commuting Hollywood clubsters. ✉ *1301 5th St., Santa Monica* ☎ *310/451–2221* ⊕ *www.zanzibarlive.com.*

COFFEEHOUSES

UnUrban Coffee House. A good place to take a break from the nonstop fun you've been having in L.A. and write about it in your journal is this funky coffeehouse. Enjoy a stiff cup of coffee or some luscious chai tea, scarf down the good but inexpensive breakfast or a sandwich, and hear the music or spoken-word performances on Sunday during the day or on weekend evenings. Open mike nights are every Wednesday and Friday. ✉ *3301 Pico Blvd., at Urban Ave., Santa Monica* ☎ *310/315–0056.*

Performing Arts

WORD OF MOUTH

"Check out the concert schedules at The Hollywood Bowl and The Greek. Both are wonderful outdoor venues and a real Southern California experience!"

—Dayle

Updated by
Alene Dawson

The outdated belief that Los Angeles is devoid of real culture continues to wither with cutting-edge performances and impresarios committed to artistic expression who call this city home. Plácido Domingo has put the Los Angeles Opera on the map; the passionate, young conductor Gustavo Dudamel has excited classical music lovers in the city—and indeed around the world—as the newest Music Director of the Los Angeles Philharmonic.

And a wide variety of theater companies, such as the Actor's Gang helmed by Tim Robbins, as well as venues such as the performing arts complex REDCAT persist in pushing the boundaries of political and social expression.

The city is one of the best places in the world for seeing soon-to-be-famous rockers as well as top jazz, blues, and classical performers. And the new and unique Grammy Museum Downtown celebrates all genres with fun, interactive genius.

The concert scene in Los Angeles is as diverse as the city is sprawled out. If you're a classical music lover, the L.A Philharmonic at Walt Disney Concert Hall and at the Hollywood Bowl in summer is a festive night out. The Greek Theatre and Gibson Amphitheatre are outdoor venues that attract big acts and take advantage of the city's hospitable weather as well. The newest concert space, Nokia Live, is already a favorite concert hall to experience that full range of music up close.

Movie theaters, including those in the luxury category like Gold Class Cinemas in Pasadena that serve multicourse dinners and swanky cocktails as you watch films, are naturally well represented here, making Los Angeles a flourishing leader in the performing arts in both scope and global influence.

PERFORMING ARTS PLANNER

WHERE TO GET INFORMATION

For a thorough listing of local events, ⊕ *www.la.com, experiencela.com,* and *Los Angeles* magazine are all good sources. The Calendar section of the *Los Angeles Times* (⊕ *findlocal.latimes.com*) also lists a wide survey of Los Angeles arts events, as does the free alternative publication, *LA Weekly* (⊕ *www.laweekly.com*), which is issued every Thursday.

WHERE TO GET TICKETS

In addition to contacting venues directly—as sometimes last-minute tickets are sold at reduced prices just hours before the performance—try these sources.

Razor Gator. Sells harder-to-get tickets. ☎ *800/542–4466* ⊕ *www.razorgator.com.*

Ticketmaster. Still the all-around top dog. ☎ *213/480–3232, 213/365–3500 fine arts* ⊕ *www.ticketmaster.com.*

BEST PERFORMING ARTS EXPERIENCES

Visit a Movie Palace. Aside from Grauman's, there are plenty of beautifully preserved old theaters, such as the Orpheum on Broadway Downtown or the fabulous ArcLight.

Kick Back at the Hollywood Bowl. Of course you can see a concert here, and you should—but even if you don't have tickets there are free practice performances to attend. And don't forget your picnic!

Make a Music Hall a Must. Get wowed by Frank Gehry's architecture and Gustavo Dudamel's conducting at the Walt Disney Concert Hall, the elegant decor at the Dorothy Chandler Pavilion, or the acoustics at L.A. Live/Nokia Theater.

WHERE TO EAT AFTER THE SHOW

For the venues Downtown or in Hollywood, it's easy to grab something quick before a performance, although there aren't any pre-theater dinner places of note. There are, however, several places to choose from that stay open late and are worth a visit in their own right.

Canter's. Craving a classic corned beef on rye and a knish? There's no better place in L.A. to come for a fix.

XIV. A super hot spot on the Sunset Strip designed by Philippe Starck has a great selection of small plates to choose from.

Fred 62. If you're out in Los Feliz, check out this classic American diner has everything from burgers to pancakes with peanut butter, chocolate chips, and bananas.

Kate Mantilini. Open until midnight, this casual spot in Beverly Hills has an extensive menu of comfort food favorites.

25 Degrees. You can't go wrong with this upscale burger joint located inside the Hollywood Roosevelt Hotel, which offers a good selection of wines by the half-bottle.

Animal. This major foodie magnet in Hollywood, with a mix of local and celeb clientele, has rich food and a fantastic multi-layered bacon chocolate bar for dessert.

8

CONCERTS

Los Angeles has a legacy of rock-and-roll. The ghost of rockers past haunt the Sunset Strip and up-and-coming bands still cut their teeth at smaller venues like the Good Hurt on Venice that charge $5 covers.

There are hundreds of places to see live acts in this town catering to your love of music whether it's jazz, rock-and-roll, new age, classic rock, mega-star pop, Latin fusion, and whatever else your heart desires. Pick up an *LA Weekly* for full listings.

MAJOR CONCERT HALLS

★ **Dorothy Chandler Pavilion.** One of the Music Center's most cherished and impressive music halls, the 3,200-seat landmark remains an elegant space to see performances with its plush red seats and giant gold curtain.

It presents an array of music programs and L.A. Opera's classics from September through June. Music director Plácido Domingo encourages fresh work (in 2006, for instance, he ushered in *Grendel*, a new opera staged by the hypercreative director Julie Taymor) as much as old favorites (the 2010 season marked the world renown production of Wagner's *Der Ring des Nibelungen* or *Ring Cycle* that ran in conjunction with *Ring Festival L.A.*—a celebration of the arts and L.A. style). There's also a steady flow of touring ballet and modern ballet companies. ⊠ *135 N. Grand Ave., Downtown* ☎ *213/972–7211.*

Gibson Amphitheater. Adjacent to Universal Studios, this 6,250-seat space hosts more than 100 performances a year, including star-studded benefit concerts and all-star shindigs for local radio station KROQ 106.7. ⊠ *100 Universal City Plaza, Universal City* ☎ *818/622–4440.*

Greek Theatre. In the beautiful tree-enclosed setting of Griffith Park, this open-air auditorium in Los Feliz is in the company of stunning Hollywood Hills homes and the nearby Griffith Observatory shining atop the hill. The Greek has hosted some of the biggest names in entertainment across all genres. Open from May through November, 2011 marks its 80th year.

Go for the laid-back California experience and the unique opportunity to experience your favorite performers in the warm western air with a view of the sparkling lights of the city flats splayed at your feet.

After the concert go for a later-night snack or cocktail in the hipster neighborhood hot spots nearby. ⊠ *2700 N. Vermont Ave., Los Feliz* ☎ *323/665–5857.*

Fodor'sChoice **Hollywood Bowl.** Ever since it opened
★ in 1920, in a park surrounded by mountains, trees, and gardens, the Hollywood Bowl has been one of the world's largest and most atmospheric outdoor amphitheaters. Its season runs from May through

September; the L.A. Philharmonic spends its summers here. There are performances daily except Monday (and some Sundays); the program ranges from jazz to pop to classical.

Concertgoers usually arrive early and bring picnic suppers (picnic tables are available). Additionally, a moderately priced outdoor grill and a more upscale restaurant are among the dining options operated by the Patina Group. ■TIP➜ Be sure to bring a sweater—it gets chilly here in the evening. You might also bring or rent a cushion to apply to the wood seats. Avoid the hassle of parking by taking one of the Park-and-Ride buses, which leave from various locations around town; call the Bowl for information. ⊠ *2301 Highland Ave., Hollywood* ☎ *323/850–2000* ⊕ *www. hollywoodbowl.com.*

Kodak Theatre. This jewel in the crown of Hollywood & Highland was created as the permanent host of the Academy Awards, and the lavish 3,500-seat theater is also used for music concerts and ballets. Awe-inspiring Cirque Du Soleil just began a decade-long run here. Seeing a show at the Kodak is worthwhile just to witness the gorgeous, crimson-and-gold interior, with its box seating and glittering chandeliers. ⊠ *6801 Hollywood Blvd., Hollywood* ☎ *323/308–6363* ⊕ *www.kodaktheatre.com.*

Nokia Theatre L.A. Live. This theater maintains bragging rights to what its creators call the best sight lines and acoustics of any live music venue in L.A.—including the Staples Center across the street.

Nokia is part of the 4-million-square-foot, $2.5-billion L.A. Live project Downtown, which also includes an array of residential, retail, entertainment spaces, and dining options, including the famous sushi spot, Katsuya. In winter the ice-skating rink is another big-draw attraction as is the not-to-be-missed Grammy Museum next door. ⊠ *777 Chick Hearn Court, Downtown* ☎ *213/763–6030* ⊕ *www.nokiatheatrelalive.com.*

Shrine Auditorium. Former home of the Oscars, the 6,300-seat Arabic-inspired space was built in 1926 as Al Malaikah Temple. Touring companies from all over the world perform here as well as do assorted gospel and choral groups, and other musical acts. High-profile awards shows, including SAG and NAACP Image Awards are still televised on-site. ⊠ *665 W. Jefferson Blvd., Downtown* ☎ *213/748–5116.*

Staples Center. Although it's used mainly for sporting events where the Lakers, Clippers, and Kings all call it home, blockbuster concerts are also booked here. Everyone from U2 to Justin Timberlake to Barbra Streisand have performed in this massive auditorium. ⊠ *1111 S. Figueroa St., Downtown* ☎ *213/742–7300* ⊕ *www.staplescenter.com.*

Fodor'sChoice ★ **Walt Disney Concert Hall.** Built in 2003 as a grand addition to L.A.'s Music Center, the 2,265-seat architectural wonder is now the home of the Los Angeles Master Chorale as well as the Los Angeles Philharmonic, under the direction of passionate, new Music Director Gustavo Dudamel, an international celebrity conductor extraordinaire.

The theater, a sculptural monument of gleaming, curved steel designed by master architect Frank Gehry, is part of a complex that includes a public park, gardens, and shops as well as two outdoor amphitheaters

8

The Los Angeles Master Chorale onstage at the Walt Disney Concert Hall.

for children's and preconcert events. ■TIP→ In the main hall, the audience completely surrounds the stage, so it's worth checking the seating chart when buying tickets to gauge your view of the performers. ⊠ *111 S. Grand Ave., Downtown* ☎ *323/850–2000.*

Wiltern LG Theater. This green terra-cotta, art deco masterpiece constructed in 1930, is a fine place to see pop, rock, jazz, and dance performances. The main space is standing room only, but there are a few seating areas available. ⊠ *3790 Wilshire Blvd., Mid-Wilshire* ☎ *213/388–1400.*

DANCE

The dance scene in Los Angeles has faced its challenges, with lackluster ticket sales at the top of the list. Though there may not be much of an audience here for ballet, forms of more modern dance are quite popular—after all, most music videos are filmed here. You can see many of the Industry's choreographers and backup grinders at theaters *listed above* and at various clubs around town.

Cal State L.A.'s Dance Department. This college presents several prominent dance events each year. Check the Web site for the schedule. ⊠ *5151 State University Dr., East Los Angeles* ☎ *323/343–4118* ⊕ *www. calstatela.edu/academic/al.*

The REDCAT (Roy and Edna Disney Cal Arts Theater). International dance companies often perform at this 260-seat space, including avant-garde dance troupes. ⊠ *631 W. 2nd St., Downtown* ☎ *213/237–2800.*

UCLA Live. There are dance performances in Royce Hall and Gloria Kaufman Hall here. Check the Web site for the schedule (⊕ *www. uclalive.org*). Purchase tickets at central ticket office on campus or at venue box office (☎ *310/825–4401*).

FILM

Spending two hours at a movie while visiting Los Angeles doesn't have to mean taking time out from sightseeing; in fact, seeing a film here is almost like paying tribute to the temple of entertainment. The city has historic and beautiful theaters, and they host both first-run and revival films.

ART AND REVIVAL HOUSES

The American Cinemathèque Independent Film Series. Screen classics are shown here, plus recent independent films, sometimes with question-and-answer sessions with the filmmakers. The main venue is the Lloyd E. Rigler Theater, within the 1922 Egyptian Theater, which combines an exterior of pharaoh sculptures and columns with a modern, high-tech design inside. The Cinemathèque also screens movies at the 1940 **Aero Theater** ⊠ *1328 Montana Ave., Santa Monica* ☎ *323/466–3456* ⊠ *6712 Hollywood Blvd., Hollywood* ☎ *323/466–3456* ⊕ *american-cinematheque.com*.

Cinespace. Taking the concept of dinner and a movie to a whole new level, this theater is now mostly reserved for private screenings but on special occasions such as Valentine's Day you can still catch classics and alternative flicks in its digital theater-restaurant open to the public. Also, the space doubles several times a week as a nightclub with DJ-provided music and a smoking patio that hovers over bustling Hollywood Boulevard and attracts indie lovers and rockers. ⊠ *6356 Hollywood Blvd., Hollywood* ☎ *323/817–3456* ⊕ *www.cinespace.info*.

New Beverly Cinema. The best of Hollywood classics and kitsch, foreign films, and, occasionally, documentaries are on tap. There's always a double bill here. ⊠ *7165 Beverly Blvd., Los Angeles* ☎ *323/938–4038*.

Nuart. This is the best-kept of L.A.'s revival houses. It shows current movies as well and has good seats, an excellent screen, and special midnight shows. ⊠ *11272 Santa Monica Blvd., West L.A.* ☎ *310/281–8223*.

★ **The Silent Movie Theatre.** A treasure of pretalkies and nonsilent films (the artier the better) are screened here. Live musical accompaniment and shorts precede some films. Each show is made to seem like an event in itself, and it's just about the only theater of its kind. The schedule—which also offers occasional DJ and live music performances—varies, but you can be sure to catch silent screenings every Wednesday. ⊠ *611 N. Fairfax Ave., Fairfax District* ☎ *323/655–2510* ⊕ *www.cinefamily.org*.

UCLA and the Hammer Museum. The museum, part of the university, presents several fine film series including those curated by the UCLA Film & Television archive. The programs of the **Billy Wilder Theater** (⊠ *10899 Wilshire Blvd., Westwood* ☎ *310/206–8013* ⊕ *www.cinema.ucla.edu*) might cover the works of major directors, documentaries, children's films, horror movies—just about anything. **School of Film & Television** uses the James Bridges Theater (⊠ *Melnitz Hall, Sunset Blvd. and*

8

Hilgard Ave., Westwood ☎ *310/206–8365* ⊕ *www.tft.ucla.edu/facilities/james-bridges-theater*) and has its own program of newer, avant-garde films. Enter the campus at the northeastern most entrance. Street parking is available on Loring Avenue (a block east of the campus) after 6 pm, or park for a fee in Lot 3 (go one entrance south to Wyton Drive to pay at the kiosk before 7, after 7 at the lot itself). ⊕ *www.tft.ucla.edu.*

MOVIE PALACES

★ **The ArcLight.** The centerpiece of this popular moviegoing, date-night destination is the geodesic Cinerama Dome, the first theater in the United States designed specifically for the large screen and sound system that went with Cinerama.

The complex now includes 14 additional screens, a shopping area, and a restaurant and bar. The first theater in L.A. to begin movies with greetings and background commentary by theater staff, the ArcLight also designates some screenings as "premium," which lets you reserve the best seats for an extra fee. "Over 21" shows let you bring cocktails into designated screening rooms. ⊠ *6360 Sunset Blvd., Hollywood* ☎ *323/464–4226.* ⊕ *www.arclightcinemas.com*

Ⓒ **Grauman's Chinese Theatre.** Open since 1927, this historic and cultural
Fodor's Choice   landmark resembling a giant, red Chinese pagoda is perhaps the world's
★ best-known theater where glamorous red carpet Hollywood movie premiers are still hosted.

The famous Hollywood Walk of Fame and concrete walkway marked by movie stars' hand- and footprints are in front. Next to the not-to-be-missed Madame Tussauds Hollywood Wax Museum and the Hollywood & Highland shopping complex, strap yourself in for the cast of street characters who greet you as you walk down Hollywood Boulevard toward the theater: Wait—is that Marilyn Monroe? Is that Spiderman? It's all part of the Grauman's Chinese Theatre experience. Inside it's all plush red and gold interiors. There are additional, smaller screens at the Mann Chinese Six, in the adjoining Hollywood & Highland Complex. ⊠ *6925 Hollywood Blvd., Hollywood* ☎ *323/464–6266.*

Ⓒ **Pacific's El Capitan.** Across the street from Grauman's this building is an Art Deco masterpiece meticulously renovated by Disney. First-run movies alternate with Disney revivals, and the theater often presents live stage shows in conjunction with Disney's animated pictures. ⊠ *6838 Hollywood Blvd., Hollywood* ☎ *323/467–7674.*

Pasadena Gold Class Theatre. Plush recliners, cozy blankets and yes, even plump pillows, this ultraluxe 40-seat theater will spoil you with an upscale dinner and a movie all in one. The server escorts you to your seats where you can be treated to dinner and cocktails while watching your cinematic favorites on the big screen. ⊠ *42 Miller Alley, Pasadena* ☎ *626/639–2260.*

Vista Theater. At the intersection of Hollywood and Sunset boulevards, this 1923 theater now shows first-run films but was once Bard's Hollywood Theater, used for vaudeville shows in the '20s. A Spanish-style facade leads to an ornate, Egyptian-style interior. ⊠ *4473 Sunset Dr., Los Feliz* ☎ *323/660–6639.*

THEATER

Los Angeles isn't quite the "Broadway of the West," as some have claimed—the scope of theater here doesn't compare to that in New York. Still, the theater scene's growth has been impressive.

Small theaters are all over town, and the larger houses, despite price hikes to as much as $70 for a single ticket, are usually full. Even small productions might include big names from the entertainment industry.

LA Stage Alliance. LA Stage Alliance also gives information on what's playing in Los Angeles, albeit with capsules that are either noncommittal or overly enthusiastic. Its LAStageTIX service allows you to buy tickets online the day of the performance at roughly half price. ⊕ *www. lastagealliance.com.*

MAJOR THEATERS

Geffen Playhouse. Jason Robards and Nick Nolte got their starts here. This acoustically superior, 498-seat theater offers new plays in summer—primarily musicals and comedies and many of the productions are on their way to or from Broadway. ⊠ *10886 Le Conte Ave., Westwood* ☎ *310/208–5454* ⊕ *www.geffenplayhouse.com.*

John Anson Ford Amphitheater. In addition to theater performances there is also a wide variety of other events happening here. Lectures, children's programs, summer jazz, dance, cabaret, and occasionally Latin and rock concerts all take place at this 1,250-seat outdoor venue in the Hollywood Hills. Winter shows are typically staged at the smaller indoor theater, **Inside the Ford.** ⊠ *2580 Cahuenga Blvd. E, Hollywood* ☎ *323/461–3673* ⊕ *www.fordamphitheater.org.*

★ **The Music Center.** Three theaters—known as the Center Theatre Group—are part of this big Downtown complex. The 2,140-seat **Ahmanson Theatre** presents both classics and new plays. The 760-seat **Mark Taper Forum** presents new works that often go on to Broadway, such as Rajiv Joseph's *Bengal Tiger at the Baghdad Zoo.* The third theater, the **Kirk Douglas Theatre,** is located in Culver City (⊠ *9820 Washington Blvd.*) and is a 317-venue. ☎ *213/628–2772* ⊕ *www.centertheatregroup. org* ⊠ *135 N. Grand Ave., Downtown* ☎ *213/972–7211* ⊕ *www. musiccenter.org.*

Pantages Theatre. The home of the Academy Awards telecast from 1949 to 1959, this is a massive (2,600-seat) and splendid example of high-style Hollywood art deco, presenting large-scale Broadway musicals such as *The Lion King* and *Wicked.* ⊠ *6233 Hollywood Blvd., Hollywood* ☎ *323/468–1770* ⊕ *www.broadwayla.org.*

Ricardo Montalbán Theatre. There's an intimate feeling here despite its 1,038-seat capacity. Plays, concerts, seminars, and workshops with an emphasis on Latin culture are all presented. ⊠ *1615 N. Vine St., Hollywood* ☎ *323/463–0089* ⊕ *www.themontalban.com.*

SMALLER THEATERS

Acting Studio at Edgemar. Architect Frank Gehry designed this industrial-styled complex of two theaters, offices, and classrooms where the non-profit performance group holds dramatic performances, dance, music, and film events, as well as outreach programs and workshops. It has

The musical comedy *Minsky's* had its world premier at the Ahmanson Theater in 2009.

such supporters as Neil Simon, Jason Alexander, and Kate Capshaw in its corner. ✉ *2437 Main St., Santa Monica* 🖼️ *310/399–3666* ⊕ *www.edgemarcenter.org.*

The Actors' Gang. Founded in 1981 by actors including Tim Robbins who is also the group's artistic director, it's one of the oldest-ensemble based theaters in Los Angeles, and they have also performed internationally. Productions generally lean toward the experimental, political, and socially conscious. ✉ *9070 Venice Blvd., Culver City* 🖼️ *310/838–4264* ⊕ *www.theactorsgang.com.*

Bob Baker Marionette Theater. A staple for L.A. youth since 1963, this theater allows kids to sit on a carpeted floor and get a close-up view of the intricate puppets; ice cream and juice are served after the shows. ✉ *1345 W. 1st St., at Glendale Blvd., Downtown* 🖼️ *213/250–9995* ⊕ *www.bobbakermarionettes.com.*

Deaf West Theater. Come here to experience productions that are simultaneously spoken and signed, and therefore accessible to both hearing and deaf audience members, in its own home space. Its ingenious (and award-winning) revivals include *A Streetcar Named Desire*, the musical *Oliver!*, and *Big River*. ✉ *5112 Lankershim Blvd., North Hollywood* 🖼️ *818/762–2998* ⊕ *www.deafwest.org.*

East West Players. East West Players is a well-respected, small theater company dedicated to the Asian-American voice, with performances that include original works and musical revivals. ✉ *120 Judge John Aiso St., Little Tokyo* 🖼️ *213/625–7000* ⊕ *www.eastwestplayers.org.*

Falcon Theatre. This well-appointed theater is the brainchild of TV and movie producer-director-writer Garry Marshall (*Laverne & Shirley, Pretty Woman*) and is a stone's throw from the Warner Bros. lot; you can often find one of Marshall's cronies looking to have fun on stage again in works like *Arsenic and Old Lace.* ✉ *4252 Riverside Dr., Burbank* ☎ *818/955–8101* ⊕ *www.falcontheatre.com.*

Fremont Center Theatre. Though not in the most accessible neck of the woods, it has nonetheless turned out its share of critically appreciated revivals and more obscure dramas. ✉ *1000 Fremont Ave., Pasadena* ☎ *626/441–5977* ⊕ *www.fremontcentretheatre.com.*

Hudson Theatres. This space is actually three performance venues and a coffee bar in one and popular with TV actors longing to tread the boards during their summer vacations. What's more, the resident company, the Hudson Guild, has a reputation for some of the finest traditional theater in town—with raves for its reinterpretations of the likes of *Twelfth Night* and *Hedda Gabler*—as well as more experimental theater. ✉ *6539 Santa Monica Blvd., Hollywood* ☎ *323/856–4249* ⊕ *www. hudsontheatre.com.*

Interact Theatre Company. Whether putting on classic Chekhov or more obscure, current productions, their plays continue to earn nominations and awards although they no longer have a permanent home. ☎ *818/765–8732* ⊕ *www.interactla.org.*

★ **Kirk Douglas Theatre.** With a strong reputation for well-staged contemporary drama and comedy, near the Culver City strip restaurants, it makes for a good night out on the town without a lot of driving. It's got solid backing, too, as it's in the same family as the Ahmanson and the Mark Taper Forum. ✉ *9820 Washington Blvd., Culver City* ☎ *213/628–2772* ⊕ *www.centertheatregroup.org.*

Odyssey Theater. The Odyssey Theater presents largely traditional dramas (plays you may not know but should) in an intimate space, typically with astute direction and taut, powerful acting. ✉ *2055 S. Sepulveda Blvd., West L.A.* ☎ *310/477–2055.*

Pacific Resident Theatre. They've earned more than 30 L.A. Drama Critics Awards since their first season as an actors' co-op in '85 and hone in on topical dramas and comedies. ✉ *703 Venice Blvd., Venice* ☎ *310/822–8392* ⊕ *www.pacificresidenttheatre.com.*

The Pasadena Playhouse. This playhouse mainly offers well-done, middle-of-the-road show that occasionally star name TV and film actors. ✉ *39 S. El Molino Ave., Pasadena* ☎ *626/356–7529* ⊕ *www. pasadenaplayhouse.org.*

Santa Monica Playhouse. A 99-seat house, the theater is worth visiting for its cozy, librarylike atmosphere, as well as its high-quality comedies, dramas, and musicals like *Funny You Don't Look Like a Grandmother* and children's programs such as *Hansel and Gretel.* ✉ *1211 4th St., Santa Monica* ☎ *310/394–9779* ⊕ *www.santamonicaplayhouse.com.*

Theatre of NOTE. This theater company has made a critical impact with both full-length plays (classic and new) and evenings of one-act works. ✉ *1517 Cahuenga Blvd., north of Sunset Blvd., Hollywood* ☎ *323/856–8611* ⊕ *www.theatreofnote.com.*

🕑 **Theatre West.** Founded in 1962, the nonprofit theater co-op has produced a lauded body of work. Its plays have gone on to Broadway (*Spoon River Anthology*) and been made into films such as *A Bronx Tale*. Stars like the late Carroll O'Connor and Richard Dreyfuss have acted with the company. Its interactive **Storybook Theater** (for three- to nine-year-olds) is a long-running favorite. ✉ *3333 Cahuenga Blvd. W, Los Angeles* ☎ *323/851–7977, 818/761–2203* ⊕ *www.theatrewest.org.*

THEATER ENSEMBLES

★ **Circle X.** One of the most lauded and loved acting groups in the city. The traveling troupe continues to win local theater awards thanks to its continuing quest to find and mount exciting new works on a shoestring budget. ☎ *213/973–3241* ⊕ *www.circlextheatre.org.*

Cornerstone Theater Company. They don't need a home of their own, instead they integrate drama into locations like city buses and shopping malls. Having hopped through rural communities in 10 states since its founding, the company is now based in L.A., where it covers everything from Shakespeare adaptations to exploratory faith-theme productions. ☎ *213/613–1700* ⊕ *www.cornerstonetheater.org.*

Shopping

WORD OF MOUTH

"Take your daughter to the Robertson Boulevard shopping district. Just north of 3rd Street, just south of Beverly Boulevard. You'll find a couple blocks of fashionable and very popular boutiques. Some of the places are very expensive, but some are a little more reasonable, and you'll find interesting, fashion-forward stuff here."

—Erin74

Updated by
Alene Dawson

Los Angeles is known as the City of Angels, and it really is heaven for shopping. Thanks to L.A. being a sprawling city, the various neighborhoods offer different things for different people. Residents generally split the city in two—by East side (the Hollywood side) and Westside (the beach side)— but many enclaves between are peppered with shops you won't want to miss.

The sun-and-sand beach culture and Hollywood stars provide big influences on the shopping scene. Stylists are always on the lookout for the newest trends and looks for the pretty young things they dress, and emerging designers take inspiration from what's being worn on the street.

Paparazzi are right there to capture the looks of the stylish starlets the second they're worn, whether they're parading on a red carpet or seen emerging from a hot spot. Together the stylemakers set the cutting-edge pace—what you see here on the racks will be big back home but maybe not for another six months.

"Sunny and 70" is the weather forecast for a good part of the year, and the climate means that most shopping centers are open-air, to allow you to park you car and walk from shop to shop. This foot traffic also means that good eateries open near good shops, and you can always find somewhere delicious to dine and covertly star-watch.

Those new to Los Angeles usually start at Rodeo Drive in Beverly Hills, not far from Hollywood. This tourist hot spot is a destination for window-shopping along the cluster of blocks and can provide a few hours of entertainment—or, if you're looking for a designer logo bag or red-carpet wear, get ready to do some serious spending.

Then you can hop in your car and really get your shop on in the city's numerous areas: finding down-and-dirty bargains downtown, hitting funky West Hollywood, kicking back with the laid-back beach vibe of Santa Monica and Venice, or going edgy in Silver Lake, Echo Park, or Los Feliz. Let the games begin.

SHOPPING PLANNER

PARKING TIPS

Parking in Santa Monica is next to impossible on Wednesday, when some streets are blocked off for the farmers' market, but there are several parking structures with free parking for an hour or two.

There are several well-marked, free (for two hours) parking lots around the core shopping area around Beverly Hills.

OPENING HOURS

Call stores for specific hours, but in general you can count on most malls, stores, and boutiques being open from 10 am to 7 pm. Sales tax is 9.75%.

TOP L.A. SHOPPING EXPERIENCES

3rd Street and The Grove. Stores on 3rd Street range from independent designer boutiques to chic houseware havens. And just blocks away, The Grove, an open-air shopping area, has brand name stores, restaurants, the adjoining Farmers Market, and celebrity sighting.

Main Street, Santa Monica. Three blocks away from the ocean, this is the choice for easy Sunday shopping after the Farmers Market or when you'd like to also visit the Santa Monica Pier. An added draw is the variety of street performers who are actually quite good.

Melrose Avenue, Melrose Place, and Nearby Robertson. This is clothing for it-girls and it-guys and the paparazzi who chase them. Come for unique purchases that say "I'm on the list" even before the bouncer opens the red rope to let you in.

Rodeo Drive. There are a surprising variety of shops that are reasonably priced on the surrounding streets—but Rodeo Drive is not to be missed for the quintessential Beverly Hills experience.

Sunset Boulevard in Silver Lake. If you have an "alternative" heart, a hipster attitude, and want to see how locals really live, this shopping area is for you. Silver Lake is like the East Village in NYC whereas Los Feliz is more of an upscale residential neighborhood.

BEST CELEB SPOTTING

Seeing your favorite celeb out toting an armful of shopping bags is a fairly common experience in these parts, so be camera-ready when visiting these places.

Kitson: ⊠ *115 South Robertson Boulevard, Los Angeles* ☎ *310/859–2652.*

The Lumber Yard in Malibu: ⊠ *3939 Cross Creek Road, Malibu.*

The Grove: ⊠ *189 The Grove Drive, Los Angeles* ☎ *323/900–8080.*

SAMPLE SALE KNOW-HOW

Sales pop year-round (Billion Dollar Babes and Sassy City Chicks host frequent ones) and the showrooms downtown in the fashion district often open their doors for sales (California Market Center, the New Mart, and Gerry Building, near 9th and California streets). Check LA.com, Luckymag.com, DailyCandy.com, and Hautelook.com, and in local publications (the *L.A. Times* and *Los Angeles* magazine) for listings.

"Benefit shopping" at sales that support various causes is also popular. Although most are private events, keep your eyes peeled for announcements of public sales.

BEVERLY HILLS

Rodeo Drive. New York City has Fifth Avenue, but L.A. has famed Rodeo Drive. The triangle, between Santa Monica and Wilshire boulevards and Beverly Drive, is one of the city's biggest tourist attractions and is lined with shops featuring the biggest names in fashion.

Rodeo is home of the well-coifed, well-heeled ladies toting multiple packages to their Mercedes and paparazzi staking out street corners. Although the dress code in L.A. is considerably laid-back, with residents wearing flip-flops year-round, you might find them to be jewel-encrusted on Rodeo.

Steep price tags on designer labels make it a "just looking" experience for many residents and tourists alike, but salespeople are used to the ogling and window shopping. In recent years, more midrange shops have opened up on the strip and surrounding blocks. Keep in mind that some stores are by appointment only.

BOOKS AND STATIONERY

Taschen. Philippe Starck designed the space to evoke a cool 1920s Parisian salon—a perfect showcase for the coffee-table books about architecture, travel, culture, and (often racy) photography. A suspended glass-cube gallery space in back shows rotating art, photo exhibits, and limited-edition books. ⊠ *354 N. Beverly Dr., Beverly Hills* ☎ *310/274–4300.*

DEPARTMENT STORES

Barneys New York. This is truly an impressive one-stop shop for high fashion. The Co-op section of this store reliably introduces indie designers before they make it big. Shop for beauty, shoes, and accessories on the first floor, then wind your way up the staircase for couture and Co-op floors for women and men; and keep your eyes peeled for fabulous and/or famous folks eating deli-style lunch at Barney Greengrass on the top floor. ⊠ *9570 Wilshire Blvd., Beverly Hills* ☎ *310/276–4400.*

★ **Henri Bendel.** This chic, beloved New York boutique has found its way to Los Angeles replete with high-end gift items and cult beauty products. There's no apparel at this location but go and be delighted at all of the happy, pretty niche offerings. Although home is the Beverly Center that caters a good deal to middle-of-the-road retailers, high-end shoppers can do damage at mall neighbors Gucci, Louis Vuitton, and Prada. ⊠ *8500 Beverly Blvd., Beverly Hills* ☎ *310/273–4741.*

Neiman Marcus. Luxury shopping at its finest. The couture salon frequently trots out designer trunk shows and most locals go right for the shoe department. ⊠ *9700 Wilshire Blvd., Beverly Hills* ☎ *310/550–5900.*

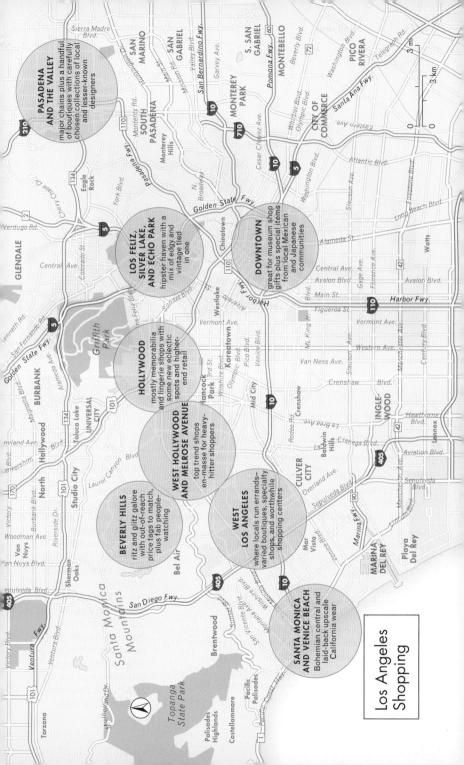

PASADENA AND THE VALLEY
major chains plus a handful of boutiques with carefully chosen collections of local and lesser-known designers

LOS FELIZ, SILVER LAKE, AND ECHO PARK
hipster haven with a mix of edgy and vintage tied in one

DOWNTOWN
great for museum shop gifts plus special items from local Mexican and Japanese communities

HOLLYWOOD
mostly memorabilia and lingerie shops with some new eclectic spots and higher-end retail

WEST HOLLYWOOD AND MELROSE AVENUE
top trend shops en-masse for heavy-hitter shoppers

BEVERLY HILLS
ritz and glitz galore with out-of-reach price tags to match, plus fab people-watching

WEST LOS ANGELES
where locals run errands—varied boutiques, specialty shops, and worthwhile shopping centers

SANTA MONICA AND VENICE BEACH
Bohemian central and laid-back upscale California wear

Los Angeles Shopping

MELROSE PLACE

Melrose Place is an in-the-know haven to savvy Los Angeles fashionistas and a charming anecdote to the city's addiction to strip-malls and megashopping centers.

(above) Minimalist design gets a splash of color at Me & Ro. (right) Boutique Marni.

Offering luxuries less bohemian than Los Feliz and Silver Lake and more upscale than Abbot Kinney but without the pretentiousness of Rodeo, it's easy to be seduced by its youthful sophistication and leafy, ivy-laden exteriors.

Not to be confused with the cheaper and trendier Melrose Avenue, Melrose Place is a chic Mid-City enclave three blocks long, east of La Cienega, one block north of Melrose Avenue.

Reminiscent of the best of West Village shopping in New York, here haute couture meets pedestrian-friendly, tree-lined walkways. Melrose Place also offers an opportunity to pampering like wealthy and famous Angelenos do: by the hands of some of the most renowned celebrity hair stylists and facialists on the planet.

Melrose Place can easily be part of your day visiting the Pacific Design Center, the shops on Robertson, Fred Segal Melrose Avenue, vintage shop Decades, and the Beverly Center.

PARKING

Pay attention to street signs here because, if you have to venture deeper into the residential section of the neighborhood beyond the parking meters, there are various restrictions that change from one side of the street to the other. Certain stores and salons on Melrose Place offer to park your car for you, so look for shop-specific valet podiums that have the names of the stores they represent written on them.

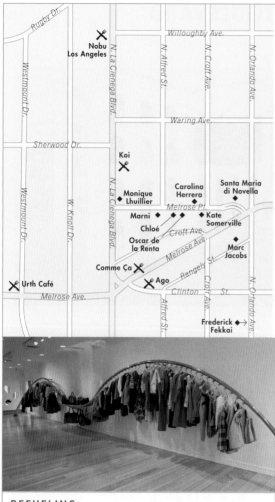

REFUELING

Eat With the Locals. A three-minute drive from Melrose Place, **Urth Caffé** (✉ *8565 Melrose Ave.*) has healthy, casual fare and is the week-end lunch it-spot for pretty scenesters. Nearby **Comme Ça** (✉ *8479 Melrose Ave.*) is David Myers' take on the classic French brasserie and at night hums with an attractive Industry-type happy crowd.

Eat Like a Celebrity. If you shop until dinnertime, **Nobu Los Angeles** (✉ *903 N. La Cienega Blvd.*), **Ago** (✉ *8478 Melrose Ave.*) owned by Robert De Niro and the Weinstein Brothers, and paparazzi outpost **Koi** (✉ *730 N. La Cienega Blvd.*) are within walking distance.

WHAT YOU'LL WANT

RED CARPET GLAMOUR
Carolina Herrera. Evening gowns and smart dresses share space with bridal gowns.

Oscar de la Renta. Signature socialite stylings encompassing elegant and ladylike ready-to-wear.

Monique Lhuillier. Neutral tones provide a brilliant backdrop to seductive red carpet gowns.

AU COURANT STAPLES
Marc Jacobs. Flouncy feminine separates and chic accessories.

Chloé. This French luxury import is devoted to youthful, casual separates.

Marni. Bohemian luxury-wear in a modernist space.

GET PAMPERED
Kate Somerville. This med-clinic is known for their Red Carpet ready treatments.

Frederick Fekkai. A two-story mecca salon for the luxury hair experience.

BEST HOSTESS GIFTS
Santa Maria di Novella. Pick up the rose water and potpourri at this Italian-centric apothecary.

9

ROBERTSON BOULEVARD

Robertson is the hot spot for celebrities who crave publicity, the paparazzi who chase them, and the public who has an insatiable appetite to be up close and personal to the show.

Christian Louboutin's Robertson Boulevard boutique. (right) The lunch hotspot Ivy.

As infamous as Rodeo Drive is famous, on Robertson the world sees celebrities broadcast on television as they dash in and out of trend-setting boutique Kitson and landmark restaurant The Ivy. But don't underestimate what's here. In addition to the Hollywood-ness of it all, this isn't just where it-girls and it-guys come to clad their A-list bodies. There's memorable shopping to round out your Los Angeles experience.

The main concentration of stores is between Beverly Boulevard and 3rd Street, with high-end boutiques such as D&G and Chanel in contrast to more eclectic and quirky Moods of Norway, Curve boutique, gauzy Vionnet, and rock-and-roll-inclined All Saints Spitalfields.

A bit farther north is the tiny two-story Christian Louboutin, celebrity favorite Maxfield, and Kinara skin clinic known for their Red Carpet facial. Robertson a bit south of 3rd Street is coming to life as well; American Apparel is a newer arrival to the west side of the street.

PARKING

Parking along Robertson isn't nearly as bad as some other popular shopping areas in the city.

The exception is on weekends, when the brunch crowd comes out in full force to lounge over a meal and then hit the streets to shop it off.

Even if parking on Robertson itself is tough, there's usually plenty on surrounding streets as well as in garages.

Rosewood Ave.
Stella McCartney ◆
↑ Kinara
◆ Christian Louboutin

Beverly Blvd.
◆ Vionnet
Beverly Pt.

Chanel ◆
Kitson ◆
All Saints ◆
◆ Spitalfields
Cedars-Sinai Medical Center
Tori Burch ◆→

N. Swall Dr.
N. Robertson Blvd.
S. San Vicente Blvd.
N. La Cienega Blvd.

Alden Dr.
Gracie Allen Dr.
Beverly Shopping Center

The Ivy ✕
◆ Kitson For Kids
◆ Intermix
Moods of Norway ◆
◆ Lisa Kline
D&G

W. 3rd St.

S. Sherbourne Dr.

American Apparel ◆

Burton Way
Burton Way

S. Swall Dr.
S. Clark Dr.
S. Robertson Blvd.
S. Hanet Rd.
S. Wilaman Dr.
S. Sherbourne Dr.
S. Holt Ave.
S. Le Doux Rd.
S. La Cienega Blvd.

◆ Maxfield
Clifton Way
S. Amaz Dr.
S. Stanley Dr.

LADIES WHO LUNCH

The Ivy. The epitome ladies-who-lunch destination—or at the very least ladies and men who want to be photographed—celebrities flock to this restaurant. What's lovely about the Ivy isn't just its white picket fence and charming interior but that the food is actually quite good and not outrageously overpriced considering the healthy portions. Make sure to procure a table on the patio and let the paparazzi guess at your pedigree.

WHAT YOU'LL WANT

TRENDS BORN HERE

Intermix. A virtual candy store of designer labels from Marchesa to Missoni.

Kitson. Paparazzi central with fun housewares, gifts such as chic coffee-table books, and a large array of beauty products.

Lisa Kline. Her celebrity-magnet flagship boutique is stocked with trendy yet grown-up designer confections and accessories with a decidedly Hollywood casual flair.

Maxfield. Postmodern fashion to antique jewelry in a shop with gallerylike quality.

Stella McCartney. This two-story ivy-covered boutique houses her cruelty-free ready-to-wear.

Tori Burch. Preppy, stylish, and colorful clothes appropriate for a road trip to Palm Springs or a flight to Palm Beach.

BUDDING FASHIONISTAS

Kitson for Kids. Miniature designer duds, toys, and furniture for newborn jet-setters to trend-obsessed tweens.

9

DID YOU KNOW?

Rodeo Drive is the main drag of the chic shopping district bordered by Santa Monica Boulevard, Wilshire Boulevard, and Beverly Drive.

HOME FURNISHINGS AND GIFTS

American Tea Room. Some like it hot; some like it iced. Silver tins lining the walls contain 250 varieties of tea, with each color-coded by the tea's region of origin. Gifts like tea baskets, box sets, and teapots make unique souvenirs. ✉ *401 N. Canon Dr., at Brighton Way, Beverly Hills* ☎ *310/271–7922.*

Del Mano Gallery. One of the best sources for wood turnings, this store also specializes in fine fiber arts, ceramics, jewelry, and art teapots by contemporary American and international artisans. ✉ *2001 Westwood Blvd., Beverly Hills* ☎ *310/441–2001.*

Gearys of Beverly Hills. Since 1930, this has been the ultimate destination for those seeking the most exquisite fine china, crystal, silver, and jewelry, mostly from classic sources like Steuben, Baccarat, and Royal Crown Derby. (Another location is on Rodeo Drive.) ✉ *351 N. Beverly Dr., Beverly Hills* ☎ *310/273–4741.*

SHOES

Jimmy Choo. Find splurge-worthy heels and equally glamorous colorful handbags from the line made famous on *Sex and the City.* ✉ *240 N. Rodeo Dr., Beverly Hills* ☎ *310/860–9045.*

Bottega Veneta. Buttery, stylish leather goods in rich colors and chic designs that never falter into being overly trendy. ✉ *457 N. Rodeo Dr., Beverly Hills* ☎ *310/858–6533.*

SHOPPING CENTERS AND MALLS

★ **Beverly Center.** This is one of the more traditional malls in L.A., with eight levels of stores, including Macy's, Bloomingdale's, and the newer addition: luxury retailer Henri Bendel. Fashion is the biggest draw and there's a little something from everyone, from D&G to H&M, and many shops in the midrange, including Banana Republic, Club Monaco, and Coach. Look for accessories at Aldo and inexpensive accessories and fun fashion at Forever 21, and there's even a destination for the race car–obsessed at the Ferrari Store.

For a terrific view of the city, head to the top-floor terrace and roof-top food court. Next door is Loehmann's, which offers a huge selection of discounted designer wear. ✉ *8500 Beverly Blvd., bounded by Beverly, La Cienega, and San Vicente Blvds. and 3rd St., Beverly Hills* ☎ *310/854–0071.*

VINTAGE CLOTHING

Lily et Cie. Rita Watnick's red-carpet shop is more a museum of Hollywood's golden-era garments than a run-of-the-mill vintage boutique. Oh, you can shop all right, but you might find a price tag marked $100,000 on the selection of one-of-a-kind frocks that date from 1900, from Chanel cocktail dresses to Givenchy evening gowns. ✉ *9044 Burton Way, Beverly Hills* ☎ *310/724–5757.*

WOMEN'S AND MEN'S BOUTIQUES

All Saints Spitalfields. The British store recently invaded Robertson and is Rock & Rock edge albeit with a black leather and studs meets the manor mix. Look for furry vests, tough shoes, skull embellishments,

The Best of Rodeo Drive

Buckle up for the Rodeo tour, which begins at **Via Rodeo,** a cobblestoned one-block section of Rodeo closest to Wilshire Boulevard (at Dayton Way).

Leaving the V of Via Rodeo, you'll walk the palm tree–lined street and spot all the big names in international fashion.

But it's not all about the luxury outfitters here. A few mid-range stores are mixed in among the couture designers.

Versace. With its temple dome ceiling and recherché design, this is just the place for a dramatic red-carpet gown. ⊠ *248 N. Rodeo Dr., Beverly Hills* ☎ *310/205–3921.*

Smythson of Bond Street. This Brit import sells luxurious leather calendars, day planners, wallets, and notebooks. ⊠ *222 N. Rodeo Dr., Beverly Hills* ☎ *310/550–1901.*

Louis Vuitton. Holding court on the corner, LV carries its recognizable monogram on all manner of accessories and leather goods. ⊠ *295 N. Rodeo Dr., Beverly Hills* ☎ *310/859–0457.*

Christian Dior. Fans of the French label can browse the latest fashions, accessories, fragrances, and beauty

products in a sparkling glass-fronted space. ⊠ *309 N. Rodeo Dr., Beverly Hills* ☎ *310/859–4700.*

Dolce & Gabbana. Pity the wet bar is just for celeb clients, but outside the VIP fitting room there's plenty of attire and accessories to quench your thirst for D&G at the adjoining men's and women's boutiques. ⊠ *312 and 314 N. Rodeo Dr., Beverly Hills* ☎ *310/888–8701.*

Yves Saint Laurent. Adorned with a simple YSL, this spacious boutique carries an extensive collection of ready-to-wear fashions. ⊠ *326 N. Rodeo Dr., Beverly Hills* ☎ *310/271–4110.*

Fendi. Karl Lagerfield's latest designs have more subtle branding, but the signature Double F logo can still be found on some of the fashions and accessories at this West Coast outpost. ⊠ *355 N. Rodeo Dr., Beverly Hills* ☎ *310/276–8888.*

Roberto Cavalli. With wild prints and sexy designs, this decadent Italian style is perfect for the men and women of the club scene. *362 N. Rodeo Dr., Beverly Hills* ☎ *310/276–6006.*

CLOSE UP

Chanel. Ladylike classics—tailored tweed suits and Chanel No. 5 perfume—from this bright white corner flagship are sure to be staples for years to come. ⊠ *400 N. Rodeo Dr., Beverly Hills* ☎ *310/278–5500.*

Giorgio Armani. Heavy-hitter Armani is known for great tailoring and fine fabrics in both mens- and womenswear. ⊠ *436 N. Rodeo Dr., Beverly Hills* ☎ *310/271–5555.*

Gucci. Part of the "epicenter" with Prada, Gucci goes for the stridently modernist aesthetic, with lean, sexy, and mainly black clothing upstairs and cube displays for signature bags downstairs. ⊠ *347 N. Rodeo Dr., Beverly Hills* ☎ *310/278–3451.*

Prada. The Rem Koolhaas–designed Italian showcase is so cool it doesn't even have a sign out front, but its 20-foot-wide staircases and funhouse curves offer an inviting way to see the classy clothes, shoes, and bags. ⊠ *343 N. Rodeo Dr., Beverly Hills* ☎ *310/278–8661.*

Cartier. Cartier has a bridal collection to sigh for in its chandeliered and respectfully hushed showroom, along with more playful colored stones and an Asian-inspired line. ⊠ *370 N. Rodeo Dr., Beverly Hills* ☎ *310/275–4272.*

Tiffany & Co. There's a bauble for everyone at Tiffany's, with three floors for its classic and contemporary jewelry and watches, crystal, silver, china, and somewhat-more-accessible sterling silver finds. ⊠ *210 N. Rodeo Dr., Beverly Hills* ☎ *310/273–8880.*

Bulgari. Bold, contemporary Italian jewelry, watches, and other luxurious necessities are the order of the day at Bulgari. ⊠ *201 N. Rodeo Dr., Beverly Hills* ☎ *310/858–9216.*

Van Cleef & Arpels. In business for more than a century, Van Cleef & Arpels still designs elegant and distinctive pieces, with lots of pavé floral designs. ⊠ *300 N. Rodeo Dr., Beverly Hills* ☎ *310/276–1161.*

Harry Winston. Perhaps the most locally famous jeweler is Harry Winston, *the* source for Oscar-night jewelry loans. The three-level space, with a bronze sculptural facade, velvet-panel walls, private salons, and a rooftop patio, is as glamorous as the gems. ⊠ *310 N. Rodeo Dr., Beverly Hills* ☎ *310/271–8554.*

Juicy Couture. Wearing drawstring pants and matching hoodies in bright colors only became acceptable on Rodeo after Juicy hit the fashion scene. ⊠ *456 N. Rodeo Dr., Beverly Hills* ☎ *310/550–0736.*

BCBG Max Azria. BCBG Max Azria offers more affordable designs that attract young celebs: romantic dresses, teeny toppers, halters, and fun accessories. ⊠ *443 N. Rodeo Dr., Beverly Hills* ☎ *310/275–3024.*

Theodore. One of the few indie clothing stores in the area, Theodore is a haven for the young and perhaps rebellious to find James Perse skinny tees, jeans of all labels, and hoodies aplenty. Upstairs, browse the avant-garde designer wear (Ann Demeulemeester, Jean Paul Gaultier). Next door, Theodore Man has faux-scruffy tees, jeans, and leather jackets for the guys. ⊠ *336 N. Camden, Beverly Hills* ☎ *310/276–0663.*

9

DID YOU KNOW?

The three-tiered staircase off Via Rodeo was built to resemble the Spanish Steps at the heart of Rome's most famous high-end shopping district.

denim and khaki skirts, which worn correctly still let them know you're with the band. ✉ *100 N. Robertson Blvd.* ☎ *310–432-8484.*

Anto Distinctive Shirt Maker. This atelier has been in the custom shirt-making business since the 1950s and has an impressive list of clients, from Frank Sinatra to Arnold Schwarzenegger. ✉ *258 N. Beverly Dr., Beverly Hills* ☎ *310/278–4500.*

Burberry. Here's proof that everything old can be new again, as British designer Christopher Bailey made the distinctive plaid—on tot-size kilts and sexy swimwear, for example. Another location is in the Beverly Center mall. ✉ *9560 Wilshire Blvd., Beverly Hills* ☎ *310/550–4500.*

Carroll & Co. Dapper is the name of the game at this long-standing, full-service, traditional men's clothing store, which has dressed such icons as Cary Grant and Clark Gable. You can still find quality goods, excellent service, and styles that endure. Another branch is in Pasadena. ✉ *425 N. Canon Dr., Beverly Hills* ☎ *310/273–9060.*

Curve. Chains from the ceiling hold wood bars for hanging garments at this shop that features layers of chiffon, lace, silk, mesh, and leather separates that will take you beyond jeans and a tank. Curve's own line rubs elbows with fresh designers like Inhabit and Michelle Mason. ✉ *154 N. Robertson Blvd., between Beverly Hills and West Hollywood* ☎ *310/360–8008.*

Emporio Armani. Sleek suits, separates, and accessories are the draw at this spot that offers Armani cachet for every day. ✉ *9533 Brighton Way, Beverly Hills* ☎ *310/271–7790.*

Intermix. The new addition of NY-based Intermix on Robertson is giving already established area boutiques a run for their money. Racks feature looks that are both femme and fierce, with brightly colored options from Vince, Robert Rodriguez, D-Squared, and more. The dress selection is especially notable. ✉ *110 N. Robertson Blvd., Beverly Hills* ☎ *310/860–0113.*

★ **Kitson.** Stars that want to be seen (and seen shopping) come here to choose from piles of jeans, tops, hoodies, Pucci scarves, sequined Converse, thongs with "naughty" bejeweled across the front, and unusual pampering products. It's pure girly glitz. Across the street, **Kitson Kids** (☎ *310/657–0450*)provides mini-me versions of trends. **Kitson Men** (✉ *146 N. Robertson* ☎ *310/358–9550*)has walls of jeans, plenty of hoodies, plus cool sneakers and accessories like a sleeping eye mask printed with "PIMP." ✉ *115 S. Robertson Blvd., Beverly Hills* ☎ *310/859–2652.*

Lisa Kline. For that Hollywood look that's trendy but grown-up, visit this dependable, celebrity-friendly shop for Angelica, Adriano Gold-schmied, Twelfth Street by Cynthia Vincent, and those all-important underpinnings for revealing outfits. Lisa Kline Men and Lisa Kline Kids have also opened on the same strip. ✉ *138 S. Robertson Blvd., Beverly Hills* ☎ *310/246–0907.*

★ **MAC on Robertson.** Not just your ordinary MAC store, this beauty emporium is what's called a "professional" MAC store with products not available at its regular outlets. This is also a place to book an appointment for makeup lessons or all-out makeovers or even to pre-pare for red carpet or other special events. The artists here are fashion show and award season veterans. ⊠ *133 N. Robertson Blvd.Beverly Hills* ☎ *310/271–9137.*

Ron Herman. You might recognize the name from the city's Fred Segal stores. This stand-alone shop is more relaxed but just as plugged in, with an eclectic mix of local and European designs. ⊠ *325 N. Beverly Dr., Beverly Hills* ☎ *310/550–0910.*

Ted Baker. Rich cord, tweed, and velvet suiting and wild striped shirts are showcased here. ⊠ *131 N. Robertson Blvd., between Beverly Hills and West Hollywood* ☎ *310/550–7855.*

Traffic Men. Those with a taste for luxe without stuffiness come here for Paul Smith, Costume National, or Helmut Lang. **Traffic Women.** Sister store Traffic Women has brands such as Citizens of Humanity Jeans and Alexander McQueen. ☎ *310/659–3438* ⊠ *Beverly Center, 6th fl., 8500 Beverly Blvd., between Beverly Hills and West Hollywood* ☎ *310/659–4313.*

WEST LOS ANGELES

This is L.A.'s errand central, where entertainment executives and Indus-try types do their serious shopping. In general, it's more affordable than Beverly Hills.

A nascent art scene is blossoming in Culver City, along the intersection of La Cienega and Washington boulevards and the Santa Monica Free-way, and down side streets like Comey Avenue. To the west, Westwood is dominated by its largest resident, UCLA.

BOOKS AND STATIONERY

Children's Book World. One of the city's largest bookstores is as loved by parents and teachers as it is by kids. The Saturday-morning storytelling series is a huge hit. It's just southwest of Century City. ⊠ *10580½ W. Pico Blvd., West Los Angeles.* ☎ *310/559–2665.*

Mystery Bookstore. There's no mystery behind this store's success. Fan of this genre flock here for a comprehensive selection of new and col-lectible titles, plus author events and writer workshops. Employees are helpful aficionados of every subgenre. ⊠ *1036-C Broxton Ave., between Weyburn and Kinross Aves., Westwood* ☎ *310/209–0415.*

HOME FURNISHINGS AND GIFTS

Room & Board. Think of this furniture store as Crate & Barrel's more fashion forward (but equally expensive) sister offering chic home acces-sories and living room pieces with mid-century modern appeal. This 36,400-square-foot warehouse emporium recently opened in the his-toric Helms Bakery space a stone's throw away from H.D. Buttercup. ⊠ *8707 Washington Blvd., between Venice and Washington Blvds., Culver City* ☎ *310/736–9100.*

Day of the Dead figures in a shop on Olvera Street.

SHOPPING MALLS

★ **H.D. Buttercup.** The renovated and expanded art deco Helms Bakery space is a shopping mecca that's more like a showroom than a traditional store. Manufacturers offer furniture, home decor, gifts, fashion accessories, antiques, books, artwork, bedding and textiles, lighting, candles and soaps, and more. Across the street, a newly opened **Backroom at Buttercup** features outlet prices on remainder stock. ✉ *3225 Helms Ave., between Venice and Washington Blvds., Culver City* ☎ *310/558–8900.*

Westfield Century City. Known locally as the Century City Mall, this open-air shopping center is set among office buildings on what used to be the back-lot of Twentieth Century Fox studios. Find a mix of luxury retailers (Louis Vuitton, Tourneau), mid-range shops (Gap, Zara), department stores (Macy's, Bloomingdale's), and trendy shops (Planet Funk, Justin Timberlake's William Rast), and Cusp, the hip Neiman Marcus spin-off featuring of-the-moment fashions. ✉ *10250 Santa Monica Blvd., Century City* ☎ *310/277–3898.*

SPECIALTY FOODS

★ **Surfas.** You're likely to rub elbows with area chefs in their work whites at this spacious and well-organized restaurant supply store that's open to the public. Find aisles of spices (priced wholesale) and jarred delicacies along with all the pots, pans, bowls, and tools you'll need to be your own Top Chef. The adjoining café serves salads, sandwiches, hot specials, gourmet teas, and baked goods. ✉ *8777 Washington Blvd., at National Blvd., Culver City* ☎ *310/559–4770.*

TOYS AND GAMES

Allied Model Trains. We know both big kids and little ones light up when visiting this huge shop that celebrates trains old and new. Operating trains choo-choo inside along with model trains, Department 56 Snow Villages, Thomas the Tank Engine, and Playmobil toys. ✉ *4371 S. Sepulveda Blvd., Culver City* ☎ *310/313–9353.*

WINE SHOPS

★ **Wally's.** It may be known as the wine store to the stars, but regular folks also delve into the vast selection of wines and liquor, fine chocolates, imported cheeses, and the impressive assortment of cigars. Saturday-afternoon wine tastings make a visit all the sweeter. ✉ *2107 Westwood Blvd., West Los Angeles* ☎ *310/475–0606.*

The Wine House. This beverage warehouse in the shadow of I–405 carries everything from $10 table wines to $500 first-growth Bordeaux—and the right cigars to go with them. The scope of the selection can be daunting, but friendly staffers help neophytes find the perfect bottle at the perfect price. Check the schedule for nightly classes and tastings and also visit the wine bar upstairs. ✉ *2311 Cotner Ave., between Pico and Olympic Blvds., West Los Angeles* ☎ *310/479–3731.*

WOMEN'S AND MEN'S BOUTIQUES

Last Chance. It looks like a regular boutique, but the price tags show sample sale prices. Score past-season separates from established and emerging designers Laila Azhar, Zac Posen, Rebecca Taylor, Twelfth Street by Cynthia Vincent, and lots of premium denim choices (True Religion, Blue Cult), and accessories. The bottom line? Pay less than half on the regular retail prices. ✉ *8712 Washington Blvd., between La Cienega and National Blvds., Culver City* ☎ *310/287–2333.*

DOWNTOWN

Downtown L.A. is dotted with ethnic neighborhoods (Olvera Street, Chinatown, Koreatown, Little Tokyo) and several large, open-air shopping venues (the Fashion District, the Flower Market, Grand Central Market, the Toy District, and the Jewelry District).

It offers an urban bargain hunter's dream shopping experience if you know precisely what you're looking for (like diamonds and gems from the Jewelry District) or if you're willing to be tempted by unexpected finds (piñatas from Olvera Street, slippers from Chinatown, or lacquered chopsticks from Little Tokyo).

HOME FURNISHINGS AND GIFTS

Museum of Contemporary Art Store. Find Ed Ruscha beach towels, Keith Haring watches, Comme des Garçons wallets, children's toys, and jewelry, plus tees featuring art from exhibits, art posters, architectural pop-up books, other books and magazines and more. The store's branch at **MOCA Store Geffen Contemporary** (✉ *152 N. Central Ave., Little Tokyo* ☎ *213/633–5323*).has similar contemporary art and design items, but if you're looking for the largest variety, head to the main museum store on Grand for purchases. ✉ *250 S. Grand Ave., Downtown* ☎ *213/621–1710.*

CLOSE UP

Downtown's Fashion District

For visiting fashionistas, the name "Fashion District" may seem alluring. But be warned. The term "fashion" here is subject to interpretation. Also, be aware that while designers troll this 90-block garment district for wholesale deals on fabrics, you'll need a merchant's license for full access to most showcase buildings.

However, special shopping events and frequent sample sales are open to the public. If shopping is your M.O., bring your bargain-hunting instincts and your patience to **Santee Alley** (⊠ *Santee St. and Maple Ave. from Olympic Blvd. to 12th St.*), where vendors are crammed side by side selling items such as faux designer sunglasses, handbags, sweatshirts, jewelry, and cell phones.

Shop owners crammed into the little strip cater to their large clientele of bargain-hunting Latino families by blasting Spanish and hip-hop music from boom boxes perched at store entrances, making for a vibrant but ear-blistering scene.

The whole Fashion District area can be overwhelming in its expansiveness. If you don't know what direction to turn, the **LA Fashion District Business Improvement District** (*BID* ☎ *213/488–1153* ⊕ *www. fashiondistrict.org*) can provide maps, info, and assistance.

If you really want to know where to locate the high-fashion finds in this insider-driven district, take a tour with shopping pro Christine Silvestri of **Urban Shopping Adventures** (☎ *213/683–9715* ⊕ *www. urbanshoppingadventures.com*), who offers a three-hour walking–shopping tour Monday–Saturday for $36 or a customized, hourly-rate VIP tour.

Or plan your visit on the last Friday of the month, when you can quench your taste for high fashion by hitting the mega sample sales in the **California Market Center** (⊠ *110 E. 9th St.* ☎ *213/630–3600*), a trade market housing 1,500 showrooms, and the neighboring **New Mart** (⊠ *127 E. 9th St.* ☎ *213/627–0671* ⊕ *www.newmart. net*), where cutting-edge designers sell off one-of-a-kind pieces, overstocks, and prototypes for the next big trends. This sale is cash-only and quite popular.

Project Runway hopefuls may also want to walk a few blocks over to the **Fashion Institute for Design and Merchandising** (*FIDM* ⊠ *919 S. Grand Ave.* ☎ *213/624–1201*) where future fashion and interior designers, graphic artists, and entertainment industry stylists get their start. The school has a scholarship store with discounted clothing, fabric, and special-occasion wear.

9

MARKETS

Grand Central Market. For almost 100 years, this open-air market has tempted Angelenos with all kinds of produce, fresh meats and seafood, spices, and fresh tortillas. Overstuffed *pupusas*, Cuban sandwiches, and kebabs satisfy shoppers on the go. ⊠ *317 S. Broadway, between 3rd and 4th Sts., Downtown* ☎ *213/624–2378.*

An in-house performance at Amoeba Records.

SHOPPING STREETS AND DISTRICTS

The Jewelry District. This area resembles a slice of Manhattan, with the crowded sidewalks, diverse aromas, and haggling bargain hunters. Expect to save 50% to 70% off retail for items, including wedding band. The more upscale stores are along Hill Street between 6th and 7th streets. There's a parking structure next door on Broadway. ⊠ *Between Olive St. and Broadway from 5th to 8th St., Downtown* ⊕ *www.lajd.net.*

Fodor's Choice
★

Olvera Street. Historic buildings line this redbrick walkway overhung with grape vines. At dozens of clapboard stalls you can browse south-of-the-border goods—leather sandals, bright woven blankets, devotional candles, and the like—as well as cheap toys and tchotchkes. With the musicians and cafés providing background noise, the area is constantly lively. ⊠ *Between Cesar Chavez Ave. and Arcadia St., Downtown.*

The Toy District. This 14-block area of wholesale toy dealers is for the adventurous bargain hunter looking for knock-off versions of popular toys. Find stuffed animals you can buy for loose change or electronic games and gas-powered pocket bikes for bigger bills. Most vendors sell wholesale only, but plenty will also sell to individuals bearing cash. ⊠ *Between 3rd and 5th Sts., and Los Angeles and San Pedro Sts., Downtown.*

HOLLYWOOD

Local shops may be a mixed bag, but at least you can read the stars below your feet as you browse along Hollywood Boulevard. In the past, lingerie and movie memorabilia stores have predominated here, but now there are numerous options in the retail-hotel-dining-entertainment complex Hollywood & Highland welcome addition to the scene.

Hollywood impersonators (Michael Jackson, Marilyn Monroe, Johnny Depp's Jack Sparrow) join break-dancers and other street entertainers in keeping tourists entertained on Hollywood Boulevard's sidewalks near the Kodak Theatre, home to the Oscars.

Along La Brea Avenue, there is plenty of trendy, quirky, and hip merchandise, from records to furniture and clothing.

BOOKS AND MUSIC

Fodor's Choice ★ **Amoeba Records.** Touted as the "World's Largest Independent Music Store," Amoeba is a playground for music-lovers with a knowledgeable staff and a "Homegrown" display to highlight local artists. Catch in-store appearances by artists and bands that play sold-out shows at venues down the road several times a week. Find a rich stock of used CDs and DVDs, an impressive cache of rarities and collectibles (like the Beatles' "Butcher" cover), an encyclopedic range of indie releases, and walls filled with posters for sale. ☒ *6400 W. Sunset Blvd., at Cahuenga Blvd., Hollywood* ☏ *323/245–6400.*

Larry Edmunds Bookshop. After more than 60 years on the boulevard, this cinema and theater bookstore maintains old-school courtesy and charm. Books on movies and about the craft of moviemaking are the main draw, but you can also find thousands of movie posters (no, really), from *Ain't Misbehavin'* to *Zelig* and countless photographs. ☒ *6644 Hollywood Blvd., Hollywood* ☏ *323/463–3273.*

Lost & Found. The owner, a former stylist, describes this place as "Alice in Wonderland meets Jimi Hendrix." Visit for trippy boys' and girls' clothing (up to size 12) from Asia, Europe, and beyond. ☒ *6314 Yucca Ave., Hollywood* ☏ *323/856–0921.*

★ **Meltdown.** The largest comic-book store on the West Coast is a monument to the artistry, wit, and downright weirdness of comics (from Ghost World to Booty Babe). Toys, art books, graphic novels, tees, posters, and a gallery with comic-related art and photography supplement the scores of comic books. ☒ *7522 Sunset Blvd. Hollywood* ☏ *323/851–7223* ⊕ *www.meltcomics.com.*

HOME FURNISHINGS AND GIFTS

Lost & Found, etc. For adults who just want to have fun, this colorful auxiliary to the nearby children's store has men and women's clothing, one-of-a-kind gifts, art, textiles, and tchotchkes. Choices include brass jewelry from France, African silk batiks, Stella Forest clothing, and other goodies handpicked from around the world. ☒ *6320 Yucca St., Hollywood* ☏ *323/856–5872.*

9

The Hollywood & Highland shopping center, around the corner from the Kodak Theatre.

SHOPPING CENTERS AND STREETS

Hollywood & Highland. Dozens of stores, eateries, a bowling alley, and the Kodak Theatre fill this outdoor complex, which mimics cinematic glamour. Find designer shops (Coach, Louis Vuitton) and chain stores (Victoria's Secret, Fossil, Sephora, and the Hard Rock Cafe).

From the upper levels, there's a camera-perfect view of the famous Hollywood Sign. On the second level, next to the Kodak Theatre, is a **Visitor Information Center** (☎ 323/467–6412) with a multilingual staff, maps, attraction brochures, and information about services.

The streets nearby provide the setting for the Sunday Hollywood Farmer's Market, where you're likely to spot a celebrity or two picking up fresh produce or stopping to eat breakfast from the food vendors. ✉ *Hollywood Blvd. and Highland Ave., Hollywood* ☎ *323/817–0220.*

Space 15 Twenty. A unique retail space and Urban Outfitters "project" concept in the heart of Hollywood anchored by an Urban Outfitters store that's flanked by gallery spaces, unique boutiques such as We the Free—a store associated with the brand Free People—What Goes Around Comes Around vintage store from NYC, Hennessey + Ingalls art and architecture book store, and other film and art venues all connected by an outside courtyard near the Sunday Hollywood Farmer's Market. ✉ *1520 N. Cahuenga, at Cahuenga Blvd., Hollywood* ☎ *323/465–1893.*

VINTAGE CLOTHING

Jet Rag. Be prepared to dig for treasure. Racks and stacks are filled with worn-in rock tees, bell-bottom jeans, polyester tops, and weathered leather jackets. Known for its reasonable prices, Jet Rag takes it one step further on Sunday from 11:30 to dusk with a big parking-lot sale. All items go for $1. ✉ *825 N. La Brea Ave. Hollywood* ☎ *323/939–0528.*

LOS FELIZ, SILVER LAKE, AND ECHO PARK

There's a hipster rock-and-roll vibe to this area, which has grown in recent years to add just the slightest shine to its edge. Come for home-grown, funky galleries, vintage shops, and local designers' boutiques. Shopping areas are concentrated along Vermont Avenue and Hollywood Boulevard in Los Feliz; Sunset Boulevard in both Silver Lake (known as Sunset Junction) and Echo Park; and Echo Park Avenue in Echo Park.

■TIP➜ Keep in mind that things are spread out enough to necessitate a couple of short car trips, and many shops in these neighborhoods don't open until noon but stay open later, so grab dinner or drinks at one of the area's über-cool spots after shopping.

ANTIQUES

Peter Vanstone, Inc. Decorators and dealers visit this courteous merchant for his eclectic selection of art, antiques, and furnishings priced from $5 to $4,000. ✉ *2211 Sunset Blvd., Silver Lake* ☎ *213/413–5964.*

BOOKS AND STATIONERY

Secret Headquarters. This could be the coolest comic-book store on the planet, with a selection to satisfy both the geekiest of collectors and those more interested in artistic and literary finds. Rich wood floors, framed comic book art, and a leather chair near the front window mark the sophisticated setting, which features wall displays neatly organized with new comics and filing cabinets marked DC and Marvel. Along with classics like Superman, you can find Buffy and Halo here as well. ✉ *3817 W. Sunset Blvd., Silver Lake* ☎ *323/666–2228.*

Skylight Books. A neighborhood bookshop through and through, Skylight has excellent coverage of L.A. travel, current affairs, children's books, fiction, and film, plus 'zines and journals and a section devoted to urban culture. The owners play host to book discussion groups and present panels and author readings with hip literati. ✉ *1818 N. Vermont Ave., Los Feliz* ☎ *323/660–1175.*

CHILDREN'S BOUTIQUES

La La Ling. This shop offers more than your run-of-the-mill clothes for kiddies, with a particularly hip take on tot-size versions of adult staples (Splendid tees, J Brand jeans) and cutesy tees ("Gucci Coo"), plus stylish slings and diaper bags for moms. ✉ *1810 N. Vermont Ave., Los Feliz* ☎ *323/664–4400.*

COSMETICS

Le Pink & Co. This small and friendly apothecary-style beauty shop is decorated with vintage perfume bottles. In stock are cult beauty brands such as Dr. Hauschka, Rosebud Salve, Caswell Massey, and hard-to-find brands such as Eminence Organics. ✉ *3820 West Sunset Blvd., Silver Lake* ☎ *323/661–7465.*

9

The Farmers Market in the Fairfax District, an L.A. institution.

HOME FURNISHINGS AND GIFTS

★ **Soap Plant Wacko/La Luz de Jesus Gallery.** This pop-culture supermarket offers a wide range of items, including rows of books on art and design and, uh, "deviant literature." But it's the novelty stock that makes the biggest impression, with Mexican wrestling masks, Marilyn Manson dolls and novelties such as X-ray specs and hula dancer lamps. The in-store gallery in the back focuses on underground and "lowbrow" art. ✉ *4633 Hollywood Blvd., Los Feliz* ☎ *323/663–0122, 323/666–7667.*

★ **Yolk.** Stocked with a little bit of everything you'll want to get or give, this home–gift shop has a spot-on selection of fresh designed goods. Find Voluspa candles, Marimekko bags, and Design House Stocklm barware, and a back room with kid stuff that includes organic cotton clothing, bedding, and nontoxic wood toys. Also find handcrafted jewelry by local designers and art on the walls by local artists. ✉ *1626 Silver Lake Blvd., Silver Lake* ☎ *323/660–4315.*

Y-Que Trading Post. It's kitsch-central here, with mostly pop culture tees, including ones with celebrity mug shots, as well as naughty novelties and gag gifts (Sarah Palin toilet paper, Sea Monkeys on Mars). A custom press in the back allows you to choose your own tee design, too. On weekends, crowds of revelers often shop here until midnight. ✉ *1770 N. Vermont Ave., Los Feliz* ☎ *323/668-0117.*

LINGERIE

Panty Raid. It's all about the fun and functional undergarment here, with an ample selection of favorites, including low-rise thongs from Cosabella and Hanky Panky. The salesgirl is likely to guess a bra size on sight, too. ✉ *1953 Hillhurst Ave., Los Feliz* ☎ *323/668–1888.*

Bittersweet Butterfly. If a shop could represent Valentine's Day, this would be it. Here you'll find frilly lingerie, fresh-cut flowers and accessories for romantic getaways. Ooh la la. ⊠ *1406 Micheltorena, Silver Lake* ☎ *323/660–4303.*

VINTAGE CLOTHING

Flounce Vintage. Scarves, rhinestone baubles, and a great stock of floral dresses and beaded cardigans await in this girlishly sweet store. ⊠ *1555 Echo Park Ave., Echo Park* ☎ *213/481–1975.*

SquaresVille. Vintage and recent recyclables share rack space at this shop with a rockin' vibe. Buy, sell, trade. ⊠ *1800 N. Vermont Ave., Los Feliz* ☎ *323/669–8464.*

WINE SHOPS

Silver Lake Wine. Boutique, small-production wineries from 'round the world provide this shop with bottles that fill vertical racks from floor to ceiling. The knowledgeable staff might look unassuming dressed in jeans and tees but they can steer you to the right wine or spirits for any occasion. You can wet your whistle at tastings on Sunday, Monday, and Thursday and look for their summer social events at nearby Barnsdall Art Park. ⊠ *2395 Glendale Blvd., Silver Lake* ☎ *323/662–9024.*

WOMEN'S AND MEN'S BOUTIQUES

Lake. Styles here are for the sophisticated East Sider: a little edgy and always comfortably chic. Find Cynthia Vincent dresses, Pila March handbags, and apothecary and gift items, including French soaps and John Derian decoupage trinkets. ⊠ *1618 1/2 Silverlake Blvd., Silver Lake* ☎ *323/664–6522.*

WEST HOLLYWOOD AND MELROSE AVENUE

West Hollywood is prime shopping real estate. And as they say with real estate, it's all about location, location, location. Depending on the street address, West Hollywood has upscale art, design, and antiques stores, clothing boutiques for the ladies-who-lunch set, megamusic stores, and specialty book vendors.

Melrose Avenue, for instance, is part bohemian-punk shopping district (from North Highland to Sweetzer) and part upscale art and design mecca (upper Melrose Avenue and Melrose Place). Discerning locals and celebs haunt the posh boutiques around Sunset Plaza (Sunset Boulevard at Sunset Plaza Drive), on Robertson Boulevard (between Beverly Boulevard and 3rd Street), and along upper Melrose Avenue.

The huge, blue Pacific Design Center, on Melrose at San Vicente Boulevard, is the focal point for this neighborhood's art- and interior design–related stores, including many on nearby Beverly Boulevard. The Beverly–La Brea neighborhood also claims a number of trendy clothing stores. Perched between Beverly Hills and West Hollywood, 3rd Street (between La Cienega Boulevard and Fairfax Avenue) is a magnet for small, friendly designer boutiques.

Finally, the Fairfax District, along Fairfax Avenue below Melrose Avenue, encompasses the flamboyant, historic Farmers Market, at Fairfax

Avenue and 3rd Street; the adjacent shopping extravaganza, The Grove; and some excellent galleries around Museum Row at Fairfax Avenue and Wilshire Boulevard.

ANTIQUES

Blackman Cruz. Browse among David Cruz and Adam Blackman's off-beat pieces (like 1940s New York subway signs) as well as fine Continental and Asian furniture from the 18th- to the mid-20th century. ⊠ *836 N. Highland Ave., West Hollywood* ☎ *310/657–9228.*

BOOKS AND MUSIC

Bodhi Tree Bookstore. Incense wafts around a huge selection of spiritual (more Buddhist than Christian) books, gifts, music, and videos. Psychic readings, signings, lectures, and workshops are held regularly. Behind the store, Bodhi's used-book shop also sells herbs and teas. ⊠ *8585 Melrose Ave., West Hollywood* ☎ *310/659–1733.*

Fodor's Choice
★

Book Soup. One of the best independent bookstores in the country, Book Soup has been serving Angelinos for more than 30 years. Given its Hollywood pedigree, it's especially deep in books about film, music, art, and photography. Fringe benefits include an international newsstand, a bargain-book section, and author readings several times weekly. ⊠ *8818 Sunset Blvd., West Hollywood* ☎ *310/659–3110.*

Traveler's Bookcase. A massive collection of travel titles fills this shop, with tabletop books, maps, guides, literatures, and gifts for travelers (notebooks, pens, luggage tags, compact clocks). ⊠ *8375 W. 3rd St. West Hollywood* ☎ *323/655–0575.*

CAMERAS AND ELECTRONICS

Samy's Camera. This is a we'll-meet-or-beat-any-price kind of place, with cameras, video equipment, lighting, and studio equipment, used wares, collectibles, rentals and repairs, and digital imaging services. But locals know the real reason to come back is the knowledgeable staff. Other branches are in Culver City and Pasadena. ⊠ *431 S. Fairfax Ave., south of W. 3rd St., Fairfax District* ☎ *323/938–2420.*

Jonathan Adler. Gabe, a pug, greets visitors at this mecca for fans of the New York–based kitsch-tastic designer. Mid-century and country club styles get retooled in pottery, fun pillows, graphic textiles, and a furniture line. ⊠ *8125 Melrose Ave., West Hollywood* ☎ *323/658–8390.*

HOME FURNISHINGS AND GIFTS

Kidrobot. Underground art is the draw at this toy boutique for grown-ups. Ugly dolls, Dunnys, Ice-Bots, and other limited-edition figures draw collectors and the curious. ⊠ *7972 Melrose Ave., Hollywood* ☎ *323/782–1411.*

★ **Moss at SLS Beverly Hills.** For home design that's a notch above luxurious, Moss can't be beat—here, high design is high art. Inside of the SLS hotel, next to the lauded restaurant Baazar, Moss's offerings are both whimsical and surreal. A square pedestal of Moliere? An artisan model boat? Be surprised at how much you just may think that you need them. ⊠ *465 S. La Cienega, Beverly Hills* ☎ *310/246–5565.*

The Santa Monica location of Fred Segal, a magnet for L.A. fashionistas.

O.K. An über–gift shop, O.K. stocks the classy (Scandinavian stemware, vintage candelabras) and specializes in architecture and design books. ⌧ *8303 W. 3rd St., West Hollywood* ☎ *323/653–3501.*

Santa Maria Novella. This shop has high-end soaps, tonics, candles, perfumes, and other gift-friendly offerings, many from Italy, in a friendly boutique. ⌧ *8411 Melrose Pl., West Hollywood* ☎ *323/651–3754.*

Soolip. As though the desk accoutrements, custom letterpress stationery, and handmade papers from nearly 50 countries weren't enough, this *paperie* also does a brisk business in couture wrapping. The space includes a bungalow with clothing, accessories, furnishings, and gifts, as well as a florist service. ⌧ *8646 Melrose Ave., West Hollywood* ☎ *310/360–0545.*

JEWELRY AND ACCESSORIES

Alpha. This spacious shop answers every guy's shopping quandry: What to wear to work? What to wear on a date? What to use for serving takeout? What to put on the coffee table? (Super-cool and -styish accessories abound.) And what to buy yourself for a holiday gift. ⌧ *8625 Melrose Ave., West Hollywood* ☎ *310/855–0775.*

SHOES

Boot Star. A huge selection of boots here spells heaven to urban cowboys and cowgirls. There's calfskin, alligator, and turquoise cobra skin, as well as hand-tooled skulls and crossbones. Most boots are handmade in Mexico and Texas and custom sizing is available. ⌧ *8493 Sunset Blvd., West Hollywood* ☎ *323/650–0475.*

9

Kate Somerville, where stars go to get their skin red-carpet ready

Sigerson Morrison. The strappy sandals, polished flats, and mod boots from this British designer have inspired many a pedicure. ✉ *8307 W. 3rd St. West Hollywood* ☎ *323/655–6133.*

SHOPPING CENTERS

Fodor's Choice
★

Farmers Market and The Grove. The granddaddy of L.A. markets dates to 1935, and the amazing array of clapboard stalls (selling everything from candy to hot sauce, fresh fruit to fresh lamb), wacky regulars, and a United Nations of food choices must be experienced to be appreciated.

Employees from the nearby CBS studios mingle with hungover clubbers and elderly locals at dozens of eateries, movie theaters and shops under one huge roof. The green trolley shuttles visitors between the Farmers Market and the nearby **Grove,** a wildly popular outdoor mall with an ersatz European feel and a fabulous people-watching scene.

Although many of the stores are familiar in any mall (Nordstrom, Abercrombie & Fitch, the Apple Store, American Girl Place), the elaborate setting with cheerful winding tile walkways, the central fountain that has "dancing" water choreographed to music, and during the holidays even man-made "snow" (!) that falls accompanied by holiday music, put this shopping center over the top.

Oh, and if you happen to be in the Glendale area of Los Angeles, the same development team that brought you this temple to shopping and the easy–breezy outdoor California lifestyle opened a bright, shiny complex called the Americana at Brand that is very similar. ✉ *6333 W. 3rd St., at Fairfax Ave., Fairfax District* ☎ *323/933–9211 Farmers Market, 323/900–8080 The Grove.*

VINTAGE CLOTHING

★ **Decades.** Stylists and A-listers come here to scour the racks for dresses for award season. Owner Cameron Silver's stellar selection includes dresses by Pucci and Ossie Clark, and Hermès bags. On the street level, the newly expanded **Decades Two** resells contemporary designer and couture clothing (often worn once by celeb clientele) and accessories at up to 80% off. ☎ *323/655–1960* ✉ *8214 Melrose Ave., West Hollywood* ☎ *323/655–0223.*

Resurrection. There's a spot-on selection of high-quality 1960s–'80s vintage wear from the likes of Halston, YSL, and Pucci, as well as vintage Levi's, Gucci accessories, and more—all neatly arranged by color and style. ✉ *8006 Melrose Ave., West Hollywood* ☎ *323/651–5516.*

The Way We Wore. Overlook the over-the-top vintage store furnishings to find one of the city's best selections of well-cared-for and one-of-a-kind items, with a focus on sequins and beads. Upstairs, couture from Halston, Dior, and Chanel can cost up to $20,000. ✉ *334 S. La Brea, Beverly–La Brea* ☎ *323/937–0878.*

WOMEN'S AND MEN'S BOUTIQUES

Fodor's Choice **American Rag Cie.** Half the store features new clothing from established
★ and emerging labels and of-the-moment denim lines, and the other side is stocked with well-preserved vintage clothing, neatly organized by color and style. Also find shoes and accessories. Adjoining store World Denim Bar stocks jeans galore. Browse the mainly French home furnishings and European CDs in another store annex, **Maison Midi,** which also has a bistro–café with a lively lunch scene. ☎ *323/935–3157* ✉ *150–160 S. La Brea Ave., Beverly–La Brea* ☎ *323/935–3154.*

Bleu. Ever dream of getting a fresh look without lifting a finger? The friendly, style-savvy staff will size you up in minutes and deliver just the right edgy basics for day or flirty party frocks for night (with the jewelry, shoes, and undies to match) to your dressing room. ✉ *454 S. La Brea Ave., Beverly–La Brea* ☎ *323/939–2228.*

Diane von Furstenberg. This famous designer's classic wrap dresses and line of resort wear in distinctive geometric prints can be found here. ✉ *8407 Melrose Ave., West Hollywood* ☎ *323/951–1947.*

Fodor's Choice **Fred Segal.** The ivy-covered building and security guards in the parking
★ lot might tip you off that this is *the* place to be. Go during the lunch hour to stargaze at the super-trendy café. This longtime L.A. fashion landmark is subdivided into miniboutiques that range from couture clothing to skateboard fashions. The entertainment industry's fashion fiends are addicted to the exclusive goods here, some from overseas, others from cult L.A. designers just making their marks. ✉ *8100 Melrose Ave., at Crescent Heights Blvd., West Hollywood* ☎ *323/651–4129.*

Hillary Rush. The shopkeeper here is third-generation, and her expertise shows. Edgy and sleek separates, the latest skinny jeans, soft tees by local line L.A. Made, plus just the right accessories are spot-on L.A. ✉ *8222 W. 3rd St., West Hollywood* ☎ *323/852–0088.*

H. Lorenzo. Funky, high-end designer clothes (Ohne Titel, Junya Watanabe, Jaded by Knight) attract stylists and a young Hollywood crowd, people who don't blink at paying $250 for jeans. Next door, **H. Men** provides the same hot styles for the guys. ☎ *310/652–7039* ⊠ *8660 Sunset Blvd., West Hollywood* ☎ *310/659–1432.*

James Perse. The soft cotton tees (and sweaters and fleece) are quintessentially L.A. Find them here in an immaculate gallerylike space, with sleek white- and light-wood furnishings. ⊠ *8914 Melrose Ave., West Hollywood* ☎ *310/276–7277.*

Kate Somerville. A skin emporium where the stars go for facials and prep their skin to get Red Carpet ready. Their historic space is airy and chic in hues of light blue and white as seen in Vogue—a space that transports you to spa heaven. Her well-known products are on sale here as well. ⊠ *8428 Melrose Pl., West Hollywood* ☎ *323/655–7546.*

Lotta. True bohemian glamour prevails here, with halters and tunics in bright colors from the shop's line and other hippie-chic designers. Piles of accessories complete the look. Walls and shelves are adorned with magazine tear sheets of celebs wearing the same styles you see on the racks. ⊠ *8372 W. 3rd St. West Hollywood* ☎ *323/852–0520.*

Madison/Diavolina. These two veteran Los Angeles staples—Madison for clothing and Diavolina for shoes—have joined together in one boutique to showcase what is hot right this minute. Fendi shares shelf space with Uggs, but what's in common is that it's all stylish. ⊠ *8741 and 8745 W. 3rd St., West Hollywood* ☎ *310/275–1930, 310/550–1341.*

Marc Jacobs. He brings his fresh, forward-thinking look to four boutiques in West Hollywood. One for his women's collection, one for his men's line, and the third for his more affordable Marc by Marc line. Bookmarc, featuring his accessories line, opened in November 2010. ⊠ *8400 Melrose Pl. West Hollywood* ☎ *310/653–5100.*

Fodor's Choice ★ **Maxfield.** Enter the modern concrete structure for one of L.A.'s too-cool-for-school sources for high fashion, with sleek-as-can-be offerings from Chanel, Roland Mouret, Balmain, and Rick Owen. For serious shoppers (or gawkers) only. ⊠ *8825 Melrose Ave., at Robertson Blvd., West Hollywood* ☎ *310/274–8800.*

MILK. Milk bottles and old trunks and suitcases line the shelves at this spacious shop, which has become a destination for new trends. Tees and jeans top the tables and racks feature well-edited picks, from silky dresses and lacy tops to luxe sweaters. Part of the back is devoted to menswear. ⊠ *8209 W. 3rd St., West Hollywood* ☎ *323/951–0330.*

Paul Smith. You can't miss the shocking fuchsia "shoebox" that houses Paul Smith's fantastical collection of clothing, luggage, boots, hats, and objets d'art, where photos and art line the walls above shelves of tomes on pop culture, art, and Hollywood. The clothing vibrates in signature colors like hot pink and mustard yellow, and Smith's signature stripes on socks to notebooks. ⊠ *8221 Melrose Ave., West Hollywood* ☎ *323/951–4800.*

Satine. This small shop has a retro feel to it, matched by the selection of clothing by indie designers you won't find elsewhere and more well-known ones (Tom Ford, Alexander McQueen). A vintage-loving style permeates the air, with a playful touch of little-girl-grown-up. ✉ *8134 W. 3rd St., West Hollywood* ☎ *323/655–2142.*

South Willard. Hit this store–design lab, which stocks mostly menswear for the man not shy about wearing well-cut high-style designs from mostly European lines. ✉ *8038 W. 3rd St., West Hollywood* ☎ *323/653–6153.*

Ten Over Six. If you love accessories, this is the place for you. This boutique stocks highly acclaimed designers such as Alexander Wang, Comme Des Garçons, and Band of Outsiders for fun, out of the box shopping and original pieces blurring the boundaries between art and commerce. ✉ *8425 Melrose Ave. West Hollywood* ☎ *323/330–9355.*

Theory. Sleek and sophisticated separates and suits for urban living offered in an open airy space. ✉ *8428 Melrose Ave Blvd., West Hollywood* ☎ *323/782–0163.*

Trina Turk. Interior designer Kelly Wearstler put her stamp on this beautiful space, with mod furnishings providing a perfect setting for Turk's bohemian-chic line. The place has a resort feel, with mannequins wearing big sunglasses and print scarves. ✉ *8008 W. 3rd St., West Hollywood* ☎ *323/651–1382.*

SANTA MONICA AND THE BEACHES

The breezy beachside communities of Santa Monica and Venice are ideal for leisurely shopping. Scads of tourists (and some locals) gravitate to the Third Street Promenade, a popular pedestrians-only strolling–shopping area that is within walking range of the beach and historic Santa Monica Pier. The newly refurbished Santa Monica Place, at the south end of the promenade, draws the young and hip.

A number of modern furnishings stores are nearby on 4th and 5th streets. Main Street between Pico Boulevard and Rose Avenue offers upscale chain stores, cafés, and some original shops, while Montana Avenue is a great source for distinctive clothing boutiques and child-friendly shopping, especially between 7th and 17th streets.

In Venice, Abbot Kinney Boulevard is abuzz with mid-century furniture stores, art galleries and boutiques, and cafés.

BOOKS AND MUSIC

Arcana. A treasure trove for artists and filmmakers, this store boasts a serious collection of new and out-of-print books on art, architecture, design, and fashion—with an especially impressive selection on photography. ✉ *1229 3rd St. Promenade, Santa Monica* ☎ *310/458–1499.*

Hennessey + Ingalls Bookstore. A stop here would make a perfect end to a day at the Getty. In L.A., this is the largest collection of books on graphic design, art, architecture, and photography. ✉ *214 Wilshire Blvd., between 2nd and 3rd Sts., Santa Monica* ☎ *310/458–9074.*

CHILDREN'S BOUTIQUES

★ **Acorn.** Remember when toys didn't require computer programming—and weren't recalled for containing lead? Ellen West's old-fashioned shop sparks kids' imaginations with dress-up clothes, books, and hand-painted wooden toys: no batteries or plastic allowed. ✉ *1220 5th St., Wilshire Blvd., Santa Monica* ☎ *310/451–5845.*

Every Picture Tells a Story. This well-stocked children's bookstore doubles as an art gallery with framed pieces from classic books, from Dr. Seuss, Maurice Sendak, Charles Schulz, and others hanging on the walls above the shelves of old and new titles. ✉ *1333 Montana Ave., Santa Monica* ☎ *310/451–2700.*

Jenny Bec's. This children's toy store is jam-packed with puzzles, books, and crafts, as well as classics like Slinkies and bubbles. There are special sections throughout (for pirates, fairies), with a back baby room. Bonus: colorful gift-wrapping and shipping services. ✉ *11710 San Vicente Blvd., Brentwood* ☎ *310/395–9505.*

COSMETICS

Palmetto. This shelves and counters at this long-standing shop are literally crammed with bath, body, and beauty treats from little-known and sought-after lines, with a focus on products that are made with natural ingredients. ✉ *1034 Montana Ave., Santa Monica* ☎ *310/395–6687.*

Strange Invisible Perfumes. A custom-made fragrance by botanical perfumer Alexandra Balahoutis might run you in the thousands, but you can pick up ready-made scents from her exotic line, along with body lotions, washes, and candles in her exquisitely designed shop that is both modern and romantic. ✉ *1138 Abbot Kinney Blvd.* ☎ *310/314–1505.*

HOME FURNISHINGS AND GIFTS

Colcha. This gem-filled Abbot Kinney spot moved to a more spacious location up the block to better showcase its home decor and gifts, with John Derian plates, Burn candles, leather-bound journals, glassware, art books, and furniture. ✉ *1416 Abbot Kinney Blvd., Venice* ☎ *310/392–3600.*

SHOPPING CENTERS AND STREETS

Brentwood Country Mart. A preservationist has restored this faux country market with its red-barn backdrop and cobblestone courtyards, and it still has an old-school charm. The dozen or so stores include Calypso (for beachy, boho brights), Turpan (for luxury home goods and gifts), Marie Mason Apothecary (for beauty), James Perse (for laid-back cotton knits), and Sugar Paper (for letterpress cards and paper goods), and the recently opened Broken English (for exotic and fine jewelry). Grab a chicken basket at Reddi Chik and eat on the open-air patio. ✉ *225 26th St., at San Vicente Blvd., Santa Monica.*

★ **The Lumberyard.** This new Malibu shopping complex is equally a window into luxe, beachfront California living. Its slick dark wood design is as chic and relaxed as Malibu's lifestyle, with stores such as James Perse, Alice + Olivia, celebrity magnet Maxfield, and one of the most boutiquelike J. Crew stores ever seen.

You can start your shopping by picking up a sandwich or salad at Malibu Country Mart across the way—another spot for star spotting—or drive farther up PCH and pay a visit to in-the-know El Matador beach and feast on fresh seafood at Neptune's Net—a shack that's one part

Kites and spinners on display at Venice Beach.

biker stop, one part Vogue spread, and one part hangout for surfers. ✉ *3939 Cross Creek Rd., Malibu.*

★ **Third Street Promenade.** Whimsical dinosaur-shaped, ivy-covered fountains, and buskers of every stripe set the scene along this pedestrians-only shopping stretch. Stores are mainly the chain variety (Restoration Hardware, Urban Outfitters, Apple), but there are also Quiksilver and Rip Curl outposts for cool surf attire. Movie theaters, bookstores, pubs, and restaurants ensure that virtually every need is covered. ✉ *3rd St. between Broadway and Wilshire Blvd.*

WOMEN'S AND MEN'S BOUTIQUES

Fodor'sChoice **Fred Segal.** The West Hollywood branch might draw more celebrities, ★ but this location is larger and decidedly more laid-back. Across-the-street shops in two buildings feature mini-boutiques for the latest denim styles, handbags, and more. The beauty selection at the Apothia mini-boutique is particularly impressive. The trendy Umami Burger and a hair salon provide reprieves from shopping. ✉ *500 and 420 Broadway, Santa Monica* ☎ *310/458–8100.*

Heist. Owner Nilou Ghodsi sends thank-you notes to customers and employs a sales staff that is friendly and helpful but not at all overbearing at this warm, box-shaped boutique that is small but never claustrophobic. A table at the center of the store is surrounded by racks of fetching separates (from American designers such as Nili Lotan and Gary Graham to hard-to-find French and Italian designers) and a loft room upstairs features denim, tees, and sale items. ✉ *1104 Abbot Kinney Blvd.* ☎ *310/450–6531.*

Fabulous Flea Markets

Flea markets are a fantastic resource for those who love all things vintage. Flea market culture has a few rules: arrive early (the "great finds" tend to go fast), polite haggling is allowed, and remember that what you see is what you get (no, those Pumas from the '70s don't come in other colors).

Melrose Trading Post. Held every Sunday 9–5 in Fairfax High School's parking lot, the Melrose Trading Post is hip, fairly junk-free, and popular with Hollywood denizens, and you're likely to find a recycled rock tee or some vinyl to fill your collection. Live music and fresh munchies entertain vintage hunters and collectors. The market benefits Fairfax High's clubs and organizations. Parking is free, but admission is $2. ⊠ *Fairfax Blvd. and Melrose Ave.* ☎ *323/655–7679* ⊕ *www.melrosetradingpost.org.*

Rose Bowl Flea Market. Huge and hyped, the Rose Bowl Flea Market happens on the second Sunday of every month, rain or shine. This extremely popular market attracts more than 2,500 vendors looking for top dollar for their antiques, crafts, and new furniture. It's an especially good source for pop culture odds and ends (like a $100 *Partridge Family* lunchbox). Admission is $8 from 9 to 3; more expensive special passes

The Levi's Store. Step into the Fit Locator booth here for a full body scan and printout of your best fit and size. This is the largest Levi's outlet in Southern California, with thousands of jeans in various colors and configurations. Vests, jackets, shirts, and boots break up the sea of denim. ⊠ *1409 3rd St. Promenade, Santa Monica* ☎ *310/393–4899.*

★ **Planet Blue.** The quintessential Malibu style is found here, with baskets on the floor filled with flip-flops and an abundance of jeans, cute tops, dresses, and accessories. It does hippie-beach-chic best, hands-down. Another location is on Montana Avenue. ⊠ *2940 Main St., Santa Monica* ☎ *310/396–1767.*

Principessa. A recent renovation of this warm and homey boutique means more space for comfy and oh-so-cool clothes from Ella Moss, Rebecca Taylor, Vince, and more. An ample selection of jeans and jewelry, some from local designers, completes the look. The adjoining shop Vamp features deals on its stock, with everything marked $100 or less. ⊠ *1104 Abbot Kinney Blvd.* ☎ *310/450–6696.*

Sean. A stop for the stylish guy who doesn't want to look like he's trying too hard: Emile Lafaurie's clean and classic house-line features clothes with just enough polish: button-downs with a narrow cut, boxy painter's jackets, sedate suits. **Station 25**, an in-store shoe boutique, provides the finishing touches. ⊠ *1107 Montana Ave., Santa Monica* ☎ *310/260–5616.*

Wasteland. This vintage emporium, one block from the 3rd Street Promenade, also sells recently recycled items for both women and men in good condition. Find everything from wide-lapelled polyester shirts to last year's Coach bag. Another location is on Melrose Avenue. ⊠ *1338 4th St., Santa Monica* ☎ *310/395–2620.*

ZJ Boarding House. One of the area's best surf, skate, and snow shops has a smaller shop for women next door. Both offer gear and essentials for board sports (from wax to boards and wet suits) but also an ample selection of apparel from the best lines. ⊠ *2619 Main St., Santa Monica* ☎ *310/392–5646.*

PASADENA AND THE VALLEY

Over "the Hill" and into the San Fernando Valley, Studio City's Ventura Boulevard is the vital artery of Valley shopping. Mimicking Hollywood, stars line this shopping drag, but here they honor past TV shows. Only 20 freeway minutes over another hill east of Hollywood are the San Gabriel Valley communities of Burbank and Pasadena.

In Pasadena, the stretch of Colorado Boulevard between Pasadena Avenue and Arroyo Parkway, known as Old Town, is a popular pedestrian shopping mecca, with retailers such as Crate & Barrel and H&M, and Tiffany's, which sits a block away from Forever 21. A few blocks east on Colorado, the open-air "urban village" known as Paseo Colorado mixes residential, retail, dining, and entertainment spaces along Colorado Boulevard between Los Robles and Marengo avenues. Enter on Colorado or Marengo for free parking.

BOOKS AND STATIONERY

Storyopolis. This huge children's bookstore features sections for "world of classics" and "land of possibilities"; plenty of seating and a back room art gallery and side room for readings and other events; and a toy room with paint-by-numbers and crafts plus plush toys. ⊠ *14945 Ventura Blvd., Studio City* ☎ *818/509–5600.*

Vroman's Bookstore. Southern California's oldest and largest (27,000 square feet) independent bookseller is justly famous for great service. An attached newsstand, café, and adjacent gift and stationery store boost the total shopping experience. Some 400 author events annually, plus a fab kids' zone with a play area, make this a truly outstanding spot. ⊠ *695 E. Colorado Blvd., Pasadena* ☎ *626/449–5320.*

MEN'S AND WOMEN'S BOUTIQUES

Belle Gray. Everything in actress Lisa Rinna's recently expanded boutique is comfortable but chic, with a range of styles that are casual (their own drawstring sweats and thin tees) and more luxe (cashmere sweaters, Alice + Olivia dresses). The new shoe room in back is particularly inviting. ⊠ *13812 Ventura Blvd.* ☎ *818/789–4021.*

Dari. Bohemian kicked up a notch is what you'll get at this boutique, which offers separates in warm, rich colors from the likes of Philip Lim. ⊠ *12184 Ventura Blvd.* ☎ *818/762–3274.*

Elisa B. Elisa's small but well-edited collection of up-and-coming L.A. designers (Wasabi) and established favorites (Michael Stars, Tracey Reese) draw women of all ages to this friendly Old Town boutique. ⊠ *12 Douglas Alley, Pasadena* ☎ *626/792–4746.*

Faire Frou Frou. It's a lingerie shop first and foremost but the pretty shop also stocks pieces to be worn on the outside, including lace-trimmed chemises, silk camisoles, and bustiers. Find lacy and racy underthings along with more practical-but-still-sexy options from La Perla and Fleur de England. ⊠ *13017-A Ventura Blvd., near Coldwater Canyon Ave.* ☎ *818/783–4970.*

It's a Wrap. Looking for castoffs from *Hannah Montana, All My Children, Star Trek,* or dozens of other productions? The wardrobe departments of movie and TV studios and production companies ship clothes here daily. A "letter of authenticity" accompanies each bargain (that's 35%–95% off retail). Another store is open near Beverly Hills, on South Robertson Boulevard. ⊠ *3315 W. Magnolia Blvd., at California St., Burbank* ☎ *818/567–7366.*

Playclothes Vintage Fashions. This gigantic off-the-beaten-path shop offers vintage clothing from all eras and an especially impressive selection of accessories found in cases and on display throughout the store. ⊠ *3100 W. Magnolia Blvd.* ☎ *818/557–8447.*

Where to Eat

WORD OF MOUTH

"Dinner on Friday night was at A.O.C., which serves small plates
suitable for sharing (or solo dining), and has a great wine list."
                                                              —goddessintl

Updated by
Cindy Arora

Los Angeles may be known for its beach living and celebrity-infused backdrop, but it was once a farm town. The hillsides were covered in citrus orchards and dairy farms, and agriculture was a major industry. These days, although L.A. is urbanized, the city's culinary landscape has re-embraced a local, sustainable, and seasonal philosophy at many levels—from fine dining to street snacks.

With a growing interest in farm-to-fork, the city's farmers' market scene has exploded, becoming popular at big-name restaurants and small eateries alike. In Hollywood and Santa Monica you can often find high-profile chefs scouring farm stands for fresh produce.

Yet the cache of the celebrity chef continues to carry weight around this town. People follow the culinary zeitgeist with the same fervor as celebrity gossip. You can queue up with the hungry hordes at **Mozza** to catch a glimpse of Mario Batali or Nancy Silverton, or snag a seat at **Street** to chat with chef Susan Feniger—also of Border Grill. Elsewhere, Zoe Nathan has caused a huge ripple with her seasonally driven bakery **Huckleberry** in Santa Monica, and in Culver City chef Roy Choi (of Kogi BBQ fame) has turned a run-down International House of Pancakes into the DJ thumping and ski chalet inspired **A-Frame Tavern**. The newest addition into the "who's who" of celebrity chefs is Thomas Keller who opened **Bouchon Bistro** in Beverly Hills.

Ethnic eats continue to be a backbone to the L.A. dining scene. People head to the San Gabriel Valley for dim sum and ramen, Koreatown for epic Korean cooking, and West L.A. for phenomenal sushi. Latin food is well represented in the city, making it tough to choose between Guatemalan eateries, Peruvian restaurants, nouveau Mexican bistros, and Tijuana-style taco trucks. With so many dining options, sometimes the best strategy is simply to drive and explore. Just don't mind the traffic.

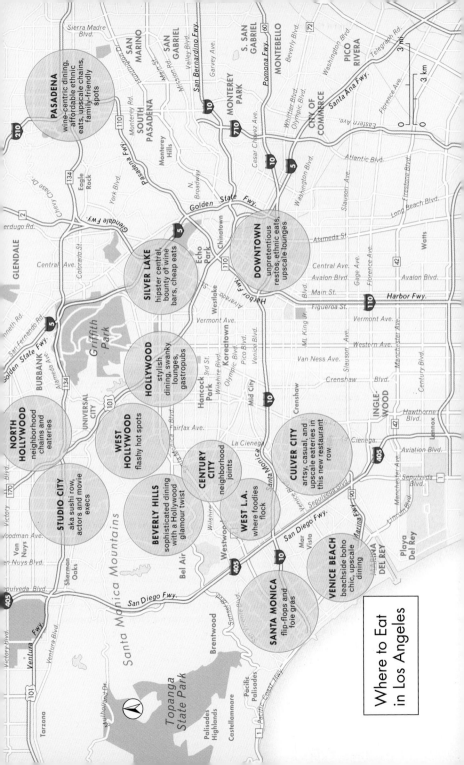

Where to Eat in Los Angeles

PASADENA
wine-centric dining, affordable ethnic eats, upscale chains, family-friendly spots

SILVER LAKE
hipster central, bounty of wine bars, cheap eats

DOWNTOWN
unpretentious restos, ethnic eats, upscale lounges

HOLLYWOOD
stylish dining, swanky lounges, gastropubs

NORTH HOLLYWOOD
neighborhood chains and eateries

WEST HOLLYWOOD
flashy hot spots

CENTURY CITY
neighborhood joints

CULVER CITY
artsy, casual, and upscale eateries in this new restaurant row

STUDIO CITY
aka sushi row, actors and movie execs

BEVERLY HILLS
sophisticated dining with a Hollywood glamour twist

WEST L.A.
where foodies flock

SANTA MONICA
flip-flops and foie gras

VENICE BEACH
beachside boho chic, upscale dining

LOS ANGELES DINING PLANNER

EATING OUT STRATEGY

Where should we eat? With thousands of Los Angeles eateries competing for your attention, it may seem like a daunting question. But fret not—our expert writers and editors have done most of the legwork. The selections here represent the best this city has to offer—from hot dogs to haute cuisine. Search "Best Bets" for top recommendations by price, cuisine, and experience. Sample local flavor in the neighborhood features. Or find a review quickly in the alphabetical listings. Dive in, and enjoy!

CHILDREN

Although it's unusual to see children in the dining rooms of L.A.'s most elite restaurants, dining with youngsters here does not have to mean culinary exile. Many of the restaurants reviewed in this chapter are excellent choices for families, and are marked with a ☾ symbol.

SMOKING

Smokers should keep in mind that California law forbids smoking in all enclosed areas, including bars.

RESERVATIONS

You'll be happy to hear it's getting easier to snag a desired reservation, but it's still a good idea to plan ahead. Some renowned restaurants are booked weeks or even months in advance. If that's the case, you can get lucky at the last minute if you're flexible—and friendly. Most restaurants keep a few tables open for walk-ins and VIPs. Show up for dinner early (6 pm) or late (after 9 pm) and politely inquire about any last-minute vacancies or cancellations.

Occasionally, an eatery may ask you to call the day before your scheduled meal to reconfirm: don't forget or you could lose out. While making your reservation, also inquire about parking. You'll find most places, except small mom-and-pop establishments, provide valet parking at dinner for reasonable rates (often around $5, plus tip).

DINING HOURS

Despite its veneer of decadence, L.A. is not a particularly late-night city for eating. (The reenergized Hollywood dining scene is emerging as a notable exception.) The peak dinner times are from 7 to 9, and most restaurants won't take reservations after 10 pm. Unless otherwise noted, the restaurants listed in this guide are open daily for lunch and dinner. Generally speaking, restaurants are closed either Sunday or Monday; a few are shuttered both days. Most places—even the upscale spots—are open for lunch on weekdays, since many of Hollywood megadeals are conceived at that time.

WHAT TO WEAR

Dining out in Los Angeles tends to be a casual affair, and even at some of the most expensive restaurants you're likely to see customers in jeans (although this is not necessarily considered in good taste). It's extremely rare for L.A. restaurants to actually require a jacket and tie, but all of the city's more formal establishments appreciate a gentleman who dons a jacket—let your good judgment be your guide.

TIPPING AND TAXES

In most restaurants, tip the waiter 16%–20%. (To figure out a 20% tip quickly, just move the decimal point one place to the left on your total and double that amount.) Note that checks for parties of six or more sometimes include the tip already. Tip at least $1 per drink at the bar, and $1 for each coat checked. Never tip the maître d' unless you're out to impress your guests or expect to pay another visit soon. Also, be prepared for a sales tax of 9.75% to appear on your bill.

PRICES

If you're watching your budget, be sure to ask the price of daily specials recited by the waiter. The charge for specials at some restaurants is noticeably out of line with the other prices on the menu. Beware of the $10 bottle of water; ask for tap water instead. And always review your bill.

If you eat early or late, you may be able to take advantage of a prix-fixe deal not offered at peak hours. Most upscale restaurants are offering great lunch deals with special menus at cut-rate prices designed to give customers a true taste of the place.

Credit cards are accepted unless otherwise noted in the review. While many restaurants do accept credit cards, some smaller places accept only cash. If you plan to use a credit card it's a good idea to double-check its acceptability when making reservations or before sitting down to eat.

WHAT IT COSTS					
	¢	$	$$	$$$	$$$$
Restaurants	under $10	$10–$17	$18–$24	$25–$35	over $35

Prices are per person for a main course or equivalent combination of smaller plates (e.g., tapas, sushi), excluding 9.75% sales tax.

10

BEST BETS FOR LOS ANGELES DINING

With thousands of restaurants to choose from, how will you decide where to eat? Fodor's writers and editors have selected their favorite restaurants by price, cuisine, and experience in the Best Bets lists below. You can also search by neighborhood—just peruse the following pages to find specific details about a restaurant in the full reviews later in the chapter.

Fodor's Choice★

Angelini Osteria $$$, p. 272

A.O.C. $$$, p. 272

The Apple Pan $, p. 276

Bouchon Bistro $$$, p. 264

Bottega Louie $$, p. 247

Cube Café and Marketplace $$, p. 257

Little Dom's $$, p. 251

Mélisse, $$$, p. 284

Philippe the Original ¢, p. 249

Pizzeria Mozza $$, p. 259

Providence $$$$, p. 259

Spago Beverly Hills $$$, p. 267

Urasawa $$$$, p. 269

Yuca's Hut $, p. 252

By Price

¢

Pink's Hot Dogs, p. 259

Philippe the Original, p. 249

Zankou Chicken, p. 260

$

The Apple Pan, p. 276

Artisan Cheese Gallery, p. 261

Father's Office, p. 283

La Serenata Gourmet, p. 277

Little Flower Candy Company, p. 287

Porto's Bakery, p. 253

Wood Spoon, p. 250

Yuca's Hut, p. 252

$$

Bombay Café, p. 276

Bottega Louie, p. 247

Cube Café and Marketplace, p. 257

Gjelina, p. 285

Little Dom's, p. 251

Pizzeria Mozza, p. 259

Tanzore, p. 268

$$$

Angelini Osteria, p. 272

Animal, p. 256

A.O.C., p. 272

Bouchon Bistro, p. 264

Campanile, p. 273

Cobras & Matadors, p. 273

Enoteca Drago, p. 266

Oliverio, p. 267

Osteria Mozza, p. 258

Spago Beverly Hills, p. 267

Water Grill, p. 250

$$$$

Gordon Ramsay at The London, p. 274

Providence, p. 259

Urasawa, p. 269

By Cuisine

AMERICAN

The Apple Pan, p. 276

Philippe the Original, p. 249

CHINESE

Mandarette, p. 275

FRENCH

Comme Ça, p. 274

Mélisse, p. 284

Patina, p. 249

INDIAN

Bombay Café, p. 276

Tanzore, p. 268

ITALIAN

Angelini Osteria, p. 272

Cube Café and Marketplace, p. 257

Osteria Mozza, p. 258

Pecorino, p. 269

Pizzeria Mozza, p. 259

Valentino, p. 285

JAPANESE

Asanebo, p. 261

Matsuhisa, p. 267

Mori Sushi, p. 277

Urasawa, p. 269

Wa Sushi & Bistro, p. 276

KOREAN

Gyenari, p. 271

MEDITERRANEAN

A.O.C., p. 272
Campanile, p. 273
Fraîche, p. 271

MEXICAN

La Serenata Gourmet, p. 277
Lotería! Grill Hollywood, p. 258
Monte Alban, p. 277
Yuca's Hut, p. 252

NEW AMERICAN

Craft Los Angeles, p. 270
The Foundry, p. 274
Lucques, p. 275
Spago Beverly Hills, p. 267
XIV, p. 276

SEAFOOD

Providence, p. 259
Water Grill, p. 250

SPANISH

Bar Pintxo, p. 282
The Bazaar by José Andrés, p. 263
Cobras & Matadors, p. 273

STEAK

BLT Steak, p. 273
CUT, p. 264
Nick & Stef's Steakhouse, p. 248

VIETNAMESE

Crustacean, p. 264
Gingergrass, p. 252

By Experience

BAR SCENE

Blue Velvet, p. 247
Father's Office, p. 283
The Foundry, p. 274
Fraîche, p. 271
Nobu Malibu, p. 278

BRUNCH

The Belvedere, p. 263
Bottega Louie, p. 247
Campanile, p. 273
Oliverio, p. 267

CELEB-SPOTTING

Bouchon Bistro, p. 264
Craft Los Angeles, p. 270
CUT, p. 264
The Grill on the Alley, p. 266
Matsuhisa, p. 267

Nobu Malibu, p. 278
Spago Beverly Hills, p. 267

CHILD-FRIENDLY

Border Grill, p. 282
Fred 62, p. 251
Little Flower Candy Company, p. 287
Lotería! Grill Hollywood, p. 258
Philippe the Original, p. 249
Porto's Bakery, p. 253

GOOD FOR GROUPS

A.O.C., p. 272
Bottega Louie, p. 247
Craft Los Angeles, p. 270
Little Dom's, p. 251
Gordon Ramsay at The London, p. 274
25 Degrees, p. 260

GREAT VIEW

Beau Rivage, p. 278
Blue Velvet, p. 247
Encounter, p. 278
Gladstone's Malibu, p. 279

HISTORIC

Campanile, p. 273
Cicada, p. 248
Engine Co. No. 28, p. 248
Musso & Frank Grill, p. 258
Philippe the Original, p. 249
Pink's Hot Dogs, p. 259

Santa Monica Seafood, p. 284

LATE-NIGHT DINING

Animal, p. 256
Canter's, p. 273
Fred 62, p. 251
Kate Mantilini, p. 267
25 Degrees, p. 260
XIV, p. 276

MOST ROMANTIC

A.O.C., p. 272
Bouchon Bistro, p. 264
Cicada, p. 248
Gjelina, p. 285
Mélisse, p. 284
Patina, p. 249

10

DOWNTOWN
WITH LOS FELIZ AND SILVER LAKE

There was a time when heading Downtown for dinner was a strange concept. But, oh how times have changed. The area has experienced a restaurant renaissance in the last few years, propelling Downtown and its neighboring 'hoods into the culinary spotlight.

(opposite bottom) Tender Greens. (opposite right) Bottles at City Sip.

Long known for its cheap urban eats, roaming taco trucks, and street vendors, these neighborhoods have raised the bar of quality eats while staying true to their edgy spirit. Downtown has a diverse mix of wine bars, hot spots, and casual hangouts. In neighboring Silver Lake, the area is a smidgen rough on the exterior, but artistic at its core. Here you can find indie bistros, vintage shops, and bakeries for the hipster crowd that flocks to Sunset Boulevard. For a bit of sophistication, Los Feliz Village is a hodgepodge of French bistros, Italian trattorias, and upscale restaurants. It's still an artsy hub, no doubt about it, but with a decidedly high-end feel.

DINE AND DASH

Snap up some treats on the fly from these hotspots. At **Nickel Diner** (✉ 524 S. Main St. ☎ 213/623–8301) downtown, loyal suitors come in search of the maple-bacon doughnut. If cheeses and charcuterie are your passion, head to the **Cheesestore of Silverlake** (✉ 3926 W. Sunset Blvd. ☎ 323/644–7511) and grab a panini to go.

RETURN OF THE SALAD

Salad-centric eateries have been springing up all over urban Los Angeles, but let's be clear these aren't your average salad bars from the 1980s. Gone are the days of sub-par croutons and shredded processed cheese—the salad has gone couture and is never going back. Here are some of the favorite spots around town.

TENDER GREENS

This casual eatery is loved by locals who can't get enough of the leafy greens brought in every morning from a gourmet lettuce farm in Ventura County. Red, green, butter, frisée, mesclun...there's a whole world of high-end lettuce out there. Order from the Big Salad section of the menu and try the grilled flank steak salad served with red and green butter lettuce, blue cheese crumbles, and red and yellow beets tossed with horseradish vinaigrette (⊠ 6290 Sunset Blvd. ☎ 323/382–0380 ⊕ www.tendergreensfood.com).

FORAGE L.A.

Chef James Kim pays homage to the urban farmer at his Silver Lake casual eatery where fresh fruits, vegetables, and herbs are foraged from local Los Angeles neighbors to create an affordable California seasonal menu. The dining space is airy and simple with long wooden tables and vintage school chairs and the service is semi-cafeteria style, with orders taken at counter and oversized metal trays you take to your table. Local favorites include chicken salad with cucumbers, red onions, and lemon-tahini dressing, and the marinated steak salad with tarragon-buttermilk dressing. (☎ 3823 W. Sunset Blvd. ☎ 323/663–6885 ⊕ www.foragela.com).

GREENLEAF GOURMET CHOP SHOP

This green-friendly and health conscious salad joint offers a slew of specialty salads made with fresh, locally-grown veggies and meats, and gourmet toppings. Be as healthy—or as indulgent—as you want to be. (⊠ 1888 Century Park East ☎ 424/239–8700 ⊕ www.greenleafchopshop.com)

ICE CREAM

L.A. ice cream makers have tapped into the people's love for artisanal ice cream that no longer sticks to the basics. Chocolate, vanilla, and strawberry? Forget it; ice cream aficionados are falling head over spoon for flavors that are far from ordinary. A handful of new ice cream shops in L.A. are meeting the taste challenge. In Brentwood, **Sweet Rose Creamery** (⊠ 225 26th Ave. ☎ 310/260–2663) is crafting small batches of homemade ice cream. Try a salted caramel sundae or malted chocolate with toasted hazelnut praline cone. **Scoops** (⊠ 712 N. Heliotrope Dr. ☎ 323/906–2649) has an unstoppable cult following with loyal fans who come in for fanciful flavors like rosewater pistachio, and Guinness chocolate cheesecake. In Pasadena, **Carmela Ice Cream** (⊠ 2495 E. Washington Blvd. ☎ 323/319–6084) is the newest kid in town, offering fresh farmers' market–inspired batches of ice cream and sorbet such as lavender-honey and strawberry-buttermilk.

10

HOLLYWOOD
AND THE STUDIOS

(above) Sweet treats at Gelato Bar. (opposite bottom) Locali makes great sandwiches. (opposite right) Big Sugar Bakeshop.

Irreverent independent restaurants, late-night wine bars, upscale chains, congested tourist hubs, and swanky hotel restaurants dominate Hollywood's dining scene.

Expect to see tattooed musicians, tourists taking pictures along the strip, studio executives, and families who ventured down from the Hollywood Hills and the Valley. Sure, Hollywood is congested with traffic, parking can be tough (bring your quarters), and the culinary scene can be a little heavy on chains. But Hollywood still has strong roots in old-world glamour and rock 'n' roll—you just have to look past the big-box pop-ups. Along the gateway into Hollywood is Franklin Boulevard, where quaint diners, coffeehouses, and restaurants cater to locals. Edging into Hollywood Boulevard, stop at Hollywood & Highland to refuel with lunch. The eastern portion of Sunset Boulevard has many new bistros, gourmet markets, waffle houses, and lounges. And Melrose Avenue continues to offer cutting-edge eateries and innovative bakeries.

VALLEY VISIT

Just over the hill sits the Valley, a neighborhood often overlooked because of its suburban disposition and saturation of mini-malls. But in this hub of movie studios, there are also a number of foodie haunts like **Big Sugar Bake Shop** (⊠ 12182 Ventura Blvd. ☎ 818/508–5855), **Caioti Pizza Café** (⊠ 4346 Tujunga Ave. ☎ 818/761–3588), and **Gelato Bar** (⊠ 4342½ Tujunga Ave. ☎ 818/487–1717).

SEASONAL LOS ANGELES

While Los Angeles may seem like a concrete jungle, Hollywood is actually home to one of the largest farmers' markets in the city. Held every Sunday morning along Ivar Street and Selma Avenue, the **Hollywood Farmers' Market** (☎ 323/463–3171 ⊕ www.hollywoodfarmersmarket.net) is packed with throngs of moms pushing strollers, incognito celebrities, local dwellers, and chefs in search of seasonal bounty. Packed with farmers and food artisans, the market sells fruits and vegetables, freshly cut flowers, homemade jams, free-range chickens, naturally raised bison burgers, and seasonal ice creams. The market—one of the largest in the state—is put together by the Sustainable Economic Enterprise of Los Angeles (SEE-L.A.), a nonprofit that educates people about agriculture. When you're here, it's easy to forget you're in Hollywood—until you see a camera crew filming a reality show next to the organic pears.

SEE-L.A. recently opened the **Farmer's Kitchen** (✉ 1555 North Vine St. ☎ 323/467–7600), a seasonal-driven lunch spot that is inspired by what's sold in the farmers' market. Found in the Sunset + Vine complex on the corner of Selma Avenue and Morningside Court, the affordable menu changes every week and ranges from market sandwiches, soups, roasted vegetables, and salads. Parking is difficult, but you can take the Metro and exit at the Hollywood and Vine stop.

LOCALI YOURS

With the arrival of **Locali** (✉ 5825 Franklin Blvd. ☎ 323/466–1360 ⊕ www.localiyours.com), a sustainable locally driven neighborhood market in Hollywood's charming Franklin Village, convenience is now eco-friendly. The conscious quick stop carries sandwiches, candy, chocolate, and hot pretzels made by L.A. food artisans. Stop in for a pint of butternut squash ice cream made by Carmela Ice Cream, a local who makes seasonally inspired creations.

SUNSET DISTRICT

Restaurateur and New York transplant George Abou-Daoud has made it his personal mission to revive the eastern side of Sunset Boulevard, which has often been overshadowed by the glitzier center of town. With a slew of new bars and restaurants opened by Abou-Daoud, the Sunset District is now becoming its own destination. Stop into **Delancey's** (✉ 5936 Sunset Blvd. ☎ 323/469–2100), an Italian gastropub that serves up one amazing thin crust pizza, or **Tamarind Deli** (✉ 1471 Tamarind Blvd. ☎ 323/960–2451) for a hot brisket sandwich and cherry limeade. Grab a burger at the **Bowery** (✉ 6268 Sunset Blvd. ☎ 323/465–3400), a New York–style bistro, or head over to the newest restaurant on the strip the **Mercantile** (✉ 6600 Sunset Blvd. ☎ 323/962–3202), an unpretentious eatery, wine bar, and gourmet market that serves up a K-Town sandwich and buttered-popcorn ice cream. These restaurants are all walking distance to each other, which make for excellent bar-hopping.

10

SANTA MONICA
AND THE BEACHES

Yoga teachers, surf instructors, real estate moguls, and beach-loving celebrities call Santa Monica and its neighboring cities home.

(above) Stop into a restaurant along the Venice Beach Boardwalk for the city's best people-watching.

In Santa Monica, Wilshire Boulevard and Montana Avenue are pedestrian-friendly streets where locals walk to upscale haunts like **Andrew's Cheese** store (⊠ *728 Montana Ave.* ☎ *310/393–3308*) or **Vanilla Bake Shop** (⊠ *512 Wilshire Blvd.* ☎ *310/458–6644*).

Closer to the beaches, try 4th Street, Broadway, and Main Street for bars, fast-casual chains, and shopping at the Third Street Promenade. Stop for a late afternoon nosh at **Blue Plate Oysterette** (⊠ *1355 Ocean Ave.* ☎ *310/576–3474*) or **La Monarca Bakery** (⊠ *1300 Wilshire Blvd.* ☎ *310/451–1114*) for fruit-filled sweet taquito. On Wednesday mornings there's the **Santa Monica Farmers' Market** (⊠ *Arizona and Main Sts.* ☎ *310/458–8712*).

Venice Beach from Main Street to Abbot Kinney is home to gelato stores, vintage shops, coffeehouses, and a few notable dinner spots like **Chaya Venice** (⊠ *110 Navy St.* ☎ *310/396–1179*), just above Main Street. For breakfast, try the *très* chic **3 Squares Café and Bakery** (⊠ *1121 Abbot Kinney Blvd.* ☎ *310/399–6504*) known for its delicious pretzel bread.

SWEET SPOT

Pastry chef Zoe Nathan sent foodies into a frenzy when she opened her bakery **Huckleberry** (⊠ *1014 Wilshire Blvd.* ☎ *310/451–2311*). The café has found itself instantly beloved by Angelenos who make the trek, wait in line, and hope to snag a spot at the communal table. Breakfast offerings include fried egg sandwiches and maple-bacon biscuits. The lunch menu features turkey meatball sandwiches and seasonal salads.

INSIDE L.A.'S FOOD SCENE

Carrie Kommers
Editor, www.dineLA.com

As editor of dineLA, a program created by the Los Angeles Convention and Visitors Bureau to promote the city's diverse food community, Carrie Kommers is tapped in to the beating heart—and stomach—of Los Angeles. Here, she shares a few tips with Fodor's readers.

Q: How does dineLA stay on top of dining trends in the Los Angeles area?
A: I'd say that about 75% of what makes dineLA work is the relationship building. I love talking to journalists, chefs, owners, event producers—so many amazing people contribute to L.A.'s food culture and it's crucial to be directly in conversation with them.

Q: What is the best way for visitors to discover the world of food here in Los Angeles?
A: Thankfully, now we are seeing a boom in local culinary tours. **Melting Pot Tours** (⊕ www.meltingpottours. com) really paved the way with their wonderful farmers' market tours and then came **Six Taste** (⊕ www.sixtaste. com) and **Foody Field Trips** (⊕ www.foodyfieldtrips. com). They're great primers for visitors *and* locals. I did Six Taste's San Gabriel dim sum walking tour and went home knowing that I could never have found those little places on my own. It

would have taken me weeks of research and even then I would have had trouble knowing what to order—or how to pronounce it.

Q: When you have guests in town, what are some of your favorite spots to take friends and family in Santa Monica?
A: Santa Monica is a really interesting mix of locals and tourists. It's a fairly concentrated area with loads of really good restaurants and a ton of variety and it's nice because you can stay on foot the whole time if you want to, which is unusual in L.A. For burgers I like **Chez Jay** (⊠ 1657 Ocean Ave. ☎ 310/395–1741). For oysters and a glass of rosé I go to **Santa Monica Seafood Café** (⊠ 1000 Wilshire Blvd. ☎ 310/393–5244).

Q: What do you think would surprise people the most about food and dining in Los Angeles?
A: Probably how indulgent the menus currently are. I think there are aspects to the "rabbit food and salad" stereotype that still persist about L.A., but I try to explain to people that pork belly, fried chicken, and burgers have taken over. I think it might also surprise people simply to know how much variety there is here. You just can't possibly begin to take it all in.

LOCAL FAVES

To rub elbows with Angelenos in their natural habitats, try one of these spots:
Locals from Venice Beach and Santa Monica come to **Library Ale House** (⊠ 2911 Main St. ☎ 310/314–4855) for the craftsman beer and affordable comfort food. It's a boisterous scene during peak hours with regulars noshing on fish tacos and tipping back pints.
The casual restaurant and gourmet market **La Grande Orange** (⊠ 2000 Main St. ☎ 310/396–9145) offers breakfast, lunch, and dinner in a relaxed, neighborhood setting—it's a perfect spot for sipping a margarita and nibbling on shrimp ceviche.
Sunday mornings at the seasonal bistro **Fig** (⊠ Fairmont Miramar, 101 Wilshire Blvd. ☎ 310/319–3111) are known around town thanks to its "Kegs and Eggs" special. A weekly brunch that costs $37 for an egg dish of your choice and all you can drink pints of draft beer.

10

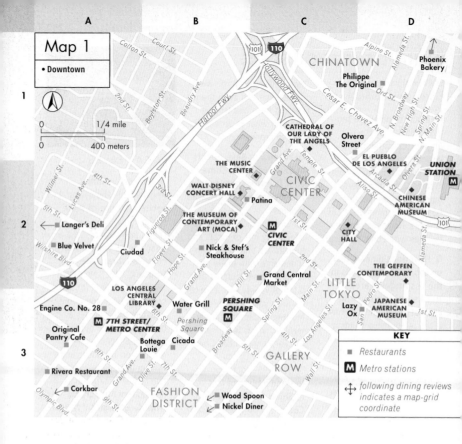

Map 1
• Downtown

| | A | B | C | D |

CHINATOWN

Phoenix Bakery

Philippe The Original ■

Colton St. · Court St. · Cesar E. Chavez Ave. · Alpine St. · Ord St. · N. Broadway · New High St. · N. Main St. · Spring St. · Alameda St.

CATHEDRAL OF OUR LADY OF THE ANGELS

Olvera Street

EL PUEBLO DE LOS ANGELES

UNION STATION Ⓜ

THE MUSIC CENTER ■

WALT·DISNEY CONCERT HALL ◆ Patina ■

CHINESE AMERICAN MUSEUM

CIVIC CENTER

◆← Langer's Deli

THE MUSEUM OF CONTEMPORARY ART (MOCA) ◆

Ⓜ **CIVIC CENTER**

CITY HALL ◆

■ Blue Velvet

Ciudad ■

■ Nick & Stef's Steakhouse

THE GEFFEN CONTEMPORARY ◆

Grand Central Market ■

LITTLE TOKYO

LOS ANGELES CENTRAL LIBRARY ◆

Water Grill ■

PERSHING SQUARE

Ⓜ

JAPANESE AMERICAN MUSEUM ◆

Engine Co. No. 28 ■

Lazy ■ Ox

Pershing Square

Original Pantry Cafe ■

Ⓜ **7TH STREET/ METRO CENTER**

Bottega Cicada Louie ■ ■

GALLERY ROW

■ Rivera Restaurant

←■ Corkbar

FASHION DISTRICT

←■ Wood Spoon
←■ Nickel Diner

Olympic Blvd.

KEY

■ Restaurants

Ⓜ Metro stations

✢ following dining reviews indicates a map-grid coordinate

0 ——— 1/4 mile
0 ——— 400 meters

RESTAURANT REVIEWS

Listed alphabetically within neighborhoods; use the coordinate (✢ 1:B2) at the end of each listing to locate a site on the corresponding map.

DOWNTOWN WITH LOS FELIZ AND SILVER LAKE

The Eastside is home to L.A.'s boho community a mixture of aspiring artists, musicians, scribes, and young families who grow their own vegetables and motor around on vintage Vespas. The neighborhood has been changing the last few years as Downtown's culinary renaissance has rippled through the area, making it a popular dining destination where people come in search of the edgy and creative menus that celebrate the artistic spirit of these communities. Here you'll find plenty of cozy wine bars, quaint bistros, historical landmarks, ethnic eats, and upscale restaurants that lack pretension.

The pastry case at Bottega Louie

DOWNTOWN

$$$ ✕**Blue Velvet.** Carved out of an abandoned Holiday Inn in an eco-
NEW AMERICAN conscious apartment building, this hip poolside restaurant reflects the
dynamic changes occurring in downtown L.A. Featuring striking views
of the new $2.5 billion L.A. Live project, a lively lounge, and a contem-
porary menu from a daring kitchen, cosmopolitan Blue Velvet oozes
sex appeal. The mostly small-plate menu offers crispy Kurobuta pork
belly with squash puree, hamachi sashimi with apple sauce, and hanger
steak with onion rings, all enhanced with organic herbs from a rooftop
garden, making Blue Velvet one cool green scene. ✉ *750 S. Garland
Ave., Downtown* ☎ *213/239–0061* ⊕ *www.bluevelvetrestaurant.com*
🍴 *Reservations essential* ⊘ *No lunch; closed Sun. and Mon.* ✛ *1:A2.*

$$ ✕**Bottega Louie.** This former Brooks Brothers suit store was reincarnated
ITALIAN into a lively Italian restaurant and gourmet market in 2008 and quickly
Fodor'sChoice crowned Downtown's new culinary darling. Vast open space, stark
★ white walls and long windows that stretch from floor to ceiling give it
a grand and majestic appeal. An army of stylish servers weave in-and-
out of the crowds carrying bowls of pasta, trays of bubbly prosecco and
thin-crust pizzas. Pick and choose from a bevy of salads, pastas, pizzas,
and entrées that range from wild Italian sea bass to a *bistecca arrabiata*
(seared steak with long peppers and tomatoes). Or simply order from
its small plates menu with favorites; asparagus with fried egg, jambon
Serrano, heirloom carrots, tomato bruschetta, and fried calamari. Don't
let the crowd of people waiting for a table deter you, order a cocktail
from the bar, peruse the gourmet market, and nibble on a brightly colored macaroon. ✉ *700 S. Grand Ave., Downtown* ☎ *213/802–1470.*

$$$$ ╳ **Cicada.** Certainly one of the most romantic and architecturally dra-
ITALIAN matic dining venues in L.A., Cicada occupies the ground floor of the
1928 art deco Oviatt Building. Carved maple columns soar two stories
to a gold leaf ceiling, and from the mezzanine a glamorous bar overlooks the spacious dining room. The menu leans on Italy, but with
global influences, featuring dishes like tuna carpaccio with lemon-ginger
sauce, and lamb chops with rosemary-mirin sauce. Fans rave about the
restaurant's Lalique glass accents, live music, and widely spaced tables.
Others complain about its banquet hall feel and so-so food. ⊠ *617 S.
Olive St., Downtown* ☎ *213/488–9488* ⊕ *www.cicadarestaurant.com*
⊘ *Closed Mon. No lunch* ✛ *1:B3.*

$$ ╳ **Engine Co. No. 28.** A lovingly restored 1912 fire station, where every-
AMERICAN thing—even the original brass sliding pole—has been preserved, now
⟲ rushes out solid, old-fashioned comfort food. The long bar is a popular
hangout for Downtown workers delaying their rush-hour commute.
The kitchen does a fine job with crab cakes, chili, macaroni and cheese,
and thick slabs of terrific meat loaf. Specials showcase recipes inspired
by firehouse cooking across the country. ⊠ *644 S. Figueroa St., Down-
town* ☎ *213/624–6996* ⊕ *www.engineco.com* ⊘ *No lunch weekends*
✛ *1:A3.*

¢ ╳ **Langer's Deli.** With fluorescent lighting and Formica tables, Langer's
DELI has the look of a no-frills Jewish deli back in New York. The draw here
⟲ is the hand-cut pastrami, which is relatively lean, peppery, and robust in
flavor—those who swear it's the best in town have a strong case. Some
regulars opt for the legendary #19 (pastrami with Swiss and coleslaw
piled high on twice-baked rye), but purists prefer it straight up with
Russian dressing. The neighborhood is rough around the edges, but
the nearby metro station brings plenty of businesspeople and adven-
turous foodies who come in search of this James Beard award-winning
spot. ⊠ *704 S. Alvarado St., Downtown* ☎ *213/483–8050* ⊕ *www.
langersdeli.com* ⌲ *Reservations not accepted* ⊘ *Closed Sun. No din-
ner* ✛ *1:A2.*

$$ ╳ **Lazy Ox Canteen.** Found in the artsy Little Tokyo section of down-
ECLECTIC town Los Angeles, Lazy Ox Canteen is a neighborhood favorite often
filled with downtown dwellers who come in and tuck themselves into
a communal table for the night. The lively dimly lit restaurant brings
together flavorful food, great wine, and moderate prices along with an
outdoor patio for enjoying L.A.'s sunny weather. The kitchen is led by
chef Josef Centeno, whose diverse culinary background has resulted in
a hodgepodge of seasonal eats that range from caramelized onion soup
to beef tongue ravioli. Order the duck breast with crushed yams, the
whole roasted branzino, or the Lazy Ox burger with cantal cheese and
green peppercorn mustard. Specials change daily, such as a pork porter-
house with pancetta gravy for two. Stick around for dessert: you won't
be disappointed. ⊠ *241 S. San Pedro, Downtown* ☎ *213/626–5299*
⊕ *www.lazyoxcanteen.com* ✛ *1:D3.*

$$$ ╳ **Nick & Stef's Steakhouse.** The contemporary beef palace of restaurateurs
STEAK Joachim and Christine Splichal, named after their twin boys, has been so
successful they've replicated the concept in other cities. Despite a sleek
modern aesthetic, elements of the traditional steak house—comfortable

A "vegetable mosaic" from Patina.

booths, crisp white linen, and wood accents—remain. The premium steaks come from a glassed-in, on-site aging chamber; build up your order by choosing from a diverse array of sauces, starches, and vegetables that give honored steak-house traditions a little sex appeal. The wine list, deep in California reds, is predictably strong. ⊠ *330 S. Hope St., Downtown* ☎ *213/680–0330* ⊕ *www.patinagroup.com* ⌂ *Reservations essential* ☉ *No lunch on weekends* ✛ *1:B2.*

$$$ ✕**Patina.** In a bold move, chef-owner Joachim Splichal moved his
FRENCH flagship restaurant from Hollywood to Downtown's striking Frank Gehry–designed Walt Disney Concert Hall. His gamble paid off—the contemporary space, surrounded by a rippled "curtain" of rich walnut, is an elegant, dramatic stage for the acclaimed restaurant's contemporary French cuisine. Specialties include copious amounts of foie gras, butter-poached lobster, and medallions of venison served with lady apples. Finish with a hard-to-match cheese tray (orchestrated by a genuine *maître fromager*) and an apple tatin with a crisp Granny Smith apple sorbet served as its companion. ⊠ *Walt Disney Concert Hall, 141 S. Grand Ave., Downtown* ☎ *213/972–3331* ⊕ *www.patinagroup.com* ⌂ *Reservations essential* ☉ *Closed Mon. Lunch Tues.–Sun.* ✛ *1:B2.*

¢ ✕**Philippe the Original.** L.A.'s oldest restaurant (1908), Philippe claims
AMERICAN the French dip sandwich originated here. You can get one made with
☺ beef, pork, ham, lamb, or turkey on a freshly baked roll; the house hot
Fodor'sChoice mustard is as famous as the sandwiches. Its reputation is earned by
★ maintaining traditions, from sawdust on the floor to long communal tables where customers debate the Dodgers or local politics. The home cooking—orders are taken at the counter where some of the motherly servers have managed their long lines for decades—includes huge

The classic French dip sandwich from Philippe the Original.

breakfasts, chili, pickled eggs, and an enormous pie selection. The best bargain: a cup of java for 10¢ including tax. ✉ *1001 N. Alameda St., Downtown* ☎ *213/628–3781* ⊕ *www.philippes.com* ⌫ *Reservations not accepted* ▭ *No credit cards* ✛ *1:D1.*

$$$
SEAFOOD

✕ **Water Grill.** There's a bustling, enticing rhythm here as platters of glistening shellfish get whisked from the oyster bar to the cozy candlelit booths. Start with a roasted beet salad with lavender cured feta or the Tahitian albacore served with chili sauce, ruby-red grapefruit and mint leaves. For entrees, explore the king salmon with a poached egg and polenta, the sturgeon with a beet risotto and the big eyed tuna elegantly paired with a dried cranberry quinoa. A sesaonlly driven and sophisticated menu that brings all the seafood greats together in one amazing menu. Excellent desserts and a fine wine list round out this top-notch dining experience. ✉ *544 S. Grand Ave., Downtown* ☎ *213/891–0900* ⊕ *www.watergrill.com* ⌫ *Reservations essential* ☾ *No lunch weekends* ✛ *1:B3.*

$
BRAZILIAN

✕ **Wood Spoon.** There's no sign for this cozy bistro in Downtown's Fashion District, just a big wood spoon that locals have come to know as the beacon for great Brazilian food. Loved by students from the fashion institute, Brazilian expats and concertgoers heading to the Orpheum Theatre for a show, this place is an affordable gem in a high-priced dining area. Order from the small plate's selection, such as *coxinha* (a Brazilian street snack made with chicken), calabreza sausage with potatoes, and the hearts of palm frittata. The house favorite is a Brazilian chicken potpie or pork burger served with yam fries. ✉ *107 W. 9th St., Downtown* ☎ *213/629–1765* ⊕ *www.woodspoonla.com* ⌫ *Reservations essential* ☾ *Closed Sun.* ✛ *1:B3.*

LOS FELIZ

¢ ✕**Cha Cha Cha.** Left-of-center Cha
CARIBBEAN Cha Cha attracts an eclectic crowd.
It's hip without being pretentious
or overly trendy. A giant map on
the wall suggests the restaurant's
Caribbean influences. You can sit
in the small dining room or on the
enclosed tropical patio where Car-
men Miranda would feel at home.
Standard options include empana-
das, Jamaican jerk chicken or pork,
curried shrimp, fried plantain chips,
and paella. Sangría is the drink of
choice. ✉ *656 N. Virgil Ave., Los
Feliz* ☎ *323/664–7723* ✛ *2:H3.*

¢ ✕**Fred 62.** A tongue-in-cheek take
AMERICAN on the American diner created by
☺ funky L.A. chef-restaurateur Fred
Eric. The usual burgers and shakes
are joined by choices like grilled
salmon, Southern-style brisket, and

a "Poorest Boy" sandwich (crispy fried chicken, onions, and rémoulade
on a French roll). Toasters sit on every table and breakfasts range from
tofu scrambles to "Hunka Hunka Burnin' Love"—pancakes made with
peanut butter, chocolate chips, and banana. Like the neighborhood
itself, nobody is out of place here, with everybody from button-down
businesspeople to tattooed musicians showing up at some point during
its 24/7 cycle. ✉ *1850 N. Vermont Ave., Los Feliz* ☎ *323/667–0062*
⊕ *www.fred62.com* ✍ *Reservations not accepted* ✛ *2:H1.*

$$ ✕**Little Dom's.** With a $15 Monday night supper, a vintage bar with
ITALIAN a barkeep who mixes up seasonally inspired retro cocktails and an
Fodor's Choice attached Italian deli where one can pick up a pork cheek sub, it's not
★ surprising why Little Dom's is a neighborhood favorite. Cozy and invit-
ing with big leather booths one can sink into for the night, the menu
blends classic Italian fare with a modern sensibility, with dishes like
the baked ricotta and wild boar soppressatta, classic pappardelle with
homemade sausage, whitefish picatta, and a New York strip steak with
fennel béarnaise. This is a terrific spot for weekend brunch; grab a shot
of rich hot chocolate and take a seat on the sidewalk patio. ✉ *2128 Hill-
hurst Ave., Los Feliz* ☎ *323/661–0055* ⊕ *www.littledoms.com* ✍ *Reser-
vations essential* ☉ *Breakfast and lunch served to 3 pm daily* ✛ *2:H1.*

$ ✕**Umami Burger.** There's sweet, salty, bitter, and sour, and now, there's
AMERICAN Umami. This burger joint, named after the pleasant savory taste dis-
covered by the Japanese, has found a loving following by L.A. locals
who come here for gourmet burgers that awaken all the senses. A sim-
ple dining room with lively music creates a casual environment that's
home to locals, gourmets, and families who come in search of a savory
burger with unique fixings. Go for the Umami burger made with a juicy
patty and served medium rare with a Parmesan crisp and the signature

10

ketchup that's both sweet and savory. Or try the SoCal burger that's made with oven-dried tomato spread, butter lettuce, and house-made American cheese. Add a side of sweet potato fries or ask for the off-the-menu cheesy tater tots that come with jalapeño ranch dressing. Other locations exist throughout the city. ⊠ *4655 Hollywood Blvd., Los Feliz* ☎ *323/669–3922* ⊕ *www.umamiburger.com* ✛ *2:H2.*

$$$
NEW AMERICAN

✕ **vermont.** This stylish eatery kicked off a renaissance on its colorful namesake street. Vaulted ceilings, Persian rugs, and fresh flowers make the interior graceful and inviting. The modern menu starts with the likes of crab cakes with mustard–lemon aïoli, or duck salad with ginger–soy vinaigrette, then moves on to crispy whitefish with basil sauce, flatiron steak with a fiery peppercorn sauce, and vegetarian risotto. Well-suited for quiet business lunches, vermont becomes lively during dinner. An alluring lounge adjoins the restaurant attracting everyone from Armani-clad studio suits to bohemian artists. ⊠ *1714 N. Vermont Ave., Los Feliz* ☎ *323/661–6163* ⊕ *www.vermontrestaurantonline.com* ⊘ *No lunch weekends* ✛ *2:H1.*

$
MEXICAN
☕
Fodor's Choice
★

✕ **Yuca's Hut.** Blink and you can miss this place, whose reputation far exceeds its size (it may be the tiniest place to have ever won a James Beard award). It's known for carne asada, carnitas, and *cochinita pibil* (Yucatán-style roasted pork) tacos, burritos, and banana leaf-wrapped tamales. This is a fast-food restaurant in the finest tradition—independent, family-owned, and sticking to what it does best. The liquor store next door sells lots of Coronas to Hut customers soaking up the sun on the makeshift parking-lot patio. There's no chance of satisfying a late-night craving, though; it closes at 6 pm. ⊠ *2056 N. Hillhurst Ave., Los Feliz* ☎ *323/662–1214* ✍ *Reservations not accepted* ▬ *No credit cards* ⊘ *Closed Sun.* ✛ *2:H1.*

SILVER LAKE

$
VIETNAMESE
☕

✕ **Gingergrass.** Traditional Vietnamese favorites emerge from this café's open kitchen, sometimes with a California twist. With a minimalist decor marked by tropical wood banquettes, Silver Lake's bohemian past and über-trendy present converge at Gingergrass. Consider classic crispy-skinned imperial rolls (filled with chicken, veggies, or crab and shrimp, served with lettuce and mint for wrapping), variations on *pho* (Vietnam's ubiquitous noodle soup), and Cal-light versions of *bánh mì* (baguette sandwiches that fuse French and Southeast Asian traditions), along with a refreshing basil-lime elixir. ⊠ *2396 Glendale Blvd., Silver Lake* ☎ *323/644–1600* ⊕ *www.gingergrass.com* ✍ *Reservations not accepted* ✛ *2:H2.*

$$
CAFÉ

✕ **LAMILL Coffee Boutique.** With a sleek, neoclassical design, and menu designed by Providence chef Michael Cimarusti and his acclaimed pastry chef Adrian Vasquez, this is no ordinary neighborhood coffeehouse. For coffee connoisseurs, LAMILL features the finest beans from around the world, brewed in a French press or through a siphon apparatus that looks like it was salvaged from the laboratory of a mad scientist. For foodies, house-cured Tasmanian sea trout with wasabi crème fraîche, steak frites, or chai-spiced duck with *vadouvan* (a garlicky Indian masala) and black olive-rosemary honey are followed by exquisitely presented desserts like chocolate lollipops and an exotic Asian twist

Cube Café & Marketplace.

on s'mores. ✉ *1636 Silver Lake Blvd., Silver Lake* ☎ *323/663–4441* ⊕ *www.lamillcoffee.com* ✛ *2:H2.*

HOLLYWOOD AND THE STUDIOS

Hollywood has two faces. Although a hub for tourists who come here to take photos along the Hollywood Walk of Fame, it is still in touch with its irreverent rock-and-roll roots. The result is a complex dining scene made up of upscale eateries, overpriced chains, cheap fast food, and provocative hot spots helmed by celebrity chefs. Just over the hill in the studios, the slower-paced, slightly suburban area is known for its sushi, gastropubs, and bakeries that are well worth a visit.

BURBANK

$ ✕ **Porto's Bakery.** Waiting in line at Porto's is as much as part of the expe-
CAFÉ rience as is indulging in a roasted pork sandwich and chocolate-dipped
☺ croissant. Locals love this neighborhood bakery and café that has been an L.A. staple for 35 years. This is its second location just minutes away from the studios and makes for a great spot to take a stroll and peruse the consignment shops run by former movie stylists. The crowded café bustles with an ambitious lunch crowd, but counter service is quick and efficient. Go for one of its tasty Cuban sandwiches like the media noche or the potato sandwich (potato stuffed with ground beef), or order the house specialty: chorizo pie. Skipping dessert here would just be wrong. Your sweet tooth will thank you later. ✉ *3614 W. Magnolia Blvd., Burbank* ☎ *818/846–9100* ⊙ *Mon.–Sat., 6:30 am–7:30 pm, Sun. 6:30 am–5:30 pm* ✛ *3:D1.*

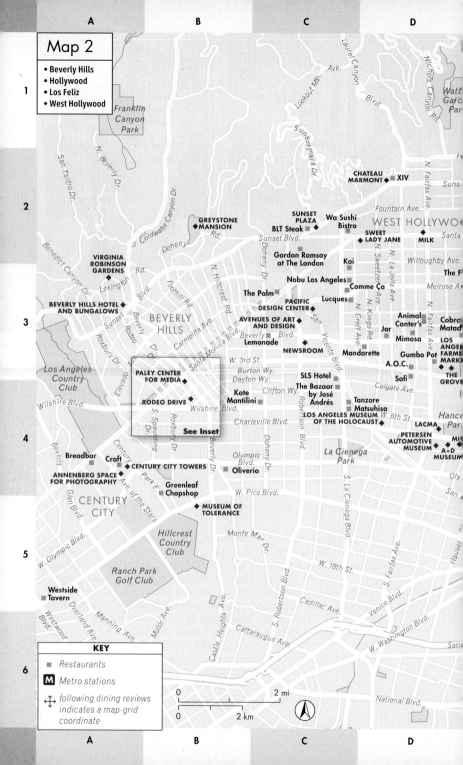

HOLLYWOOD

$$
AMERICAN

✕ **Ammo.** This hip canteen proves that the designers and photographers (aka the regulars here) have good taste in food as well as fashion. Lunch might be French lentil salad; a prosciutto, mozzarella, and arugula sandwich; or a really great burger. Start dinner with one of the kitchen's market-fresh salads, then follow up with a baby artichoke pizza, a solid burger, or a grilled hanger steak. The crisp, minimal setting is cool but not chilly. ✉ *1155 N. Highland Ave., Hollywood* ☎ *323/871–2666* ⊕ *www.ammocafe.com* ✛ *2:E2.*

$$$
AMERICAN

✕ **Animal.** When foodies in Los Angeles need a culinary thrill, they come to this minimalist restaurant in the Fairfax District, which is light on the flash but heavy on serious food. The James Beard award–winning restaurant is owned by Jon Shook and Vinny Dotolo, two young chefs who shot to fame with a stint on *Iron Chef* and later with their own Food Network show, *Two Dudes Catering.* With a closing time of 2 am, the small restaurant is an L.A. anomaly. That assessment is also true for the restaurant's diverse clientele, which ranges from neighborhood dwellers to young Hollywood celebrities to food snobs in search of their new favorite dish. The daily menu consists of small plates and entrées that make it easy to explore many items, like barbecue pork belly sandwiches, *poutine* with oxtail gravy, foie gras *loco moco* (a hamburger topped with foie gras, quail egg, and Spam), and fried quail served with maple *au jus.* For dessert, the house specialty is a multilayered bacon-chocolate crunch bar. ✉ *435 N. Fairfax Ave., Los Angeles* ☎ *323/782–9225* ⊕ *www.animalrestaurant.com* ☾ *No lunch* ✛ *2:D3.*

$$$
LATIN AMERICAN

✕ **Beso.** Celebrity chef Todd English takes on Hollywood, collaborating with television star Eva Longoria at this stylish, Latin-theme restaurant with a name that means "kiss" in Spanish. Glittering chandeliers dangle over a dramatic scene: young hipsters sipping mojitos at a marble bar, and tourists sliding into cozy booths with a view of the prominent exhibition kitchen. Begin with one of the inventive appetizers, such as the taqueria taster (skirt steak, plantain, tuna tartare), the artichoke guacamole, or addictive crispy lamb ribs with peanut-chipotle sauce. For the main course, move on to a steak with chimichurri sauce, paella, or wild striped bass with grilled asparagus. Churros with chocolate and *dulce de leche* dipping sauces make for the sweetest finale. Beso is pure Hollywood, but because it doesn't take itself too seriously, it adds plenty of fun to the legendary neighborhood. ✉ *6350 Hollywood Blvd., Hollywood* ☎ *323/467–7991* ⊕ *www.besohollywood.com* ⌕ *Reservations essential* ☾ *Closed Sun. No lunch.* ✛ *2:E2.*

$$$
MEDITERRANEAN

✕ **Cleo.** Hollywood's nightlife and revitalized dining landscape continues to thrive especially with spots like this hip Mediterranean restaurant that pays homage to Cleopatra. Tucked away in the newly revamped Redbury Hotel, Cleo bumps with energy and life in both its ambience and fresh approach to Mediterranean cuisine. Small-plate offerings allow for plenty of sampling. Start with a trio of dips including hummus with tahini, *lebaneh* (thick yogurt) with feta, and *muhammara* (walnut garlic spread) that comes with fresh-from-the-oven flatbread. Chicken and lamb kebabs are an ideal segue into the proteins, as is a perfectly roasted lamb shank or moussaka made with eggplant, beef ragù, and

One of Pizzeria Mozza's renowned pies.

feta, and sprinkled with pine nuts. Get your veggie allowance with the Brussels sprouts made with capers, parsley, and almonds, or mushrooms with hazelnuts and dates. The thoughtful cocktail menu, decent wine list, and enthusiastic staff make Cleo a great place to spend the evening—Hollywood style. ⊠ *1717 Vine St., Hollywood* ☎ *323/962–1711* ⊕ *www.cleorestaurant.com* ✦ *2:F2.*

$$ ✕ **Cube Café & Marketplace.** Cheese, charcuterie, and pasta lovers take
ITALIAN heed: this dark and cozy Italian restaurant will ruin you for all the oth-
Fodor'sChoice ers. With more than 85 varieties of cheese, an enviable salami selection,
★ pasta made in-house, and a passionate and earnest staff, this former
pasta company turned upscale café and gourmet market is one of L.A.'s
more affordable culinary gems. Take a seat at the cheese bar and order
the *Sleepless in Salumi* plate or the *When in Rome* and pair it with a
glass of Italian wine. For dinner, order the antipasti of braised octopus,
and then move onto the seasonally driven pasta dishes, like the wild
boar gnocchi, veal ravioli, or pumpkin-stuffed pasta. ⊠ *615 N. La Brea
Blvd., Hollywood* ☎ *323/939–1148* ⊙ *Mon.–Sat. 11 am–10:30 pm.
Closed Sun.* ✦ *2:D3.*

$ ✕ **El Cholo.** The first of what's now a small chain, this landmark south of
MEXICAN Hollywood has been packing them in since the 1920s. A hand-painted
adobe ceiling and an outdoor patio with a fountain create a partylike
atmosphere, which the bar's legendary margaritas can only enhance.
The fare includes all kinds of Cal–Mex standards, including tacos,
chicken enchiladas, *carnitas* (shredded fried pork), and—from July
through October—their famous green-corn tamales. ⊠ *1121 S. West-
ern Ave., Hollywood* ☎ *323/734–2773* ⊕ *www.elcholo.com* ✦ *2:G5.*

10

$ **✕Guelaguetza.** Catering to a largely
MEXICAN Spanish-speaking clientele, the
spare decor at this in-the-know spot
is compensated by a festive mood
and exotic scents filling the small,
cheerful space. Surely one of L.A.'s
best Mexican eateries, it serves the
complex but not overpoweringly
spicy cooking of Oaxaca, one of
Mexico's most renowned culinary
capitals. The standouts are the
moles, whose intense flavors come
from intricate combinations of
nuts, seeds, spices, chiles, and bit-
ter chocolate. But be sure to check
out barbecued-goat tacos or pizza-
like *clayudas* topped with white cheese and *tasajo* (dried beef) or *cecina*
(chili-marinated pork) and chorizo. ⊠ *3337½ W. 8th St., Hollywood*
☎ *213/427–0601* ⊕ *www.guelaguetzarestaurante.com* ✛ *2:H4.*

$ **✕Lotería! Grill Hollywood.** After drawing an almost cultlike following
MEXICAN from a stand in the Farmers Market, Lotería! takes on Hollywood
☺ with a sleek sit-down restaurant with essentially the same time-tested
menu. Start with banana squash and corn soup or *chicharron de queso*
(a crunchy, paper-thin sheet of addictive griddle-toasted cheese) with
guacamole while sipping on the tequila you've selected from a long list.
Then tuck into tacos or burritos stuffed with *epazote*-spiced mushrooms
and cheese, meatballs in tomato-chipotle sauce, or *cochinita pibil* (Yuca-
tán-style pork). To tame the heat, nothing soothes the palate like its
homemade Mexican ice cream. ⊠ *6627 Hollywood Blvd., Hollywood*
☎ *323/465–2500* ⊕ *www.loteriagrill.com* ✛ *2:F1.*

$$ **✕Musso & Frank Grill.** Liver and onions, lamb chops, goulash, shrimp
AMERICAN Louis salad, dry gin martinis, gruff waiters—you'll find all the old favor-
ites here in Hollywood's oldest restaurant. A film-industry hangout
since it opened in 1919, Musso & Frank still attracts the working studio
set to its maroon faux-leather booths, along with tourists and locals
nostalgic for Hollywood's golden era. Great breakfasts are served all
day, but the kitchen's famous "flannel cakes" (pancakes) are served only
until 3 pm. ⊠ *6667 Hollywood Blvd., Hollywood* ☎ *323/467–7788*
☺ *Closed Sun. and Mon.* ✛ *2:F1.*

$$$ **✕Osteria Mozza.** Born from the immensely popular collaboration
ITALIAN between celebrated bread maker Nancy Silverton (founder of L.A.'s
La Brea Bakery and Campanile) and Iron Chef Mario Batali, Osteria
Mozza features candlelit, linen-clad tables surrounding a central mar-
ble-topped mozzarella bar, ideal for solo diners. From that bar come
several presentations of velvety *burrata* cheese and perfectly dressed
salads, while the kitchen turns out an oversize *raviolo* oozing ricotta
and egg in brown butter sauce, blissful sweetbreads piccata and grilled
whole *orata* (Mediterranean sea bream), capped off with Italian cheeses
and delicious rosemary–olive oil cakes. If you can't score a reservation
here, treat yourself to the partners' pizzeria next door. ⊠ *6602 Melrose*

Ave., Hollywood ☎ *323/297–0100* ⊕ *www.mozza-la.com* ⌂ *Reservations essential* ⊙ *No lunch* ✛ *2:E3.*

¢ ✕ **Pink's Hot Dogs.** Orson Welles ate 18 of these hot dogs in one sitting,
AMERICAN and you, too, will be tempted to order more than one. The chili dogs are
⟳ the main draw, but the menu has expanded to include a Martha Stewart
Dog (a 10-inch frank topped with mustard, relish, onions, tomatoes,
sauerkraut, bacon, and sour cream). Since 1939, Angelenos and tourists alike have been lining up to plunk down some modest change for
one of the greatest guilty pleasures in L.A. Pink's is open until 3 am
on weekends. ⊠ *709 N. La Brea Ave., Hollywood* ☎ *323/931–4223*
⊕ *www.pinkshollywood.com* ⌂ *Reservations not accepted* ▬ *No credit
cards* ✛ *2:E3.*

$$ ✕ **Pizzeria Mozza.** The other, more casual half of Batali and Silverton's
ITALIAN partnership (the first being Osteria Mozza), this casual venue gives
Fodor's Choice newfound eminence to the humble "pizza joint." With traditional
★ Mediterranean items like white anchovies, lardo, squash blossoms, and
Gorgonzola, Mozza's pies—thin-crusted delights with golden, blistered
edges—are much more Campania than California, and virtually every
one is a winner. Antipasti include simple salads, roasted bone marrow,
and platters of *salumi*. All sing with vibrant flavors thanks to superb
market-fresh ingredients, and daily specials may include favorites like
lasagna. Like the menu, the wine list is both interesting and affordable.
⊠ *641 N. Highland Ave., Hollywood* ☎ *323/297–0101* ⌂ *Reservations
essential* ✛ *2:E3.*

$$$$ ✕ **Providence.** Chef-owner Michael Cimarusti has elevated Providence
SEAFOOD to the ranks of America's finest seafood restaurants. The elegant dining
Fodor's Choice room, outfitted with subtle nautical accents, is smoothly overseen by co-
★ owner–general manager Donato Poto. Obsessed with quality and freshness, the meticulous chef maintains a network of specialty purveyors,
some of whom tip him off to their catch before it even hits the dock.
This exquisite seafood then gets the Cimarusti treatment of French technique, traditional American themes, and Asian accents, often presented
in elaborate tasting menus. Pastry chef Adrian Vasquez's exquisite desserts are not to be missed; consider a three- to eight-course dessert tasting menu. ⊠ *5955 Melrose Ave., Hollywood* ☎ *323/460–4170* ⊙ *No
lunch Mon.–Thurs. and weekends* ✛ *2:F3.*

¢ ✕ **Roscoe's House of Chicken 'n Waffles.** Don't be put off by the name of
SOUTHERN this casual eatery, which honors a late-night combo popularized in
⟳ Harlem jazz clubs. Roscoe's is *the* place for real down-home Southern cooking. Just ask the patrons, who drive from all over L.A. for
Roscoe's bargain-price fried chicken, wonderful waffles (which, by the
way, turn out to be a great partner for fried chicken), buttery chicken
livers, and toothsome grits. Although Roscoe's has the intimate feel
of a smoky jazz club, those musicians hanging out here are just taking five. ⊠ *1514 N. Gower St., Hollywood* ☎ *323/466–7453* ⊕ *www.
roscoeschickenandwaffles.com* ⌂ *Reservations not accepted* ✛ *2:F2.*

$$$ ✕ **STREET.** Celebrity chef Susan Feniger pays homage to her love of travel
INTERNATIONAL and street food at her new restaurant in the heart of Hollywood. The
unpretentious locale has tapped into the wanderlust of diners with
its eclectic menu of small plate offerings, salads, entrées, and desserts

10

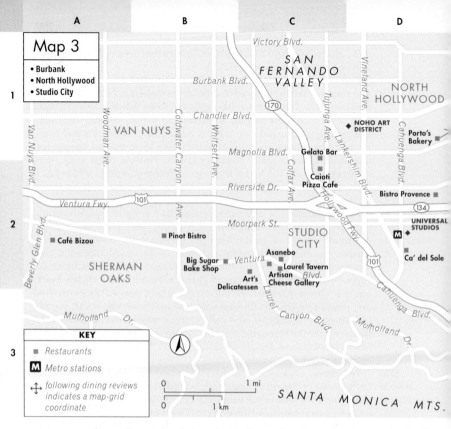

Map 3

- Burbank
- North Hollywood
- Studio City

Victory Blvd.

SAN FERNANDO VALLEY

NORTH HOLLYWOOD

Burbank Blvd.

Chandler Blvd.

VAN NUYS

Magnolia Blvd.

Riverside Dr.

NOHO ART DISTRICT

Porto's Bakery

■ Gelato Bar

■ Caioti Pizza Cafe

■ Bistro Provence

Ventura Fwy.

Moorpark St.

STUDIO CITY

UNIVERSAL STUDIOS

🅼

■ Café Bizou

■ Pinot Bistro

SHERMAN OAKS

■ Big Sugar Bake Shop

Ventura

■ Asanebo

■ Laurel Tavern

■ Artisan Cheese Gallery

Blvd.

■ Ca' del Sole

■ Art's Delicatessen

Mulholland Dr.

Mulholland Dr.

KEY

■ Restaurants

🅼 Metro stations

✛ following dining reviews indicates a map-grid coordinate

0   1 mi

0   1 km

SANTA MONICA MTS.

---

from all over the globe. Choose from Ukranian spinach *varenky* (fried dumplings made with spinach and salted cheese), curried mussels with chorizo, Vietnamese-spiced corn, Korean rice salad, or hearty Singapore chili crab. Finish up with Turkish donuts and a cup of Hong Kong milk tea. While this place is often milling with celebrities who call L.A. home, the atmosphere is decidedly friendly and casual. ✉ *742 N. Highland Blvd., Hollywood* ☎ *323/203–0500* ⊕ *www.eatatstreet.com* ✛ *2:F3.*

\$

AMERICAN

✕ **25 Degrees.** Named after the difference in temperature between a medium-rare and well-done burger, this upscale burger joint sits in one of Hollywood's hippest hotels. The action at 25 Degrees revolves around a counter constructed of rich oak instead of Formica, and cabernet is favored over cola. Order the #1 (caramelized onions, Gorgonzola and Crescenza cheeses, bacon, arugula, and Thousand Island dressing) or create your own masterpiece from a selection of premium meats, artisanal cheeses, and house-made condiments. A long list of half-bottles makes wine pairings easy for solo diners. They're open 24 hours—and mercifully do offer other items, including a good fried egg sandwich, if you're unsure about burgers for breakfast. ✉ *Hollywood Roosevelt Hotel, 7000 Hollywood Blvd., Hollywood* ☎ *323/785–7244* ⊕ *www.25degreesrestaurant.com* ⌂ *Reservations not accepted* ✛ *2:E2.*

¢

MIDDLE EASTERN

✕ **Zankou Chicken.** Forget the Colonel. Zankou's aromatic, Armenian-style rotisserie chicken with perfectly crisp, golden skin is one of L.A.'s truly great budget meals. It's served with pita bread, veggies, hummus, and unforgettable garlic sauce. If this doesn't do it for you, try the kebabs, falafel, or sensational *shawarma* (spit-roasted lamb or chicken) plates. ✉ *5065 W. Sunset Blvd., Hollywood* ☎ *323/665–7845* ⊕ *www. zankouchicken.com* ⌕ *Reservations not accepted* ✛ *2:H2.*

NORTH HOLLYWOOD

$$ ⨯ **Ca' del Sole.** With antique wood hutches, copper moldings, and a fire-
ITALIAN place, this studio-area establishment draws a diverse clientele in search of grilled octopus drizzled with a lemon vinaigrette, soulful spaghetti carbonara, pumpkin-filled *mezzelune* (half moon–shaped ravioli), and classic osso buco. The wine list is moderately priced and, weather permitting, you can sit in the walled patio that, despite its proximity to L.A. traffic, feels wonderfully escapist. ✉ *4100 Cahuenga Blvd., North Hollywood* ☎ *818/985–4669* ⊕ *www.cadelsole.com* ⊘ *No lunch Sat.* ✛ *3:D2.*

STUDIO CITY

$ ⨯ **Artisan Cheese Gallery.** Taste your way through triple creams, blues,
DELI goats milk, and stinky cheeses from all over the globe at this charming
☾ locale that offers cheese and charcuterie plates, sandwiches, oversize salads, and hot panini sandwiches. Taste-testing is encouraged, so don't be shy to ask. Grab a table in small outdoor patio and enjoy the neighborhood scenery; it's a great way to experience the Valley. ✉ *12023 Ventura Blvd., Studio City* ☎ *818/762–1221* ⊕ *www.artisancheesegallery.com* ⌕ *Reservations not accepted* ✛ *3:C2.*

$$$ ⨯ **Asanebo.** Don't let its nondescript minimal location deter you:
JAPANESE Asanebo is one of L.A.'s finest Japanese restaurants—and still relatively undiscovered. Once strictly a sashimi bar, this congested but inviting establishment introduced top-quality sushi to satisfy increasing local demand and also offers a wealth of innovative dishes. From a simple morsel of pristine fish dusted with sea salt to intricately cooked items, Asanebo continues to impress. The affable chefs will introduce you to memorable specialties such as a caviar-topped lobster cocktail and succulent seared *toro* (tuna belly) drizzled with a light garlic cream. ✉ *11941 Ventura Blvd., Studio City* ☎ *818/760–3348* ⌕ *Reservations essential* ⊘ *Closed Mon. No lunch weekends* ✛ *3:C2.*

¢ ⨯ **Laurel Tavern.** This rustic modern pub found along traffic-heavy Ven-
AMERICAN tura Boulevard replaced one of the swankier nightclubs along the strip. But locals—who work in the film and television industry in the area—quickly pledged their allegiance to this classic American pub that serves gourmet bar food and craft beers. The eatery comes in one handsome package of exposed brick, leather padded walls, and two huge picture windows. The menu is classic burgers, beers, and fries, but with a gourmet twist. Top choices include chorizo sliders, pork belly skewers, the Laurel Burger, and roasted marrowbones. There are 10 beers on draft that range from $5 to $6 handpicked by the restaurant's "beer chick." ✉ *11938 Ventura Blvd., Studio City* ☎ *818/506–0777* ⊕ *www. laureltavern.net* ⊘ *No lunch* ✛ *3:C2.*

$$$$ ⨯ **Vibrato Grill, Jazz, etc.** Co-owned by trumpeter Herb Albert, Vibrato
AMERICAN takes a high-road approach to a jazz club: this is a stylish, acoustically

10

Snacking at the Market

The landmark Los Angeles Farmers Market, at the corner of 3rd Street and Fairfax Avenue, is crammed with delicious food from all corners of the globe. Most spots are fast-food–style eateries sharing a common seating area—good for people-watching. An authentic *croque monsieur* sandwich, as well as crepes both savory and sweet, are available at the **French Crepe Company** (☎ 323/934-3113 ⊕ www.frenchcrepe.com). You can find more French specialties like coq au vin or beef bourguignon at the cozy, sit-down **Monsieur Marcel** (☎ 323/939-7792 ⊕ www.mrmarcel.com) wine bar and bistro. For a taste of the Mediterranean, stop by **Ulysses Voyage** (☎ 323/939-9728 ⊕ www. ulyssesvoyage.com), another full-service charmer, for classics like spanakopita and moussaka. Some of the city's best tacos, wrapped in freshly made tortillas, are found at **Lotería! Grill Hollywood** (☎ 323/930-2211 ⊕ www.loteriagrill.com), and folks line up for the bold flavors of Louisiana—including decent jambalaya and one of the few authentic New Orleans–style muffuletta sandwiches in L.A.—at the **Gumbo Pot** (☎ 323/933-0358 ⊕ www.thegumbopotla.com). **Bob's Coffee & Doughnuts** (☎ 323/933-8929) is legendary for its raspberry-filled bismarck donuts, and some of L.A.'s most beloved pies are peddled at **Du-par's** (☎ 323/933-8446).

The original spirit of the Farmers Market has been preserved despite the aggressive development of some adjoining commercial property. At **The Grove** shopping center next door, restaurants include **Morels** (☎ 323/965-9595), a French bistro and steak house with a winning patio, and **La Piazza** (☎ 323/933-5050 ⊕ www.lapiazzaonline.com), where thin-crusted pizzas are the best bet. Also adjacent to the Farmers Market is **Wood Ranch BBQ & Grill** (☎ 323/937-6800 ⊕ www. woodranch.com), where hordes of devotees line up at the door for heaping portions of ribs.

perfect venue where every table has a sight line to the stage. The kitchen is as notable as the music; it turns out contemporary American fare such as sea bass with parsley *pistou*, macaroni and cheese with bacon-brioche crust, and USDA Prime steaks. Art on the walls was painted by the Grammy-winning owner himself. ⊠ *2930 Beverly Glen Circle, Bel Air* ☎ *310/474–9400* ⊕ *www.vibratogrilljazz.com* ⌂ *Reservations essential* ⊙ *Closed Mon. No lunch.* ✛ *4:D1.*

BEVERLY HILLS AND THE WESTSIDE

Never short on sophistication, these two neighborhoods are known for their high-profile eateries that often have paparazzi camped outside. Beverly Hills, which has taken a hit during the economic times, still has some of the most expensive restaurants in town. From upscale steak houses and French bistros to sushi establishments that top their sashimi with caviar, this neighborhood doesn't skimp on decadence. The Westside has a cutting-edge dining scene that's slightly more family-friendly, with more moderate and casual spots.

BEVERLY HILLS

$$
DELI
✕ **Barney Greengrass.** Unlike your corner lox-and-bagel joint, this haute deli on the fifth floor of Barneys department store has an appropriately runway-ready aesthetic: limestone floors, mahogany furniture, and a wall of windows. On the outdoor terrace, at tables shaded by large umbrellas, you can savor flawless smoked salmon, sturgeon, and white-fish flown in fresh from New York. The deli closes at 6 pm. ⊠ *Barneys, 9570 Wilshire Blvd., Beverly Hills* ☎ *310/777–5877* ✛ *2:H6.*

$$$$
SPANISH
✕ **The Bazaar by José Andrés.** Celebrity Spanish chef José Andrés conquers L.A. with a multifaceted concept that includes two dining rooms (one classic, one modern, each with a tapas bar), a cocktail bar stocked with liquid nitrogen, and a flashy pâtisserie. There are even roaming pushcarts dispensing foie gras wrapped in cotton candy. Half of the menu is dedicated to traditional Spanish tapas: creamy chicken croquetas, *bacalao* (salt cod) fritters with honey aïoli, and plates of chorizo or prized jamón Ibérico. The other half involves some wild inventions of molecular gastronomy inspired by Andrés' mentor Ferran Adrià of world-famous El Bulli restaurant in Spain. Among the latter are "liquid" olives (created through a technique called spherification), and an ethereal version of the traditional tortilla Española in which an egg is cooked slowly at 63 degrees, just short of coagulation. A splendid list of Spanish wines is offered. For dessert, items like beet meringue with pistachios and chocolate lollipops await. ⊠ *SLS Hotel at Beverly Hills, 465 S. La Cienega Blvd., Beverly Hills* ☎ *310/246–5555* ⊕ *www.thebazaar.com* ⌂ *Reservations essential* ✛ *2:C3.*

$$$$
AMERICAN
✕ **The Belvedere.** In the entertainment industry's A-list hotel, the Peninsula, you're sure to be rubbing elbows with power brokers. The refined

10

cooking here elevates the opulent Belvedere far above the usual hotel dining room. You may want to start with the signature house-smoked salmon with scallion pancakes, chive crème fraîche, and caviar, then indulge in osso bucco, Kansas City strip steak, or grilled Alaskan halibut with pomegranate gastrique. At lunch, deal makers convene over whimsical small bites (e.g., tuna and hamachi lollipops with mango-sesame sauce), salads, and "glamburgers" like sautéed salmon with pinot noir–cured onions. Of course, the execs who favor this place are prone to special ordering—and the staff graciously obliges. ⊠ *9882 S. Santa Monica Blvd., Beverly Hills* ☎ *310/788–2306* ⊕ *www.peninsula.com* ✛ *2:F6.*

$$$
FRENCH
Fodor's Choice
★

✕ **Bouchon Bistro.** Famed chef Thomas Keller finally made it to Los Angeles and has set up his French bistro in swanky Beverly Hills. Grand and majestic, but still casual and friendly, there is nothing about a night at Bouchon that doesn't make you feel pampered. With little details that separate it from the pack, there's filtered Norwegian water served at every table, a twig-shaped baguette made fresh in the kitchen, and an expansive wine list celebrating California wines. It's a foodie scene that welcomes L.A.'s high-profile chefs, celebrities, and locals. Start with its classic onion soup that arrives with a bubbling lid of cheese or the salmon rillettes, which are big enough to share. For dinner, there's a traditional steak and frites, roasted chicken, steamed Maine mussels, and a delicious grilled *croque madame*. Bouchon Bistron is also known for its beautiful French pastries. For a sweet bite, order an espresso and the profiteroles or the Bouchons (bite-size brownies served with homemade vanilla ice cream). Ask for a tour of the kitchen for a sneak peek inside the operation. ⊠ *235 N. Canon Dr., Beverly Hills* ☎ *310/271–9910* ⊕ *www.bouchonbistro.com* ⌂ *Reservations essential* ✛ *2:H6.*

$$$$
VIETNAMESE

✕ **Crustacean.** A perennially hot scene, this head-turning venue of San Francisco's An family is a surreal reproduction of colonial Vietnam. Exotic fish swim in a floor-to-ceiling aquarium and through a glass-topped "river" sunk into the marble floor underfoot, which meanders toward the bar. The French-influenced Southeast Asian menu includes lemongrass–scented bouillabaisse and filet mignon with ponzu glaze. Colossal tiger prawns and whole Dungeness crab simmered in sake, Chardonnay, and Cognac parade out of the "secret kitchen" where only An family members are allowed, thereby protecting treasured recipes. ⊠ *9646 Santa Monica Blvd., Beverly Hills* ☎ *310/205–8990* ⊕ *www. anfamily.com* ⌂ *Reservations essential* ☽ *No lunch weekends* ✛ *2:G5.*

$$$$
STEAK

✕ **CUT.** In a true collision of artistic titans, celebrity chef Wolfgang Puck presents his take on steak-house cuisine in a space designed by Getty Center architect Richard Meier. The restaurant's contemporary lines and cold surfaces recall few of the comforts of this beloved culinary tradition. And, like Meier's design, Puck's fare doesn't dwell much on the past; a thoroughly modern Crab Louis salad is the closest thing to nostalgia on the menu. Playful dishes like bone-marrow flan take center stage before diners dive into perfectly dry-aged and seared hunks of Nebraskan sirloin—a few bites prove that the Austrian-born super-chef understands our beefy American love affair. ⊠ *Regent Beverly Wilshire, 9500 Wilshire Blvd., Beverly Hills* ☎ *310/276–8500* ⊕ *www.*

CLOSE UP

Local Chains Worth Stopping For

It's said that the drive-in burger joint was invented in L.A., probably to meet the demands of an ever-mobile car culture. Burger aficionados line up at all hours outside **In-N-Out Burger** (⊕ *www.in-n-out.com*, multiple locations), still a family-owned operation whose terrific made-to-order burgers are revered by Angelenos. Visitors may recognize the chain as the infamous spot where Paris Hilton got nabbed for drunk driving, but locals are more concerned with getting their burger fix off the "secret" menu, with variations like "Animal Style" (mustard-grilled patty with grilled onions and extra spread), a "4 x 4" (four burger patties and four cheese slices, for big eaters) or the bun-less "Protein Style" that comes wrapped in a bibb of lettuce. The company's Web site lists explanations for other popular secret menu items.

Tommy's sells a delightfully sloppy chili burger; the original location (✉ *2575 Beverly Blvd., Los Angeles* ☎ *213/389–9060*) is a no-frills culinary landmark. For rotisserie chicken that will make you forget the Colonel forever, head to **Zankou Chicken** (✉ *5065 Sunset Blvd., Hollywood* ☎ *323/665–7845* ⊕ *www.zankouchicken.com*), a small chain noted for its golden crispy-skinned birds, potent garlic sauce, and Armenian specialties. Homesick New Yorkers will appreciate **Jerry's Famous Deli** (✉ *10925 Weyburn Ave., Westwood* ☎ *310/208–3354* ⊕ *www. jerrysfamousdeli.com*), where the massive menu includes all the classic deli favorites. With a lively bar scene, good barbecued ribs, and contemporary takes on old favorites, the more upscale **Houston's** (✉ *202 Wilshire Blvd., Santa Monica* ☎ *310/576–7558* ⊕ *www.hillstone.com*) is a popular local hangout. And **Señor Fish** (✉ *422 E. 1st St., Downtown* ☎ *213/625–0566* ⊕ *www.senor-fish.com*) is known for its healthy Mexican seafood specialties, such as scallop burritos and ceviche tostadas.

10

The *croque madame* from Bouchon Bistro.

wolfgangpuck.com ⚓ *Reservations essential* ⊘ *Closed Sun. No lunch* ✛ *2:H6.*

$$ ✕**Da Pasquale.** In a neighborhood dominated by the likes of Gucci and
ITALIAN   Prada, an affordable meal is harder to spot than a pair of sensible shoes.
And that's one reason to visit Da Pasquale. An even better reason is the
wonderful thin-crust pizza topped with ingredients like fresh tomato,
garlic, and basil or three cheeses with prosciutto. The kitchen also excels
at familiar pastas and roasted chicken. Despite talent-agency regulars,
the homey Old Napoli interior and friendly staff makes everybody feel
welcome. ⊠ *9749 S. Santa Monica Blvd., Beverly Hills* ☎ *310/859–
3884* ⊕ *www.dapasqualecaffe.com* ⊘ *Closed Sun. and Mon. No lunch
Sat.* ✛ *2:G6.*

$$$ ✕**Enoteca Drago.** High-flying Sicilian chef Celestino Drago scores with
ITALIAN   this sleek but unpretentious version of an *enoteca* (a wine bar serving
small snacks). It's an ideal spot for skipping through an Italian wine
list—more than 50 wines are available by the glass—and enjoying a
menu made up of small plates such as stuffed olives, an assortment of
cheeses and *salumi*, ricotta-stuffed zucchini flowers, or *crudo* (Italy's
answer to ceviche) from the raw bar. Although the miniature mush-
room-filled ravioli bathed in foie gras–truffle sauce is a bit luxurious
for an enoteca, it's one of the city's best pasta dishes. Larger portions
and pizzas are also available here, but the essence of an enoteca is preserved. ⊠ *410 N. Cañon Dr., Beverly Hills* ☎ *310/786–8236* ⊕ *www.
celestinodrago.com* ⚓ *Reservations essential* ✛ *2:H5.*

$$$ ✕**The Grill on the Alley.** Beverly Hills restaurants can take you many
AMERICAN places, from Provence to Polynesia, but in this case it's just up the
Golden State Freeway to a traditional San Francisco–style grill with

dark-wood paneling and brass trim. This clubby chophouse, where movie industry execs power-lunch creates tasty, simple American fare, including steaks, chicken potpies, and Cobb salad. If you've really made it in Hollywood, you've got your usual booth at the Grill. ✉ *9560 Dayton Way, Beverly Hills* ☎ *310/276–0615* ⊕ *www.thegrill.com* ⬧ *Reservations essential* ⊘ *No lunch Sun.* ✛ *2:H6.*

$$ ✕ **Kate Mantilini.** Casual but cool, this is a good place to remember for

AMERICAN brunch on weekends or a late-night snack (open until midnight on weekends). The lengthy menu lines up all-American staples like New England clam chowder, macaroni and cheese, meat loaf, and a white chili made with white beans and chicken. Despite its truck stop/diner–style comfort food, the cavernous ultramodern space exudes a hip urban vibe and prices are much more Beverly Hills than *Smallville.* ✉ *9101 Wilshire Blvd., Beverly Hills* ☎ *310/278–3699* ✛ *2:C4.*

$$$ ✕ **Matsuhisa.** Freshness and innovation are the hallmarks of this flagship

JAPANESE restaurant of Nobu Matsuhisa's empire. The prolific chef-restaurateur had planned on closing it in favor of his newer, more glamorous Nobu up the street, but ultimately bowed to clamoring protests from loyal patrons. The surprisingly modest-looking place draws celebrities and serious sushi buffs alike. Here you can encounter such dishes as the Chilean sea bass with foie gras, fresh scallop sashimi with black garlic sauce and kiwi, or kampachi served with *agua de chili.* Reflecting his past stint in Peru, Matsuhisa incorporates intriguing Latin ingredients into traditional Japanese cuisine. Daring diners should ask for the *omakase,* a seven-course chef selected menu for an amazing culinary experience (with a tab to match). ✉ *129 N. La Cienega Blvd., Beverly Hills* ☎ *310/659–9639* ⊕ *www.nobumatsuhisa.com* ⬧ *Reservations essential* ⊘ *No lunch weekends* ✛ *2:C4.*

$$$ ✕ **Oliverio.** This restaurant in the Avalon Hotel, an eco-friendly property

ITALIAN in a renovated 1950s apartment complex, feels straight out of the *Valley of the Dolls* movie. Mid-century design gives vintage appeal that blends in with the restaurant's modern Italian cuisine and Californian sensibility. Fresh food concepts are created by chef Mirko Padernois who uses seasonal ingredients inspired from the hotel's rooftop garden. Enjoy a starter of fritto misto or a cauliflower soufflé, for dinner try the braised lamb tortelli, beef short ribs, or a risotto Milanese. Reserve a private cabana poolside to eat your dessert underneath the stars while enjoying Southern California's patio lifestyle. ✉ *9400 W. Olympic Ave., Beverly Hills* ☎ *310/277–5221* ⊕ *www.avalonbeverlyhills.com* ✛ *2:B4.*

10

$$$ ✕ **Spago Beverly Hills.** The famed flagship restaurant of Wolfgang Puck

NEW AMERICAN is justifiably a modern L.A. classic. Spago centers on a buzzing out-

Fodor's Choice door courtyard shaded by 100-year-old olive trees. From an elegantly

★ appointed table inside, you can glimpse the exhibition kitchen and, on rare occasions, the affable owner greeting his famous friends (these days, compliments to the chef are directed to Lee Hefter). The people-watching here is worth the price of admission, but the clientele is surprisingly inclusive, from the biggest Hollywood stars to Midwestern tourists to foodies more preoccupied with vintages of Burgundy than with faces from the cover of *People.* Foie gras has disappeared, but the daily-changing menu might offer a four-cheese pizza topped with

Good Morning, L.A.

In L.A., many a big-screen mega-hit has been conceived over a breakfast of yogurt-and-granola or huevos rancheros.

Hugo's. At Hugo's, one of the city's top morning destinations, breakfast specialties include pumpkin pancakes and "Pasta Mama" (pasta scrambled with eggs, garlic, and Parmesan cheese). ✉ *8401 Santa Monica Blvd., West Hollywood* ☎ *323/654-3993* ⊕ *www.hugosrestaurant.com.*

Culina. A new favorite amongst healthy Hollywood is Culina. Order from its versatile breakfast menu that offers whole-wheat pancakes with pomegrante maple syrup and a sinless Eggs Benedict. ✉ *Four Seasons Hotel, 300 S. Doheny Dr., Beverly Hills* ☎ *310/273-2222* ⊕ *www. culinarestaurant.com.*

Griddle Café. Big breaks might be found at the Griddle Café. Tuck into "Black Magic" flapjacks (filled with Oreo cookie crumbs) or the red velvet panCake topped with swirls of cream cheese frosting. ✉ *7916 Sunset Blvd., Hollywood* ☎ *323/874-0377* ⊕ *www. thegriddlecafe.com.*

John O'Groats. For a thoroughly unpretentious L.A. morning experience, head over to the Westside's John O'Groats, where the good old-fashioned American breakfasts are accompanied by signature homemade biscuits. ✉ *10516 W. Pico Blvd., West L.A.* ☎ *310/204-0692* ⊕ *www. ogroatsrestaurant.com.*

Euro Pane Bakery. In Pasadena, folks line up at Euro Pane Bakery, a cozy French bakery and café. ✉ *950 E. Colorado Blvd., Pasadena* ☎ *626/577-1828.*

Clementine. Over in Century City a modest café called Clementine reels in fans with fresh scones and buttermilk biscuit sandwiches stuffed with egg and ham. ✉ *1751 Ensley Ave.* ☎ *310/552-1080* ⊕ *www. clementineonline.com.*

Nate 'n Al. In Beverly Hills, New York expats huddle at Nate 'n Al over matzo brei or corned beef hash. ✉ *414 N. Beverly Dr.* ☎ *310/274-0101.*

Azalea Restaurant & Bar. For a Japanese breakfast, head to Azalea Restaurant & Bar at Little Tokyo's Kyoto Grand Hotel and Gardens. ✉ *120 S. Los Angles St.* ☎ *213/253-9235.*

---

truffles, *côte de boeuf* with Armagnac-peppercorn sauce, Cantonese-style duck, and some traditional Austrian specialties. Acclaimed pastry chef Sherry Yard works magic with everything from an ethereal apricot soufflé to Austrian *kaiserschmarrn* (crème fraîche pancakes with fruit). ✉ *176 N. Cañon Dr., Beverly Hills* ☎ *310/385-0880* ⊕ *www. wolfgangpuck.com* ⚱ *Reservations essential* ⊘ *No lunch Sun.* ✛ *2:H6.*

$$ ✕ **Tanzore.** The design and menu of a venerable traditional Indian restaurant has been dramatically transformed to create a totally new experience. Now lighter contemporary fare prepared with seasonal California ingredients—like coriander-crusted tuna with avocado raita (a yogurt-based condiment), tandoori sea bass, and wok-fried tofu masala—dominates the menu, while its colorful spaces encompass sleek blond wood surfaces, water features, a showy glass-ensconced wine cellar, and an

INDIAN

ultrahip lounge. ⊠ *50 N. La Cienega Blvd., Beverly Hills* ☎ *310/652–3894* ⊕ *www.tanzore.com* ⚖ *Reservations essential* ✛ *2:C4.*

$$$$
JAPANESE
Fodor'sChoice
★

✕ **Urasawa.** Shortly after celebrated sushi chef Masa Takayama packed his knives for the Big Apple, his soft-spoken protégé Hiroyuki Urasawa settled into the master's former digs. The understated sushi bar has few precious seats, resulting in incredibly personalized service. At a minimum of $350 per person for a strictly *omakase* (chef's choice) meal, Urasawa remains the priciest restaurant in town, but the endless parade of masterfully crafted, exquisitely presented dishes renders few regrets. The maple sushi bar, sanded daily to a satin-like finish, is where most of the action happens. You might be served velvety bluefin toro paired with beluga caviar, slivers of foie gras to self-cook *shabu shabu* style, or egg custard layered with *uni* (sea urchin), glittering with gold leaf. This is also the place to come during fugu season, when the legendary, potentially deadly blowfish is artfully served to adventurous diners. ⊠ *2 Rodeo, 218 N. Rodeo Dr., Beverly Hills* ☎ *310/247–8939* ⚖ *Reservations essential* ⊗ *Closed Monday. No lunch* ✛ *2:H6.*

BRENTWOOD

$$$
JAPANESE

✕ **Katsuya.** Katsuya indulges Angelenos' sushi bars mania, catering to a beautiful, trend-conscious clientele. This place ups the ante with a seductive, ultramodern look created by celebrated designer Philippe Starck, in which walls are lined with backlit murals of a geisha's face—glossy lips kiss the room's clientele from one wall, while kohl-rimmed eyes peer out from behind the sushi bar on another. Highly regarded sushi chef Katsuya Uechi turns out spicy tuna atop crispy rice, whimsical wonton cones filled with scoops of mousselike crab and tuna tartare, and larger plates like miso-marinated black cod. Don't neglect the plates from the *robata* bar, where skewers of veggies, seafood, and meats are grilled over hot coals. ⊠ *11777 San Vicente Blvd., Brentwood* ☎ *310/207–8744* ⊕ *www.sbe.com/katsuya* ⚖ *Reservations essential* ⊗ *No lunch weekends* ✛ *4:C2.*

$$$
ITALIAN

✕ **Pecorino.** San Vicente Boulevard is lined with trendy trattorias, but Pecorino presents a delightful compromise between old-world charm and modern L.A. sensibilities. Wrought-iron chandeliers hang from a beamed ceiling above a room dressed up with white-linen tablecloths and red velvet curtains while the pleasures of the namesake sheep's milk cheese are explored in simply sauced pastas and Abruzzese–style lamb casserole. A huge baked onion filled with eggplant, raisins, and pine nuts is a terrific vegetarian beginning; a plate of pecorino cheeses from every corner of Italy is a perfect finish. ⊠ *11604 San Vicente Blvd., Brentwood* ☎ *310/571–3800* ⊕ *www.pecorinorestaurant.com* ⚖ *Reservations essential* ⊗ *No lunch Sun.* ✛ *4:C2.*

CENTURY CITY

$$
ECLECTIC

✕ **Breadbar.** The art of bread hasn't always been celebrated in cardio-happy LA, but at Breadbar it's all grains and glory. Breadbar is known for its tasty house-made artisanal breads—redwood rye, Parmesan lavash, golden fig loaf, and a traditional rustic white. These loaves star (or co-star) in an appetizing array of sandwiches, salads and entrée dishes. Start with a bread basket and a cheese plate or an order of

10

Brandade from A.O.C.

steamed mussels in white wine sauce–perfect for dipping crusty bread. Order a grilled cheese, the signature corned beef, or a chopped frisée salad made with hazelnuts and feta cheese. Pair these with a crisp glass of white wine or a jasmine iced tea for a lazy lunch. Stop in for dinner and try the roasted chicken breast with mushroom sauce or tandoori chicken brochettes. A lively coffee bar makes this a great place to charge up before heading out for some L.A. shopping. ⊠ *10250 Santa Monica Blvd, Century City* ☎ *310/277–3770* ⊕ *www.breadbar.net* ⊹ *2:A4.*

$$$
NEW AMERICAN

✕ **Craft Los Angeles.** Prominent New York chef Tom Colicchio (star judge of TV's *Top Chef*) expands his burgeoning empire with this sleek Southern California outpost. Thanks to Century City's growing legions of Hollywood agents and lawyers, Craft has emerged as a major film industry hangout. In its open, airy dining room vaguely reminiscent of an elegant special-events tent, deals are brokered over lunches featuring seasonal, artisanal ingredients. In the evening, Craft is ideal for groups sharing plates from Colicchio's signature à la carte menu that changes daily to encompass the likes of roasted Peruvian octopus in *zatar* yogurt and roasted pineapple, braised beef short ribs, and veal sweetbreads with plums. Boutique produce goes into a plethora of side dishes, and desserts may include butterscotch pudding with dates and hazelnuts or beignets with blackberry honey and chocolate. The endless, non-descriptive menu can be frustrating and some dishes miss the mark— but just as many sparkle. ⊠ *10100 Constellation Blvd., Century City* ☎ *310/279–4180* ⊕ *www.craftrestaurant.com* ⌂ *Reservations essential* ☾ *No lunch weekends* ⊹ *2:A4.*

CULVER CITY

$$ ✕ **Fraîche.** Further fueling the transformation of unglamorous Culver
MEDITERRANEAN City into a not-to-be-missed dining destination is this smart-looking
restaurant where Gino Angelini (Angelini Osteria) protégé Jason Travi
celebrates flavors from both the French and Italian countryside. Ebul-
lient patrons begin with platters of cold seafood, boudin noir with
Dijon-crème fraîche, or porcini salad before moving on to pastas, lamb
spezzatino stew, or steak frites. The soul-warming fare is enhanced by
50-plus wines under $50 and desserts designed by Travi's wife, Miho.
The casually sophisticated stone-clad dining room, with tables spilling
onto the sidewalk, suits varied occasions. ✉ *9411 Culver Blvd., Culver
City* ☎ *310/839–6800* ⊕ *www.fraicherestaurant.com* ⌂ *Reservations
essential* ⊘ *No lunch weekends* ✛ *4:E3.*

$$$ ✕ **Gyenari.** Korean cuisine is emerging from L.A.'s Koreatown to the
KOREAN delight of a dining public craving a healthy, interactive experience,
and Gyenari is among a flurry of new mainstream Korean restaurants.
Named for a flower that blooms just once a year—a mural featuring
the blossom dominates a whole wall—this is a sleek, stylish restaurant
whose custom-made tables feature down-draft burners (excellent for
fanning away smokiness). While California influences appear, you can
find traditional "jap chae" cellophane noodles, *mandoo* (dumplings),
an ample selection of seafood, the requisite kimchi, and marinated
meats ranging from Wagyu beef to pork belly. ✉ *9540 Washington
Blvd., Culver City* ☎ *310/838–3131* ⊕ *www.gyenari.com* ⌂ *Reservations essential* ✛ *4:E3.*

¢ ✕ **Honey's Kettle Fried Chicken.** This family-operated business has updated
SOUTHERN the old-fashioned practice of kettle-cooking—frying its chicken with
intense heat in stainless steel drums, allowing the juices to be sealed
beneath a crackly, generously battered skin. This is soulful Southern
goodness, and for folks who appreciate this kind of food—it's a bit
greasy, but you can say that about any respectable fried chicken—Honey's is well worth a visit. In addition to the golden bird, the menu offers
a satisfying fried catfish, hot cakes, and some of the fluffiest biscuits
in town. Hang out on the patio with a glass of homemade lemonade
and observe the hipsters filing into the high-end eateries that surround
unpretentious Honey's. ✉ *9537 Culver Blvd., Culver City* ☎ *310/202–
5453* ⊕ *www.honeyskettle.com* ⌂ *Reservations not accepted* ✛ *4:E3.*

$ ✕ **Tender Greens.** Here, in the center of Culver City's burgeoning res-
AMERICAN taurant district, veterans from posh hotel kitchens turn out the kind of
fast food your mom, accountant, and nutritionist would unanimously
approve of—emphasizing health and value without compromising quality. After you stand in line for a bit, locally produced greens are tossed
in front of you in a big metallic bowl, plated with perfectly grilled
meats or fish. Enjoy a grilled-chicken Cobb salad or chipotle-barbecue
chicken salad with creamy lime dressing while sitting on the sidewalk
patio with a glass of homemade lemonade. ✉ *9523 Culver Blvd., Culver
City* ☎ *310/842–8300* ⊕ *www.tendergreensfood.com* ⌂ *Reservations
not accepted* ✛ *4:E3.*

$$ ✕ **Waterloo & City.** Found in a renovated, greasy spoon in the outskirts
BRITISH of downtown Culver City, Waterloo & City is a British gastropub that

10

has fine-dining lineage from its owners and kitchen staff. But the mood here is decidedly casual and definitely easygoing. A communal table anchors the lounge area, vintage mirrors adorn the walls, and suede banquettes make for cozy seating. Start your night with a pint or a cocktail and order from the beloved one-of-a-kind charcuterie menu, which has given this restaurant meat-curing street cred. Order the rabbit and pistachio terrine, duck and walnut paté, and pig trotters. Balance out the rich meats with an arugula salad tossed with roasted almonds, tangerines, and Parmesan cheese. The fettuccini with spicy Thai lobster, mussels, and lime is a fresh approach to pasta, and the lamb "bangers" and carrot "mash" is a great spin to an English classic. The sticky toffee pudding with salted caramel is an absolute must. ⊠ *12517 W. Washington Blvd., Culver City* ☎ *310/391–4222* ✛ *3:D4.*

WEST HOLLYWOOD

$$$
ITALIAN
Fodor'sChoice
★

✕ **Angelini Osteria.** You might not guess it from the modest, rather congested dining room, but this is one of L.A.'s most celebrated Italian restaurants. The key is chef-owner Gino Angelini's thoughtful use of superb ingredients, evident in dishes such as a salad of lobster, apples, and pomegranate; and pumpkin tortelli with butter, sage, and asparagus. An awesome lasagna verde, inspired by Angelini's grandmother, is not to be missed. Whole branzino, crusted in sea salt, and boldly flavored rustic specials (e.g., tender veal kidneys, rich oxtail stew) consistently impress. An intelligent selection of mostly Italian wines complements the menu, and desserts like the open-face chocolate tart with coffee cream and hazlenut gelato are baked fresh daily. ⊠ *7313 Beverly Blvd., West Hollywood* ☎ *323/297–0070* ⊕ *www.angelinoosteria.com* ☾ *Closed Mon. No lunch weekends* ✛ *2:E3.*

$$$
MEDITERRANEAN
Fodor'sChoice
★

✕ **A.O.C.** Since it opened in 2002, this restaurant and wine bar has revolutionized dining in L.A., pioneering the small-plate format that has now swept the city. The space is dominated by a long, candle-laden bar serving more than 50 wines by the glass. There's also a charcuterie bar, an L.A. rarity. The tapas-like menu is perfectly calibrated for the wine list; you could pick duck confit, warm salt cod tart with orange salad, an indulgent slab of pork rillettes (a sort of pâté), or just plunge into one of the city's best cheese selections. Named for the acronym for Appellation d'Origine Contrôlée, the regulatory system that ensures the quality of local wines and cheeses in France, A.O.C. upholds the standard of excellence. ⊠ *8022 W. 3rd St., West Hollywood* ☎ *323/653–6359* ⊕ *www.aocwinebar.com* ⚅ *Reservations essential* ☾ *No lunch* ✛ *2:D3.*

$$
AMERICAN

✕ **BLD.** Chef Neal Fraser leaves his high-end cuisine behind at Grace, just down the street, to concentrate on simple, approachable fare at this casual yet sophisticated eatery open from morning to night. With its versatile menu, you can enjoy a vegan Benedict (house-smoked tofu bacon, veggie patty, wilted arugula, dairy-free hollandaise) or ricotta-blueberry pancakes in the morning; snack on an excellent selection of cheeses and charcuterie, enjoy a Vietnamese Ribeye Bahn Mi sandwich, or an all-American burger for lunch; and then tuck into a steak at dinner. Prices are reasonable, too, which helps explain the line out the door. ⊠ *7450 Beverly Blvd., West Hollywood* ☎ *323/930–9744* ⊕ *www.bldrestaurant.com* ✛ *2:E3.*

$$$
STEAK

✕ **BLT Steak.** BLT Steak now occupies the Sunset Strip building formerly home to legendary film industry hangout Le Dôme; the space is now more casual and sparingly decorated, with a hip vibe and a vague bistro essence. Certified Angus beef is the main attraction here, which should be enjoyed after a refreshing start of oysters from the raw bar or kampachi sashimi spiked with yuzu and kumquats. Pass on the domestic Wagyu (which lacks the consistency of the Japanese product) and hanger steak (too chewy). Instead, enjoy a big red wine with the bone-in rib eye or fillet with a Béarnaise sauce worthy of a real French bistro, and finish with a killer peanut butter–chocolate mousse. ⊠ *8720 Sunset Blvd., West Hollywood* ☎ *310/360–1950* ⊕ *www.bltrestaurants. com* ⌂ *Reservations essential* ⊗ *No lunch* ✛ *2:C2.*

$$
ITALIAN

✕ **Ca' Brea.** Starters steal the show at this reliable spot—try the *formaggio*—baked goat cheese wrapped in pancetta and served atop a Popeye-size mound of spinach. Among the entrées, look for osso buco or the lamb chops with black truffle-spiked mustard sauce. A 2007 renovation after a fire resulted in warm blend of stone, brick, and Venetian plaster. ⊠ *346 S. La Brea Ave., West Hollywood* ☎ *323/938–2863* ⊕ *www. cabrearestaurant.com* ⊗ *Weekend brunch* ✛ *2:E4.*

$$$
MEDITERRANEAN

✕ **Campanile.** Chef-owner Mark Peel has mastered the mix of robust Mediterranean flavors with homey Americana. The 1926 building (which once housed the offices of Charlie Chaplin) exudes a lovely Renaissance charm and Campanile is one of L.A.'s most acclaimed and beloved restaurants. Appetizers may include fried risotto pancakes or a grapefruit and fennel salad, while pan-seared black cod with white bean–eggplant puree and grilled prime rib with tapenade are likely to appear as entrées. Thursday night, grilled cheese sandwiches are a huge draw, as the beloved five-and-dime classic is morphed into exotic creations. For an ultimate L.A. experience, come for weekend brunch on the enclosed patio. ⊠ *624 S. La Brea Ave., West Hollywood* ☎ *323/938–1447* ⊕ *www.campanilerestaurant.com* ⌂ *Reservations essential* ⊗ *No dinner Sun.* ✛ *2:E4.*

$
DELI
☾

✕ **Canter's.** This granddaddy of L.A. delicatessens (it opened in 1928) cures its own corned beef and pastrami and has an in-house bakery. It's not the best deli in town, or the friendliest, but it's a true L.A. classic and open 24/7. Next door is the Kibitz Room, where there's live music every night. ⊠ *419 N. Fairfax Ave., Fairfax District* ☎ *323/651–2030* ⊕ *www.cantersdeli.com* ⌂ *Reservations not accepted* ✛ *2:D3.*

10

$$$
SPANISH

✕ **Cobras & Matadors.** A bustling storefront spot whose cramped tables and long bar channel the aura of a Madrid side street, Cobras & Matadors hits the mark with quality ingredients and value-oriented pricing. Among the numerous appetizers and tapas are favorites like grilled squid salad, crispy green lentils, and charred green asparagus with walnut vinaigrette. Larger plates include the grilled Angus steak, pan-roasted white fish, and homemade paella. There's no wine list here, but no corkage fee either—bring a bottle from your own cellar or buy one from the owner's wine shop next door, where the intriguing inventory leans heavily toward Spanish vino. ⊠ *7615 Beverly Blvd., West Hollywood* ☎ *323/932–6178* ⊗ *No lunch* ✛ *2:D3.*

$$$
FRENCH

✕ **Comme Ça.** This brasserie from Sona chef David Myers, with polished service and a menu with something for everyone, is styled for those craving a decidedly French joie de vivre. Simple tables covered in butcher paper offset elegant antique mirrors, and a long chalkboard doubles as a wall. Comme Ça can't help but encourage an affair with food and wine. Savor specialties like tarte flambée, steak frites, and the Monday night special of perfectly roasted chicken for two. Drain a carafe of Côtes du Rhône with French cheeses before concluding with profiteroles or a chocolate-whiskey soufflé while you longingly imagine yourself in Montparnasse (at least your dollar stretches farther here). ⊠ *8479 Melrose Ave., West Hollywood* ☎ *323/782–1104* ⊕ *www. commecarestaurant.com* ⌕ *Reservations essential* ✛ *2:C3.*

$$$
NEW AMERICAN

✕ **The Foundry.** Ex-Patina chef Eric Greenspan is a bear of a young man whose passion is reflected in every aspect of his Streamline Moderne–inspired restaurant, from the live music in the lounge to his work station on the dining room side of an open kitchen, allowing him direct access to guests and immediate feedback. After starters like grape-glazed pork belly or the popular potato soup (made with leek-bacon bread pudding and Gruyère, and topped with a fried egg), Greenspan impresses with main courses such as monkfish adorned with carrots, sweet potato, and blood sausage, and a glammed-up rendition of beef short ribs. For a more relaxed environment, head to the covered patio, warmed by a fireplace and order a glass of wine and indulge in a butterscotch brulee. ⊠ *7465 Melrose Ave., West Hollywood* ☎ *323/651–0915* ⊕ *www.thefoundryonmelrose.com* ⌕ *Reservations essential* ◔ *No lunch* ✛ *2:E3.*

$$$$
FRENCH

✕ **Gordon Ramsay at the London.** The foul-mouthed celebrity chef from Fox's *Hell's Kitchen* demonstrates why he nevertheless ranks among the world's finest chefs at this fine-dining restaurant in a West Hollywood boutique hotel. Two pastel-color dining rooms with city views flank a formidable white marble bar, creating a space that feels trendy yet surprisingly unpretentious. A menu of small plates accommodates both light suppers and indulgent feasts alike. Highlights include crisp pork with figs, flilet mignon and braised short ribs, and a Maine Lobster with coconut froth and mushroom ravioli. To maximize the experience, consider one of the flexible tasting menus ($95 or $110), artfully crafted by Ramsay's local culinary team and orchestrated by a polished, gracious serving staff. ⊠ *The London, 1020 N. San Vicente Blvd., West Hollywood* ☎ *310/358–7788* ⌕ *Reservations essential* ✛ *2:C2.*

$$$
AMERICAN

✕ **Jar.** At this modern chophouse, refined style meets classic, comfort-food favorites. Chef Suzanne Tracht cooks up a hit parade of all-American dishes, executed with a refined touch. After crab-accented deviled eggs, dressed-up fried clams, or endive Caesar salad, consider a rack of lamb, roasted salmon, or a massive slab of tender pot roast that's a few steps above Mom's recipe. Appropriately, steaks also are stellar, and well-priced to boot. Homey desserts like rich chocolate pudding or banana cream pie summon a sweet ending. ⊠ *8225 Beverly Blvd., West Hollywood* ☎ *323/655–6566* ⊕ *www.thejar.com* ◔ *No lunch Mon.–Sat.* ✛ *2:D3.*

¢ ✕**Lemonade.** Take a seat on the patio of this charming L.A. eatery that
AMERICAN caters to locals in search of unique salads, fresh and comforting braised
meats, pot roast sandwiches, and—of course—fresh-squeezed lemon-
ade. Its seasonally driven menu pulls straight from the Farmer's Market. Try salads like fig, arugula, blue cheese, and balsamic dressing;
green tomato, sweet corn, pepitas, and ancho-chili dressing; or poached
chicken, green mango, jicama, and spicy dressing. The traditional short
rib sandwich hits the comfort food spot. Tangy and savory chicken
curries and stews round out the wonderfully diverse menu. ✉ *9001
Beverly Blvd, West Hollywood* ☎ *310/247–2500* ⊕ *www.lemonadela.
com* ✛ *2:C3.*

$$$ ✕**Lucques.** Formerly silent-film star Harold Lloyd's carriage house, this
NEW AMERICAN brick building has morphed into a chic restaurant that has elevated
chef/co-owner Suzanne Goin to national prominence. In her veggie-
intense contemporary American cooking, Goin uses finesse to balance
tradition and invention. Consider the Italian heirloom pumpkin soup
with sage and chestnut cream, Alaskan black cod with acorn squash
and chorizo–golden raisin vinaigrette, and short ribs with horseradish
cream. Finish with the likes of acacia honey panna cotta with blood
orange granita. ✉ *8474 Melrose Ave., West Hollywood* ☎ *323/655–
6277* ⊕ *www.lucques.com* ✍ *Reservations essential* ☾ *No lunch Sun.
and Mon.* ✛ *2:C3.*

$ ✕**Mandarette.** Clad in warm wood and copper finishes, this inviting
CHINESE café began as a casual spin-off of the Mandarin in Beverly Hills, but
Ⓒ the casual concept has outlasted its high-end originator. Start with
cucumber salad with spicy peanut dressing, scallion pancakes, or cur-
ried chicken dumplings before indulging in kung pao scallops or crispy
sesame beef. ✉ *8386 Beverly Blvd., West Hollywood* ☎ *323/655–6115*
⊕ *www.mandarettecafe.com* ✛ *2:D3.*

$$$ ✕**The Palm.** All the New York elements are present at this West Coast
STEAK replay of the famous Manhattan steak house—mahogany booths, tin
ceilings, a boisterous atmosphere, and no-nonsense waiters rushing you
through your cheesecake (flown in from the Bronx). This is where you'll
find the biggest and best lobster; good steaks, prime rib, and chops; and
great French-fried onion rings. ✉ *9001 Santa Monica Blvd., West Hollywood* ☎ *310/550–8811* ⊕ *www.thepalm.com* ✍ *Reservations essential*
☾ *No lunch weekends* ✛ *2:C3.*

$$$ ✕**Red O.** Rick Bayless's Los Angeles venture was met with a tinge of
MEXICAN cynicism upon its arrival, but with a luxurious resort setting, fun tequila
lounge, loveseat swings by the main bar, and a menu that blends classic
Mexican food with innovative ingredients, it's clear Red O has won over
the hearts and palates of everyone in town. Scoring a seat at Red O—a
celebrity hotbed often milling with young Hollywood types—makes
you privy to some of the best people-watching in town. Pull up a
white wicker chair and start your evening with a margarita made with
serrano pepper-infused syrup, and ask for the yellowtail ceviche that
comes with homemade tortilla chips. Small-plate offerings allow for
sampling: try the soft tacos made with braised short rib, and Sonoma
County lamb Colorado dish. The fresh corn and goat cheese tamales
are a tasty rendition of a Mexican classic and the shrimp empanaditas

10

seal the deal. ✉ *8155 Melrose Ave., West Hollywood* ☎ *323/655–5009* ⊕ *www.redorestaurant.com.*

$$
GREEK

✗ **Sofi.** Hidden from bustling, increasingly hip 3rd Street, this friendly little taverna offers all the Greek classics: dolmades, *taramasalata* (a creamy, salty dip made from fish roe), spanakopita, and souvlaki. The smart, casual dining room is more than comfortable, but consider sitting outside on the lovely bougainvillea-shaded garden patio. All that's missing is a view of the Aegean Sea. ✉ *8030¾ W. 3rd St., West Hollywood* ☎ *323/651–0346* ⊕ *www.sofisrestaurant.com* ✛ *2:D3.*

$$$
NEW AMERICAN

✗ **XIV.** Superchef Michael Mina and partners give an old Sunset Strip nightclub a glitzy makeover by über-designer Philippe Starck; it combines stainless steel, marble, and polished wood to arrive at a 21st-century urban château. Here diners select from a menu of intriguing, globally inspired but classically prepared small plates to create indulgent tasting menus. Consider dishes like crispy nuggets of pork belly with cashew puree, or duck breast paired with foie gras and lavender-honey jus. Generally just a few bites each, dishes are elegantly presented. Inventively composed cheese courses and desserts make lasting final impressions. A vegetarian counterpart is available for every menu selection. Truly ambitious diners opt for a taste of all 35 items, a culinary marathon priced at $250. ✉ *8117 Sunset Blvd., West Hollywood* ☎ *323/656–1414* ⊕ *www.xivla.com* ✍ *Reservations essential* ⊗ *No lunch* ✛ *4:D2.*

$$$
JAPANESE

✗ **Wa Sushi & Bistro.** Founded by three alums from trendsetting Matsuhisa, Wa offers a more personalized experience with comparable high-quality sushi and intriguing Japanese cooking. Particularly enticing are dishes enhanced with French-inspired sauces. For instance, Chilean sea bass is layered with foie gras and bathed in a port reduction, while Santa Barbara prawns crowned with uni are dosed with a perfect beurre blanc prepared on a rickety range behind the sushi bar. Although casual, Wa's second-story hillside location allows for seductive city views from a small handful of tables dressed up with linen and candles. ✉ *1106 N. La Cienega Blvd., West Hollywood* ☎ *310/854–7285* ✍ *Reservations essential* ⊗ *Closed Mon. No lunch* ✛ *2:D2.*

WEST LOS ANGELES

$
AMERICAN
Fodor's Choice
★

✗ **The Apple Pan.** A burger-insider haunt since 1947, this unassuming joint with a horseshoe-shaped counter—no tables here—turns out one heck of a good burger topped with Tillamook cheddar, plus an excellent hickory burger with barbecue sauce. You can also find great fries and, of course, an apple pie indulgent enough to christen the restaurant (although many regulars argue that the banana cream deserves the honor). Be prepared to wait, but the veteran countermen turn the stools at a quick pace. In the meantine, grab a cup of Sanka and enjoy a little L.A. vintage. ✉ *10801 W. Pico Blvd., West L.A.* ☎ *310/475–3585* ✍ *Reservations not accepted* ▭ *No credit cards* ⊗ *Closed Mon.* ✛ *4:D2.*

$$
INDIAN

✗ **Bombay Café.** Some of the menu items at Bombay Café are strictly authentic, others have been lightened up a bit to suit Southern California sensibilities, and a few are truly innovative (e.g., ginger margarita, California tandoori salad with lemon-cilantro dressing). Regulars (and there are many) swear by the chili-laden lamb *frankies* (burritolike snacks sold by vendors on the beaches of Bombay), *sev puri* (wafers topped with onions, potatoes, and chutneys), and Sindhi chicken, a complex poached-then-sautéed recipe with an exotically seasoned crust. ✉ *12021 W. Pico Blvd., West L.A.* ☎ *310/473–3388* ⊕ *www.bombaycafe-la.com* ✛ *4:C3.*

$ ✕ **La Serenata Gourmet.** With uncom-

MEXICAN   fortable chairs and crowds from the nearby Westside Pavilion boosting decibel levels, this branch of the East L.A. original isn't ideal for leisurely conversation. But the restaurant scores big points for its boldly flavored Mexican cuisine. Pork dishes and moles are delicious, but seafood is the real star—there are chubby *gorditas* (cornmeal pockets stuffed with shrimp), juicy shrimp enchiladas in tomatillo sauce, and flavorful grilled fish with cilantro or garlic sauce. If your experience with Mexican food has been on the Tex-Mex end of the spectrum, come here to broaden your taste buds' horizons. ✉ *10924 W. Pico Blvd., West L.A.* ☎ *310/441–9667* ⊕ *www.laserenataonline.com* ✛ *4:D2.*

$ ✕ **Monte Alban.** This family-owned café serves the subtle cooking of one

MEXICAN   of Mexico's most respected culinary regions, Oaxaca. Flavors here are

☯   intense without being fiery. Try their version of *chiles rellenos* (bright green chili peppers stuffed with chicken, raisins, and groundnuts); any of the complex moles ladled over chicken, pork, or salmon; or extra-tender stewed goat. For dessert, there's fried, sliced sweet plantains topped with crème fraîche that's *delicioso.* ✉ *11927 Santa Monica Blvd., West L.A.* ☎ *310/444–7736* ✛ *4:C2.*

$$ ✕ **Mori Sushi.** Only a small fish logo identifies the facade of this res-

JAPANESE   taurant, but many consider it the best sushi bar in L.A. and Mori-hiro Onodera one of the great sushi masters in America. The austere whitewashed space stands in contrast to the chef's artful presentations of pristine morsels of seafood, all served on ceramic plates he makes himself. Allow him to compose an entire meal for you—this can be an expensive proposition—and he'll send out eye-popping presentations of sushi or sashimi accented with touches of rare sea salts, yuzu, and freshly ground wasabi, as well as intricately conceived salads, housemade tofu, and soups. ✉ *11500 Pico Blvd., West L.A.* ☎ *310/479–3939* ⊕ *www.morisushi.org* ☯ *Closed Sun. No lunch Sat.* ✛ *4:D3.*

$$ ✕ **Mr. Cecil's California Ribs.** A rib-loving movie-studio exec opened this

SOUTHERN   eatery in a tiny, circular hatbox of a building. The meaty, tender St.

☯   Louis–style ribs are particularly outstanding, with a spirited but not overpowering sauce. Aficionados of pecan pie should also beat a path here. Bonus: It's the only rib joint in town where you can order a bottle of Château Lafite Rothschild. ✉ *12244 W. Pico Blvd., West L.A.* ☎ *310/442–1550* ⊕ *www.mrcecilscaribs.com* ✛ *4:C3.*

$ ✕ **Versailles.** Despite its no-frills dining room in which noise echos off

CUBAN   Formica surfaces and art is an afterthought, people line up outside the

☯   door for Versailles's respectable, bargain-price Cuban food. Most are crazy about the citrusy *mojo*-marinated chicken seasoned with loads

10

of garlic. Others prefer flank steak, *ropa vieja* (shredded beef), and paella. ⊠ *10319 Venice Blvd., West L.A.* ☎ *310/558–3168* ⊕ *www. versaillescuban.com* ⌦ *Reservations not accepted* ✛ *4:E3.*

$$
NEW AMERICAN
☺

✕ **Westside Tavern.** It's not all that typical for a restaurant in a mall to make a culinary splash, but this modern-day gastropub has created a casual, lively, and engaging space without cutting corners on well-executed food. A large comfy bar is your first stop; grab a white peach-and-basil gimlet before being escorted to your dinner table. Then start with the ceviche of the day or maybe a platter of fried green beans. If you are craving a sandwich, order the lamb French dip, a BLT with a soft fried egg, or an open-faced portabella melt. Main entrées include Niman Ranch flat-iron steak and fried halibut-and-chips. For a sweet finish, try the cinnamon sugar donuts that arrive with raspberry and chocolate dipping sauces. ⊠ *Olympic Collection, 10850 Pico Blvd., West L.A.* ☎ *310/470–1539* ⊕ *www.westsidetavernla.com* ☻ *Bar open until midnight Fri. and Sat.* ✛ *4:D2.*

SANTA MONICA AND THE BEACHES WITH LOS ANGELES AIRPORT

In these neighborhoods, choose from a diverse collection of eateries—from taco stands to upscale seafood houses—that that cater to the healthy and active lifestyle of locals. But beware of overpriced eateries betting that an ocean view will help you forget about substandard value and quality. Fortunately, they're easy to avoid by sticking to our list here. As for budget eats, there are plenty of cafés, burger shacks, and casual chains that won't raise an eyebrow when you walk in with your sandy flip-flops.

LOS ANGELES INTERNATIONAL AIRPORT

$$$
NEW AMERICAN
☺

✕ **Encounter.** If you're flying to L.A., you can begin or end your trip with a stop by the dramatic Theme Building for a meal with a runway view. Designers from Walt Disney Imagineering whipped up the intergalactic atmosphere. Choices such as tuna tartare, Peking-style duck, and roasted chicken with a mustard cream sauce certainly beat airplane fare. The place, with its colorful, futuristic design and close encounters with rumbling 747s, is a delight for kids and kids-at-heart. ⊠ *209 World Way, LAX* ☎ *310/215–5151* ⊕ *www.encounterlax.com* ✛ *4:E6.*

MALIBU

$$$
MEDITERRANEAN

✕ **Beau Rivage.** One of the few Malibu restaurants with a view of the beach and ocean, this romantic Mediterranean villa–style dining room has copper domes and lush landscaping. The expansive menu includes filet mignon with a three-mustard sauce, salmon steak with a Champagne-raspberry sauce, and a strong lineup of pastas, risotto, and gnocchi. In contrast to trendier Malibu haunts, the staff here is warm and welcoming. ⊠ *26025 Pacific Coast Hwy., Malibu* ☎ *310/456–5733* ⊕ *www.beaurivagerestaurant.com* ⌦ *Reservations essential* ☻ *Closed Mon. and Tues. No lunch. Saturday and Sunday brunch from 11 am–4 pm* ✛ *4:A6.*

$$$
JAPANESE

✕ **Nobu Malibu.** At famous chef-restaurateur Nobu Matsuhisa's coastal outpost, the casually chic clientele sails in for morsels of the world's

The Jetson's-styled Encounter at LAX.

finest fish. In addition to stellar sushi, Nobu serves many of the same ingenious specialties offered at his original Matsuhisa in Beverly Hills or glitzy Nobu in West Hollywood. You can find exotic species of fish artfully accented with equally exotic South American peppers, ultratender Kobe beef, and a broth perfumed with matsutake mushrooms. Elaborate omakase dinners start at $90. ✉ *3835 Cross Creek Rd., Malibu* ☎ *310/317–9140* ⊕ *www.noburestaurants.com* ⌱ *Reservations essential* ⊙ *No lunch* ✛ *4:B6.*

$$$

ITALIAN

✕ **Tra di Noi.** The name means "among us," and Malibu natives are trying to keep this simple *ristorante* just that—a local secret. A Tuscan villa–inspired hideaway, the homey Tra di Noi draws everyone from movie stars to well-heeled neighborhood regulars. Nothing too fancy or *nuovo* on the menu, just generous salads, hearty lasagna and other freshly made pastas, short ribs braised in Chianti wine, and a whole two-pound branzino served with herb sauce. An Italian buffet is laid out for Sunday brunch. ✉ *3835 Cross Creek Rd., Malibu* ☎ *310/456–0169* ⊕ *www.tradinoimalibu.com* ✛ *4:B6.*

10

PACIFIC PALISADES

$$$

SEAFOOD

☙

✕ **Gladstone's Malibu.** Gladstone's is one of the most popular restaurants along the Southern California coast; its demand has even spawned a sister restaurant in Universal Studios' CityWalk (though the lack of beachfront makes it far less attractive). The food is notable mostly for its oversize portions: giant bowls of crab chowder, lobsters up to six pounds, spectacular seafood towers and the famous mile-high chocolate cake, which can easily feed a small regiment. But the real reason to visit Gladstone's is the glorious vista of sea, sky, and beach. Sip on one

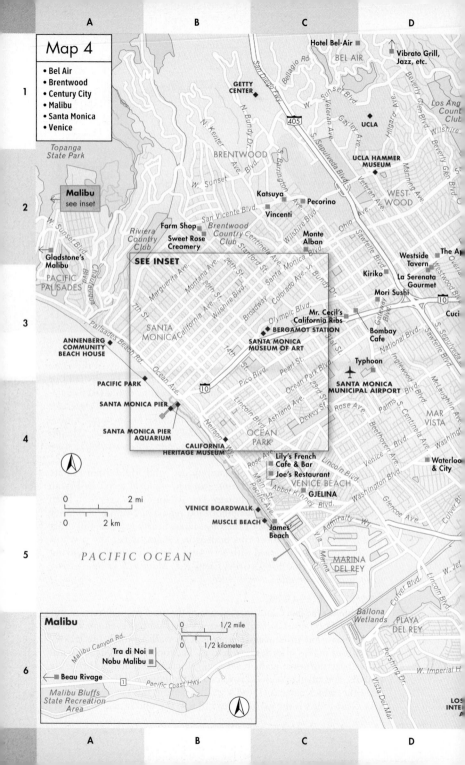

Map 4

- Bel Air
- Brentwood
- Century City
- Malibu
- Santa Monica
- Venice

A   B   C   D

1

Hotel Bel-Air ■
BEL AIR
Vibrato Grill, ■
Jazz, etc.

GETTY ◆
CENTER

San Diego Fwy.
Bellagio Rd.
Sunset Blvd.
405
N. Bundy Dr.
N. Kenter Ave.
Veteran Ave.
Gayley Ave.
Hilgard Ave.
S. Sepulveda Blvd.
Beverly Glen Blvd.
Los Ang
Count
Club
Wilshire

UCLA ◆

BRENTWOOD

Topanga
State Park

UCLA HAMMER ■
MUSEUM
Manning Ave.
WEST-
WOOD

2

Malibu
see inset ←

Katsuya ■
Pecorino ■
Vincenti ■
Monte ■
Alban

W. Sunset Ave.
San Vicente Blvd.
Wilshire Blvd.
Ohio Ave.
Sawtelle Blvd.

Westside ■
Tavern
The A

Riviera
Country
Club
Farm Shop ■
Sweet Rose ■
Creamery
Brentwood
Country
Club
26th St.
Stanford St.
Santa Monica
S. Bundy Dr.

Kiriko ■
La Serenata ■
Gourmet
Mori Sushi ■
Cuci

W. Sunset Blvd.
Chautauqua

Gladstone's ■
Malibu

PACIFIC
PALISADES

3

SEE INSET

Marguerita Ave.
Montana Ave.
20th St.
California Ave.
Wilshire Blvd.
7th St.
Broadway
Colorado Ave.
Olympic Blvd.
Mr. Cecil's ■
California Ribs

10

ANNENBERG ■
COMMUNITY
BEACH HOUSE

SANTA
MONICA

BERGAMOT STATION ◆
SANTA MONICA ◆
MUSEUM OF ART

Bombay ■
Cafe
National Blvd.
S. Sepulveda Blvd.

PACIFIC PARK ◆

14th
Pico Blvd.
Pearl St.
31st St.

Typhoon ■
SANTA MONICA ■
MUNICIPAL AIRPORT

Inglewood Blvd.
McLaughlin Ave.
Washing

SANTA MONICA PIER ◆

Palisades Beach Rd.
Ocean Ave.
Lincoln Blvd.
Ocean Park Blvd.
23rd St.
Ashland Ave.
Dewey St.
Rose Ave.
Palms
S. Centinela Blvd.
Beethoven Ave.

MAR
VISTA

4

SANTA MONICA PIER
AQUARIUM

OCEAN
PARK

Venice Ave.
Glencoe Ave.
Culver Bl

Waterloo ■
& City

CALIFORNIA ◆
HERITAGE MUSEUM

Nielson Way
Main St.
Abbot Kinney Blvd.

Lily's French ■
Cafe & Bar
Joe's Restaurant ■

VENICE BEACH

GJELINA ■

Washington Blvd.

VENICE BOARDWALK ◆

Pacific Ave.

MUSCLE BEACH ◆

James' ■
Beach

Via Marina
S. Via Marina

MARINA
DEL REY

W. Jef

Culver Blvd.
Lincoln Blvd.

5

PACIFIC OCEAN

0   2 mi
0   2 km

Ballona
Wetlands

PLAYA
DEL REY

Pershing Dr.
Vista Del Mar

W. Imperial H

LOS
INTE
A

6

Malibu

0   1/2 mile
0   1/2 kilometer

Malibu Canyon Rd.
Tra di Noi ■
Nobu Malibu ■

Beau Rivage ■ ←
1
Pacific Coast Hwy.

Malibu Bluffs
State Recreation
Area

A   B   C   D

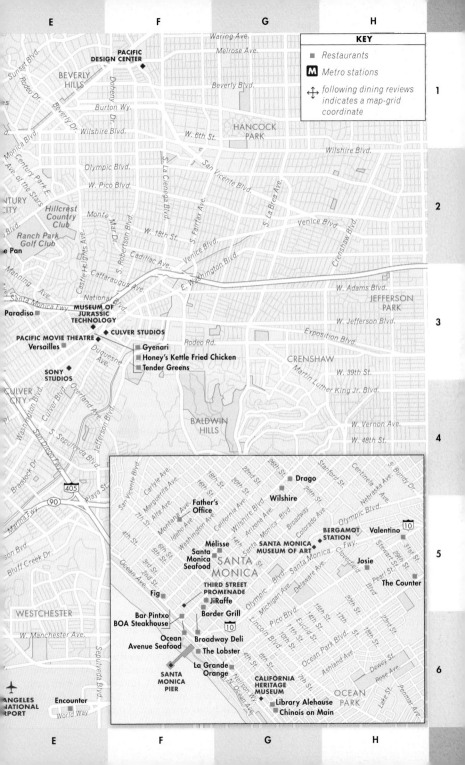

of their iconic mojitos and watch the sun dip into the ocean at sunset. It's also a good weekend breakfast spot. ⊠ *17300 Pacific Coast Hwy., at Sunset Blvd., Pacific Palisades* ☎ *310/454–3474* ⊕ *www.gladstones. com* ✛ *4:A2.*

SANTA MONICA

$$
SPANISH

✕ **Bar Pintxo.** Inspired by his trips to Spain, chef Joe Miller (of Joe's restaurant in Venice) opened this lively, warmly appointed tapas bar. In the Basque region, tapas are called *pintxos*, and this narrow slice of the Iberian Peninsula carries the spirit of the genuine article, despite having a view of the Pacific—the Bay of Biscay would be more appropriate—and being occupied by SoCal surfer dudes and struggling screenwriters taking advantage of the good values. Sip a glass of Albariño or sangría while snacking on *croquetas de pollo y jamón, morcilla* (blood sausage), or paprika-laden chorizo with fried quail eggs. A bowl of Andalusian gazpacho is perfect on a hot California evening. ⊠ *109 Santa Monica Blvd., Santa Monica* ☎ *310/458–2012* ⌥ *Reservations not accepted* ✛ *4:F6.*

$$$
STEAK

✕ **BOA Steakhouse.** This is not your father's steak house; businesspeople and somber mahogany have been swapped out for a fun-loving crowd bathed in multicolor lights from avant-garde fixtures. But you can still start with a prawn cocktail or a traditional Caesar salad prepared tableside before slicing your Laguiole knife into a dry-aged prime New York strip or rib eye (genuine Japanese Wagyu and certified organic beef are also available). Although the steaks are delicious without any frills, you can opt for an embellishment such as a blue cheese rub or cabernet reduction sauce. ⊠ *101 Santa Monica Blvd., Santa Monica* ☎ *310/899–4466* ⊕ *www.boasteak.com* ⌥ *Reservations essential* ✛ *4:F6.*

$$
MEXICAN
☾

✕ **Border Grill.** Massive, colorful murals are a perfect complement to modern interpretations of this busy restaurant's ancient Mayan dishes such as *cochinita pibil* (achiote-marinated pork). Other favorites include a wild-mushroom quesadilla, green corn tamales, plantain empanadas, and daily ceviche specials. Celebrity chef-owners Mary Sue Milliken and Susan Feniger display a passion for Mexican cuisine here, but they do mellow the dishes to suit a broad audience. ⊠ *1445 4th St., Santa Monica* ☎ *310/451–1655* ⊕ *www.bordergrill.com* ✛ *4:F6.*

¢
AMERICAN
☾

✕ **Broadway Deli.** The name tells just half the story. This lively, cavernous place is a cross between a European brasserie and an upscale diner. The huge menu goes way beyond corned beef and pastrami sandwiches to include pizzas, an ostrich burger, shepherd's pie, and even duck enchiladas. Breads are baked on-site, and there's a kids' menu. ⊠ *1457 3rd St. Promenade, Santa Monica* ☎ *310/451–0616* ⊕ *www.broadwaydeli. com* ⌥ *Reservations not accepted* ✛ *4:F6.*

$$$
ASIAN

✕ **Chinois on Main.** A once-revolutionary outpost in Wolfgang Puck's repertoire, this is still one of L.A.'s most crowded—and noisy—restaurants. The jazzy interior is just as loud as the clientele. Although the menu has expanded, the restaurant's happy marriage of Asian and French cuisines shows best in its signature dishes such as Chinois chicken salad, Shanghai lobster with spicy ginger-curry sauce, and Cantonese duck with fresh plum sauce. ⊠ *2709 Main St., Santa Monica* ☎ *310/392–9025* ⊕ *www. wolfgangpuck.com* ⌥ *Reservations essential* ☾ *No lunch* ✛ *4:G6.*

¢
BURGERS

The Counter. Angelenos still adore the venerable Apple Pan, but they've also embraced its upscale, contemporary burger-joint counterpart. Here, by checking off your preferences on a sushi bar–style order sheet, you can select beef, turkey, or veggie patties, then specify your preferred cheeses, toppings, one of 18 different sauces (anything from spicy sour cream to sweet BBQ sauce), and bun (or, for carb counters, a "burger-in-a-bowl"). Even with the slick surroundings and wild combinations, this emerging chain is a nostalgic reminder of L.A.'s ongoing love affair with the burger. ✉ *2901 Ocean Park Blvd., Santa Monica* ☎ *310/399–8383* ⊕ *www.thecounterburger.com* ⌂ *Reservations not accepted* ✛ *4:H5.*

$$$
ITALIAN

Drago. Native Sicilian Celestino Drago's home-style fare is carefully prepared and attentively served in stark designer surroundings. White walls and white linen–covered tables line both sides of a floating service station dressed up with a towering arrangement of fresh flowers. The menu adds sophisticated finishes to rustic foundations in dishes such as pappardelle tossed in a pheasant and morel mushroom sauce, pan-roasted veal chop in truffle sauce, or grilled boneless quail served with polenta. ✉ *2628 Wilshire Blvd., Santa Monica* ☎ *310/828–1585* ⊕ *www.celestinodrago.com* ✆ *No lunch weekends* ✛ *4:G4.*

$
AMERICAN

Farmshop. Tucked away inside of the Brentwood Country Mart, the new seasonal and California-inspired culinary darling Farmshop was invented by Jeffrey Cerciello, formerly the culinary director of Thomas Keller's casual restaurants. The Southern California native brought a little Napa Valley home with this classic spot that pays attention to the little details, but also keeps things refreshingly simple. Breads and pastries are made everyday on-site, which is one detail that makes breakfast epic. Order the buttermilk biscuits served with quince preserves, French toast with pear marmalade and raisins, and the shirred eggs with wild greens, fennel cream, and flavorful sourdough toast. Lunch is a blend of farm-fresh salads, soups, and sandwiches. Try the warm Dungeness crab salad made with butter lettuce, sunchokes, and curly mustard greens, or the smoked salmon tartine dressed with caper berries and pickled vegetables on rye bread. ✉ *225 26th St., Santa Monica* ☎ *310/566–2400* ⊕ *www.farmshopla.com* ✆ *Open for breakfast and lunch only.* ✛ *3:B2*

$
AMERICAN

Father's Office. With a facade distinguished only by a vintage neon sign, Father's Office is a congested, gentrified pub famous for handcrafted beers and what is widely regarded as L.A.'s best burger. Topped with Gruyère and Maytag blue cheeses, arugula, caramelized onions, and applewood-smoked bacon compote, the "Office Burger" is a guilty pleasure worth waiting in line for (which is usually required). Other options include steak frites and Spanish tapas, with side orders of addictive sweet potato fries served in a miniature shopping cart with aïoli— don't even think of asking for ketchup, because FO enforces a strict no-substitutions policy. So popular is the Office Burger that chef-owner Sang Yoon has recently opened a second location in Culver City. Note: Because Father's Office is a bar, it's strictly 21 and over. ✉ *1018 Montana Ave., Santa Monica* ☎ *310/393–2337* ⊕ *www.fathersoffice.com* ⌂ *Reservations not accepted* ✆ *No lunch weekdays* ✛ *4:F5.*

$$$
NEW AMERICAN

JiRaffe. The two-story California bistro with ceiling-high windows and polished dark-wood accents is as handsome as the menu is tasteful.

10

Chef-owner Raphael Lunetta, who is also an accomplished surfer, turns out seasonal appetizers such as a delicate roasted-tomato tart or a roasted-beet salad with caramelized walnuts and dried Bing cherries. They're worthy preludes to main dishes like a truly memorable crispy-skinned salmon with parsnip puree, braised fennel, and sweet balsamic reduction. ⊠ *502 Santa Monica Blvd., Santa Monica* ☎ *310/917–6671* ⊕ *www.jirafferestaurant.com* ⌦ *Reservations essential* ⊘ *No lunch* ✛ *4:F5.*

$$$
AMERICAN

✕ **Josie.** Done in understated taupe hues with generously spaced tables, this cosmopolitan establishment feels like it belongs in San Francisco instead of laid-back L.A. The kitchen, however, blends that sophistication with inspirations from the Great Outdoors, resulting in "campfire trout" cooked in a cast-iron skillet, bacon wrapped quail, and its signature foie-gras topped buffalo burger with truffle fries. ⊠ *2424 Pico Blvd., Santa Monica* ☎ *310/581–9888* ⊕ *www.josierestaurant.com* ⌦ *Reservations essential* ⊘ *No lunch* ✛ *4:H5.*

$$$
SEAFOOD

✕ **The Lobster.** Anchoring the beach end of the festive Santa Monica Pier, the Lobster usually teems with locals and tourists alike, who come here for the jubilant scene, the great view, and the comfort seafood of chef Allyson Thurber. Start with lobster cocktail with tarragon-lemon aïoli, lobster clam chowder, or lobster salad with sweet corn pancakes. For entrées, the theme continues with both Maine and Pacific spiny varieties—but dishes like king salmon in herb sauce are equally satisfying. Weather permitting, request a table on the terrace, both for the views and an escape from the high-decibel interior. ⊠ *1602 Ocean Ave., Santa Monica* ☎ *310/458–9294* ⊕ *www.thelobster.com* ⌦ *Reservations essential* ✛ *4:F6.*

$$$
FRENCH
Fodor's Choice
★

✕ **Mélisse.** In a city where informality reigns, this is one of L.A.'s more dressy, but not stuffy, restaurants. The dining room is contemporary yet elegant, with well-spaced tables topped with flowers and Limoges china. The garden room loosens up with a stone fountain and a retractable roof. Chef-owner Josiah Citrin enhances his modern French cooking with seasonal California produce. Consider seared sweet white corn ravioli in brown butter–truffle froth, lobster bolognese, slow cooked rabbit, or duck confit. The cheese cart is packed with domestic and European selections. ⊠ *1104 Wilshire Blvd., Santa Monica* ☎ *310/395–0881* ⊕ *www.melisse.com* ⌦ *Reservations essential* ⊘ *Closed Sun. and Mon. No lunch* ✛ *4:F5.*

$$
SEAFOOD
♻

✕ **Santa Monica Seafood.** The Cigliano family began their modest seafood business along the Santa Monica Pier in the early 1930s. More than 70 years later, it remains a Southern California food icon and also a popular seafood purveyor for many of L.A.'s top chefs. Recently celebrating its 70th anniversary, the family moved into spacious digs along swanky Wilshire Boulevard. They expanded the retail market and made room for a café where oysters and champagne can be enjoyed while wearing jeans and flip-flops. The menu is simple with touches of Italian flavors like the steamed Mediterranean mussel, cioppino, and grilled shrimp panzanella. There are also sandwiches, soups, and a kids' menu. Take time to walk around the market, read up on the history and enjoy the free tastings of the latest specials. ✉ *1000 Wilshire Blvd., Santa Monica* ☎ *310/393–5244* ⊕ *www.santamonicaseafood.com* ✛ *4:F5.*

$$$
ITALIAN

✕ **Valentino.** Renowned as one of the country's top Italian restaurants, Valentino has a truly awe-inspiring wine list. With nearly 2,800 labels consuming 130 pages, backed by a cellar overflowing with nearly 100,000 bottles, this restaurant is nothing short of heaven for serious oenophiles. In the 1970s, suave owner Piero Selvaggio introduced L.A. to his exquisite modern Italian cuisine, and he continues to impress guests with dishes like a timballo of wild mushrooms with rich Parmigiano-Reggiano–saffron *fonduta*, squid ink–tinted risotto with Maine lobster, a memorable osso buco, and sautéed branzino with lemon emulsion. A welcome addition is its more casual wine bar for wine tasting and nibbles like *crudo* and carpaccio. ✉ *3115 Pico Blvd., Santa Monica* ☎ *310/829–4313* ⊕ *www. valentinorestaurantgroup.com* ⋟ *Reservations essential* ⊙ *Closed Sun. No lunch Sat. and Mon.–Thurs.* ✛ *4:H5.*

$$$
NEW AMERICAN

✕ **Wilshire.** The woodsy patio at Wilshire is one of the most coveted spaces on the L.A. dining circuit—its candlelight, firelight, and gurgling fountain reel in a hip crowd beneath a cloud of canvas. A passion for organic, market-fresh ingredients is reflected in dishes like lobster bisque with lemongrass cream and duck breast with dried cherry chutney. The eclectic wine list is first-rate, and there's a lively bar scene here, too. ✉ *2454 Wilshire Blvd., Santa Monica* ☎ *310/586–1707* ⊕ *www. wilshirerestaurant.com* ⋟ *Reservations essential* ⊙ *Closed Sun. No lunch weekends. Hrs change in summer* ✛ *4:H4.*

VENICE

$$
AMERICAN

✕ **Gjelina.** This handsome restaurant comes alive with personality the minute you walk through its oversize rustic wooden door. There are long communal tables, hanging light fixtures that soften the room and make it glow, and an outdoor patio. The menu is smart and seasonal with small plates, cheese and charcuterie, pastas, and pizza. Begin with a mushroom, goat cheese and truffle oil pizza, spinach heirloom salad, mussels with chorizo, or grilled Monterey squid with fingerling potatoes. For the main course, there's the chicken with saffron quinoa or the Niman Ranch pork chop with mixed mushrooms. Typically crowded and noisy, it is a great spot that dazzles all four senses. ✉ *1429 Abbot Kinney Blvd., Venice* ☎ *310/450–1429* ⊕ *www.gjelina.com* ⋟ *Reservations essential* ⊙ *Open until midnight daily* ✛ *4:C5.*

$$$
AMERICAN

✕ **Joe's Restaurant.** In what was originally a turn-of-the-20th-century beach house, Joe Miller has created the definitive neighborhood restaurant with a citywide reputation. His imaginative French-influenced California cooking focuses on fresh ingredients. Start with tuna tartare or porcini ravioli in mushroom-Parmesan broth, and continue with Berkshire pork *crépinette* (a type of sausage) or potato-crusted red snapper in port wine sauce. For dessert, try the chocolate crunch cake with hazelnuts and house-made coffee ice cream. Lunch is a terrific value—all entrées are $18 or less and come with soup or salad. ✉ *1023 Abbott Kinney Blvd., Venice* ☎ *310/399–5811* ⊕ *www.joesrestaurant. com* ⊙ *Closed Mon.* ✛ *4:C4.*

10

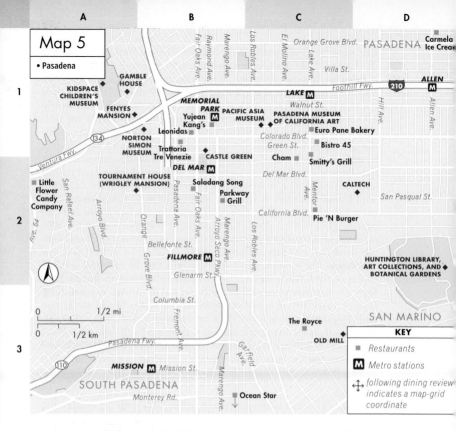

Map 5

• Pasadena

A B C D

KIDSPACE CHILDREN'S MUSEUM
GAMBLE HOUSE
FENYES MANSION
Leonidas
NORTON SIMON MUSEUM
Trattoria Tre Venezie
TOURNAMENT HOUSE (WRIGLEY MANSION)
Little Flower Candy Company

MEMORIAL PARK
Yujean Kang's
PACIFIC ASIA MUSEUM
DEL MAR
Saladang Song
Parkway Grill
CASTLE GREEN

FILLMORE

PASADENA
Carmela Ice Cream
ALLEN
LAKE
Walnut St.
PASADENA MUSEUM OF CALIFORNIA ART
Euro Pane Bakery
Bistro 45
Cham
Smitty's Grill
CALTECH
Pie 'N Burger

Orange Grove Blvd.
Villa St.
Foothill Fwy.
Colorado Blvd.
Green St.
Del Mar Blvd.
California Blvd.

HUNTINGTON LIBRARY, ART COLLECTIONS, AND BOTANICAL GARDENS

Bellefonte St.
Glenarm St.
Columbia St.

0 1/2 mi
0 1/2 km
Pasadena Fwy.

The Royce
OLD MILL
SAN MARINO

MISSION Mission St.

SOUTH PASADENA
Monterey Rd.
Ocean Star

KEY
▪ Restaurants
Ⓜ Metro stations
✢ following dining review indicates a map-grid coordinate

$ ✕ **Lilly's French Café & Bar.** Forget haute cuisine—Lilly's celebrates the
FRENCH robust flavors of French bistro cooking. Start with *flamiche* (a northern
French goat cheese and leek tart) or escargots with garlic-herb butter.
Then move on to roasted duck breast with orange sauce or entrecôte
steak with Béarnaise sauce, and finish with profiteroles or a lemon tart.
The daily prix-fixe lunch is a great value: soup or salad plus a gorgeous
sandwich or omelet for about $12. No reservations are accepted for
lunch, but be sure to call ahead for dinner. ⊠ *1031 Abbot Kinney Blvd.,
Venice* ☎ *310/314–0004* ⊕ *www.lillysfrenchcafe.com* ✢ *4:C4.*

PASADENA AND ENVIRONS

Pasadena is a charming suburb home to picturesque foothills, vintage
Craftsman bungalows, the Rose Bowl Flea Market, and an evolving
dining scene that's breaking out of its retail chain doldrums. With the
revitalization of Old Town Pasadena and a new rail system that brings
visitors in from downtown L.A., Hollywood, and the Valley, more
people are discovering the beauty of Rose City. They mingle at bistros,
upscale eateries, and taco trucks, but are also discovering the newer
innovative dining spots that are giving Pasadena a hipper feel.

PASADENA

$
INDIAN

✕**All India Cafe.** Reflecting the eclectic scene of Old Pasadena is this authentic Indian eatery. Ingredients are fresh, and flavors are bold without depending on overpowering spiciness. Start with the *bhel puri,* a savory puffed rice-and-potato dish. In addition to meat curries and tikkas, there are many vegetarian selections and some hard-to-find items such as the burrito-like frankies, a favorite Bombay street food. The prices are as palatable as the meals: a full lunch still costs less than $15. ⊠ *39 S. Fair Oaks Ave., Pasadena* ☎ *626/440–0309* ⊕ *www. allindiacafe.com* ✛ *5:B1.*

$$$
FRENCH

✕**Bistro 45.** One of Pasadena's most stylish and sophisticated dining spots, Bistro 45 blends traditional French themes with modern concepts to create fanciful California hybrids that delight locals and visitors alike. Seared ahi tuna with a black-and-white-sesame crust, and duck with tamari-ginger sauce incorporate Pacific Rim accents. The art deco bungalow has been tailored into a sleek environment. Oenophiles, take note: in addition to having one of the best wine lists in town, owner Robert Simon regularly hosts lavish winemaker dinners. ⊠ *45 S. Mentor Ave., Pasadena* ☎ *626/795–2478* ⊕ *www.bistro45.com* ⌢ *Reservations essential* ⊙ *Closed Mon. No lunch weekends* ✛ *5:C1.*

$
KOREAN

✕**Cham.** The name of this restaurant, which translates to "meal for workers," is a healthy fast-casual eatery that takes traditional Korean food and turns it into seasonally driven tasty tapas, stews, and *ssam* (barbecue and garden platters). Its arrival in charming tree-filled Pasadena signals the areas growing dining culture that is evolving to match the diverse locals who are tired of driving to Hollywood for urban eats. Relaxed and inviting, Cham is a neighborhood spot that is approachable with clean and simple wood furnishing and oversized tables that make for comfy dining. A boutique wine list, craft beers, and Korean cocktails are all handpicked to match the lively flavors of the food. Order the hot chicken or steak bibimbap that arrives with crunchy rice or the barbecue garden platter that comes with meat or vegetables that you can fold into fresh lettuce for a healthy Korean taco-esque nosh. ⊠ *851 Cordova St., Pasadena* ☎ *626/792–2474* ⊕ *www. chamkoreanbistro.com* ✛ *5:C2.*

$
CAFÉ
☺

✕**Little Flower Candy Company.** Just off the beaten path of Old Town Pasadena sits this quaint café that has charmed the hearts and taste buds of locals with its seasonally driven menu of sandwiches, salads, fresh soups, and incredible baked goods. The café is owned by Christine Moore, who made a name for herself in the candy world as a creator of addicting sea salt caramels and oversize sugar marshmallows. She opened shop a few years ago to sell her sweets, but also ended up creating a neighborhood hub for northeast Los Angeles. The café is nestled up against the sloping hills for a small-town feel even though downtown LA is a few miles away. It's a terrific place to grab a coffee, a fig pastry, or a light lunch before heading out for an afternoon of shopping. ⊠ *1424 W. Colorado Blvd., Pasadena* ☎ *626/304–4800* ⊕ *www.littleflowercandyco.com* ⊙ *Mon.–Sat. 7–5, Sun. 7–4* ✛ *5:A2.*

$$$
INTERNATIONAL

✕**Parkway Grill.** This ever-popular, influential restaurant (once referred to as the Spago of Pasadena) sports all-American fixtures like brick

10

walls, a carved-wood bar, and a prominent fireplace. The food wanders farther afield, incorporating influences from Italian to Japanese. In one sitting you might have black bean soup or a tiger shrimp corn dog with Thai aïoli, then filet mignon or whole fried catfish with yuzu–ponzu sauce, followed by s'mores for dessert. ☒ *510 S. Arroyo Pkwy., Pasadena* ☎ *626/795–1001* ⊕ *www.theparkwaygrill.com* ⚞ *Reservations essential* ⊙ *No lunch weekends* ✛ *5:B2.*

¢ ✕ **Pie 'N Burger.** A legendary Caltech hangout, this place serves up a
AMERICAN burger that the locals justifiably worship, plus potpies, a bargain lov-
ꙅ er's steak, traditional fountain drinks, and tasty pies (especially peach, pecan, and peanut butter). There are only a few tables, but you'll be treated right at a long counter filled with astrophysicists. ☒ *913 E. California Blvd., Pasadena* ☎ *626/795–1123* ⊕ *www.pienburger.com* ⚞ *Reservations not accepted* ▭ *No credit cards* ✛ *5:C2.*

¢ ✕ **Saladang Song.** The owners of Saladang, a standard Thai restaurant
THAI next door, concoct a more interesting menu here, going well beyond the usual satays and pad thai. It's a striking Thai-tech pavilion surrounded by outdoor tables and towering, ornamental pierced-steel panels that put this eatery in its own graciously hermetic world. For lunch or dinner, consider the spicy fish cakes or salmon with curry sauce. Or for a rarer treat, come for a Thai breakfast, with *kao-tom-gui* (rice soup with or without various meats and seafood) and *joak* (the Thai-style rice porridge), with sweet potato, taro, and pumpkin. ☒ *383 S. Fair Oaks Ave., Pasadena* ☎ *626/793–5200* ✛ *5:B2.*

$$$ ✕ **The Royce.** Slightly off the well-beaten path, the Langham Hotel is
FRENCH nestled in one of Pasadena's most prestigious neighborhoods. Arriving here, you'll feel enveloped in California-style luxury. The same can be said for its new upscale restaurant The Royce, a light, bright, and not nearly as formal restaurant as what was once here—but still decidedly fresh, seasonal, and French. The innovative menu is created by David Féau and the experience is thoughtful dining, heavy on distinct tastes that are best enjoyed slowly and leisurely and with a glass of wine selected by the savvy sommeliers. The menu is divided into easy-to-read catergories: cold and warm; hot and raw; fish and shellfish; meat and poultry. A great option is the two five-course tasting menus that allow for a sampling of the entire menu. ☒ *The Langham Huntington, 1401 S. Oak Knoll Ave., Pasadena* ☎ *626/585–6410* ⊕ *www.roycela. com* ✛ *5:C3.*

$$$ ✕ **Trattoria Tre Venezie.** Much more than a neighborhood trattoria, this
ITALIAN unexpected ristorante excels in specialties from a trio of Italy's northernmost regions along the Austrian border, collectively referred to as Tre Venezie. Sparked with unusual ingredients and sauces, the menu can challenge your preconceptions about Italian food. Start with *jota* (a traditional smoky pork-and-bean soup) before enjoying the signature smoked pork chop with sauerkraut and a light Gorgonzola sauce. ☒ *119 W. Green St., Pasadena* ☎ *626/795–4455* ⊙ *Closed Mon. No lunch Tues. or weekends* ✛ *5:B1.*

Where to Stay

WORD OF MOUTH

"Make your decision on where to stay based on what you are going to do. If you are amusement parking at Disney and Knott's, stay in Anaheim. . . . Driving from area to area in L.A. is so time-consuming that you do not want to spend most of your three days on the freeway."

—Stumpworks73

Updated
by Kathy A.
McDonald

When it comes to finding a place to stay, travelers have never been more spoiled for choice in today's Los Angeles. From luxurious digs in Beverly Hills to budget boutiques along the coast, hotels are stepping up service, upgrading amenities, and throwing in perks like free Wi-Fi, in-room espresso makers, and spa-quality bath products.

The ambitious revitalization of the city's downtown, anchored around the L.A. Live complex, includes a new 54-tower that holds both a Ritz-Carlton and JW Marriott offering a new set of grand hotel restaurants and services close to the convention center. Other downtown hotels, such as the Westin Bonaventure Hotel & Suites and the Omni Los Angeles Hotel at California Plaza, have upgraded their rooms and lobbies to rival this newly built competition.

Along with the bigger multistory hotels, smaller inns and lodges have also opened for low-key, eco-minded stays, built via green construction, as sustainable stays become an increasing trend. Consider booking one of the three charming Venice Beach Eco-Cottages, or a homey casita at the Loz Feliz Lodge, where innkeepers stock the kitchen with organic mint tea and the bathrooms with bamboo-fiber towels.

Hollywood's already trendy nightlife scene now has party-friendly hotels in the W Hollywood and The Redbury. Both offer full bars in-room as well as vibrant restaurants that appeal to a younger crowd. The W also has a rooftop nightclub Drai's that brings Vegas glitz to the heart of Hollywood and comes with dramatic city views. Rooftop socializing continues at The London West Hollywood where the backdrop is spectacular vistas of downtown Los Angeles and Century City.

For the best in-town getaway, the new resort at Terranea's oceanfront spa promises relaxation within sight of frolicking dolphins and seasonally migrating whales. While newer hotels kick it up, classics like the splendidly refreshed Four Seasons Los Angeles, and even more storied Beverly Hills Hotel seem to only get better with time, anticipating all a guest might need and want with seamless perfection.

WHERE SHOULD I STAY?

11

	NEIGHBORHOOD VIBE	PROS	CONS
Downtown	High-rises, office towers, commercial districts, and cultural institutions, with a growing residential scene.	Affordable hotels within walking distance of art museums, concert halls, and the new L.A. Live complex.	Homeless encampments, with some sketchy areas at night.
Hollywood	Historic theaters and the Walk of Fame, but much of the area is overly touristy.	Heart of the city's night-life and see-and-be-seen spots, from lively night-clubs to popular eateries.	Steep parking fees, quirky celebrity-obsessed crowd, overpriced everything.
Studio City, Universal City, and North Hollywood	Residential and suburban feel, with some commer-cial (strip-mall) spots.	Safe, family-friendly, affordable accommoda-tions, plentiful dining options.	Requires a car to get anywhere, even a nearby coffee shop.
Beverly Hills	Upscale—one of the city's best addresses, with classy and elegant hotels.	Great shopping, celeb-spotting, numerous restaurants all near quiet residential areas.	Big bucks to stay, dine, and shop here; limited diversity.
Century City and Culver City	Businesses mixed with residential buildings; cen-trally located.	Easy access to all points on the Westside; pedestrian-friendly strip in Culver City.	Some strictly office areas, no beach or ocean views.
Bel Air, Brent-wood, West Hollywood	Coveted neighbor-hood for elite; boutique hotels abound in West Hollywood.	Close proximity to Getty Center; ambitious restau-rants and fun nightspots in West Hollywood.	Stuffy attitudes in Bel Air; spendy stays in West Hollywood.
LAX vicinity	Concentration of office towers and commercial buildings.	Convenient location near airport; incredibly affordable.	Little activity, dull nearby strip malls with restau-rants and shopping.
Santa Monica and Malibu	Laid-back beach towns with waterfront hotels, cottages, and inns.	Ocean breezes, super-safe, family-friendly; walkable pockets with restaurants, cafés, and boutiques.	Some bars, but limited nightlife; steep prices for an ocean view.
Venice, Man-hattan, Her-mosa, Marina Del Rey, Long Beach	Edgy, artsy in Venice; residential in Manhattan Beach; sailing and biking in Marina del Rey.	Diverse neighbor-hoods but close to the ocean without Malibu's spendiness. Long Beach airport is a great travel alternative.	Mostly residential in some pockets; traffic along Highway 1 means long driving times.
Pasadena	Residential with walkable strip of shops and cafés.	Charming small town feel, family-friendly, historic.	Removed from Westside and beaches; lengthy driving time into the city.

LOS ANGELES LODGING PLANNER

LODGING STRATEGY

Where should I stay? With hundreds of Los Angeles hotels, it may seem like a daunting question. But fret not—our expert writers and editors have done most of the legwork. The selections here represent the best this city has to offer—from the best budget motels to the sleekest designer hotels. Scan "Best Bets" on the following pages for top recommendations by price and experience. Or find a review quickly in the listings—search by neighborhood, then alphabetically. Happy hunting!

NEED A RESERVATION?

Hotel reservations are an absolute necessity when planning your trip to Los Angeles—although rooms are easier to come by these days. Competition for clients also means properties undergo frequent improvements, so when booking ask about any renovations, lest you get a room within earshot of construction. In this ever-changing city travelers can find themselves temporarily, and most inconveniently, without commonplace amenities such as room service or spa access if their hotel is upgrading.

SERVICES

Most hotels have air-conditioning, cable TV, and in-room irons and ironing boards. Those in the moderate and expensive price ranges often have voice mail, coffeemakers, bathrobes, and hair dryers as well. Most also have high-speed Internet access in guest rooms, with a 24-hour use fee (though at a number of hotels it's free). Wireless access (Wi-Fi) is now common even at budget properties. Southern California's emphasis on being in shape means most hotels have fitness facilities; if the one on-site is not to your liking, ask for a reference to a nearby sports club or gym.

If a particular amenity is important to you, ask for it; many hotels will provide extras upon request. Also double-check your bill at checkout. These days, hotels are fond of tacking on charges such as a "minibar restocking fee" or cleaning charges for smokers. If a charge seems unreasonable, ask to remedy it at checkout. If you're traveling with pets, note that pet policies do change and some hotels require substantial cleaning fees. A cautionary note to smokers: most hotels are entirely smoke-free, meaning that smoking on the property—even outdoors—is frowned upon or prohibited.

STAYING WITH KIDS

From Disneyland to the beach cities, laid-back Los Angeles definitely has a reputation as a family-friendly destination. Resorts and hotels along the coast, in particular, attract plenty of beach-going family vacationers looking for sun and sandcastles. Some properties provide such diversions as in-room movies and video games; others have suites with kitchenettes and foldout sofa beds. Hotels often provide cribs, rollaway beds and references to babysitting services, but make arrangements when booking the room, not when you arrive. Properties that are especially kid-friendly are marked with ☾ throughout the chapter.

PARKING

Exploring Los Angeles, a sprawling city of wide boulevards and five-lane freeways, pretty much requires a car. Though you might stroll Rodeo Drive on foot or amble along the Hollywood Walk of Fame, to get from one part of town to another, you'll need wheels. Thankfully, there's street parking in most areas (read signs carefully as some neighborhoods are by permit only) and many public parking lots offer the first hour or two free. Though a few hotels have free parking, most charge for the privilege, and some resorts only have valet parking, with fees as high as $40 per night.

PRICES

Tax rates for the area will add 10% to 15.5% to your bill depending on where in Los Angeles County you stay; some hoteliers tack on energy, service, or occupancy surcharges—ask about customary charges when you book your room.

When looking for a hotel, don't write off the pricier establishments immediately. Price categories here are determined by "rack rates"—the list price of a hotel room—which is often higher than those you'll find online or by calling the hotel directly. Specials abound, particularly downtown on the weekends. Many hotels have packages that include breakfast, theater tickets, spa services, or exotic rental cars. Pricing is competitive, so always check out the hotel Web site in advance for current special offers.

Finally, when making reservations, don't forget to check the hotel's Web site for exclusive Internet specials.

WHAT IT COSTS					
	¢	$	$$	$$$	$$$$
Hotels	under $100	$100–$199	$200–$299	$300–$400	over $400

The lodgings we list are the top selections of their type in each price category. Price categories are assigned based on the range between the least and most expensive standard double rooms in nonholiday high season, on the European Plan (no meals) unless otherwise noted. Taxes (10%–15.5%) are extra. In listings, we always name the facilities available, but we don't specify whether they cost extra. When pricing accommodations, always ask what's included.

HOTEL REVIEWS

For expanded hotel reviews, visit Fodors.com.

Use the coordinate (✛ 1:B2) at the end of each listing to locate a site on the corresponding map.

DOWNTOWN WITH LOS FELIZ AND SILVER LAKE

For expanded reviews, visit Fodors.com.

An ongoing revitalization in downtown, anchored around the L.A. Live complex, along with a thriving, hipster vibe in Los Feliz and artsy Silver Lake make these areas a great place to see Los Angeles in transition. Think affordable accommodations, safe streets lined with coffeehouses and edgy boutiques that can be explored on foot.

Take advantage of the proximity to the Griffith Park Observatory during the summer or burgeoning nightlife in downtown.

DOWNTOWN

$ **Figueroa Hotel.** On the outside, it feels like Spanish Colonial; on the inside, this 12-story hotel, built in 1926, is a mix of Mexican, Mediterranean, and Moroccan styles, with earth tones, hand-glazed walls, and wrought-iron beds. **Pros:** a short walk to Nokia Theatre, L.A. Live, Convention Center; well-priced; great poolside bar. **Cons:** somewhat funky room decor; small bathrooms; gentrifying neighborhood. ⊠ *939 S. Figueroa St., Downtown* ☎ *213/627–8971, 800/421–9092* ⊕ *www.figueroahotel.com* ⇨ *285 rooms, 6 suites* ♿ *In-room: a/c, Wi-Fi. In-hotel: restaurant, bar, pool, parking* ✢ *1:A3.*

$$$ **Hilton Checkers Los Angeles.** Opened as the Mayflower Hotel in 1927,
Fodor's Choice Checkers retains much of its original character; its various-size rooms
★ all have charming period details, although they also have contemporary luxuries like pillow-top mattresses, coffeemakers, 24-hour room service, and plasma TVs. **Pros:** historic charm; business-friendly; rooftop pool and spa. **Cons:** no on-street parking; some rooms compact; urban setting. ⊠ *535 S. Grand Ave., Downtown* ☎ *213/624–0000, 800/445–8667* ⊕ *www.hiltoncheckers.com* ⇨ *188 rooms, 5 suites* ♿ *In-room: a/c, Internet, Wi-Fi. In-hotel: restaurant, bar, pool, gym, spa, parking* ✢ *1:B3.*

$ **Inn at 657.** Proprietor Patsy Carter runs a homey, welcoming bed-and-breakfast near the University of Southern California. **Pros:** vintage home and quiet garden; homemade treats; you'll meet the innkeeper. **Cons:** low-tech stay; you'll have to speak to other guests; no elevator. ⊠ *657 W. 23rd St., Downtown* ☎ *213/741–2200* ⊕ *www.patsysinn657.com* ⇨ *5 rooms* ♿ *In-room: a/c, Wi-Fi. In-hotel: parking* ✢ *1:A3.*

$ **JW Marriott Los Angeles at L.A. Live.** Set in a shimmering blue-glass tower, the 878-room convention center-adjacent hotel anchors the L.A. Live entertainment complex that's home to the Nokia Theater and more than a dozen bars, nightclubs, and eateries. **Pros:** new property; higher floors have jetliner views; movie theaters, restaurants, and a pro sports arena just out the door. **Cons:** imposing and chilly lobby; expensive dining choices and valet ($38). ⊠ *900 W. Olympic Blvd., Downtown* ☎ *213/765-8600* ⊕ *www.lalivemarriott.com* ⇨ *826 rooms, 52 suites* ♿ *In-room: a/c, safe, Internet, Wi-Fi. In-hotel: restaurant, bar, pool, gym, business center, parking, some pets allowed* ✢ *1:A3.*

$$ **Los Angeles Marriott Downtown.** Near the U.S. 101 and I–110 freeways and five blocks north of the Staples Center, L.A. Live, and the L.A. Convention Center, the 14-story, glass-walled Marriott is an especially good choice if you're traveling on business. **Pros:** new luxury bedding; great city views. **Cons:** corporate feel; weekday rates higher; expensive dining. ⊠ *333 S. Figueroa St., Downtown* ☎ *213/617–1133, 800/260–0227* ⊕ *www.losangelesmarriottdowntown.com* ⇨ *400 rooms, 69 suites* ♿ *In-room: a/c, safe, Internet, Wi-Fi. In-hotel: restaurant, bar, pool, gym, business center, parking* ✢ *1:B2.*

$$$ **Millennium Biltmore Hotel.** One of downtown L.A.'s true treasures, the gilded 1923 Beaux Arts masterpiece exudes ambience and history. **Pros:** historic character; famed filming location; club-level rooms have

BEST BETS FOR LOS ANGELES LODGING

11

Fodor's offers a selective listing of lodging experiences at every price range. Here, we've compiled our top recommendations by price and experience. The very best properties are designated in the listings with the Fodor's Choice logo.

Fodor's Choice★

Beach House Hotel Hermosa Beach, $$, p. 312

Channel Road Inn, $$, p. 320

The Crescent Beverly Hills, $$, p. 307

Farmer's Daughter Hotel, $$, p. 303

Hilton Checkers Los Angeles, $$$, p. 294

Hotel Erwin, $$, p. 325

The Langham Huntington, Pasadena, $$, p. 326

Peninsula Beverly Hills, $$$$, p. 309

Renaissance Hollywood Hotel, $$, p. 303

Shorebreak Hotel, $$$, p. 314

Shutters on the Beach, $$$$, p. 325

Sunset Marquis Hotel & Villas, $$$, p. 312

Terranea, $$$, p. 318

By Price

¢

El Patio Inn, p. 305

$

Ayres Hotel, p. 315

The Beverly Garland Holiday Inn, p. 305

Figueroa Hotel, p. 294

Los Feliz Lodge, p. 298

Magic Castle Hotel, p. 303

Sea Shore Motel, p. 323

Sportsmen's Lodge, p. 305

$$

Beach House Hotel Hermosa Beach, p. 312

Cal Mar Hotel Suites, p. 320

Channel Road Inn, p. 320

The Crescent Beverly Hills, p. 307

Crowne Plaza Redondo Beach & Marina Hotel, p. 318

Farmer's Daughter Hotel, p. 303

Hotel Erwin, p. 325

The Langham Huntington, Pasadena, p. 326

Renaissance Hollywood Hotel, p. 303

Sheraton Gateway Los Angeles Hotel, p. 315

The Standard, Downtown L.A., p. 298

$$$

Hilton Checkers Los Angeles, p. 294

Hotel Amarano Burbank, p. 299

Shorebreak Hotel, p. 314

Sunset Marquis Hotel & Villas, p. 312

Terranea, p. 318

$$$$

Beverly Wilshire, a Four Seasons Hotel, p. 307

Four Seasons Hotel, Los Angeles at Beverly Hills, p. 307

Le Merigot Beach Hotel & Spa, p. 323

Peninsula Beverly Hills, p. 309

Shutters on the Beach, p. 325

By Experience

BEST DESIGN

Avalon, p. 306

Figueroa Hotel, p. 294

Mondrian, p. 311

Mosaic Hotel, p. 309

Oceana, p. 323

The Standard, Downtown L.A., p. 298

Viceroy, p. 325

BEST SPAS

Beverly Hills Hotel, p. 306

Four Seasons Hotel, Los Angeles at Beverly Hills, p. 307

Montage Beverly Hills, p. 307

Renaissance Hollywood Hotel, p. 303

Shutters on the Beach, p. 325

Westin Bonaventure Hotel & Suites, p. 298

GREEN FOCUS

The Ambrose, p. 320

Hotel Palomar Los Angeles–Westwood, p. 312

Hotel Shangri-La, p. 323

Los Feliz Lodge, p. 298

Venice Beach Eco-Cottages, p. 325

MOST KID-FRIENDLY

Casa Malibu Inn on the Beach, p. 315

Loews Santa Monica Beach Hotel, p. 323

Magic Castle Hotel, p. 303

Renaissance Hollywood Hotel, p. 303

Sheraton Universal, p. 305

Shutters on the Beach, p. 325

Terranea, p. 318

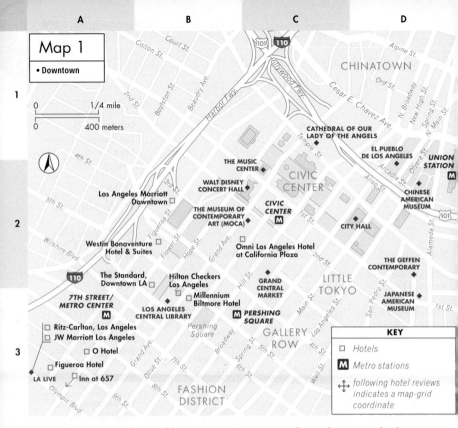

A   **B**   **C**   **D**

many hospitable extras. **Cons:** pricey valet parking; standard rooms are truly compact. ✉ *506 S. Grand Ave., Downtown* ☎ *213/624–1011, 866/866–8086* ⊕ *www.thebiltmore.com* ➟ *635 rooms, 48 suites* ⚭ *In-room: a/c, Internet, Wi-Fi. In-hotel: restaurant, bar, pool, gym, business center, parking* ⊕ *1:B3.*

$ 🏨 **O Hotel.** A former residential hotel, the O has been completely cleaned up and redone in a minimalist, Zen-modern style. **Pros:** boutique, European city-style hotel; ambitious restaurant cuisine; rapidly gentrifying neighborhood. **Cons:** boxy, almost monastic cell-like rooms and few views; gentrifying neighborhood means numerous homeless people, and deserted streetscapes come nightfall. ✉ *819 S. Flower St., Downtown* ☎ *213/623–9904* ⊕ *www.ohotelgroup.com* ➟ *67 rooms* ⚭ *In-room: a/c, Internet. In-hotel: restaurant, bar, gym, business center, parking* ⊕ *1:A3.*

$$ 🏨 **Omni Los Angeles Hotel at California Plaza.** The 17-story Omni is in
☾   downtown's cultural and business heart, just steps from the Museum of Contemporary Art and the Los Angeles Philharmonic's home, Walt Disney Concert Hall. **Pros:** western-facing rooms have stunning views including Disney Hall; a short walk to most downtown culture and courthouses; all-new decor in 2011. **Cons:** confusing lobby layout (entrances on different floors); Olive Street super-traffic-y and not pedestrian-friendly; $30 valet parking. ✉ *251 S. Olive St., Downtown*

CLOSE UP

Spa Specialists

In a city where image is everything, spas are urban sanctuaries, but also places of pampering and rejuvenating for those willing to pay the price. A one-hour massage can set you back as much as $160 (up to $410 for the Spa Montage's tandem treatment by two massage therapists). Along with massages, spas emphasize anti-aging treatments since everyone's after the fountain of youth here.

When booking a massage, specify your preference for a male or female therapist. Prices vary but consider a package of treatments to try out several services. Give yourself time to arrive early and relax via steam, sauna, or Jacuzzi depending on the spa. You should tip at least 15% to 20%.

Beverly Hills Hotel Spa by La Prairie. Close to the hotel's famed pool, the Beverly Hills Hotel Spa by La Prairie is discreetly tucked away. Treatments here are all about the bling: skin treatments involving caviar, gold, and diamonds. ⊠ *9641 Sunset Blvd., Beverly Hills* ☎ *310/887–2505.*

Bliss. Want that red-carpet glow? Bliss's super-hydrating triple-oxygen-treatment facial plumps and reinvigorates even the most blah skin in super-slick, all-white treatment rooms. ⊠ *6250 Hollywood Blvd., Hollywood* ☎ *877/862-5477.*

Huntington Spa. At the Huntington Spa, Chinese medicine–influenced therapies help restore balance and harmony to the body via meditative breathing rituals and acupressure. ⊠ *1401 S. Oak Knoll Ave., Pasadena* ☎ *626/585–6414.*

One. Hollywood skin-care guru Ole Henriksen is behind the treatments at One, in Santa Monica. Body treatments here, such as sea-mineral scrubs, turn skin silky soft using Henriksen's all-natural tonics. ⊠ *Shutters on the Beach, 1 Pico Blvd., Santa Monica* ☎ *310/587–1712.*

Peninsula Spa at the Peninsula Beverly Hills. The Peninsula Spa at the Peninsula Beverly Hills is an exclusive rooftop retreat; rarefied treatments here include massages with oils laced with pulverized precious stones. ⊠ *9882 S. Santa Monica Blvd., Beverly Hills* ☎ *310/551–2888.*

Spa at the Beverly Wilshire. Chill out under a fabulous rain shower—cascades vary from a cool mist to a brisk Atlantic storm, at the Spa at the Beverly Wilshire. A super-size, mosaic-tile steam room is just one of the elegant spa's calming touches. Celeb facialist Kate Somerville's products are featured; intensive 20-minute treatments help soothe techie-neck and, for PDA users, "crampberry" spasms. ⊠ *9500 Wilshire Blvd., Beverly Hills* ☎ *310/385–7023.*

Spa at the Four Seasons, Beverly Hills. The Spa at the Four Seasons, Beverly Hills concentrates on traditional body treatments in small, seasonally scented private quarters. Choose your own soundtrack in the deluxe treatment rooms; try the fabulous Manipura experience body treatment that begins with a Himalayan salt scrub and ends with a body massage with argan oil. ⊠ *300 S. Doheny Dr., Beverly Hills* ☎ *310/273–2222, 310/786–2229.*

Spa Montage. The Moroccan decor, ornate steam room, glass-walled sauna, coed mineral pool, and indoor Jacuzzi at this hidden Casbah of pampering will keep you relaxed for hours. ⊠ *225 N. Canon Dr., Beverly Hills* ☎ *310/860–7840.*

☎ *213/617–3300, 800/843–6664* ⊕ *www.omnihotels.com* ⇀ *439 rooms, 14 suites* ⚏ *In-room: a/c, Wi-Fi. In-hotel: restaurant, bar, pool, gym, spa, business center, parking, some pets allowed* ✛ *1:B2.*

$$ ⌂ **The Ritz-Carlton, Los Angeles.** This citified Ritz-Carlton is on the 23rd and 24th floors of a 54-story tower within downtown's L.A. Live entertainment complex. **Pros:** designer spa with a *Jetsons*-esque relaxation room; well soundproofed; impressive views and dining at WP24. **Cons:** somewhat confusing layout; expensive valet parking and room service. ⌧ *900 West Olympic Blvd., Downtown* ☎ *213/742–6855* ⊕ *www. ritzcarlton.com* ⇀ *109 rooms, 14 suites* ⚏ *In-room: a/c, Internet, Wi-Fi. In-hotel: restaurant, bar, pool, gym, spa, business center, parking, some pets allowed* ✛ *1:A3.*

$$ ⌂ **The Standard, Downtown L.A.** Built in 1955 as Standard Oil's company's headquarters, the building was completely revamped under the sharp eye of owner André Balazs. **Pros:** on-site Rudy's barbershop for grooming; 24/7 coffee shop for dining; rooftop pool and lounge for fun. **Cons:** disruptive party scene weekends and holidays; street noise; hipper-than-thou scene in lounge. ⌧ *550 S. Flower St., Downtown* ☎ *213/892–8080* ⊕ *www.standardhotel.com* ⇀ *171 rooms, 36 suites* ⚏ *In-room: a/c, Internet, Wi-Fi. In-hotel: restaurant, bar, pool, gym, business center, parking, some pets allowed* ✛ *1:A2.*

$$$ ⌂ **Westin Bonaventure Hotel & Suites.** L.A.'s largest hotel has five towers, each mirrored, cylindrical, and 35 stories tall. **Pros:** numerous restaurants including Korean barbecue; an Asian-theme spa offers shiatsu or chair massage; revolving rooftop lounge is a classic experience. **Cons:** lacking personal touch; mazelike lobby and public areas. ⌧ *404 S. Figueroa St., Downtown* ☎ *213/624–1000, 866/716–8132* ⊕ *www. westin.com* ⇀ *1,354 rooms, 135 suites* ⚏ *In-room: a/c, safe, Internet, Wi-Fi. In-hotel: restaurant, bar, pool, gym, spa, business center, parking, some pets allowed* ✛ *1:A2.*

LOS FELIZ

$ ⌂ **Los Feliz Lodge.** Checking into this bungalow-style lodge is like crashing at an eco-minded and artsy friend's place: you let yourself into an apartment with fully stocked kitchen, washer and dryer, and a communal patio. **Pros:** homey feel; walking distance to restaurants. **Cons:** no on-site restaurant or pool. ⌧ *1507 N. Hoover St., Los Feliz* ☎ *323/660– 4150* ⊕ *www.losfelizlodge.com* ⇀ *4 rooms* ⚏ *In-room: a/c, kitchen, Internet, Wi-Fi. In-hotel: laundry facilities* ✛ *2:H2.*

HOLLYWOOD AND THE STUDIOS

For expanded reviews, visit Fodors.com.

For easy access to the Walk of Fame, attractions like Madame Tussaud's and trendy nightlife, Hollywood is the best bet. Movie buffs may take days exploring the vicinity, but most travelers usually spend some time walking along Hollywood Boulevard, which is a congested strip of historic theaters, bars, restaurants and kitschy (and sometimes tacky) shops. Many hotels in the area, however, offer great views of the Hollywood sign and Universal Studios theme park is one or two Metro stops away.

The Beverly Hills Hotel Spa by La Prairie.

BURBANK

$ **Coast Anabelle Hotel.** This small hotel's location on Burbank's main drag is handy, especially for those on studio business since it's a straight-shot mile from NBC and 3 mi from Warner Bros. **Pros:** near studios; free Burbank airport shuttle; use of pool. **Cons:** soundproofing issues; average restaurant and room decor. ⊠ *2011 W. Olive Ave., Burbank* 🕾 *818/845–7800, 800/782–4373* ⊕ *www.coasthotels.com* ⇆ *40 rooms, 7 suites* ⚘ *In-room: a/c, Internet, Wi-Fi. In-hotel: restaurant, bar, gym, laundry facilities, parking* ✛ *4:D1.*

$$$ **Hotel Amarano Burbank.** Close to Burbank's TV and movie studios, the smartly designed Amarano feels like a Beverly Hills boutique hotel. **Pros:** boutique style in a Valley location; pleasant breakfast room. **Cons:** no pool to cool off during scorching summertime; Pass Avenue street noise. ⊠ *322 N. Pass Ave., Burbank* 🕾 *818/842–8887, 888/956–1900* ⊕ *www.hotelamarano.com* ⇆ *91 rooms, 10 suites* ⚘ *In-room: a/c, kitchen, Internet, Wi-Fi. In-hotel: restaurant, bar, gym, business center, parking, some pets allowed* ✛ *4:D1.*

$ **Los Angeles Marriott Burbank Airport.** Across the street from the Burbank's Bob Hope Airport, this hotel is a comfortable choice for business travelers. **Pros:** closest hotel to Burbank's airport with free shuttle; large gym; Daily Grill restaurant on-site. **Cons:** nearby restaurants limited to fast-food outlets; airport noise. ⊠ *2500 N. Hollywood Way, Burbank* 🕾 *818/843–6000, 800/736–9712* ⊕ *www.marriott.com/burap* ⇆ *392 rooms, 93 suites* ⚘ *In-room: a/c, Internet, Wi-Fi. In-hotel: restaurant, bar, pool, gym, laundry facilities, business center, parking, some pets allowed* ✛ *4:D1.*

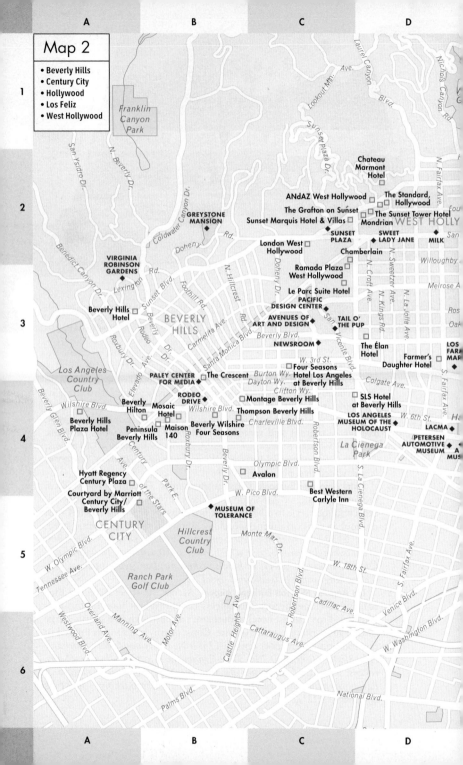

Farmer's Daughter Hotel

Renaissance Hollywood Hotel

HOLLYWOOD

$$
Fodor's Choice
★
Farmer's Daughter Hotel. Tongue-in-cheek country style is the name of the game at this motel: rooms are upholstered in blue gingham with denim bedspreads, and farm tools serve as art. **Pros:** great central city location; across from the cheap eats of the Farmers Market and The Grove's shopping and entertainment mix. **Cons:** pricey restaurant; roadside motel-size rooms; shaded pool; less than stellar service. ☒ *115 S. Fairfax Ave., Farmers Market* ☎ *323/937–3930, 800/334–1658* ⊕ *www. farmersdaughterhotel.com* ➷ *63 rooms, 2 suites* ⚟ *In-room: a/c, Wi-Fi. In-hotel: restaurant, pool, parking, some pets allowed* ✛ *2:D3.*

$
Hollywood Heights Hotel. Formerly a Holiday Inn, this budget hotel delivers bang for your buck in a primo location without the chain-y feel. **Pros:** great location near Hollywood sights and Metro stop; value for money. **Cons:** hefty parking fee. ☒ *2005 N. Highland Ave., Hollywood* ☎ *323/876–8600, 866/696–3157* ⊕ *www.hollywoodheightshotel.com* ➷ *160 rooms* ⚟ *In-room: a/c, Internet, Wi-Fi. In-hotel: restaurant, bar, pool, gym, business center, parking, some pets allowed* ✛ *2:F1.*

$$$
Hollywood Roosevelt Hotel. Think hip bachelor pad when considering the Roosevelt. **Pros:** in the heart of Hollywood's action; lively social scene; great burgers at hotel's restaurant, 25 Degrees. **Cons:** reports of noise and staff attitude; stiff parking charges. ☒ *7000 Hollywood Blvd., Hollywood* ☎ *323/466–7000, 800/950–7667* ⊕ *www. hollywoodroosevelt.com* ➷ *305 rooms, 48 suites* ⚟ *In-room: a/c, Internet, Wi-Fi. In-hotel: restaurant, bar, pool, gym, parking* ✛ *2:E2.*

$
☾
Magic Castle Hotel. Close to the action (and traffic) of Hollywood, this former apartment building faces busy Franklin Avenue and is a quick walk to the nearby Red Line stop at Hollywood & Highland. **Pros:** remarkably friendly and able staff; free Wi-Fi; good value. **Cons:** traffic-y locale; no elevator; small bathrooms. ☒ *7025 Franklin Ave., Hollywood* ☎ *323/851–0800, 800/741–4915* ⊕ *www.magiccastlehotel. com* ➷ *7 rooms, 33 suites* ⚟ *In-room: a/c, kitchen, Internet, Wi-Fi. In-hotel: pool, laundry facilities, parking* ⒢ *Breakfast* ✛ *2:E1.*

$$
The Redbury. In the heart of Hollywood's nightlife, near the intersection of Hollywood and Vine, the Redbury's dark hues and suites (the smallest is 750 square feet) are designed to appeal to everyone's inner Bohemian. ☒ *1717 Vine St., Hollywood* ☎ *323/962–1717, 977/962–1717* ⊕ *www.theredbury.com* ➷ *57 suites* ⚟ *In-room: a/c, kitchen, Internet, Wi-Fi. In-hotel: restaurant, bar, laundry facilities, parking, some pets allowed* ✛ *2:F1.*

$$
☾
Fodor's Choice
★
Renaissance Hollywood Hotel. Part of the massive Hollywood & Highland shopping and entertainment complex, this 20-story Renaissance is at the center of Hollywood's action. **Pros:** large rooms with new contemporary-styled furniture; Red Line Metro–station adjacent. **Cons:** corporate feeling; very touristy. ☒ *1755 N. Highland Ave., Hollywood* ☎ *323/856–1200, 800/769–4774* ⊕ *www.renaissancehollywood.com* ➷ *604 rooms, 33 suites* ⚟ *In-room: a/c, Internet, Wi-Fi. In-hotel: restaurant, bar, pool, gym, spa, business center, parking* ✛ *2:E1.*

$$$$
W Hollywood. Just off the historic intersection of Hollywood and Vine and above a busy Metro station, the W Hollywood is ultramodern and outfitted for the wired traveler. **Pros:** Metro stop outside the front door;

CLOSE UP Kid-Friendly Hotels

Most hotels in Los Angeles allow children under a certain age to stay in their parents' room at no extra charge, but others charge for them as extra adults; be sure to find out the cutoff age for children's discounts.

Hotel pools are dependable distractions for kids, but some are better than others. The **Beverly Hilton Hotel** has an almost-Olympic-size pool that's perfect for splash time. Santa Monica's **Le Merigot Beach Hotel & Spa** has a small pool and even bigger beach out the back door. At the **Beverly Hills Hotel** there are a lifeguard and swimming lessons and pool toys for children. Turndown for kids includes cookies, milk, and a teddy bear. On the sand, experienced swimmers can go native and use **Casa Malibu Inn on the Beach's** boogie boards or opt for board rentals from a nearby surf shop.

More economical choices include the Kids' suites at the **Beverly Garland Holiday Inn**, which come with bunk beds and video games. Also in the Valley, the venerable **Sportsmen's**

Lodge is close to Universal Studios, but a world unto itself: there's plenty of room for kids to roam safely and a family friendly coffee shop. Prior to arrival at the **Loews Santa Monica Beach Hotel** a family concierge can suggest family-friendly vacation ideas. The hotel also offers childproofing kits and special children's menus. **Shutters on the Beach** has boogie board and bike rentals, and keeps kid-appropriate DVDs on hand. Teens will like the **Renaissance Hollywood Hotel,** which links directly to Hollywood & Highland's shopping and Mann Theaters. The **Magic Castle Hotel,** more reasonably priced, is also close to Hollywood's action; kids can attend the famed magic show here only at Sunday brunch. And downtown amid skyscrapers, the **Omni Los Angeles Hotel** welcomes kids with a special goodie bag, lends out toys and games, and offers a special room service menu. The outdoor rooftop pool is sized just right. **Terranea** has a waterslide, splash fountains, and well-outfitted children's center plus supervised teen zone.

you'll be equipped for an in-room party—from ice to cocktail glasses. **Cons:** small pool; pricey dining and valet parking; soundproofing issues. ⊠ *6250 Hollywood Blvd., Hollywood* ☏ *323/798–1300, 888/625–4955* ⊕ *www.whotels.com/hollywood* ➾ *265 rooms, 40 suites* ⌂ *In-room: a/c, Internet, Wi-Fi. In-hotel: restaurant, bar, pool, gym, spa, business center, parking* ✛ *2:F2.*

NORTH HOLLYWOOD

$ ⊡ **The Beverly Garland Holiday Inn.** The Hollywood connection starts in the lobby where framed photos of hotel namesake actress Beverly Garland decorate the lobby. **Pros:** large pool and play area; unpretentious and friendly feel; on-site Wi-Fi café. **Cons:** small bathrooms; touristy; $14 self-parking lot charge. ⊠ *4222 Vineland Ave., North Hollywood* ☏ *818/980–8000, 800/238–3759* ⊕ *www.beverlygarland.com* ➾ *238 rooms, 17 suites* ⌂ *In-room: a/c, Internet, Wi-Fi. In-hotel: restaurant, bar, pool, tennis court, gym, laundry facilities, parking* ✛ *4:C2.*

STUDIO CITY

¢   ⊡ **El Patio Inn.** Behind a classic hacienda-style adobe and neon-lighted facade, El Patio Inn is a throwback to 1960s-era roadside motels. **Pros:** close to Universal Studios and a Metro line stop; Ventura Boulevard has an endless supply of restaurants; low rates. **Cons:** no pool; service matches the low rates; zero amenities. ⊠ *11466 Ventura Blvd., Studio City* ☏ *818/508–5828* ⊕ *www.elpatioinn.com* ➾ *16 rooms* ⌂ *In-room: a/c, Internet. In-hotel: parking, some pets allowed* ✛ *4:B2.*

$ ⊡ **Sportsmen's Lodge.** The sprawling five-story hotel is under new ownership and management, and the lobby, bar, and popular coffee shop now have a contemporary look. **Pros:** close to Ventura Boulevard's plentiful restaurants; free shuttle and discounted tickets to Universal Hollywood; garden-view rooms are quietest. **Cons:** $11 daily self-parking fee. ⊠ *12825 Ventura Blvd., Studio City* ☏ *818/769–4700, 800/821–8511* ⊕ *www.slhotel.com* ➾ *177 rooms, 13 suites* ⌂ *In-room: a/c, Internet, Wi-Fi. In-hotel: restaurant, bar, pool, gym, laundry facilities, parking* ✛ *4:A2.*

UNIVERSAL CITY

$$ ⊡ **Sheraton Universal.** Because of its large meeting spaces and veteran staff, this Sheraton buzzes year-round. **Pros:** woodsy location straddling Hollywood Hills; Metro access; all new room furnishings. **Cons:** average in-house restaurant; touristy. ⊠ *333 Universal Hollywood Dr., Universal City* ☏ *818/980–1212, 888/627–7184* ⊕ *www.sheratonuniversal.com* ➾ *451 rooms, 31 suites* ⌂ *In-room: a/c, Internet, Wi-Fi. In-hotel: restaurant, bar, pool, gym, laundry facilities, business center, parking, some pets allowed* ✛ *4:C2.*

BEVERLY HILLS AND THE WESTSIDE

For expanded reviews, visit Fodors.com.

A dream location (and zip code), posh Beverly Hills and the Westside are likely the most central for accessing the beaches, the Getty Center, and mid-city. The prime address means hotels here, including stylish newcomers like the Thompson and SLS, come with a hefty price tag.

The silver lining—walkable pockets of Beverly Hills, so you'll spend less time in a car.

BEL AIR

$ ▦ **Hotel Angeleno.** A thoroughly up-to-date remake of the landmark 1970s mod, cylindrical tower hotel, this building conveniently sits at the crossroads of Sunset Boulevard and I–405. **Pros:** complimentary shuttle to nearby Getty Center; free Wi-Fi; intriguing design throughout. **Cons:** compact rooms; small, shaded pool; somewhat isolated location. ⊠ *170 N. Church La., Brentwood* ☎ *310/476–6411, 866/264–3536* ⊕ *www. jdvhotels.com/angeleno* ⤳ *205 rooms, 3 suites* ⚹ *In-room: a/c, Wi-Fi. In-hotel: restaurant, bar, pool, gym, business center, parking* ✛ *3:C1.*

$$$$ ▦ **Luxe Hotel Sunset Boulevard.** On seven landscaped acres near the Getty Center, the Luxe feels like a secluded country club—but it's also next to I–405 for easy freeway access. **Pros:** country-club feel; oversize rooms; central for Westside business meetings. **Cons:** some freeway noise; off an extremely busy intersection; a car almost essential. ⊠ *11461 Sunset Blvd., Bel Air* ☎ *310/476–6571, 800/468–3541* ⊕ *www.luxehotels. com* ⤳ *110 rooms, 51 suites* ⚹ *In-room: a/c, Internet, Wi-Fi. In-hotel: restaurant, bar, pool, tennis court, gym, spa, business center, parking, some pets allowed* ✛ *3:C1.*

BEVERLY HILLS

$$$ ▦ **Avalon.** Interior decorator Kelly Wearstler put her Midas touch on this mid-century Beverly Hills hotel, mixing original classic pieces by George Nelson and Charles Eames with her chic custom designs. **Pros:** stylish; Beverly Hills location. **Cons:** poolside social scene can be noisy. ⊠ *9400 W. Olympic Blvd., Beverly Hills* ☎ *310/277–5221, 800/670–6183* ⊕ *www.avalonbeverlyhills.com* ⤳ *76 rooms, 10 suites* ⚹ *In-room: a/c, kitchen, Internet, Wi-Fi. In-hotel: restaurant, bar, pool, gym, laundry facilities, parking, some pets allowed* ✛ *2:B4.*

$ ▦ **Best Western Carlyle Inn.** A gussied-up Best Western, the Carlyle is adjacent to Beverly Hills and Century City. **Pros:** full breakfast available indoors or outside. **Cons:** smallish rooms and street noise from busy Robertson and nearby Pico boulevards; weekends often sell out—book ahead. ⊠ *1119 S. Robertson Blvd., Beverly Hills* ☎ *310/275–4445, 800/322–7595* ⊕ *www.carlyle-inn.com* ⤳ *32 rooms* ⚹ *In-room: a/c, safe, Wi-Fi. In-hotel: gym, business center, parking* ❆ *Breakfast* ✛ *2:C4.*

$$$$ ▦ **Beverly Hills Hotel.** Remarkably still at the top of her game, the "Pink ♺ Palace" continues to attract Hollywood's elite after 100 years. **Pros:** pool, spa, and legendary, retro 20-seat Fountain Coffee room. **Cons:** average and pricey fare at the Polo Lounge. ⊠ *9641 Sunset Blvd., Beverly Hills* ☎ *310/276–2251, 800/283–8885* ⊕ *www.beverlyhillshotel. com* ⤳ *145 rooms, 38 suites, 23 bungalows* ⚹ *In-room: a/c, kitchen, Internet, Wi-Fi. In-hotel: restaurant, bar, pool, gym, spa, parking, some pets allowed* ✛ *2:A3.*

$ ▦ **Beverly Hills Plaza Hotel.** With a precious courtyard surrounding the pool, the well-maintained, all-suites Beverly Hills Plaza has a look that would be right at home in the south of France. **Pros:** European ambience; amiable staff. **Cons:** lowest-priced suites are accessible via stairs only; no services or restaurants close-by, so car is a must. ⊠ *10300*

Wilshire Blvd., Beverly Hills ☎ *310/275–5575, 800/800–1234* ⊕ *www. beverlyhillsplazahotel.com* ➫ *116 suites* ⌂ *In-room: a/c, kitchen, Internet, Wi-Fi. In-hotel: restaurant, bar, pool, gym, business center, parking* ✛ *2:A4.*

$$$ 🏨 **Beverly Hilton.** Home of the Golden Globe Awards, the Beverly Hilton is as polished as its glitzy address after some pricey renovation. **Pros:** walking distance to Beverly Hills; complimentary car service for short jaunts; one of L.A.'s largest hotel pools. **Cons:** corporate feel; some rooms feel tired; unremarkable dining. ⊠ *9876 Wilshire Blvd., Beverly Hills* ☎ *310/274–7777, 877/414–8018* ⊕ *www.beverlyhilton. com* ➫ *468 rooms, 101 suites* ⌂ *In-room: a/c, Internet, Wi-Fi. In-hotel: restaurant, bar, pool, gym, spa, business center, parking, some pets allowed* ✛ *2:A4.*

$$$$ 🏨 **Beverly Wilshire, a Four Seasons Hotel.** Built in 1928, the Italian Renaissance–style Wilshire wing of this fabled hotel is replete with elegant details: crystal chandeliers, oak paneling, walnut doors, crown moldings, and marble. **Pros:** chic location; top-notch service; and refined vibe. **Cons:** small lobby; valet parking backs up at peak times; expensive dining choices. ⊠ *9500 Wilshire Blvd., Beverly Hills* ☎ *310/275–5200, 800/427–4354* ⊕ *www.fourseasons.com/beverlywilshire* ➫ *258 rooms, 137 suites* ⌂ *In-room: a/c, Internet, Wi-Fi. In-hotel: restaurant, bar, pool, gym, spa, business center, parking, some pets allowed* ✛ *2:B4.*

$$ 🏨 **The Crescent Beverly Hills.** Built in 1926 as a dorm for silent film actors, the Crescent is now a sleek boutique hotel within the Beverly Hills shopping triangle. **Pros:** the on-site restaurant CBH's tasty cuisine and convivial happy hour; the lobby is fashionista central. **Cons:** dorm-size rooms; gym an additional fee and only accessed outside hotel via Sports ClubLA; no elevator. ⊠ *403 N. Crescent Dr., Beverly Hills* ☎ *310/247–0505* ⊕ *www.crescentbh.com* ➫ *35 rooms* ⌂ *In-room: a/c, Wi-Fi. In-hotel: restaurant, bar, parking* ✛ *2:B3.*

Fodor's Choice
★

$$$$ 🏨 **Four Seasons Hotel, Los Angeles at Beverly Hills.** High hedges and patio gardens make this hotel a secluded retreat that even the hum of traffic can't permeate. **Pros:** expert concierge; deferential service; celebrity magnet. **Cons:** Hollywood scene in bar and restaurant means rarefied prices. ⊠ *300 S. Doheny Dr., Beverly Hills* ☎ *310/273–2222, 800/332–3442* ⊕ *www.fourseasons.com/losangeles* ➫ *185 rooms, 100 suites* ⌂ *In-room: a/c, kitchen, Internet, Wi-Fi. In-hotel: restaurant, bar, pool, gym, spa, business center, parking, some pets allowed* ✛ *2:C3.*

$$ 🏨 **Maison 140.** Colonial chic reigns in this three-story, 1930s spot, Beverly Hills' most grandly designed boutique hotel. **Pros:** ultimate boutique stay; eye-catching design; short walk to all Beverly Hills shopping. **Cons:** few amenities; room service from another hotel; 100% smoke-free. ⊠ *140 S. Lasky Dr., Beverly Hills* ☎ *310/281–4000, 800/670–6182* ⊕ *www.maison140beverlyhills.com* ➫ *43 rooms* ⌂ *In-room: a/c, Internet, Wi-Fi. In-hotel: bar, gym, business center, parking, some pets allowed* ✛ *2:B4.*

$$$$ 🏨 **Montage Beverly Hills.** The new kid on a posh block, the Montage Beverly Hills, which opened in late 2008, is a nine-story, Mediterranean-style palazzo dedicated to welcoming those who relish the highest-end stay. **Pros:** a feast for the senses; architectural details include crown

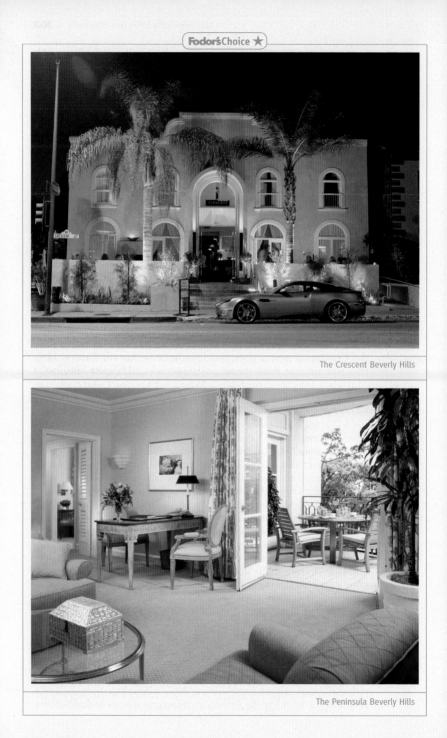

The Crescent Beverly Hills

The Peninsula Beverly Hills

moldings and muted colors; the highly trained staff is most obliging. **Cons:** all this finery adds up to a hefty tab. ✉ *225 N. Canon Dr., Beverly Hills* ☎ *310/860–7800, 888/860–0788* ⊕ *www.montagebeverlyhills. com* ⌲ *146 rooms, 55 suites* ⊡ *In-room: a/c, kitchen, Internet, Wi-Fi. In-hotel: restaurant, bar, pool, gym, spa, business center, parking, some pets allowed* ✛ *2:B4.*

$$$ ⊞ **Mosaic Hotel.** Stylish, comfortable, and decked out with the latest electronics, the Mosaic is on a quiet side street that's central to Beverly Hills's business district. **Pros:** intimate and cozy; friendly service; free Wi-Fi and local shuttle service. **Cons:** small and shaded pool; tiny lobby. ✉ *125 S. Spalding Dr., Beverly Hills* ☎ *310/278–0303, 800/463–4466* ⊕ *www.mosaichotel.com* ⌲ *44 rooms, 5 suites* ⊡ *In-room: a/c, Internet, Wi-Fi. In-hotel: restaurant, bar, pool, gym, business center, parking, some pets allowed* ✛ *2:B4.*

$$$$ ⊞ **Peninsula Beverly Hills.** This French Rivera–style palace is a favorite of Hollywood boldface names, but all kinds of visitors consistently

Fodor's Choice ⭐ describe their stay as near perfect—though expensive. **Pros:** central, walkable Beverly Hills location; stunning flowers; one of the best concierges in the city. **Cons:** serious bucks required to stay here. ✉ *9882 S. Santa Monica Blvd., Beverly Hills* ☎ *310/551–2888, 800/462–7899* ⊕ *www.beverlyhills.peninsula.com* ⌲ *142 rooms, 36 suites, 16 villas* ⊡ *In-room: a/c, Internet, Wi-Fi. In-hotel: restaurant, bar, pool, gym, spa, business center, parking, some pets allowed* ✛ *2:B4.*

$$$$ ⊞ **SLS Hotel at Beverly Hills.** Imagine dropping into Alice in Wonderland's rabbit hole: this is the colorful, textured, and tchotke-filled lobby of the SLS from design maestro Philippe Starck. **Pros:** a vibrant newcomer with lofty ambitions; excellent design and cuisine. **Cons:** standard rooms are compact but you pay for the scene; pricey hotel dining. ✉ *465 S. La Cienega Blvd., Beverly Hills* ☎ *310/247–0400* ⊕ *www. slshotels.com* ⌲ *236 rooms, 61 suites* ⊡ *In-room: a/c, Internet, Wi-Fi. In-hotel: restaurant, bar, pool, gym, spa, business center, parking, some pets allowed* ✛ *2:C4.*

$$$$ ⊞ **Thompson Beverly Hills.** The Beverly Hills outpost of New York's Thompson Hotels has smoky-sexy interiors, and lacquered all-black corridors are by designer Dodd Mitchell who makes the most of the '70s-era boxy-rooms, filling them with texture and reflective surfaces (slim mirrored panels on the ceiling). **Pros:** visually enticing interiors; party scene on the rooftop. **Cons:** compact rooms. ✉ *9360 Wilshire Blvd., Beverly Hills* ☎ *310/273–1400* ⊕ *www.thompsonhotels.com* ⌲ *91 rooms, 16 suites* ⊡ *In-room: a/c, Internet, Wi-Fi. In-hotel: restaurant, bar, pool, gym, parking* ✛ *2:B4.*

CENTURY CITY

$ ⊞ **Courtyard by Marriott Century City/Beverly Hills.** Minutes from Beverly Hills, this Marriott has is adjacent to Century City's businesses and medical center. **Pros:** friendly hotel staff; daily breakfast buffet; close to cosmetic medical centers. **Cons:** compact, basic rooms; constant traffic out the front door; no pool. ✉ *10320 W. Olympic Blvd., Century City* ☎ *310/556–2777, 800/750–0953* ⊕ *www.courtyard.com* ⌲ *135 rooms* ⊡ *In-room: a/c, Internet, Wi-Fi. In-hotel: restaurant, gym, laundry facilities, business center, parking* ✛ *2:A5.*

$$ ⊡ **Hyatt Regency Century Plaza.** For more than 40 years, the Century Plaza has been one of L.A.'s most frequented business hotels. **Pros:** on-site power gym, Equinox Fitness Club and Spa, open to guests for an extra fee; stunning views to west; lower weekend rates. **Cons:** large, corporate hotel; isolated location in Century City. ⊠ *2025 Ave. of the Stars, Century City* 📞 *310/228–1234, 800/233–1234* ⊕ *www.centuryplaza. hyatt.com* ⤴ *687 rooms, 39 suites* 🛇 *In-room: a/c, safe, Internet, Wi-Fi. In-hotel: restaurant, bar, pool, gym, spa, business center, parking, some pets allowed* ✛ *2:A4.*

WEST HOLLYWOOD

$$ ⊡ **ANdAZ West Hollywood.** On the north side of the Sunset Strip and reopened in 2009, the ANdAZ is a complete update of the former Hyatt West Hollywood. **Pros:** sleek new interiors with the latest gadgets like free Wi-Fi throughout and sizable flat-screen TVs; ambitious hotel dining and bar concepts; excellent gym overlooks Sunset Boulevard's nonstop action. **Cons:** traffic congestion impedes access; Sunset Strip is wildly popular weekends and holidays. ⊠ *8401 Sunset Blvd., West Hollywood* 📞 *323/656–1234, 800/233–1234* ⊕ *www.andaz.com* ⤴ *219 rooms, 19 suites* 🛇 *In-room: a/c, Internet, Wi-Fi. In-hotel: restaurant, bar, pool, gym, business center, parking, some pets allowed* ✛ *2:C2.*

$$$ ⊡ **Chamberlain.** On a leafy residential side street, the Chamberlain is steps from Santa Monica Boulevard and close to the Sunset Strip, bringing in young business types, the fashion–design crowd, and 24-hour party people looking to roam West Hollywood and the Strip. **Pros:** excellent guests-only dining room and bar; pleasing design; close to Strip without the hassle. **Cons:** compact bathrooms. ⊠ *1000 Westmount Dr., West Hollywood* 📞 *310/657–7400, 800/201–9652* ⊕ *www. chamberlainwesthollywood.com* ⤴ *114 suites* 🛇 *In-room: a/c, kitchen, Internet, Wi-Fi. In-hotel: restaurant, bar, pool, gym, business center, parking, some pets allowed* ✛ *2:C2.*

$$$$ ⊡ **Chateau Marmont Hotel.** Celebs like Johnny Depp appreciate this swanky hotel for its secluded cottages, bungalows, and understated suites and penthouses. **Pros:** walking distance to all of Sunset Strip's action; great food and vibe at Bar Marmont; guaranteed celeb spotting. **Cons:** plenty of attitude from staff; ancient elevators. ⊠ *8221 Sunset Blvd., West Hollywood* 📞 *323/656–1010, 800/242–8328* ⊕ *www. chateaumarmont.com* ⤴ *11 rooms, 63 suites* 🛇 *In-room: a/c, kitchen, Internet, Wi-Fi. In-hotel: restaurant, bar, pool, gym, parking, some pets allowed* ✛ *2:D2.*

$$ ⊡ **The Élan Hotel.** Small and modest, and a favorite of international travelers, this hotel has an enviable location within walking distance of some of the city's best restaurants and the Beverly Center. **Pros:** friendly staff; free Wi-Fi; central location with many great restaurants nearby. **Cons:** super-compact

> ## WORD OF MOUTH
>
> "We stayed at the Élan Hotel, within walking distance of the Beverly Center, in a neighborhood full of small shops and dining spots. It's a small boutique hotel. Very nice staff and comfortable rooms. Our rate included an extensive breakfast and evening wine and snacks in the lobby!"
>
> —lcuy

rooms; no pool. ⊠ *8435 Beverly Blvd., West Hollywood* ☎ *323/658–6663, 866/203–2212* ⊕ *www.elanhotel.com* ⤶ *46 rooms, 3 suites* ⚐ *In-room: a/c, Internet, Wi-Fi. In-hotel: business center, parking* ❄ *Breakfast* ✛ *2:D3.*

$$$ 🏨 **The Grafton on Sunset.** It's easy to tap into the Sunset Strip energy here, especially at the hotel's new Olive Kitchen + Bar restaurant and rock-n-roll–styled lounge, the Cutting Room. **Pros:** playful amenities; snazzy suites; heart of Strip's action. **Cons:** higher-priced weekend stays; Strip traffic; small standard rooms. ⊠ *8462 W. Sunset Blvd., West Hollywood* ☎ *323/654–4600, 800/821–3660* ⊕ *www.graftononsunset.com* ⤶ *105 rooms, 3 suites* ⚐ *In-room: a/c, Internet, Wi-Fi. In-hotel: restaurant, bar, pool, gym, business center, parking, some pets allowed* ✛ *2:C2.*

$$ 🏨 **Le Parc Suite Hotel.** On a tree-lined residential street close to CBS Television City and the Pacific Design Center, this congenial low-rise hotel aims to make guests feel coddled, with extremely personalized service and a strong commitment to privacy. **Pros:** great views from rooftop pool deck; lighted tennis court. **Cons:** small lobby. ⊠ *733 W. Knoll Dr., West Hollywood* ☎ *310/855–8888, 800/578–4837* ⊕ *www.leparcsuites.com* ⤶ *154 suites* ⚐ *In-room: a/c, kitchen, Internet, Wi-Fi. In-hotel: restaurant, bar, pool, tennis court, gym, laundry facilities, parking, some pets allowed* ✛ *2:C3.*

$$ 🏨 **The London West Hollywood.** Just off the Sunset Strip, cosmopolitan and chic in design, the London WeHo is a remake of 1984-built Bel Age. **Pros:** perfectly designed interiors; hillside and city views in generous-size suites all with balconies and steps from the Strip. **Cons:** too refined for kids to be comfortable; lower floors have mundane views. ⊠ *1020 N. San Vicente Blvd., West Hollywood* ☎ *310/854–1111, 866/282–4560* ⊕ *www.thelondonwesthollywood.com* ⤶ *200 suites* ⚐ *In-room: a/c, Internet, Wi-Fi. In-hotel: restaurant, bar, pool, gym, business center, parking, some pets allowed* ✛ *2:C2.*

$$$ 🏨 **Mondrian.** A city club attitude pervades at the spendy Mondrian. **Pros:** pool, spa, and nighttime social scene mean never having to leave the property. **Cons:** $32 per night valet parking only; late-night party scene; inflated prices. ⊠ *8440 Sunset Blvd., West Hollywood* ☎ *323/650–8999, 800/606–6090* ⊕ *www.mondrianhotel.com* ⤶ *54 rooms, 183 suites* ⚐ *In-room: a/c, Internet, Wi-Fi. In-hotel: restaurant, bar, pool, gym, spa, parking, some pets allowed* ✛ *2:D2.*

$$ 🏨 **Ramada Plaza West Hollywood.** Popular with tour groups, this Ramada outlet has a prime West Hollywood location, close to the Sunset Strip. **Pros:** free Wi-Fi; close to nightlife; friendly staff. **Cons:** street noise and soundproofing issues; shaded pool; parking fees. ⊠ *8585 Santa Monica Blvd., West Hollywood* ☎ *310/652–6400, 800/272–6232* ⊕ *www.ramadaweho.com* ⤶ *131 rooms, 45 suites* ⚐ *In-room: a/c, Internet, Wi-Fi. In-hotel: restaurant, bar, pool, gym, laundry facilities, business center, parking* ✛ *2:D2.*

$$ 🏨 **The Standard, Hollywood.** Hotelier André Balazs created this playful Sunset Strip hotel out of a former retirement home. **Pros:** on-site, decent 24-hour coffee shop; poolside scene; live DJs. **Cons:** extended party place for twentysomethings; staff big on attitude rather than service. ⊠ *8300 Sunset Blvd., West Hollywood* ☎ *323/650–9090* ⊕ *www.*

standardhotel.com ⤳ *137 rooms, 2 suites* ☖ *In-room: a/c, Internet, Wi-Fi. In-hotel: restaurant, bar, pool, business center, parking, some pets allowed* ✛ *2:D2.*

$$$ 🏨 **Sunset Marquis Hotel & Villas.** If you're in town to cut your new hit

Fodor'sChoice single, you'll appreciate the two on-site recording studios here. **Pros:**

★ superior service; discreet setting just off the Strip; clublike atmosphere; free passes to Equinox nearby. **Cons:** standard suites are somewhat small. ⊠ *1200 N. Alta Loma Rd., West Hollywood* ☎ *310/657–1333, 800/858–9758* ⊕ *www.sunsetmarquis.com* ⤳ *102 suites, 52 villas* ☖ *In-room: a/c, kitchen, Internet, Wi-Fi. In-hotel: restaurant, bar, pool, gym, spa, business center, parking, some pets allowed* ✛ *2:C3.*

$$$ 🏨 **The Sunset Tower Hotel.** A clubby style infuses the 1929 art deco landmark once known as the Argyle. **Pros:** sunset Strip's diversions right out the door; Tower Bar a favorite of Hollywood's elite; incredible city views. **Cons:** wedged into the Strip—driveway a challenge; small standard rooms. ⊠ *8358 Sunset Blvd., West Hollywood* ☎ *323/654–7100, 800/225–2637* ⊕ *www.sunsettowerhotel.com* ⤳ *20 rooms, 44 suites* ☖ *In-room: a/c, Internet, Wi-Fi. In-hotel: restaurant, bar, pool, gym, spa, business center, parking, some pets allowed* ✛ *2:D2.*

WESTWOOD

$$ 🏨 **Hotel Palomar Los Angeles–Westwood.** A convivial lobby and smartly designed rooms set this Kimpton-managed hotel apart. **Pros:** visually appealing room design; in-room luxe touches like Frette linens and Aveda toiletries; friendly staff. **Cons:** isolated on a busy thoroughfare. ⊠ *10740 Wilshire Blvd., Westwood* ☎ *310/475–8711, 800/472–8556* ⊕ *www.hotelpalomar-lawestwood.com* ⤳ *238 rooms, 26 suites* ☖ *In-room: a/c, Internet, Wi-Fi. In-hotel: restaurant, bar, pool, gym, business center, parking, some pets allowed* ✛ *3:D2.*

SANTA MONICA AND THE BEACHES

For expanded reviews, visit Fodors.com.

L.A.'s laid-back beach towns are the ideal place from which to enjoy the trifecta of coastal living: sun, sand, and surf. From moneyed Malibu to the original surf city Huntington Beach, each city retains a character and feel of its own, but collectively, these beach towns are family-friendly, scenic, and dotted with waterfront hotels (try the Huntley or Viceroy in Santa Monica for nighttime drinks at least, if you're not staying in the area). The farther south you venture, however, the more likely you are to encounter traffic while driving to the city's main attractions.

HERMOSA BEACH

$$ 🏨 **Beach House Hotel Hermosa Beach.** Sitting right on the sand, border-

Fodor'sChoice ing the Strand (SoCal's famous beach bike and walk path), the Beach

★ House looks like a New England sea cottage from a century ago. **Pros:** on the beach; great outdoorsy activities; ample space. **Cons:** Continental breakfast only; noise from the busy Strand; no pool. ⊠ *1300 The Strand, Hermosa Beach* ☎ *310/374–3001, 888/895–4559* ⊕ *www.beach-house.com* ⤳ *96 suites* ☖ *In-room: a/c, kitchen, Internet, Wi-Fi. In-hotel: gym, beach, business center, parking* 🍽️ *Breakfast* ✛ *3:D6.*

Poolside Perks

11

Beverly Hills Hotel

By day or night, splashy pools are so L.A.—with a pomegranate mojito in hand, of course. From ritzy Beverly Hills and buzzing West Hollywood to the beach towns of Hermosa Beach and Santa Monica, pools are where guests socialize, lounge, and generally soak up the sun.

Undoubtedly, Beverly Hills hotels have some of the city's best pools. Among the newcomers, the trendy **Thompson Beverly Hills** has a two-story deck and heated pool that's a sleek retreat in the middle of the metropolis (☎ 310/273–1400 ⊕ www. thompsonhotels.com). At the Philippe Starck–designed **SLS Hotel at Beverly Hills** (☎ 310/247–0400 ⊕ www. slshotels.com), the pool's artsy look includes oversized metallic frames meant to do just that—frame views of the skyline. Private cabanas here come equipped with DVD players, video-on-demand, and fully stocked minibars. Elegant and intimate, the rooftop garden and pool at the **Peninsula Beverly Hills** (☎ 310/551–2888 ⊕ www.beverlyhills.peninsula. com) is the ideal spot for a delicious breakfast of homemade granola and berries or afternoon cocktails.

In West Hollywood, the scene-y **Mondrian** (☎ 323/650–8999 ⊕ www. mondrianhotel.com) offers underwater music at its rooftop pool; meanwhile, divans and beds are flanked by larger-than-life flower pots. High above everything else in the neighborhood, the **London West Hollywood** (☎ 310/854–1111 ⊕ www. thelondonwesthollywood.com) allows for panoramic views of downtown and Century City. Have a pool "concierge" arrange for a spa treatment in your cabana, or on hot days, bring you complimentary orange wedges and smoothie samples.

In Long Beach, the **Hotel Maya**'s pool is family-friendly though design-obsessed will love its saffron-hued cabanas and teakwood deck area (☎ 562/435–7676 ⊕ www.hotelmaya. doubletree.com). At Santa Monica's **Hotel Shangri-La** (☎ 310/394–2791 ⊕ www.shangrila-hotel.com), the black-and-white courtyard pool is surrounded by designer-perfect cabanas; live music is also part of the scene on weekend nights.

And, of course, you can't miss the biggest pool of them all: the nearby Pacific Ocean.

HUNTINGTON BEACH

$$$
Fodor's Choice
★

Shorebreak Hotel. Across the street from Huntington Beach, this recently opened property from Joie de Vivre hotels is a surfer's haven, but with all the creature comforts. **Pros:** great location; laid-back vibe; good dining. **Cons:** some rooms face interior courtyard; limited parking in garage lot. ⊠ *500 Pacific Coast Hwy., Huntington Beach* ☎ *714/861–4470, 877/744–1117* ⊕ *www.shorebreakhotel.com* ➪ *118 rooms, 39 suites* ⌂ *In-room: a/c, Internet, Wi-Fi. In-hotel: restaurant, bar, gym, beach, water sports, business center, parking, some pets allowed* ✢ *3:D6.*

LONG BEACH

$$
Hotel Maya–a Doubletree Hotel. Formerly the Coast Long Beach, this waterfront property set on 11 acres gets a second lease on life as Hotel Maya. **Pros:** low-key vibe; dedicated staff. **Cons:** location is slightly confusing for first-time visitors. ⊠ *700 Queensway Dr., Long Beach* ☎ *562/435–7676* ⊕ *www.hotelmaya.doubletree.com* ➪ *196 rooms, 1 suite* ⌂ *In-room: a/c, Internet, Wi-Fi. In-hotel: restaurant, bar, pool, tennis court, gym, business center, parking, some pets allowed* ✢ *3:D6.*

$
Hotel Queen Mary. Experience the golden age of transatlantic travel without the seasickness: a 1936–art deco style reigns on the *Queen Mary,* from the ship's mahogany paneling to its nickel-plated doors to the majestic Grand Salon. **Pros:** walking the historic Promenade deck; views from Long Beach out to the Pacific; art deco details. **Cons:** spotty service; no soundproofing. ⊠ *1126 Queens Hwy., Long Beach* ☎ *562/435–3511, 877/342–0742* ⊕ *www.queenmary.com* ➪ *305 state-rooms, 9 suites* ⌂ *In-room: a/c, Internet, Wi-Fi. In-hotel: restaurant, bar, gym, spa, parking* ✢ *3:D6.*

$$
Renaissance Long Beach Hotel. Set in the heart of Long Beach's business district, directly across from the Long Beach Convention Center's entrance, the Renaissance's updated lobby is mix of bold green, orange, and yellow with digital images floating on screens behind the check-in desk. **Pros:** easy walk to convention center; Shoreline Village dining and Aquarium of the Pacific. **Cons:** rooms facing south have best views; definite corporate vibe. ⊠ *111 E. Ocean Blvd., Long Beach* ☎ *562/437–5900, 888/236–2427* ⊕ *www.renaissancelongbeach.com* ➪ *360 rooms, 14 suites* ⌂ *In-room: a/c, Internet, Wi-Fi. In-hotel: restaurant, bar, pool, gym, business center, parking, some pets allowed* ✢ *3:D6.*

LOS ANGELES INTERNATIONAL AIRPORT

$
Custom Hotel. Close enough to LAX to see the runways, the Custom Hotel is a playful and practical redo of a 12-story, mid-century modern tower by famed L.A. architect Welton Beckett (of Hollywood's Capitol Records' building and the Dorothy Chandler Pavilion). **Pros:** close to LAX and beach areas; designer interiors; and free Wi-Fi. **Cons:** at the desolate end of Lincoln Boulevard. ⊠ *8639 Lincoln Blvd., Los Angeles International Airport* ☎ *310/645–0400, 877/287–8601* ⊕ *www.customhotel.com* ➪ *248 rooms, 2 suites* ⌂ *In-room: a/c, Internet, Wi-Fi. In-hotel: restaurant, bar, pool, gym, business center, parking, some pets allowed* ✢ *3:E6.*

$ ⬚ **Radisson Los Angeles Westside.** Just 3 mi north of LAX, the Radisson Westside is close to freeways and a good value for those who want to fly in and check in to a hotel right away. **Pros:** within walking distance of Howard Hughes Promenade's numerous shops, restaurants, and cinemas; park-and-fly packages and free Internet access. **Cons:** unremarkable dining. ✉ *6161 Centinela Ave., Los Angeles International Airport* ☎ *310/649–1776, 888/201–1718* ⊕ *www.radissonwestside.com* ⌁ *365 rooms, 3 suites* ⌂ *In-room: a/c, Internet, Wi-Fi. In-hotel: restaurant, bar, pool, gym, laundry facilities, business center, parking, some pets allowed* ✛ *3:F5.*

$$ ⬚ **Sheraton Gateway Los Angeles Hotel.** LAX's coolest-looking hotel is so swank that guests have been known to ask to buy the black-and-white photos hanging behind the front desk. **Pros:** weekend rates significantly lower; free LAX shuttle. **Cons:** convenient to airport but not much else. ✉ *6101 W. Century Blvd., Los Angeles International Airport* ☎ *310/642–1111, 800/325–3535* ⊕ *www.sheratonlosangeles. com* ⌁ *714 rooms, 88 suites* ⌂ *In-room: a/c, Internet, Wi-Fi. In-hotel: restaurant, bar, pool, gym, business center, parking, some pets allowed* ✛ *3:F6.*

MALIBU

$ ⬚ **Casa Malibu Inn on the Beach.** Catch an early-morning surf break or
☾ just hang out all day on Casa Malibu's private stretch of beach that's raked smooth every morning. **Pros:** stellar location; low-key beachy vibe; close to most of Malibu's best restaurants. **Cons:** summer weekends and holidays book up months in advance; small tidy bathrooms. ✉ *22752 Pacific Coast Hwy., Malibu* ☎ *310/456–2219, 800/831–0858* ⌁ *19 rooms, 2 suites* ⌂ *In-room: some a/c, kitchen, Internet, Wi-Fi. In-hotel: beach, parking* ✛ *3:A3.*

$$$ ⬚ **Malibu Beach Inn.** Set right on exclusive and private Carbon Beach, the hotel is home to all manner of the super-rich: the location doesn't get any better than this. **Pros:** live like a billionaire in designer-perfect interiors right on the beach. **Cons:** noise of PCH; no pool, gym, or hot tub; billionaire's travel budget also required. ✉ *22878 Pacific Coast Hwy., Malibu* ☎ *310/456–6444* ⊕ *www.malibubeachinn.com* ⌁ *41 rooms, 6 suites* ⌂ *In-room: a/c, Internet, Wi-Fi. In-hotel: restaurant, bar, beach, parking* ✛ *3:A3.*

MANHATTAN BEACH

$ ⬚ **Ayres Hotel.** The rates may be relatively modest, but the style here
☾ is grand. **Pros:** free parking, Wi-Fi and breakfast **Cons:** on the edge of Manhattan Beach; requires drive to the ocean. ✉ *14400 Hindry Ave., Manhattan Beach* ☎ *310/536–0400, 800/675–3550* ⊕ *www. ayresmanhattanbeach.com* ⌁ *173 rooms* ⌂ *In-room: a/c, kitchen, Internet, Wi-Fi. In-hotel: restaurant, pool, laundry facilities, parking* ⧉ *Breakfast* ✛ *3:D6.*

$$$ ⬚ **shade.** Super-contemporary design makes this place feel like an adults-only playground. **Pros:** lively bar scene at Zinc; a quick walk to the beach and dozens of restaurants. **Cons:** sharp-edged furniture; recommended for adults or older kids only; small dipping pool. ✉ *1221 N. Valley Dr., Manhattan Beach* ☎ *310/546–4995, 866/742–3377* ⊕ *www.*

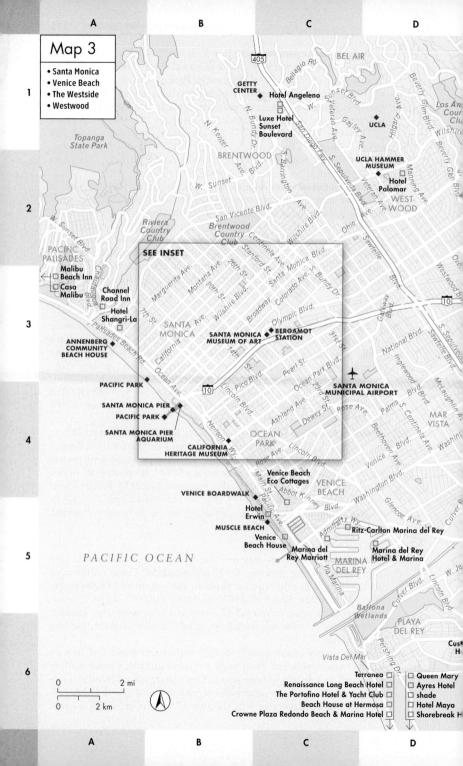

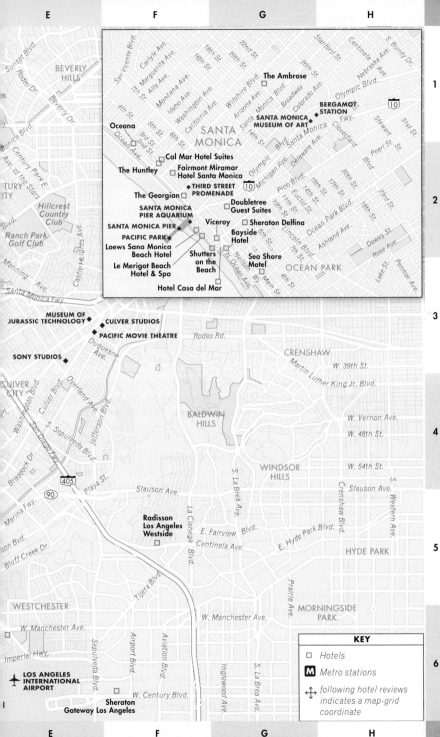

shadehotel.com ⌑ *33 rooms, 5 suites* ⌂ *In-room: a/c, Internet, Wi-Fi. In-hotel: restaurant, bar, pool, gym, business center, parking* ⎟⊙⎟ *Breakfast* ✛ *3:D6.*

MARINA DEL REY

$ ⊞ **Marina del Rey Hotel.** The balconies, patios, and harbor-view rooms take full advantage of the hotel's waterfront position. **Pros:** free parking and Wi-Fi; generous-size rooms, some with great marina views. **Cons:** long pending update means tired decor; check for construction. ⊠ *13534 Bali Way, Marina del Rey* ☏ *310/301–1000, 800/882–4000* ⊕ *www.marinadelreyhotel.com* ⌑ *150 rooms, 3 suites* ⌂ *In-room: a/c, Internet, Wi-Fi. In-hotel: restaurant, bar, pool, business center, parking* ✛ *3:C5.*

$$ ⊞ **Marina del Rey Marriott.** A jazzy lobby with plush couches, armchairs, and a welcoming bar is inside; outside is Glow, the hotel's popular lounge. **Pros:** 15 minutes to LAX; outdoor lounge for nighttime socializing; bike rentals and quiet beach across the street. **Cons:** traffic and noise from busy Admiralty Way; small gym. ⊠ *4100 Admiralty Way, Marina del Rey* ☏ *310/301–3000, 800/228–9290* ⊕ *www.marriotthotels.com* ⌑ *332 rooms, 38 suites* ⌂ *In-room: a/c, Internet. In-hotel: restaurant, bar, pool, gym, business center, parking* ✛ *3:C5.*

$$$$ ⊞ **The Ritz-Carlton Marina del Rey.** You might have a sense of déjà vu here since this resort, overlooking L.A.'s largest marina, is a favorite location of dozens of TV and film productions. **Pros:** sparkling gym; waterside location; resortlike amenities in town. **Cons:** formal dining only (poolside eatery, summers only); $35 valet parking. ⊠ *4375 Admiralty Way, Marina del Rey* ☏ *310/823–1700, 800/241–3333* ⊕ *www.ritzcarlton. com* ⌑ *281 rooms, 23 suites* ⌂ *In-room: a/c, Internet, Wi-Fi. In-hotel: restaurant, bar, pool, tennis court, gym, business center, parking, some pets allowed* ✛ *3:C5.*

RANCHO PALOS VERDES

$$$ ⊞ **Terranea.** L.A.'s only full-service oceanfront resort straddles 102 terraced acres at land's end on the scenic Palos Verdes Peninsula. **Pros:**
♨ resort near town with faraway feel; blissful oceanfront spa; saline pools
Fodor'sChoice and hot tubs. **Cons:** service needs to work kinks out; pricey and aver-
★ age on-site dining. ⊠ *100 Terranea Way Dr., Rancho Palos Verdes* ☏ *310/265–2800* ⊕ *www.terranea.com* ⌑ *326 rooms, 34 suites, 20 bungalows, 50 casitas, 32 villas* ⌂ *In-room: a/c, kitchen, Internet, Wi-Fi. In-hotel: restaurant, bar, golf course, pool, gym, spa, beach, children's programs, business center, parking, some pets allowed* ⛳ *9 holes, par 3* ✛ *3:D6.*

REDONDO BEACH

$$ ⊞ **Crowne Plaza Redondo Beach & Marina Hotel.** Redondo Beach's manmade seaside lagoon is a short walk from this contemporary five-story hotel. **Pros:** numerous resort amenities; steps from bike path, beach, and pier. **Cons:** large; corporate stay; best dining off-site. ⊠ *300 N. Harbor Dr., Redondo Beach* ☏ *310/318–8888, 800/972–2576* ⊕ *www. cpredondobeachhotel.com* ⌑ *334 rooms, 5 suites* ⌂ *In-room: a/c, Internet, Wi-Fi. In-hotel: restaurant, bar, pool, tennis court, gym, spa, laundry facilities, business center, parking* ✛ *3:C6.*

Lodging Alternatives

11

Shutters on the Beach

For your trip to Los Angeles, you may want a beachfront location and more space than a typical hotel can provide. Some travelers consider apartment and beach house rentals, but we tend to recommend hotel suites and B&Bs instead. Why? Unfortunately, rental scams are prevalent. In some cases, potential guests have arrived to find that the apartment they rented does not exist, or that they are paying for an illegal sublet. Unfortunately, travelers have also lost their deposit money, or their prepaid rent in the past. Note: Never wire money to an individual's account.

There are few reputable providers of short-term rentals, noted below. But many Fodorites have turned to suite hotels, lodges, and B&Bs with apartmentlike accommodations to guard themselves from possible scams.

Vacation rentals from reputed Web sites like **HomeAway** (⊕ *www. homeaway.com*) and its affiliate Web sites like **VRBO** (⊕ *www.vrbo. com*) come with the Carefree Rental Guarantee (for a fee), which protects travelers in sticky situations, whether the home has been foreclosed on, or the owner has double booked guests,

misrepresented a property, or withheld a security deposit.

From Malibu in the north to Long Beach farther south, most of the city's beach towns have waterfront hotels and inns with spacious suites and rooms. Some favorites include the pricey **Malibu Beach Inn** and **Shutters on the Beach** in Santa Monica, while the New England cottage–styled, all-suites **Beach House at Hermosa** and **Hotel Erwin, Venice** are comparative bargains with great ocean breezes.

Also consider cottages and B&Bs like the beloved **Inn at 657**, near the University of Southern California in L.A.'s downtown, or the **Los Feliz Lodge** close to the modern bohemian neighborhoods of Silver Lake and Echo Park. And off hip Abbot Kinney Boulevard, the **Venice Beach Eco-Cottages** marry form with eco-friendly practices.

"There are some lovely B&Bs in the Pasadena area as well, including the Bissell House (⊕ *www.bissellhouse. com*), Artists' Inn (⊕ *www.artistsinns. com*) and Arroyo Vista Inn (⊕ *www. arroyovistainn.com*)." —Jean

$$ 　The Portofino Hotel & Yacht Club. Open your balcony door and listen to the sounds of a naturally occurring Sea World at the Portofino. **Pros:** bike or walk to beach; relaxing stay; some ocean views. **Cons:** higher rates in summer and for ocean-view rooms. ✉ *260 Portofino Way, Redondo Beach* ☎ *310/379–8481, 800/468–4292* ⊕ *www.hotelportofino.com* ⊷ *161 rooms, 5 suites* ⚅ *In-room: a/c, Wi-Fi. In-hotel: restaurant, pool, gym, water sports, business center, parking* ✛ *3:C6.*

SANTA MONICA

$$ 　The Ambrose. An air of tranquillity pervades the four-story Ambrose, which blends right into its mostly residential Santa Monica neighborhood. **Pros:** L.A.'s most eco-conscious hotel with nontoxic housekeeping products and recycling bins in each room. **Cons:** quiet, residential area of Santa Monica; no restaurant on-site. ✉ *1255 20th St., Santa Monica* ☎ *310/315–1555, 877/262–7673* ⊕ *www.ambrosehotel.com* ⊷ *77 rooms* ⚅ *In-room: a/c, Internet, Wi-Fi. In-hotel: gym, business center, parking* ✛ *3:G1.*

$$ 　Bayside Hotel. Tucked snugly into a narrow corner lot, the supremely casual Bayside's greatest asset is its prime spot directly across from the beach, within walkable blocks from the Third Street Promenade and Santa Monica Pier. **Pros:** cheaper weeknight stays; beach access and views. **Cons:** homeless encampments nearby; some rooms without air-conditioning; basic bedding. ✉ *2001 Ocean Ave., Santa Monica* ☎ *310/396–6000, 800/525–4447* ⊕ *www.baysidehotel.com* ⊷ *45 rooms* ⚅ *In-room: a/c, kitchen, Internet, Wi-Fi. In-hotel: parking* ✛ *3:G2.*

$$ 　Cal Mar Hotel Suites. On a residential street one block from the Third Street Promenade and within a short walk to the beach, this low-profile, two-story, all-suites hotel is a comparative bargain. **Pros:** lower off-season rates; full kitchens; low-key vibe. **Cons:** street noise; no a/c but ocean breeze is present. ✉ *220 California Ave., Santa Monica* ☎ *310/395–5555, 800/776–6007* ⊕ *www.calmarhotel.com* ⊷ *36 suites* ⚅ *In-room: no a/c, Wi-Fi. In-hotel: pool, laundry facilities, parking* ✛ *3:F2.*

$$ 　Channel Road Inn. A quaint surprise in Southern California, the Channel Road Inn is every bit the country retreat B&B lovers adore, with four-poster beds with fluffy duvets and a cozy living room with fireplace. **Pros:** quiet residential neighborhood close to beach; free Wi-Fi and evening wine and hors d'oeuvres. **Cons:** no pool. ✉ *219 W. Channel Rd., Santa Monica* ☎ *310/459–1920* ⊕ *www.channelroadinn.com* ⊷ *15 rooms* ⚅ *In-room: a/c, Internet, Wi-Fi. In-hotel: business center, parking* ⏍ *Breakfast* ✛ *3:A3.*

Fodor'sChoice ★

$$ 　Doubletree Guest Suites. Sunlight streams through the glass-enclosed atrium and spills into the lobby. **Pros:** spacious suites appeal to families, as do many diversions nearby; on the Tide Shuttle route; walk to new restaurants and shops of Santa Monica Place. **Cons:** somewhat dated decor. ✉ *1707 4th St., Santa Monica* ☎ *310/395–3332, 800/222–8733* ⊕ *www.doubletree.com* ⊷ *253 suites* ⚅ *In-room: a/c, Wi-Fi. In-hotel: restaurant, bar, pool, gym, laundry facilities, business center, parking* ✛ *3:G2.*

Beach House Hotel at Hermosa

Channel Road Inn

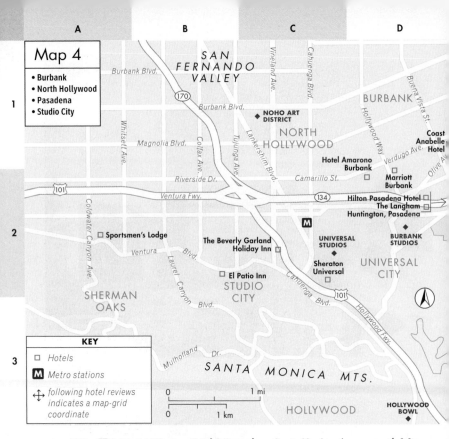

Map 4

- Burbank
- North Hollywood
- Pasadena
- Studio City

SAN FERNANDO VALLEY

BURBANK

NOHO ART DISTRICT

NORTH HOLLYWOOD

Coast Anabelle Hotel

Hotel Amarono Burbank

Marriott Burbank

Hilton Pasadena Hotel
The Langham Huntington, Pasadena

Sportsmen's Lodge

The Beverly Garland Holiday Inn

UNIVERSAL STUDIOS

BURBANK STUDIOS

Sheraton Universal

UNIVERSAL CITY

El Patio Inn

STUDIO CITY

SHERMAN OAKS

SANTA MONICA MTS.

HOLLYWOOD BOWL

HOLLYWOOD

KEY

☐ Hotels

Ⓜ Metro stations

⊹ following hotel reviews indicates a map-grid coordinate

0   1 mi
0   1 km

$$$$ 🏨 **Fairmont Miramar Hotel & Bungalows Santa Monica.** A mammoth Moreton Bay fig tree dwarfs the main entrance; the modernized lobby lounge opens onto a heated patio. **Pros:** walking distance to beach and Third Street Promenade shopping and dining. **Cons:** pricey in-house dining. ✉ *101 Wilshire Blvd., Santa Monica* ☎ *310/576–7777, 866/540–4470* ⊕ *www.fairmont.com/santamonica* 🛏 *251 rooms, 51 suites, 32 bungalows* ♿ *In-room: a/c, Internet, Wi-Fi. In-hotel: restaurant, bar, pool, gym, spa, business center, parking, some pets allowed* ⊹ *3:F2.*

$$$ 🏨 **The Georgian Hotel.** Driving by, you can't miss the Georgian: the art deco exterior is aqua, with ornate bronze grillwork and a charming oceanfront veranda. **Pros:** many ocean-view rooms; front terrace a great people-watching spot; free Wi-Fi. **Cons:** "vintage" bathrooms; unremarkable views from some rooms. ✉ *1415 Ocean Ave., Santa Monica* ☎ *310/395–9945, 800/538–8147* ⊕ *www.georgianhotel.com* 🛏 *56 rooms, 28 suites* ♿ *In-room: a/c, Internet, Wi-Fi. In-hotel: restaurant, bar, gym, business center, parking, some pets allowed* ⊹ *3:F2.*

$$$$ 🏨 **Hotel Casa del Mar.** In the 1920s it was a posh beach club catering to the city's elite; now the Casa del Mar is one of SoCal's most luxurious and pricey beachfront hotels, with three extravagant two-story penthouses, a raised deck and pool, and an elegant ballroom facing the sand. **Pros:** excellent dining at Catch; lobby socializing; gorgeous beachfront rooms. **Cons:** no room balconies; without a doubt, one of L.A.'s most pricey beach stays. ⊠ *1910 Ocean Way, Santa Monica* ☎ *310/581–5533, 800/898–6999* ⊕ *www.hotelcasadelmar.com* ⤙ *113 rooms, 16 suites* ⚏ *In-room: a/c, Internet, Wi-Fi. In-hotel: restaurant, bar, pool, gym, spa, beach, parking, some pets allowed* ⊹ *3:G2.*

$$$ ⊞ **Hotel Shangri-La.** Across from Santa Monica's scenic Palisades Park, the 1939-built, art deco–styled Shangri-La is now in tune with the 21st century. **Pros:** admirable rehabilitation of deco-styled building now with up-to-date conveniences like soundproofing and iPod docks. **Cons:** some rooms are tight like cruise-ship quarters. ⊠ *301 Ocean Ave., Santa Monica* ☎ *310/394–2791* ⊕ *www.shangrila-hotel.com* ⤙ *36 rooms, 35 suites* ⚏ *In-room: a/c, kitchen, Internet, Wi-Fi. In-hotel: restaurant, bar, pool, gym, business center, parking, some pets allowed* ⊹ *3:A3.*

$$$ ⊞ **Huntley Santa Monica Beach.** A school of 300 ceramic fish crossing a lobby wall sets the tone at this stylish property. **Pros:** ocean views; fun social scene, and great views (and drinks) at the Penthouse, the hotel's top floor restaurant. **Cons:** no pool. ⊠ *1111 2nd St., Santa Monica* ☎ *310/394–5454* ⊕ *www.thehuntleyhotel.com* ⤙ *188 rooms, 16 suites* ⚏ *In-room: a/c, Wi-Fi. In-hotel: restaurant, bar, gym, business center, parking* ⊹ *3:F2.*

$$$$ ⊞ **Le Merigot Beach Hotel & Spa.** Steps from Santa Monica's expansive ☾ beach, Le Merigot caters largely to a corporate clientele. **Pros:** steps from the beach and pier; welcoming to international travelers; walk to Third Street Promenade. **Cons:** small shaded pool. ⊠ *1740 Ocean Ave., Santa Monica* ☎ *310/395–9700, 800/539–7899* ⊕ *www.lemerigothotel. com* ⤙ *160 rooms, 15 suites* ⚏ *In-room: a/c, Internet, Wi-Fi. In-hotel: restaurant, bar, pool, gym, spa, beach, business center, parking, some pets allowed* ⊹ *3:F2.*

$$$ ⊞ **Loews Santa Monica Beach Hotel.** Walk to the ocean side of the soar- ☾ ing atrium here and you feel like you're on a cruise ship. **Pros:** resort vibe; walk to beach; pet- and kid-friendly. **Cons:** small pool. ⊠ *1700 Ocean Ave., Santa Monica* ☎ *310/458–6700, 800/235–6397* ⊕ *www. loewshotels.com* ⤙ *325 rooms, 17 suites* ⚏ *In-room: a/c, Internet, Wi-Fi. In-hotel: restaurant, pool, gym, spa, beach, business center, parking, some pets allowed* ⊹ *3:F2.*

$$$$ ⊞ **Oceana.** Generous-size suites, soundproofed windows, an open-air courtyard and pool, and ocean proximity add up to a delightful boutique hotel. **Pros:** walk to prime shopping on Montana Avenue, the Palisades park, or the beach. **Cons:** small pool. ⊠ *849 Ocean Ave., Santa Monica* ☎ *310/393–0486, 800/777–0758* ⊕ *www.hoteloceanasantamonica.com* ⤙ *70 suites* ⚏ *In-room: a/c, kitchen, Internet, Wi-Fi. In-hotel: restaurant, pool, gym, business center, parking* ⊹ *3:F2.*

$ ⊞ **Sea Shore Motel.** On Santa Monica's busy Main Street, the Sea Shore is a throwback to Route 66 and to '60s-style, family-run roadside motels. **Pros:** close to beach and great restaurants; free Wi-Fi and parking. **Cons:** street noise; motel-style decor and beds. ⊠ *2637 Main St., Santa Monica* ☎ *310/392–2787* ⊕ *www.seashoremotel.com* ⤙ *19 rooms, 5 suites* ⚏ *In-room: a/c, kitchen, Internet, Wi-Fi. In-hotel: restaurant, laundry facilities, business center, parking, some pets allowed* ⊹ *3:G3.*

$$$ ⊞ **Sheraton Delfina.** Not far from I–10 and most Westside businesses, this hotel appeals to business types during the week. **Pros:** four blocks

Shutters on the Beach

The Langham Huntington, Pasadena

from beach; spacious rooms; designer touches. **Cons:** away from Santa Monica's main dining and shopping. ⊠ *530 Pico Blvd., Santa Monica* ☎ *310/399–9344, 888/627–8532* ⊕ *www.sheratondelfina.com* ↪ *299 rooms, 11 suites* ⛄ *In-room: a/c, Internet, Wi-Fi. In-hotel: restaurant, bar, pool, gym, business center, parking, some pets allowed* ✢ *3:G2.*

$$$$ ⊡ **Shutters on the Beach.** Set right on the sand, this gray-shingle inn
◐   has become synonymous with in-town escapism. **Pros:** romantic; dis-
Fodor'sChoice creet; residential vibe. **Cons:** service not as good as it should be. ⊠ *1*
★   *Pico Blvd., Santa Monica* ☎ *310/458–0030, 800/334–9000* ⊕ *www.
shuttersonthebeach.com* ↪ *186 rooms, 12 suites* ⛄ *In-room: a/c, Internet, Wi-Fi. In-hotel: restaurant, bar, pool, gym, spa, beach, business
center, parking* ✢ *3:G2.*

$$$ ⊡ **Viceroy.** Whimsy abounds at this stylized seaside escape—just look
at the porcelain dogs as lamp bases and Spode china plates mounted
on the walls. **Pros:** eye-catching design; lobby social scene; pedestrian-
friendly area. **Cons:** super-pricey bar and dining; pool for dipping not
laps. ⊠ *1819 Ocean Ave., Santa Monica* ☎ *310/260–7500, 800/622–
8711* ⊕ *www.viceroysantamonica.com* ↪ *162 total rooms, 5 suites*
⛄ *In-room: a/c, Internet, Wi-Fi. In-hotel: restaurant, bar, pool, gym,
business center, parking, some pets allowed* ✢ *3:G2.*

VENICE

$$ ⊡ **Hotel Erwin.** Formerly a Best Western, this now bona fide boutique
Fodor'sChoice hotel just off the Venice Beach boardwalk had a major face-lift in 2009.
★   **Pros:** great location, great food; close to Santa Monica without hefty
prices. **Cons:** some rooms face a noisy alley; no pool. ⊠ *1697 Pacific
Ave., Venice* ☎ *310/452–1111, 800/786–7789* ⊕ *www.hotelerwin.com*
↪ *119 rooms* ⛄ *In-room: a/c, kitchen, Internet, Wi-Fi. In-hotel: restaurant, bar, gym, beach, business center, parking, some pets allowed*
✢ *3:C5.*

$$ ⊡ **Venice Beach Eco-Cottages.** Husband and wife owners Cynthia Fos-
ter and Karel Samson bring style and solar power together at these
charming cottages in kitschy Venice, steps from Abbot Kinney's trendy
restaurants and shops. **Pros:** charming cottage living; family-friendly;
environmentally friendly practices. **Cons:** no restaurant, pool, or tra-
ditional hotel services. ⊠ *447 Grand Blvd., Venice* ☎ *866/802–3110*
⊕ *www.venicebeachecocottages.com* ↪ *3 suites* ⛄ *In-room: no a/c,
kitchen, Internet, Wi-Fi. In-hotel: laundry facilities, some pets allowed*
↺ *3-night minimum stay* ✢ *3:C4.*

$ ⊡ **Venice Beach House.** A vestige of Venice's founding days, the Venice
Beach House was one of the seaside enclave's first mansions. **Pros:**
historic home with many charms; steps from beach and bike bath.
Cons: privacy and noise issues; parking $14; full prepayment required
with cancellation penalties. ⊠ *15 30th Ave., Venice* ☎ *310/823–1966*
⊕ *www.venicebeachhouse.com* ↪ *4 rooms without baths, 5 suites*
⛄ *In-room: a/c, Internet, Wi-Fi. In-hotel: beach, parking* ⦿*Breakfast*
✢ *3:C5.*

PASADENA AND ENVIRONS

For expanded reviews, visit Fodors.com.

Most famous for the annual Tournament of Roses, Pasadena is not only an easy detour from Los Angeles, but also a charming and historic city that can serve as your base while visiting the area. This small-town feel means a relaxing, slow pace, with the attractions of the city still nearby. It is more residential and conservative than the city though.

$ **Hilton Pasadena Hotel.** Two blocks south of busy Colorado Boulevard, the Hilton Pasadena is still within walking distance of the city's vast convention center and close to the shops and plentiful restaurant choices of Old Town. **Pros:** amiable and helpful staff; central downtown Pasadena location. **Cons:** compact bathrooms; so-so dining options; small pool. ⊠ *168 S. Los Robles Ave., Pasadena* ☎ *626/577–1000, 800/445–8667* ⊕ *www.hiltonpasadena.com* ⇆ *285 rooms, 11 suites* ⚒ *In-room: a/c, Internet, Wi-Fi. In-hotel: restaurant, bar, pool, gym, business center, parking, some pets allowed* ✛ *3:D2.*

$$ **The Langham Huntington, Pasadena.** An azalea-filled Japanese garden and the unusual Picture Bridge, with murals celebrating California's history, are just two of this grande dame's picturesque attributes. **Pros:** great for romantic escape; excellent restaurant; top-notch spa. **Cons:** set in a suburban neighborhood far from local shopping and dining. ⊠ *1401 S. Oak Knoll Ave., Pasadena* ☎ *626/568–3900* ⊕ *www. pasadena.langhamhotels.com* ⇆ *342 rooms, 38 suites* ⚒ *In-room: a/c, Internet, Wi-Fi. In-hotel: restaurant, bar, pool, tennis court, gym, spa, business center, parking, some pets allowed* ✛ *3:D2.*

Fodor's Choice ★

Disneyland and Knott's Berry Farm

WORD OF MOUTH

"Knott's Berry Farm has a good mix of rides, including some intense thrill rides. It has a bit of retro charm to it as well. My kids prefer it over Disneyland."

—lvk

Updated By
Laura Randall

Disneyland and Knott's Berry Farm have been the entertainment anchors of Anaheim and all of inland Orange County since opening amid orange groves and farmland in the middle of the 20th century. Each is surrounded by hotels, restaurants, and fun-based entertainment options that survive and often thrive in the shadows of these two popular amusement parks. Though they share similar humble beginnings (not to mention quirky founders with revolutionary ideas), the parks today operate in different stratospheres with their own unique personalities and charms.

Disneyland, with its three park-adjacent hotels and downtown promenade, is by far the bigger and shinier powerhouse. Walking down **Main Street, U.S.A.** with **Sleeping Beauty Castle** straight ahead, you really will feel like you've landed on one of the happiest places on earth. Trolleys cling-clang merrily beside you, little girls skip down the thoroughfare in princess gowns while the sounds of peppy, hummable tunes float through the air. You can't help but let your inner child escape for a few hours, or days. When you need a dose of adulthood, visit Johnny Depp's rock-star pirate, Jack Sparrow, on the new and improved **Pirates of the Caribbean** ride, or head over to **California Adventure** for a breathtaking ride on **Soarin' Over California** or a wine flight and hand-sliced prosciutto at the Wine Country Trattoria.

A 10-minute drive away, **Knott's Berry Farm** is Disney's louder, somewhat rowdier neighbor. Before even passing through the gate, you'll hear the gleeful screams of people being pulled and suspended and twisted into oblivion on the park's many high-tech thrill rides. Although the park seems to increasingly focus on bigger, better, and faster rides, there's a softer, cornier side as well. This includes the skill-based carnival games that draw cheering crowds, **Camp Snoopy's** pint-size kiddie rides, and the **Western Trails Museum,** home to coins and guns from the Old West, menus from the original chicken dinner restaurant, and Mrs. Knott's antique button collection.

PLANNING

WHEN TO GO
Beat the crowds and the heat by visiting in winter, spring, or fall. School holidays and the entire spring break window of late March and April can also be mobbed.

Disneyland and Disney's California Adventure are open daily, 365 days a year; hours vary, depending on the season, but typically Disneyland opens at 8 am and Disney's California Adventure at 10 am.

Guests at Disney hotels and those with a multiple-day Park Hopper pass are often allowed in an hour ahead of the official opening time. Disneyland stays open as late as midnight on weekends and in summer, but it's always a good idea to check the Web site or call ahead.

Knott's Berry Farm is open daily. Hours vary—call ahead to check—but it's usually open from 10 am to between 5 and 8 on weeknights and until midnight on weekends.

You can see the park in a day, but plan to start early and finish fairly late. Traffic can be heavy, so factor in time for delays.

GETTING HERE AND AROUND
DISNEYLAND
Disney is about a 30-mi drive from either LAX or downtown. From LAX, follow Sepulveda Boulevard south to the I–105 freeway and drive east 16 mi to the I–605 north exit. Exit at the Santa Ana Freeway (I–5) and continue south for 12 mi to the Disneyland Drive exit. Follow signs to the resort. From downtown, follow I–5 south 28 mi and exit at Disneyland Drive. **Disneyland Resort Express** (☎ 714/978–8855 ⊕ graylineanaheim.com) offers daily nonstop bus service between LAX, John Wayne Airport, and Anaheim. Reservations are not required. The cost is $20 one-way for adults, $17 for children, for LAX, and $15 and $12 one-way for John Wayne Airport.

KNOTT'S BERRY FARM
From Disney, Knott's Berry Farm is an easy 10-minute drive, or a 30-minute drive from downtown Los Angeles. Take I–5 to Beach Boulevard and head south 3 mi; follow the park entrance signs on the right.

SAVING TIME AND MONEY
If you plan to visit for more than a day, you can save money by buying three-, four-, and five-day Park Hopper tickets that grant same-day "hopping" privileges between Disneyland and Disney's California Adventure. You get a discount on the multiple-day passes if you buy online through the Disneyland Web site.

A one-day Park Hopper pass costs $101 for anyone 10 or older, $91 for kids ages 3–9. Admission to either park (but not both) is $76 or $68 for kids 3–9; kids 2 and under are free.

In addition to tickets, parking is $15–$20 (unless your hotel has a shuttle or is within walking distance), and meals in the parks and at Downtown Disney range from $10 to $30 per person.

If you're staying in a hotel near the park, ask if any discount packages are available when you book.

If you think you'll only need a few hours at Knott's Berry Farm, you can save money by coming after 4 pm, when admission fees drop to $28. This deal is offered any day the park is open after 6.

A full-day pass for adults is $56.99; Southern California residents pay $46.99 and children three and older, up to 48 inches tall, are $24.99. Tickets can be purchased online and printed out ahead of time, to avoid waiting in line.

In addition to tickets, you'll need to pay $12 for parking. Meals are about $10–$14 per person. The Laser Tag attraction is an extra $10, and the Big Swing ride is an additional $5.

RESTAURANTS AND HOTELS

WHAT IT COSTS					
	¢	$	$$	$$$	$$$$
Restaurants	under $7	$7–$12	$13–$22	$23–$32	over $32
Hotels	under $75	$75–$125	$126–$200	$201–$325	over $325

Restaurant prices are per person for a main course, excluding 9.75% sales tax. Hotel prices are for two people in a standard double room in nonholiday high season on the European Plan (no meals) unless otherwise noted. Taxes (9%–14%) are extra. In listings, we always name the facilities available, but we don't specify whether they cost extra. When pricing accommodations, always ask about what's included.

VISITOR INFORMATION

Anaheim Orange County Visitor & Convention Bureau. The Anaheim Orange County Visitor & Convention Bureau is a good source for maps and news on the area.

Visitor Information ⊠ *800 W. Katella Ave., Anaheim* ☎ *714/765–8888* ⊕ *www.anaheimoc.org.*

DISNEYLAND RESORT

26 mi southeast of Los Angeles, via I–5.

The snowcapped Matterhorn, the centerpiece of the Magic Kingdom, punctuates the skyline of Anaheim. Since 1955, when Walt Disney chose this once-quiet farming community for the site of his first amusement park, Disneyland has attracted more than 450 million visitors and thousands of workers, and Anaheim has been their host.

To understand the symbiotic relationship between Disneyland and Anaheim, you need only look at the $4.2 billion spent in a combined effort by the Walt Disney Company and Anaheim, the latter to revitalize the city's tourist center and run-down areas, the former to expand and renovate the Disney properties into what is known now as Disneyland Resort.

The resort is a sprawling complex that includes Disney's two amusement parks; three hotels; and Downtown Disney, a shopping, dining, and entertainment promenade. Anaheim's tourist center includes Angel Stadium of Anaheim, home of baseball's World Series Champion Los

Angeles Angels of Anaheim; Arrowhead Pond, which hosts concerts and the hockey team the Anaheim Ducks; and the enormous Anaheim Convention Center.

DISNEYLAND

12

☺ **Disneyland.** One of the biggest misconceptions people have about Disneyland is that they've "been there, done that" if they've visited either Florida's mammoth Walt Disney World or one of the Disney parks overseas. But Disneyland, opened in 1955 and the only one of the kingdoms to be overseen by Walt himself, has a genuine historic feel and occupies a unique place in the Disney legend. There's plenty here that you won't find anywhere else: for example, Storybook Land, with its miniature replicas of animated Disney scenes from classics such as *Pinocchio, Alice in Wonderland,* and the Indiana Jones Adventure ride.

Fodor's Choice
★

Characters appear for autographs and photos throughout the day; guidebooks at the entrances give times and places. You can also meet some of the animated icons at one of the character meals served at the three Disney hotels (open to the public). Belongings can be stored in lockers just off Main Street; purchases can also be sent to the package pickup desk, at the front of the park.

DISNEY LANDS

Neighborhoods for Disneyland are arranged in geographic order.

MAIN STREET, U.S.A.
Walt's hometown of Marceline, Missouri, was the inspiration behind this romanticized image of small-town America, circa 1900. The sidewalks are lined with a penny arcade and shops that sell everything from tradable pins to Disney-theme clothing and photo supplies. It opens half an hour before the rest of the park, so it's a good place to explore if you're getting an early start to beat the crowds (it's also open an hour after the other attractions close, so you may want to save your shopping for the end of the day). **Main Street Cinema** offers a cool respite from the crowds and six classic Disney animated shorts, including *Steamboat Willie.* There's rarely a wait to enter. Board the **Disneyland Railroad** here to save on walking; it tours all the lands, plus offers unique views of Splash Mountain and the Grand Canyon and Primeval World dioramas.

NEW ORLEANS SQUARE
A mini–French Quarter with narrow streets, hidden courtyards, and live street performances, this is home to two iconic attractions and the Cajun-inspired Blue Bayou restaurant. **Pirates of the Caribbean** now features Jack Sparrow and the cursed Captain Barbossa, in a nod to the blockbuster movies of the same name, plus enhanced special effects and battle scenes (complete with cannonball explosions). Nearby **Haunted Mansion** continues to spook guests with its stretching room and "doombuggy" rides (plus there's now an expanded storyline for the beating-heart bride). Its *Nightmare Before Christmas* holiday overlay is an annual tradition. This is a good area to get a casual bite to eat; the clam chowder in sourdough bread bowls, sold at the French Market Restaurant and Royal Street Veranda, is a popular choice.

FRONTIERLAND
Between Adventureland and Fantasyland, Frontierland transports you to the wild, wild West with its rustic buildings, shooting gallery,

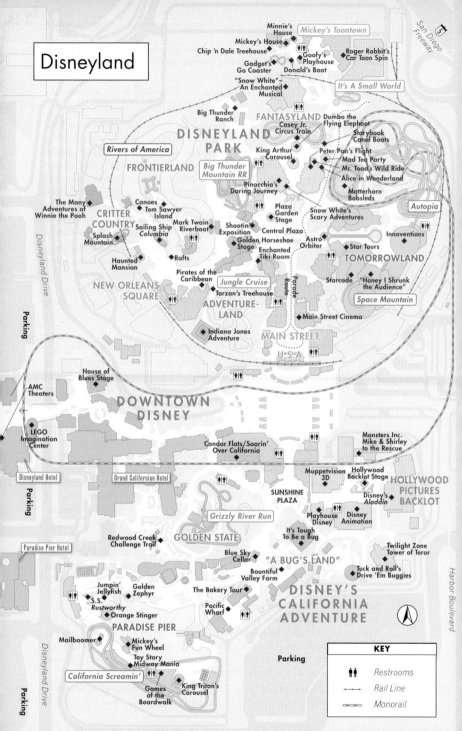

Disneyland

Mickey's Toontown
Minnie's House
Mickey's House
Chip 'n Dale Treehouse
Gadget's Go Coaster
Goofy's Playhouse
Roger Rabbit's Car Toon Spin
Donald's Boat
It's A Small World

"Snow White" An Enchanted Musical

Big Thunder Ranch

FANTASYLAND
Dumbo the Flying Elephant
Casey Jr. Circus Train
Storybook Canal Boats
King Arthur Carousel
Peter Pan's Flight
Mad Tea Party
Mr. Toad's Wild Ride
Alice in Wonderland
Matterhorn Bobsleds

DISNEYLAND PARK

Rivers of America

FRONTIERLAND

Big Thunder Mountain RR

Pinocchio's Daring Journey

Plaza Garden Stage

Snow White's Scary Adventures

Autopia

The Many Adventures of Winnie the Pooh

CRITTER COUNTRY
Canoes
Tom Sawyer Island
Mark Twain Riverboat
Sailing Ship Columbia
Splash Mountain

Shootin' Exposition
Central Plaza
Golden Horseshoe Stage
Enchanted Tiki Room

Innoventions

Astro Orbiter
Star Tours
TOMORROWLAND

Haunted Mansion
Rafts

Starcade
"Honey I Shrunk the Audience"

Pirates of the Caribbean

NEW ORLEANS SQUARE
Jungle Cruise
Tarzan's Treehouse

Space Mountain

ADVENTURE-LAND

Indiana Jones Adventure

Main Street Cinema

MAIN STREET, U.S.A.

Parade Route

House of Blues Stage

AMC Theaters

DOWNTOWN DISNEY

LEGO Imagination Center

Monsters Inc. Mike & Shirley to the Rescue

Disneyland Hotel

Grand Californian Hotel

Condor Flats/Soarin' Over California

Muppetvision 3D
Hollywood Backlot Stage
HOLLYWOOD PICTURES BACKLOT

SUNSHINE PLAZA
Disney's Aladdin

Grizzly River Run

Playhouse Disney
Disney Animation

Paradise Pier Hotel

Redwood Creek Challenge Trail

GOLDEN STATE

It's Tough To Be a Bug

Blue Sky Cellar

"A BUG'S LAND"

Twilight Zone Tower of Teror

Bountiful Valley Farm

Tuck and Roll's Drive 'Em Buggies

Jumpin' Jellyfish
Golden Zephyr
The Bakery Tour
DISNEY'S CALIFORNIA ADVENTURE

S.S. Rustworthy
Orange Stinger
Pacific Wharf

Mailboomer
Mickey's Fun Wheel
Toy Story Midway Mania
PARADISE PIER

California Screamin'

King Triton's Carousel

Games of the Boardwalk

Parking

San Diego Freeway

Harbor Boulevard

Disneyland Drive

Katella Avenue

KEY	
🚻	Restrooms
↔	Rail Line
⬯	Monorail

12

mountain range, and foot-stompin' dance hall. The marquee attraction, **Big Thunder Mountain Railroad,** is a relatively tame roller coaster ride (no steep descents) that takes the form of a runaway mine car as it rumbles past desert canyons and an old mining town. Tour the Rivers of America on the **Mark Twain Riverboat** in the company of a grizzled old river pilot or circumnavigate the globe on the **Sailing Ship Columbia,** though its operating hours are usually limited to weekends. You can also raft over from here to Pirate's Lair on **Tom Sawyer Island,** which now features pirate-theme caves, treasure hunts, and music along with plenty of caves and hills to climb and explore. If you don't mind tight seating, have a snack at the Golden Horseshoe Restaurant while enjoying the always-entertaining comedy and bluegrass show of Billy Hill and the Hillbillies. Children won't want to miss **Big Thunder Ranch,** a small petting zoo of real pigs, goats, and cows beyond Big Thunder Mountain.

> ### DISNEY'S TOP ATTRACTIONS
>
> **Finding Nemo:** Board a yellow submarine and view a 3-D animated adventure.
>
> **Haunted Mansion:** A "doom-buggy" takes you through a spooky old plantation mansion.
>
> **Pirates of the Caribbean:** Watch buccaneers wreak havoc as you float along in a rowboat.
>
> **Space Mountain:** This scary-but-thrilling roller coaster is indoors—and mostly in the dark!
>
> **Matterhorn Bobsleds:** At the center of the Magic Kingdom, this roller coaster simulates bobsleds.

CRITTER COUNTRY Down-home country is the theme in this shady corner of the park, where Winnie the Pooh and Davy Crockett make their homes. Here you can find **Splash Mountain,** a classic flume ride accompanied by music and appearances by Brer Rabbit and other characters from Song of the South. Don't forget to check out your photo (the camera snaps close-ups of each car just before it plunges into the water) on the way out. The patio of the popular Hungry Bear Restaurant has great views of Tom Sawyer's Island and Davy Crockett's Explorer Canoes.

ADVENTURELAND Modeled after the lands of Africa, Polynesia, and Arabia, this tiny tropical paradise is worth braving the crowds that flock here for the ambience and better-than-average food. Sing along with the animatronic birds and tiki gods in the **Enchanted Tiki Room,** sail the rivers of the world with joke-cracking skippers on **Jungle Cruise,** and climb the Disneyodendron semperflorens (aka always-blooming Disney tree) to **Tarzan's Treehouse,** where you can walk through scenes, some interactive, from the 1999 animated film. Cap off the visit with a wild jeep ride at **Indiana Jones Adventure,** where the special effects and decipherable hieroglyphics distract you while you're waiting in line. The kebabs at Bengal Barbecue and pineapple whip at Tiki Juice Bar are some of the best fast-food options in the park.

FANTASYLAND Sleeping Beauty Castle marks the entrance to Fantasyland, a visual wonderland of princesses, spinning teacups, flying elephants, and other classic storybook characters. Rides and shops (such as the princess-theme Once Upon a Time and Gepetto's Toys and Gifts) take precedence over

DID YOU KNOW?

Apparently, the plain purple tea cup in Disneyland's Mad Tea Party ride spins the fastest—though no one knows why.

BEST TIPS FOR DISNEYLAND

Buy entry tickets in advance. Many nearby hotels sell park admission tickets; you can also buy them through the Disney Web site. If you book a package deal, such as those offered through AAA, tickets are included, too.

The lines at the ticket booths can take more than an hour on busy days, so you'll definitely save time by buying in advance, especially if you're committed to going on a certain day regardless of the weather.

Come midweek. Weekends, especially in summer, are a mob scene. A winter weekday is often the least crowded time to visit.

Plan your times to hit the most popular rides. If you're at the park when the gates open, make a beeline for the top rides before the crowds reach a critical mass. Another good time is the evening, when the hordes thin out somewhat, and during a parade or other show. Save the quieter attractions for midafternoon.

Look into Fastpasses. These passes allow you to reserve your place in line at some of the most crowded attractions (only one at a time). Distribution machines are posted near the entrances of each attraction. Feed in your park admission ticket, and you'll receive a pass with a printed time frame (generally up to 1–1½ hours later) during which you can return to wait in a much shorter line.

Plan your meals to avoid peak mealtime crowds. Start the day with a big breakfast so you won't be too hungry at noon, when restaurants and vendors get swarmed. Wait to have lunch until after 1.

If you want to eat at the **Blue Bayou** in New Orleans Square, it's best to make reservations in person as soon as you get to the park. Another (cheaper) option is to bring your own food. There are areas with picnic tables set up for this. And it's always a good idea to bring water and a few nonmeltable snacks with you.

Check the daily events schedule online or at the park entrance. During parades, fireworks, and other special events, sections of the parks clog with crowds. This can work for you or against you. An event could make it difficult to get around a park—but if you plan ahead, you can take advantage of the distraction to hit popular rides. The Web site also lists rides that are closed for repairs or renovations, so you know what to expect before you go.

Send the Teens Next Door: Disneyland's newer sister park, California Adventure, features more intense rides suitable for older kids (Park Hopper passes include admission to both parks).

restaurants in this area of the park, but outdoor carts sell everything from churros to turkey legs. Tots love the **King Arthur Carousel, Casey Jr. Circus Train,** and **Storybook Land Canal Boats.** This is also home to **Mr. Toad's Wild Ride, Peter Pan's Flight,** and **Pinocchio's Daring Journey,** classic, movie-theater-dark rides that immerse riders in Disney fairytales and appeal to adults and kids alike. The Abominable Snowman pops up on the **Matterhorn Bobsleds,** a roller coaster that twists and turns you up and around a made-to-scale model of the real Swiss mountain. Anchoring the east end of Fantasyland is **it's a small world,** a smorgasbord of dancing animatronic dolls, cuckoo clock–covered walls, and variations of the song everyone knows, or soon *will* know, by heart. A 2008 renovation added beloved Disney characters like Ariel from *The Little Mermaid* to the mix.

MICKEY'S TOONTOWN Geared toward small fry, this lopsided cartoonlike downtown, complete with cars and trolleys that invite exploring, is where Mickey, Donald, Goofy, and other classic Disney characters hang their hats. One of the most popular attractions is **Roger Rabbit's Car Toon Spin,** a twisting, turning cab ride through the Toontown of *Who Framed Roger Rabbit?* You can also walk through **Mickey's House** to meet and be photographed with the famous mouse, take a low-key ride on **Gadget's Go Coaster,** or bounce around the fenced-in playground in front of **Goofy's House.**

TOMOR-ROWLAND This popular section of the park underwent a complete refurbishment in 1998 and has continued to tinker with its future, adding and enhancing rides regularly. One of the newest attractions, **Finding Nemo's Submarine Voyage,** updates the old Submarine Voyage ride with the exploits of Nemo, Dory, Marlin, and other characters from the Pixar film. Try to visit this popular ride early in the day if you can and be prepared for a wait. The interactive **Buzz Lightyear Astro Blasters** lets you zap your neighbors with laser beams and compete for the highest score. Hurtle through the cosmos on **Space Mountain,** refurbished in 2005 or check out mainstays like the futuristic **Astro Orbiter** rockets, **Innoventions,** a self-guided tour of the latest toys of tomorrow, and **Honey, I Shrunk the Audience,** a 3-D film featuring Rick Moranis. Disneyland Monorail and Disneyland Railroad both have stations here. There's also a video arcade and dancing water fountain that makes a perfect playground for kids on hot summer days.

Besides the eight lands, the daily live-action shows and parades are always crowd-pleasers. **Fantasmic!** is a musical, fireworks, and laser show in which Mickey and friends wage a spellbinding battle against Disneyland's darker characters. ■TIP→ Arrive early to secure a good view; if there are two shows scheduled for the day, the second one tends to be less crowded. A fireworks display sparks up Friday and Saturday evenings. Brochures with maps, available at the entrance, list show and parade times.

DISNEY'S CALIFORNIA ADVENTURE

🕐
★ **Disney's California Adventure.** The sprawling 55-acre Disney's California Adventure, right next to Disneyland (their entrances face each other), pays tribute to the Golden State with four theme areas. In 2007 the park began a major five-year overhaul aimed at infusing more of Walt Disney's spirit throughout the park.

New attractions include World of Color, a nighttime water-effects show and Toy Story Mania!, an interactive adventure ride hosted by Woody, Buzz Lightyear, and friends, which opened in 2008. Ariel's Undersea Adventure and a 12-acre section called Cars Land based on the Pixar film

Mickey as the Sorcerer's Apprentice.

are also in the works. ✉ *Disneyland Dr. between Ball Rd. and Katella Ave., Anaheim* ☎ *714/781–4565* ⊕ *www.disneyland.com* ⊗ *Hrs vary.*

DISNEY LANDS

GOLDEN STATE   Celebrate California's history and natural beauty with nature trails, a winery, and a tortilla factory (with free samples). The area of Condor Flats has **Soarin' Over California,** a spectacular simulated hang-glider ride over California terrain, and the **Redwood Creek Challenge Trail,** a challenging trek across net ladders and suspension bridges. **Grizzly River Run** simulates the river rapids of the Sierra Nevadas; be prepared to get soaked. The Wine Country Trattoria is a great place for a relaxing outdoor lunch.

HOLLYWOOD PICTURES BACKLOT   With a main street modeled after Hollywood Boulevard, a fake blue-sky backdrop, and real soundstages, this area celebrates California's most famous industry. **Disney Animation** gives you an insider's look at the work of animators and how they create characters. **Turtle Talk with Crush** lets kids have an unrehearsed talk with computer-animated Crush, a sea turtle from *Finding Nemo.* The Hyperion theater hosts **Aladdin—A Musical Spectacular,** a 45-minute live performance with terrific visual effects. ■TIP➜ Plan on getting in line about half an hour in advance: the show is well worth the wait. On the latest film-inspired ride, **Monsters, Inc. Mike & Sulley to the Rescue,** you climb into taxis and travel the streets of Monstropolis on a mission of safely returning Boo to her bedroom. A major draw for older kids is the looming **Twilight Zone Tower of Terror,** which drops riders 13 floors.

A BUG'S LAND   Inspired by the 1998 film *A Bug's Life,* this section skews its attractions to an insect's point of view. Kids can spin around in giant takeout

Chinese food boxes on **Flik's Flyers,** and hit the bug-shaped bumper cars on **Tuck and Roll's Drive 'Em Buggies.** The short show *It's Tough to Be a Bug!* gives you a 3-D look at insect life.

PARADISE PIER This section re-creates the glory days of California's seaside piers. If you're looking for thrills, the **California Screamin'** roller coaster takes its riders from 0 to 55 mph in about four seconds and proceeds through scream tunnels, steeply angled drops, and a 360-degree loop. **Mickey's Fun Wheel,** a giant Ferris wheel, provides a good view of the grounds at a more leisurely pace. There's also carnival games, a fish-theme carousel, and Ariel's Grotto, where future princesses can dine with the mermaid and her friends (reservations a must).

OTHER ATTRACTIONS

Downtown Disney. Downtown Disney is a 20-acre promenade of dining, shopping, and entertainment that connects the Disneyland Resort hotels and theme parks. Restaurant-nightclubs here include the **House of Blues,** which spices up its Delta-inspired ribs and seafood with various live music acts on an intimate two-story stage. At **Ralph Brennan's Jazz Kitchen** you can dig into New Orleans–style food and music. Sports fans gravitate to **ESPN Zone,** a sports bar–restaurant–entertainment center with American grill food, interactive video games, and 175 video screens telecasting worldwide sports events.

There's also an **AMC** multiplex movie theater with stadium-style seating that plays the latest blockbusters and, naturally, a couple of kids' flicks. Promenade shops sell everything from Disney goods to antique jewelry; don't miss **Vault 28,** a hip boutique that sells one-of-kind vintage and couture clothes and accessories from Disney, Betsey Johnson, and other designers. ⊠ *Disneyland Dr. between Ball Rd. and Katella Ave., Anaheim* ☎ *714/300–7800* ⊕ *www.disneyland.com* 🎟 *Free* ☾ *Daily 7 am–2 am; hrs at shops and restaurants vary.*

Muzeo. This stunning 20,000-square-foot exhibition hall is housed in the Carnegie Library, built in 1908. It hosts touring art and cultural exhibitions about everything from Napoleon to the Mississippi Delta blues; there are kids' programs tied to the exhibits on weekends. There's also a small permanent exhibit on Anaheim and north Orange County. ⊠ *241 S. Anaheim Blvd., North Anaheim, Anaheim* ☎ *714/956–8936* ⊕ *www.muzeo.org* 🎟 *$13* ☾ *Daily 10 am–5 am.*

Anaheim ICE. The Anaheim Ducks hockey team train at this facility. Practices are open to the public from mid-September to mid-April; call ahead for info. The rink also has public skating sessions, adult and youth hockey games, and lessons. ⊠ *300 W. Lincoln Ave., Anaheim* ☎ *714/535–7465* ⊕ *www.anaheimice.com* 🎟 *$9* ☾ *Daily 7 am–2 am; public skate times vary.*

WHERE TO EAT

$$$ ✕ **Anaheim White House.** Several small dining rooms are set with crisp
ITALIAN linens and candles in this flower-filled 1909 mansion. The northern Italian menu includes steak, rack of lamb, and fresh seafood. Try the Gwen Stefani Ravioli, lobster-filled pasta on a bed of ginger and citrus. A three-course prix-fixe "express" lunch, served weekdays, costs

$22. ⊠ *887 S. Anaheim Blvd., Anaheim* ☎ *714/772–1381* ⊘ *No lunch weekends.*

$$$
MEDITERRANEAN

✕ **Catal Restaurant & Uva Bar.** Famed chef Joachim Splichal of L.A.'s Patina empire takes a more casual approach at this bi-level Mediterranean spot—with tapas breaking into the finger-food territory. At the Uva (Spanish for "grape") bar on the ground level you can graze on olives and Spanish ham, choosing from 40 wines by the glass. Upstairs, Catal's menu spans paella, rotisserie chicken, and salads. ⊠ *1580 S. Disneyland Dr., Suite 103, Anaheim* ☎ *714/774–4442.*

$$
ITALIAN

✕ **Luigi's D'Italia.** Despite the simple surroundings—red vinyl booths and plastic checkered tablecloths—Luigi's serves outstanding Italian cuisine: spaghetti marinara, veal Parmesan, homemade pizza, and other classics. Kids will feel right at home here; there's even a children's menu. It's an easy five-minute drive from Disneyland, but less crowded and expensive than many restaurants adjacent to the park. ⊠ *801 S. State College Blvd., Anaheim* ☎ *714/490–0990.*

$$$$
CONTINENTAL

✕ **Morton's.** This upscale steak-house chain is a block from the convention center. Besides its usual menu of prime aged beef and seafood, the place features Bar 12*21, which has two flat-screen TVs, extensive martini list, and snack menu featuring mini-cheeseburgers and filet mignon sandwiches. ⊠ *1895 S. Harbor Blvd., Anaheim* ☎ *714/621–0101* ⊘ *No lunch.*

$$
AMERICAN

✕ **Mr. Stox.** Intimate booths and linen tablecloths create a sophisticated, old-school setting at this family-owned restaurant. Prime rib, Maryland crab cakes, and fresh fish specials are excellent; the pasta, bread, and pastries are made in-house; and the wine list is wide-ranging. ⊠ *1105 E. Katella Ave., Anaheim* ☎ *714/634–2994* ⊘ *No lunch weekends.*

$$$$
AMERICAN
★

✕ **Napa Rose.** In sync with its host hotel, Disney's Grand Californian, this restaurant is done in a lovely Arts and Crafts style. The contemporary cuisine here is matched with an extensive wine list (600 bottles on display). For a look into the open kitchen, sit at the counter and watch the chefs as they whip up signature dishes such as Gulf of California rock scallops in a sauce of lemon, lobster, and vanilla and spit-roasted prime rib of pork with ranch-style black beans. The four-course $85 prix-fixe menu changes weekly. ⊠ *Disney's Grand Californian Hotel, 1600 S. Disneyland Dr., Anaheim* ☎ *714/300–7170.*

WHERE TO STAY

The Anaheim area has more than 50,000 rooms in hotels, family-style inns, and RV parks. ■TIP➔ One handy perk of staying in a Disney hotel: you can charge anything you buy in either park, such as food and souvenirs, to your room, so you don't have to carry around a lot of cash. (This doesn't hold true for Downtown Disney, though.)

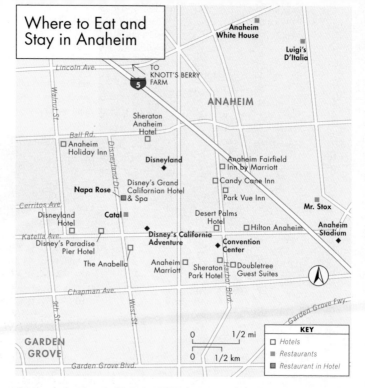

Where to Eat and Stay in Anaheim

Anaheim White House

Luigi's D'Italia

Lincoln Ave.

TO KNOTT'S BERRY FARM 5

ANAHEIM

Walnut St.

Sheraton Anaheim Hotel

Ball Rd.

Anaheim Holiday Inn

Disneyland Dr.

Disneyland

Anaheim Fairfield Inn by Marriott

Candy Cane Inn

Napa Rose

Disney's Grand Californian Hotel & Spa

Park Vue Inn

Cerritos Ave.

Mr. Stox

Disneyland Hotel

Catal

Desert Palms Hotel

Anaheim Stadium

Katella Ave.

Disney's Paradise Pier Hotel

Disney's California Adventure

Hilton Anaheim

Convention Center

The Anabella

Anaheim Marriott

Sheraton Park Hotel

Doubletree Guest Suites

Chapman Ave.

9th St.

West St.

Harbor Blvd.

Garden Grove Fwy.

GARDEN GROVE

Garden Grove Blvd.

0   1/2 mi
0   1/2 km

KEY
□ Hotels
■ Restaurants
▣ Restaurant in Hotel

An Anaheim Resort Transit (ART) bus can take you around town for $4. The buses run every 10 minutes during peak times, 20 minutes otherwise. They go between major hotels, Disney attractions, the Anaheim Convention Center, and restaurants and shops. See the ART Web site (⊕ *www.rideart.org*) for more information. In addition, many hotels are within walking distance of the Disneyland Resort.

$ 🏨 **The Anabella.** This Spanish Mission–style hotel on the convention center campus is a good value. The suites are spacious and elegant with hardwood floors, granite bathrooms, and sleeper sofas. Interior rooms (away from Katella Avenue) are quieter. The hotel's Oasis, with a hot tub and pool, plus an adults-only pool, is a perfect place for relaxing. **Pros:** attentive service; landscaped grounds; pet-friendly rooms. **Cons:** some say the room walls are thin; it's a bit removed from the action. ✉ *1030 W. Katella Ave., Anaheim* ☎ *714/905–1050, 800/863–4888* 🖷 *714/905–1054* ⊕ *www.anabellahotel.com* ➦ *358 rooms, 124 suites* ⚒ *In-room: Wi-Fi. In-hotel: restaurant, bar, pool, gym, spa, laundry facilities, parking.*

$ 🏨 **Anaheim Fairfield Inn by Marriott.** Attentive service and proximity to Disneyland (a 10-minute walk away) make this high-rise hotel a big draw for families. Most of the spacious rooms come with sleeper sofas as well as beds. In summer keep an eye out for the magician who roams the premises, entertaining adults and kids alike. **Pros:** free off-site parking with shuttle; close to many restaurants; the lobby offers fruit-infused drinking water and a TV showing Disney movies. **Cons:** small pool abuts the parking lot; lack of green space. ✉ *1460 S. Harbor Blvd., Anaheim* ☎ *714/772–6777, 800/228–2800* 📠 *714/999–1727* ⊕ *www.marriott.com* ⇢ *467 rooms* ♿ *In-room: Wi-Fi. In-hotel: restaurant, pool, laundry facilities, parking.*

¢ 📺 **Anaheim Holiday Inn.** The warmth of Old California is found in this Holiday Inn, where the walls are furnished with historic photos and water paths snake through the grounds. Rooms are on the small side, but the residential location makes for quiet evenings. **Pros:** attractive pool; friendly, personal service despite large size. **Cons:** confusing layout; it's a 10-minute drive to Disneyland's main entrance and many off-property restaurants. ✉ *1240 S. Walnut Ave., Anaheim* ☎ *714/535–0300, 800/824–5459* 📠 *714/491–8953* ⊕ *www.hianaheim.com* ⇢ *255 rooms, 28 suites* ♿ *In-hotel: restaurant, bar, pool, parking.*

$ 📺 **Anaheim Marriott.** Rooms at this busy convention hotel are well equipped for business travelers, with desks, two phones, and data ports. Spacious rooms have one king or two double beds; some have balconies. Disneyland is about a 30-minute walk away; shuttles are available. Fodor's readers say you won't find as many small children here as you may at other Disney-area hotels. **Pros:** efficient, attentive service; rooms are spacious. **Cons:** it's a long walk to Disneyland's main gate and off-property restaurants; conventioneers often take over the place. ✉ *700 W. Convention Way, Anaheim* ☎ *714/750–8000, 800/228–9290* 📠 *714/750–9100* ⊕ *www.marriott.com* ⇢ *1,031 rooms* ♿ *In-room: Internet, Wi-Fi. In-hotel: restaurant, bar, pool, gym, laundry facilities, business center, parking.*

$$ 📺 **Candy Cane Inn.** One of the Disneyland area's first hotels (deeds were
★ executed Christmas Eve, hence the name), the Candy Cane is one of Anaheim's most relaxing properties. Rooms are spacious and understated, while the palm-fringed pool is especially inviting. Premium rooms have two queen beds, microwaves, and coffeemakers. The hotel is just around the corner from Disneyland's main gate. A free Disneyland shuttle runs every half hour. **Pros:** proximity to Disneyland; friendly service; well-lighted, landscaped property. **Cons:** rooms and lobby are on the small side; all rooms face parking lot. ✉ *1747 S. Harbor Blvd., Anaheim* ☎ *714/774–5284, 800/345–7057* 📠 *714/772–5462* ⊕ *www.candycaneinn.net* ⇢ *171 rooms* ♿ *In-room: Wi-Fi. In-hotel: pool, spa, laundry facilities, parking* ⊖| *Breakfast.*

$ 📺 **Desert Palms Hotel and Suites.** This hotel midway between Disneyland and the convention center is a great value, with some one-bedroom suites that can accommodate a group of four or more. Book well in advance, especially when large conventions are in town. **Pros:** lobby is large and welcoming; free breakfast buffet; central location. **Cons:** drab exterior fronts busy Katella Avenue; small pool gets limited sun. ✉ *631 W. Katella Ave., Anaheim* ☎ *714/535–1133, 888/788–0596* 📠 *714/491–7409* ⊕ *www.desertpalmshotel.com* ⇢ *59 rooms, 128 suites* ♿ *In-hotel: pool, laundry facilities, parking* ⊖| *Breakfast.*

$$$ ☷ **Disneyland Hotel.** Not surprisingly, the first of Disney's three hotels is the one most full of Magic Kingdom magic, with Disney-theme memorabilia and Disney music. Check out the Peter Pan–theme pool, with its wooden bridge, 110-foot waterslide, and relaxing whirlpool. The cove pools' sandy shores are great for sunning and playing volleyball. East-facing rooms in Dreams Tower have the best views of the park, while west-facing rooms look over gardens. At Goofy's Kitchen, kids can dine with Disney characters. Room-and-ticket packages are available. In 2009, the hotel began a three-year multiphase renovation aimed at modernizing the entire facility with wireless Internet, noise-filtering windows, and a new water play area. Updated guest rooms will have flat-screen TVs and new Disney-theme decor such as headboards featuring Sleeping Beauty Castle. **Pros:** Disney theme is everywhere; great kids activities; 10-minute walk from main gate and near monorail. **Cons:** lots of kids means the noise level is high at all hours. ☒ *1150 Magic Way, Anaheim* ☎ *714/778–6600* 🖷 *714/956–6582* ⊕ *www.disneyland. com* ☞ *905 rooms, 60 suites* ♿ *In-room: Internet. In-hotel: restaurant, bar, pool, gym, spa, children's programs, parking.*

$$$ ☷ **Disney's Grand Californian Hotel & Spa.** The newest of Disney's Anaheim hotels, this Craftsman-style luxury property has guest rooms with views of the California Adventure park and Downtown Disney. They don't push the Disney brand too heavily; rooms are done in dark woods with amber-shaded lamps and just a small Bambi image on the shower curtain. Restaurants include the Napa Rose dining room and Storytellers Cafe, where Disney characters entertain children at breakfast. Of the three pools, the one shaped like Mickey Mouse is just for kids, plus there's an evening child activity center and portable cribs in every room. Room-and-ticket packages are available. The Mandara spa has a couple's suite with Balinese-inspired art and textiles. In 2009 the resort added a new wing with 50 Disney Vacation Club villas, most of which have full kitchens, balconies or patios, and laundry facilities, as well as 200 new rooms. **Pros:** large, gorgeous lobby; direct access to California Adventure. **Cons:** the self-parking lot is across the street from the hotel; standard rooms are on the small side. ☒ *1600 S. Disneyland Dr., Anaheim* ☎ *714/956–6425* 🖷 *714/300–7701* ⊕ *www.disneyland. com* ☞ *901 rooms, 44 suites, 50 villas* ♿ *In-room: Internet. In-hotel: restaurant, bar, pool, gym, children's programs, parking.*

Fodor's Choice
★

$$$ ☷ **Disney's Paradise Pier Hotel.** The Paradise Pier has many of the same Disney touches as the Disneyland Hotel, but it's a bit quieter and tamer. From here you can walk to Disneyland or pick up a shuttle or monorail. SoCal style manifests itself in seafoam-green guest rooms with lamps shaped like lifeguard stands, and surfboard motifs. A wooden roller coaster–inspired waterslide takes adventurers to a high-speed splashdown. Room-and-ticket packages are available. **Pros:** first-rate concierge; friendly service. **Cons:** small pool area; it's a 15-minute walk to Disneyland despite its location within the Disney resort area. ☒ *1717 S. Disneyland Dr., Anaheim* ☎ *714/999–0990* 🖷 *714/776–5763* ⊕ *www. disneyland.com* ☞ *470 rooms, 25 suites* ♿ *In-room: Internet. In-hotel: restaurant, bar, pool, gym, children's programs, parking.*

12

$$ ⊞ **Doubletree Guest Suites.** This upscale hotel near the Convention Center
★ caters to business travelers and families alike. Rooms have soundproof
walls, high-quality linens, large desks, and data ports. The one-bedroom
suites have flat-screen TVs and sleeper sofas. There's also a heated pool
and spa, fitness center, and video arcade. Disneyland is a 20-minute
walk away. **Pros:** huge suites; elegant lobby; within walking distance
of a variety of restaurants. **Cons:** some say the hotel seems far-removed
from Disneyland; pool area is small. ⊠ *2085 S. Harbor Blvd., Ana-
heim* ☎ *714/750–3000, 800/215–7316* 🖷 *714/750–3002* 🛏 *50 rooms,
202 suites* ⚴ *In-hotel: restaurant, pool, spa, laundry facilities, parking*
†⊙† *Breakfast.*

$$ ⊞ **Hilton Anaheim.** Next to the Anaheim Convention Center, this busy
Hilton is one of the largest hotels in Southern California with a restau-
rant and food court, cocktail lounges, a full-service gym, and its own
Starbucks. A $60-million renovation in 2008 updated the central lobby
and guest rooms, which are appointed in handsome beiges and browns.
A shuttle runs to Disneyland, or you can walk there in a few blocks.
Pros: friendly efficient service; great seasonal kids' programs. **Cons:**
huge size can be daunting; $14 fee to use health club. ⊠ *777 Conven-
tion Way, Anaheim* ☎ *714/750–4321, 800/445–8667* 🖷 *714/740–4460*
⊕ *www.anaheim.hilton.com* 🛏 *1,572 rooms, 93 suites* ⚴ *In-hotel: restaurant, bar, pool, gym, parking.*

$ ⊞ **Park Vue Inn.** This bougainvillea-trimmed two-story Spanish-style inn
is one of the closest hotels you can find to Disneyland's main gate.
Rooms were renovated in 2007 and most feature two queen beds, desks,
and large TVs; breakfast is included in the rate. **Pros:** easy walk to Disneyland and many restaurants; good value. **Cons:** all rooms face the
parking lot; some complain about early-morning street noise. ⊠ *1570 S.
Harbor Blvd., Anaheim* ☎ *714/772–3691, 800/334–7021* 🖷 *714/956–
4736* ⊕ *www.parkvueinn.com* 🛏 *76 rooms, 8 suites* ⚴ *In-hotel: pool,
gym, spa, laundry facilities, parking.*

$$ ⊞ **Sheraton Anaheim Hotel.** If you're hoping to escape from the commer-
★ cial atmosphere of the hotels near Disneyland, consider this sprawling
replica of a Tudor castle. In the flower- and plant-filled lobby you're
welcome to sit by the grand fireplace, watching fish swim around in
a pond. Rooms are sizable; some first-floor rooms open onto interior
gardens and a pool area. A shuttle to Disneyland is available. **Pros:**
large, attractive lobby; game room; spacious rooms with comfortable
beds. **Cons:** confusing layout; hotel sits close to a busy freeway and is
not within walking distance of Disneyland. ⊠ *900 S. Disneyland Dr.,
Anaheim* ☎ *714/778–1700, 800/325–3535* 🖷 *714/535–3889* ⊕ *www.
starwoodhotels.com* 🛏 *460 rooms, 29 suites* ⚴ *In-room: Wi-Fi. In-
hotel: restaurant, bar, pool, gym, laundry facilities, parking.*

$$ ⊞ **Sheraton Park Hotel at the Anaheim Resort.** Sheraton took over this hotel
in 2006 and freshened up the decor in guest rooms and public spaces.
The handsome rooms are decorated in rich navy and brown and have
private balconies with views of Disneyland or the surrounding area. You
can also relax in the nicely landscaped outdoor area or take a dip in the
oversize pool. It's about a 15-minute walk to Disneyland. **Pros:** luxury
lodging; large fitness center overlooks pool; most rooms have excellent

views. **Cons:** impersonal lobby; elevators can be slow when it's busy. ✉ *1855 S. Harbor Blvd., Anaheim* ☎ *714/750–1811, 800/716–6199* 🖨 *714/971–3626* ⊕ *www.starwoodhotels.com/sheraton* 🛏 *483 rooms, 7 suites* ♿ *In-room: Wi-Fi. In-hotel: restaurant, bar, pool, gym, laundry facilities, parking.*

SPORTS

Los Angeles Angels of Anaheim. Pro baseball's Los Angeles Angels of Anaheim play at Angel Stadium of Anaheim. An "Outfield Extravaganza" celebrates great plays on the field, with fireworks and a geyser exploding over a model evoking the California coast. ✉ *2000 Gene Autry Way, East Anaheim, Anaheim* ☎ *714/940–2000* ⊕ *www.angelsbaseball.com*

Anaheim Ducks. The National Hockey League's Anaheim Ducks, winners of the 2007 Stanley Cup, play at Honda Center. ✉ *Formerly Arrowhead Pond, 2695 E. Katella Ave., East Anaheim, Anaheim* ☎ *714/704–2400* ⊕ *ducks.nhl.com*

USA Men's National Volleyball Team. The USA Men's National Volleyball Team moved from Colorado to Anaheim in 2006. The team practices at American Sports Centers. ✉ *1500 S. Anaheim Blvd., Anaheim* ☎ *714/917–3600* ⊕ *www.americansportscenters.com/volleyball.htm*

KNOTT'S BERRY FARM

25 mi south of Los Angeles, via I–5, in Buena Park.

🕐 ★ **Knott's Berry Farm.** The land where the boysenberry was invented (by crossing red raspberry, blackberry, and loganberry bushes) is now occupied by Knott's Berry Farm. In 1934 Cordelia Knott began serving chicken dinners on her wedding china to supplement her family's income. Or so the story goes. The dinners and her boysenberry pies proved more profitable than husband Walter's berry farm, so the two moved first into the restaurant business and then into the entertainment business.

The park is now a 160-acre complex with 100-plus rides, dozens of restaurants and shops, and even a brick-by-brick replica of Philadelphia's Independence Hall. Although it has some good attractions for small children, the park is best known for its roster of awesome thrill rides. And, yes, you can still get that boysenberry pie (and jam, juice—you name it). ✉ *8039 Beach Blvd.* ✛ *Between La Palma Ave. and Crescent St., 2 blocks south of Hwy. 91* ☎ *714/220–5200* ⊕ *www.knotts.com.*

PARK NEIGHBORHOODS

BOARDWALK   Not-for-the-squeamish thrill rides and skill-based games dominate the scene at **Boardwalk.** Go head over heels on the **Boomerang** roller coaster, then do it again—backward. The **Perilous Plunge,** billed as the world's tallest, steepest, and—thanks to its big splash—wettest thrill ride, sends riders down an almost-vertical chute. Windseeker, opening in late 2011, whisks passengers on an unforgettable gondola ride 300 feet above the park. Boardwalk is also home to a string of test-your-skill games that are fun to watch whether you're playing or not, and Johnny Rockets, the park's newest restaurant.

CAMP SNOOPY It can get gridlocked on weekends, but small fry love this miniature High Sierra wonderland where the *Peanuts* gang hangs out. They can push and pump their own mini-mining cars on **Huff and Puff**, zip around a pint-size racetrack on **Charlie Brown Speedway**, and hop aboard **Woodstock's Airmail**, a kids' version of the park's Supreme Scream ride. Most of the rides here are geared toward kids only, leaving parents to cheer them on from the sidelines. **Sierra Sidewinder**, a roller coaster that opened near the entrance of Camp Snoopy in 2007, is aimed at older children with spinning saucer-type vehicles that go a maximum speed of 37 mph.

FIESTA VILLAGE Over in **Fiesta Village** are two more musts for adrenaline junkies: **Montezooma's Revenge**, a roller coaster that goes from 0 to 55 mph in less than five seconds, and **Jaguar!**, which simulates the motions of a cat stalking its prey, twisting, spiraling, and speeding up and slowing down as it takes you on its stomach-dropping course. There's also **Hat Dance**, a version of the spinning teacups but with sombreros, and a 100-year-old Dentzel Carousel, complete with an antique organ and menagerie of hand-carved animals.

> ## KNOTT'S BERRY FARM'S TOP ATTRACTIONS
>
> **Silver Bullet:** Let your legs dangle on this Western-themed roller coaster that rises 146 feet and then plunges 109 feet.
>
> **Supreme Scream:** This thrill ride lifts you up 254 feet…then drops you at 50 mph.
>
> **Boomerang:** Don't eat right before riding this stomach-churning, whiplash-inducing roller coaster.
>
> **GhostRider:** This classic wooden roller coaster speeds along at 56 mph and reaches a height of 118 feet.
>
> **Xcelerator:** This hydraulically launched roller coaster rockets to 82 mph…in just 2.3 seconds.

GHOST TOWN Clusters of authentic old buildings relocated from their original mining-town sites mark this section of the park. You can stroll down the street, stop and chat with a blacksmith, pan for gold (for a fee), crack open a geode, check out the chalkboard of a circa-1875 schoolhouse, and ride an original Butterfield stagecoach. Looming over it all is **GhostRider**, Orange County's first wooden roller coaster. Traveling up to 56 mph and reaching 118 feet at its highest point, the park's biggest attraction is riddled with sudden dips and curves, subjecting riders to forces up to three times that of gravity. On the Western-theme **Silver Bullet**, riders are sent to a height of 146 feet and then back down 109 feet. Riders spiral, corkscrew, fly into a cobra roll, and experience overbanked curves. The **Calico Mine** ride descends into a replica of a working gold mine. The **Timber Mountain Log Ride** is a worthwhile flume ride, especially if you're with kids who don't make the height requirements for the flumes at Disneyland. Also found here is the park's newest thrill ride, the **Pony Express**, a roller coaster that lets riders saddle up on packs of "horses" tethered to a platforms that take off on a series of hairpin turns and travel up to 38 mph. Don't miss the **Western Trails Museum**, a dusty old gem full of Old West memorabilia, plus menus from the original chicken restaurant, and Mrs. Knott's antique button collection. **Calico**

DID YOU KNOW?

On the Silver Bullet roller coaster at Knott's Berry Farm, riders spiral, corkscrew, and plunge 109 feet, with nothing between them and the ground but air.

12

BEST TIPS FOR KNOTT'S BERRY FARM

Look for Web-only Deals: Log onto the park's home page for special discounts.

Arrive Late: After 4 pm, adult admission is only $28.

Cool Off: If it's a hot day, bring your bathing suit—Knott's Soak City water park ($31.99 adults; $21.99 kids and seniors) is just next door.

Avoid Peak Times: Be aware that the park—especially Camp Snoopy—is packed during summer and on holiday weekends. As with most theme parks, visiting off-season and/or during the week is the way to go.

Get your Chicken Dinner to Go: The famous chicken dinners (and boysenberry pie) served at Mrs. Knott's Chicken Dinner Restaurant— just outside the park entrance—are delicious, but the wait for a seat can be long. Order yours as takeout, and have a picnic.

Railroad departs regularly from Ghost Town station for a round-trip tour of the park (bandit holdups notwithstanding).

WILD WATER WILDERNESS Just like its name implies, this section is home to **Big Foot Rapids,** a splash-fest of white-water river rafting over towering cliffs, cascading waterfalls, and wild rapids. Don't miss the visually stunning show at **Mystery Lodge,** which tells the story of Native Americans in the Pacific Northwest with lights, music, and beautiful images.

Knott's Soak City Water Park is directly across from the main park on 13 acres next to Independence Hall. It has a dozen major water rides; the latest is **Pacific Spin,** an oversize waterslide that drops riders 75 feet into a catch pool. There's also a children's pool, 750,000-gallon wave pool, and funhouse. Soak City is open daily after Memorial Day; weekends only after Labor Day.

WHERE TO EAT AND STAY

$$
AMERICAN

✕ **Mrs. Knott's Chicken Dinner Restaurant.** Cordelia Knott's fried chicken and boysenberry pies drew crowds so big that Knott's Berry Farm was built to keep the hungry customers occupied while they waited. The restaurant's current incarnation (outside the park's entrance) still serves crispy fried chicken, along with fluffy biscuits, corn, mashed potatoes, and Mrs. Knott's signature chilled cherry-rhubarb compote. The wait, unfortunately, can be two-plus hours on weekends; another option is to order a bucket of the same tasty chicken from the adjacent takeout counter and have a picnic at the duck pond next to Independence Hall across the street. ✉ *Knott's Berry Farm Marketplace Area, 8039 Beach Blvd.* ☎ *714/220–5080.*

$$$$
AMERICAN

✕ **Pirate's Dinner Adventure.** During this interactive pirate-theme dinner show, 150 actors/singers/acrobats (some quite talented) perform on a galleon while you eat a three-course meal. Food—barbecue pork, roast chicken, salad, veggies, rice, and unlimited soda and coffee—is mediocre and seating is tight, but kids love making a lot of noise to cheer on their favorite pirate, and the action scenes are breathtaking. ✉ *7600 Beach Blvd.* ☎ *866/439–2469.*

$$ ⛰ **Knott's Berry Farm Resort Hotel.** Knott's Berry Farm runs this convenient high-rise hotel on park grounds. The second-floor "camp rooms" are decorated in a Camp Snoopy motif and come with telephone bedtime stories. Shuttle service to Disneyland is available. Ask about packages that include entry to Knott's Berry Farm. **Pros:** easy access to Knott's Berry Farm; plenty of kids' activities; basketball court. **Cons:** lobby and hallways can be noisy and chaotic. ⊠ *7675 Crescent Ave.* ☎ *714/995–1111, 866/752–2444* 🖨 *714/828–8590* ⊕ *www.knottshotel.com* ⤴ *320 rooms* ♿ *In-room: Internet. In-hotel: restaurant, bar, pool, tennis court, gym, laundry facilities, parking.*

The South Coast
and Catalina Island

WORD OF MOUTH

"Laguna Beach is a wonderful place to spend the weekend sunning and strolling through the many quaint galleries and shops."

—ECinSF

WELCOME TO THE SOUTH COAST AND CATALINA ISLAND

TOP REASONS TO GO

★ **Catalina Island:** Just a short hydrofoil away, Catalina Island feels a thousand miles away from the rest of the state of California. Wander around charming Avalon, or explore the unspoiled beauty of the island's wild interior.

★ **Newport Beach:** Water enthusiasts delight in this sophisticated coastal town's endless yachting and boating options.

★ **Huntington Beach:** With more than 50 annual surf competitions, there's always lots of sporty oceanfront action.

★ **Laguna Beach:** Come here for SoCal's best stretches of beach, posh resorts, and quirky art scene.

★ **Mission San Juan Capistrano:** Like many of the missions throughout the state, this one offers a fascinating glimpse into California's rich history.

1 The Coast. Orange County's magnificent coastline is lined with a variety of vibrant communities, from unpretentious surf towns like Seal Beach to glamorous oceanfront enclaves like Corona del Mar. All share spectacular Pacific views buffered by generous swaths of protected beachfronts and plenty of recreational opportunities. And after a stunning sunset, both biker bars and romantic bistros await their respective clienteles.

2 Inland Orange County. Culturally diverse and cosmopolitan, the major cities of Orange County—Santa Ana and Costa Mesa—offer world-class arts venues, and beguiling ethnic neighborhoods, and great shopping.

13

GETTING ORIENTED

Like Los Angeles, Orange County stretches over a large area, lacks a singular focal point, and has limited public transportation. Every community in the region has a distinct personality, from Vietnamese-influenced Westminster to Huntington Beach, where blond surfer dudes and babes still rule. You'll need a car and a sensible game plan to make the most of your visit. There are many options for lodging throughout the county, but if you can afford it, staying at the beach is always recommended.

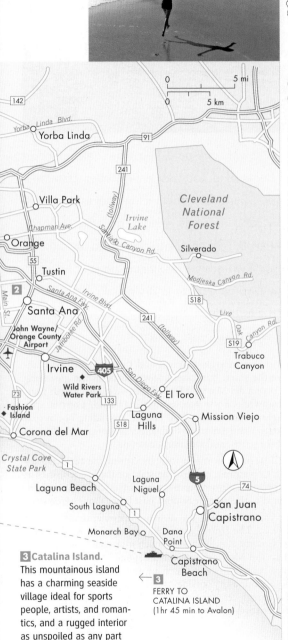

0   5 mi
0   5 km

142
Yorba Linda Blvd.
Yorba Linda
91
241
Villa Park
(Tollway)
Irvine
Lake
Cleveland
National
Forest
Chapman Ave.
Orange
Santiago Canyon Rd.
Silverado
55
Tustin
Modjeska Canyon Rd.
2
Santa Ana Fwy.
Irvine Blvd.
S18
Santa Ana
John Wayne/
Orange County
Airport
241
(Tollway)
Live
Oak Canyon Rd.
S19
Irvine
405
San Diego Fwy.
Jamboree Rd.
Trabuco
Canyon
73
Wild Rivers
Water Park
133
El Toro
Fashion
Island
Laguna
Hills
Mission Viejo
Corona del Mar
S18
Crystal Cove
State Park
1
Laguna Beach
Laguna
Niguel
5
74
South Laguna
1
Monarch Bay
Dana
Point
San Juan
Capistrano
Capistrano
Beach
3 Catalina Island.
This mountainous island has a charming seaside village ideal for sports people, artists, and romantics, and a rugged interior as unspoiled as any part of the Golden State.

← **3**
FERRY TO
CATALINA ISLAND
(1hr 45 min to Avalon)

Updated by
Laura Randall

With its tropical flowers and palm trees, the stretch of coast between Seal Beach and San Clemente is often called the California Riviera. Sure, few of the citrus groves that gave Orange County (OC) its name remain, and this region—south and east of Los Angeles—is now ruled by affluent subdivisions, high-tech businesses, theme parks, and shopping malls. But Orange County is still bucolic and refined enough to hold lots of appeal to both outdoor enthusiasts and culture vultures alike.

Exclusive Newport Beach, artsy Laguna, and the surf town of Huntington Beach are the stars, but lesser-known gems on the glistening coast—such as Corona del Mar and Dana Point—are also worth visiting. Offshore, meanwhile, lies gorgeous Catalina Island, a terrific spot for diving, snorkeling, and hiking. And despite a building boom that began in the 1980s, it's still a place to find wilderness preserves, canyon trails, greenbelt bike paths, and stunning coastline.

Get an evocative dose of California history by visiting the 18th-century Mission San Juan Capistrano, or enjoying state-of-the-art acoustics at one of America's premier performing arts centers (which, in quintessential OC form, is next to the massive South Coast Plaza shopping center).

Some of Orange County's towns are now high-profile, thanks to TV shows like *The O.C., The Hills, Laguna Beach,* and *The Real Housewives of Orange County.* But life here is much more multicultural and sophisticated than the McMansion world depicted on TV. A strong Mexican influence contributes to the cuisine and architecture, and the largest Vietnamese community outside Asia is that of Westminster's Little Saigon. And although Orange County has long been one of California's conservative bastions, it's also becoming more politically diverse.

PLANNING

WHEN TO GO

Like in the rest of Southern California, the sun shines year-round in Orange County.

However, in early summer there are the "June gloom" days that can easily extend from May to July, when skies are overcast, particularly before noon. Clear, warm, sunny days are the rule in fall and winter.

GETTING HERE AND AROUND

13

BUS TRAVEL

The Orange County Transportation Authority will take you virtually anywhere in the county, but it will take time; OCTA buses go from Knott's Berry Farm and Disneyland to Huntington Beach and Newport Beach. Bus 1 travels along the coast; buses 701 and 721 provide express service to Los Angeles.

Orange County Transportation Authority (OCTA) ☎ *714/636–7433* ⊕ *www.octa.net.*

CAR TRAVEL

The San Diego Freeway (I–405), the coastal route, and the Santa Ana Freeway (I–5), the inland route, run north–south through Orange County. South of Laguna I–405 merges into I–5 (called the San Diego Freeway south from this point). A toll road, the 73 Highway, runs 15 mi from Newport Beach to San Juan Capistrano; it costs $3.75–$5.50 (lower rates are for weekends and off-peak hours) and is usually less jammed than the regular freeways. Do your best to avoid all Orange County freeways during rush hours (6–9 am and 3:30–6:30 pm). Highway 55 leads to Newport Beach. The Pacific Coast Highway (Highway 1) allows easy access to beach communities and is the most scenic route.

FERRY TRAVEL

There are two ferries that service Catalina Island; Catalina Express runs from Long Beach (about 90 minutes) and from Newport Beach (about 75 minutes). Reservations are advised for summers and weekends.

TRAIN TRAVEL

When planning train travel, consider where the train stations are in relation to your ultimate destination. You may need to make extra transportation arrangements once you've arrived in town. From the station in San Juan Capistrano you can walk through the historic part of town. Amtrak makes daily stops in Orange County at all major towns. Metrolink is a weekday commuter train that runs to and from Los Angeles and Orange County.

Amtrak ☎ *800/872–7245* ⊕ *www.amtrak.com.*

Metrolink ☎ *800/371–5465* ⊕ *www.metrolinktrains.com.*

For more information on Getting Here and Around, see Travel Smart Los Angeles.

RESTAURANTS

Much like L.A., restaurants in Orange County are generally casual, and you'll rarely see men in jackets and ties. However, at top resort hotel dining rooms, many guests choose to dress up.

Of course, there's also a swath of super-casual places along the beach-fronts—fish-taco takeout, taquerias, burger joints—that won't mind if you wear flip-flops. Reservations are recommended for the nicest restaurants.

Many places don't serve past 11 pm, and locals tend to eat early. Remember that according to California law, smoking is prohibited in all enclosed areas.

HOTELS

Along the coast there's been a flurry of luxury resort openings in recent years; Laguna's Montage elevated expectations and was followed by the renovation of Dana Point's Ritz-Carlton and the debut of the Resort at Pelican Hill on the Newport Coast, among others.

As a rule, lodging prices tend to rise the closer the hotels are to the beach. If you're looking for value, consider a hotel that is inland along the I–405 freeway corridor.

In most cases, you can take advantage of some of the facilities of the high-end resorts, such as restaurants and spas, even if you aren't an overnight guest

WHAT IT COSTS					
	¢	$	$$	$$$	$$$$
RESTAURANTS	under $7	$7–$12	$13–$22	$23–$32	over $32
HOTELS	under $75	$75–$125	$126–$200	$201–$325	over $325

Restaurant prices are per person for a main course, excluding 9.75% sales tax. Hotel prices are for two people in a standard double room in nonholiday high season on the European Plan (no meals) unless otherwise noted. Taxes (9%–14%) are extra. In listings, we always name the facilities available, but we don't specify whether they cost extra. When pricing accommodations, always ask about what's included.

VISITOR INFORMATION

The Anaheim-Orange County Visitor and Convention Bureau is an excellent resource for both leisure and business travelers and can provide materials on many area attractions. It's on the main floor of the Anaheim Convention Center.

The Orange County Tourism Council's Web site is also a useful source of information.

Anaheim-Orange County Visitor and Convention Bureau ✉ *Anaheim Convention Center, 800 W. Katella Ave., Anaheim* ☎ *714/765–8888* ⊕ *www.anaheimoc.org.*

Orange County Tourism Council ⊕ *www.visitorangecounty.net.*

THE COAST

Running along the Orange County coastline is scenic Pacific Coast Highway (Highway 1, known locally as PCH). Older beachfront settlements, with their modest bungalow-style homes, are joined by posh new gated communities. The pricey land between Newport Beach and

Laguna Beach is where Laker Kobe Bryant, novelist Dean Koontz, and a slew of Internet and finance moguls live.

Though the coastline is rapidly being filled in, there are still a few stretches of beautiful, protected open land. And at many places along the way you can catch an idealized glimpse of the Southern California lifestyle: surfers hitting the beach, boards under their arms.

LONG BEACH AND SAN PEDRO

About 25 mi southeast of Los Angeles, I–110 south.

Aquarium of the Pacific. Sea lions, nurse sharks, and octopuses, oh my!— this aquarium focuses primarily on ocean life from the Pacific Ocean, with a detour into Australian birds. The main exhibits include lively sea lions, large tanks of various sharks and sting rays, and ethereal sea dragons, which the aquarium has successfully bred in captivity. Most impressive is the multimedia attraction, *Whales: A Journey With Giants.* This panoramic film shows in the aquarium's Great Hall, and when the entire core of the aquarium goes dark, you suddenly feel as if you're swimming with the giants. Ask for showtimes at the information desk.

For a nonaquatic experience, head over to Lorikeet Forest, a walk-in aviary full of the friendliest parrots from down under. Buy a cup of nectar and smile as you become a human bird perch. Be sure to say hello to newest resident Ollie, a sea otter rescued off the Santa Cruz coast as a baby in 2010. If you're a true tropical animal lover, book an up-close-and-personal Animal Encounters Tour ($90) to learn about and assist in care and feeding of the animals; or find out how aquarium functions with the extensive Behind the Scenes Tour ($34.95). ⊠ *100 Aquarium Way, Long Beach* ☎ *562/590–3100* ⊕ *www.aquariumofpacific.org* 🔒 *$24.95* ☉ *Daily 9–6.*

★ **Cabrillo Marine Aquarium.** Dedicated to the marine life that flourishes off the southern California coast, this Frank Gehry–designed center gives an intimate and instructive look at local sea creatures. Head to the Exploration Center and S. Mark Taper Foundation Courtyard for kid-friendly interactive exhibits and activity stations. Especially fun is the "Crawl In" aquarium, where you can be surrounded by fish without getting wet. ■TIP➔ **From March through July the aquarium organizes a legendary grunion program, when you can see the small, silvery fish as they come ashore at night to spawn on the beach.** After visiting the museum, you can stop for a picnic or beach stroll along Cabrillo Beach. ⊠ *3720 Stephen M. White Dr., San Pedro, Los Angeles* ☎ *310/548–7562* ⊕ *www.cabrilloaq.org* 🔒 *$5 suggested donation, parking available in adjacent lot at reduced rate of $1 for museumgoers* ☉ *Tues.–Fri. noon–5, weekends 10–5.*

Queen Mary. The reason to see this impressive example of 20th-century cruise ship opulence is because it's the last of its kind. And there's a saying among staff members that the more you get to know the *Queen Mary,* the more you realize she has an endearing personality to match her wealth of history.

A mural at Huntington Beach.

The beautifully preserved ocean liner was launched in 1934 and made 1,001 transatlantic crossings before finally berthing in Long Beach in 1967. It has gone through many periods of renovations since, but in 1993, the RMS Foundation took over ownership and restored its original art deco style. Delaware North Companies took over management in 2009 with plans to continue restoration and renovation of the ship.

On board, you can take one of 12 tours, such as the informative Behind the Scenes walk or the downright spooky Haunted Encounters tour. (Spirits have been spotted in the pool and engine room.) You could stay for dinner at one of the ship's restaurants, listen to live jazz in the original first-class lounge, or even spend the night in one of the wood-paneled rooms.

The ship's neighbor, a geodesic dome originally built to house Howard Hughes's *Spruce Goose* aircraft, now serves as a terminal for Carnival Cruise Lines, making the *Queen Mary* the perfect pit stop before or after a cruise. And anchored next to the *Queen* is the *Scorpion*, a Russian submarine you can tour for a look at Cold War history. ⊠ *1126 Queens Hwy., Long Beach* ☎ *877/342–0738* ⊕ *www.queenmary.com* ⊠ *Tours $24.95–$32.95, includes a self-guided audio tour* ☉ *Call for times and frequency of guided tours.*

HUNTINGTON BEACH

40 mi southeast of Los Angeles, I–5 south to I–605 south to I–405 south to Beach Blvd.

Once a sleepy residential town with little more than a string of rugged surf shops, Huntington Beach has transformed itself into a resort destination. The town's appeal is its broad white-sand beaches with often-towering waves, complemented by a lively pier, shops, and restaurants on Main Street and a growing collection of luxurious resort hotels.

13

A draw for sports fans and partiers of all stripes is the U.S. Open professional surf competition, which brings a festive atmosphere to town each July. There's even a Surfing Walk of Fame, with plaques set in the sidewalk around the intersection of PCH and Main Street.

ESSENTIALS

Visitor and Tour Information Huntington Beach Conference and Visitors Bureau ⊠ *301 Main St., Suite 208* ☎ *714/969–3492, 800/729–6232* ⊕ *www. surfcityusa.com.*

EXPLORING

Huntington Pier. Huntington Pier stretches 1,800 feet out to sea, well past the powerful waves that made Huntington Beach reach for the title of "Surf City U.S.A." A farmers' market is held on Friday; an informal arts fair sets up most weekends. **Ruby's** (☎ *714/969–7829* ⊕ *www.rubys. com*). At the end of the pier sits Ruby's, part of a California chain of 1940s-style burger joints.

Pierside Pavilion. The Pierside Pavilion has shops, restaurants, and bars with live music. The best surf-gear source is **HSS Pierside** (☎ *714/841–4000*), next to the pier, staffed by true surf enthusiasts. ⊠ *PCH across from Huntington Pier.*

International Surfing Museum. Just up Main Street from the pier, the International Surfing Museum pays tribute to the sport's greats with the Surfing Hall of Fame, which has an impressive collection of surfboards and related memorabilia. They've even got the Bolex camera used to shoot the 1966 surfing documentary *The Endless Summer.* ⊠ *411 Olive St.* ☎ *714/960–3483* ⊕ *www.surfingmuseum.org* ▨ *Free, $1 suggested donation for students, $2 for adults* ☉ *Year-round weekdays noon–5, Tuesdays until 9, weekends 11–6.*

★ **Bolsa Chica Ecological Reserve.** This impressive reserve beckons wildlife lovers and bird-watchers with an 1,180-acre salt marsh where 321 out of Orange County's 420 bird species—including great blue herons, snowy and great egrets, and brown pelicans—have been spotted in the past decade. Throughout the reserve are trails for bird-watching, including a comfortable 1½-mi loop. Free guided tours depart from the walking bridge the second Saturday of each month at 10 am. ⊠ *Entrance on PCH 1 mi south of Warner Ave., opposite Bolsa Chica State Beach at traffic light* ☎ *714/846–1114* ⊕ *www.bolsachica.org* ▨ *Free* ☉ *Daily dawn–dusk.*

WHERE TO EAT

$$$ ✕ **Duke's.** Oceanfront vistas and fresh-caught seafood reign supreme
SEAFOOD at this homage to surfing legend Duke Kahanamoku, which is a prime
people-watching spot right at the beginning of the pier. Choose from
several fish-of-the-day selections—many Hawaiian—prepared in one
of eight ways. Or try the crispy coconut shrimp or seven-spice ahi
tuna. Duke's mai tai is not to be missed. ⊠ *317 PCH* ☎ *714/374–6446*
⊕ *www.dukeshuntington.com.*

$$ ✕ **Lou's Red Oak BBQ.** You won't find any frills at Lou's Red Oak BBQ—
AMERICAN just barbecue pork, grilled linguica, rotisserie chicken, and a lot of beef.
Try the tri-tip (either as an entrée or on a toasted bun smothered with
garlic butter) or a Hawaiian teriyaki plate to get into the surfing spirit.
⊠ *21501 Brookhurst St.* ☎ *714/965–5200* ⊕ *www.lousbbq.com.*

¢ ✕ **Wahoo's Fish Taco.** Proximity to the ocean makes these mahimahi-filled
MEXICAN tacos taste even better. This healthy fast-food chain—tagged with dozens of surf stickers—brought Baja's fish tacos north of the border to
quick success. ⊠ *120 Main St.* ☎ *714/536–2050* ⊕ *www.wahoos.com.*

WHERE TO STAY

$ ▦ **Best Western Regency Inn.** This moderately priced, tidy Tudor-style
hotel is near PCH and close to the main drag and its restaurants and
shops. Rooms are cookie-cutter, but some have private whirlpools.
Forgo an ocean view and you can save a lot of money. Breakfast is
included in the room rate. **Pros:** great value; large rooms (some with
Jacuzzi tubs); free Internet; complimentary Continental breakfast.
Cons: 10-minute drive to beach; unglamorous location on busy thoroughfare; a bit dated. ⊠ *19360 Beach Blvd.* ☎ *714/962–4244* ⊕ *www.
bestwesterncalifornia.com* ⇢ *62 rooms* ⚹ *In-room: Internet. In-hotel:
pool, gym, laundry facilities, parking.*

$$$ ▦ **Hilton Waterfront Beach Resort.** Smack-dab across the street from the
beach and within walking distance of Main Street, this Mediterra-
nean-style Hilton attracts a varied clientele—singles, families, couples,
and business travelers. All guest rooms have private balconies; ocean-
front rooms boast views of Catalina Island. A heated free-form pool,
exotic landscaping, and sand volleyball court add to the resort vibe.
Pros: within walking distance of several restaurants; excellent Sunday
brunch buffet; oceanfront views. **Cons:** no self-parking; noise can be
an issue. ⊠ *21100 PCH* ☎ *714/845–8000, 800/822–7873* ⊕ *www.
waterfrontresort.com* ⇢ *290 rooms, 24 suites* ⚹ *In-room: Internet.
In-hotel: restaurant, bar, pool, tennis court, gym, parking.*

$$$$ ▦ **Hyatt Regency Huntington Beach Resort and Spa.** The design of this hand-
★ some property, which sprawls along PCH and incorporates courtyards
with fountains and firepots, is a nod to California's Mission period.
Nearly all of the spacious rooms offer ocean views and private balco-
nies or terraces. Beach-theme artwork by local artists enhances guest
rooms and public spaces. This Hyatt aims to create a village atmo-
sphere, with expansive common grounds and an inviting shopping area,
and to a large extent it has succeeded. Beach access is via a bridge over
PCH. **Pros:** close to beach; responsive staff; family-friendly. **Cons:** some
partial ocean-view rooms are disappointing; pesky resort and daily
valet fees. ⊠ *21500 PCH* ☎ *714/698–1234, 800/554–9288* ⊕ *www.*

Riding the waves at Newport Beach.

huntingtonbeach.hyatt.com ⟿ *517 rooms, 57 suites* ⚭ *In-room: Internet, Wi-Fi. In-hotel: restaurant, bar, gym, spa, water sports, children's programs, business center, parking.*

$$$$ 🏨 **Shorebreak Hotel.** Across the street from the beach and within the Strand retail complex, this new boutique hotel attracts a mix of families, business travelers, and the hipster-surfer crowd. Rooms are bright and stylish with high-definition TVs, writing desks, and tiled showers or bathtubs; some upper-level rooms have ocean views. All guests have access to a cozy courtyard with fire pits and the hotel's Mediterranean restaurant, Zimzala. **Pros:** proximity to beach and shops; comfortable beds; quiet rooms despite central location. **Cons:** steep valet parking fee; courtyard rooms have uninspiring alley views. ✉ *500 PCH* ☎ *714/861–4470, 877/744–1117* ⊕ *www.shorebreakhotel.com* ⟿ *157 rooms* ⚭ *In-room: Wi-Fi. In-hotel: restaurant, bar, gym, business center, parking, some pets allowed.*

SPORTS AND THE OUTDOORS

BEACHES **Huntington City Beach.** This beach each stretches for 3 mi north and south of the pier from Bolsa Chica State Beach to Huntington State Beach on the south. The beach is most crowded around the pier; amateur and professional surfers brave the waves daily on its north side. ☎ *714/536–5281* ⊕ *www.ci.huntington-beach.ca.us.*

Huntington State Beach. As you continue south, Huntington State Beach parallels Pacific Coast Highway. On the state and city beaches there are changing rooms, concessions, lifeguards, Wi-Fi, and ample parking; the state beach also has barbecue pits. ☎ *714/536–1454* ⊕ *www.parks. ca.gov/?page_id=643.*

CLOSE UP

Outdoor Activies on the Coast

Water sports rule the coast of Orange County. Those inexperienced at riding the waves along the coastline can get a feel for the waves by riding a boogie board at Seal Beach or at the Newport River jetties.

Surfing is permitted at most beaches year-round (check local newspapers or talk to lifeguards for conditions), and surfboard-rental stands line the coast.

The best waves are usually at San Clemente, Newport Beach, and Huntington Beach. From June through September the ocean temperature tops 70°F and lifeguards patrol almost every beach. Local newspapers print beach reports with wave information and notice of any closures.

Surfrider Foundation. You can also check local news on surf and water quality through the Surfrider Foundation. ⊕ www.surfrider.org.

Keep a lookout for signs warning of dangerous conditions: undertow, strong currents, and big waves can all be hazardous. Avoid swimming near surfers. When a yellow flag with a black circle is flying (known to locals as "black balling"), it means no hard boards are allowed, but swimming and bodyboarding are permitted.

If you'd like to explore the coastline by bike or on foot, the **Santa Ana Riverbed Trail** hugs the Santa Ana River for 20.5 mi between the Pacific Coast Highway (PCH) at Huntington State Beach and Imperial Highway in Yorba Linda. Joggers have an uninterrupted path the whole way. There are entrances, restrooms, and drinking fountains at all crossings. A bike path winds south from Marina del Rey all the way to San Diego with only minor breaks. Most beaches have bike-rental stands.

Irvine Ranch Conservancy. You'll usually hear the name Irvine linked to soulless suburban sprawl, but balancing that is the Irvine Ranch Conservancy. These 50,000 protected acres stretch 22 mi from Weir Canyon to the coast, where the reserve meets the Laguna Coast Wilderness Park and Crystal Cove State Park. The Conservancy and its affiliated environmental organizations sponsor many activities, from tough mountain bike rides to leisurely family picnics in regional parks. You'll need advance reservations for any of their docent-led activities. ☎ 714/508–4757 ⊕ www. irvineranchwildlands.org.

Bolsa Chica State Beach. At the northern section of the city, Bolsa Chica State Beach has barbecue pits and RV campsites and is usually less crowded than its southern neighbors. ☎ 714/846–3460 ⊕ www.parks. ca.gov/?page_id=642.

Dog Beach. Dog Beach, just north of the pier, is the rare place that encourages dogs to run and splash sans leash. You might even see a dog surfing with his owner. The beach is open daily 5 am–10 pm. ✉ 19000 PCH ☎ 714/841–8644 ⊕ www.dogbeach.org.

SURFING **Corky Carroll's Surf School.** Corky Carroll's Surf School organizes lessons, weeklong workshops, and surfing trips. ☎ 714/969–3959 ⊕ www. surfschool.net.

Dwight's. You can rent surf- or boogie boards at Dwight's, one block south of the pier. ☎714/536–8083.

Zack's Pier Plaza. Zack's Pier Plaza provides surfing lessons for individuals or groups and rents boards, wet suits, and other beach equipment. ✉ *405 PCH, at Main St.*

NEWPORT BEACH

6 mi south of Huntington Beach, PCH.

Newport Beach has evolved from a simple seaside village to an icon of chic coastal living. Its ritzy reputation comes from megayachts bobbing in the harbor, boutiques that rival those in Beverly Hills, and spectacular homes overlooking the ocean.

Newport is said to have the highest per-capita number of Mercedes-Benzes in the world; inland Newport Beach's concentration of high-rise office buildings, shopping centers, and luxury hotels drive the economy. But on the city's Balboa Peninsula, you can still catch a glimpse of a more innocent, down-to-earth beach town scattered with tackle shops and sailor bars.

ESSENTIALS

Visitor and Tour Information Newport Beach Conference and Visitors Bureau ✉ *110 Newport Center Dr., Suite 120* ☎ *949/719–6100, 800/942–6278* ⊕ *www.visitnewportbeach.com.*

EXPLORING

Balboa Pavilion. The Balboa Pavilion, on the bay side of the peninsula, was built in 1905 as a bath- and boathouse. Today it houses a restaurant and shops and it serves as a departure point for harbor and whale-watching cruises. Look for it on Main Street, off Balboa Boulevard. Adjacent to the pavilion is the three-car ferry that connects the peninsula to Balboa Island. In the blocks around the pavilion you can find restaurants, beachside shops, and the small **Fun Zone**—a local kiddie hangout with a Ferris wheel and a nautical museum. On the other side of the narrow peninsula is **Balboa Pier.** On its end is the original branch of Ruby's, a 1940s-esque burger-and-shake joint.

Balboa Peninsula. Newport's best beaches are on Balboa Peninsula, where many jetties pave the way to ideal swimming areas. The most intense bodysurfing place in Orange County and arguably on the West Coast, known as the **Wedge,** is at the south end of the peninsula. Created by accident in the 1930s when the Federal Works Progress Administration built a jetty to protect Newport Harbor, the break is pure euphoria for highly skilled bodysurfers. ■ TIP→ Since the waves generally break very close to shore and rip currents are strong, lifeguards strongly discourage visitors from attempting it—but it sure is fun to watch an experienced local ride it.

Fashion Island. Shake the sand out of your shoes to head inland to the ritzy Fashion Island outdoor mall, a cluster of arcades and courtyards complete with koi pond, fountains, and a Venetian-style carousel—plus some awesome ocean views. Although it doesn't have quite the international-designer clout of South Coast Plaza, it has the luxe department store Neiman Marcus and expensive spots like L'Occitane, Kate Spade, Ligne Roset, and Michael Stars. Chains, restaurants, and the requisite movie theater fill out the rest. ⊠ *410 Newport Center Dr., between Jamboree and MacArthur Blvds., off PCH* ☎ *949/721–2000* ⊕ *www.shopfashionisland.com.*

★ **Newport Harbor.** Newport Harbor, which shelters nearly 10,000 small boats, may seduce even those who don't own a yacht. Spend an afternoon exploring the charming avenues and surrounding alleys. Within Newport Harbor are eight small islands, including Balboa and Lido. The houses framing the shore may seem modest, but this is some of the most expensive real estate in the world. Several grassy areas on primarily residential Lido Isle have views of Newport Harbor.

Balboa Island. Balboa Island is a sliver of terra firma in Newport Harbor whose quaint streets are tightly packed with impossibly charming multimillion-dollar cottages. The island's main drag, Marine Avenue, is lined with equally attractive cafés and shops.

NEED A BREAK?

Sugar & Spice. Stop by ice cream parlor Sugar & Spice for a Balboa Bar—a slab of vanilla ice cream dipped first in chocolate and then in a topping of your choice such as hard candy or Oreo crumbs. Other parlors serve the concoction, but Sugar & Spice claims to have invented it back in 1945. ⊠ *310 Marine Ave., Balboa Island* ☎ *949/673–8907.* **Basilic.** This intimate French-Swiss bistro adds a touch of elegance to the island with its white linen and flower-topped tables. Head here for foie gras, steak au poivre, and a fine Bordeaux. ⊠ *217 Marine Ave.* ☎ *949/673–0570* ⊕ *www.basilicrestaurant.com.* **Olive Oil & Beyond.** At Olive Oil & Beyond, you can sample and purchase premium oils from around the globe. There's also a lineup of unique balsamic vinegars—some flavored with fig or tangerine—and other gourmet goodies. ⊠ *210 Marine Ave.* ☎ *949/566–9380.*

Newport Harbor Nautical Museum. This museum, in the Balboa Fun Zone (a small, historic amusement park), has exhibits on the history of the harbor as well as of the Pacific as a whole. There's a fleet of ship models, some dating to 1798; one is made entirely of gold and silver. Another fun display is a touch tank holding local sea creatures. A new exhibit features simulated and submersion experiences through live feeds from underwater archeological sites and a replicated yacht race. ⊠ *600 E. Bay Ave., Newport Beach* ☎ *949/675–8915* ⊕ *www.nhnm.org* ⌑ *$4* ☉ *Call for hours.*

Newport Pier. Newport Pier, which juts out into the ocean near 20th Street, is the heart of Newport's beach community and a popular fishing spot. Street parking is difficult at the pier, so grab the first space you find and be prepared to walk. A stroll along West Ocean Front reveals much of the town's character. On weekday mornings, head for the beach near the pier, where you're likely to encounter dory fishermen hawking their predawn catches, as they've done for generations. On weekends the walk is alive with kids of all ages on in-line skates, skateboards, and bikes dodging pedestrians and whizzing past fast-food joints, shops, and bars.

★ **Orange County Museum of Art.** Modernist paintings and sculpture by California artists and cutting-edge as well as international contemporary works can be found at this museum. Works by such key California artists as Richard Diebenkorn, Ed Ruscha, Robert Irwin, and Chris Burden are included in the collection. The museum also displays some of its digital art, Internet-based art, and sound works in the Orange Lounge, a satellite gallery at South Coast Plaza; free of charge, it's open the same hours as the mall. ⊠ *850 San Clemente Dr.* ☎ *949/759–1122* ⊕ *www. ocma.net* ⊠ *$12* ☉ *Wed. and Fri.–Sun. 11–5, Thurs. 11–8.*

13

WHERE TO EAT

$$ ✕ **Bluewater Grill.** On the site of an old sportfishing dock, this popular
SEAFOOD spot offers seafood from around the globe—from Mississippi catfish to barramundi from Australia. There's a tranquil bay view from either the dining room, which is adorned with early-1900s fishing photos, or the waterfront patio. Favorites include blue-nose sea bass, local Pacific red snapper, and calamari steak for those who miss the abalone that used to be common in the area. There's an emphasis on freshness—the menu changes daily—and wines are reasonably priced. ⊠ *630 Lido Park Dr.* ☎ *949/675–3474* ⊕ *www.bluewatergrill.com.*

$$$ ✕ **The Cannery.** This 1920s cannery building still teems with fish, but
SEAFOOD now they go into dishes on the eclectic Pacific Rim menu rather than being packed into crates. Settle in at the sushi bar, dining room, or patio before choosing between sashimi, bouillabaisse, or oven-roasted Chilean sea bass prepared with an Asian twist. The menu includes a selection of steaks, ribs, and seafood. Fodor's readers recommend the crème brûlée for dessert. ⊠ *3010 Lafayette Rd.* ☎ *949/566–0060* ⊕ *www.cannerynewport.com.*

$$$ ✕ **Gulfstream.** This trendy restaurant has an open kitchen, comfortable
AMERICAN booths, and outdoor seating on warm evenings. Especially tasty are the short ribs with mustard barbecue sauce; the most popular item is the ahi tuna burger. Salads, such as a mélange of cabbage, white beans, avocado, corn, and grapes, tend to be healthy and steaks and seafood dishes are simply prepared. It gets noisy near the bar area, so come early or retreat to the patio if you prefer quiet. ⊠ *850 Avocado Ave.* ☎ *949/718–0188* ⊕ *www.hillstone.com.*

$$ ✕ **3-Thirty-3.** If there's a nightlife "scene" to be had in Newport Beach,
AMERICAN this is it. This swank and stylish eatery attracts a convivial crowd—both young and old—for midday, sunset, and late-night dining; a long list of small, shareable plates heightens the camaraderie. Pair a cocktail with Chinese-spiced lollipop lamb chops or chicken satay while you check out the scene, or settle in for a dinner of Kobe flatiron steak or potato-crusted halibut. ⊠ *333 Bayside Dr.* ☎ *949/673–8464* ⊕ *www.3thirty3nb.com.*

WHERE TO STAY

$$$ ▦ **Balboa Bay Club and Resort.** Sharing the same frontage as the private Balboa Bay Club where Humphrey Bogart, Lauren Bacall, and the Reagans hung out, this hotel has one of the best bay views around. There's a yacht-club vibe in the public spaces, especially in the nautical dining room. The spacious rooms, which have either bay or courtyard views, have a beachy decor of rattan furniture, plantation shutters, and

tropical-pattern drapes. Duke's Place, a bar named for John Wayne, a former member and club governor, has photos of the star in his mariner-theme films. **Pros:** exquisite bayfront views; comfortable beds; romantic. **Cons:** service is helpful but can be slow; not much within walking distance. ⊠ *1221 W. Coast Hwy.* ☎ *949/645–5000, 888/445–7153* ⊕ *www.balboabayclub.com* ➳ *150 rooms, 10 suites* ☖ *In-room: Wi-Fi. In-hotel: restaurant, bar, gym, spa, some pets allowed.*

$$$ ▥ **Hyatt Regency Newport Beach.** The best aspect of this grande dame of Newport hotels is its lushly landscaped acres: 26 of them, overlooking the Back Bay. The casually elegant, low-profile architecture, spread over the generous grounds, will appeal to travelers weary of high-rise hotels. When booking your room, suite, or bungalow, let them know your preference of bay, golf course, garden, or pool views. Most rooms have patios or balconies. There's a 9-hole golf course and 16 lighted tennis courts. **Pros:** high-quality linens and bedding; centrally located for shopping. **Cons:** self-parking is far from main property; 10-minute drive to beach. ⊠ *1107 Jamboree Rd.* ☎ *949/729–1234* ⊕ *www.newportbeach. hyatt.com* ➳ *393 rooms, 9 suites, 4 bungalows* ☖ *In-room: Internet. In-hotel: restaurant, bar, golf course, pool, tennis court, gym, spa, parking.*

$$$$ ▥ **The Island Hotel.** A suitably stylish hotel in a very chic neighborhood (it's across the street from the Fashion Island shopping center), this 20-story tower caters to luxury seekers by offering weekend golf packages in conjunction with the nearby Pelican Hill golf course. Guest rooms have private balconies (usually with outstanding views), marble bathrooms, and original art. The spa does its bit for luxury with a pearl powder facial. The hotel lured Beverly Hills chef Bill Bracken, who now pampers diners at the elegant Palm Terrace with a contemporary menu of seductive small bites and entrées such as potato-encrusted Chilean sea bass. **Pros:** proximity to Fashion Island; 24-hour exercise facilities; first-class spa. **Cons:** steep valet parking prices; some rooms have views of mall; pricey. ⊠ *690 Newport Center Dr.* ☎ *949/759–0808, 866/554–4620* ⊕ *www.theislandhotel.com* ➳ *295 rooms, 83 suites* ☖ *In-room: a/c. In-hotel: restaurant, bar, pool, tennis court, gym, spa, business center, parking, some pets allowed.*

$$ ▥ **Newport Beach Marriott Hotel and Spa.** Here you'll be smack in the moneyed part of town: across from Fashion Island, next to a country club, and with a view toward Newport Harbor. The property recently underwent a $70-million makeover, and it shows. Rooms have that no-fuss contemporary look: dark wood, granite bathroom counters and welcome splashes of color; request one with a balcony or patio that provides a view of the lush gardens or faces the ocean. There are plenty of ways to pamper yourself: indulge in a massage at the full-service Pure Blu spa, cocktails at a poolside cabana, or a rib eye at the hotel's sleek steakhouse. **Pros:** four concierge floors offer enhanced amenities, complimentary breakfast, and snacks; bike rentals; fantastic spa. **Cons:** sprawling floor plan; small bathrooms; car is essential for exploring beyond shopping malls. ⊠ *900 Newport Center Dr.* ☎ *949/640–4000* ⊕ *www.marriott.com* ➳ *512 rooms, 20 suites* ☖ *In-room: Internet, Wi-Fi. In-hotel: restaurant, bar, pool, gym, spa, parking.*

13

$ 🏕 **Newport Dunes Waterfront Resort and Marina.** With more than 100 acres of private beach along Newport's Back Bay, Newport Dunes is one of the poshest RV parks in the world. Although beachfront pull-in premium sites—complete with Wi-Fi and TV plus hookups to water, electricity, and sewer—are considerably larger (and less cramped) than those a few rows back, all sites are immaculately clean. There are 55 sites for freestanding tents, as well as cottages with kitchens and porches that can accommodate up to six guests. At the Village Center you'll find a pool, a spa, and a convenience store, and the upscale Back Bay Bistro. Nonguests are able to access the park for day use to swim, surf or take a walking nature tour. **Pros:** pristine campsites; courteous staff; luxury spa products in cottage bathrooms. **Cons:** steep valet parking fees; located in busy (read: potentially loud) business district; restaurant and store operate on a limited basis in off-season. ✉ *1131 Back Bay Dr.* ☎ *949/729–3863, 800/765–7661* ⊕ *www.newportdunes.com* ⇄ *323 RV sites, 55 tent/RV sites, 24 cottages* ⚒ *In-hotel: restaurant, pool, spa, beach, laundry facilities, business center, parking.*

SPORTS AND THE OUTDOORS

BOAT RENTALS **Balboa Boat Rentals.** You can tour Lido and Balboa isles by renting kayaks ($15 an hour), sailboats ($45 an hour), small motorboats ($65 an hour), and electric boats ($75–$90 an hour) at Balboa Boat Rentals. You must have a driver's license, and some knowledge of boating is helpful; rented boats must stay in the bay. ✉ *510 E. Edgewater Ave.* ☎ *949/673–7200* ⊕ *www.boats4rent.com.*

BOAT TOURS **Catalina Passenger Service.** Located at the Balboa Pavilion, this company operates 90-minute daily round-trip passage to Catalina Island for $68. Call first; winter service is often available only on weekends. ✉ *400 Main St.* ☎ *949/673–5245* ⊕ *www.catalinainfo.com.*

Hornblower Cruises & Events. For fun out on the water, try Hornblower's three-hour weekend dinner cruise with dancing for $75 or their two-hour Sunday brunch cruise for $55. ✉ *2431 West Coast Hwy.* ☎ *949/646–0155, 888/467–6256* ⊕ *www.hornblower.com.*

GOLF **Newport Beach Golf Course.** This par-59 executive course is lighted for night play. Rates start at $17. Reservations are accepted up to one week in advance, but walk-ins are accommodated when possible. ✉ *3100 Irvine Ave.* ☎ *949/852–8681* ⊕ *www.npbgolf.com.*

SPORTFISHING **Davey's Locker.** In addition to a complete tackle shop, Davey's Locker operates sportfishing trips starting at $40, as well as private charters and, in winter, whale-watching trips for $30. ✉ *Balboa Pavilion, 400 Main St.* ☎ *949/673–1434* ⊕ *www.daveyslocker.com.*

CORONA DEL MAR

2 mi south of Newport Beach, via Hwy. 1.

A small jewel on the Pacific Coast, Corona del Mar (known by locals as "CDM") has exceptional beaches that some say resemble their majestic Northern California counterparts. South of CDM is an area referred to as the Newport Coast or Crystal Cove—whatever you call it, it's another dazzling spot on the California Riviera.

ESSENTIALS

Visitor and Tour Information Newport Beach Conference and Visitors Bureau ✉ *110 Newport Center Dr., Suite 120, Newport Beach* ☎ *949/719–6100, 800/942–6278* ⊕ *www.visitnewportbeach.com.*

EXPLORING

Corona del Mar State Beach. This beach is actually made up of two beaches, Little Corona and Big Corona, separated by a cliff. Facilities include fire pits, volleyball courts, a restaurant, restrooms, and parking. ■TIP➜ Two colorful reefs (and the fact that it's off-limits to boats) make Corona del Mar great for snorkelers and for beachcombers who prefer privacy. Also, parking in the lot is a steep $15, $25 on holidays, but you can often find a spot on the street on weekdays. ☎ *949/644–3151* ⊕ *www.parks.ca.gov.*

Fodor'sChoice
★

Crystal Cove State Park. Midway between Corona del Mar and Laguna, stretching along both sides of Pacific Coast Highway, Crystal Cove State Park is a favorite of local beachgoers and wilderness trekkers. It encompasses a 3½-mi stretch of unspoiled beach and has some of the best tide-pooling in southern California. Here you can see starfish, crabs, and other sea life on the rocks. The park's 2,400 acres of backcountry are ideal for hiking, horseback riding, and mountain biking, but stay on the trails to preserve the beauty. Environmental camping is allowed in one of the three campgrounds. Bring water, food, and other supplies; there's a pit toilet but no shower. Open fires and pets are forbidden. Parking costs $10.

Inside the park, the **Crystal Cove Historic District** holds a collection of 46 handmade historic cottages (14 of which are available for overnight rental), decorated and furnished to reflect the 1935–55 beach culture that flourished here. On the sand above the high tide line and on a bluff above the beach, the cottages offer a funky look at beach life 50 years ago. ☎ *949/376–8762* ☎ *949/494–3539* ⊕ *www.crystalcovestatepark. com* ⊘ *Daily 6–dusk.*

▌ **NEED A BREAK?**

For a bite to each while at the park, check out Beachcomber at Crystal Cove Café, with its deck just a few steps above the white sand. ☎ *949/376–6900* ⊕ *www.thebeachcombercafe.com*

Crystal Cove Promenade. Further adding to Orange County's overwhelming supply of high-end shopping and dining is Crystal Cove Promenade, which might be described as the toniest strip mall in America. The storefronts of this Mediterranean–inspired center are lined up across the street from Crystal Cove State Park, with the shimmering Pacific waters in plain view. There is plenty of sidewalk and courtyard seating at this center that is both a regional destination and dog-friendly neighborhood hangout for the lucky locals.

A whimbrel hunts for mussels at Crystal Cove State Park.

Sherman Library and Gardens. Sherman Library and Gardens, a 2½-acre botanical garden and library specializing in the history of the Pacific Southwest, makes a good break from the sun and sand. You can wander among cactus gardens, rose gardens, a wheelchair-height touch-and-smell garden, and a tropical conservatory. There's a good gift shop, too. Café Jardin serves lunch on weekdays plus Sunday brunch. ⊠ 2647 E. PCH ☎ 949/673–2261, 949/673–0033 *lunch reservations* ⊕ *www.slgardens.org* ☜ *$3* ☉ *Daily 10:30–4.*

WHERE TO EAT AND STAY

$
MEDITERRANEAN

✕ **Caffe Panini.** For fresh, reasonably priced food and outstanding espresso drinks with an Italian flair, this cozy café packs a lot of punch for your dining dollars. Think straight-from-the-oven breads, pizzas, pastas, and grilled panini like roast beef with onions and provolone cheese. It's a breakfast-time favorite among locals; at dinner, Mediterranean entrées include moussaka and kebabs. ⊠ *2333 E. Coast Hwy.* ☎ *949/675–8101* ⊕ *www.mypaninicafe.com* ☉ *Daily 7 am–10 pm.*

$
AMERICAN

✕ **Pacific Whey Cafe & Baking Company.** The ovens rarely get a break here; everything is made from scratch daily. Pick up a B.L.T.A. (a BLT with avocado) for a picnic across the street at Crystal Cove State Park. Or stay—at a communal table inside or in the courtyard, which has an ocean view—for the likes of lemon soufflé pancakes or grilled salmon with citrus sauce. ⊠ *7962 E. Coast Hwy., Crystal Cove Promenade* ☎ *949/715–2200* ⊕ *www.pacificwhey.com.*

$$$
NEW AMERICAN
★

✕ **Sage on the Coast.** Between Newport and Laguna in the Crystal Cove Promenade, chef and owner Rich Mead offers contemporary American cuisine in an expansive stainless-steel and glass setting, set off by a warm fireplace and garden area. The ever-changing menu, which has equal European and Asian influences, may include roasted duck breast with pomegranate syrup, swordfish with a pinot noir reduction, and rib eye with green peppercorn sauce. The grilled beef fillet medallion with portobello mushrooms and Gorgonzola is recommended. Mead uses only the finest ingredients, which he sources from local farmers and fishermen. ✉ *7862 E. Coast Hwy.* ☎ *949/715–7243* ⊕ *www. sagerestaurant.com.*

$$$$ ▢ **The Resort at Pelican Hill.** This new ultra-glam resort, which opened
☺ in 2008, allows golfers to stay at Pelican Hill, one of the state's most
★ renowned links with 36 championship holes designed by Tom Fazio. Adjacent to Crystal Cove State Park, the resort has 204 bungalow suites, each a minimum of 847 square feet with Italian limestone fireplaces and marble baths, built into terraced hillsides overlooking the Pacific; the resort's 128 villas are larger than most suburban homes and staffed with butlers 24/7. With its wraparound terraces, the Coliseum Pool (inspired by the Roman landmark) is a spectacular focal point. Soothe sore muscles at a 23,000-square-foot spa after a day on the course before enjoying a sunset dinner from the Andrea Ristorante, one of the area's most opulent dining rooms. Kids are treated like VIPs, too; Camp Pelican, a separate facility, has all sorts of games and activities for young 'uns. **Pros:** paradise for golfers; a gracious, attentive staff. **Cons:** sky-high prices, even for a swanky resort; common areas can feel cold. ✉ *22701 Pelican Hill Rd. S, Newport Coast* ☎ *949/467–6800* ⊕ *www. pelicanhill.com* ⇥ *204 bungalows and suites, 128 villas* ☐ *In-room: kitchen, Wi-Fi. In-hotel: restaurant, bar, golf course, pool, gym, spa, children's programs, parking.*

LAGUNA BEACH

Fodor's Choice *10 mi south of Newport Beach on Hwy. 1, 60 mi south of Los Angeles,*
★   *I–5 south to Hwy. 133, which turns into Laguna Canyon Rd.*

Even the approach tells you that Laguna Beach is exceptional. Driving in along Laguna Canyon Road from the I–405 freeway gives you the chance to cruise through a gorgeous coastal canyon, large stretches of which remain undeveloped. You'll arrive at a glistening wedge of ocean, at the intersection with PCH.

Laguna's welcome mat is legendary. For decades in the mid-20th century a local booster, Eiler Larsen, greeted everyone downtown. (There's now a statue of him on the main drag.) On the corner of Forest and Park avenues you can see a 1930s gate proclaiming, "This gate hangs well and hinders none, refresh and rest, then travel on." A gay community has long been established here; until relatively recently, this was quite the exception in conservative Orange County. The Hare Krishnas have a temple where they host a Sunday vegetarian feast, environmentalists rally, artists continue to gravitate here—there seems to be room for everyone.

There's a definite creative slant to this tight-knit community. The California plein air art movement coalesced here in the early 1900s; by 1932 an annual arts festival was established. Art galleries now dot the village streets, and there's usually someone daubing up in Heisler Park, overlooking the beach. The town's main street, Pacific Coast Highway, is referred to as either South Coast or North Coast Highway, depending on the address. From this waterfront, the streets slope up steeply to the residential areas. All along the highway and side streets, you'll find dozens of fine art and crafts galleries, clothing boutiques, jewelry shops, and cafés.

ESSENTIALS

Visitor and Tour Information Laguna Beach Visitors Bureau ⊠ *252 Broadway* ☎ *949/497–9229, 800/877–1115* ⊕ *www.lagunabeachinfo.org.*

EXPLORING

Main Beach Park. Laguna's central beach gives you a perfect slice of local life. A stocky 1920s lifeguard tower marks Main Beach Park, at the end of Broadway at South Coast Highway. A wooden boardwalk separates the sand from a strip of lawn. Walk along this, or hang out on one of its benches, to watch people bodysurfing, playing sand volleyball, or scrambling around one of two half-basketball courts. The beach also has children's play equipment, picnic areas, restrooms, and showers. Across the street is a historic Spanish Renaissance movie theater.

Laguna Art Museum. The Laguna Art Museum displays American art, with an emphasis on California artists from all periods. Special exhibits change quarterly. ■TIP→ The museum, along with galleries throughout the city, stays open until 9 for Art Walk on the first Thursday of each month (⊕ *www.firstthursdaysartwalk.com*). A free shuttle service runs from the museum to galleries and studios. ⊠ *307 Cliff Dr.* ☎ *949/494–8971* ⊕ *www.lagunaartmuseum.org* 🎫 *$12* ☉ *Daily 11–5.*

WHERE TO EAT

$ ✕ **Café Zinc & Market.** Families flock to this small Laguna Beach institution for well-priced breakfast and lunch. Try the signature quiches or poached egg dishes in the morning, or swing by later in the day for healthy salads, quesadillas, lasagna, or one of their pizzettes. The café also has great artisanal cheese and gourmet goodies to go, and your four-legged friends are welcome in the outdoor patio area. ⊠ *350 Ocean Ave.* ☎ *949/494–6302* ⊕ *www.zinccafe.com* ☉ *No dinner.*

VEGETARIAN

$$$ ✕ **French 75.** Locals love this bistro and champagne bar, inspired by Paris supper clubs of the 1940s, for its intimate, opulent feel. It's definitely a change from the usual bright, casual restaurant look; the space has low lighting, dark-wood paneling, and a mural of cherubs spritzing bubbly. The menu focuses on bistro classics like escargots, moules frites, and coq au vin, with the occasional curveball, like Tasmanian sea trout with blood-orange vinaigrette. One constant: the Callebaut chocolate soufflé. ⊠ *1464 S. Coast Hwy.* ☎ *949/494–8444* ⊕ *www.french75.net* ☉ *No lunch.*

FRENCH

$$$ ✕ **Mosun & Club M.** This is the "it" spot for the young and fabulous sushi-loving crowd, who come to dance, to dine, or to canoodle with a date over cocktails. At this restaurant-cum-nightclub, if it's Monday night, you're partying with all-you-can-eat sushi for $22; at Sushi Sessions on Tuesday, Thursday, and Sunday nights, you can order $6 rolls and $6 sake bombs. The wide-ranging menu offers much more, however:

JAPANESE

Looking for shells on Laguna Beach, one of the nicest stretches of sand in Southern California.

panko-crusted halibut in an Asian-inspired beurre blanc, Kobe beef, and spicy sesame chicken. It's wise to call ahead for reservations. ✉ *680 S. Coast Hwy.* ☎ *949/497–5646* ⊕ *www.mosunclubm.com* ◷ *No lunch.*

$$$
INTERNATIONAL

✕ **Sapphire Laguna.** This Laguna Beach establishment is part gourmet pantry (a must-stop for your every picnic need) and part global dining adventure. Iranian-born chef Azmin Ghahreman takes guests on a journey through Europe and Asia with dishes like Hong Kong–style salt and pepper shrimp, Kurobuta pork shank, and Moroccan chicken tagine. Nearly a dozen beers from around the world and an extensive, fittingly eclectic wine list rounds out the experience. The dining room is intimate and earthy but infused with local style. Brunch is fast becoming a favorite with locals, as well—enjoy it on the patio in good weather. ✉ *The Old Pottery Place, 1200 S. Coast Hwy.* ☎ *949/715–9888* ⊕ *www.sapphirellc.com.*

$
VEGETARIAN

✕ **The Stand.** If an eatery can be called typically Laguna, this is it. Only organic vegan ingredients are used to prepare the salads, burritos with brown rice and hummus, pita sandwiches, and smoothies. There are about 20 outdoor seats where you can eat, read the supplied tracts and newspapers, and maybe argue a point or two. ✉ *238 Thalia St., near PCH* ☎ *949/494–8101* ◷ *Daily 7–7.*

$$$$
AMERICAN
★

✕ **Studio.** In a nod to Laguna's art history, Studio has food that entices the eye as well as the palate. You can't beat the location, on a 50-foot bluff overlooking the Pacific Ocean—every table has an ocean view. And because the restaurant occupies its own Craftsman-style bungalow, it doesn't feel like a hotel dining room. The menu changes daily to reflect the finest seafood and the freshest local ingredients on hand. You might begin with Kumamoto oysters or slow-roasted pork belly with sauteed Napa cabbage before moving on to rack of lamb or wild Alaskan salmon scallopini. The wine list here is bursting, with nearly 2,000 labels. ⊠ *Montage Hotel, 30801 S. Coast Hwy.* ☎ *949/715–6420* ⊕ *www.studiolagunabeach.com* ⚐ *Reservations essential* ⊙ *Closed Mondays. No lunch.*

13

$ ✕**Taco Loco.** This may look like a fast-food taco stand, and the hemp
MEXICAN brownies on the menu may make you think the kitchen's *really* laid-back, but the quality of the food here equals that in many higher-price restaurants. Some Mexican standards get a Louisiana twist, like Cajun-spiced seafood tacos. Other favorites include blackened lobster tacos and the mushroom-and-tofu burgers. It stays open late on Friday and Saturday, until 2 am. ⊠ *640 S. Coast Hwy.* ☎ *949/497–1635.*

$$$ ✕**Ti Amo Ristorante.** An intimate setting, creative Mediterranean cuisine
ITALIAN and a celebrity clientele have earned this place favorable notoriety. The several charming dining areas here have tall candles and cozy booths and contribute to the restaurant's legendary sense of romance—there's also a grand fireplace in the main room. You can also request a table in the enclosed garden out back. Try the Linguine ai Frutti di Mare, linguine with shrimp, mussels, clams, calamari, fresh fish in a spicy tomato broth, or the veal Marsala. Service can be slow, but the views are spectacular and the food well worth it. ⊠ *31727 S. Coast Hwy.* ☎ *949/499–5350* ⊕ *www.tiamolagunabeach.com* ⊙ *No lunch.*

WHERE TO STAY

$$$ 🏨**Hotel Casa del Camino.** This historic Spanish-style hotel was built in
★ 1927 and was once a favorite of Hollywood stars. Its ace in the hole is the large rooftop terrace, with clear ocean views—an ideal spot at sunset. Rooms have warm color schemes; beds have feather duvets to ward off the seaside chill. Those on the highway side of the property are apt to be noisy. K'ya, the hotel's cozy restaurant, has a contemporary menu with French and Asian influences. **Pros:** breathtaking views from rooftop lounge; personable service; close to beach. **Cons:** decor a bit dated; frequent on-site events can make hotel busy and noisy. ⊠ *1289 S. Coast Hwy.* ☎ *949/497–2446, 888/367–5232* ⊕ *www.casacamino. com* ⚑ *26 rooms, 10 suites* ⚐ *In-room: Wi-Fi. In-hotel: restaurant, bar, gym, parking, some pets allowed.*

$$ 🏨**Hotel Laguna.** The oldest hotel in Laguna (opened in 1888) has manicured gardens, beach views, and an ideal location downtown adjacent to Main Beach. Accommodations take second stage to the outdoor ambience, so expect rooms to be small, short on amenities, and somewhat tired in terms of decor (drab, dated furnishings). Among the perks is access to the hotel's private beach, where guests are provided with lounges, umbrellas, and towels and can order lunch or cocktails from the Beach Club menu. **Pros:** fantastic location; lovely views from restaurant; clean rooms. **Cons:** in need of an upgrade; street noise. ⊠ *425 S. Coast Hwy.* ☎ *949/494–1151, 800/524–2927* ⊕ *www.hotellaguna.*

com 63 *rooms, 2 minisuites* In-room: no a/c, Wi-Fi. In-hotel: res-
taurant, bar, beach, parking Breakfast.

$$ Inn at Laguna Beach. On a bluff overlooking the ocean, this inn is
steps from Main Beach and the surf. You can walk to the art museum,
shops, galleries, and restaurants, and even the Festival of Arts grounds.
Rooms have a beachy feel, and most have full or partial ocean views
and balconies. Those on the highway side are apt to be noisy. Proximity
to the beach makes this a good hotel for children. Continental break-
fast, delivered to the room, is included in the price and Las Brisas, a
restaurant famous for its view, is located next door. **Pros:** large rooms;
complimentary Continental breakfast; oceanfront location. **Cons:**
ocean-view rooms are pricey; foot traffic on nearby public walkway
can be noisy. ⊠ *211 N. Coast Hwy.* ☎ *949/497–9722, 800/544–4479*
⊕ *www.innatlagunabeach.com* 70 *rooms* In-room: Wi-Fi. In-hotel:
pool, beach, parking.

$$$$ Montage Resort & Spa. Laguna's connection to the Californian plein
Fodor'sChoice air artists is mined for inspiration at this head-turning, lavish hotel. The
★ Montage uses the local Craftsman style as a touchstone. Shingled build-
ings ease down a bluff to a sandy cove; inside, works by contemporary
and early-20th-century California artists snare your attention. Guest
rooms balance ease and refinement; all have ocean views and amenities
such as CD/DVD players and extra-deep tubs. Of the restaurants, Stu-
dio is the fanciest, with more sweeping Pacific views and a refined con-
temporary menu. At the 20,000-square-foot oceanfront spa and fitness
center, you can indulge in a sea-salt scrub, take a yoga class, or hit the
lap pool. **Pros:** top-notch service; idyllic coastal location; special pro-
grams for all interests, from art to marine biology. **Cons:** pricey; food
inconsistent given the prices. ⊠ *30801 S. Coast Hwy.* ☎ *949/715–6000,*
888/715–6700 ⊕ *www.montagelagunabeach.com* 190 *rooms, 60*
suites In-room: a/c, Wi-Fi. In-hotel: restaurant, bar, pool, gym, spa,
beach, water sports, children's programs, parking.

$$$$ Surf & Sand Resort. One mile south of downtown, this Laguna Beach
★ property has been made over and is now even more fantastic than long-
time locals remember. On an exquisite stretch of beach with thunder-
ing waves and gorgeous rocks, this is a getaway for those who want a
boutique hotel experience without all the formalities. Expect elegant
beige and white decor in the rooms, private balconies, slumber-worthy
beds within earshot of the ocean, and a small yet full service spa—all
within walking distance of downtown Laguna. The seasonal Califor-
nia cuisine at Splashes is top-notch. **Pros:** easy beach access; intimate
property; central location slightly removed from Main Street crowds.
Cons: expensive valet parking; surf is quite loud. ⊠ *1555 S. Coast*
Hwy. ☎ *949/497–4477, 888/869–7569* ⊕ *www.surfandsandresort.*
com 155 *rooms, 13 suites* In-room: no a/c, Internet. In-hotel:
restaurant, bar, pool, gym, spa, beach, children's programs, parking.

NIGHTLIFE AND THE ARTS

Laguna Playhouse. The Laguna Playhouse, dating to the 1920s, mounts
a variety of productions, from classics to youth-oriented plays. ⊠ *606*
Laguna Canyon Rd. ☎ *949/497–2787* ⊕ *www.lagunaplayhouse.com.*

Sandpiper Lounge. The Sandpiper Lounge, a hole-in-the-wall joint with live music, attracts an eclectic crowd. ✉ *1183 S. Coast Hwy.* ☎ *949/ 494–4694.*

Sawdust Arts Festival. The Sawdust Arts Festival, held from late June to late August opposite the Festival of the Arts amphitheater, always hosts musicians and entertainers. ☎ *949/494–3030* ⊕ *www.sawdust-artfestival.org.*

White House. White House, a hip club on the main strip, has nightly entertainment and dancing. ✉ *340 S. Coast Hwy.* ☎ *949/494–8088* ⊕ *www.whitehouserestaurant.com.*

SPORTS AND THE OUTDOORS

BEACHES There are a handful of lovely beaches around town besides the Main Beach.

Aliso Creek County Beach. Aliso Creek County Beach, in south Laguna, has a playground, fire pits, parking, food stands, and restrooms. ☎ *949/923–2280* ⊕ *www.ocparks.com/alisobeach.*

1,000 Steps Beach. 1,000 Steps Beach, off South Coast Highway at 9th Street, is a hard-to-find locals' spot with great waves. There aren't really 1,000 steps down (but when you hike back up, it'll certainly feel like it).

Wood's Cove. Wood's Cove, off South Coast Highway at Diamond Street, is especially quiet during the week. Big rock formations hide lurking crabs. Climbing the steps to leave, you can see a Tudor-style mansion that was once the home of Bette Davis.

GOLF **Aliso Creek Inn & Golf Course.** This course offers a 9-hole facility whose stunning views and challenging par-fours elevate it well above most executive courses. Greens fees are $27–$36 with discounts for twilight play (after 2 pm in winter or 4 pm during Daylight Saving Time); pull carts cost $3, electric ones are $8. Reservations are accepted up to 30 days in advance. ✉ *31106 S. Coast Hwy.* ☎ *949/499–1919* ⊕ *www. alisocreekinn.com.*

HIKING **Laguna Coast Wilderness Park.** For some of the area's best hiking, Laguna Coast Wilderness Park is spread over 19 acres of fragile coastal terri- tory, including the canyon. The trails are great for hiking and moun- tain biking and are open daily, weather permitting. Docent-led hikes are given regularly; call for information. ☎ *949/923–2235* ⊕ *www. lagunacanyon.org.*

WATER **Hobie Sports.** Because its entire beach area is a marine preserve, Laguna
SPORTS Beach is ideal for snorkelers. Scuba divers should head to the Marine Life Refuge area, which runs from Seal Rock to Diver's Cove. Rent bodyboards at Hobie Sports. ✉ *294 Forest Ave.* ☎ *949/497–3304* ⊕ *www.hobie.com.*

SHOPPING

Coast Highway, Forest and Ocean avenues, and Glenneyre Street are full of art galleries, fine jewelry stores, and clothing boutiques.

Art for the Soul. A riot of color, Art for the Soul has hand-painted fur- niture, crafts, and unusual gifts. ✉ *272 Forest Ave.* ☎ *949/497–8700* ⊕ *www.art4thesoul.com.*

Candy Baron. Get your sugar fix at the time-warped Candy Baron, filled with old-fashioned goodies like gumdrops, bull's-eyes, and more than a dozen barrels of saltwater taffy. ⊠ *231 Forest Ave.* ☎ *949/497–7508* ⊕ *www.thecandybaron.com.*

La Rue du Chocolat. La Rue du Chocolat dispenses hand-crafted chocolates in flavors like baked apple streudel and caramel-chile. ⊠ *Peppertree La., 448 S. Coast Hwy., Suite B, Laguna Beach* ☎ *949/494–2372.*

Crystal Image. The Crystal Image has an almost overwhelming trove of rare minerals, meteorites, fossils, jewelry, and art. ⊠ *225 Forest Ave.* ☎ *949/497–3399* ⊕ *www.thecrystalimage.com.*

Fetneh Blake. Hit Fetneh Blake for pricey, Euro-chic clothes. The emerging designers found here lure Angelenos to make the trek south. ⊠ *427 N. Coast Hwy.* ☎ *949/494–3787.*

Adam Neeley Fine Art Jewelry. Be prepared to be dazzled at Adam Neeley Fine Art Jewelry where young artisan proprietor Adam Neeley creates one-of-a-kind modern pieces. ⊠ *353 N. Coast Hwy.* ☎ *949/715–0953.*

Trove. At Trove you can rummage for 18th- to 20th-century furniture, chandeliers, and odd, whimsical finds. ⊠ *370 Ocean Ave.* ☎ *949/376–4640* ⊕ *www.trovelaguna.com.*

ART GALLERIES Most South Village art galleries line up along the South Coast Highway in the 900 to 2000 blocks.

DeRu's Fine Art. This gallery specializes in California impressionist works by artists such as Edgar Payne, William Wendt, and others. ⊠ *1590 S. Coast Hwy.* ☎ *949/376–3785* ⊕ *www.derusfinearts.com.*

Redfern Gallery. Another top source for California impressionists, the Redfern Gallery also houses some of its collection at the Montage Resort. ⊠ *1540 S. Coast Hwy.* ☎ *949/497–3356* ⊕ *www.redferngallery.com.*

Mandarin Fine Art Gallery. Check out this gallery if you're in the market for stunning contemporary Chinese art. ⊠ *1294 S. Coast Hwy., Suite C* ☎ *949/376–9608* ⊕ *www.mandarinfineart.com.*

DANA POINT

10 mi south of Laguna Beach, via PCH.

Dana Point's claim to fame is its small-boat marina tucked into a dramatic natural harbor and surrounded by high bluffs.

ESSENTIALS

Visitor and Tour Information Dana Point Chamber of Commerce. The Dana Point Chamber of Commerce offers a useful visitor's guide. ☎ *949/496–1555* ⊕ *danapoint-chamber.com.*

Dana Point Harbor. This harbor was first described more than 100 years ago by its namesake, Richard Henry Dana, in his book *Two Years Before the Mast.* At the marina are docks for private boats and yachts, marine-oriented shops, restaurants, and boat and bike rentals. In early March the **Dana Point Festival of Whales** celebrates the passing gray whale migration with concerts, 40-foot-long balloon whales on parade,

DID YOU KNOW?

Dana Point is named for the author Richard Henry Dana, who described the area in his book *Two Years Before the Mast.*

films, sports competitions, and a weekend street fair. ☎ 949/472–7888, 888/440–4309 ⊕ www.festivalofwhales.org ☎ 949/923–2255 ⊕ www. danapointharbor.com.

Doheny State Beach. At the south end of Dana Point, Doheny State Beach is one of Southern California's top surfing destinations, but there's a lot more to do within this 61-acre area. Divers and anglers hang out at the beach's western end, and during low tide, the tide pools beckon both young and old. You'll also find five indoor tanks and an interpretive center devoted to the wildlife of the Doheny Marine Refuge.

There are food stands and shops, picnic facilities, volleyball courts, and a pier for fishing. The beachfront campground here is one of the most popular in the state with 120 no-hookup sites that rent for $30–$35 per night; essential reservations from **Reserve America** (☎ 800/444–7275). ■TIP→ Be aware that the waters here periodically do not meet health standards established by California (warning signs are posted if that's the case). ☎ 949/496–6172, 714/433–6400 water quality information ⊕ www. dohenystatebeach.org.

☪ **Ocean Institute.** Two indoor tanks at the Ocean Institute contain touchable sea creatures, an accessible man-made tide pool, as well as the complete skeleton of a gray whale. Anchored near the institute is *The Pilgrim*, a full-size replica of the square-rigged vessel on which Richard Henry Dana sailed. You can tour the boat Sunday 10–3:30. Weekend cruises are also available. In addition, marine-mammal exploration cruises are given January through March. ⊠ 24200 Dana Point Harbor Dr. ☎ 949/496–2274 ⊕ www.ocean-institute.org ⚏ $6.50, $35 marine mammal cruises ☉ Weekends 10–3.

WHERE TO EAT

$$$ ╳ **Gemmell's.** Accomplished chef Byron Gemmell's moderately priced
FRENCH bistro is a welcome change from the fish houses that dominate this town, particularly around the harbor. In a laid-back but romantic setting, you can begin with escargots or French onion soup before moving on to rack of lamb with thyme demi-glace or roasted duck in a seductive rum-banana liquor reduction. Finish with a soufflé—either classic chocolate or Grand Marnier. The wine list includes some reasonably priced Bordeaux. The food is rich, but a meal here won't break the bank. ⊠ 34471 Golden Lantern St., Dana Point ☎ 949/234–0063 ⊕ www. gemmellsrestaurant.com ⚏ Reservations essential ☉ No dinner Sun.

$$ ╳ **Luciana's Ristorante.** This intimate family-owned eatery serves simply
ITALIAN prepared, tasty Italian food. Try one of the homemade soups or gnocchi classico—Grandma's homemade potato dumplings with marinara sauce. If you don't have a reservation, be prepared to wait at the bar with a glass of one of the many reasonably priced Italian wines, chatting with the predominantly local clientele. ⊠ 24312 Del Prado Ave. ☎ 949/661–6500 ⊕ www.lucianas.com ☉ No lunch.

$$ ╳ **Turk's.** This neighborhood joint—its detractors might call it a dive—
AMERICAN is a remnant of the days when Dana Point was a crusty fishing village, not a posh resort town. You'll find steaks, chicken, fish-and-chips, and seafood at this old school bar and grill, and at great prices. Once owned by Hollywood bit player and strongman Turk Varteresian, Turk's is

now run by his daughter Candy. Overhead, clear-bottom aquariums create a nautical feel; the walls are adorned with old pictures of Turk's movie days and various celebrities. It stays open until 2 am, and has an old-fashioned jukebox. ⊠ *34683 Golden Lantern St.* ☎ *949/496–9028.*

$$ ✕**Wind & Sea.** An unblocked marina view makes this a particularly great
AMERICAN place for lunch or a sunset dinner. Among the entrées, the macadamia-crusted mahimahi and the shrimp-stuffed halibut with lobster sauce stand out. On warm days, patio tables beckon you outside, and looking out on the Pacific might put you in the mood for a retro cocktail like a mai tai. ⊠ *34699 Golden Lantern St.* ☎ *949/496–6500* ⊕ *www. windandsearestaurants.com.*

13

WHERE TO STAY

$$$ ⊞**Blue Lantern Inn.** Combining New England–style architecture with a
★ Southern California setting, this white-clapboard B&B rests on a bluff overlooking the harbor and ocean. A fire warms the intimate, inviting living area and cozy library, where you can enjoy complimentary hors d'oeuvres and wine or play backgammon every afternoon. Don't miss the sweeping harbor and ocean view from the inn's patio dining area. The spacious Nantucket-style guest rooms also have fireplaces and updated bathrooms with whirlpool tubs. The top-floor Tower Suite has a 180-degree ocean view. Forgot your toothbrush? Don't worry, the staff will take care of you. **Pros:** gas fireplaces; amazing harbor views from Room 304; afternoon wine and cheese; breakfast buffet. **Cons:** nearby restaurant can be noisy; understaffed compared to larger resorts. ⊠ *34343 St. of the Blue Lantern* ☎ *949/661–1304, 800/950–1236* ⊕ *www.bluelanterninn.com* ↬ *29 rooms* ⌂ *In-room: Internet. In-hotel: gym, parking* ⏐◎⏐*Breakfast.*

$$$$ ⊞**Ritz-Carlton, Laguna Niguel.** Take Ritz-Carlton's top-tier level of service
Fodor'sChoice coupled with an unparalleled view of the Pacific and you're in the lap
★ of complete luxury at this opulent resort. Rooms are well-appointed and spacious; tricked out with oversize plasma TVs, private balconies, and posh marble bathrooms. Splurge for the Club Level where the list of included extra amenities is exhaustingly long. Service is impeccable for all guests, as every need is anticipated. Enjoy the panoramic views at Raya, where the focus is on Latin American coastal cuisine, or bone up on your wine knowledge at ENO, the property's wine, cheese, and chocolate tasting room. Guests can leisurely stroll through opulent gardens, and down perfectly manicured trails to the pristine white-sand beach. **Pros:** beautiful grounds and views; luxurious bedding; seamless service. **Cons:** some rooms are small for the price; culinary program has room to grow. ⊠ *1 Ritz-Carlton Dr.* ☎ *949/240–2000, 800/240–2000* ⊕ *www.ritzcarlton.com* ↬ *363 rooms, 30 suites* ⌂ *In-room: Internet, Wi-Fi. In-hotel: restaurant, bar, pool, tennis court, gym, spa, beach, children's programs, parking.*

SPORTS AND THE OUTDOORS

Rental stands for surfboards, windsurfers, small powerboats, and sailboats can be found near most of the piers.

Swim Beach. Inside Dana Point Harbor, Swim Beach has a fishing pier, barbecues, food stands, parking, restrooms, and showers.

Dana Wharf Sportfishing & Whale Watching. This company runs charters and whale-watching excursions from early December to late April. Tickets cost $29; reservations are required. ⊠ *34675 Golden Lantern St.* ☎ *949/496–5794* ⊕ *www.danawharf.com.*

Hobie Sports. This shop is one of the area's best bets for surfboard and boogie board rentals. ⊠ *24825 Del Prado* ☎ *949/496–2366* ⊕ *www. hobie.com.*

Capt. Dave's Dolphin & Whale Safari. On Capt. Dave's Dolphin & Whale Safari, you have a good chance of getting a water's-eye view of resident dolphins and migrating whales if you take one of these tours on a 35-foot catamaran. Dave, a marine naturalist–filmmaker, and his wife run the safaris year-round. The endangered blue whale is sometimes seen in summer. Reservations are required for the safaris, which last 2½ hours and cost $55. ⊠ *24440 Dana Point Harbor Dr.* ☎ *949/488–2828* ⊕ *www.dolphinsafari.com.*

SAN JUAN CAPISTRANO

5 mi north of Dana Point, Hwy. 74, 60 mi north of San Diego, I–5.

San Juan Capistrano is best known for its historic mission, where the swallows traditionally return each year, migrating from their winter haven in Argentina, but these days they are more likely to choose other local sites for nesting. St. Joseph's Day, March 19, launches a week of fowl festivities. After summering in the arches of the old stone church, the swallows head south on St. John's Day, October 23. Charming antiques stores, which range from pricey to cheap, line Camino Capistrano.

If you arrive by train, which is far more romantic and restful than battling freeway traffic, you'll be dropped off across from the mission at the San Juan Capistrano depot. With its appealing brick café and preserved Santa Fe cars, the depot retains much of the magic of early American railroads. If driving, park near Ortega and Camino Capistrano, the city's main streets.

ESSENTIALS

Visitor and Tour Information San Juan Capistrano Chamber of Commerce and Visitors Center ⊠ *31421 La Matanza St.* ☎ *949/493–4700* ⊕ *www. sanjuanchamber.com.*

EXPLORING

Fodor's Choice
★

Mission San Juan Capistrano. This mission, founded in 1776 by Father Junípero Serra, was one of two Roman Catholic outposts between Los Angeles and San Diego. The Great Stone Church, begun in 1797, is the largest structure created by the Spanish in California. Many of the mission's adobe buildings have been preserved to illustrate mission life, with exhibits of an olive millstone, tallow ovens, tanning vats, metalworking furnaces, and the padres' living quarters. The gardens, with their fountains, are a lovely spot in which to wander. The bougainvillea-covered Serra Chapel is believed to be the oldest church still standing in California and is the only building remaining in which Fr. Serra actually led Mass. Mass takes place daily at 7 am in the chapel. ⊠ *Camino*

Mission San Juan Capistrano.

Capistrano and Ortega Hwy. ☎ *949/234–1300* ⊕ *www.missionsjc.com*
✉ *$9* ⊘ *Daily 8:30–5.*

San Juan Capistrano Library. Near Mission San Juan Capistrano is the San Juan Capistrano Library, a postmodern structure built in 1983. Architect Michael Graves combined classical and Mission styles to striking effect. Its courtyard has secluded places for reading. ✉ *31495 El Camino Real* ☎ *949/493–1752* ⊕ *www.sanjuancapistrano.org* ⊘ *Mon.– Wed. 10–8, Thurs. 10–6, Sat. 10–5, Sun. noon–5. Closed Fri.*

WHERE TO EAT

$$
AMERICAN
☾

✕ **Cedar Creek Inn.** Just across the street from the Mission, this restaurant's location is ideal for visiting families, with a patio perfect for a late lunch or a romantic dinner. The menu is fairly straightforward, dishes are tasty, and portions are substantial—try the Monte Cristo or a burger at lunch, or splurge on the rack of lamb for dinner. The patio, which has a waterfall and a view of the mission, is irresistible in warm weather. Don't miss the Toll House pie for dessert. ✉ *26860 Ortega Hwy.* ☎ *949/240–2229* ⊕ *www.cedarcreekinn.com.*

$$$
FRENCH

✕ **L'Hirondelle.** Locals have romanced at cozy tables for more than 25 years at this delightful restaurant. Classic Belgian dishes such as escalope of veal with Béarnaise sauce and rabbit with white wine and prune sauce are the hallmark of this French and Belgian restaurant, whose name means "the little swallow" in French. The extensive wine list is matched by an impressive selection of Belgian beers. You can dine in the cozy dining room or on the lovely patio, which is perfect for the superb Sunday brunch. ✉ *31631 Camino Capistrano* ☎ *949/661–0425* ⊕ *www.lhirondellesjc.com.*

$$ ✕ **The Ramos House Cafe.** It may be worth hopping the Amtrak for San
AMERICAN Juan Capistrano just for the chance to have breakfast or lunch at one
of Orange County's most beloved restaurants. Here's your chance to
visit one of Los Rios Historic District's simple, board and batten homes
dating back to 1881. This café sits practically on the railroad tracks
across from the depot—nab a table on the patio and dig into a hearty
breakfast, such as the mountainous wild-mushroom scramble. The $35
weekend brunch includes champagne, memorable mac-and-cheese with
smoked veggies, and huckleberry coffee cake. Every item on the menu
illustrates chef-owner John Q. Humphreys' creative hand. ⊠ *31752
Los Rios St.* ☎ *949/443-1342* ⊕ *www.ramoshouse.com* ☉ *Closed Mon.
No dinner.*

NIGHTLIFE

Coach House. This roomy, casual club with long tables and a dark-wood
bar, draws crowds of varying ages for dinner and entertainment ranging
from hip new bands to jazz guitarist Lee Ritenour. ⊠ *33157 Camino
Capistrano* ☎ *949/496–8930* ⊕ *www.thecoachhouse.com.*

Swallows Inn. Prayer and misbehavior lie cheek by jowl; across the way
from the mission you can find a line of Harleys in front of the Swallows
Inn. Despite a somewhat tough look, it attracts all kinds—bikers, surf-
ers, Marines from nearby Camp Pendleton, grandparents—for a drink,
a casual bite, and some rowdy live music. There's no cover charge.
⊠ *31786 Camino Capistrano* ☎ *949/493–3188* ⊕ *www.swallowsinn.
com.*

▌ OFF THE
  BEATEN
  PATH

San Clemente. Travelers who shun the throngs in favor of a low-key
beach experience—the part of the OC coast that Hollywood doesn't
base TV series on—should drive 10 mi south of Dana Point on Pacific
Coast Highway to San Clemente. There, 20 square mi of prime bicy-
cling terrain await. Camp Pendleton, the country's largest Marine Corps
base, welcomes cyclists to use some of its roads—just don't be sur-
prised to see a troop helicopter taking off right beside you. Surfers favor
San Clemente State Beach, which has camping facilities, RV hookups,
and fire rings. **San Onofre State Beach,** just south of San Clemente, is
another surfing destination. Below the bluffs are 3½ mi of sandy beach,
where you can swim, fish, and watch wildlife. ☎ *949/492–3156* ⊕ *www.
parks.ca.gov.com*

INLAND ORANGE COUNTY

If you can tear yourself away from Orange County's lush coast, you'll
be rewarded with a variety of cultural attractions inland, from Bowers
Museum of Cultural Arts to the wonders of Little Saigon to the con-
certs and musicals held at the Orange County Performing Arts Center.

SANTA ANA AND COSTA MESA

39 mi south of downtown Los Angeles via I–5, I–605, and I–405 to South Coast Plaza.

Ethnically diverse Santa Ana is the region's largest city and the governmental hub of Orange County (the county's administrative offices and courts are here). It adjoins Costa Mesa, the OC's cultural epicenter and home to one of Southern California's toniest and most expensive shopping centers, South Coast Plaza. This designer-dominated mall is connected by sky bridge to the Orange County Performing Arts Center, which has evolved into one of America's premier cultural entertainment complexes. City lines blur here, making it hard to tell exactly where you are, but the bottom line is, this is where you can catch a glimpse of Orange County's cosmopolitan face.

ESSENTIALS

Visitor and Tour Information Costa Mesa Conference and Visitors Bureau ⊠ *Box 5071, Costa Mesa* ☎ *714/786-8585, 888/588-9417* ⊕ *www.travelcostamesa.com.*

EXPLORING

☺ **Bowers Museum of Cultural Art.** Santa Ana's premier cultural asset is the Bowers Museum of Cultural Art, which exhibits collections from both the British Museum and Beijing's Palace Museum Permanent. Exhibits include Pacific Northwest wood carvings; beadwork of the Plains cultures; clothing, cooking utensils, and silver-adorned saddles used on early California ranches; and California impressionist paintings. Special exhibits such as a show of Egyptian mummies rotate through on a regular basis. A $15-million addition accommodates an Asian art gallery and 300-seat auditorium. Enjoy a salad, pasta dish, or French-inspired lamb shank beneath abundant skylights at Tangata, the museum's outstanding café.

The neighboring **Bowers Kidseum** (⊠ *1802 N. Main St.*) has interactive exhibits geared toward kids ages 6–12, in addition to classes, storytelling, and arts-and-crafts workshops. Admission is included in the general museum ticket. ⊠ *2002 N. Main St., off I–5* ☎ *714/567–3600* ⊕ *www.bowers.org* 🖾 *$12; permanent exhibits, additional charges for special exhibits* ☉ *Tues.–Sun. 10–4.*

☺ **Discovery Science Center.** With a 108-foot tilting architectural cube beckoning from the I–5 freeway, the Discovery Science Center is easy to spot. The hands-on exhibits are for kids from preschool through teens (they especially like the Virtual Volleyball). Children with an interest in dinosaurs will hit the jackpot: there are life-size dinosaur models, a giant walk-through Argentinosaurus, a fossil dig, and online game of Dinosaur Quest. Other fun activities include lying on a bed of nails, climbing a rock wall, and making tidal waves. ⊠ *2500 N. Main St., Santa Ana* ☎ *714/542–2823* ⊕ *www.discoverycube.org* 🖾 *$12.95* ☉ *Daily 10–5; closed Thanksgiving and Christmas.*

OFF THE
BEATEN
PATH

Little Saigon. Little Saigon encompasses much of the city of Westminster, but the heart of the action is around Magnolia and Bolsa streets, where the colorful Asian Garden Mall tempts shoppers with jewelry and gift shops (bargaining on the prices is expected), Asian herbalists, and informal family restaurants. For a snack, try the *pho* (Vietnam's signature beef and noodle soup) at Pho 79. Note that the mall gets extremely crowded on weekends and is total madness around the Chinese New Year. ⊠ *Bolsa St. between Bushard and Magnolia Sts., Westminster.*

★ **South Coast Plaza.** If you look at the where-to-buy listings at the bottom of couture ads in glossy magazines, you'll often see, sandwiched between listings of shops in Paris and Beverly Hills, the name of Costa Mesa's most famous landmark, South Coast Plaza. This immense complex gets ritzier by the year as international designer boutiques jostle for platinum-card space. The original section has the densest concentration of shops: Gucci, Armani, Burberry, La Perla, Hermès, Versace, Chloé, and Prada. You can also find all the familiar mall stores like Victoria's Secret and Banana Republic.

Major department stores, including Saks and Bloomingdale's, flank the exterior, and restaurants range from fast-food to haute cuisine (among the most prominent are Charlie Palmer at Bloomingdale's and the acclaimed contemporary bistro Marché Moderne). A pedestrian bridge crosses Bear Street to the second wing, a smaller offshoot with a Room & Board store and several galleries and restaurants. ⊠ *3333 S. Bristol St., off I–405, Costa Mesa* ☎ *714/435–2000, 800/782–8888* ⊕ *www. southcoastplaza.com* ⊙ *Weekdays 10–9, Sat. 10–8, Sun. 11–6:30.*

WHERE TO EAT

$$$ ✗ **Onotria.** In a soaring space that has the feel of an Italian village piazza,
MEDITERRANEAN   chef and owner Massimo Navarretta celebrates the wine country cuisine of his native Campania and adopted California. You can see Navarretta's own vegetable garden and miniature vineyard through the windows. Begin with velvety *burrata*, a fresh cheese made with mozzarella and cream, paired with blood orange and drizzled with passion-fruit syrup, or poached octopus with artichokes and fennel. For hearty entrées, consider a contemporary curry-scented cassoulet with beef and lamb meatballs or risotto with lobster and veal sausage in a saffron sauce. The wine list offers innumerable choices for seasoned oenophiles and enthusiastic novices alike. ⊠ *2831 Bristol St., Costa Mesa* ☎ *714/641– 5952* ⊕ *www.onotria.com* ⌑ *Reservations essential* ⊙ *Closed Sun. No lunch Sat.*

$$ ✗ **Plum's Café.** Salmon hash and Plum's famous Dutch baby, a deep-dish
AMERICAN   skillet-baked pancake, keep the locals coming back to start their days at Oregon transplant Kim Jorgenson's Pacific Northwest–inspired eatery. Coconut French toast and hazelnut pancakes are also popular breakfast picks, especially with kids; lunch and dinner specialties include the Lamburger with feta and couscous and the filet mignon in a Washington cabernet reduction. Dine at the bar, in the casual dining room, or on the patio. ⊠ *369 E. 17th St., Costa Mesa* ☎ *949/722–7586* ⊕ *www. plumscafe.com.*

¢   ✗ **Taco Mesa.** If fresh, fast Mexican fare is what you want, this frill-free,
MEXICAN   small chain of always-packed taquerias serves up huge burritos (try it
★   "wet," bathed in enchilada sauce) and *carnitas pibil* (a specialty from the Yucatan) and makes its salsa fresh daily. Personable service, festive ambience, and healthy menu options have given this joint a statewide

reputation (there are now several branches in the O.C. but this is the original). Try the fresh-squeezed juices. ✉ *647 W. 19th St., Costa Mesa* ☎ *949/642–0629* ⊕ *www.tacomesa.net.*

$$$
MEDITERRANEAN
★
✕**Zov's Bistro.** There's a well-worn path to both sides of Zov's. The restaurant out front prepares bistro favorites with a deft Middle Eastern spin, such as rack of lamb with pomegranate sauce or a Moroccan-inspired seafood *tagine* (mussels, clams, prawns, and grape leaf-wrapped halibut with couscous). Locals flock to the separate, more modestly priced café and bakery (open for breakfast and lunch) for fresh pastries, *meze* (small plates), or burgers. Both the bistro and the café have patio tables. Zov's has branches in Newport and Irvine, but this is the original. ✉ *Enderle Center, 17440 E. 17th St., Tustin* ☎ *714/838–8855* ⊕ *www.zovs.com.*

WHERE TO STAY

$$
🛏 **Westin South Coast Plaza.** Ideal for business travelers, this high-rise hotel adjoins the South Coast Plaza complex—within just a few steps, your every retail therapy need can be met. Modern, spacious rooms are outfitted with flat-screen TVs, deliciously comfortable beds with feather duvets, and spalike showers. Tennis aficionados will appreciate the convenience of nearby courts. The hotel is steps from the Orange County Performing Arts Center. **Pros:** contemporary decor; business-friendly; close to shopping, dining, and the arts. **Cons:** spotty concierge service; Internet costs extra. ✉ *686 Anton Blvd., Costa Mesa* ☎ *714/540–2500,* ⊕ *www.westin.com* ⮑ *393 rooms, 5 suites* ♿ *In-room: Internet, Wi-Fi. In-hotel: restaurant, pool, tennis court, gym, children's programs, laundry facilities, business center, some pets allowed.*

NIGHTLIFE AND THE ARTS

Orange County Performing Arts Center. Costa Mesa's role in consumer consumption is matched by its arts venues. The Orange County Performing Arts Center holds three music venues plus the highly regarded South Coast Repertory Theater. The original 3,000-seat Henry Segerstrom Concert hall offers fine acoustics for opera, ballet, symphony, and musicals. The intimate 250-seat Founders Hall is the place to hear chamber music and occasional jazz concerts. A third venue, the Henry and Renée Segerstrom Concert Hall, is home to the Pacific Symphony and Philharmonic Society of Orange County.

This acclaimed César Pelli–designed structure, which was unveiled in 2006, has state-of-the-art sound equipment, a 30-ton organ with 4,322 pipes, and a modern, upscale dining room called Leatherby's Café Rouge. Richard Lippold's enormous *Firebird*, an angular metal sculpture, extends outward from the glass-enclosed lobby of the original Seagerstrom concert hall. ✉ *600 Town Center Dr., east of Bristol St.* ☎ *714/556–2787* ⊕ *www.ocpac.org.*

OFF THE BEATEN PATH
Richard Nixon Presidential Library and Birthplace. Yorba Linda's main claim to fame is the Richard Nixon Presidential Library and Birthplace, final resting place of the 37th president and his wife, Pat. Exhibits illustrate the checkered career of Nixon, from heralded leader of the free world to beleaguered resignee. Now run by the National Archives and Records Administration, it includes the so-called smoking-gun tape from the

Watergate days, among hundreds of other recorded conversations. Life-size sculptures of foreign world leaders, gifts Nixon received from international heads of state, and a large graffiti-covered section of the Berlin Wall are on display.

You can also visit Pat Nixon's tranquil rose garden and the small farmhouse where Richard Nixon was born in 1913. Don't miss the bookstore, selling everything from birdhouses to photos of Nixon with Elvis. ⊠ *18001 Yorba Linda Blvd., at Imperial Hwy., Yorba Linda* ☎ *714/993–5075* ⊕ *www.nixonlibraryfoundation.org* ⊠ *$9.95* ⊙ *Mon.–Sat. 10–5, Sun. 11–5.*

CATALINA ISLAND

Fodor'sChoice ★   Just 22 mi out from the L.A. coastline, across from Newport Beach and Long Beach, Catalina has virtually unspoiled mountains, canyons, coves, and beaches; best of all, it gives you a glimpse of what undeveloped Southern California once looked like.

Water sports are a big draw, as divers and snorkelers come for the exceptionally clear water surrounding the island. The main town, Avalon, is a charming, old-fashioned beach community, where yachts bob in the crescent bay. Wander beyond the main drag and find brightly painted little bungalows fronting the sidewalks, with the occasional golf cart purring down the street.

Perhaps it's no surprise that Catalina has long been a destination for filmmakers and movie stars. In its earlier past, however, the island also sheltered Russian fur trappers (seeking sea-otter skins), pirates, gold miners, and bootleggers (carrier pigeons were used to communicate with the mainland).

In 1919, William Wrigley Jr., the chewing-gum magnate, purchased a controlling interest in the company developing Catalina Island, whose most famous landmark, the Casino, was built in 1929 under his orders. Because he owned the Chicago Cubs baseball team, Wrigley made Catalina the team's spring training site, an arrangement that lasted until 1951.

In 1975, the Santa Catalina Island Conservancy, a nonprofit foundation, acquired about 86% of the island to help preserve the area's natural flora and fauna, including the bald eagle and the Catalina Island fox. These days the conservancy is restoring the rugged interior country with plantings of native grasses and trees. Along the coast you might spot oddities like electric perch, saltwater goldfish, and flying fish.

GETTING HERE AND AROUND

FERRY TRAVEL   Two companies offer ferry service to Catalina Island. The boats have both indoor and outdoor seating and snack bars. Excessive baggage is not allowed, and there are extra fees for bicycles and surfboards. The waters around Santa Catalina can get rough, so if you're prone to seasickness, come prepared.

Catalina Express makes an hour-long run from Long Beach or San Pedro to Avalon and a 90-minute run from Dana Point to Avalon with

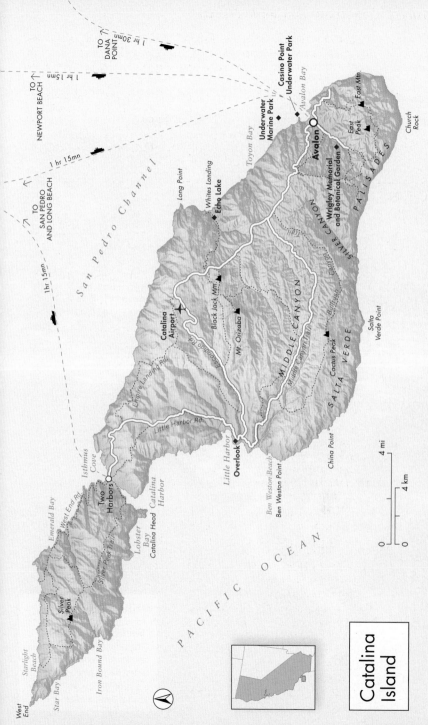

Catalina Island

DID YOU KNOW?

There's no gambling at the Casino on Avalon Bay. The circular Art Deco building is famed for its ballroom, where big band dances are held several times a year.

some stops at Two Harbors. Round-trip fares begin at $68.50, with discounts for seniors and kids. On busy days, a $15 upgrade to the Commodore Lounge, when available, is worth it. Service from Newport Beach to Avalon is available through Catalina Passenger Service. Boats leave from Balboa Pavilion at 9 am (in season), take 75 minutes to reach the island, and cost $68 round-trip. Return boats leave Catalina at 4:30 pm. Reservations are advised in summer and on weekends for all trips. ■TIP→ Keep an eye out for dolphins, which sometimes swim alongside the ferries.

13

GOLF CARTS Golf carts constitute the island's main form of transportation for sightseeing in the area, but they can't be used on the streets in town. You can rent them along Avalon's Crescent Avenue and Pebbly Beach Road for about $40 per hour with a $30 deposit, payable via cash or traveler's checks only.

HELICOPTER TRAVEL Island Express helicopters depart hourly from San Pedro and Long Beach (8 am–dusk). The trip takes about 15 minutes and costs $86 one-way, $164 round-trip (plus tax). Reservations a week in advance are recommended.

TIMING

Although Catalina can be seen in a day, several inviting hotels make it worth extending your stay for one or more nights. A short itinerary might include breakfast along the boardwalk, a tour of the interior, a snorkeling excursion at Casino Point, and a romantic waterfront dinner in Avalon.

After late October, rooms are much easier to find on shorter notice, rates drop dramatically, and many hotels offer packages that include transportation from the mainland and/or sightseeing tours. If you'd rather stay at a charming freestanding cottage or home, contact a local real estate office such as Catalina Island Vacation Rentals.

TOURS

Santa Catalina Island Company runs the following Discovery Tours: a summer-only coastal cruise to Seal Rocks; the *Flying Fish* boat trip (summer evenings only); a comprehensive inland motor tour (which includes an Arabian horse performance); a tour of Skyline Drive; a Casino tour; a scenic tour of Avalon; a glass-bottom-boat tour, an undersea tour on a semisubmersible vessel; and a tour of the Botanical Garden. Reservations are highly recommended for the inland tours. Tours cost $16 to $99. There are ticket booths on the Green Pleasure Pier, at the Casino, in the plaza, and at the boat landing. Catalina Adventure Tours, which has booths at the boat landing and on the pier, arranges similar excursions at comparable prices.

The Santa Catalina Island Conservancy organizes custom ecotours and hikes of the interior. Naturalist guides drive open Jeeps through some gorgeously untrammeled parts of island. Tours start at $98 per person for a three-hour trip (three-person minimum); you can also book half- and full-day tours. The tours run year-round.

ESSENTIALS

Helicopter Contacts Island Express ☎ *800/228–2566* ⊕ *www. islandexpress.com.*

Ferry Contacts Catalina Express ☎ 800/481–3470 ⊕ www.catalinaexpress.com.

Catalina Passenger Service ☎ 949/673–5245, 800/830–7744 ⊕ www. catalinainfo.com.

Golf Cart Rentals Island Rentals ✉ 125 Pebbly Beach Rd., Avalon ☎ 310/510–1456.

Vacation Rentals Catalina Island Vacation Rentals, Inc. ✉ 119 Sumner Ave., Suite B, Avalon ☎ 310/510–2276 ⊕ www.catalinavacations.com.

Visitor and Tour Information Catalina Adventure Tours ✉ Box 92766, Long Beach ☎ 877/510–2888 ⊕ www.catalinaadventuretours.com.

Catalina Island Chamber of Commerce & Visitors' Bureau ✉ #1 Green Pleasure Pier, Avalon Box 217 ☎ 310/510–1520 ⊕ www.catalinachamber.com.

Santa Catalina Island Company ✉ Box 737, Long Beach ☎ 310/510–2800, 800/626–1496 ⊕ www.scico.com.

Santa Catalina Island Conservancy ✉ 125 Claressa Ave., Avalon ✉ Box 2739 ☎ 310/510-2595 ⊕ www.catalinaconservancy.org.

AVALON

A 1- to 2-hr ferry ride from Long Beach, Newport Beach, or San Pedro; a 15-min helicopter ride from Long Beach or San Pedro.

Avalon, Catalina's only real town, extends from the shore of its natural harbor to the surrounding hillsides. Its resident population is about 3,500 but it swells with tourists on summer weekends. Most of the city's activity, however, is centered on the pedestrian mall on Crescent Avenue, and most sights are easily reached on foot. Private cars are restricted and rental cars aren't allowed, but taxis, trams, and shuttles can take you anywhere you need to go. Bicycles and golf carts can be rented from shops along Crescent Avenue.

EXPLORING

Crescent Avenue. A walk along Crescent Avenue is a nice way to begin a tour of the town. Vivid art deco tiles adorn the avenue's fountains and planters—fired on the island by the now-defunct Catalina Tile Company, the tiles are a coveted commodity.

Green Pleasure Pier. Head to the Green Pleasure Pier, at the center of Crescent Avenue, for a good vantage point of Avalon. At the top of the hill you'll spot a big white building, the Inn at Mt. Ada, now a top-of-the-line B&B but originally built by William Wrigley Jr. for his wife. On the pier you can find the Catalina Island Chamber of Commerce, snack stands, the Harbor Patrol, and scads of squawking seagulls.

★ **Casino.** On the northwest point of Avalon Bay (looking to your right from Green Pleasure Pier) is the majestic landmark Casino. This circular white structure is one of the finest examples of art deco architecture anywhere. Its Spanish-inspired floors and murals gleam with brilliant blue and green Catalina tiles. In this case, *casino,* the Italian word for "gathering place," has nothing to do with gambling. Rather, Casino life revolves around the magnificent ballroom.

Santa Catalina Island Company leads tours of the Casino, lasting about 55 minutes, for $16. You can also visit the **Catalina Island Museum,** in the lower level of the Casino, which investigates 7,000 years of island history; or stop at the **Casino Art Gallery** to see works by local artists. First-run movies are screened nightly at the **Avalon Theatre,** noteworthy for its classic 1929 theater pipe organ. The same big-

band dances that made the Casino famous in the 1930s and '40s still take place several times a year. The New Year's Eve dance is hugely popular and sells out well in advance. ⊠ *1 Casino Way* ☎ *310/510–2414 museum, 310/510–0179 Avalon Theatre* ⊕ *www.catalinamuseum.com* 🖾 *Museum $5* ⊘ *Call for hours.*

Casino Point Underwater Park. In front of the Casino are the crystal clear waters of the Casino Point Underwater Park, a marine preserve protected from watercraft where moray eels, bat rays, spiny lobsters, halibut, and other sea animals cruise around kelp forests and along the sandy bottom. It's a terrific site for scuba diving, with some shallow areas suitable for snorkeling. Scuba and snorkeling equipment can be rented on and near the pier. The shallow waters of **Lover's Cove,** east of the boat landing, are also good for snorkeling.

Wrigley Memorial and Botanic Garden. Two miles south of the bay via Avalon Canyon Road is Wrigley Memorial and Botanic Garden. Here you can find plants native to Southern California, including several that grow only on Catalina Island: Catalina ironwood, wild tomato, and rare Catalina mahogany. The Wrigley family commissioned the garden as well as the monument, which has a grand staircase and a Spanish mausoleum inlaid with colorful Catalina tile. (The mausoleum was never used by the Wrigleys, who are buried in Los Angeles.) Taxi service from Avalon is available, or you can take a tour bus from the downtown Tour Plaza or ferry landing. ⊠ *Avalon Canyon Rd.* ☎ *310/510–2897* 🖾 *$5* ⊘ *Daily 8–5.*

WHERE TO EAT

$$$
STEAK
✕ **Catalina Country Club.** The beautifully restored California Mission-style structure, which was built in 1921 as a spring-training clubhouse for the Chicago Cubs, is now a restaurant with dark wood, white linen, and an air of formality that's unusual on this casual island. This is the place on the island for a special occasion. The menu emphasizes organic and sustainable ingredients; offerings might include scallops in vanilla beurre blanc, filet mignon, and local sand dabs meunière. The adjacent bar, which connects to the old Cubs locker room and is filled with memorabilia, is great for an after-dinner drink. ⊠ *1 Country Club Dr.* ☎ *310/510–7404* 🍴 *Reservations essential.*

¢
AMERICAN
✕ **Eric's on the Pier.** This little snack bar has been an Avalon family–run institution since the 1920s. A favorite of Fodor's readers, it's a good place to people-watch while munching a breakfast burrito, hot dog,

or signature buffalo burger. Most of the action (and seating) is outside, but you can also sit down at a table inside and dine on a bowl of homemade clam chowder in a baked bread bowl or an order of fish-and-chips. ☒ *Green Pier No. 2* ☎ *310/510–0894* ☒ *Closed Thurs. No dinner Nov.–May.*

$$$　✕ **Steve's Steakhouse.** Within a stone's throw of the bay and most Cata-
STEAK　lina hotels, this second-floor steak-centric restaurant keeps hungry diners happy with USDA Choice steaks and slow-cooked baby back ribs, as well as ample seafood such as locally caught swordfish and the popular Avalon-style shrimp. The sultry black-and-blue decor and old-fashioned supper club feel create a romantic, retro atmosphere that's enhanced by the restaurant's stunning harbor views. ☒ *417 Crescent Ave.* ☎ *310/510–0333* ⊕ *www.stevessteakhouse.com.*

WHERE TO STAY

$$$　🏨 **Aurora Hotel & Spa.** In a town dominated by historic properties, the Aurora is refreshingly contemporary, with a hip attitude more reminiscent of Hollywood than Avalon. Standard rooms are small but appointed with mod chocolate and blue furniture and flat-screen TVs, while suites have Jacuzzi tubs or elaborate showers—the spacious Aurora Suite is a great splurge. There are striking ocean views from the rooftop deck. Unwind after a day of hiking or boating with a Mermaid's Kiss massage—a blend of Swedish, Japanese, and Thai techniques—at the spa. A complimentary Continental breakfast is served and the front desk loans out laptops, binoculars, and GPS units to guests. **Pros:** trendy design; quiet location off main drag yet still close to restaurants. **Cons:** standard rooms are small, even by Catalina standards. ☒ *137 Marilla Ave., Avalon* ☎ *310/510–0454* ⊕ *www.auroracatalina. com* ⇌ *15 rooms, 3 suites* ⌂ *In-room: Internet, Wi-Fi. In-hotel: spa.*

$　🏨 **Hermosa Hotel and Catalina Cottages.** With plenty of charm and character, this historic 1890s hotel offers small rooms with shared baths. If you're looking for luxury or amenities, this may not be the place for you. Cottages with basic kitchen facilities and cooking essentials are more spacious and comfortable; you can also request one of the more updated rooms, which have heat, a/c, and private baths. A few suites with private entrances, full kitchens, and private baths sleep six and are ideal for families or groups. The beach is half a block away. **Pros:** quiet enforced after 10 pm; kitchenettes available; reasonably priced; nearby grocery store. **Cons:** no frills; some shared bathrooms; some rooms lack heating and/or a/c. ☒ *131 Metropole St.* ☎ *310/510–1010, 888/684–1313* ⊕ *www.hermosahotel.com* ⇌ *27 rooms, 19 cottages, 5 suites* ⌂ *In-room: no a/c (some), kitchen, no TV.*

$$　🏨 **Hotel Metropole and Market Place.** This romantic hotel evokes the former look of New Orleans's French Quarter. Some guest rooms have balconies overlooking a flower-filled courtyard holding restaurants and shops; others have ocean views. Many have fireplaces. Room 102, an oceanfront suite with vaulted ceilings and lavish bath, is a pricey indulgence. For a stunning panorama, head for the rooftop deck. **Pros:** family-friendly; outdoor Jacuzzi and sundeck; convenient location. **Cons:** some rooms on small side; nearby grocery store deliveries make some rooms noisy in morning. ☒ *205 Crescent Ave.* ☎ *310/510–1884,*

800/541–8528 ⊕ www.hotel-metropole.com ⟿ 44 rooms, 8 suites ⟳ In-room: Wi-Fi ⟨⟨⟩ Breakfast.

$ 🏨 **Hotel Villa Portofino.** Steps from the beach and the Pleasure Pier, this hotel has a European flair and creates an intimate feel with brick courtyards and walkways. Rooms are decorated in deep jewel tones and suites are named after Italian cities. Some ocean-facing rooms have open balconies, fireplaces, and marble baths. You can sunbathe on the private deck, or ask for beach towels and chairs to take to the cove. **Pros:** romantic; close to beach; incredible sundeck. **Cons:** though quiet in general, ground floor rooms can be noisy; some rooms are on small side; no elevator. ✉ *111 Crescent Ave.* ☎ *310/510–0555, 800/346–2326 ⊕ www.hotelvillaportofino.com ⟿ 35 rooms ⟳ In-room: Wi-Fi. In-hotel: restaurant ⟨⟨⟩ Breakfast.*

$$$ 🏨 **Hotel Vista del Mar.** On the middle of Main Street, this beautiful prop-
★ erty is just steps from the beach, where complimentary towels, chairs, and umbrellas await guests. The 14 rooms and suites are aligned along a lovely glass-covered promenade. Modern Mediterranean decor, nightly milk and cookies, and in-room fireplaces and whirlpool tubs make the hotel a popular spot for honeymooners and couples seeking a quiet getaway. **Pros:** comfortable king beds; central; modern decor. **Cons:** no restaurant or spa facilities; only two rooms have ocean views or balconies; no elevator. ✉ *417 Crescent Ave.* ☎ *310/510–1452, 800/601–3836 ⊕ www.hotel-vistadelmar.com ⟿ 11 rooms, 3 suites ⟳ In-room: Wi-Fi ⟨⟨⟩ Breakfast.*

$$$$ 🏨 **Inn on Mt. Ada.** If you stay in the mansion where Wrigley Jr. once
Fodor's Choice lived, you'll enjoy all the comforts of a millionaire's home—at a mil-
★ lionaire's prices. Nightly rates, which start at $400 in summer, include breakfast, lunch, beverages, and snacks (note that the restaurant does not serve dinner), plus use of a golf cart. The guest rooms are traditional and elegant; some have fireplaces and all have water views. The hilltop view of the curve of the bay is spectacular; the Windsor Room, with views of both the ocean and bay, is among the most coveted. Service is gracious and attentive, and a stay at this enchanting property is memorable. **Pros:** timeless charm; shuttle from heliport and dock; first-class service. **Cons:** smallish rooms and bathrooms; pricey. ✉ *398 Wrigley Rd.* ☎ *310/510–2030, 800/608–7669 ⊕ www.innonmtada.com ⟿ 6 rooms ⟳ In-room: no a/c, Wi-Fi. In-hotel: restaurant, some age restrictions ⟨⟨⟩ Some meals.*

SPORTS AND THE OUTDOORS

BICYCLING To bike beyond the paved roads of Avalon, you must buy an annual permit from the Catalina Conservancy. Individual passes start at $35; family passes cost $125. You may not ride on hiking paths.

Bike rentals are widely available in Avalon starting at $5 per hour and $12 per day.

Brown's Bikes. Look for rentals on Crescent Avenue and Pebbly Beach Road such as Brown's Bikes. ✉ *107 Pebbly Beach Rd., next to Island Rentals* ☎ *310/510–0986* 🖷 *310/510–0747 ⊕ www.catalinabiking.com.*

DIVING AND The Casino Point Underwater Park, with its handful of wrecks, is best
SNORKELING suited for diving. Lover's Cove is better for snorkeling (no scuba diving

allowed, but you'll share the area with glass-bottom boats). Both are protected marine preserves.

Catalina Divers Supply. Catalina Divers Supply rents equipment, runs guided scuba and snorkel tours, gives certification classes, and more. It has an outpost at Casino Point. ⊠ *Green Pleasure Pier, Avalon* ☎ *310/510–0330* ⊕ *www.catalinadiverssupply.com.*

HIKING   **Santa Catalina Island Conservancy.** Permits from the Santa Catalina Island Conservancy are required for hiking into Catalina Island's interior. ■ TIP➔ If you plan to backpack overnight, you'll need a camping reservation. The interior is dry and desertlike; bring plenty of water and sunblock. The permits are free and can be picked up at the main house of the conservancy or at the airport. You don't need a permit for shorter hikes, such as the one from Avalon to the Botanical Garden. The conservancy has maps of the island's east-end hikes, such as Hermit's Gulch Trail. It's possible to hike between Avalon and Two Harbors, starting at the Hogsback Gate, above Avalon, though the 28-mi journey has an elevation gain of 3,000 feet and is not for the weak. ■ TIP➔ For a pleasant 4-mi hike out of Avalon, take Avalon Canyon Road to Wrigley Gardens and follow the trail to Lone Pine. At the top, you'll have an amazing view of the Palisades cliffs and, beyond them, the sea. ⊠ *125 Claressa Ave. Box 2739* ☎ *310/510–2595* ⊕ *www.catalinaconservancy.org.*

Airport Shuttle Bus. Another hike option is to take the Airport Shuttle Bus from Avalon to the airport for $17 round-trip. The 10-mi hike back to Avalon is mostly downhill, and the bus is an inexpensive way to see the interior of the island. ☎ *310/510–0143.*

Travel Smart Los Angeles

WORD OF MOUTH

"You do not want your introduction to beautiful California to be Los Angeles's morning rush hour traffic. Ughhh!!! Traffic starts around 6 am and continues until at least 10 am or so and then starts again around 1–2 pm until 6 pm. Traffic is still really busy even during the off hours. You will love California, but not the L.A. traffic."

—michele_d

GETTING HERE AND AROUND

Los Angeles has more than 12 million residents, so be prepared to rent a car and fight for space on the freeway (especially at rush hour) to make your way along the array of destinations that span from the carefree beaches of the coastline to the glitz and glamour of Beverly Hills shops, the nightlife of Hollywood, and the film studio action of the Valley. It's worth it. Nowhere else in the country can you spot celebrities over breakfast, sunbathe on the beach in the afternoon, and head out to the slopes for skiing within hours.

▊ AIR TRAVEL

Nonstop flights from New York to Los Angeles take about six hours; with the three-hour time change, you can leave JFK by 8 am and be in L.A. by 11 am. Some flights may require a midway stop, making the total excursion between 7½ and 8½ hours. Many of the flights out of Chicago are nonstop with a duration of four hours. Nonstop times are approximately 3 hours from Dallas, and 10 hours from London.

The city's main airport, Los Angeles International Airport (LAX) is quite busy although flights are generally not delayed due to weather. Because of heavy traffic around the airport (not to mention the city's extended rush hours) and difficult parking, however, you should allow plenty of time prior to scheduled departure or arrival times. Some hotels near LAX offer air-travel perks, such as free shuttles to the airport. There are three other nearby airports that serve L.A. County; they're smaller and have more limited services but are worth investigating when booking flights. For instance, the Long Beach airport is a hub for the low-cost domestic airline jetBlue (which also flies out of Burbank and LAX), while Southwest has a big presence at the Burbank (Bob Hope), Ontario, and Orange County airports.

Plan to arrive at the airport about two hours before your scheduled departure time for domestic flights and 2½ to 3 hours before international flights. You may need to arrive earlier if you're flying from LAX or during peak air-traffic times.

Airlines and Airports Airline and Airport Links.com. Check for links to many of the world's airlines and airports. ⊕ *www. airlineandairportlinks.com.*

Airline Security Issues Transportation Security Administration. The TSA has answers for almost every question that might come up. ⊕ *www.tsa.gov.*

AIRPORTS

All Los Angeles International Airport (LAX) departures are from the upper level, and arrivals are on the lower level. LAX is serviced by more than 85 major airlines and is the sixth-largest airport in the world in terms of passenger traffic. Make the best of long delays or layovers by heading to Encounter, the intergalactic-theme restaurant and cocktail lounge just across the street from Terminals 1 and 2 on the lower level (reservations are recommended for lunch and dinner; ☎ *310/215–5151* ⊕ *www.encounterlax.com*).

For longer delays, several hotels are a five-minute walk or shuttle ride away, including Courtyard Marriott and Radisson. They have spa services and restaurants. Ontario International Airport, about 35 mi east of Los Angeles, serves the San Bernardino–Riverside area with a dozen airlines. Burbank's Bob Hope Airport serves the San Fernando Valley with seven airlines. Six airlines use Long Beach Airport. John Wayne/Orange County Airport serves Orange County with 11 airlines, including three commuter carriers.

SECONDARY AIRPORTS

It's generally easier to navigate the secondary airports than to get through sprawling LAX. Bob Hope Airport in Burbank is closest to downtown L.A., and domestic flights to it can be cheaper than flights to LAX—it's definitely worth checking out. From Long Beach Airport it's equally convenient to go north to central Los Angeles or south to Orange County. Flights to Orange County's John Wayne Airport are often more expensive than those to the other secondary airports.

Airport Information Bob Hope Airport (*BUR*) ☎ 818/840-8830 ⊕ www.bobhopeairport. com. **John Wayne/Orange County Airport** (*SNA*) ☎ 949/252-5006 ⊕ www.ocair.com. **Long Beach Airport** (*LGB*) ☎ 562/570-2600 ⊕ www.lgb.org. **Los Angeles International Airport** (*LAX*) ☎ 310/646-5252 ⊕ www.lawa. org or www.airport-la.com. **Ontario International Airport** (*ONT*) ☎ 909/937-2700 ⊕ www.lawa.org.

GROUND TRANSPORTATION

LAX provides free bus service from one terminal to another, and the car-rental companies also have gratis shuttles to their nearby branches. Some hotels, especially those near the airport, provide free airport shuttles for their guests.

Driving. Driving times from LAX to different parts of the city vary considerably: it will take you at least 45 minutes to get downtown, 20 minutes to get to Santa Monica, 30 minutes to Beverly Hills, and 45 minutes to an hour to Van Nuys or Sherman Oaks (the central San Fernando Valley). With traffic, particularly on the 405 freeway, it can take much longer. From Burbank, it's 30 minutes to downtown, 40 minutes to Santa Monica, 45 minutes to Beverly Hills, and 15 minutes to the central San Fernando Valley. The drive from downtown L.A. to the Ontario or Orange County airports takes at least an hour; plan on at least 45 minutes for the drive to Long Beach Airport.

Taxis. If not renting a car, taxis are the most convenient way to get between the city and the airports. It's a $50 flat rate between downtown L.A. and LAX in either direction, plus a $2.50 surcharge. Taxis to and from Ontario Airport run on a meter and can cost up to $60 and

$70 depending on traffic; taxis between downtown and Bob Hope Airport are also metered and can cost $40 to $50. From Long Beach Airport to Long Beach hotels, some taxis offer a $24 flat rate; trips to downtown L.A. are metered and cost roughly $65.

Shuttles. For two or three travelers—particularly if you're going a longish distance, for example, to the San Fernando Valley from LAX—shuttle services are economical, $16–$22 per person. However, an individual traveler, depending on the destination, may end up paying more than by cab. Shuttle ride costs are determined by postal codes; fares increase depending on how many postal-code areas you pass. A shuttle ride generally takes longer than a cab ride. These big vans typically circle the airport repeatedly to fill up with passengers. Your travel time will be determined in part by how many other travelers are dropped off before you. At LAX, Prime Time and SuperShuttle allow walk-on shuttle passengers without prior reservations; otherwise, you'll need to make a reservation at least 24 hours in advance for a ride either to or from an airport.

FlyAway buses. In 2006 the Los Angeles World Airports group started a nonstop bus service between Union Station in downtown L.A. and LAX and between Van Nuys, Westwood, now Irvine, and LAX. The cost is $5–$7 ($25 for Irvine). Buses run 24 hours a day: every half hour between 5 am and 1 am, then every hour from downtown, or every 15 minutes between 4:45 am and 9:30 am from Van Nuys. They've got luggage bays on board. If you're on a domestic flight, you can avoid lines at the airport by checking your luggage and getting your boarding pass before getting on the bus. ⊕ www.lawa.org/flyaway.

Public transportation. If you don't have much to carry, are not in a hurry, and know your destination is near a bus or subway stop, consider taking public transit from LAX into L.A. Free shuttles take passengers from the arrivals levels of each terminal to public transit points; shuttle C will take you to parking lot C and MTA bus connections, while shuttle G goes to the Metro Rail Green Line Aviation station. The Green Line trains run every 15–20 minutes until 1 am. Several bus lines include the airport, but they often don't stick to their schedule. It may take four times as long as it would by car, but the fare is usually $5 or less. From Burbank's airport, meanwhile, you can connect with Metrolink or Amtrak train service for a 20-minute trip to downtown Union Station. The fare is $6, but you may have to wait up to an hour between trains. There's no direct public transportation from the Ontario or Long Beach airports into Los Angeles proper.

AIRPORT TRANSFERS

Shuttles Prime Time ☎ 800/733–8267 ⊕ www.primetimeshuttle.com. **Xpress Shuttle** ☎ 800/427–7483 ⊕ www.execucarexpress.com. **SuperShuttle** ☎ 323/775–6600, 310/782–6600, 800/258–3826 ⊕ www.supershuttle.com.

FLIGHTS

Delta and American have the most nonstop and direct flights to Los Angeles International Airport (LAX) from U.S. cities. Jet-Blue Airways, a low-fare domestic airline, has daily nonstop flights from LAX to New York and Boston, and between Long Beach and Oakland; Burbank; Sacramento; Seattle; Chicago; Salt Lake City; Las Vegas; New York City; Boston; Washington, D.C.; Austin, Texas; Portland, Oregon; and Fort Lauderdale; it also recently added nonstop flights between Burbank and New York and Las Vegas. Low-fare Southwest Airlines serves the LAX, Ontario, Burbank, and Orange County airports.

Major Airlines American Airlines ☎ 800/433–7300 ⊕ www.aa.com. **Continental Airlines** ☎ 800/523—3273 ⊕ www.continental.com. **Delta Airlines** ☎ 800/221–1212 ⊕ www.delta.com. **jetBlue** ☎ 800/538–2583 ⊕ www.jetblue.com. **Southwest Airlines** ☎ 800/435–9792 ⊕ www.southwest.com. **United Airlines** ☎ 800/864–8331 ⊕ www.united.com. **US Airways** ☎ 800/428–4322 ⊕ www.usairways.com.

❚ BUS TRAVEL

TO AND FROM LOS ANGELES

The duration of a bus trip from other parts of California or nearby states can be comparable to the time it takes to take a plane, preflight waiting considered. The only Greyhound terminal is in an industrial area of downtown L.A., off Alameda Street. The waiting room and restrooms are clean, and there are individual pay TVs. The terminal is not close to other transit stations but by taking MTA Bus 58 you can get to Union Station. Taxis are also available at the terminal.

Greyhound has dozens of daily routes serving Los Angeles. It often has promotional fares from other West Coast cities to L.A. You can buy tickets by phone, on the Greyhound Web site, or in person at the terminal. The online purchasing service is called Will Call; you'll need to make the transaction at least two hours before departure.

WITHIN LOS ANGELES

Inadequate public-transportation systems have been an L.A. problem for decades. That said, many local trips can be made, with time and patience, by bus. In certain cases, it may be your best option; for example, visiting the Getty Center, going to Universal Studios and/or the adjacent CityWalk, or venturing into Downtown. There's also a special Metropolitan Transit Authority (MTA) bus that goes between Union Station and Dodger Stadium for Friday night home games. It doesn't save money, but it can save you time and parking-related stress.

For the fastest MTA service, look for the red-and-white Metro Rapid buses; these stop less frequently and are able to extend green lights. At this writing, there were 21 Rapid routes including routes on Wilshire and Vermont boulevards. The Metropolitan Transit Authority DASH (Downtown Area Short Hop) minibuses cover six different circular routes in Hollywood, Mid-Wilshire, and the downtown area. The buses stop every two blocks or so. The

Santa Monica Municipal Bus Line, also known as the Big Blue Bus, is a pleasant and inexpensive way to move around the Westside, where the MTA lines leave off. There's also an express bus to and from downtown L.A. Culver CityBus Lines run seven routes through Culver City.

MTA schedules are available through the information line below, but heavy local traffic can make them unreliable. Service is available at all hours. An MTA bus ride for both standard and Rapid service costs $1.50, plus 35¢ for each transfer between buses or from bus to subway.

At this writing, a one-day pass costs $6, and a weekly pass $20 for unlimited travel on all Metro buses and trains (biweekly and monthly passes are also available). Passes are valid from Sunday through Saturday.

DASH buses make pickups at five-minute intervals. You pay 35¢ every time you get on. Buses generally run weekdays 6 am–7 pm and Saturday 10 am–5 pm; a few downtown weekend routes run on Sunday as well. Note: The Downtown Discovery Route (DD) makes a continuous loop among downtown sites; Route E is a shopper's tour with stops in the Broadway, Jewelry, and Fashion districts, as well as at two downtown malls.

The Santa Monica Municipal Bus Line (the Big Blue Bus) costs $1. Transfers are free from one Big Blue Bus to another; to MTA or Culver CityBus it's 50¢. You can also use a prepaid Metrocard, the Little Blue Card, and get the same discounted rate for multiple rides (70¢ per ride). The Big Blue buses generally run from 5 am to midnight.

Culver CityBus is $1 and runs 6 am–midnight. The Santa Monica bus line's Metrocard can be used on this system but not Big Blue Bus tokens. Culver CityBuses also accept MTA tokens but not MTA passes. Children and people over 65 always pay less on all lines.

You can pay your fare in cash on MTA, Santa Monica, and Culver City buses, but you must have exact change. You can buy MTA passes and tokens throughout the city at MTA customer centers and some convenience stores and grocery stores. Metrocards or tokens for the Santa Monica buses can be purchased at local libraries and retailers. Call or check the pertinent bus Web site for the retail location nearest you.

Bus Information Commute Smart ⊕ *www. commutesmart.info.* **Culver CityBus Lines** ☎ 310/253–6500 ⊕ *www.culvercity.org.* **DASH** ☎ 213/626–4455, 310/808–2273 ⊕ *www. ladottransit.com/dash.* **Metropolitan Transit Authority (MTA)** ☎ 213/626–4455 ⊕ *www. mta.net.* **Santa Monica Municipal Bus Line** ☎ 310/451–5444 ⊕ *www.bigbluebus.com.*

▮ CAR TRAVEL

Picture L.A. and you might see a hectic mesh of multilane freeways with their hypnotic streams of cars. Once you've joined the multitudes you'll be caught up in the tempos of traffic: frustration, exhilaration, and crushing boredom. "Freeway culture" is one of the city's defining traits.

GASOLINE

In L.A., as of this writing, gasoline costs around $3 a gallon. Most stations offer both full and self-service stations. There are plenty of stations in all areas; most stay open late, and some are open 24 hours. To find the stations with the lowest gas prices in town, visit ⊕ *www.losangelesgasprices. com.* Prices are updated every 36 hours by a network of volunteer spotters.

NAVIGATING LOS ANGELES

Finding your way by car in Los Angeles can be a piece of cake or a nightmare. If you're used to urban driving, you shouldn't have too much trouble, but if you're unused to driving in big cities, L.A. can be unnerving. The city may be sprawling and traffic clogged, but at least it has evolved with the automobile in mind. Streets are wide and parking garages abound, so it's more driver-friendly than many older big cities.

There are plenty of identical or similarly-named street in L.A. (Beverly Boulevard and Beverly Drive, for example), so be as specific as you can when getting or checking directions. Also, some smaller streets seem to exist intermittently for miles, so unless you have good directions, stick to major streets, where you'll be less subject to detours.

Expect sudden changes in street-address numbering, as streets pass through neighborhoods, then incorporated cities, then back into neighborhoods. This can be most bewildering on Robertson Boulevard, an otherwise useful north–south artery that, by crossing through L.A., West Hollywood, and Beverly Hills, dips in and out of several such numbering shifts in a matter of miles.

In Santa Monica, odd numbers switch over from the north and west sides of streets to the south and east sides.

Try to get clear directions and stick to them. The *Thomas Guide,* a hefty, spiral-bound, super-thorough street guide and directory, is published annually and is available at bookstores, grocery stores, and the like. It's worth the money if you're planning to stay longer than a week and spend the majority of your time navigating the area in your car, but for most visitors the compact L.A. city maps available at auto clubs and retail shops are more manageable and work just fine.

If you get discombobulated while on the freeway, remember the rule of thumb: even-numbered freeways run east and west, odd-numbered freeways run north and south.

PARKING

For some shops and many restaurants and hotels in L.A., valet parking is virtually assumed. The cost is usually $4–$6 and/or an optional tip; keep small bills on hand for the valets.

But there are also some inexpensive and easy garage and lot parking options. For instance, the underground facility at the Hollywood & Highland entertainment and shopping complex, at 6801 Hollywood Boulevard, charges $2 for the first

four hours and a maximum of $10 for the day; no validation is required.

In Beverly Hills, the first two hours are free at several lots on or around Rodeo Drive (for a detailed map, visit ⊕ *www. beverlyhills.org*). There's never a parking fee or a long wait to enter and exit at the Westside Pavilion's open-access garage at 10800 Pico Boulevard.

Parking in downtown L.A. can be tough, especially on weekdays, but the garage at the 7+Fig retail complex at Ernst & Young Plaza (⊠ 725 S. Figueroa St.) is spacious, reasonable, and visitor-friendly. Validation from a shop or restaurant gets you three hours free; otherwise, it's $7 before 9 am and $8 after 4 pm and on weekends.

Parking rules are strictly enforced in Los Angeles, so make sure you check for signs. Illegally parked cars are ticketed or towed quickly. Parking is generally available in garages or parking lots; some public lots are free all or part of the day; otherwise prices vary from 25¢ (in the public lots) to $2 per half hour or from a few dollars to $30 per day. Downtown and Century City garage rates may be as high as $25 an hour, though prices tend to drop on weekends.

Sometimes businesses will offer validated parking if you've parked in an affiliated lot; validation will give you free parking for a certain time period. At a restaurant, for instance, ask for parking validation from the host or hostess. Metered parking is also widely available; meter rates vary from 25¢ for 15 minutes in the most heavily trafficked areas to 25¢ for one hour; have a bunch of change available. In some areas, metered parking is free on weekends or on Sunday. Another bonus: If a meter is out of order (for example, if it is flashing the word *FAIL* where the time remaining would appear), parking is free for the posted time limit.

Street parking in L.A. can be confusing because of varying restrictions (during the day, only at night, once a week during street-cleaning hours, etc.).

ROAD CONDITIONS

Beware of weekday rush-hour traffic, which is heaviest from 7 am to 10 am and 3 pm to 7 pm. KNX has frequent traffic reports; the Los Angeles city Web site and southern California CommuteSmart Web site have real-time traffic information maps, and the California Highway Patrol has a road-conditions line. To encourage carpooling, some crowded freeways reserve an express lane for cars carrying more than one passenger.

Parallel streets can often provide viable alternatives to jam-packed freeways, notably Sepulveda Boulevard for I–405; Venice and Washington boulevards for I–10 from Mid-Wilshire west to the beach; and Ventura Boulevard, Moorpark Street, and/or Riverside Drive for U.S. 101 through the San Fernando Valley.

Information California Highway Patrol ☎ 800/427–7623 for road conditions. **City of Los Angeles** ⊕ www.sigalert.com. **CommuteSmart** ⊕ www.commutesmart.info.

ROADSIDE EMERGENCIES

For lesser problems on L.A.'s freeways (being out of gas, having a blown tire, needing a tow to the nearest phone), Caltrans (California's Department of Transportation) has instituted the Freeway Service Patrol (FSP) 6:30 am–7 pm. More than 145 tow trucks patrol the freeways offering free aid to stranded drivers.

If your car breaks down on an interstate, try to pull over onto the shoulder and either wait for the state police to find you or, if you have other passengers who can wait in the car, walk to the nearest emergency roadside phone and call the state police.

When calling for help, note your location according to the small green mileage markers posted along the highway. Other highways are also patrolled but may not have emergency phones or mileage markers.

Emergency Services Freeway Service Patrol ☎ 213/922–2957 general information, 323/982–4900 for breakdowns.

RULES OF THE ROAD

The use of seat belts for all passengers is required in California, as is the use of car seats for children five years old or younger or 60 pounds or less. The speed limit is 25–35 mph on city streets and 65 mph on freeways unless otherwise posted.

Turning right on a red light after a complete stop is legal unless otherwise posted. Many streets in downtown L.A. are one-way, and a left turn from one one-way street onto another is okay on a red light after a complete stop. On some major arteries, left turns are illegal during one or both rush hours (watch for signs). Certain car-pool lanes, designated by signage and a white diamond, are reserved for cars with more than one passenger. Freeway on-ramps often have stop-and-go signals to regulate the flow of traffic, but cars in high occupancy vehicle (HOV) lanes can pass the signal without stopping.

As of July 2008, California law began requiring that all drivers use hands-free devices when talking on cell phones.

Some towns, including Beverly Hills and Culver City, use photo radar at stoplights to try to reduce speeding (these intersections are always identified with signs). LAX is notorious for handing out tickets to drivers circling its busy terminals; avoid the no-parking zones and keep loading or unloading to a minimum.

Also keep in mind that pedestrians always have the right of way in California; not yielding to them, even if they're jaywalkers, may well result in a $100 ticket.

Speeding can earn you a fine of up to $500. It is illegal to drive in California with a blood alcohol content of 0.08% or above (0.01% if you're under 21); the cost of driving while intoxicated can be a $390–$1,000 fine plus 48 hours to six months in jail for first offenders.

Parking infractions can result in penalties starting at $30 for a ticket on up to having your vehicle towed and impounded (at an ultimate cost of nearly $200 even if you pay up immediately, more if you don't).

In California, radar detectors aren't illegal, but "scanners" (which receive police radio signals) *are*; per the FCC, "jammers" (which interfere with signals) are illegal throughout the United States.

CAR RENTAL

In Los Angeles, a car is a necessity. When renting one, keep in mind that you'll likely be spending a lot of time in it, and options like a CD player or power windows that might seem unnecessary may make a significant difference in your day-to-day comfort.

Major-chain rates in L.A. begin at $35 a day and $110 a week, plus 9.75% sales tax. Luxury and sport utility vehicles start at $69 a day. Open-top convertibles are a popular choice for L.A. visitors wanting to make the most of the sun. Note that the major agencies offer services for travelers with disabilities, such as hand-controls, for little or no extra cost.

Beverly Hills Budget Car Rental, with six locations, offers the widest range of vehicle rentals, including Hummers, convertibles, minivans, and economy cars. Daydreaming of a restored classic Chevy or the latest Porsche? Beverly Hills Rent-A-Car, a rental facility with branches in Santa Monica, Beverly Hills, Hollywood, and near LAX, rents exotics, classic cars, luxury models, economy cars (including Mini Coopers), vans, and SUVs. Midway Car Rental, with eight offices on the Westside, in the Valley, and in Mid-Wilshire, has the usual, plus some extra-large vans and, in its "executive class," Lexus, BMW, Mercedes, and so on. Possibly the handiest in the lower-price range is Enterprise, with two dozen branches in the area (some have luxury vehicles as well). You can rent an eco-friendly electric or hybrid car through Budget; for more information contact EV Rental Cars.

In California you must be 21 and have a valid credit card, often with $200–$300 available credit on it (regardless of how you ultimately pay), to rent a car; rates may be higher if you're under 25. There's no upper age limit.

Automobile Associations American Automobile Association (AAA). Most contact with the organization is through state and regional members. ☎ 315/797–5000 ⊕ www.aaa.com. **National Automobile Club.** Membership is open to California residents only. ☎ 650/294–7000 ⊕ www.thenac.com.

Major Agencies Alamo ☎ 800/462–5266 ⊕ www.alamo.com. **Avis** ☎ 800/230–4898 ⊕ www.avis.com. **Budget** ☎ 800/527–0700 ⊕ www.budget.com. **Hertz** ☎ 800/654–3131 ⊕ www.hertz.com. **National Car Rental** ☎ 800/227–7368 ⊕ www.nationalcar.com.

▌ METRO RAIL TRAVEL

Metro Rail covers a limited area of L.A.'s vast expanse, but what there is, is helpful and frequent. The underground Red Line runs from Union Station downtown through Mid-Wilshire, Hollywood, and Universal City on its way to North Hollywood, stopping at the most popular tourist destinations along the way.

The light commuter rail Green Line stretches from Redondo Beach to Norwalk, while the partially underground Blue Line goes from downtown to the South Bay (Long Beach/San Pedro). The Green and Blue lines are not often used by visitors, though the Green is gaining popularity as an alternative, albeit time-consuming, way to reach LAX. The monorail-like Gold Line stretches from Pasadena and Sierra Madre to Union Station; in 2009, it extended east to Atlantic Boulevard in Monterey Park, serving Little Tokyo, Boyle Heights and east L.A. The Orange Line, a 14-mi bus corridor connecting the North Hollywood subway station with the western San Fernando Valley, opened in 2005.

There's service from about 4:30 am to 12:30 am, every 5–15 minutes, depending on time of day and location. Buy a ticket from any station's vending machines (use bus tokens, coins, or $1 or $5 bills). It costs $1.50 plus 35¢ per transfer, or $6 for an all-day pass. The machines print your tickets and make change. (If you have a valid Metro Pass for buses, you don't need a ticket.) Metro Rail operates on the honor system; officers make periodic checks for valid tickets or passes on board. Bicycles are not allowed during rush hours and other times only with permits, but you can store them on a rack (free) or in a locker (fee). The Web site is the best way to get info on Metro Rail.

TICKET/PASS	PRICE
Single Fare	$1.50
All-Day Pass	$6

ZONE	PRICE
A	$1.50
B	$3
C	$4.50

Metro Rail Information Metropolitan Transit Authority (MTA) ☎ 800/266–6883, 213/626–4455 ⊕ www.mta.net.

▌ TAXI AND LIMO TRAVEL

Don't even try to hail a cab on the street in Los Angeles. Instead, phone one of the many taxi companies. The metered rate is $2.70 per mi, plus a $2.85 per-fare charge. Taxi rides from LAX have an additional $2.50 surcharge. Be aware that distances between sights in L.A. are vast, so cab fares add up quickly. On the other end of the price spectrum, limousines come equipped with everything from a full bar and telephone to a hot tub. If you open any L.A.–area yellow pages, the number of limo companies will astound you. Most charge by the hour, with a three-hour minimum.

Limo Companies ABC Limousine & Sedan Service ☎ 818/980–6000, 888/753–7500. **American Executive** ☎ 800/927–2020. **Black & White Transportation Services** ☎ 800/924–1624. **Chauffeur's Unlimited** ☎ 888/546–6019 ⊕ www.chaufusa.com. **Dav**

El Chauffeured Transportation Network ☎ 800/922–0343 ⊕ www.davel.com. **First Class Limousine Service by Norman Lewis** ☎ 800/400–9771 ⊕ www.first-classlimo.com. **ITS** ☎ 800/487–4255.

Taxi Companies Beverly Hills Cab Co. ☎ 800/273–6611. **Checker Cab** ☎ 800/300–5007. **United Independent Taxi** ☎ 800/411–0303, 800/822–8294. **Yellow Cab/LA Taxi Co-Op** ☎ 800/200–1085, 800/200–0011.

▌ TRAIN TRAVEL

Union Station in downtown Los Angeles is one of the great American railroad stations. The interior is well kept and includes comfortable seating, a restaurant, and snack bars. As the city's rail hub, it's the place to catch an Amtrak train. Among Amtrak's Southern California routes are 13 daily trips to San Diego and seven to Santa Barbara. Amtrak's luxury *Coast Starlight* travels along the spectacular coastline from Seattle to Los Angeles in just a day and a half (though it's often a little late). The *Sunset Limited* goes to Los Angeles from Florida (via New Orleans and Texas), and the *Southwest Chief* from Chicago.

You can make reservations in advance by phone or at the station. As with airlines, you usually get a better deal the farther in advance you book. You must show your ticket and a photo ID before boarding. Smoking is not allowed on Amtrak trains.

Information Amtrak ☎ 800/872–7245 ⊕ www.amtrak.com. **Union Station** ✉ 800 N. Alameda St. ☎ 213/683–6979.

ESSENTIALS

▌ DAY TOURS AND GUIDES

You can explore L.A. from many vantage points and even more topical angles. Not surprisingly, lots of guides include dollops of celebrity history and gossip. Most tours run year-round, and most require advance reservations.

BUS AND VAN TOURS

Guideline Tours gives sightseeing tours all around L.A., including downtown, stars' homes, Universal Studios, and Hollywood. L.A. Tours and Sightseeing has several tours ($49–$109) by van and bus covering various parts of the city, including downtown, Hollywood, and Beverly Hills. The company also operates tours to Disneyland, Universal Studios, Six Flags Magic Mountain, beaches, and stars' homes. Starline Tours of Hollywood ($18–$129) picks up passengers from area hotels and from Grauman's Chinese Theatre. Universal Studios, Knott's Berry Farm, stars' homes, and Disneyland are some of the sights on this popular tour company's agenda.

Fees and Schedules Guideline Tours ☎ 323/461–0156, 800/604-8433 ⊕ www.tourslosangeles.com. **L.A. Tours and Sightseeing** ☎ 323/460–6490 ⊕ www.latours.net. **Starline Tours of Hollywood** ☎ 323/463–3333, 800/959–3131 ⊕ www.starlinetours.com.

HELICOPTER TOURS

If you want an aerial tour, lift off with Orbic Helicopters. It offers two 30-minute tours (a general L.A. tour and a scenic shoreline/Westside tour) and a 45-minute tour combining those itineraries. Orbic's been flying its two- and four-passenger helicopters for more than a dozen years, and the pilots each have 16 or more years of flying experience.

Flights cost $160 per person ($225 if you book two tours; custom tours are $280 per hour); reserve via credit card and cancel within 24 hours at no charge (no-shows pay full fare).

Fees and Schedules Orbic Helicopters ☎ 818/988–6532 ⊕ www.orbichelicopters.com.

SCOOTER TOURS

For an unusual perspective on L.A.'s attractions, you can take a tour of the city via the Segway, the electric scooter and "human transporter" that debuted on city sidewalks in 2003.

Tours are $89 per person, and there are six different areas or themes from which to choose, including the UCLA campus, Santa Monica, and downtown L.A. All tours begin with an instruction session, followed by a guided ride, totaling just over two hours.

Fees and Schedules Segway Tours ☎ 310/358–5900 ⊕ www.segwow.com.

SPECIAL-INTEREST TOURS

With Architecture Tours L.A., you can zip all over the city in a 1960s Cadillac on a private tour with an architectural historian. Rates start at $68. Architours customizes walking and driving tours for architecture buffs; these can include interior visits with architects, artists, and designers. A three-hour driving tour is $85; a downtown walking tour is $35.

The city of Beverly Hills operates year-round trolley tours that are focused on art and architecture and local sights. They last 40 minutes and run from 11 am to 4 pm every Saturday. Tickets cost $10. Soak up the shimmer and glow of classic neon signs from an open double-decker bus on one of the Museum of Neon Art's tours; tours and cruises $55 (offered June through November).

The Next Stage also has an innovative take on the city; it takes people by foot, bus, van, train, and helicopter on its tours. Favorites (mostly in the $40–$70 range) include the Insomniac's Tour, a chocolate-covered L.A. tour, and a culinary tour. Take My Mother Please will arrange lively, thematic combination walking and driving tours; for instance, you could explore sights associated with Raymond Chandler's detective novels. Custom tours are also available. Rates start at $350 for up to three people for a half day.

Fees and Schedules Architecture Tours L.A
☎ 323/464–7868 ⊕ www.architecturetoursla. com. **Architours** ☎ 323/294–5821 ⊕ www. architours.com. **City of Beverly Hills Trolley Tours** ☎ 310/285–2438 ⊕ www.beverlyhills. org/attractions/trolley.asp). **Neon Art Tours** ☎ 213/489–9918 ⊕ www.neonmona.org. **The Next Stage** ☎ 626/577–7880 ⊕ www. nextstagetours.com. **Take My Mother Please** ☎ 323/737–2200 ⊕ www.takemymotherplease. com.

WALKING TOURS

Red Line Tours offers daily one- and two-hour walking tours of Hollywood behind the scenes and historic and contemporary downtown Los Angeles. Tours, which cost $25, are led by a docent, and include live audio headsets to block out street noise.

The Los Angeles Conservancy's walking tours (each about 2½ hours long at a cost of $10 per person) chiefly cover the downtown area. The Historic Core tour showcases the city's art deco and beaux arts past.

Fees and Schedules Los Angeles Conservancy ☎ 213/623–2489 ⊕ www. laconservancy.org. **Red Line Tours** ☎ 323/402–1074 ⊕ www.redlinetours.com. **Santa Monica Visitors Information Center** ☎ 310/319–6263, 800/544–5319 ⊕ www. santamonica.com.

▌ HEALTH

Air pollution in L.A. may affect sensitive people in different ways. During particularly bad days in summer (the media update pollution levels each day), it's a good idea to plan a day indoors or on a windy beach. The sun can burn even on overcast days, and the dry heat can dehydrate, so wear hats, sunglasses, and sunblock and carry water with you.

Do not fly within 24 hours of scuba diving, or you'll put your lungs at risk by going from a high-pressure environment to a low-pressure one.

▌ HOURS OF OPERATION

Los Angeles is not a 24-hour city like New York, but through much of the area, business extends well into the evening, especially for the bigger stores and chains and malls. On Monday certain restaurants, nightclubs, and shops (such as outdoor sports–gear rental stores) are closed.

Many L.A. museums are closed on Monday and major holidays. However, a few of the preeminent art museums, including the Norton Simon and Los Angeles County Museum of Art, stay open on Monday. Instead, the Norton Simon is closed Tuesday, the Los Angeles County museum on Wednesday. Most museums close around 5 pm or 6 pm, and most stay open late at least one night a week, often Thursday. Many museums, large and small, have weekly or monthly free days or hours when no admission is charged.

Most stores in Los Angeles are open 10 to 6, although many stay open until 9 pm or later, particularly those in trendy areas such as Melrose Avenue and in Santa Monica. Amoeba Music in East Hollywood, for example, is open until 11 pm most nights. Shops along Melrose, Abbot Kinney Boulevard in Venice, and in Los Feliz often don't get moving until 11 am or noon. Most shops are open on Sunday at least in the afternoon.

▌ MONEY

Although not inexpensive, costs in Los Angeles tend to be a bit lower than in other major cities such as New York and San Francisco. For instance, in a low-key local diner, a cup of coffee might cost a dollar. In high-profile or trendy establishments, though, costs escalate; a cup of coffee in an upscale restaurant can cost as much as $5.

FOR INTERNATIONAL TRAVELERS

CURRENCY

The dollar is the basic unit of U.S. currency. It has 100 cents. Coins are the penny (1¢); the nickel (5¢), dime (10¢), quarter (25¢), half-dollar (50¢), and the rare golden $1 coin and rarer silver $1. Bills are denominated $1, $5, $10, $20, $50, and $100, all mostly green and identical in size; designs and background tints vary. A $2 bill exists but is extremely rare.

CUSTOMS

Information U.S. Customs and Border Protection ⊕ www.cbp.gov.

DRIVING

Driving in the United States is on the right. Speed limits are posted in miles per hour (usually between 55 mph and 70 mph). In small towns and on back roads limits are usually 30 mph to 40 mph. Most states require front-seat passengers to wear seat belts; children should be in the back seat and buckled up. In major cities, rush hours are 7 to 10 am and 4 to 7 pm. Some freeways have high-occupancy vehicle (HOV) lanes, ordinarily marked with a diamond, for cars carrying two people or more.

Highways are well paved. Interstates—limited-access, multilane highways designated with an "I–" before the number—are fastest. Interstates with three-digit numbers circle urban areas, which may also have other expressways, freeways, and parkways. Limited-access highways sometimes have tolls.

Gas stations are plentiful, except in rural areas. Most stay open late (some 24 hours). Along larger highways, roadside stops with restrooms, fast-food restaurants, and sundries stores are well spaced. State police and tow trucks patrol major highways. If your car breaks down, pull onto the shoulder and wait, or have passengers wait while you walk to a roadside emergency phone (most states). On a cell phone, dial *55.

ELECTRICITY

The U.S. standard is AC, 110 volts/60 cycles. Plugs have two flat pins set parallel to each other.

EMERGENCIES

For police, fire, or ambulance, dial 911 (0 in rural areas).

HOLIDAYS

New Year's Day (Jan. 1); Martin Luther King Day (3rd Mon. in Jan.); Presidents' Day (3rd Mon. in Feb.); Memorial Day (last Mon. in May); Independence Day (July 4); Labor Day (1st Mon. in Sept.); Columbus Day (2nd Mon. in Oct.); Thanksgiving Day (4th Thurs. in Nov.); Christmas Eve and Christmas Day (Dec. 24 and 25); and New Year's Eve (Dec. 31).

MAIL

You can buy stamps and send letters and parcels in post offices. Stamp-dispensing machines can occasionally be found in airports, bus and train stations, office buildings, drugstores, convenience stores, and in ATMs. U.S. mailboxes are stout, dark-blue steel bins; pickup schedules are posted inside the bin (pull the handle). Mail parcels over a pound at a post office.

A first-class letter weighing 1 ounce or less costs 44¢; each additional ounce costs 17¢. Postcards cost 28¢. Postcards or 1-ounce airmail letters to most countries cost 98¢; postcards or 1-ounce letters to Canada or Mexico cost 79¢.

To receive mail on the road, have it sent c/o General Delivery to your destination's main post office. You must pick up mail in person within 30 days with a driver's license or passport for identification.

Contacts DHL ☎ *800/225–5345* ⊕ *www.dhl.com.* **FedEx** ☎ *800/463–3339* ⊕ *www.fedex.com.* **Mail Boxes, Etc./The UPS Store** ☎ *800/789–4623* ⊕ *www.mbe.com.* **USPS** ⊕ *www.usps.com.*

PASSPORTS AND VISAS

Visitor visas aren't necessary for citizens of the United Kingdom, or most citizens of EU countries coming for tourism and staying for under 90 days. A visa is $100, and waiting time can be substantial. Apply for a visa at the U.S. consulate in your place of residence.

Visa Information Destination USA ⊕ *travel.state.gov/visa/visa_1750. html.*

PHONES

Numbers consist of a three-digit area code and a seven-digit local number. In Los Angeles, the area codes are 310, 818, and 323. Within many local calling areas, dial just seven digits. In others, dial "1" first and all 10 digits; this is true for calling toll-free numbers—prefixed by "800," "888," "866," and "877." Dial "1" before "900" numbers, too, but know they're very expensive.

For international calls, dial "011," the country code, and the number. For help, dial "0" and ask for an overseas operator. Most phone books list country codes and U.S. area codes. The country code for Australia is 61, for New Zealand 64, for the United Kingdom 44. Calling Canada is the same as calling within the United States (country code: 1).

For operator assistance, dial "0." For directory assistance, call 555–1212 or 411 (free at many public phones). To call "collect" (reverse charges), dial "0" instead of "1" before the 10-digit number.

Instructions are generally posted on pay phones. Usually you insert coins in a slot (usually 25¢–50¢ for local calls) and wait for a steady tone before dialing. On long-distance calls the operator tells you how much to insert; prepaid phone cards, widely available, can be used from any phone. Follow the directions to activate the card, then dial your number.

CELL PHONES

The United States has several GSM (Global System for Mobile Communications) networks, so multiband mobiles from most countries (except for Japan) work here. It's almost impossible to buy just a pay-as-you-go mobile SIM card in the U.S.—needed to avoid roaming charges—but cell phones with pay-as-you-go plans are available for well under $100. AT&T (GoPhone) and Virgin Mobile have the cheapest with national coverage.

Contacts AT&T ☎ *888/333–6651* ⊕ *www.wireless.att.com.* **T-Mobile** ☎ *877/453–1304* ⊕ *www.t-mobile. com.* **Verizon** ☎ *800/922–0204* ⊕ *www.verizon.com.*

ITEM	AVERAGE COST
Cup of Coffee	$1.75
Glass of Wine	$8
Glass of Beer	$6
Sandwich	$8
15-Minute Taxi Ride	$14
Museum Admission	$8

Prices throughout this guide are given for adults. Substantially reduced fees are almost always available for children, students, and senior citizens.

CREDIT CARDS

AE, American Express; D, Discover; DC, Diners Club; MC, MasterCard; and V, Visa.

Reporting Lost Cards American Express ☎ 800/992–3404 in U.S. ⊕ www.americanexpress.com. **Diners Club** ☎ 800/234–6377 in U.S. ⊕ www.dinersclub.com. **Discover** ☎ 800/347–2683 in U.S. ⊕ www.discovercard.com. **MasterCard** ☎ 800/622–7747 in U.S. ⊕ www.mastercard.com. **Visa** ☎ 800/847–2911 in U.S. ⊕ www.visa.com.

▌ RESTROOMS

You can assume that gas stations along the highways outside of town will have a bathroom available, but this isn't true of every station in L.A. itself. Restrooms in parks are often dirty. Restaurants and bars may have signs that read "For Patrons Only" so that you're obliged to buy something to use the facilities. Better bets for relatively clean, obligation-free restrooms are those in department stores and large chain bookstores.

▌ SAFETY

The most concentrated homeless population in the city is Downtown, and on some blocks panhandling is common. Hollywood and Santa Monica are other areas where you're most likely to be approached for money or food.

After years in decline, gang-related violent crime has recently been on the rise, prompting aggressive new antigang initiatives. Gang-related street violence is concentrated in certain neighborhoods; South L.A., Compton, and Watts should be avoided, particularly at night.

Of the Metro lines, the Red and Green lines are the safest and are more heavily patrolled. The Blue Line can be sketchy after dark. Avoid riding in empty cars, and move with the crowd when going from the station to the street.

EARTHQUAKES

Very minor earthquakes occur frequently in Southern California; most of the time they're so slight that you won't notice them at all. If you do feel a stronger tremor, follow basic safety precautions. If you're indoors, take cover in a doorway or under a table or desk—whichever is closest to you. Protect your head with your arms. Stay clear of windows, mirrors, or anything that might fall from the walls. Do not use elevators. If you're in an open space, move away from buildings, trees, and power lines. If you're outdoors near buildings, duck into a doorway. If you're driving, slow down and pull over to the side of the road, avoiding overpasses, bridges, and power lines, and stay inside the car. Expect aftershocks; if you feel a smaller quake following a larger tremor, take cover again.

▌ TAXES

The sales tax in Los Angeles is 9.75%, one of the highest in California. There's none on most groceries, but there is on newspapers (unless bought from a coin-operated machine) and magazines. The tax on hotel rooms ranges from 13%–15.5%.

▌ TIME

Los Angeles is in the Pacific time zone, two hours behind Chicago, three hours behind New York, and eight hours behind London.

⊕ www.worldtimezone.com can help you figure out the correct time anywhere in the world.

▌TIPPING

The customary tip rate is 15%–20% for waiters and taxi drivers and 10%–15% for hairdressers and barbers. Bellhops and airport baggage handlers receive $1–$2 per bag; parking valets are usually tipped $1–$2. Bartenders are generally tipped $1 per drink. Hotel maids should generally receive $1–$3 per day of the stay. In upscale establishments, they should receive at least 4% of the room rate before taxes, unless the hotel charges a service fee that includes a gratuity. In restaurants, a handy trick for estimating the tip is to move the decimal point one space and then double that to get 20%.

▌VISITOR INFORMATION

L.A. Inc./The Convention and Visitors Bureau (CVB) publishes an annually updated general information packet with suggestions for entertainment, lodging, dining, and a list of special events. There are two L.A. visitor information centers, on Figueroa downtown and in the Hollywood & Highland complex. The Santa Monica CVB run a drop-in visitor information center on Main Street, which is open daily 9–5, and three kiosks at Palisades Park, the Santa Monica Pier, and the Third Street Promenade; call for hours.

City and State Contacts California Office of Tourism ☎ 916/444–4429, 800/862–2543 ⊕ visitcalifornia.com. **L.A. Inc./The Convention and Visitors Bureau** ☎ 213/624–7300, 800/228–2452 ⊕ discoverlosangeles.com.

Neighborhood Contacts Beverly Hills Conference and Visitors Bureau ☎ 310/248–1000, 800/345–2210 ⊕ beverlyhillschamber. com, beverlyhillsbehere.com. **Hollywood Chamber of Commerce Info Center** ☎ 323/469–8311 ⊕ www.hollywoodchamber. net. **Long Beach Area Convention and Visitors Bureau** ☎ 562/436–3645 ⊕ www. visitlongbeach.com. **Pasadena Convention; Visitors Bureau** ☎ 626/795–9311 ⊕ www. pasadenacal.com. **Redondo Beach Visitors Bureau** ☎ 310/376-6911, 800/282–0333 ⊕ www.visitredondo.com. **Santa Monica Convention; Visitors Bureau** ☎ 310/319–6263, 800/544–5319 ⊕ www.santamonica. com. **West Hollywood Convention and Visitors Bureau** ☎ 310/289–2525, 800/368–6020 ⊕ www.visitwesthollywood.com.

INDEX

PHOTO CREDITS

1, Hendrik Holler / age fotostock. 2, Paul Fisher/iStockphoto. 5, ames sf/Flickr. Chapter 1: Experience Los Angeles: 8–9, Jose Gil/iStockphoto. 10, Christopher Hudson/iStockphoto. 11 (left), Jose Gil/Shutterstock. 11 (right), Andrea Wyner. 12, Kinetic Imagery/Shutterstock. 13 (left), scoutingstock/Shutterstock. 13 (right), Michel Stevelmans/Shutterstock. 16 (left), Ted Chi/Flickr. 16 (top center), Boomer/LACVB. 16 (top right), Diana Lundin/Shutterstock. 16 (bottom right), Joe Shlabotnik/Flickr. 17 (left), Lee Pettet/iStockphoto. 17 (top right), S. Greg Panosian/iStockphoto. 17 (bottom right), Famke Backx/iStockphoto. 18, Douglas H. Kim/iStockphoto. 19 (left), pointnshoot/Flickr. 19 (right), Sean Goebel/iStockphoto. 20, Stanislav Khrapov/Shutterstock. 21 (left), Jay Spooner/iStockphoto. 21 (right), Adan Garcia/Flickr. 22, La Citta Vita/Flickr. 23, vmiramontes/Flickr. 24, Ted Chi/Flickr. 25, Rennett Stowe/Flickr. 26, kristin_a (Meringue Bake Shop)/Flickr. 27 (left), maveric2003/Flickr. 27 (right), pink_fish13/Flickr. 28, UCLA Hammer Museum. 29 (left), Richard Ross with the courtesy of the J. Paul Getty Trust. 29 (right), slick_monkey/Flickr. 30, Nickolay Stanev/Shutterstock. 31 (left), joevare/Flickr. 31 (right), Ilpo's Sojourn/wikipedia.org. 32, Flickr. 33, afternoon/Flickr. 34, Yogma/Flickr. 35, Randy Plett/iStockphoto. 36, wisely/Flickr. 37 (top), Ron Diggity/Flickr. 37 (bottom), Gonzalo Rivero/wikipedia.org. 40, Heeb Christian / age fotostock. 41 (top), Neil Emmerson / age fotostock. 41 (bottom), stevelyon/Flickr. 42 (top), IK's World Trip/Flickr. 42 (bottom), Kjetil Ree/Wikimedia Commons. 43 (top left), Stepan Mazurov/Flickr. 43 (bottom left), Hyatt. 43 (top right), The Key Club. 44 (top), Mike Simpson/iStockphoto. 44 (bottom), **viv**/Flickr. Chapter 2: Downtown Los Angeles: 45, Robert Holmes. 47, Luis Lopez/Flickr. 48, Ned Raggett/Flickr. 49 (top), the_toe_stubber/Flickr. 49 (bottom), ricardodiaz11/Flickr. 50, Larry Brownstein/PhotoDisc/Getty Images. 52, adamsofen/Flickr. 55, S. Greg Panosian/iStockphoto. 56, Epic Stock/Shutterstock. 59, Adrian Miles/Flickr. 60, Gerry Boughan/Shutterstock. 61, Brett Shoaf/Artistic Visuals. 64, Jose Gil/Shutterstock. 65, Omar Omar/Flickr. Chapter 3: Hollywood and the Studios: 69, Robert Holmes. 71, Byron W.Moore/Shutterstock. 72, Andy Z./Shutterstock. 73 (top), Thomas Nord/Shutterstock. 73 (bottom), Juan Camilo Bernal/Shutterstock. 74, Universal Studios Hollywood. 75 (top), Micah May/Shutterstock. 75 (bottom), star5112/Flickr. 76 and 77, Universal Studios Hollywood. 78, David Livingston/iStockphoto. 79 (top), Clinton Steeds/Flickr. 79 (bottom), wolfsavard/Flickr. 80, PeterPhoto/iStockphoto. 81, David Liu/iStockphoto. 82, Clinton Steeds/Flickr. 85, Robert Holmes. 89, RoidRanger/Shutterstock. 90, Universal Studios Hollywood. 93, Brett Shoaf/Artistic Visuals. 96, Robert Holmes. 98–99, Allstar Picture Library/Alamy. Chapter 4: Beverly Hills and the Westside: 101, David Liu/iStockphoto. 103, Lee Pettet/iStockphoto. 104, Andy Hwang/iStockphoto. 105, Brett Shoaf/Artistic Visuals. 106, prayitno/Flickr. 111, Douglas Williams / age fotostock. 113, Robert Holmes. 114–15, Scott Leigh/iStockphoto. 117, Brett Shoaf/Artistic Visuals. 118, Lee Pettet/iStockphoto. 123, Karin Lau/iStockphoto. Chapter 5: Santa Monica and the Beaches: 125, thelastminute/Flickr. 127, Jose Gil/Shutterstock. 128, SIME/Giovanni Simeone/eStock Photo. 130, jonrawlinson/Flickr. 132, NOIZE Photography/Flickr. 134, Naki Kouyioumtzis / age fotostock. 135 (top left), Pygmy Warrior/Flickr. 135 (top right), alonzoD/Flickr. 135 (center right), Anton J. Geisser / age fotostock. 135 (bottom right), ames sf/Flickr. 137 (top), Ivan Solis/iStockphoto. 137 (bottom), Jeremy Edwards/iStockphoto. 138 (top left), Kenna Love/LACVB. 138 (top right), Lee Pettet/iStockphoto. 138 (center), Dr EG/Flickr. 138 (bottom left), JustASC/Shutterstock. 139 (top), Daniel Sofer/hermosawave.net/iStockphoto. 141, Richard Ross with the courtesy of the J. Paul Getty Trust. Chapter 6: Pasadena and Environs: 145, prayitno/Flickr. 147, The Huntington Library, Art Collections, and Botanical Gardens. 148, maveric2003/Flickr. 150–51, Brett Shoaf/Artistic Visuals. 153, wikipedia.org. 157, Lowe Llaguno/Shutterstock. Chapter 7: Nightlife: 159, sunny_J/Flickr. 160, Epic Stock/Shutterstock. 163, LOOK Die Bildagentur der fotografen GmbH/Alamy. 165, sunny_J/Flickr. 167 (top), Trujillo Paumie. 167 (bottom), michael balderas/iStockphoto. 168 (top left), Tamsin Slater/Flickr. 168 (top right), tannazie/Flickr. 168 (bottom center), Trujillo Paumie. 168 (bottom right), CV Photography / Alamy. 168 (bottom), Trujillo Paumie. 169 (top left), Chez Jay. 169 (bottom left), Kibitz Room. 169 (bottom center), stevendamron/Flickr. 169 (top right), bORjAmATiC/Flickr. 169 (bottom right), wikipedia.org. 169 (bottom), Never Cool in School / Leslie Kalohi/Flickr. 170 (top left), Musso & Frank Grill. 170 (bottom left), Howard Wise. 170 (top center), Never Cool in School / Leslie Kalohi/Flickr. 170 (top right), rawblog.blogspot.com/flickr. 170 (bottom right), arnold l inuyaki/flickr. 170 (bottom), Musso & Frank Grill. 172, d.neuman/Flickr. 174, Heeb Christian / age fotostock. 177, Naki Kouyioumtzis / age fotostock. 179, Stepan Mazurov/Flickr. 181, ricardodiaz11/Flickr. Chapter 8: Performing Arts: 185, WDCH, Music Center of Los Angeles County. Photo by Alex Pitt. 186, Monika Rittershaus. 190, Steve Cohn. 194, Craig Schwartz Photography. Chapter 9: Shopping: 197, Ian Cumming / age fotostock. 198, M. Ariano 202, John Robinson. 203, Donato Sardella. 204, Eric Laignel. 205, ChrisYunker/Flickr.. 206, Stella Levi/iStockphoto. 208, Andy Z./Shutterstock. 210, RENAULT Philippe / age fotostock. 213, Loren Javier/Flickr. 216, Never Cool in School / Leslie Kalohi/Flickr.